Enterprise Information Systems Design, Implementation and Management:

Organizational Applications

Maria Manuela Cruz-Cunha
Polytechnic Institute of Cavado and Ave, Portugal

Joao Varajao
University of Tras-os-Montes e Alto Duoro, Portugal

A volume in the Advances in Business
Information Systems and Analytics
(ABISA) Book Series

Director of Editorial Content:	Kristin Klinger
Director of Book Publications:	Julia Mosemann
Acquisitions Editor:	Lindsay Johnston
Development Editor:	Christine Bufton
Publishing Assistant:	Travis Gundrum
Typesetter:	Casey Conapitski
Production Editor:	Jamie Snavely
Cover Design:	Lisa Tosheff

Published in the United States of America by
Information Science Reference (an imprint of IGI Global)
701 E. Chocolate Avenue
Hershey PA 17033
Tel: 717-533-8845
Fax: 717-533-8661
E-mail: cust@igi-global.com
Web site: http://www.igi-global.com

Library of Congress Cataloging-in-Publication Data

Enterprise information systems design, implementation and management : organizational applications / Maria Manuela Cruz-Cunha and Joao Varajao, editors.
     p. cm.
  Includes bibliographical references and index.
  Summary: "This book investigates the creation and implementation of enterprise information systems, covering a wide array of topics such as flow-shop scheduling, information systems outsourcing, ERP systems utilization, Dietz transaction methodology, and advanced planning systems"--Provided by publisher.
  ISBN 978-1-61692-020-3 (hardcover) -- ISBN 978-1-61692-021-0 (ebook) 1. Management information systems. 2. Information technology--Management. I. Cruz-Cunha, Maria Manuela, 1964- II. Varajão, João, 1972- III. Title.

HD30.213.E583 2010
658.4'038011--dc22

                            2010006618

This book is published in the IGI Global book series Advances in Business Information Systems and Analytics (ABISA) Book Series (ISSN: 2327-3275; eISSN: 2327-3283)

British Cataloguing in Publication Data
A Cataloguing in Publication record for this book is available from the British Library.

All work contributed to this book is new, previously-unpublished material. The views expressed in this book are those of the authors, but not necessarily of the publisher.

Advances in Business Information Systems and Analytics (ABISA) Book Series

Madjid Tavana
La Salle University, USA

ISSN: 2327-3275
EISSN: 2327-3283

MISSION

The successful development and management of information systems and business analytics is crucial to the success of an organization. New technological developments and methods for data analysis have allowed organizations to not only improve their processes and allow for greater productivity, but have also provided businesses with a venue through which to cut costs, plan for the future, and maintain competitive advantage in the information age.

The **Advances in Business Information Systems and Analytics (ABISA) Book Series** aims to present diverse and timely research in the development, deployment, and management of business information systems and business analytics for continued organizational development and improved business value.

COVERAGE

- Big Data
- Business Decision Making
- Business Information Security
- Business Process Management
- Business Systems Engineering
- Data Analytics
- Data Management
- Decision Support Systems
- Management Information Systems
- Performance Metrics

IGI Global is currently accepting manuscripts for publication within this series. To submit a proposal for a volume in this series, please contact our Acquisition Editors at Acquisitions@igi-global.com or visit: http://www.igi-global.com/publish/.

The Advances in Business Information Systems and Analytics (ABISA) Book Series (ISSN 2327-3275) is published by IGI Global, 701 E. Chocolate Avenue, Hershey, PA 17033-1240, USA, www.igi-global.com. This series is composed of titles available for purchase individually; each title is edited to be contextually exclusive from any other title within the series. For pricing and ordering information please visit http://www.igi-global.com/book-series/advances-business-information-systems-analytics/37155. Postmaster: Send all address changes to above address. Copyright © 2011 IGI Global. All rights, including translation in other languages reserved by the publisher. No part of this series may be reproduced or used in any form or by any means – graphics, electronic, or mechanical, including photocopying, recording, taping, or information and retrieval systems – without written permission from the publisher, except for non commercial, educational use, including classroom teaching purposes. The views expressed in this series are those of the authors, but not necessarily of IGI Global.

Titles in this Series

For a list of additional titles in this series, please visit: www.igi-global.com

Managing Enterprise Information Technology Acquisitions Assessing Organizational Preparedness
Harekrishna Misra (Institute of Rural Management Anand, India) and Hakikur Rahman (University of Minho, Portugal)
Business Science Reference • copyright 2013 • 345pp • H/C (ISBN: 9781466642010) • US $185.00 (our price)

Information Systems and Technology for Organizations in a Networked Society
Tomayess Issa (Curtin University, Australia) Pedro Isaías (Universidade Aberta, Portugal) and Piet Kommers (University of Twente, The Netherlands)
Business Science Reference • copyright 2013 • 432pp • H/C (ISBN: 9781466640627) • US $185.00 (our price)

Cases on Enterprise Information Systems and Implementation Stages Learning from the Gulf Region
Fayez Albadri (ADMO-OPCO, UAE)
Information Science Reference • copyright 2013 • 370pp • H/C (ISBN: 9781466622203) • US $185.00 (our price)

Business Intelligence and Agile Methodologies for Knowledge-Based Organizations Cross-Disciplinary Applications
Asim Abdel Rahman El Sheikh (The Arab Academy for Banking and Financial Sciences, Jordan) and Mouhib Alnoukari (Arab International University, Syria)
Business Science Reference • copyright 2012 • 370pp • H/C (ISBN: 9781613500507) • US $185.00 (our price)

Business Intelligence Applications and the Web Models, Systems and Technologies
Marta E. Zorrilla (University of Cantabria, Spain) Jose-Norberto Mazón (University of Alicante, Spain) Óscar Ferrández (University of Alicante, Spain) Irene Garrigós (University of Alicante, Spain) Florian Daniel (University of Trento, Italy) and Juan Trujillo (University of Alicante, Spain)
Business Science Reference • copyright 2012 • 374pp • H/C (ISBN: 9781613500385) • US $185.00 (our price)

Electronic Supply Network Coordination in Intelligent and Dynamic Environments Modeling and Implementation
Iraj Mahdavi (Mazandaran University of Science and Technology, Iran) Shima Mohebbi (University of Tehran, Iran) and Namjae Cho (Hanyang University, Korea)
Business Science Reference • copyright 2011 • 434pp • H/C (ISBN: 9781605668086) • US $180.00 (our price)

Enterprise Information Systems Design, Implementation and Management Organizational Applications
Maria Manuela Cruz-Cunha (Polytechnic Institute of Cavado and Ave, Portugal) and Joao Varajao (University of Tras-os-Montes e Alto Duoro, Portugal)
Information Science Reference • copyright 2011 • 622pp • H/C (ISBN: 9781616920203) • US $180.00 (our price)

www.igi-global.com

701 E. Chocolate Ave., Hershey, PA 17033
Order online at www.igi-global.com or call 717-533-8845 x100
To place a standing order for titles released in this series, contact: cust@igi-global.com
Mon-Fri 8:00 am - 5:00 pm (est) or fax 24 hours a day 717-533-8661

List of Reviewers

Albert Boonstra, *University of Groningen, The Netherlands*
Antonio Guevara, *University of Malaga, Spain*
António Trigo, *Polytechnic Institute of Coimbra, Portugal*
Bart H.M. Gerritsen, *TNO N. Org. for App. Scientific Research, The Netherlands*
Carlos Ferrás Sexto, *Universidad de Santiago de Compostela, Spain*
Cesar Alexandre de Souza, *University of São Paulo, Brazil*
Dimitrios Koufopoulos, *Brunel University, UK*
Duminda Wijesekera, *George Mason University, USA*
George Leal Jamil, *FUMEC/BH, Brazil*
João Varajão, *University of Trás-os-Montes e Alto Douro, Portugal*
José L. Leiva, *University of Malaga, Spain*
Klara Antlova, *Technical University of Liberec, Czech republic*
Malihe Tabatabaie, *University of York, UK*
Maria Manuela Cruz Cunha, *Polytechnic Institute of Cávado and Ave, Portugal*
Nuno Lopes, *Polytechnic Institute of Cávado and Ave, Portugal*
Ozden Ustun, *Dumlupinar University, Turkey*
Patrícia Gonçalves, *Polytechnic Institute of Cávado and Ave, Portugal*
Paulo Martins, *University of Trás-os-Montes e Alto Douro, Portugal*
Rinaldo C. Michekini, *PMAR Lab of the University of Genova, Italy*
Roberto Razzoli, *PMAR Lab of the University of Genova, Italy*
Rui Dinis Sousa, *University of Minho, Portugal*
Vítor Basto Fernandes, *Polytechnic Institute of Leiria, Portugal*
Vladanka Acimovic-Raspopovic, *University of Belgrade, Serbia*
Vojko Potocan, *University of Maribor, Slovenia*
Wai Ming Cheung, *University of Bath, UK*

Table of Contents

Section 1
Information Systems Architectures

Section 2
Business Process Modelling

Section 3
Organizational Knowledge

Section 4
EIS Design, Application, Implementation and Impact

Section 5
EIS Adoption

Section 6
EIS Social Aspects

Section 7
IT/IS Management

Section 8
Collaborative, Networked and Virtual Organizations

Chapter 31
Hans-Henrik Hvolby, Aalborg University, Denmark
Kenn Steger-Jensen, Aalborg University, Denmark
Erlend Alfnes, Norwegian University of Science and Technology, Norway
Heidi C. Dreyer, Norwegian University of Science and Technology, Norway

Detailed Table of Contents

Section 1
Information Systems Architectures

The three chapters of Section 1 focus on IS/IT architectures, aiming at its alignment with business regarding management support and increased competitiveness

    Tariq Mahmoud, Carl von Ossietzky University, Germany
    Jorge Marx Gómez, Carl von Ossietzky University, Germany

Nowadays, it becomes more and more critical and essential for the vendors in the business-related markets to tailor their products and software to meet the needs of the Small and Medium Businesses (SMB) since their market share has been enormously raised and the issues related to the Business-to-Business (B2B) environment are becoming great challenges to be considered. The semantic Service-Oriented Architecture (SOA)-based model involves Semantic Web Services to be applied in business environments in order to have a consistent framework that makes the data understandable for both humans and machines. The ultimate goal of the authors' proposed model is to transfer the enterprise Web into a medium through which data and applications can be automatically understood and processed. The main components of the proposed model and the vision of applying it to one of the business solutions area illustrated in order to show how these components can work together to overcome the traditional SOA-based solutions weakness.

    António Gonçalves, Trás-os-Montes University, Portugal
    Natália Serra, Polytechnic Institute of Setúbal, Portugal
    José Serra, OLISIPO, Portugal
    Pedro Sousa, Instituto Superior Técnico, Portugal

In the second chapter, the authors demonstrate, by using a case study, how it is possible to achieve the alignment between business and Information Technology (IT). They describe several phases of project development, from planning strategy, enterprise architecture, development of businesses supporting tools and keeping dynamic alignment between the business and the IT. The authors also propose a framework, framed under an enterprise architecture that guarantees a high level of response to the applications development or configuration as improves its alignment to business by solving some limitations of traditional software development solutions namely: difficulty in gathering clients requirements, which should be supported by the applications; difficulty to connect the organisation processes used to answer the client, which must also be integrated in the applications and the difficulty to develop the applications that can follow the business cycle. To test the approach, this was applied to a real case study consisting in the configuration of an application that manages the relationship with the clients.

Chapter 3

Luis Fernando Ramos Molinaro, Universidade de Brasília, Brazil
Karoll Haussler Carneiro Ramos, Universidade de Brasília, Brazil
Humberto Abdalla Jr., Universidade de Brasília, Brazil
João Mello da Silva, Universidade de Brasília, Brazil
Flávio Elias Gomes de Deus, Universidade de Brasília, Brazil
Annibal Affonso Neto, Universidade de Brasília, Brazil

The third chapter aims to present a proposal for a model that supports organizational governance through the alignment of business with Information Technology - IT. Firstly, it was observed that there are some paradigms which limit the use of enterprise architectures and hinder governance functions. Secondly, it focuses on the IT unit, where IT systems and subsystems are interrelated and the performance levels of the organization are aggregated, creating a macro-structure system capable of supporting corporate governance and IT. Finally, the IBM's Component Business Model - CBM® was applied to represent relationships of IT unit with the organization, through decomposing the organization into business components that supply and demand services to facilitate their governance and management.

Section 2
Business Process Modelling

The second section of the book includes four chapters devoted to enterprise/business modelling and supporting representation methodologies and technologies.

Chapter 4

Carlos Páscoa, INOV - INESC Inovação, Portuga &Estado-Maior da Força Aérea, Portugal
Pedro Sousa, INOV - INESC Inovação, Portuga &Estado-Maior da Força Aérea, Portugal
José Tribolet, INOV - INESC Inovação, Portuga &Estado-Maior da Força Aérea, Portugal

Ontologies, being "an explicit specification of a conceptualization", have tried to capture knowledge within the aspects of concepts (used to represent a domain entity), relations (representing an interaction between the domain concepts), functions (a special case of relations), axioms (which represent true statements) and instances (used to represent domain elements). The Enterprise Ontology can be seen as a collection of terms and definitions relevant to business enterprises that can be used as a basis for decision making. The fourth chapter presents a new concept of Enterprise Ontology, proposed by Dietz, and defined as the realization and implementation essence of an enterprise proposing a distinction world ontology and system ontology. The traditional way to model processes, like the BPMN, draw events, activities and data in a sequence of symbols that may not represent completely all the actions in presence and, above all, does not detect and identify consistency between actors and actions. However, BPMN diagrams can also be used to represent various actions and models proposed by Dietz as the transaction, "Process" and "State" diagrams. Both ways of representing have advantages and disadvantages and can be used, either isolated or together to give a deep representation of reality.

Chapter 5

Masakazu Ohashi, Chuo University, Japan
Mayumi Hori, Hakuoh University, Japan

In chapter five, the authors propose to incorporate the authentication roaming technology with existing social infrastructures from the perspective of users instead of that of service providers. By conducting experiments in the Business to Consumer (B to C) environment, the authors' research demonstrated and confirmed the effectiveness of the authentication roaming technology to realize a safe and convenient network society. This technology contributes to the construction of a citizen-centric, reassuring system especially for mobile and transportation by proposing a cooperation system for the mobile information services based on the XML Web Services technology. The aim is to enable mobile users to access a variety of essential information for maintaining safety and comfortable management of networks and enable them to make an educated decision regarding the treatment they may receive in case of trouble.

Chapter 6

Rebecca Angeles, University of New Brunswick, Canada

Rebecca Angeles looks at the perceived ability of two variables, reciprocal investments and relational interaction, to moderate the relationship between the independent variables, components of IT infrastructure integration and supply chain process integration, and two dependent radio frequency identification (RFID) system variables, exploitation and exploration. Using the moderated regression procedure, the study presented seeks to test the ability of both reciprocal investments and relational interaction to moderate the relationship between the independent and dependent variables using data gathered from 87 firms using an online survey. Results show that relational interaction is an effective moderator between the dependent variable, exploitation, and the following independent variables: data consistency, cross-functional application integration, financial flow integration, physical flow integration, and information flow integration. Neither reciprocal investments nor relational interaction effectively moderated the independent variables, IT infrastructure integration and supply chain process integration and the other dependent variable, exploration.

In the current context of globalization and with the increasing need to automate the work, modelling business processes has become essential. Modelling helps not only to understand processes but also to anticipate changes and build a flexible structure. In chapter seven, the authors adopt from software engineering the concept of reverse-engineering. For organizations with unmodelled BP, reverse-engineering is a way to provide process models ready for improvement or usage in other stages of the business process lifecycle. This chapter proposes a method for business process reverse-engineering fulfilling these requirements. It consists of a multi-view metamodel, covering all perspectives of a process, and a detailed approach to guide the business process modeller. The approach was tested on a web application from the French academic Information Systems.

Section 3
Organizational Knowledge

Managing and exploiting organizational knowledge regarding the needs to support business decision are concerns addressed in the five chapters of Section 3.

Chapter 8 proposes concepts for designing and developing decision support systems that acknowledge, explore and exploit the fact that conversations among people are the top-level "supporting device" for decision-making. The goal is to design systems that support, configure and induce increasingly effective and efficient decision-making conversations. The proposal sees the sum total of decisions being taken in an organization as the global decision process of the organization. The global decision process of the organization is structured in decision processes corresponding to organizational domains. Each organizational domain has associated a unit decision process. If the organizational domain contains organizational sub-domains, then its compound decision process is the union and composition of its unit decision process and the unit decision processes of its sub-domains. The proposal can be seen as extending, enlarging and integrating group decision support systems into an organization-wide system. The resulting organizational decision support system, by its conversational nature, may become the kernel decision support system of an organization or enterprise. In this way, the global decision process of the organization may be made explicit and monitored.

Chapter 9

Max E. Stachura, Medical College of Georgia, USA

Joseph Wood, Dwight D. Eisenhower Army Medical Center, USA

Fjorentina Angjellari-Dajci, Paine College, USA

James M. Grayson, Augusta State University, USA

Elena V. Astapova, Medical College of Georgia, USA

Hui-Lien Tung, Paine College, USA

Donald Sofge, Naval Research Laboratory, USA

William F. Lawless, Paine College, USA

In chapter nine, the authors review a model of the conservation of information (COI) applied to organizations. Following this review, the chapter includes a brief review of the mathematics in support of this model and its implications for the development of theory. Then the model is applied to a review of the status of telemedicine and e-health in Georgia, which the authors had begun to study last year. After the reviews, they discuss future steps and draw conclusions about the model and its benefit to organizational attention and decision-making.

Chapter 10

Meira Levy, Ben-Gurion University of the Negev, Israel

A firm's capability to transfer its existing knowledge to various stakeholders and translate knowledge into action determines its success in today's volatile global business environment. However, while many firms systematically manage data and information, managing knowledge remains a controversial issue. One of the reasons for this is inconclusiveness about what knowledge is and whether it can be managed. In order to more precisely define knowledge and its management, the author proposes a knowledge warehouse conceptual model (KW-CM) for practically and systematically assimilating of knowledge within organizational business processes. This conceptual model integrates aspects of knowledge that encompass business processes, stakeholders and other organizational information systems within the existing data warehouse (DW) conceptual model. In addition, the chapter presents a formal architecture, definitions and guidelines that describe the KW components and processes for leveraging data and information into knowledge. The proposed KW-CM is demonstrated with an example of a DW which handles information regarding customer product usage.

Chapter 11

Rick Tijsen, Utrecht University, The Netherlands

Marco Spruit, Utrecht University, The Netherlands

Martijn van de Ridder, Capgemini Nederland, The Netherlands

Bas van Raaij, Capgemini Nederland, The Netherlands

Over the years many organizations have invested in Business Intelligence (BI) systems. While BI-software enables organization-wide decision support, problems are encountered in the "fit" between systems' provision and changing requirements of a growing amount of BI (end-) users. Chapter eleven aims at investigating the factors that influence the "fit" between Business Intelligence (BI) end-users, tasks and technologies (BI-FIT). Based on an extensive literature study on the elements of BI-FIT, in this research the BI-FIT Framework is developed that shows the most relevant factors and the interrelationships between BI end-users, tasks and technologies. The framework can be used to help organizations to identify and fulfil the needs of BI end-users, thereby improving adoption and increasing satisfaction of the BI end-user base.

Gabriela Alves, FEAD, Brazil
Jorge Neves, UFMG, Brazil

Chapter twelve aims to present specific features concerning information management in the Continuous Improvement area of the Americas Long Carbon sector in ArcelorMittal. The aim is also to learn what the informational resources related to continuous improvement area are and describe how the process of managing information actually happens. The study was based on theoretical models of Davenport (1998) and Choo (2006) and tried to understand how the efficient management of information can aid in decision making at organizations. The result of the documentary research revealed the existence of initiatives throughout the different units in the Americas and also revealed corporate tools for information management. The field research results indicate the need for a structured and formalized model of information management that responds to users in adequate time, while alert to the need for policies that encourage the sharing of information related to the improvement of processes, products and services.

Section 4
EIS Design, Application, Implementation and Impact

The five chapters of Section 4 address the tremendous challenge associated to the design and implementation of Enterprise Information Systems in organizations.

Ricardo Almeida, Universidade do Porto, Portugal
Américo Azevedo, Universidade do Porto, Portugal

The new market trends are forcing companies to constantly reorganize their business processes so that they can react quickly to the new economic challenges. Although not always, enterprise information systems provide an appropriate response to these situations due to several reasons, such as technology failure, lack of adaptable configuration tools or even the financial investment required, which makes it unaffordable to companies. Chapter thirteen presents a functional model for ERP systems (called FME) that would guarantee a baseline structure to build solutions which would provide a complete configuration and, therefore, a timely reaction to market fluctuations. This model also summarizes some of the most used functionalities of the available ERP systems.

Quality is, in real-life, a multidimensional notion. A schedule is described and valued on the basis of a number of criteria, for example: makespan, work-in-process inventories, idle times, observance of due dates, etc. An appropriate schedule cannot be obtained unless one observes the whole set of important criteria. The multidimensional nature of the scheduling problems leads us to the area of Multicriteria Optmization. Thus considering combinatorial problems with more than one criterion is more relevant in the context of real-life scheduling problems. Research in this important field has been scarce when compared to research in single-criterion scheduling. The proliferation of metaheuristic techniques has encouraged researchers to apply them to combinatorial optimization problems. The chapter presents a review regarding multicriteria flow-shop scheduling problem, focusing on Multi-Objective Combinatorial Optimization theory, including recent developments considering more than one optimization criterion, followed by a summary discussion on research directions.

Research about ERP post-implementation and ERP assimilation is very limited. Similarly, scant research investigated ERP experiences in developing countries. Based on a qualitative research methodology grounded in the diffusion of innovations theory, the study presented in chapter 15 aims at investigating the determining contextual factors for ERP assimilation. A cross-case study analysis of four firms in a developed and a developing country suggests that in both contexts, the primary factor for encouraging a successful ERP assimilation is top management support. Other factors such as post-implementation training and education, IT support, organizational culture, managers and users involvement, strategic alignment, external pressures and consultant effectiveness are also identified as factors that influence ERP assimilation. Several assimilation impediments that should be watched are also specified.

A large number of firms worldwide have made major investments in the application of ERP systems to modify their business model and be able to offer better processes. When firms implement ERP systems they try to integrate and optimize their processes in what they consider their key areas. The present chapter tries to offer a view centred on the main reasons why Spanish firms have implemented ERP systems in the last ten years and what have been their main critical success factors and their main failure factors too. For that, the authors apply a model based in 5 main groups of variables. Firms were inquired about their perceptions and final results provided by the variables affecting their change processes in the ERP implementation.

    Emad Abu-Shanab, Yarmouk University, Jordan
    Heyam Al-Tarawneh, Ministry of Education, Jordan

Enterprise systems are becoming more important as they support the efficiency and effectiveness of operations and reduce cost. Chapter 17 explores the literature related to production information systems (PIS), enterprise systems, and other applications and their influence in an industrial zone in Jordan. Constructs from the Innovation Diffusion Theory were used, where results indicated that the adoption rate is acceptable and all variables have high means with respect to their evaluation by managers, but only two variable significantly predicted intention to use. In a second study that explored the status of IT usage in manufacturing firms using a different sample, results indicated that accounting information systems were widely used and distribution systems and manufacturing aiding systems were the least used.

Section 5
EIS Adoption

Section 5 is concerned with studying and measuring the utilization, impact, and difficulties associated with Enterprise Information Systems adoption, along its four chapters.

    Hedman Jonas, Copenhagen Business School, Denmark
    Johansson Björn, Lund University, Sweden

As the deployment of ERP systems within enterprises is increasing, it is of extreme interest to measure the degree of utilization of ERP systems. One reason for this interest is that no benefits are realized if the systems are not used; since ERPs are massive investments, they need to show benefits, or at least be able to measure the benefits. However, to be able to do so, there is a need to explain ERP systems utilization and the factors that influence ERP utilization. Chapter 18 provides an explanation of factors influencing ERP systems utilization by testing a research model building on four dimensions: volume, breadth, diversity, and depth. The contributions of the research are: First, it provides support for the notion of diffusion found in the theory of network externalities where a critical mass is necessary to achieve benefits. This can be used to better understand failures in ERP projects. Second, the use of volume, breadth and depth provide insights for use as a construct and the need to treat it more rigorously. Third, the study contributes to our understanding of the many aspects of use of IT, such as ERPs, and potentially contributes to value and firm performance from ERP utilization.

    Ahmed Elragal, German University in Cairo, Egypt
    Dalia Birry, Alexandria University, Egyptt

There has been an increasing interest in ERP systems in both research and practice in the last decade. But unfortunately in many occasions a lot of companies have stopped using these systems after they went-live with the implementation. Chapter 19 is an attempt to reveal the factors influencing users' intention to continue using the ERP system. A survey was sent to respondent gaining a number of 223 responses. A hypothesized model was developed based on three theories; TAM, ECT, and TPB. The model was tested using regression analysis of the collected responses. Results showed that users' intension to continue using the ERP systems are affected by: perceived usefulness, satisfaction, subjective norm, and perceived behavior control. Meanwhile, perceived usefulness is affected by confirmation and subjective norm while satisfaction is affected by perceived usefulness and confirmation.

Chapter 20 proposes a possible model of criteria for ERP system selection. The proposed model consists of four groups of ERP system selection criteria: the ERP systems benefits criteria, the system quality criteria, the vendor related criteria and the ERP system package criteria. The data were collected in companies in Slovenia. Research results have confirmed internal consistency of ERP selection criteria in each group. For each criterion the importance is evaluated by small, medium-sized and large companies. Beside that also company size, implemented information strategy, representation of the IT department on the board level in the company and turnover impact on importance of each criterion is evaluated and presented. The model presented in this chapter could be useful for ERP system providers to better understand companies' needs and to provide systems tailored for individual needs of the company. The model could also be useful for companies considering ERP system implementation to avoid high costs of failed implementations.

Nowadays, the WWW is playing a vital role in the business world. Most enterprises are becoming digital. Content management systems provide an effective method to improve the development of web applications and make the maintainer's job easier. The purpose of this work is to study the advantages that the use of web technologies can represent for an SME company when they are applied to integrate their work techniques and procedures. The authors have also tried to use it to provide their customers with several services, and to make easier the company expansion process. The framework developed includes a security system for the access to the contents based on the RBAC model. The use of the

INOVA framework has provided a benefit as much for INOVA itself, as for its customers, by including in a centralized way document resources and toolkits that can be accessed remotely.

Section 6
EIS Social Aspects

The social and professional side of EIS plays a central role in EIS adoption as demonstrated in the two chapters of this Section 6.

Chapter 22

    Vojko Potocan, University of Maribor, Slovenia
    Matjaz Mulej, University of Maribor, Slovenia

Modern business environments require innovated business concepts. Meeting them in enterprises' functioning depends also on creation and implementation of appropriate information support. In terms of contents, information support and information must be reliable to not be misinformation; information and communication technology is not enough for it because information means impact. Potential errors on the long path from data to information must hence be prevented. A one-sided approach, which belongs to the practices of professionals as narrow specialists, can prevent errors and misinformation rarely – when rather one-sided information is enough. More complex situation and processes require a more holistic approach that, in its turn, requires interdisciplinary creative co-operation of specialists of various interdependent professions. Chapter 22 contributes to the discussion about reliability of information by thinking how can one tackle the data-to-information-to-decision process in order to diminish dangers of poor reliability of information/decision.

Chapter 23

    Jonatan Jelen, Parsons The New School for Design, USA
    Marko Kolakovic, University of Zagreb, Croatia

Google, eBay, Amazon, Facebook, Myspace, Craig's List and their foreign equivalents, such as the Chinese QQ and Baidu, for example, are ostensibly complex, and – more troublesome - their attitudes are becoming increasingly contradictory, controversial, and conflicted: For one, Tom Malone's decade-old predictions of a decentralized network of a multitude of small, cooperating firms did not materialize; to the contrary and counter to the spirit of the democratic nature of information and information technology, these e-giants are defining their own industries and defying regulation, submitting the participants in their respective markets to proprietary rules via three central tenets: regulatory capture, regulatory arbitrage, and regulatory opportunism. Chapter 23 is critical and explores these traits of the Complex Information Technology-Intensive firms and formulate elements of a framework for their ambiguous nature that may lead to social cost exceeding their initially glorified social value creation.

Section 7
IT/IS Management

The five chapters of Section 7 explore strategies, processes and tools for information systems and information technology implementation and management.

Over the past decade, Contact Centers have experienced exceptional growth. In UK and USA Contact Centers employ about three percent of the working population. Contact Center's projects are complex because occur in a multidisciplinary area with multiple actors and constraints. Information systems play a decisive role in these projects. However, several studies indicate a low success level of information and communications technology projects leading to research opportunities for their improvement. In their previous research, authors have identified a framework with the key factors to be considered in these projects. Due to the highly dynamic reality of the Contact Centers, the framework must evolve in order to maintain its usefulness for project managers and other center professionals. Focus groups are interactive discussion groups used for generating knowledge and hypotheses, exploring opinions, attitudes and attributes. In this way, the study presented in this chapter aims to verify, expand and actualize the existent framework, using a focus group with professionals in the area.

As World economy lingers it is increasingly more important to justify any investment so that available corporate funds are spent wisely. However, estimating the value of ITIL investments is not an easy task, which means that most CIOs do not invest in large-scale ITIL projects as much as it would be desirable. Instead, CIOs prefer to embark on quick win implementations (e.g. solely implement the incident management process). In this chapter the authors propose an ITIL Value Estimator. This estimator is based on an estimation process that quantifies the project's total cost, along with each process' benefits. The outcome of the ITIL Value Estimator is a Monte Carlo simulation whose result provides CIOs with a justification of the value of large-scale ITIL implementations, which can be used to gain the upper hand during the decision-making process.

Information Systems (IS) Outsourcing has emerged as a strategic option to be considered and has been increasingly adopted by managers. However, many contracts still fail during their initial years, meaning that Outsourcing has also been subject to strong criticism. There are advantages to Outsourcing but also significant risks associated to it, and the assessment of both is therefore of great relevance for informed decision-making. The objective of chapter 26 is to determine to what extent a common view about risks and benefits associated to IS Outsourcing is shared by the Portuguese market players – Service Providers, Clients and Opinion Makers. In order to accomplish this, an on-line Delphi study was conducted, combined with the Q-sort technique, which allowed to obtain the perspective of each player on the risks and benefits IS Outsourcing. Comparing these perspectives it was possible to understand that the market players don't share the same point of view.

Chapter 27

The main objective of chapter 27 is to present an innovative tool for innovation management with emphasis to the information technology-IT management called INMATE. In order to arrive at this tool an analysis on the current market tools was conducted. This analysis observed that none of the existent tools gives the due importance to the role of information technology-IT for the innovation process. In this way, the chapter presents a brief discussion of two of these market tools: an international, called TEMAGUIDE, and a Brazilian, called NUGIN. And then it introduces the INMATE tool with its main dimensions and gives detailed account on how the IT management is dealt inside INMATE, which is done via the concept of Enterprise Architecture, a concept from the Computing Science and Engineering. From this concept the chapter presents a methodology, in an analogy to the Structure-Conduct-Performance Paradigm (that is traditionally used on the empirical market analysis), which identifies the firm according to three linear connected approaches: its architecture, its governance, and its growth strategy.

Chapter 28

Corporate governance is a key element today in organizations and companies. IT Governance, as a part of corporate governance, plays its role in aligning IT with the business and obtaining the maximum value, minimizing the risks. Several frameworks and guidelines have been published in order to set the basis for this discipline. The recent release of the ISO 38500 ads an effort to standardize the different elements of IT governance. Despite these efforts, none of the different frameworks or guidelines is focused on the specific characteristics of small and medium companies (SMOs), although the authors consider that their conclusions are universal. Furthermore, there is no research so far that analyzed the status of IT governance in Spanish organizations. Chapter 28 presents a research to identify the state of the art of IT governance in the Spanish small and medium organizations.

Section 8
Collaborative, Networked and Virtual Organizations

Organizations no longer live inside their four walls. Section 8 presents collaboration tools and environments regarding the exploitation of the concept of distributed, virtual and collaborative organizational models.

Chapter 29
George Draghici, Politehnica University of Timisoara, Romania
Anca Draghici, Politehnica University of Timisoara, Romania

Today, product development is a result of a collaborative networked design process. Taking into consideration this fact, a National Research Network for Integrated Product and Process Engineering (IN-PRO) has been created. Chapter 29 presents the relevant items for building a PLM multisite platform for collaborative integrated product development based on the common researches developed in the INPRO project and network. Authors discuss this approach by presenting the collaborative distributed design process, the product model and the PLM multisite platform for collaborative integrated product development. Based on these was built a collaborative multisite platform that join together the methodology, methods and tools for Product Lifecycle Management (PLM), Knowledge Management (KM) and Human Resources Management (HRU), examples of good practice. The core of the proposed approach is the product lifecycle model which is the base for the proposed collaborative product development methodology and the multisite PLM platform architecture.

Chapter 30
Anca Draghici, "Politehnica" University of Timisoara, Romania
Monica Izvercianu, "Politehnica" University of Timisoara, Romania
George Draghici, "Politehnica" University of Timisoara, Romania

Chapter 30 presents a preliminary approach for building a virtual center for entrepreneurship development that will be implemented in a university research network in Romania. The authors argue the most relevant aspects that conduct them to an organizational information system design, implementation and management with double role: education (entrepreneurial skills development in the case of students) and research (new competencies development by a-learning future programs). The following items are presented: (1) the training needs for business creation - based on a preliminary market research developed with subjects with technical and economical background and that allow the identification of the entrepreneurial knowledge; (2) the university entrepreneurial education as a process of knowledge transfer; (3) preliminary design and architecture of the virtual center for entrepreneurship. Finally, some relevant conclusions and the future researches directions are presented.

Chapter 31

Hans-Henrik Hvolby, Aalborg University, Denmark
Kenn Steger-Jensen, Aalborg University, Denmark
Erlend Alfnes, Norwegian University of Science and Technology, Norway
Heidi C. Dreyer, Norwegian University of Science and Technology, Norway

The focus of manufacturing planning and control has gradually expanded from (in-house) production activities towards all manufacturing and logistics activities in the supply chain. Planning of in-house operations is still very important, but the trends towards increased use of outsourcing and mass customisation require that customers and suppliers are able to exchange information frequently to cut down costs and lead time while quickly adapting their manufacturing and logistics operations to market/customer requirements. Many vendors offer systems to plan and control in-house operations, whereas only a few large vendors (such as Oracle, SAP and I2) offer supply chain planning systems. This limits the ability for SMEs to exploit the supply chain planning options. Chapter 31 discusses current supply chain planning solutions and presents a more simple and adaptive concept to be used in both SMEs and larger enterprises.

Preface

ABOUT THE SUBJECT

"An enterprise system has the Herculean task of seamlessly supporting and integrating a full range of business processes by uniting functional islands and making their data visible across the organization in real time."[1]

For the last decades, it is being recognized that that enterprise computer-based solutions no longer consist of isolated or dispersedly developed and implemented MRP (Material Requirements Planning) and MRP II solutions, CRM (Customer Relationship Management) solutions, electronic commerce solutions, ERP (Enterprise Resources Planning) solutions and other, transposing the functional/technological islands to the so-called 'islands of information'. Solutions must be integrated, built on a single system, supported by a common information infrastructure central to the organization, ensuring that information can be shared across all functional levels and management, so that users can see data entered anywhere in the system in real-time and, simultaneously, seamlessly allow the integration and coordination of most (if not all) the enterprise business processes.

The topic of Enterprise Information Systems (EIS) is gaining an increasingly relevant strategic impact on global business and the world economy, and organizations are undergoing hard investments (in cost and effort) in search of the rewarding benefits of efficiency and effectiveness that this range of solutions promise. But, as we all know, this is not an easy task! It is not only a matter of financial investment! It is much more, as this book shows. EIS are at same time responsible by tremendous gains in some companies and tremendous losses in others. So, their adoption should be carefully planned and managed.

Responsiveness, flexibility, agility and business alignment are requirements of competitiveness that enterprises search for. And we hope that the models, solutions, tools and case studies presented and discussed in this book can contribute to highlight new ways to identify opportunities and overtake trends and challenges of EIS selection, adoption and exploitation.

ORGANIZATION OF THE BOOK

This book integrates the enhanced versions of 31 papers selected from the international conference CENTERIS – Conference on ENTERprise Information Systems held in Ofir, Portugal in October 2009. These selected contributions discuss the main issues, challenges, opportunities and developments related with Enterprise Information Systems from the social, managerial and organizational perspectives, in a very comprehensive way, and contribute to the dissemination of current achievements and practical solutions and applications in the field.

These 31 chapters are written by a group of 80 authors that includes many internationally renowned and experienced authors in the EIS field and a set of younger authors, showing a promising potential for research and development. Contributions came from USA, Canada, Latin America, several countries of Eastern and Western Europe, Africa and Asia. At the same time, the book integrates contributions from academe, research institutions and industry, representing a good and comprehensive representation of the state-of-the-art approaches and developments that address the several dimensions of this fast evolutionary thematic.

"Enterprise Information Systems Design, Implementation and Management: Organizational Applications" is organized in eight sections:

- "Section 1: Information Systems Architectures," includes three chapters that focus on IS/IT architectures aiming at its alignment with business regarding management support and increased competitiveness.
- "Section 2: Business Process Modelling" includes four chapters devoted to enterprise/business modeling and supporting representation methodologies and technologies.
- "Section 3: Organizational Knowledge" discusses the management and exploitation of organizational knowledge regarding the needs of business decision-making support.
- "Section 4: EIS Design, Application, Implementation and Impact" address the tremendous challenge associated to the design and implementation of Enterprise Information Systems in organizations.
- "Section 5: EIS Adoption" is concerned with studying and measuring the utilization, impact, and difficulties associated with Enterprise Information Systems adoption.
- "Section 6: EIS Social Aspects" addresses the social and professional side of EIS in EIS adoption.
- "Section 7: IT / IS Management" address the topic of information systems and information technology 8 and management methodologies and tools.
- Finally, "Section 8: Collaborative, Networked and Virtual Organizations," presents collaboration tools and environments regarding the exploitation of the concept of distributed, virtual and collaborative organizational models.

The three chapters of Section 1, *"Information Systems Architectures,"* focus on IS/IT architectures aiming at its alignment to business regarding management support and increased competitiveness.

#### Chapter 1

Nowadays, it becomes more and more critical and essential for the vendors in the business-related markets to tailor their products and software to meet the needs of the Small and Medium Businesses (SMB) since their market share has been enormously raised and the issues related to the Business-to-Business (B2B) environment are becoming great challenges to be considered. The semantic Service-Oriented Architecture (SOA)-based model involves Semantic Web Services to be applied in business environments in order to have a consistent framework that makes the data understandable for both humans and machines. The ultimate goal of the model proposed by Mahmoud and Marx Gómez in the first chapter, *"Applying Semantic SOA-Based Model to Business Applications, "* is to transfer the enterprise Web into a medium through which data and applications can be automatically understood and processed. The main components of the proposed model and the vision of applying it to one of the business solutions area illustrated in order to show how these components can work together to overcome the traditional SOA-based solutions weakness.

#### Chapter 2

In the second chapter, *"How to use Information Tecnology Effectively to Achieve Business Objectives,"* Gonçalves, N. Serra, J. Serra and Sousa demonstrate, by using a case study, how it is possible to achieve the alignment between business and Information Technology (IT). They describe several phases of project development, from planning strategy, enterprise architecture, development of businesses supporting tools and keeping dynamic alignment between the business and the IT. The authors also propose a framework, framed under an enterprise architecture that guarantees a high level of response to the applications development or configuration as improves its alignment to business by solving some limitations of traditional software development solutions namely: difficulty in gathering clients requirements, which should be supported by the applications; difficulty to connect the organization processes used to answer the client, which must also be integrated in the applications and the difficulty to develop the applications that can follow the business cycle. To test the approach, this was applied to a real case study consisting in the configuration of an application that manages the relationship with the clients.

In the third chapter , *"Governance and Management of Information Technology: Decomposing the Enterprise in Modular Building Blocks Based on Enterprise Architecture and Business Oriented Services,"* Molinaro, Carneiro Ramos, Abdalla Jr., Silva, Deus & Neto present a proposal for a model that supports organizational governance through the alignment of business with Information Technology - IT. Firstly, it was observed that there are some paradigms which limit the use of enterprise architectures and hinder governance functions. Secondly, it focuses on the IT unit, where IT systems and subsystems are interrelated and the performance levels of the organization are aggregated, creating a macro-structure system capable of supporting corporate governance and IT. Finally, the IBM`s Component Business Model - CBM® was applied to represent relationships of IT unit with the organization, through decomposing the organization into business components that supply and demand services to facilitate their governance and management.

The second section, *"Business Process Modelling"* includes four chapters devoted to enterprise / business modeling and supporting representation methodologies and technologies.

#### Chapter 4

Ontologies, being "an explicit specification of a conceptualization," have tried to capture knowledge within the aspects of concepts (used to represent a domain entity), relations (representing a interaction between the domain concepts), functions (a special case of relations), axioms (which represent true statements) and instances (used to represent domain elements). The Enterprise Ontology can be seen as a collection of terms and definitions relevant to business enterprises that can be used as a basis for decision making. In the fourth chapter, *"Ontology construction: representing Dietz "Process" and "State" models using BPMN diagrams,"* Páscoa, Sousa and Tribolet present a new concept of Enterprise Ontology, proposed by Dietz, and defined as the realization and implementation essence of an enterprise proposing a distinction world ontology and system ontology. The traditional way to model processes, like the BPMN, draw events, activities and data in a sequence of symbols that may not represent completely all the actions in presence and, above all, does not detect and identify consistency between actors and actions. However, BPMN diagrams can also be used to represent various actions and models proposed by Dietz as the transaction, "Process" and "State" diagrams. Both ways of representing have advantages and disadvantages and can be used, either isolated or together to give a deep representation of reality.

In Chapter 5 *"Security Management Services Based on Authentication Roaming between Different Certificate Authorities,"* Ohashi and Hori propose to incorporate the authentication roaming technology with existing social infrastructures from the perspective of users instead of that of service providers. By conducting experiments in the Business to Consumer (B to C) environment, the authors' research demonstrated and confirmed the effectiveness of the authentication roaming technology to realize a safe and convenient network society. This technology contributes to the construction of a citizen-centric, reassuring system especially for mobile and transportation by proposing a cooperation system for the mobile information services based on the XML Web Services technology. The aim is to enable mobile users to access a variety of essential information for maintaining safety and comfortable management of networks and enable them to make an educated decision regarding the treatment they may receive in case of trouble.

In Chapter 6, "*Perceived Moderating Ability of Relational Interaction versus Reciprocal Investments in Pursuing Exploitation versus Exploration in RFID Supply Chains,*" Rebecca Angeles looks at the perceived ability of two variables, reciprocal investments and relational interaction, to moderate the relationship between the independent variables, components of IT infrastructure integration and supply chain process integration, and two dependent radio frequency identification (RFID) system variables, exploitation and exploration. Using the moderated regression procedure, the study presented seeks to test the ability of both reciprocal investments and relational interaction to moderate the relationship between the independent and dependent variables using data gathered from 87 firms using an online survey. Results show that relational interaction is an effective moderator between the dependent variable, exploitation, and the following independent variables: data consistency, cross-functional application integration, financial flow integration, physical flow integration, and information flow integration. Neither reciprocal investments nor relational interaction effectively moderated the independent variables, IT infrastructure integration and supply chain process integration and the other dependent variable, exploration.

In the current context of globalization and with the increasing need to automate the work, modeling business processes has become essential. Modeling helps not only to understand processes but also to anticipate changes and build a flexible structure. In Chapter 7, "*A Method for Business Process Reverse-Engineering Based on a Multi-view Metamodel,*" Cheikh, Front and Rieu adopt from software engineering the concept of reverse-engineering. For organizations with unmodeled BP, reverse-engineering is a way to provide process models ready for improvement or usage in other stages of the business process lifecycle. This chapter proposes a method for business process reverse-engineering fulfilling these requirements. It consists of a multi-view metamodel, covering all perspectives of a process, and a detailed approach to guide the business process modeler. The approach was tested on a web application from the French academic Information Systems.

The five chapters of Section 3, "*Organizational Knowledge*" are concerned with managing and exploiting organizational knowledge regarding the needs to support business decision-making.

Paulo Garrido, in "*Conversation-Oriented Decision Support Systems for Organizations,*" proposes concepts for designing and developing decision support systems that acknowledge, explore and exploit the fact that conversations among people are the top-level "supporting device" for decision-making. The goal is to design systems that support, configure and induce increasingly effective and efficient decision-making conversations. The proposal sees the sum total of decisions being taken in an organization as the global decision process of the organization. The global decision process of the organization is structured in decision processes corresponding to organizational domains. Each organizational domain has associated a unit decision process. If the organizational domain contains organizational sub-domains, then its compound decision process is the union and composition of its unit decision process and the unit decision processes of its sub-domains. The proposal can be seen as extending, enlarging and integrating group decision support systems into an organization-wide system. The resulting organizational decision support system, by its conversational nature, may become the kernel decision support system of an organization or enterprise. In this way, the global decision process of the organization may be made explicit and monitored.

In Chapter 9, "*Representing organizational conservation of information: A Review of Telemedicine and e-Health in Georgia,*" Stachura, Astapova, Wood, Tung, Sofge, Grayson, Lawless and Angjellari-Dajci review a model of the conservation of information (COI) applied to organizations. Following this review, the chapter includes a brief review of the mathematics in support of this model and its implications for the development of theory. Then the model is applyed to a review of the status of telemedicine and e-health in Georgia, which the authors had begun to study last year. After the reviews, they discuss future steps and draw conclusions about the model and its benefit to organizational attention and decision-making.

A firm's capability to transfer its existing knowledge to various stakeholders and translate knowledge into action determines its success in today's volatile global business environment. However, while many firms systematically manage data and information, managing knowledge remains a controversial issue. One of the reasons for this is inconclusiveness about what knowledge is and whether it can be managed. In order to more precisely define knowledge and its management, the author proposes a knowledge warehouse conceptual model (KW-CM) for practically and systematically assimilating of knowledge within organizational business processes. This conceptual model presented in Chapter 10, "*A Conceptual Model of a Knowledge Warehouse*" by Levy integrates aspects of knowledge that encompass business processes, stakeholders and other organizational information systems within the existing data warehouse (DW) conceptual model. In addition, the chapter presents a formal architecture, definitions and guidelines that describe the KW components and processes for leveraging data and information into knowledge. The proposed KW-CM is demonstrated with an example of a DW which handles information regarding customer product usage.

Over the years many organizations have invested in Business Intelligence (BI) systems. While BI-software enables organization-wide decision support, problems are encountered in the "fit" between systems' provision and changing requirements of a growing amount of BI (end-) users. In Chapter 11, "*BI-FIT: Aligning Business Intelligence end-users, tasks and technologies*" Tijsen, Spruit, van de Ridder and van Raaij aim at investigating the factors that influence the "fit" between Business Intelligence (BI) end-users, tasks and technologies (BI-FIT). Based on an extensive literature study on the elements of BI-FIT, in this research the BI-FIT Framework is developed that shows the most relevant factors and the interrelationships between BI end-users, tasks and technologies. The framework can be used to help organizations to identify and fulfill the needs of BI end-users, thereby improving adoption and increasing satisfaction of the BI end-user base.

Chapter 12, "*Information Management Process in Continuous Improvement Area at Worldwide Steel Company,*" by Alves and Neves, presents specific features concerning information management in the Continuous Improvement area of the Americas Long Carbon sector in ArcelorMittal. The aim is also to learn what the informational resources related to continuous improvement area are and describe how the process of managing information actually happens. The study was based on theoretical models of Davenport (1998) and Choo (2006) and tried to understand how the efficient management of information can aid in decision making at organizations. The result of the documentary research revealed the existence of initiatives throughout the different units in the Americas and also revealed corporate tools for information management. The field research results indicate the need for a structured and formalized model of information management that responds to users in adequate time, while alert to the need for policies that encourage the sharing of information related to the improvement of processes, products and services.

The five chapters of Section 4 *"EIS Design, Application, Implementation and Impact"* address the tremendous challenge associated to the design and implementation of Enterprise Information Systems in organizations.

The new market trends are forcing companies to constantly reorganize their business processes so that they can react quickly to the new economic challenges. Although not always, enterprise information systems provide an appropriate response to these situations due to several reasons, such as technology failure, lack of adaptable configuration tools or even the financial investment required, which makes it unaffordable to companies. Almeida and Azevedo, in Chapter 13, *"The Needed Adaptability for ERP Systems"* present a functional model for ERP systems (called FME) that would guarantee a baseline structure to build solutions which would provide a complete configuration and, therefore, a timely reaction to market fluctuations. This model also summarizes some of the most used functionalities of the available ERP systems

Quality is, in real-life, a multidimensional notion. A schedule is described and valued on the basis of a number of criteria, for example: makespan, work-in-process inventories, idle times, observance of due dates, etc. An appropriate schedule cannot be obtained unless one observes the whole set of important criteria. The multidimensional nature of the scheduling problems leads us to the area of Multicriteria Optmization. Thus considering combinatorial problems with more than one criterion is more relevant in the context of real-life scheduling problems. Research in this important field has been scarce when compared to research in single-criterion scheduling. The proliferation of metaheuristic techniques has encouraged researchers to apply them to combinatorial optimization problems. Chapter 14, *"Multicriteria Flow-Shop Scheduling Problem"* by Mokotoff, presents a review regarding multicriteria flow-shop scheduling problem, focusing on Multi-Objective Combinatorial Optimization theory, including recent developments considering more than one optimization criterion, followed by a summary discussion on research directions.

Research about ERP post-implementation and ERP assimilation is very limited. Similarly, scant research investigated ERP experiences in developing countries. Based on a qualitative research methodology grounded in the diffusion of innovations theory, the study presented by Kouki, Pellerin and Poulin in Chapter 15, *"Beyond ERP Implementation: an Integrative Framework for Higher Success"* aims at investigating the determining contextual factors for ERP assimilation. A cross-case study analysis of four firms in a developed and a developing country suggests that in both contexts, the primary factor for encouraging a successful ERP assimilation is top management support. Other factors such as post-implementation training and education, IT support, organizational culture, managers and users involvement, strategic alignment, external pressures and consultant effectiveness are also identified as factors that influence ERP assimilation. Several assimilation impediments that should be watched are also specified.

A large number of firms worldwide have made major investments in the application of ERP systems to modify their business model and be able to offer better processes. When firms implement ERP systems they try to integrate and optimize their processes in what they consider their key areas. In Chapter 16, *"An Exploratory Analysis for ERPs Value Creation,"* C. de Pablos and M. de Pablos offer a view centred on the main reasons why Spanish firms have implemented ERP systems in the last ten years and what have been their main critical success factors and their main failure factors too. For that, the authors apply a model based in 5 main groups of variables. Firms were inquired about their perceptions and final results provided by the variables affecting their change processes in the ERP implementation.

Enterprise systems are becoming more important as they support the efficiency and effectiveness of operations and reduce cost. In Chapter 17, *"Production Information Systems Usability in Jordan,"* Abu-Shanab and Al-Tarawneh explore the literature related to production information systems (PIS), enterprise systems, and other applications and their influence in an industrial zone in Jordan. Constructs from the Innovation Diffusion Theory were used, where results indicated that the adoption rate is acceptable and all variables have high means with respect to their evaluation by managers, but only two variable significantly predicted intention to use. In a second study that explored the status of IT usage in manufacturing firms using a different sample, results indicated that accounting information systems were widely used and distribution systems and manufacturing aiding systems were the least used.

Section 5, *"EIS Adoption"* is concerned with studying and measuring the utilization, impact, and difficulties associated with Enterprise Information Systems adoption, along its four chapters.

#### Chapter 18

As the deployment of ERP systems within enterprises is increasing, it is of extreme interest to measure the degree of utilization of ERP systems. One reason for this interest is that no benefits are realized if the systems are not used; since ERPs are massive investments, they need to show benefits, or at least be able to measure the benefits. However, to be able to do so, there is a need to explain ERP systems utilization and the factors that influence ERP utilization. Jonas and Björn in *"Measuring Utilization of ERP Systems Usage in SMEs"* provide an explanation of factors influencing ERP systems utilization by testing a research model building on four dimensions: volume, breadth, diversity, and depth. The contributions of the research are: First, it provides support for the notion of diffusion found in the theory of network externalities where a critical mass is necessary to achieve benefits. This can be used to better understand failures in ERP projects. Second, the use of volume, breadth and depth provide insights for use as a construct and the need to treat it more rigorously. Third, the study contributes to our understanding of the many aspects of use of IT, such as ERPs, and potentially contributes to value and firm performance from ERP utilization.

There has been an increasing interest in ERP systems in both research and practice in the last decade. But unfortunately in many occasions a lot of companies have stopped using these systems after they went-live with the implementation. Chapter 19, *"Factors Influencing Users' Intention to Continue Using ERP Systems"* by Elragal and Birry is an attempt to reveal the factors influencing users' intention to continue using the ERP system. A survey was sent to respondent gaining a number of 223 responses. A hypothesized model was developed based on three theories; TAM, ECT, and TPB. The model was tested using regression analysis of the collected responses. Results showed that users' intension to continue using the ERP systems are affected by: perceived usefulness, satisfaction, subjective norm, and perceived behavior control. Meanwhile, perceived usefulness is affected by confirmation and subjective norm while satisfaction is affected by perceived usefulness and confirmation.

Chapter 20 *"ERP System Selection Criteria: The Case of Companies in Slovenia"* by Pucihar, Lenart and Sudzina, propose a possible model of criteria for ERP system selection. The proposed model consists of four groups of ERP system selection criteria: the ERP systems benefits criteria, the system quality criteria, the vendor related criteria and the ERP system package criteria. The data were collected in companies in Slovenia. Research results have confirmed internal consistency of ERP selection criteria in each group. For each criterion the importance is evaluated by small, medium-sized and large companies. Beside that also company size, implemented information strategy, representation of the IT department on the board level in the company and turnover impact on importance of each criterion is evaluated and presented. The model presented in this chapter could be useful for ERP system providers to better understand companies' needs and to provide systems tailored for individual needs of the company. The model could also be useful for companies considering ERP system implementation to avoid high costs of failed implementations.

Nowadays, the WWW is playing a vital role in the business world. Most enterprises are becoming digital. Content management systems provide an effective method to improve the development of web applications and make the maintainer's job easier. The purpose of Chapter 21, "*INOVA Framework: A Case Study of the use of Web Technologies for the Integration of Consulting Techniques and Procedures,*" by Borrajo Enríquez, Saco, Cotos, Casal and Larsson is to present and discuss the benefits that the use of web technologies can represent for an SME company when they are applied to integrate their work techniques and procedures. The authors have also tried to use it to provide their customers with several services, and to make easier the company expansion process. The framework developed includes a security system for the access to the contents based on the RBAC model. The use of the INOVA framework has provided a benefit as much for INOVA itself, as for its customers, by including in a centralized way document resources and toolkits that can be accessed remotely.

The social and professional side of EIS plays a central role in EIS adoption as demonstrated in the two chapters of Section 6, "*EIS Social Aspects*".

Modern business environments require innovated business concepts. Meeting them in enterprises' functioning depends also on creation and implementation of appropriate information support. In terms of contents, information support and information must be reliable to not be misinformation; information and communication technology is not enough for it because information means impact. Potential errors on the long path from data to information must hence be prevented. A one-sided approach, which belongs to the practices of professionals as narrow specialists, can prevent errors and misinformation rarely – when rather one-sided information is enough. More complex situation and processes require a more holistic approach that, in its turn, requires interdisciplinary creative co-operation of specialists of various interdependent professions. Potocan and Mulej, in "*Crucial Consequences of Un-Holistic Business Information,*" contribute to the discussion about reliability of information by thinking how can one tackle the data-to-information-to-decision process in order to diminish dangers of poor reliability of information/decision.

Google, eBay, Amazon, Facebook, Myspace, Craig's List and their foreign equivalents, such as the Chinese QQ and Baidu, for example, are ostensibly complex, and – more troublesome - their attitudes are becoming increasingly contradictory, controversial, and conflicted: For one, Tom Malone's decade-old predictions of a decentralized network of a multitude of small, cooperating firms did not materialize; to the contrary and counter to the spirit of the democratic nature of information and information technology, these e-giants are defining their own industries and defying regulation, submitting the participants in their respective markets to proprietary rules via three central tenets: regulatory capture, regulatory arbitrage, and regulatory opportunism. In Chapter 23, "*The Social Cost of Social Value Creation: An Exploratory Inquiry into the Ambivalent Nature of Complex Information Technology Intensive Firms,*" Jelen and Kolakovic criticize and explore these traits of the Complex Information Technology-Intensive firms and formulate elements of a framework for their ambiguous nature that may lead to social cost exceeding their initially glorified social value creation.

The five chapters of Section 7, "*IT/IS Management*" address strategies, processes and tools for information systems and information technology implementation and management.

Contact Centers have experienced exceptional growth over the past decade, and Contact Center's projects are complex because occur in a multidisciplinary area with multiple actors and constraints. Information systems play a decisive role in these projects. However, several studies indicate a low success level of information and communications technology projects leading to research opportunities for their improvement. In their previous research, authors have identified a framework with the key factors to be considered in these projects. Due to the highly dynamic reality of the Contact Centers, the framework must evolve in order to maintain its usefulness for project managers and other center professionals. Focus groups are interactive discussion groups used for generating knowledge and hypotheses, exploring opinions, attitudes and attributes. In this way, the study presented in *"Information systems projects in contact centers"* by Rijo, Varajão and Gonçalves aims to verify, expand and actualize the existent framework, using a focus group with professionals in the area.

As World economy lingers it is increasingly more important to justify any investment so that available corporate funds are spent wisely. However, estimating the value of ITIL investments is not an easy task, which means that most CIOs do not invest in large-scale ITIL projects as much as it would be desirable. Instead, CIOs prefer to embark on quick win implementations (e.g. solely implement the incident management process). In Chapter 25, *"A Process for Estimating the Value of ITIL Implementations,"* Oliveira, Furtado da Silva and Mira da Silva propose an ITIL Value Estimator. This estimator is based on an estimation process that quantifies the project's total cost, along with each process' benefits. The outcome of the ITIL Value Estimator is a Monte Carlo simulation whose result provides CIOs with a justification of the value of large-scale ITIL implementations, which can be used to gain the upper hand during the decision-making process.

Information Systems (IS) Outsourcing has emerged as a strategic option to be considered and has been increasingly adopted by managers. However, many contracts still fail during their initial years, meaning that Outsourcing has also been subject to strong criticism. There are advantages to Outsourcing but also significant risks associated to it, and the assessment of both is therefore of great relevance for informed decision-making. The objective of Chapter 26, *"Information Systems Outsourcing: Risks and Benefits for Organizations"* authored by André and Sampaio, is to determine to what extent a common view about risks and benefits associated to IS Outsourcing is shared by the Portuguese market players – Service Providers, Clients and Opinion Makers. In order to accomplish this, an on-line Delphi study was conducted, combined with the Q-sort technique, which allowed to obtain the perspective of each player on the risks and benefits IS Outsourcing. Comparing these perspectives it was possible to understand that the market players don't share the same point of view.

The main objective of Chapter 27, *"INMATE- Innovation Management Technique: An Innovation Management Tool with Emphasis on IT-Information Technology"* authored by Cavalcanti, is to present an innovative tool for innovation management with emphasis to the information technology-IT management called INMATE. In order to arrive at this tool an analysis on the current market tools was conducted. This analysis observed that none of the existent tools gives the due importance to the role of information technology-IT for the innovation process. The chapter presents a brief discussion of two of these market tools: an international, called TEMAGUIDE, and a Brazilian, called NUGIN. And then it introduces the INMATE tool with its main dimensions and gives detailed account on how the IT management is dealt inside INMATE, which is done via the concept of Enterprise Architecture, a concept from the Computing Science and Engineering. From this concept the chapter presents a methodology, in an analogy to the Structure-Conduct-Performance Paradigm (that is traditionally used on the empirical market analysis), which identifies the firm according to three linear connected approaches: its architecture, its governance, and its growth strategy.

Corporate governance is a key element today in organizations and companies. IT Governance, as a part of corporate governance, plays its role in aligning IT with the business and obtaining the maximum value, minimizing the risks. Several frameworks and guidelines have been published in order to set the basis for this discipline. The recent release of the ISO 38500 (ISO 2008) ads an effort to standardize the different elements of IT governance. Despite these efforts, none of the different frameworks or guidelines is focused on the specific characteristics of small and medium companies (SMOs), although the authors consider that their conclusions are universal. Furthermore, there is no research so far that analyzed the status of IT governance in Spanish organizations. In Chapter 28, *"Analysis of IT Governance in Spanish Organizations,"* Arroyo and Carrillo Verdún present a research to identify the state of the art of IT governance in the Spanish small and medium organizations.

Organizations no longer live inside their four walls. Section 8, *"Collaborative, Networked and Virtual Organizations"* presents collaboration tools and environments regarding the exploitation of the concept of distributed, virtual and collaborative organizational models.

Today, product development is a result of a collaborative networked design process. Taking into consideration this fact, a National Research Network for Integrated Product and Process Engineering (INPRO) has been created. George and Anca Draghici, in Chapter 29, *"Multisite PLM Platform: A Collaborative Design Environment"* present the relevant items for building a PLM multisite platform for collaborative integrated product development based on the common researches developed in the IN-PRO project and network. The authors discuss this approach by presenting the collaborative distributed design process, the product model and the PLM multisite platform for collaborative integrated product development. Based on these was built a collaborative multisite platform that join together the methodology, methods and tools for Product Lifecycle Management (PLM), Knowledge Management (KM) and Human Resources Management (HRU), examples of good practice. The core of the proposed approach is the product lifecycle model which is the base for the proposed collaborative product development methodology and the multisite PLM platform architecture.

In Chapter 30, *"Virtual Center for Entrepreneurship Development,"* Anca Draghici, Izvercianu and George Draghici present a preliminary approach for building a virtual center for entrepreneurship development that will be implemented in a university research network in Romania. The authors argue the most relevant aspects that conduct them to an organizational information system design, implementation and management with double role: education (entrepreneurial skills development in the case of students) and research (new competencies development by a-learning future programs). The following items are presented: (1) the training needs for business creation - based on a preliminary market research developed with subjects with technical and economical background and that allow the identification of the entrepreneurial knowledge; (2) the university entrepreneurial education as a process of knowledge transfer; (3) preliminary design and architecture of the virtual center for entrepreneurship. Finally, some relevant conclusions and the future researches directions are presented.

The focus of manufacturing planning and control has gradually expanded from (in-house) production activities towards all manufacturing and logistics activities in the supply chain. Planning of in-house operations is still very important, but the trends towards increased use of outsourcing and mass customisation require that customers and suppliers are able to exchange information frequently to cut down costs and lead time while quickly adapting their manufacturing and logistics operations to market/customer requirements. Many vendors offer systems to plan and control in-house operations, whereas only a few large vendors (such as Oracle, SAP and I2) offer supply chain planning systems. This limits the ability for SMEs to exploit the supply chain planning options. In Chapter 31 *"Collaborative Demand and Supply Planning Networks,"* Hvolby, Steger-Jensen, Alfnes and Dreyer discuss current supply chain planning solutions and presents a more simple and adaptive concept to be used in both SMEs and larger enterprises.

EXPECTATIONS

The book provides researchers, scholars, professionals with some of the most advanced research, solutions and discussions of Enterprise Information Systems design, implementation and management and is targeted to be read by academics (teachers, researchers and students of several graduate and postgraduate courses) and by professionals of Information Technology, IT managers, Information Resources managers, Enterprise managers (including top level managers), and also technology solutions developers.

We strongly hope it meets your expectations!

The Editors,

Maria Manuela Cruz-Cunha
João Eduardo Varajão

Ofir, January 2010

ENDNOTE

[1]   Strong, D. M., & Volkoff, O. (2004). A Roadmap for Enterprise System Implementation. *Computer-Aided Design & Applications, 37*(6), 22-29.

Acknowledgment

Editing a book is a quite hard but involves a set of enriching activities of discussion and exchange of ideas and experiences, process management, organization and integration of contents, and many others, with the permanent objective of creating a book that meets the public expectations. And this task cannot be accomplished without a great help and support from many sources. As editors we would like to acknowledge the help, support and believe of all who made possible this creation.

First of all, the edition of this book would not have been possible without the ongoing professional support of the team of professionals of IGI Global. We are grateful to Dr. Mehdi Khosrow-Pour, to Mrs. Kristin Klinger, Director of Editorial Content, and to Mrs. Jan Travers, Managing Director, for the opportunity. A special mention of gratitude is due to Mrs. Christine Bufton, Assistant Development Editor, for her professional support and friendly words of advice, encouragement and prompt guidance.

Special thanks go also to all the staff at IGI Global, whose contributions throughout the process of production and making this book available all over the world was invaluable.

We are grateful to all the authors, for their insights and excellent contributions, which made possible this book.

Thank you.

The Editors,

Maria Manuela Cruz-Cunha
João Eduardo Varajão

January 2010

Section 1
Information Systems Architectures

Chapter 1
Applying Semantic SOA Based Model to Business Applications

Tariq Mahmoud
Carl von Ossietzky University, Germany

Jorge Marx Gómez
Carl von Ossietzky University, Germany

ABSTRACT

Nowadays, it becomes more and more critical and essential for the vendors in the business-related markets to tailor their products and software to meet the needs of the Small and Medium Businesses (SMB) since their market share has been enormously raised and the issues related to the Business-to-Business (B2B) environment are becoming great challenges to be considered. The semantic Service-Oriented Architecture (SOA)-based model involves Semantic Web Services to be applied in business environments in order to have a consistent framework that makes the data understandable for both humans and machines. The ultimate goal for using the authors' proposed model is to transfer the enterprise Web into a medium through which data and applications can be automatically understood and processed. The main components of the proposed model and the vision of applying it to one of the business solutions will be illustrated in order to show how these components can work together to overcome the traditional SOA-based solutions weakness.

INTRODUCTION AND PROBLEM DEFINITION

Large scale, dynamics, and heterogeneity of Web Services may hinder any attempt for understanding their semantics and hence outsourcing them.

This calls for techniques to organize the Web Services in a way that they can be efficiently understood and outsourced. The Web becomes a very helpful environment to share and extract the information from multiple sources that were not accessible previously. Web data had designed in a way that it is understandable for humans and

DOI: 10.4018/978-1-61692-020-3.ch001

one of the main obstacles which have to be considered in such context is the lack of semantics that is critical to enable machines understanding and automatically processing the data which they can now only display.

A lot of companies moved their entire information infrastructures towards the Web platform by applying SOA-based solutions, offering a unified and standardized access for customers, suppliers and employees to the information and services offered by those companies (Brehm et al., 2008) (Cardoso, Hepp & Lytras, 2007).

Web-Service-enabled SOA solutions are completely depending on common Web Service (WS) technologies that allow interoperability by using standards like Universal Description Discovery and Integration (UDDI) (Clement et al., 2004), Web Service Description Language (WSDL) (Christensen et al., 2001), Simple Object Access Protocol (SOAP) (Mitra, 2003), etc.

Federated Enterprise Resource Planning (FERP) system is one of the Web-Service-enabled SOA solutions and it is developed by the Very Large Business Applications (VLBA) Department in Carl von Ossietzky University of Oldenburg (Brehm, Lübke & Marx-Gómez, 2007). It is based completely on standards. It allows the separation of local and remote functions whereby no local resources are wasted for unnecessary components. Furthermore, in FERP, single components are executable on small computers, which subsides the installation and maintenance costs by decreasing the degree of local system complexity (Brehm, Lübke & Marx-Gómez, 2007).

Since FERP is a SOA solution, it depends on typical Web Service technologies that allow interoperability by using standards like UDDI, WSDL, SOAP, etc. and it is based on the idea that business functionality is separated and published as services. In addition, this approach has some fundamental advantages that can be summarized as follows:

- Relying on standards provides a high degree of flexibility and offers an adaptable implementation;
- It becomes eventually possible to switch from a particular service to a different one without adaptions;
- The high ability of reusing the functionality.

According to this, FERP approach offers a solution to the problem of standards by avoiding the central point of integration which was often a bottleneck in the previous solutions, also it reduces the number of point-to-point adapters because each interface is based on WSDL and it can communicate with every other WSDL-enabled interface. What it does not solve is the problem of making the semantic documentation of such interfaces.

Moreover, SOA-based solutions lack (semi)-automatic service discovery, (semi)-automatic service composition, data and process interoperability. This means that nowadays the existing architecture of the enterprise Web has many defects such as lack of interoperability, massive unstructured data and an increasing number of various systems waiting to be linked (Hu et al., 2008). To address these problems, new approaches are being proposed and developed, and Semantic Web Services appears to be one of the soundest solutions as an important step on the road towards making the data understandable for both humans and machines in an automated manner.

On the one hand, Semantic Web is an evolving extension of the World Wide Web in which the semantics of information and services on the Web are well defined, making it possible for the Web to understand and satisfy the requests of people and machines to use the Web content (Berners-Lee, Hendler & Lassila, 2001). And on the other hand, research and industry have realized that the Semantic Web can facilitate the integration and interoperability of intra- and inter-business processes and systems, as well as enable the creation of global infrastructures for sharing documents and data, to ease and make the information searching and reusability more efficacious.

However, from one side the new emerging technologies in the world of Semantic Web makes the Semantic SOA techniques seem to be inaccurate to be used in terms of semanticizing the capabilities of Web Services and the requests of WS consumers because of the blurred representation of the involved ontology. And from the other side, traditional SOA-based solutions lack semantic documentation of WS interfaces (Mahmoud & Marx Gómez, 2008a), and that will return inaccurate information to the consumer.

Based on that, our proposed light weight Semantic SOA-based model will have the responsibility of splitting the semantic annotation from the core services in a way that both normal and Semantic Web Services (Studer, Grimm & Abecker, 2007) can be validated (Maximilien & Munindar, 2004) and used. This model will also provide a second level of WS classification by grouping Web Services in categories based on the area of interest named "WS clouds" which will entail their concepts from a predefined ontology, and this will be explained in details later in this chapter.

The rest of this chapter is structured as follows. As we intend to analyze the work that had been done in this domain we give an overview (section two) on the background information of SOA and its drawbacks, Semantic Web Services, main conceptual frameworks and their semantic execution environments. Afterwards, section three describes the methodology and the specifications of the proposed semantic SOA-based model we are developing as a work on progress. Section four summarizes the main outcomes behind semantic SOA-based model. Then we will provide our future research directions related to this model in section five and how we can enhance the efficiency and the performance in it, and an overall conclusion will be given in section six.

BACKGROUND

Service Oriented Architecture and its Drawbacks

Talking about Web Services, there are a lot of definitions that are describing the term of Web Services such as: a Web Service is a business function made available via the Internet by a service provider and accessible by clients that could be human users or software applications (Casati & Shan, 2001). It is defined by the W3C consortium as: a software system designed to support interoperable machine to machine interaction over a network (Booth et al., 2004). It can be also described as business functionalities that are:

- Programmatically Accessible: Web Services are mainly designed to be invoked by other Web Services and applications. They are distributed over the Web and accessible via widely deployed protocols such as HTTP and SMTP. Web Services must describe their capabilities to other services including their operations, input and output messages, and the way they can be invoked.
- Loosely Coupled: Communication among Web Services is document-based. Web Services generally communicate with each other by exchanging XML documents. The use of a document-based communication model provides loosely coupled relationships among Web Services.

Web Service is the main unit inside SOA and conceptually the main components in the SOA architecture are (Brehm et al., 2008):

- Web Service Provider: It creates a Web Service and possibly publishes its interface and access information to the service registry.

Figure 1. Activities within SOA

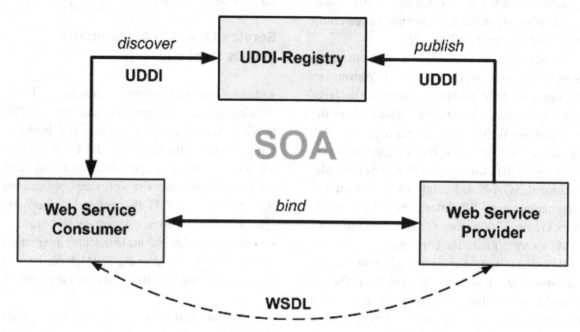

- UDDI-Registry: Also known as service broker, it is responsible for making the access information of both Web Service interface and implementation available to any potential service consumer, and categorizing the results in taxonomies. UDDI-registry defines the way to publish and discover information about Web Services.
- Web Service Consumer: The service consumer (requester) or Web Service client locates entries in the UDDI registry using various searching operations and then binds to the service provider in order to invoke one of its Web Services.

Figure 1 illustrates the mechanism of publishing, discovering and binding Web Services in SOA concept.

In this chapter, we are going to discuss the problems of the existing SOA-based solutions at the discovery and invocation phases. Firstly, traditional SOA service discovery problems can be described as follows: Web Services appear to become more widely adopted allowing much broader

intra- and inter-enterprise integration. However, developers will require automated systems for service discovery in order to enable further Web Service interactions with even less human effort. UDDI exists precisely for this reason. However, unless the service consumer knows the exact form and meaning of a service's WSDL specification in advance, the combination of UDDI with WSDL and coarse-grained business descriptions are not enough to allow fully automated service discovery and usage of Web Services.

Secondly, the service invocation problem which can be described in the terms of dealing with systems that might differ in its invocation method by providing different interfaces (public processes) for the semantical same operation (Bussler & Fensel, 2002). For example, one system offers product purchasing with one single invocation while another system requires first the process of creation a user, then activation of the user and finally the purchase of the product. Therefore, in the first system, one invocation completely defines a user whereas in the second system several interface invocations are necessary to achieve the same functionality. More important than the invocation is its specific execution messages order or process heterogeneity problem: the activation of the user cannot be achieved before the creation of this user.

By extending the concept of SOA with semantics, a formal description of the Web Service functionality will be provided to make it understandable by all the involved entities (humans and machines) and solutions for the problems discussed above are proposed.

Semantic Web Services

In the world of SOA, there is a dependency on standardized Web Services. By extending this concept with semantics, Semantic Web Services are proposed and presented. The most important tasks these semantic services have to accomplish are (OWL-S, 2004):

- Automatic Service Discovery: The ontology-enhanced searching schema is used to locate a particular WS that adheres to requested constraints;
- Automatic Service Invocation: Semantic WS description interface languages provide a set of declarative, computer interpretable APIs that are necessary for automated Web Service execution. A software agent is able to interpret the mark-up to understand what input is needed, what information will be returned, and how to execute the service automatically;
- Automatic Service Composition and Interoperation: Semantic WS description interface languages provide declarative specifications of the prerequisites and consequences of individual service. A software agent can select and compose multiple Web Services to achieve a given task automatically;
- Automatic Service Execution Monitoring: Semantic WS description interface lan-

guages aim at providing descriptors for the execution of services.

Semantic SOA Virtues

After the previous discussion about the problems of the SOA-based solutions, applying semantics on those solutions can overcome difficulties at both discovery and invocation phases.

As defined in the SOA concept, the main components in SOA architecture are service provider, registry and consumer. By extending existing SOA-based solutions with semantics, semantic SOA-based model will be provided, and this model will support the use of Semantic Web Services. In order to add semantics to these components' interactions, semantic descriptions will be added by the service providers to the Web Services they provide in order to be advertised then in the service registry. In addition, the consumer will send its request in form of a semantic goal by using the support of ontologies in order to describe the desired functionality. In this way, our proposed architecture will deal with semantic goals and matchmaking processes will be done with the available Web Services' capabilities in the registry in order to give the most related results back to the consumer and these results are based on the consumer needs by describing them as semantic goals. More details about these issues will be described later in the specifications of our proposed model with clear definition about the functionality provided by each component in it.

By extending FERP approach with semantics, we will provide a formal description of the Web Service functionality allowing the developers to make the manual integration, if necessary at all, on this knowledge about the meaning of the data (Mahmoud & Marx Gómez, 2008b).

Semantic-enriched FERP approach is actually the concept that supports the use of Semantic Web Services, and one of its duties is to overcome Web resources heterogeneity problems, since in such digital environment there is a need to deal with the differences in both ways; the way in which the consumer wants to use the functionality of a Web Service, and the way in which this functionality is made available by the Web Service back to the consumer.

In other words, one of the most important functionality of this model is to overcome the enterprise Web resources heterogeneity problems both at data and process level (Mahmoud & Marx Gómez, 2009), in addition to have a mechanism for dynamic composition of Web Services by grouping them in categories and implementing them semantically based on a predefined metadata ontology. That will ease the dynamic composition process by generating dynamic workflows that will have the responsibility of composing the desired services based on the concepts entailed from the existing ones.

In the proposed framework, light weight Semantic SOA-based solution will be used to enhance information searching and retrieving in an automated manner and the ultimate goal is to transform the enterprise Web into a medium through which data and applications can be automatically understood and processed.

Conceptual Frameworks

There are two main conceptual frameworks dealing with Semantic Web Services and defining main elements to semantically describe services: Web Service Modeling Ontology (WSMO) (Bussler et al., 2004) and Web Ontology Language for Services (OWL-S) (Burstein et al., 2004).

In addition, we are going to describe two execution environments: Internet Reasoning Service (IRS-III) (Cabral et al. 2004) and Web Service Execution Environment (WSMX) (Cimpian et al., 2005) that are following conceptual models defined in WSMO.

WSMO is a formal model for describing various aspects related to Semantic Web Services, and it is based on the Web Service Modeling Framework (WSMF) (Bussler & Fensel, 2002).

The objective of WSMO is to define a consistent technology for Semantic Web Services by providing the means for semi-automated discovery, composition and execution of Web Services based on logical inference-mechanisms. WSMO applies Web Service Modeling Language (WSML) as the underlying language based on different logical formalisms (Bussler & Fensel, 2002).

WSMO defines four main modeling elements for describing several aspects of Semantic Web Services (SWS) (Bruijn et al., 2007):

- Ontologies: Are formal explicit specifications of a shared conceptualization (Gruber, 1993). They link machine and human terminologies.
- Goals: Provide the means to express a high level description of a concrete task.
- Web Services: Define various aspects of Web Services' capabilities.
- Mediators: Bypass interpretability problems and there are four types of mediators: OO-Mediators that have the role of resolving possible representation mismatches between ontologies, GG-Mediators that have the role of linking two goals, WG-Mediators that link Web Services to goals, meaning that the Web Service can fulfill the goal to which it is linked and finally the WW-Mediators that are used for linking two Web Services in the context of automatic composition of Web Services.

OWL-S is ontology for describing Semantic Web Services represented in OWL. It combines the expressivity of description logics and the pragmatism found in the emerging Web Services standards, to describe services that can be expressed semantically and yet grounded within a well-defined data typing formalism. It is comprised of three top-level notions:

- Service Profile: Describes both the functional and non-functional properties of a

Web Service, for the purpose of service discovery (Burstein et al., 2004).

- Service Model: Contains descriptive information on the composition or orchestration of one or more services in terms of their constituent processes. This can be used for reasoning about possible compositions and controlling the service publishing and invocation.

- Service Grounding: Gives details of how to access the service, mapping from an abstract to a concrete specification for service usage.

Semantic Execution Environments

IRS-III is an infrastructure for publishing, locating, executing and composing Semantic Web Services; it is organized according to the WSMO framework.

The main features in IRS-III can be seen as follows (Cabral et al., 2005):

- It is based on SOAP messaging standard.

- It supports one-click publishing of standard programming code and it can automatically transform programming code (Java and Lisp are supported) into a Web Service, by automatically creating the appropriate wrapper.

- It supports capability-driven service execution which means that users of IRS-III can directly invoke Web Services via goals.

- It is programmable so users can substitute their own Semantic Web Services for some of the main IRS-III components, e.g. how Web Services are selected from a goal request or how complex services are executed.

IRS-III services are Web Service compatible so standard Web Services can be trivially published through the IRS-III and any IRS-III service automatically appears as a standard Web Service to other Web Service infrastructures.

Goals in IRS-III have inputs and outputs and IRS-III broker finds applicable Web Services via mediators where the mediator source is a goal. Also Web services have inputs and outputs inherited from goal descriptions and they are selected via assumption (in capability) (Cabral et al., 2005).

The difference between IRS-III and WSMO is that IRS-III has a new type of mediators called GW-Mediator that transforms goal inputs into Web Service inputs while WG-Mediator transforms Web Service output for a goal. It also has the type GInv-Mediator which mediates between two goal invocations and is specific to runtime compositions.

We had pointed IRS-III here in order to use it or to introduce similar mediator-based framework to solve the possible mismatches that might occur between Semantic Web Service descriptions and semantic goals in our proposed model.

WSMX is the last semantic execution environment about which we are going to speak. WSMX is the reference implementation of WSMO and it is an execution environment for dynamic discovery, mediation and invocation of Web Services, it offers also a complete support for interacting with Semantic Web Services. WSMX supports the interaction with non-WSMO Web Services (classical ones), ensuring that the interaction with existing Web Services is totally possible.

In our future work, we will try to find a medium in which we can include some of the relevant methods and functionalities mentioned above and to develop a mediator-based framework to solve the possible mismatches that might occur between Semantic Web Service descriptions and semantic goals.

SEMANTIC SOA-BASED MODEL

The main idea behind this model is to have an ontology that has the role of dealing with Semantic Web Services as well as representing the whole concepts of a WS; it has also category type and generic operations divided to syntactic, semantic, behavioral and qualitative operations. Starting from this point, new categorizing level has to be done by the help of cloud provider (see next paragraph) who will have the responsibility of grouping WSs in clouds. The classifying will be based on the business domain of interest, each of these clouds is itself a WS and the cloud provider will advertise them in the WS directory.

At this point the WS provider system will search in the directory for its cloud based on its business domain's interests and will register itself in one of them to later on entail the required concepts out of that cloud and implement its own WSs to be registered also in it, and if there is no cloud matches with its purposes, the service provider will ask the cloud provider to create a new one and advertise it in the directory as well, and here the concepts will be inherit from the metadata cloud ontology.

The process of adding semantic on WS request and capability will take benefits from the semantic mediator-based system functionality by submitting semantic goal to be fulfilled with SWS capability. The mediation issues will be also applied depending on the variety of mediators provided by the mediator-based system as well.

At the later stages, the model will be applied on one of the business applications like ERP to have semi-automated solution in the ERP world, and by using a workflow system we can use the market best practices by storing workflows in an internal database. Everything mentioned here will be described later on in more details in the following sections.

Component Description

The Semantic SOA-based model has the following components:

- User System: Implements functions that will be used in the end users interfaces.

This subsystem is able to generate user screens at runtime.

- Workflow System: Deals with business processes described in an appropriate XML-based workflow language.
- Web Service Consumer System: Contains XML schema definitions and functions needed for the processes of WS discovery and invocation provided by different service providers.
- Web Service Provider System: It deals with HTTP incoming and outgoing user's requests and contains functions required for providing Web Services, and has connection to WS directory to allow the publication of them. And it has also a connection to the validation system in order to validate its Web Services before being annotated with semantics.
- Web Service Directory: Its interface has the responsibility of the publication and searching for WSs following the highly defined WS requests (semantic goals) provided by the WS consumer system, it resides in the validation system and has a link to the validation repository so that it can store data about Web Services to be used for the validation process.
- Semantic Web Service System: The main two entities that have interactions with this component are the cloud ontology and the clouds. The cloud ontology is a metadata ontology that serves as a base to provide concepts leading the process of creating the clouds and the Web Services within them by enabling derivation of the concepts descriptions from the ontology. The clouds are defined by the cloud provider. Clouds are services themselves, and can be created, advertised, discovered and invoked in the traditional way. Each cloud has a category type and generic operations. In addition, clouds are published in the WS

Directory in order to let the service providers discovering them to later on register their services as members in them.

- Cloud Provider: Will define the clouds as instances of the cloud ontology by assigning values to its concepts. The cloud providers can be normal service providers or businesses that share common point of interest (non-profit and in most cases profit organizations).
- Semantic Mediator-based System: Has the responsibility of solving the heterogeneity issues that might occur between the semantic goals provided by WS consumer system and the semantic descriptions of the clouds' capabilities by performing the matchmaking and filtering results processes. The mediator-based system may be embedded in a middleware as depicted in the Figure 2, or it can be an external WS that accomplishes the mediating scenarios at run-time in a way that lessens the load of mediation process. This loose coupling promotes reusability and facilitates dynamic partner binding, especially at run-time. These issues are to be considered in our future work.
- Validator: It is the interface that has the responsibility of tunneling the communication between the WS capabilities and concepts derived from the clouds in the semantic WS system and also monitoring the non-functional properties of WS.
- Validation Repository: It has the functionality of calculating the values of the WS non-functional properties in order to forward it to the validator interface to make the proper mapping decisions and it also contains the relations between concepts that are entailed from the existing domain ontologies outside this model.
- Cloud Directory: It is the directory of clouds and it will store data about Web Services to be used for the validation, all

the clouds will be provided via the cloud provider system. For better understanding of the abovementioned specifications, Figure 2 depicts these components and the relations between them in the proposed model.

System Interactions

In this new model, the interactions can be detailed as follows:

- The cloud provider will define clouds as instances of the cloud ontology and the clouds then will be published in the cloud directory so that the WS providers can discover them.
- Via the validator's interfaces, service providers will identify the cloud of interest and register their Web Services within it after adding the semantic descriptions on them, and during this stage the provider specifies the cloud concepts that are inherited by its WSs (only some of the generic operations) and register them in the appropriate cloud together with publishing them in the WS directory after applying the proper validation (see next paragraph). In the case that the service will be shared between multiple clouds, the provider will register it in all of them.
- The workflow system will execute a workflow using an appropriate XML-based workflow engine like Yet Another Workflow Language (YAWL) (van der Aalst, ter Hofstede, 2005) or any other dynamic workflow engines and will pass the WS request to the WS consumer system.
- WS consumer system will have the responsibility of searching for desired services, and that is done by sending its request to WS directory.
- At this stage, the request will be forwarded to the semantic mediator-based framework

Figure 2. Semantic SOA-based model for business applications

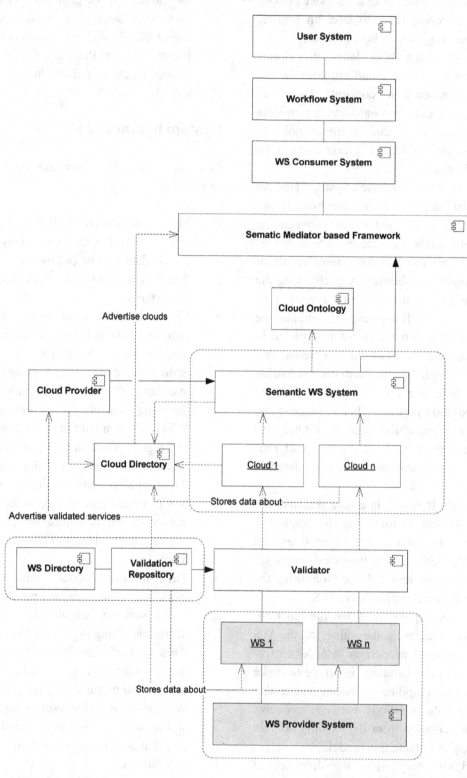

that applies semantics on the request transforming it to a semantic goal by adding, discovering or using existing suitable semantic inputs. The mediating framework then forwards the semantic goal to the WS directory and applies the matchmaking process (Agarwal & Studer, 2006) between the goals and capabilities in order to return firstly the appropriate cloud and consequently to invoke one of its Web Services (which are registered by the provider).

- It might happen that more than one WS fulfills the semantic goal, and at this point, a dynamic workflow is generated in order to compose the desired WS (if possible and depending on having such functionality in the Web Services advertised in the directory). In this case, a composite service may outsource operations that have different domains of interest and since these operations belong to two or more different clouds, the new composite service has to be registered in all of them.
- Each invocation of a cloud operation is translated into the invocation of one of its Web Services.

  The proposed architecture will be applied on FERP system that consists of components that are distributed within a computer network (Brehm & Marx Gómez, 2005) (Brehm, Marx Gómez & Strack, 2007). FERP reference architecture is based on the concepts of SOA, and it is an execution environment for discovery and invocation of enterprise Web Services, it offers also a complete support for interacting with Web Services within the enterprise space or among enterprises. Because one of the main objectives of the FERP system is to integrate business components of different vendors, all components have to comply with standards. In this approach, these standards are described as XML schema documents (Brehm & Marx Gómez, 2007).

To solve the problem of the standards in FERP system, semantics will be introduced and Semantic Web Services will be involved within the new system that will be responsible of the matchmaking, filtering results processes and applying dynamic Web Service composition.

WEB SERVICE VALIDATION WITHIN SEMANTIC SOA-BASED MODEL

Web Service Compliance

One goal of the semantic SOA-based model is to annotate information with semantic metadata. In contrast to other concepts, the annotation (Handschuh & Staab, 2003) here is not a part of the adopted Web Service itself. There is an isolated service, which is used to perform this annotation task. It is a precondition to validate the adopted WS against the external domain ontologies. The reason behind that resides in the issue that the user of an ontology expects that the service will work as the ontology describes, and the only way to insure this is to apply service validation.

We can classify the compliance of Web Services in four main different types:

- Exact: WS is able to comply with the requirements (WS properties).
- Over-Exact: WS has higher compliance than the requirements.
- Partial: WS is able to comply with the requirements fractionally.
- Failure: WS is not able to comply with the requirements.

An exact compliance is the ideal situation. In this case, a WS fulfills the expectations. An over-exact compliance is happening when the WS provides a higher level of quality more than

$$O_{request} := \{lastName, firstName, birthDate\} \qquad (1)$$

$$O_{divided} := \{d_1(lastName, firstName); d_2(email); d_3(birthDate)\} \qquad (2)$$

$$Mapping_{partial}\{d_2 \Rightarrow WS_1; d_3 \Rightarrow WS_2\} \qquad (3)$$

$$Mapping_{exact}\{d_1, d_2(WS_1), d_3(WS_2) \Rightarrow WS_3\} \qquad (4)$$

expected by the consumer. The partial compliance of a WS is happened when the requirements can be divided into logical parts. If the WS complies with a part, then it can be used to handle the information in collaboration with another Web Services. Failure compliance is happened when the WS does not comply with the request or parts of that request.

To clarify the abovementioned compliance types we can give the following example: suppose a data set about a customer that has to be validated and stored and it contains his first and last names, email and birth date. The validation of the email address and the birth date can be done partially and independently from storing the customer's information (see 2).

Web Services WS_1 and WS_2 are partially complaint to the request (see 1) where WS_1 complies with the customer's email address and WS_2 complies with his birth date (see 3). They are used to handle the validation. WS_3 (see 4) is an exact match because it complies with all of the customer's information and it will be used to store this information.

From a provider's perspective, this provides a possibility to integrate low capacity Web Services into ambitious requests by making crossing among the possible requests. But the challenge is to analyze the structure of the information by machines not by humans. To do so, the person within the ontology has to be broken down into properties.

Typically, literals are used to store information like the name of a person and in this way, a first name can be everything described as an array of characters. However, in the real world this is not totally true because there are small quantities of character combinations that are valid to be first names. Considering this fact, the correct data type for the property first name would be an enumeration or an object that contains a table of valid entries. An email address is not a random literal too and the previous example showed that the design of the ontology has to start at the level of the properties not the level of entities.

Another challenge is the reflection of an ontology to an information system. Even at the level of primitive data types, there are many possible incompatibilities. The size of an xsd:string for example is limited by the storage file system (Malhotra et al., 2009). It is not a big deal to create an xsd:string with the size of 3 Gbytes but it is not possible to load this string into a Java-based software because the Java:string length is limited to $(2^{31} - 1)$ bytes. If the data has to be stored in a database, which size is the right one for a text field? Another issues can be the handling of numbers, so if an xsd:PositiveInteger has to be handled, from one side the same problems will appear and from the other side there is no PositiveInteger data type in a lot of software platforms, and this will give the possibility to handle such invalid values from the ontology's perspective.

Design Aspects

After discussing the abovementioned issues, we can define ontologies at the lowest possible level and generalize more complex ontologies (see Figure 3). By doing so, it is important to think about two important points: Firstly, the ontology has to be implementable to work in an information system and secondly, the ontology definition has to be done by domain experts who define all the concepts that constitute such an ontology. The implementation needs to have positive and negative validation tests in order to prove the correctness of valid targeting range. Where the positive validation is occurred within the range of the targeting values and the negative validation occurs within the input values that are invalid and outside the range of targeting values.

The reader now might ask this: why should we do that? Typically, in an information system there are many layers where data are validated. The first layer is the user interface, where the user input is validated. However, even the user acts as a validator, because he knows the domain and can filter evidently wrong data. The next layer is the business logic layer that deals with the data and check the plausibility that might be repeated at the lower layers consequently.

This approach is correct, if we are working within an isolated system. But in SOA solutions, there is a good chance that different applications are using the same services, if these applications share data then the following problem might appear: an application assumes that the stored data are correct, and if the other application validates the data at a lower quality level, there is a risk to load invalid data. The only way to prevent this is to validate the data at the target service. This means, it is necessary that an object does not have only properties, attributes and methods to be existed rather it must be able to validate its own status!

Domain Specific Information

The explanation of the term domain specific information requires defining the word information. Related to the topic of semantics, we define information as data enriched by annotations. This means that the phrase <>Peter</> represents data while the phrase <firstname>Peter</firstname> represents information. Though there are still higher levels to take into account like knowledge or wisdom, but at this stage, we will only deal with information.

Semantics at the top level of the semantic SOA-based model are used to describe information while at the lower levels the difference between data and information can't be recognized easily. If the annotation of information is inaccurate then it represents only data to the user and not the user's desired information and this happens when the annotation does not represent the data in a sufficient way.

Example: If we consider this phrase: <fn>Peter</fn>, the consumer of this information can at first glance guess that the intended meaning behind this phrase is "first name", but he can't be sure. And for a computer system the interpretation is much harder, because the machine will not be able to use knowledge to process and understand the meaning of the annotation corresponding to the sample data. A solution for this problem is the involvement of semantic annotations and the ultimate goal behind its usage is to allow machines to interpret the date.

Split the Semantic Annotation from the Object

The semantic SOA-based model's validation layer provides the semantic annotation activity. Typically, a Web Service itself has the responsibility of adding the annotation. This means, the semantic information is added like the syntactic information in the Web Service response (Horrock, 2008). As

Figure 3. Type Inheritance

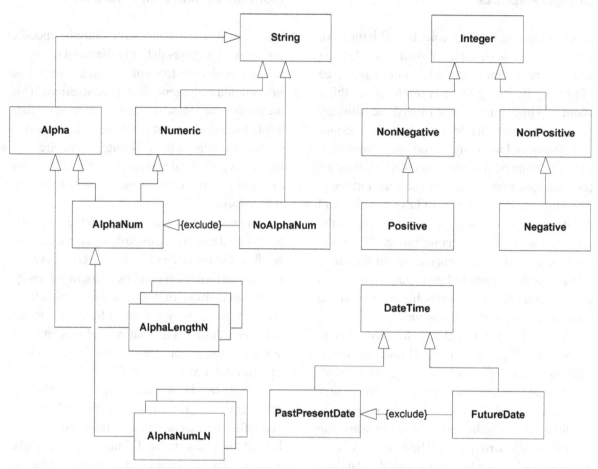

it first seemed, the separation adds no advantage to a system – it will slow down the system by having additive communication traffic.

As answer to the question of why this extra layer has been used? We have to consider some issues. First issue to consider is the reusability of existing Web Services: Normally, a Web Service does not provide any semantic annotations and in order to use it in the semantic SOA-based model, some changes have to be done on the Web Service. From the provider's perspective the problem is that there are different annotations for the used semantics and as a result, the provider has to implement different interfaces for its Web Services.

Second important point is the fulfillment of a semantic meaning: It is not correct to annotate

a Web Service in order to be adapted in the semantic SOA-based model, rather there is a need to validate whether a Web Service is dealing with information like expected or not. This means that, an annotated Web Service has to have exactly the same data ranges or data types like the annotation describes. And as a result, a Web Service needs to be validated against the semantic descriptions. The bundling of the annotation together with the test functions in a separate layer reduces the programming effort by enabling the reusability of those functionalities.

The third point to consider is the expressiveness of Web Services themselves: While data structures that are modeled to describe an object are often primitive, there is a high probability that a Web

Service is not only able to handle information for which it has been designed rather it can handle different information using different annotations.

Example:

For an application, there is the need to store data about an enterprise's employees. A manager is modeled in this way:

```
class manager:={first_
name:string,last_
name:string,born:date,job_
description:string}
```

A developer is modeled as follows:

```
class developer:={first_
name:string,last_
name:string,born:date,job_
description:string}
```

An object with the same attributes can represent both employees. In object-oriented programming (OOP) the solution would be the generalization of the class employee.

```
class employee:={first_
name:string,last_
name:string,born:date,job_
description:string}
class manager:employee
class developer:employee
```

The separation of the annotation from the Web Service itself allows using similar techniques to reduce the need of different services. Related to the previous example, the annotation created by the validator decides if an object is the representation of a manager or a developer.

Information Flow

In general, components used in SOA have to work within different applications. Consequently, the way that the validation of information performs is dissimilar to the way used in the closed systems where information is being validated at different systems layers. The first type of validation happens at the user/data interface. At the business logic layer, there are probably some functions that check the data from another perspective. At the data layer, triggers and stored procedures are used to validate the date from a third perspective. All these validations perspectives are together responsible for the validity of an object state.

At SOA, a component does not know which validation is done at which layer (or component). As a result, each component itself has to check the validity of an object state. More precisely, the object itself should be able to determine its correct state. In semantic SOA-based model, this functionality is realized in the validator component. The reason to determine the object state at this level is that it is the point where an object reaches its persistent state. An object stored in a database (represented by a Web Service) has to be in a correct state, because all the other components that are using this object expect its correctness. If an object can be interchanged between different applications, its state has to be validated too. The validator acts as a test library to support these requirements.

Each test represents an ontology or a part of it. The relation between an ontology and a test is documented using the Uniform Resource Identifier (URI) (Berners-Lee, 2005). As a result, the state of an object can be validated starting from the semantic level, which is the abstract ontology, down to the physical representation at the Web Services level.

Figure 4 illustrated this idea clearly, it shows that two different components A and B are using the same component C. Component A probably shares data via component C with component B.

The flow: {Semantic Interface → Component A → Component C → Validator} can be affected by the flow {Semantic Interface → Component B → Component C → Validator}.

Figure 4. Information flow in the semantic SOA-based model

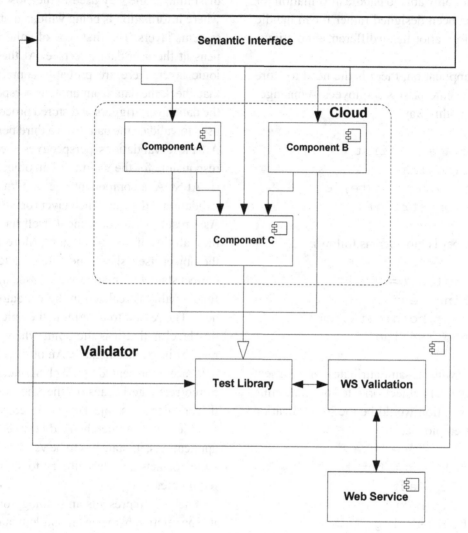

OUTCOMES OF SEMANTIC SOA-BASED MODEL

The main added values from this model over the existing related work can be summarized as follows:

1. Light Weight Semantic Solution: From one hand, the problems of SOA that occur at both discovery and invocation phases can be solved by using the proposed model and the reference architecture that will imple-ment it. From the other hand, applying light weight semantics in this model will reduce the complexity existing in Semantic SOA.

2. Reusability: The high ability of reusing the functionality in this model allows each component to be considered as a standalone system.

3. Generating Dynamic Workflows: In the process of composing a new service that does not exist in the directory, a dynamic workflow will be created in order to produce the new service, and based on the concepts that are

shared between services the desired service will be created. This approach will motivate the workflow designers to ask for new virtual Web Services that this new model can create. In addition, the workflows reusability is an important factor because the workflows will be stored in internal repositories to possibly take benefit from their functionality over and over.

4. Dynamic Composition of Web Services: Because the Web Services in this model have the same root metadata ontology, it will be easier to compose services based on semantic goals. And this dynamic composition means that the composed services will be registered within the cloud that it had been created in, and if it is shared between one or more clouds then it will be registered within all of them.

5. Categorizing of Web Services in Clouds: This will provide a second level of classification together with the traditional one in the service directories and this will make the WS searching mechanism more powerful and will improve the response time of the discovery phase activities and the performance as a whole.

6. Advertisement of New Web Services: In the case of desired functionalities absence, advertisements of new Web Services that implement such functionalities will be forwarded to the WS providers.

FUTURE RESEARCH DIRECTIONS

Our future directions will mainly focus on the model enhancement side by side with the implementation of full reference architecture out of this reference model. This will be done by checking the various data storage techniques that will be involved in the new model. Study of how to obfuscate information in order to use untrusted Web

Services within the model will be done where we can divide the WS objects into slices and forward these slices to the service providers to implement them as separate Web Services. Such a concept will be a great improvement for both consumer and provider sides.

From the consumer's perspective the main enhancements will be to find out that the security of information in the confidential context is highly enriched while from the provider's perspective the advantage is to deal with much more primitive data structures. As a result, the chance to reuse a Web Service will be highly improved.

Another important direction in our future work is how to ensure the availability of information within the model by proposing possible criteria to group Web Services like: I/O scalability or data redundancy...

Business architecture together with high-level semantic information model will be specified where the businecss architecture will act as a bridge between the adopted busines context and the semantic SOA-beased model; and the semantic information model will identify the major business entities and documents within the semantic SOA-based reference architecture.

A concrete methodology to perform dynamic Web Service composition will be defined. Trust and security issues also will be part of the future work.

CONCLUSION

In this chapter, the main focus was to introduce an ontological SOA-based model that deals with Semantic Web Services in order to apply it to one of the SOA-based business solutions like FERP system.

One of the main purposes of this model is to group the Web Services based on the actual domain that they are related to (the area of interest). All the components that are composing this model together with the interactions between them have been described in this chapter. We showed how the cloud ontology is used as a template to create clouds. Grouping Web Services in the clouds, defining semantic goals (highly defined WS requests), performing the matchmaking process between goals and Web Services, creating static and dynamic workflows and implementing them using workflow engines have been explained.

Web Service validation within this model has been clarified by defining the four types of Web Service compliance to aid ontologies design at the lowest possible level. We showed also how to split the semantic annotation from an object to reduce the need of using different services by assigning this task to the validator component in the model. Moreover, we listed the main outcomes that can be gained from adopting this model in business environments. Finally, prototype implementations of the future will show the practicability of these concepts.

REFERENCES

Agarwal, S., & Studer, R. (2006). Automatic Matchmaking of Web Services. In *International Conference on Web Services (ICWS'06)*.

Berners-Lee, T. (2005). *Uniform Resource Identifier (URI), Generic Syntax*. Retrieved from http://labs.apache.org/webarch/uri/rfc/rfc3986.html/

Berners-Lee, T., Hendler, J., & Lassila, O. (2001, May 17). The Semantic Web. *Scientific American Magazine*.

Booth, D., Champion, I. M., Ferris, C., Haas, H., McCabe, F., Newcomer, E., & Orchard, D. (2004). *Web Services Architecture*. Retrieved from http://www.w3.org/TR/ws-arch/

Brehm, N., Lübke, D., & Marx Gómez, J. (2007). Federated Enterprise Resource Planning (FERP) System . In *Handbook of Enterprise Systems Architecture in Practice* (pp. 294–297). Hershey, PA: IGI Global.

Brehm, N., Mahmoud, T., Marx-Gomez, J., & Memari, A. (2008). Towards Intelligent Discovery of Enterprise Architecture Services (IDEAS). *Journal of Enterprise Architecture, 4*(3), 26–37.

Brehm, N., & Marx Gómez, J. (2005). Standardization approach for Federated ERP systems based on Web Services. In *1st International Workshop on Engineering Service Compositions*, Amsterdam.

Brehm, N., & Marx Gómez, J. (2007). The Web Service-based combination of data and logic integration in Federated ERP systems. In *Proceedings of 18th IRMA International Conference - Managing Worldwide Operations and Communications with Information Technology (IRMA'2007)*, Vancouver, Canada (pp. 1559-1564).

Brehm, N., Marx Gómez, J., & Strack, H. (2007). Request-Response-Evaluation Infrastructure for trusted Web Service-based ERP Systems . In Rautenstrauch, C. (Ed.), *Die Zukunft der Anwendungssoftware – die Anwendungssoftware der Zukunft* (pp. 83–93). Aachen, Germany: Shaker.

Bruijn, J. D., Domingue, G., Fensel, D., Lausen, H., Polleres, A., Roman, D., & Stollberg, M. (2007). *Enabling Semantic Web Services, the Web Service Modeling Ontology*. Berlin: Springer.

Burstein, M., Martin, D., McDermott, D., McGuinness, D., McIlraith, S., Paolucci, M., et al. (2004). Bringing Semantics to Web Services: The OWL-S Approach. In *Proceedings of the First International Workshop on Semantic Web Services and Web Process Composition (SWSWPC 2004)*, July 6-9, San Diego, California, USA. Retrieved from http://www.daml.org/services/owl-s

Bussler, C., & Fensel, D. (2002). The Web Service Modeling Framework WSMF. *Electronic Commerce Research and Applications, 1*(2).

Bussler, C., Fensel, D., Keller, U., Kifer, M., Lausen, H., Oren, E., & Roman, D. (2004). *Web Service Modeling Ontology (WSMO)*. Retrieved from http://www.wsmo.org/2004/d2/v1.0/

Cabral, L., Domingue, J., Hakimpour, F., Motta, E., & Sell, D. (2004). A platform and infrastructure for creating WSMO based Semantic Web Services. In *WSMO Implementation Workshop*. Frankfurt, Germany: IRS III.

Cabral, L., Domingue, J., Hakimpour, F., Motta, E., & Sell, D. (2005). Semantic Web Service Composition in IRS III: The Structured Approach. In *International IEEE Conference on E-Commerce Technology*, Universität Münchin, Germany.

Cardoso, J., Hepp, M., & Lytras, M. (2007). *The Semantic Web: Real-World Applications from Industry*. Berlin: Springer.

Casati, F., & Shan, M.-C. (2001 May). Models and Languages for Describing and Discovering E-Services (Tutorial). In *Proceedings of the International ACM SIGMOD Conference on Management of Data*, Santa Barbara, CA.

Christensen, E., Curbera, F., Meredith, G., & Weerawarana, S. (2001). *Web services description language (WSDL) 1.1*. Retrieved from http://www.w3.org/TR/2001/NOTE-wsdl-20010315

Cimpian, E., Moran, M., Oren, E., Vitvar, T., & Zaremba, M. (2005). *Overview and Scope of WSMX*. Technical report. Retrieved from http://www.wsmo.org/TR/d13/d13.0/v0.2/

Clement, L., Hately, A., von Riegen, C., & Rogers, T. (2004). *UDDI version 3.0.2*. UDDI Spec Technical Committee Draft. Retrieved from http://uddi.org/pubs/uddi_v3.htm

Gruber, T. R. (1993). A translation approach to portable ontology specification. *Knowledge Acquisition, 5*(2), 199–220. doi:10.1006/knac.1993.1008

Handschuh, S., & Staab, S. (2003). *Annotation for the Semantic Web*.

Horrocks, I. (2008). Ontologies and the semantic web. *Communications of the ACM, 51*(12), 58–67. doi:10.1145/1409360.1409377

Hu, Y., Sun, X., Wei, P., & Yang, Q. (2008 September). Applying Semantic Web Services to Enterprise Web. In *The 6th International Conference on Manufacturing Research (ICMR08)*, Brunel University, UK.

Mahmoud, T., & Marx Gómez, J. (2008a). Semantic Web Services Process Mediation Using WSMX Concepts. In *Proceedings 20th International Conference on Systems Research, Informatics and Cybernetics (InterSymp-2008)*, Baden-Baden, Germany.

Mahmoud, T., & Marx Gómez, J. (2008b). *Integration of Semantic Web Services Principles in SOA to Solve EAI and ERP Scenarios*.

Mahmoud, T., & Marx Gómez, J. (2009). Towards Process Mediation in Semantic Service Oriented Architecture. In *Handbook of Research on Social Dimensions of Semantic Technologies and Web Services*. Hershey, PA: IGI Global.

Malhotra, A., Peterson, D., & Gao, S. Sperberg-McQueen. C. M. & Thompson, H. (2009). *W3C XML Schema Definition Language (XSD) 1.1 Part 2: Datatypes*. Retrieved from http://www.w3.org/TR/xmlschema11-2/

Maximilien, E., & Munindar, P. (2004). *Towards Autonomic Web Services Trust and Selection*. New York: ACM.

Mitra, N. (2003). *SOAP version 1.2 part 0: Primer*. W3C Recommendation. Retrieved from http://www.w3.org/TR/soap12-part0/

OWL-S. (2004). Semantic Markup for Web Services. W3C Member Submission, November 2004. Retrieved from http://www.w3.org/Submission/2004/SUBM-OWL-S-20041122/

Studer, R., Grimm, S., & Abecker, A. (2007). *Semantic Web Services: Concept, Technologies and Applications*. Heidelberg, Germany: Springer.

van der Aalst, W. M. P., & ter Hofstede, A. H. M. (2005). YAWL: Yet Another Workflow Language. *Information Systems*, *30*(4), 245–275. doi:10.1016/j.is.2004.02.002

Chapter 2
How to Use Information Technology Effectively to Achieve Business Objectives

António Gonçalves
Trás-os-Montes University, Portugal

Natália Serra
Polytechnic Institute of Setúbal, Portugal

José Serra
OLISIPO, Portugal

Pedro Sousa
Instituto Superior Técnico, Portugal

ABSTRACT

In this chapter the authors show, by using a case study, how it is possible to achieve the alignment between business and Information Technology (IT). It describes several phases of project development, from planning strategy, enterprise architecture, development of businesses supporting tools and keeping dynamic alignment between the business and the IT. The authors propose a framework, framed under an enterprise architecture that guarantees a high level of response to the applications development or configuration as improves its alignment to business by solving some limitations of traditional software development solutions namely: difficulty in gathering clients requirements, which should be supported by the applications; difficulty to connect the organisation processes used to answer the client, which must also be integrated in the applications and the difficulty to develop the applications that can follow the business cycle. To test the approach, this was applied to a real case study consisting in the configuration of an application that manages the relationship with the clients.

DOI: 10.4018/978-1-61692-020-3.ch002

Figure 1. Alignment between business and IT

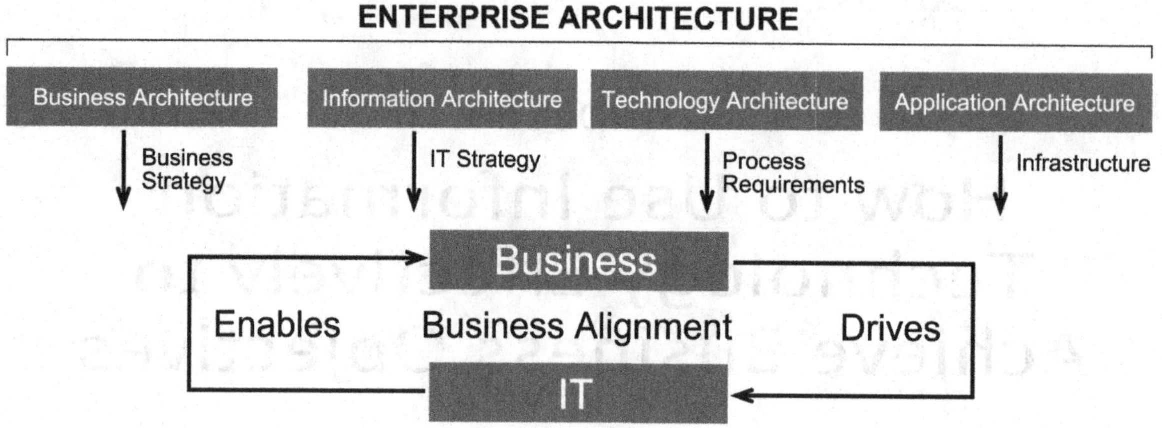

ENTERPRISE ARCHITECTURE

Business Architecture	Information Architecture	Technology Architecture	Application Architecture
Business Strategy	IT Strategy	Process Requirements	Infrastructure

Business

Enables   Business Alignment   Drives

IT

INTRODUCTION

The use made by the IT is recognised as crucial to the good performance of an organisation (Laudon, K., & Laudon, J., 2009). Different factors have been promoting and conditioning the changes on the IT namely (Spewak, S., 1993), (Henderson, J. C., & Venkatraman, N., 1993): minor duration of the company's business cycle; markets globalisation and group activities, competition and technologies revolution. Pressure for changing (Figure 1) may occur due to different reasons. For the new IT to be efficient, their development must be done in an organised way. The strategy of change of the IT must be consistent with the **business strategy**. This is the only way to justify the **investments on IT** (Amor, D, 2001) (Maes, R., 2000).

The framing of new technologies in the business offers great possibilities for the organisations that are able to benefit from the advantages of their use but it also means challenge to the IT management as the organisations become more dependent on them and their management specificity. In this complex scenario, the challenge means to identify the risks and the benefits that the IT represents to the organisation targets. In principle aspects, which are always present, are identified (Lankhorst, M.,

2009): administrative automation, rationalization of means and processes remodelling.

The main challenge of this work consists in defining frameworks that permit **aligning business strategies with applications.** For such it was used a modified version of the Hochin Kanri Matrix where the CRUD table, which allows the alignment of the business with the Information Systems, is introduced. At last, to promote the development of the applications it is proposed the introduction of some principles that may assure the success of applications, namely (Reich, B., 2000): simplify; automate and integrate.

As such, we use an approach to the development of applications that enable a continuous and fast increase in opposition to more complex and more expensive solutions whose development is prolonged over the time and represents a major risk of failure.

These works follow the concepts: what is **static alignment** and dynamic alignment between business strategy and IT. In the formulation definition phase, the alignment is made just once and sets the components of business planning and the IT components. In the next development phase, the alignment often occurs by the use of revision and control of the execution methods of the plan components defined in the previous phase.

After having a tool that promotes the alignment between business and IT in the organisation it was noted that business demand to the IT increased, new development requested occurred and changes to the existing applications. This is due to the IT exposition. In fact, the requests always existed but only now are justified and supported by a strategy and an alignment control model: the need for new applications development is based upon the trust the models give to those requesting them: the business or the infra-structure of the organisation. All this implies an increase of pressure on the IT and consequently on the computing professionals that will be liable if the business doesn't go as expected. The way a business specification, which must be supported by applications, is communicated as well as their framing on the company processes have now an important role in the IT development. Two important questions arise: How is it possible to realize an organization and how is possible to implement an enterprise?

By realization it is understood the integration of the following demands: the demand of the costumer that is what he expects from the organization; the interaction of the client with the organisation collaborators and finally the mapping of behaviour and information in the application components.

By implementation of Organization it is understood the making of the operation by means of technology.

BACKGROUND

In face of the present business environment, strongly competitive and in constant **changes** it is necessary to assure a good organisational performance. De Boer (De Boer, 2005) concludes that the enterprise business cycle passed from 7 years, in the 80s, to not more than 18 months in the 90s. The dynamic of the organisations implies giving a larger emphasis to the changing factor in planning Business and IT. Both must be flexible and adaptable. To assure the consistency of the IT

strategy with the business strategy became a goal so that investments made by the organisations to improve and optimise procedures, control costs, increase efficiency of the collaborators, develop the relationship with suppliers and partners and to improve and personify the services rendered may be justified. This concern is a challenge but it is also an area of investigation that studies the alignment between business and **information systems** (Henderson, 1993), (Mendelow, A., 1986), (Reich, 2000). Maes (Maes, 2000) pay special attention to the dynamism required to the process of alignment that is determined by a constant need of adjustment.

The known Henderson and Venkatrama **model** of alignment (Henderson, 1993) proposes several approaches to explain the relationships between the Information Technologies (IT) and the business strategy.

The model mentioned below distinguishes four main perspectives to assure the alignment between the IT and the business (see Figure 2).

Strategy development (arrow 1): This perspective sees business strategies a determinant factor to the choice of the organisation structure and the relevant infrastructure. This vision intends to valorise the position of the enterprise in the market (clients, long terms projects, competitive advantage and business range).

Technological potential (arrow 2): This perspective also sees the business strategy as a starting point. However it resorts to the potential afford by the information systems strategy to define the business processes. Here the main incidence is the position in the market through long-term technological projects and the technological range.

Competitive potential (arrow 3): In opposition to the previous perspectives that consider the business strategy as a starting point this one subjects the business strategy to the potentialities of the technology. It is the classic example of the companies that built all their business models on the exploitation of the capabilities of a certain technology. In this perspective the focus will on

Figure 2. Model of strategic alignment: Venkatraman, Henderson

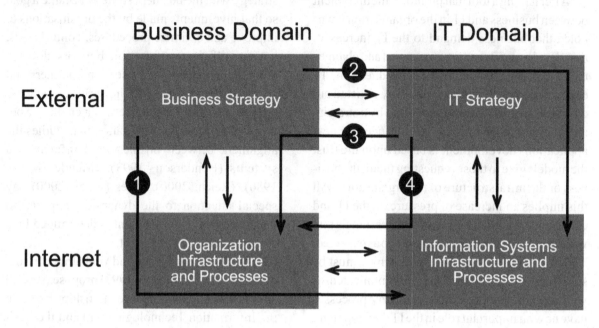

the market posture by means of long-term technological projects and technological embracing.

Service level (arrow 4): This alignment perspective implies the definition of the business processes based on the strategy of the information systems witch arise as a main trump for an effective answer in markets constantly in change.

In face of the above mentioned the following questions need to be answered:

- What do we understand by alignment between business and IT?
- In the alignment model which of the perspectives (strategy development, technological potential, competitive potential or service level) must be chosen to guaranty the alignment between IT and business?
- How is it possible to maintain the alignment once the organisations are permanently changing?
- At last which are the methodology and the tool that allows the maintenance of the alignment?

The alignment may be defined as the adjustment between the strategies and the business goals with the objectives and functions of the IT. It will bring competitive advantages and a better organisational performance conferring an accrued value to the business. If this is not verified it will be very difficult for the IT to support the business strategies.

To guarantee the alignment between the IT and the business it is our conviction that the alignment strategy based on the definition of business strategy (arrow 1, Figure 2), allows to represent the market vision of the organisation, its position among the clients, long-term business projects and search for competitive advantages within the business sphere. Therefore, the focus will be in the improvement of the organisational infrastructures. The need to support the improvement of the processes and infrastructure impels the changes in the information systems.

The methodology and the tool that may allow the adoption of the technology architecture that better applies to the enterprise reality and that permits future modifications to occur naturally

Figure 3. SWOT and Hoshin Kanri matrix

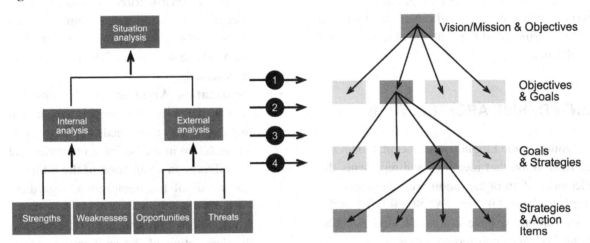

and in coherence with the adopted systems is the Business Architecture and the Thomas L. Wheelen an J.David Hunger model. The Enterprise Architecture and the model of strategic management proposed by Thomas L. Wheelen and J.David Hunger allow representing clearly all relationships between the business strategy, the information, the applications, the technology and the processes.

ENTERPRISE STRATEGY

The enterprise strategy is started by the analysis of the strengths and the enterprise weaknesses as well as the threats and opportunities resulting from a SWOT analysis. Then the strategic options of the enterprise must be set up as well as the strategic projects that will materialise those same options. For all projects the actions to be implemented must be described in detail as well as the relevant timetable and people in charge.

All elements of the **SWOT** analysis are represented in the Hoshin Kanri matrix, which is a tool that uses the concept of the **Plan-Do-Check-Act cycle** to create objectives, connecting them to targets and allowing the control of their progress.

The information is represented in the **Hoshin Kanri matrix** as follows (Figure 3): The rela-

tionship 1 represents the crossing between all the enterprise Strategic Projects and the elements identified in the SWOT (Strengths, Weaknesses, Opportunities and Threats) . That is, it shows in what way each strategic project increases the strengths and the opportunities or faces the weaknesses and the threats.

The relationship 2 represents the alignment, the relationship between the Strategic Projects with the Strategic Options of the enterprise. This means that the Strategic Projects set up are going to substantiate the Strategic Options.

Relationship 3 represents the crossing between the analysis of the enterprise (Strengths and Weaknesses) with the Strategic Options. That is in what way the Options take into consideration the specific characteristics of the enterprise.

Relationship 4 crosses the analysis of the external environment (Opportunities and Threats) with the Strategic Options. That is, in what way the Options take into consideration the elements considered as relevant within the context where the enterprise develops its activity.

Based on the Options and Strategic Objectives it is possible to define and quantify the Strategic Objectives of the Enterprise for a pre-established period.

At last, the indicators that will allow the enterprise management to follow up the evolution of the fulfilment of the strategic objectives shall be defined.

ENTERPRISE ARCHITECTURE

Considering the Engineering concept, model is a generalisation that identifies and represents the elements of an organisation with the necessary detail to the end it seeks (ANSI, 2007.). For the organisations we have an area of knowledge - the Organisational Engineering – that is focused in this subject and is based on the following assumptions (Liles D. H., 1996):

- A organisation is understood as a complex system;
- Engineering may be used in the understanding process of an organisation;
- As a system an organisation may be decomposed into subsystems;
- Engineering may be used in the process of transforming the organisation.

Based on this pretexts it is possible to model, design and implement an organisational architecture. The modulation supplies the means by which it is possible to focus the most important elements for the problem object of study within the organisation. The design is the mean by which is described how an organisation must be. The implementation permits the materialization of what was defined in the design phase (Zachman, 1997).

The elements that integrate the architecture model for an organisation are: (Sousa e al., 2005):

- **Organisational Architecture**: It considers aspects related to the definition of business strategies, its processes and functional requirements, such as: mission, vision, purpose and structure of the organisation;

- **Business Architecture**: It considers the execution of a business strategy based on business processes where the behaviour and the structure of the elements are represented;
- **Information Architecture**: It considers the passive objects (informational entities) that the organisation needs to carry out its job as set up in the business processes and it facilitates an abstraction of the information needs of the organisation regardless the technology;
- **Applications Architecture**: It considers the description of the applications which facilitate the management of the informational entities supporting the business processes;
- **Technology Architecture:** It considers the Technologies behind the implementation of the applications set up and the communications easiness necessary to the support of the business architecture.

The description of the organisation through architecture (Figure 4) having as base the modulation intends to permit the analysis of the subjects related to the alignment and its deviation among the referred to elements: organisation; business; information; application and technology.

An architecture where large deviations from alignments are verified damages directly the comprehension of the organisation. An architecture with a strong alignment may contribute to an incentive to the collection of knowledge namely under the form of structured and semi-structured documents described in the models.

As primitives of the activities modulation within an organisation the following concepts and their relationships are considered (Lankhorst, M. et al, 2005):

- **Information** Represents something that exists within the organisation. In general it

Figure 4. Enterprise architecture

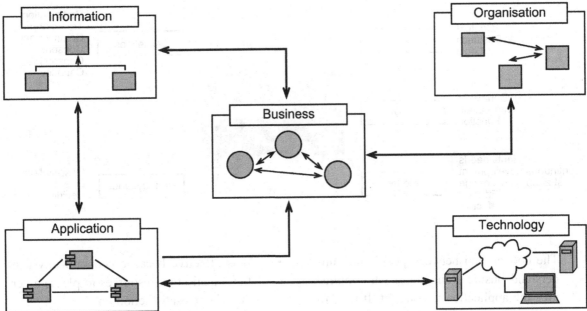

is represented by an individual (e.g. actor; department);

- **Behaviour:** Represents the **actions** that occur in the organisation by the individuals' usage. It is usually represented by a verb (e.g. send);
- **Function**: Represents a collection of particular characteristics and **behaviours** an individual shows when carrying out actions (e.g. salesman, buyer).

To be possible to chart all the applications a table was used (CRUD table) in which the business processes of the enterprise are crossed with all the informational entities. In this operation are described the actions (Read Create Update and Delete) that each process uses on each entity. This way it will be possible to identify the characteristics of the applications (associated to the group of processes) that may optimize better the CRUD table.

The found solution to align the strategic model represented in the Hochin Kanri matrix, with the applications represented in the CRUD

table, consisted in inclusion of the **CRUD table** in the representation of the model. This allows an aligned vision of the enterprise strategy with the business processes, the indicators, the organisational entities and the applications of the information systems.

SOLUTION ARCHITECTURE

The contribution of this work proposed an approach composed by a method, a **development strategy** (O-**O-D-A** LOOP) and a set of participation principles of the collaborators in the method (Figure 5).

The approach embraces some factors, which are considered as differentiate factors to the configuration or the application development under the context of Enterprise Architecture, namely:

- Emphasizes the client needs, the organisation capacity and the application potential;
- Promotes continuous development by involving all organisation collaborators.

Figure 5. Approach description

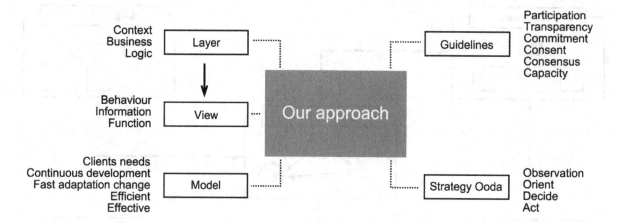

The cooperation between people that understand business and those who configures the application is constant. It tries to contour the natural difficulty in writing procedures;

- Adopts a development approach, which implies a continuous evolution and allows a fast adaptation to changes. The goals to be reached have the tendency to change with time;

- It is efficient because it tries to achieve its goals that is the necessities of the costumers and the organisation capacities considered in the application;

- It is effective because economically uses the organisation resources to please a certain client's satisfaction level.

The method was described by Don Awalt (Awalt A., McUmber R., 2004) and uses some concepts gathered from *ArchiMate* Modelling language (Lankhorst, M., 1998). The method is composed by three layers (Table 1):

- **Context:** Represents the client's vision and point of view about what he wants from the organisation and signifies the external stimulus to answer to, understand and improve the organisation internal behaviour;

Table 1. Method description

Layer	Description	Behaviour	Information	Function
Context	Describes the demand of the costumer that is what he expects from the organisation	The demands the client makes to the organisation	Information Model that needs to be understood by the costumer to complete a transaction.	Which are the organization department involved with client
Business	Describes the interaction of the client with the organisation collaborators	Describes the activities performed due to the interaction between the client and the organisation.	Model of the information that must to be understood by the client and the collaborators to complete a transaction.	Which are the organization department that are involved and that have a relationship with the client
Logical	Describes the mapping of behaviour and information in the application components	Describes how the activities are mapped in the application	Mapping between information and data application	How and whom maintain the application

Figure 6. Strategy O-O-D-A cycle

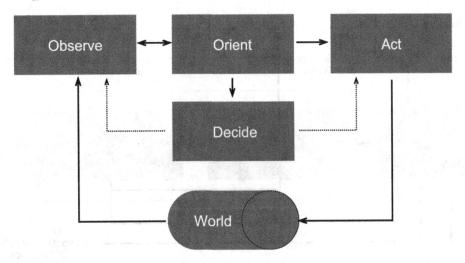

- **Business:** Represents the organisation's vision and point of view and allows to identify and promote the use of the capacities the organisation has to answer to the client stimulus;
- **Logic:** Represents the vision of the application and its point of view and permits to define the development strategy or configuration of specific software.

Each layer represents a vision of the problem with a certain detail and a diverse refining described under a form of behaviour, information and functions. Each layer encapsulates the behaviour and the information of the previous layer. Each layer is described as following:

- **Behaviour:** Describes the activities, tasks and events related to a service rendered;
- **Information:** Fragment of relevant data for a certain behaviour. It may be informal or conceptual or both;
- **Function**: Represents the responsibility it has under the behaviour of an entity (person or company department).

The strategy adopted was developed by John Bloyd (Angerman, S., 2004), known by the cycle O-O-D-A (Figure 6). Boyd said that, in a competitive environment, the entity capable of guiding the decision process formed by the cycle "observe; orient; decide and act" in a faster and efficient manner shall perform his task more successfully than his opponents.

Initially designed for military applications the concepts developed from Boyd' ideas became used in several other areas. As example of the use of this methodology in project management field can be found in (Rosa, Marcelo, 2005) and was used as a source to choose this strategy. It was necessary to frame the phases of the O-O-D-A cycle (Figure 7) in the chosen method:

1. **Observation** includes acquisition and data and information compiling: CRUD matrix, Hoshin Kanri matrix, processes diagram, entities related to the expected development, new orders made by business and the organisational frameworks, external data on existing technology to support development, background knowledge of solutions to problems raised as well as the knowledge of the organisation weakness and strengths;

2. **Guidance** consists on analysing scenarios based upon observations, experience, organisational vision, organisational culture,

Figure 7. O-O-D-A Cycle: Adapted

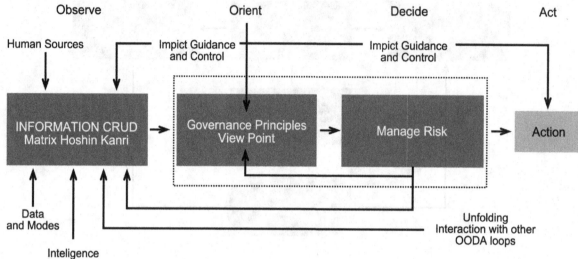

points of view, etc. Guidance results on the construction of mental diagrams that show reality in a way that the actions possible to be performed make sense. Guidance is dependent from existing view. This also means dependent from the tacit knowledge that each element has on the organization. This phase helps the team to observe and obtain a global sense of what is observable respecting the vision each element has. Guidance consists in a way to promote sharing of knowledge each individual has and which is usually difficult to be formalized or explained to third parties, as it is subjective and inherent to each individual capacity. Guidance orients decision but also considers observation and action thus allowing alternative solutions.

3. **Decision** is made from the image produced in the Guidance process and defines which adequate answer for the situation in question is. The decision will be implemented by a selected action;

4. **Action** consists in materializing the decision made. Once performed the results and their alignment towards the business, namely in what regards processes must be evaluated

periodically by different collaborators with distinct visions within the organisation especially at the level of the entities supported and also in the communication with the remaining applications. If the result is not satisfactory or it ceases to satisfy the organisation, measures to amend eventual failures and to improve quality and efficiency must be made.

Boyd presumes that the major factor to obtain the expected results does not consist in observe, guide, decide and act in the best way. The most important thing is observe, guide, decide and act quickly that is the speed reached to interact. The interaction speed wins the quality of interaction meaning the improvement on the continuous process of the solutions found.

The method also comprises a set of principles, which intend to promote: motivation, participation, capacity of decision, autonomy and collaborators participation in the development of applications. These principles are (Weill, P. & Ross. 2004):

1. **Participation:** It means that associated processes must be participated by elements dispersed in the organisation. This may occur in a direct or indirect way. The participation implies the capacity to express the strengths and weaknesses of the applications and the capacity of association in groups, with different opinions on same application and the relevant context namely how to support the processes intervening in the business and their integration with the remaining applications. The principle is viable since there are clear and specific rules assuring the proposed terms and there are initiatives within the organisation tending towards the sustenance of the terms;

2. **Transparency:** The decisions taken and their supervision are made by known rules and regulations. All data is available and directly accessible to those affected by said decisions;

3. **Commitment:** The applications and the way they are managed aim to serve the organisation as a whole. The management processes must be prepared to answer the collaborators needs within a reasonable time;

4. **Consent:** The development decisions and applications management must consider that the best solution for collaborators is the one looking for consensus among the different interests. The aim in reaching consensus must be obtaining an agreement about the best solution for the organisation as a whole. This way of obtaining decisions implies a long-term perspective so that a sustainable applications development occurs;

5. **Consensus:** The applications development must assure the equality of all groups of collaborators in view of the application targets within the organisation. The proposed path shall promote satisfaction of all groups;

6. **Capacity:** It must be assured that the applications are adequate to the organisation processes and the result goes towards its

needs and, at the same time, make the best use of the available resources. This means that recourses are used in a sustainable way and in a controlled environment.

The use of these principles and actions assures that the collaborators needs and different opinions are taken into consideration. This means the needs of all participating in the organisation are considered in the decision of IT management.

Thus, it contributes to maintain the alignment of the IT towards business, to promote the capacity and agility for new business or to make adjustments in the present ones; it makes the relation between investment in IT and the return of the data value; it maintains the risks of business under control; makes transparent the importance of the continuity of IT in the business and, at last, is a measure that promotes the constant improvement of the IT performance.

CASE STUDY RESULTS

Due to the nature of the proposed techniques their validation was done in the configuration of real software. The chosen software was Client Relationship Management(CRM) by the following reasons:

1. It allows to test the processes related to the interaction with the client;

2. CRM, more than a tool is a philosophy though it is necessary the commitment of all the organisation;

3. It allows to test the participation of the administration in the project;

4. It allows to test the communication of the collaborators within the team;

5. It allows the incorporate the collaborators skills in the development of the application they are going to use;

6. It allows the use of the O-O-D-A cycle as the development of the functionalities is

progressive and it will be necessary to adapt the system to support the business changes.

The team agreed to initiate the development of the CRM by the module regarding the sales force:

- **Accounts and Contacts Management:** permits the access to all clients data and their relationship with the contacts namely: information on clients, contacts, the role each contact has in commercial relationship, the relationship contacts have between themselves and their relationship towards the management of proposals;
- **Commercial Proposals Management:** permits the control of proposals type (layout), automatic generation of invoicing, treatment by period of proposal, automate the emailing of proposals and the control of the composition of the price of each item;
- **Invoicing Management:** once a commercial proposal is accepted it is possible to create an invoicing order and manage the other relevant aspects such as placement of orders and invoicing;
- At last the modules allowing the **Products Management** and the **Price Lists Management** of products for each client were also implemented.

Three groups were formed, one for each model layer: context, business and logic. The collaborators were shared to facilitate the communication and the passage of models between the groups. Each group can only carry out its work of analysis after receiving the analysis the previous layer. As such the business layer only initiated its work after receiving the models of processes and the entities of the context layer and, the logic level only started his work after receiving the models of the business layer.

Each work session, of each group, followed the loop O-O-D-A strategy: existing data collection for analysis; preparation of new scenarios;

analysis of different scenarios under a new information or development of models. In case there is a changing proposal in each layer (new behaviour or new information) it must be communicated to the other layers. The final changes will only be accepted after all layers include the proposed changes. The model resulting from work is briefly presented in Table 2.

The activities developed by each group of work allowed detailing, specifying and checking the models thus creating a solid base for the development of a system lined up with business. The group communications was supported by use case that describes the problems and validates the solutions regarding the changing proposals. The changing of models has created some difficulties but we understand change as a natural thing in this process.

The chosen platform supporting the logical development in the model was ZOHO CRM (Figure 8), due to the positive analysis made of the following aspects: i) the platform is available as a service software thus it stimulates the Information System Department to be constituted as a unit that passes from development and maintenance of the application to support the services that the platform offers; ii) the price of each license is substantially more economic than the other considered solutions; iii) the capacity of interaction with other applications through the **REST** communication that allows the use of a web interface using **XML** and **HTTP**, without the additional abstractions of the protocols based on patterns of exchanging messages, as the web services protocol **SOAP**; iv) the easiness to form a multidisciplinary team for the development of a solution by using O-O-D-A strategy.

Issues, Controversies, Problems

In the approach described, the alignment of the information Technologies with the business is made by the implementation of the strategy. The tools used are framed within the Organisational

Table 2. Mapping of the levels for the sales force

Description	Behaviour	Information	Function
LAYER I CONTEXT			
The client intends to contract consultants specialised in IT.	The client request the services of consultants specialized in technology IT; Client selects the consultants and closes the business, Client pays the organisation the experts' services.	Mail request with the information that describe the IT skills that they need; Receive curriculum *vitae* from organization	There are two departments involved in the client: Outsourcing department- who make the request; 'financial department- who make the payment
LAYER II BUSINESS			
Organisation processes to perform the client request.	The client sends the request to the collaborator of its own account; The collaborator researches in the catalogue and tries to find a consultant offer; The collaborator sends the commercial proposal in accordance with the agreed prices schedule; The costumer accepts the consultants; The collaborator updates the consultant catalogue; The collaborator requests the contract agreement with the selected consultant and sends data to the Human Resources department.	Consultant; catalogue; account; commercial proposal; item; request; Invoice order; Order form.	There are four departments in the organization that collaborate with client: Recruitment department. That is responsible to manager curriculum vitae database; sales department that communicate with the client Outsourcing department and account department that send invoice to client and the HR department that manage the user that will work in the client.
LAYER III LOGIC			
Describes the high level components of the application and the way it is related to the previous levels.	The following modules are using and map to other layers behaviour: Accounts; Contacts; Opportunities; Products; Price Books; Quotes; Activities & Calendar.	Map for each application module each piece of information as data	The infrastructure of the application is support by the provider of service on demand. Internally the IT department will make the necessary changes as being requested by users

Engineering with the intention to understand, modulate, develop and analyse all aspects of the business by focusing the understanding of the relationships and dependencies between strategy, processes and the information systems supporting them.

The model that represents the present scenario of the organisation is called the enterprise model as-is, in opposition to the model to-be, which reflects future modifications that may occur within the organisation. These improvements result from the well succeed implementation of the enterprise strategy that gives origin to new processes as a result of new needs or improvements in the existing processes.

From the relationship between the description of the strategy and its relationship with the processes arise the following questions:

Q1: To connect the organisation strategy with the processes is the best and more efficient method of analysis? The success of this relationship gives origin to a modification in the processes and consequently in the passage of an organisation as-is to an organisation to-be which alters the structure that is being created in the Hochin Kanri matrix and relates: projects and strategic options with indicators and targets.

Q2: What is the relevance of the processes in the strategy? To carry out the survey of the processes of an organisation is a hard job that may influence the way the organisation develops its own activities. However, the models of the real processes are those which are in the mind of their executants and are complexes and difficult to perceive.

It is not in discussion the importance of the survey of the business processes as it is one of the requirements of ISO 9000:2001, and the modulation of complex processes, with high levels of detail permits the concentration in the level

Figure 8. CRM platform

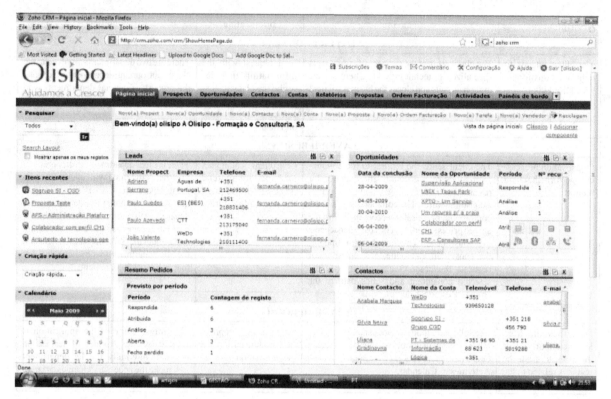

of detail that matters for each act. The notation of the model allows a more faithful description of the processes than it would happen with a description in a natural language. However, the survey of the processes is an attempt to create an organisation model with the contribution of different intervenient each with its own idea about what a process is.

We think that a possible solution will consist in a stable representation of the organisation and its nature and will serve as base for an understanding between those intervening in a certain domain. In this context, the Enterprise Ontology may contribute to the understanding of the organisation once its purpose is the specification of the conceptual model of the Organisation nature independently from its realization and implementation.

Solutions and Recommendations

Once the proposed base model relates business with the IT based on the strategy, being the relationship point of the business process the use of an Enterprise Ontology supported by a methodology, it may contribute for a solution as for each organisation there exists the same ontology which shows the main business activities, the actors and the products or services with which they cope with. As an eventual support methodology in future jobs it is proposed the **DEMO methodology** (Design and Engineering Methodology for Organization), since it cover important properties of the ontology (Dietz, 2006):

- To benefit from the work already done in the conceptual modulation in particular the work made in the area of modelling approaches based in the natural language as they link directly to the logic.

- It is concerned with the main aspects of production and communication within an organisation and not how the actors communicate (subject regarding implementation).
- It does not include lexical questions such as the name of the things and the statement of values.
- It makes a clear distinction based on solid theoretical issues between the world (states and events) and the causes of change of that work (actors and roles).
- It supplies a vocabulary to represent knowledge. This vocabulary is based on a supporting context that avoids ambiguous interpretations of said vocabulary.
- It allows the partition of knowledge. As such, if there is an ontology that models the domain of knowledge it can be shared and used by actors developing different actions within said domain.

The DEMO methodology is based on the assumption that communication between individuals constitutes a base, which is necessary, stable and sufficient for the development of the organisations theory. There is an abstraction related with the technical aspects of production of means thus in DEMO only the results of the production activities are relevant. The DEMO is based in axioms that are materialised in four models:

- **Construction Model**: regards the construction of the enterprise system (the organization), specified by transaction types, actor roles (plus initiator and executor links), and information banks (plus information links).
- **Process Model**: regards the state space and process space of the coordination world, specified by business events and business laws.

- **State Model**: regards the state space and process space of the production world, specified by business object classes, business fact types, and business laws.
- **Action Model**: regards the operation of the enterprise system, specified by business rules (that are the operational equivalent of the business laws)

CONCLUSION

This work explores the possibility to assure the alignment between business and the IT by using a strategic model that contributes to the improvement of the organisation performance.

It was identified a strategic model of execution in which it is possible to set up the requirements of the organisational infrastructure and the information systems. In this work it is proposed an interactive method that allows adapting the software to the identified requirements and consequently to cover the alignment between business, organisational infrastructure and information systems. This model is framed in the perspective of a business architecture, which is formed by a set of artefacts, which describe the details, the business, information; application and the role people must have within the organisation at different layers. Its use is important to understand an organisation and can be a support tool to the continuous improvement we intended to achieve due to business changes.

In this work a method, a strategy and guidelines that help to integrate an application under the scope of Enterprise Architecture.

The method aims to manage complexity through the analysis of the problem levels under different perspectives so that the application can contemplate all the organisation and client needs.

The loop strategy O-O-D-A triggers the process in order to look for a continuous improvement of the application maintaining business alignment.

The guidelines were introduced to promote the acceptance of the solutions found by collective responsibility of the collaborators that participated in the applications integration process.

It was possible to test the model application due to the fact it was being used in a real situation, which consisted on the configuration of a CRM platform.

One of the aspects that may be improved concerns the amount of time spend identifying the artefacts of the method to be used in future jobs to describe in a detailed and systematic way the artefacts that must be apart of each level of the submitted method, their relationships and concepts and also the improvement of their connection to the model of strategic organisation.

By this study we conclude that: there is an increase in accepting the use of technology on business; the general satisfaction of the organisation is assured by fast delivery and continuous improvement of the applications promotes the alignment once the late changes are included in the development; the constant cooperation between the people, who understand the business, those who use the application and those who program it; focus on the individuals and interactions more than in tools.

REFERENCES

American National Standards Institute (ANSI). (2007). [Industrial automation systems - Concepts and rules for enterprise models.]. *ISO, 14258*, 1998.

Amor, D. (2001). *The E-Business (R)evolution: Living and Working in an Interconnected World* (2nd ed.). Englewood Cliffs, NJ: Prentice Hall.

Angerman, W. S. (2004). *Coming Full Circle with Boyd's OODA Loop Ideas: An Analysis of Innovation Diffusion and Evolution*. Washington, DC: Storming Media.

Awalt, D., & McUmber, R. (2004). *Secrets of Great Architects*. Retrieved November 15, 2009, from http://msdn.microsoft.com/en-us/library/aa480041(lightweight).aspx

Chan, J. O. (2005). Toward a unified view of customer relationship management. *The Journal of American Academy of Business*, *6*(1), 32–38.

Checkland, P. (2000). Soft systems methodology: a thirty year retrospective. *Systems Research*, *17*(S1), S11–S58. doi:10.1002/1099-1743(200011)17:1+<::AID-SRES374>3.0.CO;2-O

De Boer, F. S., Bonsangue, M. M., Groenewegen, L. P. J., Stam, A. W., Stevens, S., & Van Der Torre, L. (2005). Change impact analysis of enterprise architectures. In *Proceedings of the 2005 IEEE International Conference on Information Reuse and Integration (IRI-2005)* (pp. 15-17).

Dietz, J. L. (2006). *Enterprise Ontology: Theory and Methodology* (1st ed.). Berlin: Springer. doi:10.1007/3-540-33149-2

Henderson, J. C., & Venkatraman, N. (1993). Strategic alignment: Leveraging information technology for transforming organizations. *IBM Systems Journal*, *32*(1), 4–16. doi:10.1147/sj.382.0472

Hoogervorst, J. (2004). Enterprise architecture: Enabling integration, agility and change. *International Journal of Cooperative Information Systems*, *13*(3), 213–233. doi:10.1142/S021884300400095X

Jackson, T. L. (2006). *Hoshin Kanri for the Lean Enterprise: Developing Competitive Capabilities and Managing Profit*. Florence, KY: Productivity Press.

Lankhorst, M. (2009). *Enterprise architecture at work: Modelling, communication and analysis*. Berlin: Springer-Verlag GmbH.doi:10.1007/978-3-642-01310-2

Laudon, K., & Laudon, J. (2009). *Management Information Systems* (11th ed.). Englewood Cliffs, NJ: Prentice Hall.

Liles, D. H., & Presley, A. R. (1996). Enterprise modeling within an enterprise engineering framework. In *Proceedings of the 28th conference on Winter simulation* (pp. 993-999). Coronado, CA: IEEE Computer Society. doi: 10.1145/256562.256882

Maes, R., Rijsenbrij, D., Truijens, O., & Goedvolk, H. (2000). *Redefining business–IT alignment through a unified framework.* White paper.

Mendelow, A. L. L. (1986). Issues in information systems planning*1. *Information & Management, 10*(5), 245–254. .doi:10.1016/0378-7206(86)90027-3

Reich, B. H., & Benbasat, I. (2000). Factors that influence the social dimension of alignment between business and information technology objectives. *Management Information Systems Quarterly, 24*(1), 81–113. doi:10.2307/3250980

Rosa, M. (2005). O Ciclo de Decisão de Boyd e o Gerenciamento de Projectos. *PMI-RS Journal,* 12.

Shpilberg, D., Berez, S., Puryear, R., & Shah, S. (2007). Avoiding the Alignment Trap in IT. *MIT . Sloan Management Review, 49*(1), 51.

Sousa, P., Pereira, C., & Marques, J. (2005). *Enterprise Architecture Alignment Heuristics.* Retrieved November 15, 2009, de http://msdn. microsoft.com/en-us/library/aa480042.aspx

Spewak, S. H. (1993). *Enterprise Architecture Planning: Developing a Blueprint for Data, Applications, and Technology.* Hoboken, NJ: Wiley.

Steenbergen, M., Berg, M., & Brinkkemper, S. (2008). A Balanced Approach to Developing the Enterprise Architecture Practice. In *Enterprise Information Systems* (pp. 240-253).

Steenbergen, M., & Brinkkemper, S. (2009). Modeling the Contribution of Enterprise Architecture Practice to the Achievement of Business Goals. In *Information Systems Development* (pp. 609-618).

Chapter 3

Governance and Management of Information Technology:
Decomposing the Enterprise in Modular Building Blocks Based on Enterprise Architecture and Business Oriented Services

Luis Fernando Ramos Molinaro
Universidade de Brasília, Brazil

Karoll Haussler Carneiro Ramos
Universidade de Brasília, Brazil

Humberto Abdalla Jr.
Universidade de Brasília, Brazil

João Mello da Silva
Universidade de Brasília, Brazil

Flávio Elias Gomes de Deus
Universidade de Brasília, Brazil

Annibal Affonso Neto
Universidade de Brasília, Brazil

ABSTRACT

This chapter aims to present a proposal for a model that supports organizational governance through the alignment of business with Information Technology - IT. Firstly, it was observed that there are some paradigms which limit the use of enterprise architectures and hinder governance functions. Secondly, it focuses on the IT unit, where IT systems and subsystems are interrelated and the performance levels of the organization are aggregated, creating a macro-structure system capable of supporting corporate governance and IT. Finally, the IBM's Component Business Model - CBM® was applied to represent relationships of the IT unit with the organization, through decomposing the organization into business components that supply and demand services to facilitate their governance and management.

DOI: 10.4018/978-1-61692-020-3.ch003

INTRODUCTION

Organizations operate as large systems composed of other systems and subsystems. Considering organizations as systems, questions are raised about the interdependence of these systems and subsystems. This is especially relevant when dealing with issues involving human activity in social systems including production organizations, in which the factors involved depend upon different fields of knowledge and different levels of research (Kasper, 2000).

In this context, Information Technology (IT) appeared in order to facilitate the systemic flow of information in organizations, initially serving as a support tool for routine operations. Nowadays, the existence of IT is an essential factor for maintaining a competitive advantage. So as to fulfill its current mission, two key concepts can be considered: enterprise architecture and the concept of business services.

The application of enterprise architecture in conjunction with business services is capable of generating a competitive advantage, since the final solution allows the attributes of interoperability, flexibility, cost-effectiveness and innovation to be better explored.

This article presents a model that applies the knowledge of enterprise architecture and business services as a way of making corporate governance and IT viable.

The objective is to promote the alignment of business with IT, decomposing the organization into business components that supply and demand services based on elements of enterprise architecture, in order to facilitate their governance and management.

A justification for this article comes from the recurring use of different paradigms of enterprise architecture to map out an organization. This vision is disaggregated due to the application of different paradigms that generates rework in enterprises, as any problem diagnosed is examined from different points of view.

The contribution here is in presenting a model that supports dimensions of organizational governance through the alignment of business with IT. It considers the three paradigms of enterprise architecture to map out the organization and the business services concept.

THEORETICAL REFERENCE

The theoretical reference presents the main knowledge base that subsidized the proposed model: the concept of performance levels; enterprise architecture and services; paradigms of enterprise architecture; IT subsystems; and business components will be presented.

Corporate Governance

In order to work, enterprises need shareholders and managers who manage resource applications to achieve the Enterprise's purposes (Pelanda, 2006). Naturally, there are conflicts of interest between managers and shareholders, when the ownership and corporations' control do not coincide.

The conflict exists because we cannot expect that Enterprise managers, being other peoples' money managers, rein in money with the same vigilance as members of a private company who care about their wealth. This conflict is called the Agency theory (Pelanda, 2006).

Administrative councils were created to decrease these conflicts. Their function is to monitor managers in order to reduce costs, mitigate conflict and align the interests of shareholders with managers.

Due to this problem, a set of control and incentive mechanisms were created, known as Corporate Governance (Pelanda, 2006).

Corporate governance is a system through which companies are addressed and monitored. The Governance system allows that mission, vision and strategy are processed according to the desired goals and outcomes. The Enterprise's dependence on information tools is too big and governance issues cannot be solved without the intensive use of information technology.

It Governance

Due to regulatory pressure from national and international markets, which generated a strong influence on the establishment of best practices for IT Governance, IT has ceased to be one of the areas least required in regulatory terms (Pelanda, 2006).

Fernandes and Abreu (2008) also emphasize that business dependence in relation to IT and regulatory agencies became important growth drivers of IT Governance in organizations.

According to Weil and Ross (2004), IT Governance seeks to meet practices defined by Corporate Governance and aims to answer the following questions: (i) Do IT capabilities improve a company's competitiveness? ii) Will the company's managers recognize their responsibilities for the effective management and use of IT - or will they assume that this is a problem only in the IT area? iii) Will IT investments meet their company's strategic objectives – or will the company only be wasting resources and investments to meet operational needs and tactical initiatives?

According to the Ministry of International Trade and Industry (1999), IT Governance is the Organization's ability to control the formulation and implementation of strategy and to guide IT in a direction that is conducive to achieving competitive advantages for the Corporation.

As Grembergen (2004) states, IT governance is the organizational capacity exerted by senior management, executive management and IT to control the formulation and implementation of IT strategy in order to align IT with the organization.

Business and IT Alignment

In general, the main concern of IT Governance is business IT alignment. According to Rezende and Abreu (2002) IT and business integration is a constant problem in organizations, generating large financial and human effort that cannot guarantee a return on available investments.

Plazaola (2006) also says that many companies are not careful with strategic planning, which should be the basis for IT and business alignment. Organizations that have already aligned IT and business are constantly buoyed by organizational effectiveness, which is not perceived in isolated areas only, but also across the entire Organization (Lankhorst et al, 2005).

The literature suggests that companies cannot be competitive or successful if their business and IT strategies are not aligned. Nowadays, the most accepted conceptual model for IT and business alignment is the model proposed by Henderson and Venkatraman, called the Strategic Alignment Model (SAM) (Plazaola, 2006).

SAM segments the organization into business and IT. In both business and IT segments, the strategy of each part should be aligned with its operational capacities. The alignment between these segments should happen both in terms of strategy and capabilities. Following this line of thought, business and IT are divided into two other segments: business strategy and organizational infrastructure (for business); and IT strategy and infrastructure (for IT).

SAM is conceived of in terms of two fundamental strategic management features: i) strategic suitability and the interrelation between external and internal domains; (ii) functional integration (between the areas of business and IT). SAM's proposal in operationalization suggests that all organizations which start with business strategy verification must contribute to formulating IT strategy and thus be in the IT infrastructure's constitution.

Schekkerman (2006) uses the SAM as a tool for holistic understanding of the Organization and through it defines the organizational architecture principles, which are "a complete expression of the enterprise; a master plan which 'acts as a collaboration force' between aspects of business planning such as goals, visions, strategies and governance principles; aspects of business operations such as business terms, organization structures, process and data; aspects of automation such as information systems and databases; and of automation such as information systems and databases; and the enabling technological infrastructure of the business such as computers, operating systems and networks " (p.13).

Performance Levels

Organizations are like systems (Harmon, 2007; Bio, 1996; Rummler & Brache, 1994) that interact with other external systems and its subsystems like department sections, cells, components and so on. Many times these subsystems are not limited to knowledge or to a single subject (Kasper, 2000).

According to Rummler & Brache (1994), there are three levels to understanding the dynamics of an organization as a system: organization; processes; and implementation.

At the organization level, the strategies, governance, structure, enterprise architecture and the use of resources are considered and evaluated, in addition to the tools that help in understanding the vision of customers, suppliers and human resources in order to improve the organization's business model.

At the process level, the business model is represented by the flow of processes and procedures.

At the implementation level there are people, technical architectures and technologies that enable the procedures to be implemented. . Regarding people, we refer to the profile of professionals that contribute to achieving the goals of the business and through this we can build the foundations for hiring policies, for defining responsibilities, for rewards and for training.

Note that the approach of Rummler & Brache (1994) has two distinct concerns: i) the definition of a current model that represents the Organization's daily operation; (ii) the definition which expresses the desired model across the organization.

Throughout these levels, there is an accumulation of knowledge across the Organization, emphasizing the importance of creating and maintaining a knowledge base. This foundation allows it to positively influence the process of learning and growth within an organization.

Enterprise Architecture

There are many concepts used to define the term Enterprise Architecture (EA). According to Dragstra (2005) EA is the fundamental setting of an enterprise; of its architectural descriptions; of its relations with each part; and the environment and the principles that guide its evolution and development.

To IFEAD (Institute for Enterprise Architecture Developments) apud Dragsta (2005), enterprise architecture is the comprehension of all the different elements used to build an organization and how these elements (people, processes, business and technology) correlate.

According to RRB (Railroad Retirement Board, Bureau of Information Services) apud Dragsta 2005, enterprise architecture is the scheme of business processes, information systems and technology used to perform the processes efficiently.

Enterprise architecture is a coherent whole of principles, methods and models that are used in the design and implementation of an enterprise structure, business process, information system and technical infrastructure (Dragstra apud IEEE 1471-2000).

In other words, Enterprise Architecture aims at communicating the essential elements that explain the operation of an organization, allowing its managers to have a clear idea of the issues that must be dealt with reaching the desired goals. Thus, the entire organization is represented, expressing and aligning goals, visions, strategies, principles of governance, operational processes, organizational structures and aspects of automation such as information systems and technology infrastructure.

This representation of enterprise architecture allows for continually refining information technology, without jeopardizing alignment with the business organization and favors the permanent retention of knowledge to facilitate decision-making.

It is necessary to understand the concept of services concurrently with the concept of enterprise architecture. A service can be defined as a functionality that some entity (system, enterprise unit, etc.) offers to its environment, which has value for certain entities in the environment (typically service users) (Lankhorst, 2005).

The importance of using the services concept in conjunction with the enterprise architecture concept arises from the fact that the services concept is widespread in different areas of an organization, allowing IT and business employees to have a common language.

Applying the services concept in conjunction with enterprise architecture can generate a competitive advantage, since the resulting solution allows a better attributes' exploitation of interoperability, flexibility, cost-effectiveness and innovation.

Enterprise Architecture Paradigms: It-Centric, Business Process-Centric, Governance-Centric

According to Dragstra (2005), there are three approaches that aim at representing an organization based on enterprise architecture elements in order to achieve the alignment of business with IT. They are IT-centric, Business process-centric and Governance-centric.

The IT-centric concept is based on using enterprise architectures to improve effectiveness and efficiency in the technological area. The IT-centric vision is a widely used approach that creates an architecture that shows different models

of IT and resources and explains how they relate (Dragstra, 2005).

Usually, this view is presented using a model of four layers made up of business, information, application, and technical infrastructure.

The business process-centric concept defines a sequence of activities and knowledge required to produce the desired results. In this case, enterprise architecture focuses on all the processes of the organization, seeking to optimize them and to create new opportunities for refinement (Dragstra, 2005).

Application architectures and infrastructure technologies are also used in this approach in a secondary role.

The governance-centric concept is interconnected with a description of the components' desired functionalities, which is represented by specifying the results to be achieved.

Since organizations are composed of a set of complex systems, there are two ways to govern them. The first way is to focus on improving management systems and control of the organization as a whole. The second divides the organization into a network of small manageable parts, called business domains.

The governance-centric vision uses a governing approach and emphasizes boundary demarcation on different levels (organization, processes and implementation) and between personnel organization and IT systems.

IT Subsystems

One of the organization's systems is the entity responsible for providing all IT services to other entities of the organization. This system can be considered an autonomous IT organization that has three cohesive subsystems, called Direct, Development and Delivery (Gibert, 2003).

These subsystems interact with the IT organization, enabling its alignment with the business (Betz, 2007).

The Direct subsystem takes care of the IT organization's strategy and its architecture. It has the function of planning and exercising high-level control; monitoring whether demands are met; defining priorities in the service portfolio and products to be developed or delivered by other subsystems.

The Development subsystem has the task of designing and building solutions, typically using the project management process, ensuring quality and configuration management in order to mitigate the development subsystem's risk.

The Delivery subsystem executes the implementation of developed projects, manages the service catalogue, and runs all of the information systems, support and equipment for operations, as well as managing maintenance programs that support these systems and equipment, such as the operation of data storage centers, help desks, e-mail service, among others.

The main concerns of each subsystem are:

- Direct subsystem:
- What are the most promising future investments in my IT portfolio?
- What are the current good investments?
- What are the current questionable investments?
- What are the current bad investments?
- What are the total costs of acquisition and operation?
- Develop subsystem:
- What are the services or systems that we need to improve?
- Which systems use a specific piece of data?
- What is the current level of change in my systems?
- Delivery subsystem:
- How am I taking advantage of my resources?
- What is the operating status and trends of the system?
- How do the metrics of incidents and problems relate to the activities of change?

The problem with these subsystems is when the features of each one cross the theoretical borders, generating an overlapping (Betz, 2007). This fact is one of the main difficulties in IT management because it promotes relationships that are difficult to manage (Betz, 2007).

Business Components

The Component Business Model - CBM® is an IBM modeling technique. It is a mechanism that enables the achievement of excellence through encapsulating services in specific business components. This view contributes to specializing services and benefits in organizations that deliver high value to its customers, employees or shareholders (IBM, 2005).

The specific business components have internal and external views. Internally, the components enable the organization to rethink how it can leverage its assets and capabilities. Externally, components help organizations to identify the expertise that they cannot create by themselves.

The components put together business activities in discrete modules that can be shared in the organization. Furthermore, the components must work together in the context of the organization's business model (Carter, 2008).

According to IBM (2005), the Component Business Model serves as a tool to identify gaps and redundancies in order that the organization be guided by business oriented services.

CBM ®, through gap analysis, identifies and consolidates activities within cohesive business units and tests them in terms of interoperability between units.

The business component map provides a basis for developing new strategic and operational ideas. By evaluating the strategic value of the map's different components, managers can determine which components require immediate attention.

Each component encompasses five dimensions: Business purpose, Activities, Resources, Governance and Business services (IBM, 2005):

- Business purpose represents the logical reason for the component's existence in the organization. This logical reason is defined by the value it provides to other components.
- In Activities, each component leads to an exclusive set of activities to achieve the business purpose.
- In Resources, each component requests resources, people, knowledge and assets that support their activities.
- In Governance, each component is managed as an independent entity based on its own governance model.
- Business services are similar to standalone businesses, where each component provides and receives business from the business services.

SUPPORT MODEL FOR GOVERNANCE DIMENSION PROPOSAL

Aiming to promote the alignment of business with IT, how the enterprise can be decomposed into business components will be shown, considering the aspects of IT organization cited previously. Moreover, a governance cycle to be applied to each component of the organization will be proposed.

Merging the three levels of performance with the three subsystems will also be covered.

Uniting the performance levels with IT subsystems will be considered in order to understand the operation of an IT organization from a business and IT point of view.

Figure 1 illustrates this union, where we have a defined set of standardized requests, application units, resulting from business demands and with a service portfolio as output. These demands can be identified and organized into four types of standard applications: idea exploration; projects; services; and incident reports.

These demands may be endogenous, from the IT area, or exogenous, external to the IT area. The service portfolio is used to manage the lifecycle of all services and includes assistance services (proposed or in development), services catalogue and discontinued services. This representation takes three areas into account: architectural structure (focusing on alignment between levels and areas), processes and functionalities to explain the operation of an IT organization.

Each level has distinct characteristics that align themselves to management models, strategies, processes, organization structures, people, technologies and knowledge.

While going through these three levels, an accumulation of knowledge occurs in the organization, resulting in the importance of creating and maintaining a knowledge base. This base will positively influence the learning process and growth inside the organization.

DIRECT COMPONENT

The Direct enterprise level plans and executes the IT area strategy. To look at how the enterprise level complies with its role in the Direct subsystem, you must consider the context in which the Direct subsystem is inserted, as well as IT Governance. In regards to the context, it is up to the IT unit to respond effectively and efficiently to their consumers' requests within the time agreed upon.

For that to happen IT must submit a list of services offered, called a service catalogue. In addition to the services catalogue, IT needs to identify the main demand patterns. According to the types of requests required by customers and users, you can observe certain demand patterns such as idea exploration requests, project requests, service requests and incident reports (Betz, 2007).

Idea exploration request does not have guaranteed funding. Its goal is to use the knowledge of the Organization to make an assessment of a product or service. In Project requests, all projects begin with a proposal that solicits an overall assessment and competitive use in relation to prioritizing or-

Figure 1. Model of systems and subsystems that comprise an IT Enterprise

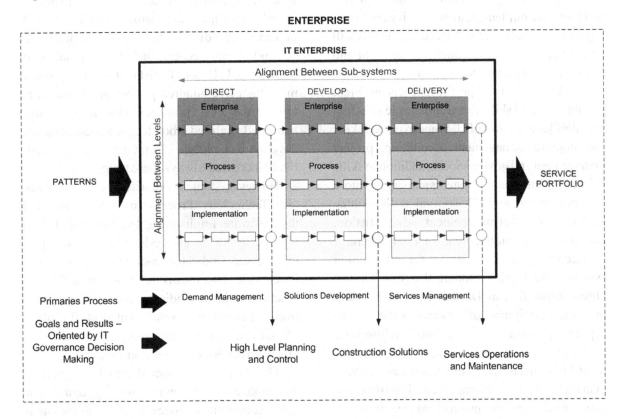

ganization resources.. Service requests can be met by the capacity of existing operational services. For example, provisioning an e-mail account for a user is a service request and the establishment of a new e-mail service is a project request. An incident report is a service where incidents or problems in existing operational services are reported and quality service is expected within the time agreed upon with its consumers.

Regardless of what the subsystem is, IT Governance monitors compliance with decisions by means of performance indicators and control objectives.

For Direct, the selected performance indicators refer to IT financial management. These indicators are obtained in COBIT, from a process called IT investment management. The goal of control can be defined as a desired outcome statement or the purpose to be achieved on the implementation

level of an IT unit. A control objective is chosen in order to mitigate risks to prevent compliance with the decisions taken. Risk mitigation is a procedure that can be used to support the identification of control objectives. So as to customize control objectives accordingly with the Direct governance's decisions, you can investigate and identify the causes of risks that generate the degradation of performance indicators or adopt and adapt control objectives or available controls in the collection of best practices from COBIT.

Control objectives chosen and adapted from COBIT for IT financial management are financial control, control of prioritizing investments, budget control, cost and benefit control. The process level includes activities that enable Macro-process Demand Management modeling, which is divided into two processes: Fulfilling Demand Requests and Customer Relationships (Betz, 2007).

The level of implementation includes features that allow the implementation of activities targeting the Direct subsystem. Amendment to this will be the approach of Personnel Management and Information systems and Support.

The IT professional profile that acts on Direct should highlight skills that stimulate the planning and high-level control of IT. Some expected skills are: domain management accounting, project management and governance, in addition to skills in handling information systems and support more common in this area. Behavioral skills include leadership, conflict management and negotiation, taking into account the organizational culture.

According to Betz (2007), the information systems and typical support that can support Direct automation are Demand Management and portfolio, monitoring of services' performance, capacity planning, organizational architecture, business continuity management, risk management, IT financial management, purchase contract management, asset management, infrastructure management and configuration management.

Develop Component

The enterprise-level plans and executes the Develop governance. To look at how the enterprise level complies with its role in the Develop subsystem, it is necessary to consider the aspects of IT Governance and Context.

The Develop subsystem has four processes: project management; design and construction solutions; quality assurance; and configuration management (Betz, 2007).

However, greater emphasis will be given to the project management process for it is considered critical to the success of the Develop subsystem. Project management supports the application of knowledge, skills and techniques to elaborate and implement activities that seek to achieve a set of predefined objectives. Performance indicators measure how the IT organization or IT department

is behaving to obtain the desired results. To define IT indicators, many companies rely on the use of performance indicators for certain best practices.

Taking into account that the IT trend is to implement ITIL and COBIT, it should manage more than five hundred performance indicators to meet these best practices. This fact generates increased qualified labor, technological resource development and the IT unit expenses consecutively increased/always increasing.

However, studies conducted by the Information Technology Process Institute (ITPI) and the Software Engineering Institute (SEI) with high-performance enterprises in IT show that performance indicators work according to the Pareto rule. This means that from all of the best practices collection indicators utilized by IT, only twenty percent are useful (Antao et al, 2005). Thus, not all controls are equally responsible for IT effectiveness, efficiency and security.

This study was conducted to analyze how high performance enterprises in IT usually control their business objectives. Processes and activities within these enterprises were analyzed to this end (Antao, 2005). It was noted that these high performance enterprises become engaged in a process of continuous improvement as a natural consequence of demands in the quest for excellence. In this research, all organizations have incorporated security increases in the IT environment. But the key data that led ITPI and SEI to conclude on the Pareto rule was the fact that surveyed enterprises have similar procedures for controlling their operating environment in order to achieve the desired outcome (Antao, 2005). ITPI and SEI high-performance indicators are presented in this chapter, distributed in the Develop and Delivery subsystems.

For the Develop performance measurement system, performance indicators and control objectives that mitigate risks are directed to project management. The strategy used to reach the goal of making Develop high-performance was to adopt the proposals of Information Technology Process Institute (ITPI) and Software Engineering Institute (SEI) (Antao, 2005).

Specifically, the project management process has identified indicators of effectiveness and efficiency: high perceived value by business; high rate of projects carried out within the time and cost; satisfactory security; low cost per project managed; and low cost of security. So as to customize the control objectives in accordance with the decisions of development (Develop governance), you can investigate and identify the causes of the risks that can cause performance indicator degradation or adopt and adapt available control objectives in the collection of best practices from COBIT.

Each objective has a distinct level of importance, which is the goal of scope change control in relation to the dominant control objectives of quantification and productivity error.

The process level includes activities that allow the macro-process solutions' Develop modeling, which is divided into four procedures: project management; design and construction solutions; quality assurance; and hardware and software configuration management (Betz, 2007).

Project management is one of the major processes of Develop, once there is a project authorized by Direct. It is commonly applied with the support of other processes. For example, in the case of a software development project, the project management process will be applied in conjunction with other processes, such as project change management, configuration management and estimates. The implementation level includes features that enable the implementation of Develop activities. For this implementation, a people management and information systems and support approach will be presented.

The IT professional that acts in the Develop subsystem is responsible for project management, design and construction of quality assurance solutions, products and services with configuration management. Some skills expected are: (i) knowledge of project management and governance, including skills in handling support and information systems; (ii) mastering the software development cycle and development tool used, for example, Java; (iii) mastering process management, with emphasis on software quality assurance. According to Betz (2007) typical information systems and support that can keep Develop automating are project management, requirements management, project inquiry management, projects estimate support and hardware and software configuration management.

Delivery Component

The enterprise-level plans and executes the Delivery governance strategy. To look at how the enterprise level complies with its role in the Delivery subsystem, it is necessary to consider the features of IT Governance and Context.

The service portfolio is the complete set of services that are managed and used to manage the entire lifecycle of all services. It includes three categories: standby service (proposed or Develop); service catalogue (in production or available for deployment) and discontinued services.

The Delivery subsystem typically develops its activities in accordance with the Direct governance guidelines and the solutions developed by Develop. The Delivery macro-process is the service management. The service management is a specialized set of organizational capacities to provide value to their consumers in the form of services (ITIL, 2007).

Delivery service management has six processes: release management; managing changes in production; fulfilling service requests; maintenance of operational services; incident and problem resolution; and configuration item management (Betz, 2007). The strategy used to reach the goal of high performance and Delivery was to adopt the proposals of the Information Technology Process Institute (ITPI) and the Software Engineering Institute (SEI) (Antao, 2005).

Specifically for Macro-process service management, the indicators identified were for: effectiveness and efficiency at the highest levels of availability and service levels; satisfactory and sustainable security; low quantity of unplanned changes; high rate of change; high rate of changes with success; lower repetition of problems found through auditing; low cost; high success rate in first time correction; low percentage of IT budget consumed in regulatory matters; and IT budget percentage consumed during the operation. Among the various settings of IT Governance, the most recurrent is one that identifies the main activity of IT Governance as support for decision making at all levels of the IT enterprise (Simonsson & Ekstedt, 2006).

To identify service management causes that create a perception of low or high quality of production, operational services were based on the Information Technology Infrastructure Library (ITIL). In addition, the results of research developed by ITPI also will be used. Specifically for the Delivery, it is worth examining the main causes discovered by ITPI, which impact the quality of IT operational services of production as perceived by its consumers.

From this research six main causes were verified that contribute to the degradation or improvement of IT operational service production as carried out by its high percentage of consumers. They are: a high rate of unplanned changes; a high rate of non-authorized accesses; low authorized release success; low efficiency in troubleshooting; high non-operating level agreements; and low correlation of configuration items. These causes contribute to the perception of poor quality services provided to IT service consumers.

The ITPI (2005) recommends implementing control objectives, change control, access control, release control, resolution control, service-level control and configuration control. Each objective

has a distinct level of importance, and the change control objectives and dominant access are more important in relation to release control objectives, resolution, service level and configuration.

The process level includes activities that allow macro-process service management modeling. The service management processes are divided into release management, managing changes in production, fulfilling service requests, maintenance of operational services, incident and problem resolution and configuration item management (Betz, 2007). Process level, the improvement of service provisioning may increase the chances of success, especially when certification service management is obtained. The level of implementation includes features that enable the implementation of the Delivery activities. This presented an approach focused on people management and information systems and support. The IT professional's profile in Delivery takes care of the Enterprise's service managing.

Some technical skills expected are governance knowledge and service management, including skills in handling support and information systems, mastering the products and tools that support the service portfolio and the process management domain, with an emphasis on quality service assurance.

Among behavioral skills, the ones that stand out are interpersonal capacity, self-motivation and self-management, collaborative work capacity, capability to identify and solve problems.

The list of information systems and typical support that can uphold the automation of IT area Delivery is change management, availability management, incident and problem resolution and configuration item management (Betz, 2007).

Components and Their Relationships

The components are related as a network with reference to the range of services offered by each. Thus, the relationship of the components is determined by the relationship of supply and

Figure 2. Relationship of supply and demand of services between components

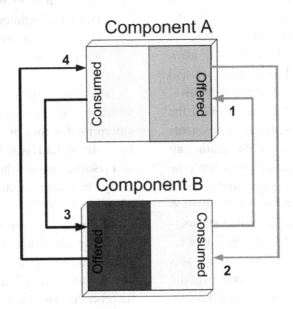

demand, in which one component supplies a service to another component and that one receives a business event at the same time it can consume a service, generating a business event for another component.

This relationship establishes that what is supplied by a component is consumed by the other and vice versa. Figure 2 illustrates this relationship, in which component A, arrow 2, provides a service to component B in response to a business event, arrow 1. The same applies to the component that generates an event for component B, arrow 3, and receives a service supplied by component B, arrow 4.

Considering an organization with multiple components, in which each one can provide services to all other components and from them receives business events, it is interesting to adopt a graphic representation that facilitates communicating the relationship between components.

In Figure 2 the arrow represents the range of services supplied by the component and the bar represents the means of communication used so that all other components can consume the services supplied.

BUSINESS COMPONENT MAP FOR ENTERPRISES

A zebra approach could be used to understand the decomposition of an organization. Initially, the entire organization is considered a system that is understood by its external interactions, as if it were a "black box". But when the external interactions are dominated, one can observe what happens within the system, and now the system is a "white box". The "white box" in turn can be decomposed into other components. These new components are seen as a "black box" until all interactions are well defined. When this happens, the ideas emerge and its contents can be observed (Hopkins & Jenkins, 2008).

Through the zebra approach and considering the CBM® aligned with the systemic characteristics presented by IT, a hypothetical architecture components map for aligning the organization with IT was produced, considering the relationships among its components. This map also has decomposition levels applied to components, establishing a hierarchical relationship. An analysis of the IT component considered the three breakdown levels in detail, as shown in Figure 3.

At the first level of decomposition, there are five components: master, business, IT, management and integration. The business, IT and administration components are all federative, meaning that they do not have a vision of the whole, so the integration and master components have the mission of guiding and integrating all other components. In the master component, the strategy of the organization is developed and in the integration component a base of information is found that integrates all the information generated by the components and its disseminations.

It is important to note that for all other levels underlying the first level, there are versions of the integration component and the master component. These versions are the link with the remaining components. Specifically, for the master components on the levels above and below, these are actually a mirror of the component from which they were originated. For example, for the IT component, it is represented by the IT master component in the second level as well as the direct component which is represented by the master direct component on the third level.

At the second level there are three components that represent the direction, development and delivery subsystems, and there are two other components: the IT master component and the integration component.

The third level consists of three components, reflecting the decomposition of the components: direct, developand delivery, where each has the components: governance, control and execution, including versions of the master and the integration components.

Following the establishment of the architecture components map for aligning the organization with IT, an analysis is performed where the components that add more value will be highlighted. This analysis consists of three phases:

1. Survey of components that add value;
2. Design of architecture;
3. Decision to invest and monitor the transformation.

In Phase 1, there are certain components which generate competitive advantages for the enterprise. For that, one can use the Theory of the Firm Resource Based View, which gives value to a resource when it has the following features: rarity, valuable, inimitable and irreplaceable, (Gottschalk, 2007).

In Phase 2, two sub-phases are established for the design of the architecture, which are the construction of strategic architecture and business architecture. Strategic architecture is responsible for procedures to transform the component, which includes moving from the current situation to the desired situation. Architecture business is responsible for representing the structure used to supply and demand services.

Both architectures, strategic and business, are composed of social architecture, business process and technical architecture. Social architecture takes into account organization structure, performance metrics, skills and organization culture. The business processes reflect the business model of the organization in terms of activity flows. The technical architecture includes systems applications and technical infrastructure (Prahalad, 2008).

Both strategic architecture and business architecture are features of enterprise architecture. Therefore, when enterprise architecture is used to perform the transition from the current situation to the desired situation, it will be called strategic architecture. If enterprise architecture is used to describe the day-to-day life of the component's operation, it will be called business architecture.

In Phase 3, the interaction of strategic and business architectures occurs considering the aspects of social architecture, business processes and technical architecture that must be applied to each business component. In this phase, investment issues have already been discussed and the

Figure 3. Architecture components map for aligning the organization with IT

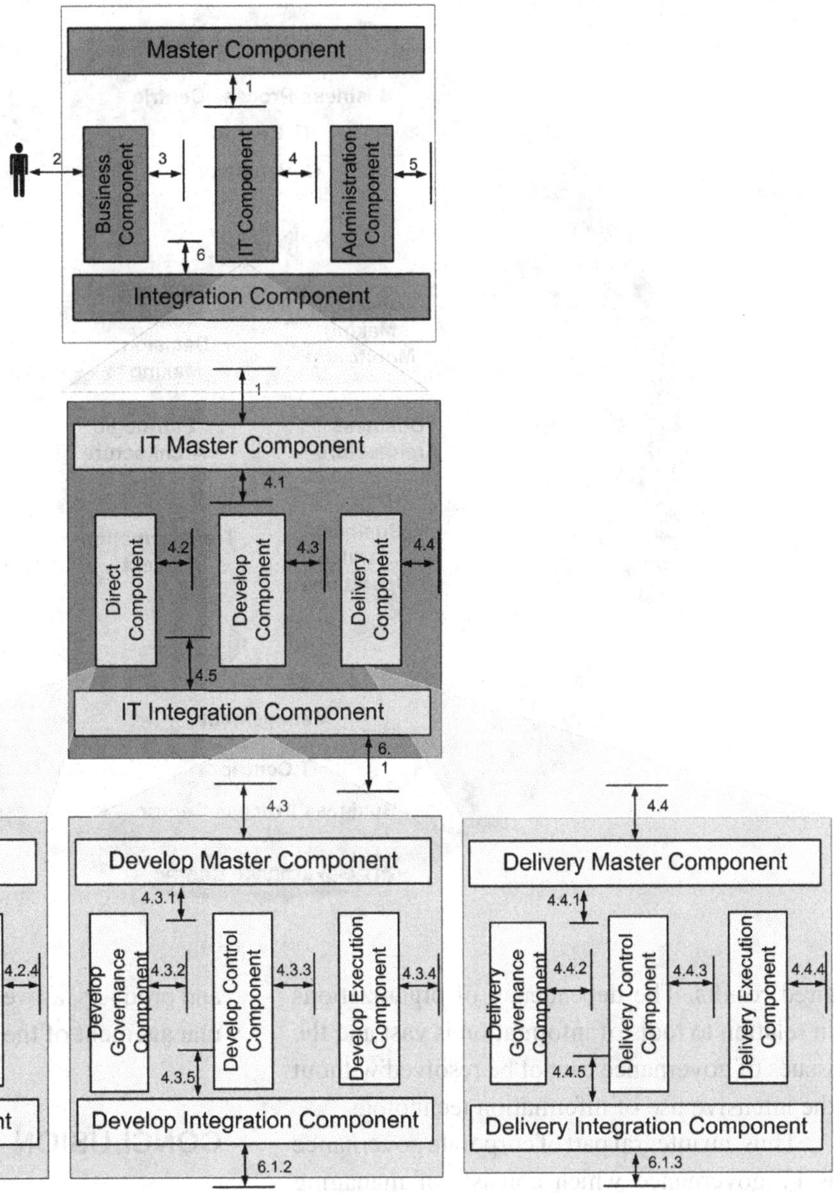

governance and management cycle are applied continuously.

The governance and management cycle, represented by Figure 4, supports the dimension of governance and management of each business component. The evaluation of business results, strategy clarification and improvement of business

models, through decision making are involved in the aspects of governance.

Governance dealt with here includes both corporate governance and IT governance. Corporate governance is a system by which companies are directed and monitored. The system of governance allows that the mission, vision, and strategy are transformed, keeping in mind the goals and de-

Figure 4. Governance and Management Cycle

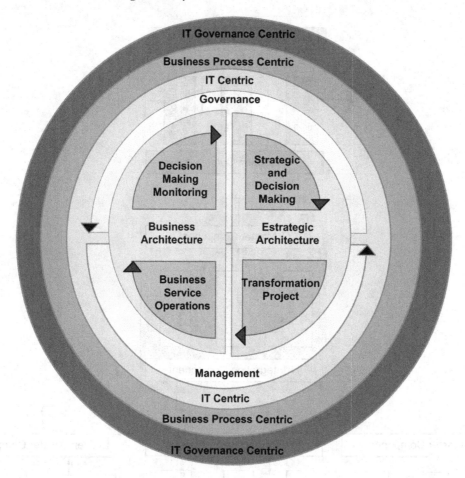

sired results. The dependency of organizations in relation to tools of information is vast and the issues of governance cannot be resolved without the intensive use of information technology.

Thus, an integral part of corporate governance is IT governance which consists of managing organization structures and processes to ensure the sustainability and expansion of the strategy and objectives of the organization (Grembergen, 2004 apud IT Governance Institute, 2001).

With respect to management, the cycle involves the design and implementation of strategic architecture and the operation of day-to-day business services. It is noteworthy that the management of IT is focused on the internal supply of IT services

and products, as well as on effective and efficient management of the current operations.

CONCLUSION

Considering organizations as systems composed of other interconnected systems and subsystems, it conditions the analysis of how these relationships are established among all organization entities. Having the knowledge of these relationships is fundamental for good decision making on all organization levels, even if the object of study is Information Technology.

Currently, organizations are applying the enterprise architecture concept as a way of aligning various organizational entities. But what has been seen so far is a focus of enterprise architectures on certain visions such as IT-centric, business process-centric or governance-centric.

This article sought to demonstrate that the alignment of business with IT can be achieved without being restricted to a single vision. Initially, a model that represents the IT systems and subsystems was considered.

In the second place, IT alignment with the organization was developed based on the Component Business Model - CBM ® by way of business components, and also a model that supports the dimension of organization governance was proposed.

Finally, it was considered how business components may be governed and managed independently, but following certain architecture and business strategy principles that aim at full integration of social aspects, processes and techniques as the best way to establish corporate governance and the IT of an organization.

REFERENCES

Antao, R., et al. (2005). *Quantifying the Value, Effectiveness, Efficiency, and Security of IT Controls.* IT Process Institute. Retrieved from http://www.itpi.org/docs/ITPI_Controls_ Bench-marking_Survey_Initial_Findings_v0817.pdf

Betz, C. T. (2007). *Architecture and Patterns for IT Service Management, Resource Planning, and Governance: making shoes for the Cobbler's children.* San Francisco, CA: Morgan Kaufman Publishers.

Bio, S. R. (1996). *Sistemas de Informação: um enfoque gerencial.* São Paulo, Brasil: Atlas.

Carter, S. (2007). *The New Language of Business. SOA & WEB 2.0.* New York: IBM Press.

Dragstra, P. (2005). *Enterprise Architecture: The select process of an Enterprise Architecture Toolset to support understanding and the governing Enterprise.* Unpublished master dissertation, Department of Mathematics and Computing Science.

Fernandes, A. A., & Abreu, V. F. (2008). *Implantando a Governança de TI: da estratégia à gestão dos processos e serviços.* São Paulo, Brasil: Brasport.

Gibert, J. (2003a). The IT Management Status Quo and the 5 Year Challenge. IT Physician Heal Thyself. *bITa-Center.* Retrieved June 20, 2007 from http://archive.bita-center.com/bitalib/bita/jg_art1.pdf

Gibert, J. (2003b). Concepts of a Unified Framework and Mapping Existing IT Frameworks.[s. l.]: IT Physician Heal Thyself. *bITa-Center.* Retrieved June 20, 2007 from http://archive.bita-center.com/bitalib/bita/jg_art2.pdf

Gibert, J. (2003c). Mapping IT Governance and the IT Value Chain onto a Unified Framework. [s. l.]: IT Physician Heal Thyself. *bITa-Center.* Retrieved June 20, 2007 from http://archive.bita-center.com/bitalib/bita/jg_art3.pdf

Gibert, J. (2003d). End to End Service Management: a case study. [s. l.]: IT Physician Heal Thyself. *bITa-Center.* Retrieved June 20, 2007 from http://archive.bita-center.com/bitalib/bita/jg_art4.pdf

Gibert, J. (2003e). The UPF Support Dimension. [s. l.]: IT Physician Heal Thyself. *bITa-Center.* Retrieved June 20, 2007 from http://archive.bita-center.com/bitalib/bita/jg_art5.pdf

Gibert, J. (2003f). The UPF Enabling Dimension. [s. l.]: IT Physician Heal Thyself. *bITa-Center.* Retrieved June 20, 2007 from http://archive.bita-center.com/bitalib/bita/jg_art6.pdf

Gibert, J. (2003g). UPF The Way Forward. [s. l.]: IT Physician Heal Thyself. *bITa-Center.* Retrieved June 20, 2007 from http://archive.bita-center.com/bitalib/bita/jg_art7.pdf

Gottschalk, P. (2007). *Business Dynamics in Information Technology.* Hershey, PA: Idea Group.

Grembergen, W. V. (2004). *Strategies for Information Technology Governance.* Hershey, PA: Idea Group Publishing.

Harmon, P. (2007). *Business Process Change: a guide for business managers and BPM and six sigma professionals.* Burlington, MA: Morgan Kaufman Publishers.

Hopkins, J. (2008). *Eating the IT Elephant: Moving from Greenfield Development to Brownfield.* New York: IBM Press.

IBM. (2005). Component Business Models: Making Specialization Real. *IBM Institute for Business Value.* Retrieved April 10, 2009, from http://www-935.ibm.com/services/us/index.wss/ibvstudy/imc/a1017908?cntxt=a1003208

ITPI. (2005). *IT Controls Benchmarking Survey: quantifying the value, effectiveness, efficiency and security of IT controls.* Retrieved February 11, 2008, from http://www.itpi.org/docs/ITPI_Controls_Benchmarking_Survey_Initial_Findings_v0817.pdf

Kasper, H. (2000). *O Processo de Pensamento Sistêmico: um estudo das principais abordagens a partir de um quadro de referencia proposto.* Unpublished master dissertation, Universidade Federal do Rio Grande do Sul.

Lankhorst, M. (2005). *Enterprise Architecture at Work.* New York: Springer.

Pelanda, M. L. (2006). *Modelos de Governança de Tecnologia da Informação adotados no Brasil: um estudo de casos múltiplos.* Unpublished master dissertation, Universidade Metodista de São Paulo, São Bernardo do Campo.

Plazaola, L., et al. (2006). A Metamodel for Strategic Business and IT. Alignment Assessment. In *Proceedings of the 41st Annual Hawaii International Conference on System Sciences (HICSS 2008),* Hawaii.

Prahalad, C. K. (2008). *The new age of innovation: Driving Co-Created Value Through Global Network.* New York: McGraw Hill.

Rezende, D. A., & Abreu, A. F. (2002). *Modelo de Alinhamento Estratégico da Tecnologia da Informação ao Negócio Empresarial.* Paper presented at the meeting of the XXII Encontro Nacional de Engenharia de Produção, Curitiba.

Rummler, G., & Brache, A. P. (1994). *Melhores Desempenhos das Empresas.* São Paulo, Brasil: Makron Books.

Section 2
Business Process Modelling

Chapter 4
Ontology Construction:
Representing Dietz "Process" and "State" Models Using BPMN Diagrams

Carlos Páscoa
INOV - INESC Inovação, Portuga &Estado-Maior da Força Aérea, Portugal

Pedro Sousa
INOV - INESC Inovação, Portugal & Instituto Superior Técnico, Portugal

José Tribolet
INOV - INESC Inovação, Portuga & Instituto Superior Técnico, Portugal

ABSTRACT

Capturing knowledge has always been an objective although known to be costly and time consuming. ontologies, being "an explicit specification of a conceptualization," have tried to capture knowledge within the aspects of concepts (used to represent a domain entity), relations (representing a interaction between the domain concepts), functions (a special case of relations), axioms (which represent true statements) and instances (used to represent domain elements). The Enterprise Ontology, which represents the work on ontologies applied to the enterprise, as proposed initially by Gruber, can be seen as a collection of terms and definitions relevant to business enterprises that can be used as a basis for decision making. A new concept of Enterprise Ontology proposed by Dietz is defined as the realization and implementation essence of an enterprise proposing a distinction world ontology and system ontology. The sequence of actions, according to Dietz can be classified as "datalogical", "infological" and "ontological" and all become under a Transaction Pattern which consists of four basic states: "request", "promise", "state" and "accept". Further more the author defines four models that can be used to verify the consistency of the actions: "Process", "Action", "State" and "Construction" models. The traditional way to model processes, like the BPMN, draw events, activities and data in a sequence of symbols that may not represent completely all the actions in presence and, above all, does not detect and identify consistency between actors and actions. However, BPMN diagrams can also be used to represent various actions and models proposed by Dietz as the transaction, "Process" and "State" diagrams. Both ways of representing have advantages and disadvantages and can be used, either isolated or together to give a deep representation of reality.

DOI: 10.4018/978-1-61692-020-3.ch004

INTRODUCTION

Ontologies have been used to capture knowledge and representing domains of interest. Since the first works, around 1990, ontologies have evolved significantly and they are used, in the present time, within a broader scope.

As the first ontologies consisted of practical examples defining syntax and semantics about a domain, today they have many formal definitions, each having advantages and disadvantages, and can define concepts, relations, functions, axioms or instances of the domain elements.

The Enterprise Ontology is a collection of terms and definitions relevant to business enterprises modeling and provides a formal way to define a particular domain: the enterprise trying to scope together some of the key organizational elements like goals, work processes, authority, positions and communication. More recently, some authors proposed a framework for modeling organizations.

Thus, the Enterprise Ontology presents several sections: Meta Ontology and Time, Activity, Plan, Capability, and Resource, Organization, Strategy and Marketing and associated concepts and relations between them. The TOVE model considers an organization to be a set of constraints on the activities performed by agents and has the objectives to produce and develop the organizational object taxonomy.

Although ontologies serve several purposes they do not identify lack of coherence between actions of a domain.

Dietz Enterprise Ontology, objectively proposes a methodology and a set of models to represent and analyze consistency of actions in a given process, while identifying three types of human abilities: "performa" (performer acts), "informa" (expressing acts) and "forma" (datalogical acts).

Dietz Transaction Pattern defines four states: "request", "promise", "state" and "accept". The existence of the four states should be considered as a universal need for every transaction. Further more, to detail exhaustively the several actions

a set of four models, with their exclusive way of representation, "Process", "Action", "State" and "Construction" are defined by the author, who ten demonstrates using the Volley example.

Although is seems that the Transaction Pattern is a convenient and universal method to state identifying the four models could be represented in a existing language, like the BPMN.

Using the Portuguese Air Force Mission Request Process, more complex than the Volley, the authors intend to assert that Dietz's Transaction Pattern also applies and demonstrate that two models, "Process" and "State", can be represented using BPMN.

Speaking of the Enterprise Ontology implies revisiting the concept of ontologies, in paragraph "ONTOLOGIES", and the particular case of the Enterprise Ontology (paragraph "ENTERPRISE ONTOLOGY"). Paragraph "DIETZ ENTERPRISE ONTOLOGY" introduces Dietz Enterprise Ontology and presents the concepts behind: the Transaction Pattern and the "Process", "Action", "State" and "Construction" models applied to the *Volley* case study. Paragraph "THE POR- TUGUESE AIR FORCE MISSION REQUEST PROCESS" discusses the Mission Request Process and the application of the Transaction Pattern in its analysis and its "Process" and "State" representation using BPMN.

BACKGROUND

Capturing knowledge has always been an objective although known to be costly and time consuming (Neches et al., 1991). Additionally, acquiring and representing the knowledge in a successful way, for a particular domain, does not mean that the captured knowledge can be reused in a new system (Swartout et al., 1994).

The work on the ontologies field goes back to the beginning of 1990. From those early years, ontology-building methodologies have evolved, and several have been proposed in order to achieve the current state of the art in ontology design (Baptista et al., 2004).

ONTOLOGIES

The first ontologies consisted in practical examples, built from scratch and made available in order to demonstrate the usefulness of such technology. By that time no methodologies or guidelines were available to lead or ease the building process. After some experience on the field, Gruber (1993), introduced some principles for the design of ontologies. Gruber's work was the first to describe the role of ontologies in supporting knowledge sharing activities, and presented a set of guidelines for the development of ontologies. The ontology-building process became clearer, with the continuous development of several other ontologies. As a consequence, the first methodologies for building ontologies appeared in 1995, leading to the emergence of the ontological engineering field (Baptista et al, 2006).

What Is an Ontology

The term "Ontology", dated circa 1721 (Merriam-Webster, 2008), in its abstract philosophical notion can be defined as "a branch of metaphysics concerned with the nature and relations of being" (Merriam-Webster, 2008), "a particular theory about the nature of being or the kinds of things that have existence" (Merriam-Webster, 2008). As early as 1900, the notion of a formal ontology has been distinguished from formal logic by the philosopher Husserl (Smith, 1998).

The term "Ontology", in Artificial Intelligence, is used to refer to the shared understanding of some domain of interest which may be used as a unifying framework to identifying important underlying concepts, define them, assign terms to them and note their important relation-ships, improving shared understanding, communication (among organizations, people and software

systems), systems specification, requirements identification, inter-operability and the potential for reuse and sharing (Uschold & Gruninger, 1996). Formal definitions include:

- *"An Ontology is an explicit specification of a conceptualization."* (Gruber 1995, pp. 907);
- *"An Ontology is a theory of what entities can exist in the mind of a knowledgeable agent."* (Wielinga and Schreiber, 1993);
- *"Ontologies are agreements about shared conceptualizations. Shared conceptualizations include conceptual frameworks for modeling domain knowledge; content-specific protocols for communication among inter-operating agents; and agreements about the representation of particular domain theories. In the knowledge-sharing context, ontologies are specified in the form of definitions of representational vocabulary. A very simple case would be a type hierarchy, specifying classes and their subsumption relationships. Relational database schemata also serve as ontologies by specifying the relations that can exist in some shared database and the integrity constraints that must hold for them"* (Gruber, 1994);
- *"An Ontology is a explicit knowledge level specification of a conceptualization, (...) which may be affected by the particular domain and task it is intended for."* (van Heijst, Schreiber and Wielinga 1996, pp. 11);
- *"An Ontology is an explicit, partial account of a conceptualization."* (Guarino & Giaretta, 1995, pp. 26);
- *"An Ontology for a body of knowledge concerning a particular task or domain describes a taxonomy of concepts for that task or domain that define the semantic interpretation of the knowledge."* (Alberts, 1993, cited by Sierra et al, pp. 34);

• "*An Ontology is an explicit, partial specification of a conceptualization that is expressible as a meta-level viewpoint on a set of possible domain theories for the purpose of modular design, redesign and reuse of knowledge-intensive system components.*" (Schreiber, Wielinga & Jansweijer, 1995, pp. 161).

Gruber's definition was further extended by Borst in 1997. In his work Construction of Engineering Ontologies (Borst, 1997) he defines ontology as: "*Ontologies are defined as a formal specification of a shared conceptualization*". Studer, Benjamins and Fensel (1998) further refined and explained this definition in 1998. In their work, the authors defined an ontology as: "*a formal, explicit specification of a shared conceptualization*" where: **Formal**: "*refers to the fact that an ontology should be machine-readable*"; **Explicit**: "*means that the type of concepts used, and the restrictions on their use are explicitly defined*". **Shared**: "*reflects the notion that the ontology captures consensual knowledge, that is, it is not the privilege of some individual, but accepted by a group*"; **Conceptualization**: *refers to an abstract model of some phenomenon in the world by having identified the relevant concepts of that phenomenon.*

The several possibilities above prove that a definition is an agreed issue, each having advantages and disadvantages (Guarino, 1996).

Ontologies provide a formal specification of a knowledge domain (Benjamins and Gómez-Pérez, 1999). Normally an ontology is composed of five components (Gruber, 1993).

• *Concepts*, used to represent a domain entity (tasks, functions, strategy, etc.);
• *Relations*, representing a interaction between the domain concepts with cardinality n:n;
• *Functions*, a special case of relations with cardinality n:1;

• *Axioms*, which represent true statements;
• *Instances*, used to represent domain elements.

THE ENTERPRISE ONTOLOGY

The motto ontologies are built to be reused (Fernandez et al., 1997) conveys in an appropriate manner the ideas originally proposed by Gruber (1993). Therefore, one of the steps taken to achieve the proposed objective was to survey existing information sources of the organization (enterprise) domain and verify their adequacy. Of these sources, some fall in the spectrum of definitions, presented by (McGuinness 2003), that details the concept of ontology introduced by Gruber (1993).

Mintzberg (1983) provides an early (and informal) analysis of organization structure distinguishing among five basic parts of an organization (strategic apex, middle line, operational core, techno-structure and logistics) and five distinct organization configurations that are encountered in practice (mutual adjustment, direct supervision, standardization of work processes, standardization of output, standardization of skills). This "ontology" includes several mechanisms that together achieve coordination, like goals, work processes, authority, positions and communication. The various parts of an organization are distinguished by the specific roles they play in achieving coordination with the above means.

The "language/action perspective" (Winograd, 1987) on cooperative work in organizations provides an ontology that emphasizes the social activity by which "agents" generate the space of cooperative actions in which they work, rather than the mental state of individuals. The basic idea is that social activity is carried out by language and communication.

In the same vein, (Auramaki et al., 1988) present a method for modeling offices as systems of communicative action through which people engage in actions by creating, modifying and deleting commitments that bind their current and future behaviors.

The work of Lee (1988) looks at language acts in the bureaucratic office, viewing language not as a mechanism for information transfer but as a mechanism for social interaction and control. He presents a logic-based representation of deontic notions - authorization, permission, prohibition and the like - and shows how this can be used to model cooperative work in the office.

Yu and Mylopoulos (1994) have proposed a framework for modeling organizations as being made of social actors that are intentional, having motivations, wants and beliefs and strategic, evaluating their opportunities and vulnerabilities with respect to each other. This formal model is used to explore alternative process designs in business reengineering.

The Enterprise Ontology is a collection of terms and definitions relevant to business enterprises modeling the enterprise in an organization wide-view manner that then can be used as a basis for decision making (Uschold and King 1995).

The major role of the Enterprise Ontology is to act as a communication medium; in particular, between: different people, including users and developers, across different enterprises and different computational systems (Uschold et al. 1996).

The Enterprise Ontology was developed as "*a collaborative effort to provide a method and a computer tool set for enterprise modeling*", using strong facilities for integration[1], communication[2], flexibility[3] and support[4], with the aim of providing and assuring a enterprise-wide view an a common understanding at all levels (Uschold et al, 1996).

The Enterprise Ontology presents several sections: Meta Ontology and Time, Activity, Plan, Capability, and Resource, Organization, Strategy and Marketing and associated concepts and relations between them.

In the same manner, ontology defined terms are presented as a core asset for term conformance within the ontology itself. Uschold et al. (1996) defined the formal terms, addressing the Enterprise Ontology, for different areas of interest (activity, organization, strategy, marketing and time).

The TOVE Enterprise Modeling project (Fox et al, 1997) intended to create the next generation Enterprise, a Common Sense Enterprise Model. The TOVE authors consider an organization to be a set of constraints on the activities performed by agents. This view follows that of Weber (1987) who views the process of bureaucratization as a shift from management based on self-interest and personalities to one based on rules and procedures.

The TOVE model considers an organization to be a set of constraints on the activities performed by agents. In particular, an organization consists of a set of divisions and subdivisions (recursive definition), a set of organization-agents (said to be members of a division of the organization), a set of roles that the members play in the organization, and an organization-goal tree that specifies the goals (and their decomposition into sub goals) the members try to achieve. An organization-agent (or in short agent) plays one or more roles. Each role is defined with a set of goals that the role is created to fulfill and is allocated with proper authority at the level that the role can achieve its goals. Agents perform activities in the organization, each of which may consume resource (e.g. materials, labors, tools, etc.) and there is a set of constraints that constrain the activities (Fox et al, 1997).

An approach to engineering ontologies begins with defining an ontology's requirements; this is in the form of questions that an ontology must be able to answer and can be referred as the competency of the ontology. The second step is to define the terminology of the ontology – its objects, attributes, and relations (Fox et al. 1997).

Therefore the resulting diagram (containing objects, attributes, and relations) can be used to represent organization actors, agents and actions and the relation between. However, it does not validate the processes in which they are involved.

Dietz proposes a "stronger" form of Enterprise Ontology. In fact, true semantic can only

Figure 1. The three production acts

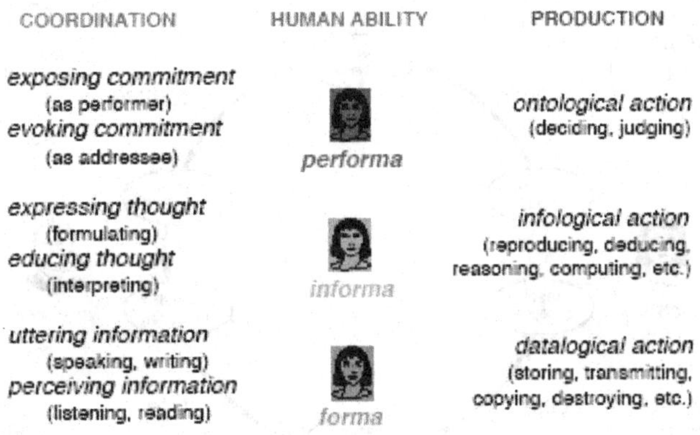

be achieved if action modeling is taken into consideration. Therefore, besides characterizing the elements that are involved in the action, Dietz also validates if the process activities are formally correct. It is the first step of a process towards implementation which, in the author's opinion, represents a complete new issue on organization design and engineering. The next chapter shows an example.

DIETZ ENTERPRISE ONTOLOGY

In chapter two of his book the Enterprise Ontology, Dietz defines Enterprise Ontology[5] "as the realization and implementation independent essence of an enterprise, in short, as the deep structure behind its observable surface structure" (Dietz, 2006).

In his analysis of the complexity of an apparent simple case – the "Volley" case, he uses a flow chart to show the sequence of actions that are performed stating that, under the axiom explained in his book (chapter 12, see Figure 1), the actions can be classified as datalogical[6], infological (both concepts as defined originally by Langefors (1977)) or ontological[7].

According to Dietz "a datalogical production[8] act is an act in which one manipulates the form of information, commonly referred to as data, so

without being concerned about its content" that are translated in acts like "copying, storing, and transmitting data" (in the case volley the act of recording an application for membership in the letter book). Datalogical acts are associated with datalogical typical coordination acts like "speaking, listening, writing, and reading"

An infological[9] act, like deciding and judging, always brings new original things and does not concern about the form but "about the content of information only" like inquiring, calculating and reasoning (e.g. calculating the membership fee). Infological acts also include formulating thoughts) written or spoken sentences) and interpreting perceived sentences (through listening or reading).

Langefors distinguished between two work areas or problems in the development of information systems: the infological problem and the datalogical problem. The infological problem is how to define the information to be provided by the information system in order to satisfy user needs. The datalogical problem is how to organize the set of data and the hardware in order to implement the information system.

Dietz defines a circular transaction pattern (where typical ontological acts are requesting and promising) and draws a flower request example (shown in Figure 2) where a bouquet is requested by the requestor with a tacit promise by the vendor

Figure 2. Dietz transaction pattern (adapted)

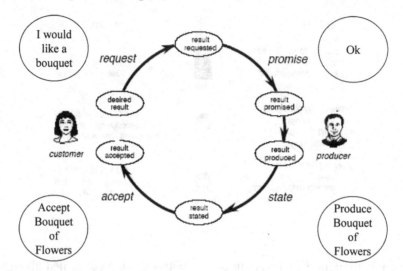

In this request there are some assumptions subjacent to the request showing that the requestor is aware of the type of bouquet that is sold by the vendor (natural flowers or plastic flowers or n flowers for each bouquet).

In the case Volley there appears to be two ontological transactions (becoming member of the tennis club and paying the membership fee – T2). The author delves into the analysis of the case Volley presenting several flow charts annotated with the several type of acts within the Transaction Pattern showing incoherencies (for example the inexistence of T01 promise and acceptance acts).

Focusing on the ontological production of the case Volley, the author defines four models: The "Process", "Action", "State" and "Construction" models.

The **"Process" Model** (shown in Figure 3) describes the basic steps of the two transactions linking the several steps within the Transaction Model. Dietz also specifies an action rule model that identifies what to be done when the producer has to deal with a request.

The **"Action" Model** (represents the collection of action rules for the enterprise. Figure 4 shows an example.

The **"State" Model** (shown in Figure 5) whose function is to show all the information items (object classes and fact types) that occur in the Action Model.

Considering the same two ontological type transactions it means that the membership starts to exist and that the first membership has been paid.

The **"Construction" Model** (Figure 6) demonstrates that the ontological models are independent of the way in which it is or might be implemented.

After presenting the several ontological aspect models, Dietz enforces the idea that the ontological fact (being very stable):

- Is fully abstracted from the current way in which it operates;
- It does not contain organization functions;
- it does not contain infological or datalogical things;
- is completely abstracts from the communication acts being totally independent from new organizational structure;
- Shown things that have no explicit implementation, like the promise and acceptance;
- Serves for proposing, analyzing and implementing organizational changes providing

Figure 3. Dietz ontological process model of volley

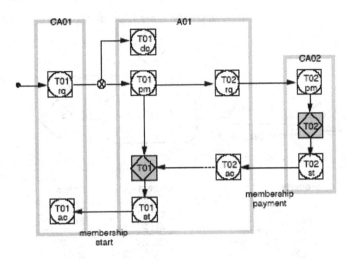

Figure 4. Dietz volley case action

```
on requested T01(M) with member(new M) = P
        if age(P) < minimal_age or
            #members(Volley)=maximum_number(current_year)
            decline T01(M)
        if age(P) < minimal_age and
            #members (Volley) < maximum_number(current_year)
            promise T01(M)
        fi
no
```

the right amount of (re)design and (re)engineering freedom;

• Is composed by a set of four aspect models that are coherent based on a theoretical foundation;

The independence of the ontological models from implementation and the usefulness of the ontological facts are valuable factors in analyzing business processes. The next chapter presents the Portuguese Air Force Mission Request Process and uses Dietz Transaction Pattern and the four

ontological models to assert the existence of all the transaction components.

However Dietz, as opposed to using conventional and well established representation languages, like BMPN, choose to lay down a new form for representing some of his diagrams. In fact he could have used BPMN to draw the entire representations.

The following chapter describes the Air Force Mission Request Process in a textual manner and analyses the same process according to Dietz transaction and ontological models and, while veri-

Figure 5. Dietz ontological "state" model of volley

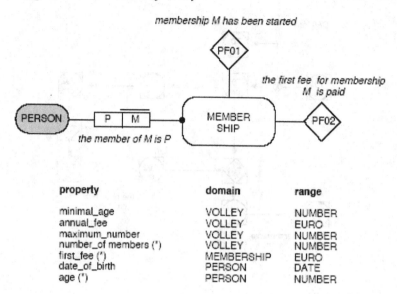

Figure 6. Dietz ontological "construction" model of volley

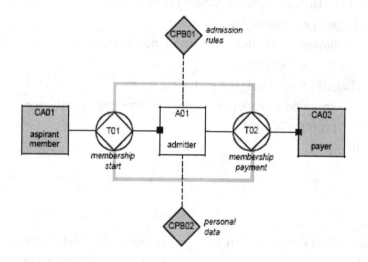

fying consistency, using BMPN to represent the "Transaction", "Process" and the "State" models.

THE PORTUGUESE AIR FORCE MISSION REQUEST PROCESS

This chapter describes the Air Force Mission Request Process and uses Dietz Transaction,

"Process" and the "State" models to concepts to characterize it. The representation is done using BMPN diagrams to show that existing representation languages can also be used to show new concepts.

Process Description

Every organization can issue a mission request for the Air Force. The mission request should be sent, by letter, fax or postal mail to the Chief Of Staff Cabinet. In that letter the requesting organization has to mention its name, telephone number, postal address, fiscal number (street, house number and zip code), the type of mission, estimated time of departure, estimated time of arrival, departure location, arrival location, number of passenger and/or cargo (number of packages, size and weight and information about the passengers (birth date and sex).

Upon receiving the request, one person inside the Chief of Staff Cabinet, the one that administrates mission requests, checks whether the information provided is complete. If not, he makes a telephone call to the sender in order to complete the data.

If the information is complete, the person adds an incoming mail number and the date, records the letter in the IT system, and archives a copy. He then checks for the existence of a memorandum of understanding (MOU) between the Air Force and the requesting that foresees the realization of such missions. If the MOU does not exist he checks the potential interest for the Air Force on accomplishing the mission. In both cases, existing MOU and Air Force interest, he checks with the Operational Command for availability of the type of aircraft and crew for the requested date and time.

Upon verification completeness, he prepares a Memo and proposes to the Chief of Air Staff whether this mission is to be performed.

If a mission request is denied (e.g., because lack of aircraft availability or because the maximum number of requested passengers or cargo exceeds the aircraft capacity), the mission administrator will send a letter in which he explains why the applicant cannot receive the requested mission.

If the decision is affirmative, the mission details are sent to the Operational Command that generates an Air Task order. This is an application with numbered missions and each new mission is entered on a new line. The line number is the mission number, by which the new mission is referenced in the Air Force.

Upon receiving the Air Task the operational unit performs the mission and reports it on the mission report format and sends it to the Operational Command that after due analysis, sends it back to the Chief of Air Force Chief of Staff Cabinet.

Next, the mission administrator calculates the mission fee that the requester has to pay. Based on existing Memorandum of Agreement or aircraft hour of flight cost, he finds the amount due. Then, he writes down the amount in the mission report and sends it the finance directorate.

Upon receiving mission report, the finance directorate issues a mission card on which are mentioned the mission number, the commencement date, the organization name, the mission date, the departure and arrival locations, and the postal address and prepares an invoice to the requester for payment. Payments have to be performed by bank transfer.

As soon as the payment is received the receipt is sent to the mission requester by postal mail or fax.

Transaction and Ontological Models Application

The Mission Request Process is more complex than the Volley. Under the perspective of the Transaction Pattern the Volley has two main stages: membership request and acceptance (which then culminates with paying the first membership). The in processing of the request is depending only in one actor and all the actions are performed within the same office. Therefore, a "request" is followed by a "promise" (of processing the request) and then a "state" that is "accepted" by the person which wants to becoming a member and paying the first membership fee.

The Mission Request is rather more complex. The requestor issues the "Request" which, as

Figure 7. The process model of PoAF's mission request

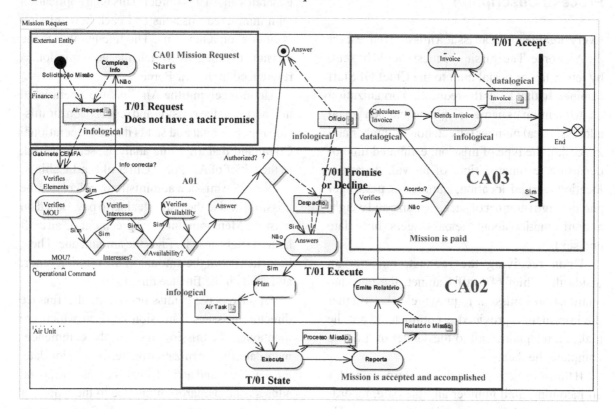

opposed to the Volley case, does not have a tacit promise. Evaluating the request is done by several persons, within one cabinet, that produce a recommendation. The final decision is given to the Chief of Air Staff. Only then there's a "Promise" and only if the answer is "yes".

The subsequent stages include preparing the mission and its accomplishment and report which, all together represents the "State" phase of the Transaction pattern. After the mission is finalized one can think that the requestor has accepted it and thus it can be considered as the "Accept" stage. However, this is not true and the "Accept" stage should only be considered when the requestor receives the invoice and pays the mission cost (for requestors that produce a memorandum of understanding with the Air Force it is considered that the mission is already under the terms agreed which include payment).

Actually, the ontological values are exactly the same in both cases. Becoming a member and pay the fist membership fee as opposed to getting the mission and paying its cost can be seen as the ontological facts of the Volley and Mission Request Process.

In sequence of what was written before, and referring to the ontological models application which is represented in BPMN (see Figure 7) of the Mission Request Process. As the Mission Request comes in (*CA01 Mission Request Starts*), the Air Force Cabinet has to verify that the necessary data is present. In Dietz transaction model this can be considered that the mission request (***T/01 Request*** is done but it does not have a tacit promise).

Upon element completeness verification, several actions have to be made internally in order to assure if the mission can be accomplished. *A01 square* shows all the actions that need to be

Figure 8. The "state" model of PoAF's mission request

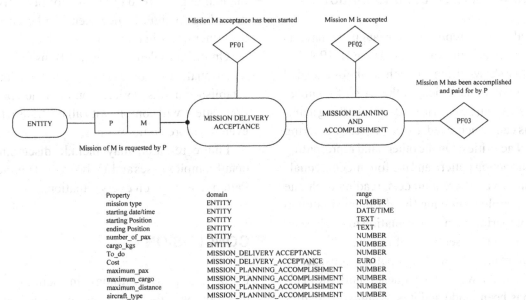

Property	domain	range
mission type	ENTITY	NUMBER
starting date/time	ENTITY	DATE/TIME
starting Position	ENTITY	TEXT
ending Position	ENTITY	TEXT
number_of_pax	ENTITY	NUMBER
cargo_kgs	ENTITY	NUMBER
To_do	MISSION_DELIVERY ACCEPTANCE	NUMBER
Cost	MISSION_DELIVERY_ACCEPTANCE	EURO
maximum_pax	MISSION_PLANNING_ACCOMPLISHMENT	NUMBER
maximum_cargo	MISSION_PLANNING_ACCOMPLISHMENT	NUMBER
maximum_distance	MISSION_PLANNING_ACCOMPLISHMENT	NUMBER
aircraft_type	MISSION_PLANNING_ACCOMPLISHMENT	NUMBER

done including verifying if there is an existing memorandum of understanding between the Air Force and the requesting entity, checking mission interest, and verifying aircraft availability.

Upon verifications finalization a proposal is submitted to the Chief of Staff decision. This stage represents a ***T01 Execute/Decline*** state in the Transaction Pattern. If the decision is affirmative, a letter is sent to the requesting entity (***T01 Promise***) and an order to execute is sent to the operational command.

Mission acceptance (***T01 State***) and accomplishment are performed in the CA02 square. Upon mission accomplishment a mission report is sent to the chief of staff cabinet that verifies the execution elements and sends (in the lack of a memorandum of understanding existence) to the finance department which produces the invoice and sends it to the requesting entity (CA03 square). The acceptance (***T/01 Accept***) stage of the Transaction Pattern is then performed by the requesting entity.

Figure 7 shows that Dietz *Transaction* and *Process Models* can be represented by a BPMN

diagram given that further elements are drawn as depicted in the diagram. Notice that, although not present, the BMPN model can represent data elements which could bring a detailed representation of data and infological aspects of the process.

What about the "State" Model? Does BPMN represent state as accurately as Dietz diagram? A "State" model for the Mission Request Process can be represented in Figure 8.

What can be seen if a comparison is made between Figure 7 ("Process" Model represented in BPMN) and Figure 8 ("State" Model) is that the states shown in Figure 8 are also shown in Figure 7 represented by the red squares. The attributes that are defined in Dietz "State" Model (*CA01 to CA03*) can also be included in the BPMN diagram if the data elements are included.

Based on the anterior text, one can assume that the BPMN representation (see Figure 7) can replace Dietz case analysis flow charts, the "Process" model (Figure 4) and the "State" model (Figure 5).

Solutions and Recommendations

Naturally, all the representation languages have its advantages and disadvantages. One BMPN diagram that shows all the actions has to be overloaded with annotations which, in the case of complex processes, can be hard to read – minimizing annotations can be achieved, for example, by coloring BPMN activities. On the other hand representing the transaction pattern and the four models equals drawing five different models, reading each one (which implies knowing five different notations) and comparing each representation to produce an understood representation of reality.

Referring the transaction pattern consistency there is no answer to the requestor until the decision has been made and it is assumed that, after the mission has been performed, that everything went according to plan. Actually, there are some elements that can jeopardize mission accomplishment such as aircraft malfunction (Air Force responsibility), weather, political rules, and third party flight authorizations (third party responsibilities). However, when the requestor receives the "State" from the Air Force he already knows that he is due to "Accept" the mission even if it is not successfully due to third party responsibilities.

FUTURE RESEARCH DIRECTIONS

Towards an understood representation of reality both models (BPMN and the "Process" and "State" models can be used. Naturally, both have advantages and disadvantages.

BPMN is a widely used and understood modeling language. Using BPMN will short the user learning process. However, BMPN diagrams when taking advantage of its full notation tend to be confusing and therefore hard to read. Future research directions include investigating new ways of using the full scope of BMPN notation while

maintaining its readability. Coloring activities according to significance seems to be one path to further investigations on this subject.

On the completeness of the Transaction Pattern to analyze the range of transactions a doubt is established in this work reasoning if the Transaction Pattern will comply with all the transactions, even the more complex ones.

Future research may include discussing in detail complex cases and analyzes the Transaction Pattern coverage on every situation.

CONCLUSION

Dietz Enterprise Ontology introduces a new methodology for representing processes and decomposes its representation into four different diagrams while also verifies, based on the Transaction Pattern, the coherence of process actions.

Chapter two and three revisit the concept of ontologies and, in particular, the Enterprise Ontology formal defined terms and the TOVE organizational object taxonomy.

Dietz Enterprise Ontology proposes a "new" form of ontology that, while characterizing the elements that are involved also validates the actions present in the Transaction Pattern that comprehends four stages: "Request", "Promise", "State" and "Accept". To fully represent a process, Dietz uses the Volley case to introduce new notations to four models ("Process", "Action", "State" and "Construction"). A question arises: do existing notations permit the models representation?

Using the Air Force Mission Request process, more complex, than the Volley, the authors propose to represent, the "Process" and "State" models using standard BPMN diagram, while applying and discussing Dietz transaction pattern. Both the Mission Request and the Volley have two ontological statements, however the inside-tasks are different as they depend on one actor that as control over everything – Volley – and on several actors that perform different tasks that end up with a recommendation for a decision – the Mission Request.

The "Request" stage is equal for both (but different on the tacit acceptance) but the "Promise" stage differs significantly in terms of what has to be done and the path that has to be followed. On the other hand, there are some explicit differences on the "State" stage. On the Volley case after the validation phase is complete the clerk can promise the requestor that he is going to be a member. On the Mission Request, although the Air Force promises to perform the mission, there could be third party reasons either for not doing it at all or to deviate from the initial plan. In this case, the requestor has to informally accept the fact the he has to "Accept" the mission even if it does match the request.

Using Dietz's Transaction Pattern proved to be very useful in analyzing and identifying process activities using the "Request", "Promise", "State" and "Accept "stages as it allows to verify consistency between activities and identify items that need to be changed in order to provide a clearer understanding of the actions performed by the process actors.

On the representation part, a BPMN diagram was used to draw both the "Process" and the "State" models (provided that the BPMN data elements are used including the one that can represent infologic aspects). The diagram, after annotation, can also represent the Transaction Pattern. Naturally there are advantages and disadvantages in using one notation to represent the complexity of a process or using five diagrams to represent a pattern and four models, as proposed by Dietz.

The way how BMPN could be used to fully represent Dietz models can be further brought to a level of more detail as people thinks about it involving more work and new ways if representing.

Dietz's universal Transaction Pattern applicability to every situation, even the more complex ones, which involve multiple decision levels and multiple actors, is brought to a reasonable doubt. Further debate methodology on this issue should identify complex cases and study thoroughly the Transaction Pattern applicability.

On both subjects, BPMN usage to replace Dietz's "Process" and "State" diagrams and the universal application of the Transaction Pattern, this paper intent is to unveil the world of possibilities making a small initial contribution.

REFERENCES

Alberts, L. K. (1993). *YMIR: An Ontology for Engineering Design*. PhD thesis, University of Twente.

Auramaki, E., Lehtinen, E., & Lyytinen, K. (1988, April). A speech-act-based office modeling approach. *ACM Transactions on Office Information Systems*, 6(2), 126–152. doi:10.1145/45941.214328

Benjamins, R., & Gomez Perez, A. (1999). Overview of Knowledge, Sharing and Reuse Components: Ontologies and Problem-Solving Methods. In *Proceedings of the IJCAI-99 workshop on Ontologies and Problem-Solving Methods (KRR5)*, Stockholm, Sweden (pp. 1-15).

Borst, W. N. (1997). *Construction of Engineering Ontologies*. Enshede, The Netherlands: Centre for Telematica and Information Technology, University of Twente.

Dietz, J. L. G. (2006). *Enterprise Ontology: Theory and Methodology*. Delft, The Netherlands: Springer. doi:10.1007/3-540-33149-2

Fernandez, M., Gomez-Perez, A., & Juristo, N. (1997 March). Methontology: from Ontological Art towards Ontological Engineering. In *Proceedings of the AAAI97 Spring Symposium Series on Ontological Engineering*, Stanford, USA (pp. 33–40).

Fox, M. S., Barbuceanu, M., Gruninger, M., & Lin, J. (1997). *An Organization Ontology for Enterprise Modeling*. Enterprise Integration Laboratory - Department of Mechanical and Industrial Engineering, University of Toronto.

Gruber, T. R. (1993). A Translation Approach to Portable Ontology Specifications. *Knowledge Acquisition, 5*(2), 199–220. doi:10.1006/knac.1993.1008

Gruber, T. R. (1993). *Welcome to the SRKB working group*. Retrieved January 15, 2008 from http://www-ksl.stanford.edu/email-archives/srkb.messages/0.html

Gruber, T. R. (1995). Toward principles for the design of ontologies used for knowledge sharing. *International Journal of Human-Computer Studies, 43*(5-6), 907–928. doi:10.1006/ijhc.1995.1081

Guarino, N. (1996). Understanding, Building, and Using Ontologies. In *Proceedings of the 10th Knowledge Acquisition for Knowledge-Based Systems Workshop*, Alberta, Canada.

Guarino, N., & Giaretta, P. (1995). Ontologies and Knowledge Bases: Towards a Terminological Clarification . In Mars, N. (Ed.), *Towards Very Large Knowledge Bases: Knowledge Building and Knowledge Sharing* (pp. 25–32). Amsterdam: IOS Press.

Langefors, B. (1977). Information System Theory. *Information Systems, 2*, 207–219. doi:10.1016/0306-4379(77)90009-6

Lee, R. M. (1988, April). Bureaucracies as deontic systems. *ACM Transactions on Office Information Systems, 6*(2), 87–108. doi:10.1145/45941.45944

McGuinness, D. L. (1998). Ontologies Come of Age . In Fensel, D., Hendler, J., Lieberman, H., & Wahlster, W. (Eds.), *Spinning the Semantic Web: Bringing the World Wide Web to Its Full Potential*. Cambridge, MA: MIT Press.

Merriam-Webster. (2008). *Ontology word In Merriam-Webster Dictionary online*. Retrieved February 1, 2009, from http://www.m-w.com/dictionary/ontology

Mintzberg, H. (1983). *Structure in Fives-Designing Effective Organizations*. Upper Saddle River, NJ: Prentice Hall Inc.

Neches, R., Fikes, R., Finin, T., Gruber, T., Patil, R., Senator, T., & Swartout, W. R. (1991). Enabling Technology for Knowledge Sharing. *AI Magazine, 12*(3), 36–56.

Ribeiro, R., Batista, F., Paulo, J., Mamede, N., & Pinto, H. S. (2006). Cooking an Ontology. In *Proceedings of the 12th International Conference on Artificial Intelligence: Methodology, Systems, Applications*.

Studer, R., Benjamins, V. R., & Fensel, D. (1998). Knowledge engineering: principles and methods. *IEEE Transactions on Data and Knowledge Engineering, 25*(1-2), 161–197. doi:10.1016/S0169-023X(97)00056-6

Swartout, W. R., Neches, R., & Patil, R. (1994). Knowledge sharing: Prospects and challenges . In Fuchi, K., & Yokoi, T. (Eds.), *Knowledge Building and Knowledge Sharing* (pp. 102–109). Amsterdam: IOS Press.

Uschold, M., & Gruninger, M. (1996). Ontologies: principles, methods and applications. *Journal of Knowledge Engineering Review, 11*(2), 93–155. doi:10.1017/S0269888900007797

Uschold, M., & King, M. (1995). Towards a Methodology for Building Ontologies. In *Proc. of IJCAI95's Workshop on Basic Ontological Issues in Knowledge Sharing*.

Uschold, M., King, M., Moralee, S., & Zorgios, Y. (1996). *The Enterprise Ontology*. Retrieved June 14, 2007, from http://www.aiai.ed.ac.uk/~oplan/documents/1996/96-enterprise-ontology.pdf van Heijst, G., Schreiber, A. T., & Wielinga, B. J. (1996). Using Explicit Ontologies in KBS Development. *International Journal of Human and Computer Studies, 46*(2/3),183-292.

Wielinga, B., Schreiber, A. T., & Jansweijer, W. F. (1995). The KACTUS View on the 'O' Word. In *IJCAI Workshop on Basic Ontological Issues in Knowledge Sharing* (pp. 159-168).

Wielinga, B. J., & Schreiber, A. T. (1993). Reusable and sharable knowledge bases: A European perspective. In *Proceedings International Conference on Building and Sharing of Very Large-Scaled Knowledge Bases* (pp. 103–115). Tokyo, Japan: Japan Information Processing Development Center.

Winograd, T. (1987). A language/action perspective on the design of cooperative work. *Human-Computer Interaction, 3*(1), 3–30. doi:10.1207/s15327051hci0301_2

Yu, E. S. K., & Mylopoulos, J. (1994). From E-R to "A-R" - Modelling strategic actor relationships for business process reengineering. In *13-th Int. Conf. on the Entity-relationship Approach*, December 13-16, 1994, Manchester, UK.

ENDNOTES

[1] "Integration must be achieved for relating information to obtain different views of the enterprise, for relating tasks to be performed to the tools that support them, and to establish connections between the tools themselves."

[2] "Communication must be achieved between people, ensuring that the enterprise models are shared within the organization, between tasks that are performed so that information can be used where it is relevant, and between the tools used to perform the tasks so that relevant data can be passed between them."

[3] "Flexibility is important to allow an organization to adapt its business processes to meet changing goals and changes in its environment; e.g. to take advantage of deregulation. It is also important to allow flexibility in the enactment of processes to ensure that people's time is used as effectively as possible, giving people the choice of what to do and when to do it."

[4] "Support must be provided, assisting the user by making clear what is going on and why, stepping them through difficult situations as well as taking care of technical details. This ensures that processes are carried out effectively and efficiently reducing risk of confusion which could arise with too much flexibility."

[5] Ontology. Generally speaking, it is the metaphysical study of the nature of being and existence. Specifically (in this book), the ontology of something is a conceptual model that satisfies the next requirements: coherent, comprehensive, consistent, concise, and essential. We distinguish between world ontology and system ontology.

[6] Datalogical. A notion related to production acts. Production acts that concern the storing, transmitting, copying, destroying etc, of data are called datalogical production acts.

[7] Ontological model. The constructional model of a (homogeneous) system that is fully independent of its implementation.

[8] Dietz defines the Operation Axiom with two acts: the Production act as the act in a transaction by which the executor establishes the production factum (or production result); the Coordination act as an act by which a coordination factum (or coordination result) is created.

[9] Infological. A notion related to production acts. Production acts that concern reproducing, deducing, computing etc. of concepts are called infological production acts.

Chapter 5
Security Management Services Based on Authentication Roaming between Different Certificate Authorities

Masakazu Ohashi
Chuo University, Japan

Mayumi Hori
Hakuoh University, Japan

ABSTRACT

The purpose of this study is to incorporate the authentication roaming technology with existing social infrastructures from the perspective of users instead of that of service providers. By conducting experiments in the Business to Consumer (B to C) environment, the authors' research demonstrated and confirmed the effectiveness of the authentication roaming technology to realize a safe and convenient network society. This technology contributes to the construction of a citizen-centric, reassuring system especially for mobile and transportation by proposing a cooperation system for the mobile information services based on the XML Web Services technology. The authors' aim to enable mobile users to access a variety of essential information for maintaining safety and comfortable management of networks and enable them to make an educated decision regarding the treatment they may receive in case of trouble.

INTRODUCTION

It is essential to reinforce citizens' health management and disease prevention as well as to reduce increasing public share of medical costs, as Japan is well on the way to an aging society. In order to achieve them, it is essential to improve the quality of the health services as unifying force (hubs) to utilize a variety of functions such as authentication, security, procedures, and procurements. As has been the pattern, individual medical institutions including clinics and hospitals had independently responded to the medical needs of citizens. Currently, there are various services available that utilize the Internet. Additionally, more and more services are newly created to meet users' diverse needs by incorporating existing services and social

DOI: 10.4018/978-1-61692-020-3.ch005

infrastructures. Nonetheless, many of the existing services are often provided with specifications unique to each service provider, making it difficult or even impossible to integrate them with existing social infrastructures. Therefore, it is essential to develop a scheme that incorporates different services and infrastructures without boundaries of specifications.

Traditionally, many services were provided by locally connecting computers. However, with the rapid and widespread diffusion of the Internet, the demand for integration remotely or globally has increased. Consequently, there emerges an increasing need for the development of technologies that incorporate different systems. However, implementing the same technology used for connecting computers locally into a system connecting computers globally is costly and time consuming. The social infrastructure is a wide concept, and it includes so many various entities. Today, not only information and communications technologies (ICT) including broadband networks and mobile phones but also the logistics and sales systems are prevailed as social infrastructures. Nonetheless, there are still few models that transcend the difference of business types and industries, and connect them altogether to provide a new service.

For the demonstration experiment, we selected the Business to Consumer (B to C) model. The model we built aims to utilize different social infrastructures, and coordinates with other services regardless of their business types and industries to offer convenient and effective services for users. We developed the Web Service that provides user-centric services as well as the authentication system essential for coordinating different systems. However, the current condition with advancing medical technology, deficit operation of medical institutions', and lack of doctors makes it nearly impossible to respond a variety of medical and healthcare needs of people. This issue is especially serious in countryside areas hence optimization of management resources for healthcare and medical services is very much in need. As a strategic solution for this issue, we propose creation of a cooperation network among municipalities, hospitals and clinics, nutrition counseling centers, corporations, and university research centers.

BACKGROUND OF THIS STUDY

With the rapid aging of population, Japan has the world's highest longevity rate today. As a result, a reform of the conventional healthcare at hospitals is required. That is, building a cooperative structure with related organizations, institutions, and citizens is strongly required to establish a total lifetime healthcare not only for sick people but also for healthy people to swiftly respond and figure out the medical, healthcare, and welfare needs of all the citizens. Conventionally, medical care has functioned specifically to diagnose and treat illness. Nonetheless, today's scope of medical care is required to include health maintenance and promotion, prevention of disease and early detection, early diagnosis and treatment, and elderly care. Furthermore, people have become more conscious about not only *cure* but also *care* to live a healthy life. It has long been difficult for patients and citizens to access a variety of information including insurance, illness, and treatment that are essential to choose appropriate medical institutions and receive proper treatment. Especially in countryside areas far from urban cities, there are much less medical resources such as healthcare centers and medical institutions.

From the perspectives of total optimization for medical and healthcare needs of people, it is essential to take a citizen-centric, patient-oriented approach to determine the appropriateness of functions and locations of medical institutions from the viewpoint of residents(Ohashi,edi,2005). In addition, it is highly important to create a cooperative network among not only medical institutions including hospitals and clinics but also among municipalities, corporations dealing with food, medicine/medical devices/care centre facilities, nutrition centers, and universities and research institutes to improve patients and residents' quality of life including health promotion, prevention of diseases, medical treatment, and rehabilitation (Hori & Ohashi,2006).

OBJECTIVES OF THIS STUDY

Our goal is to explore patient's oriented medical system, that is to say, to develop a user-friendly application that enables information workers at their desktops to use XML Web Services to access and use enterprise information in order to explore the full potential of the XML Web Services that streamlines the process of gathering information and makes it easier to reuse information throughout the organization. For proof of the concept, we introduce and review some useful health care systems which utilize the medical information services and develop solutions to meet the needs of patients and medical institutions in this study. Most healthcare organizations have almost hundreds of applications running in the enterprise. There is much information in silos across organization because these applications often do not "talk to" each other. Then clinicians find it extremely frustrating when they search information they required. In addition, every application has an extremely different user interface and work-flow. This may be especially troublesome for clinicians who travel from one hospital to another. Every hospital may have a different clinical information system that the clinician is expected to use. Therefore, it is very tiresome and too difficult for clinicians to learn how to use all these different systems with their unique user-interfaces and work flow interpretations.

Today, many key decision makers are often unable to make informed decisions because the information they need is trapped within documents or databases in another part of the organization.

So technologies such as XML Web services have been helpful in improving business processes from server to server, but till now, they have not been connected directly to information workers at their desktops. This has meant that information workers have not had a way to interact with XML Web Services directly to access and use the enterprise information that they need. Therefore, it is essential to develop a user-friendly application that enables information workers at their desktops to use XML Web Services to access and use enterprise information in order to explore the full potential of the XML Web Services that streamlines the process of gathering information and makes it easier to reuse information throughout the organization. In this paper, we discuss the potentialities and expansibility of application of the XML Web Services technology to improve the quality of the Japanese medical services.

The purpose of this study is to confirm the validity of the Web Service we developed. Through the experiment conducted in the B to C environment, we aim to demonstrate the effectiveness of the Web Service which incorporates various social infrastructures being developed by enterprises in the private sector, and to proclaim that this is the new business model requiring less time and cost. For the experiment in our study, we selected three widely diffused social infrastructures: convenience stores, Internet connection, and mobile phones. Furthermore, we intend to prove that the services utilizing the Web Service contributes to the building of the safe and convenient social system.

Another purpose of this study is to prove the effectiveness of the new roaming technology which shares authentication results among existing systems, as well as between different certificate authorities (CAs). In our experiment, the server of a convenience store and a mobile phone work together through a one-stop authentication process via the Internet connection. Our authentication roaming technology enables users to enjoy different Internet services by having different certificate authorities share their ID information. n this section we introduce the text format specifications.

EMPIRICAL METHOD AND RESULTS

We examined the possibility of collaboration among corporations, universities, and research institutions by building an information sharing environment prior to applying the XML Web Services into the data management system which utilizes the information stored within the iDC. Second, we examined the effectiveness of the data storage system and evaluated whether the external applications are capable of high-level utilization such as its proficiency of producing knowledge out of information, presenting data effectively, and storing know-how (Ohashi.edi,2003b). The following criteria were examined by the demonstration experiment utilizing the collaborative work test bed:

1). The possibility of collaboratively creating digital visual image contents in the distributed environment. All the materials in the visual library were stored, managed, and safely backed-up in an integrated fashion without making duplications at organizations within in the distributed environment.

2) The potentialities of connecting different organizations through the iDC with high-speed network and of building a system with which users can exchange large amount of data on-line and on-time. Its effectiveness of arousing an academic curiosity for the further development of high-speed, large capacity data and information exchange and sharing.

3) The capability of the iDC and the proxy servers to operate interactive control functions even when clients and their servers are located in an IP unreachable area.

4) The efficiency of collaboratively developing educational materials, reducing the process dynamics before making it available to classes, and reducing the cost of security by examining the issues in operating with modified server applications to make them more suitable and useable within the iDC. The operationalization of the dynamic image archives.

5) The validity of the data structuralization, retrieval, extraction, supply, and utilization with XML in the knowledge management systems being developed in the platform.

Especially, the capability of prompting the collaborative work while protecting the data privacy by allowing users to switch the collaborative workplaces according to their object where access is controlled by each organization so that only permitted group members have the authority to share data. One-stop services is the original goal for promoting the Health Care System. As a means to realize one-stop services that integrates variety of services, portal has been reviewed and implemented from the beginning of the stage by government and with collaboration between public and private sectors. Implementing Web Services into the interface between servers and clients, and implementing not on the portal (server) but on clients (users) would bring about a new way to realize one-stop services (Figure 1)(Web Services Initiative,2005). There are two main advantages of citizen-centric one-stop services:

1) No need of the portal systems that could be a major burden to construct

2) No need for portal to posses personal information.

Building of a portal system is very difficult. From the point of authentication and organizing interfaces, it is difficult to develop a portal after each service has been developed. Additionally, it is also difficult to build a portal before any service

Figure 1. One-stop services on smart client

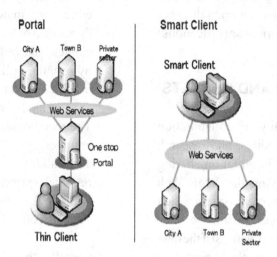

will be developed because it means to design a gigantic system from scratch.

In terms of the personal information necessary for one-stop services, though temporally, portal needs to acquire and possess all the information. On the other hand, the citizen-centric model would enable users to submit bare minimum of personal information from their PCs to receive individual service. On the other hand, the weak point is that it is required for users to equip themselves with a program that realizes one-stop services; hence it is not suited for the systems that are less used by general public. In general, portal model is suited for simple services that are less often used by general public. It is appropriate for the G2C services while citizen-centric model is suited for complicated services that are often used by specific users. Therefore, it is appropriate for the G2B services and in G services inside government offices.

Results for the Demonstration Experiment

The demonstration experiment proved that real-time discussion with sharing data and resources among the geographically-dispersed teams was possible. Furthermore, we confirmed that it is possible to collaboratively edit and process image data between remote locations using high-speed network and From the experiment, the following benefits of applying the XML Web Services were proved:

- Flexible cooperation and collaboration through sharing the ICT resources
- Flexibility in data exchange
- Automatic execution of modules
- Applicability to existing internet-based technologies (vendor independent)
- Effective utilization of existing programs
- Low cost for implementation(Ohashi edi.2003,2004)

CA Roaming Technology Description

In order to protect the security of the B to C model, we implemented the following technologies(Takeda,Y. et al,2006) (Figure2 & Figure3):

- **Authentication Roaming:** When integrating different systems with the Web Service, some systems require authentication of users. Therefore, we implemented the authentica-

Figure 2. "Fast, secure and anonymous" one-stop services are required

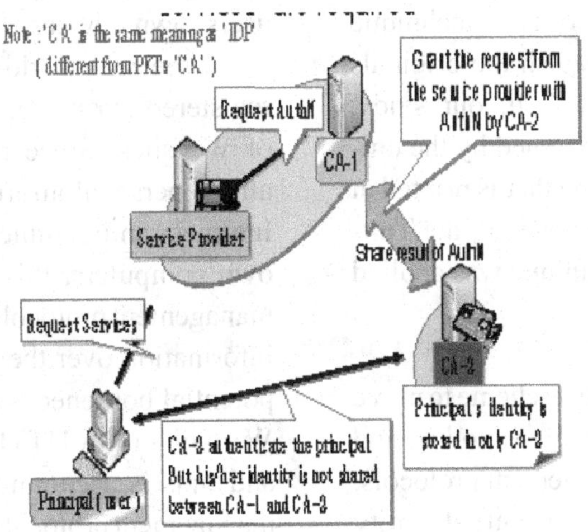

Figure 3. Allow the users to select their favorite CA's(IDPs)

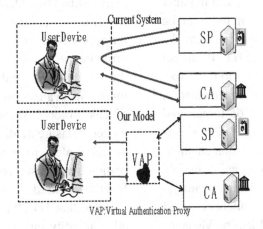

tion roaming technology which is currently under development by the NiCT. The authentication roaming is the technology that shares the information being authenticated by one Website with other Websites.

    ◦   **Biometrics for mobile phones:** The fingerprint authentication system is implemented into the mobile phone terminal in our study. With this technology, university can confirm that

the person who requests the certification is the same person as who prints the certification at the store.

    ◦   **Tint-Block Printing:** Tint-Block Printing is a special printing technique applied on a regular printing paper that shows the paper is being duplicated. When the Tint-Block Printing paper is being duplicated, the letters such as "Do Not Duplicate" show up in bold relief on the paper, confirming the duplication. This technique allows us to distinguish the originals and those duplicated. In our study, since the certificate issued by the university as well as one that is printed at the store had to be original, the Tint-Block Printing technique was applied onto the paper.

HTTP redirect is a convenient scheme to move a Web browser from one Website to another, and is widely used in identity management protocols, including newly emerging User-Centric Identity Management technologies. HTTP redirect, however, can cause a performance bottleneck in the identity management processes. Although this problem is already explored partially in OASIS SAML and the Liberty Alliance Project, this paper discusses how the approach used in them can be enhanced from the viewpoint of user centrism. We developed a new model to replace HTTP redirect with server-to-server communication. Performance evaluation of our prototype implementation shows significant improvement of turnaround time for authentication by avoiding HTTP redirect over a 64kbps wireless communication channel.

Citizen-Centrism is an emerging principle to design solutions in digital identity management. There is, however, still no widely accepted definition of Citizen-Centric Identity Management. One example definition, which might not cover all aspects, is that Citizen-Centric Identity Management is about controlling one's identity data without central repository of his or her own personal data. We believe the concept of Citizen-Centric Identity Management includes at least two types of technologies. One type, including SXIP and OpenID, is to make users specify his or her identity repository. The other type, including Windows CardSpace (formerly InfoCard) and Higgins Trust Framework Project, is to shift the control of personal information (and the physical location of some part of them) from servers to users' own devices.

In the real world, many of us have already registered our personal information on a variety of Websites. Since it is unrealistic to imagine all the personal information distributed over the Internet can be immediately gathered up on our own computers, this paper focuses on identity management protocols to pass and receive identity information over the Internet, and discusses the potential bottlenecks and our solution approach. We explain why HTTP redirect is commonly used and thus is a common problem in the identity management protocols. Previous work, which was explored by The Liberty Alliance Project and was then adopted in OASIS SAML is also illustrated. The analysis of SAML profiles shows another problem, the selection of the Identity Providers (The entities that identify or authenticate users), from the viewpoint of user-centrism. We describe our approach, an enhanced Identity Provider (IDP) proxying protocol, and the design issues including the flexibility and the security of its system model. We evaluate our prototype implementation of this protocol, showing the results of performance measurement. As the name implies, our model implementation is based on Identity Federation mechanism, but is also applicable to non federation-based identity management protocols.

Note that HTTP redirect is also used in the other identity management protocols including OASIS SAML and Liberty. The following part of this section discusses current approach used in SAML and The Liberty Alliance Project.

To avoid negative side effects of HTTP redirect, Liberty introduced an entity, Liberty Enabled Client or Proxy (LECP) to its identity federation framework (ID-FF) and a similar concept, enhanced client or proxy (ECP) was introduced to SAML2.0 later. This paper refers to the ECP profile of SAML2.0, because it was ratified later than ID-FF1.2 of Liberty, and is expected to be more up to date. Before explaining more about ECP, we briefly explain about SAML and ID-FF.

SAML was initially designed as a protocol to enable users to log on to multiple Web sites with single authentication by a Web site, exchanging the result of authentication using XML messages called assertions between the Web sites. The Liberty Alliance Project designed the initial ID-FF as the superset of SAML, and contributed it to OASIS. The efforts of these two organizations on Web single sign-on standard, along with a number of the related technologies on identity management including account linking and single logout, were then converged into the latest SAML, SAML2.0. Replace HTTP redirects with server –to-server communications (Takeda,Y. et al,2006)

CASE EXAMPLE

In this chapter we discuss the case evidence on information system about the consolidation project at Ninohe Hospital (Iwate prefecture) in the northern district in Japan. This case shows how integrating information system was promoted regional coordination of medical systems by realizing medical information system based on XML Web Services technology. And the results reveal the success in adopting and implementing the integrating information system.

Turning now to existing environment and issues of a prefectural hospital, which is controlled by local government, so hospital directors have no budget execution, this hospital has the close relationship with Iwate prefecture healthcare department and many other local hospitals and companies. As for common issues, they were as follows:

- Difficulties in coordination of existing many systems in hospital: multi-vender systems in each department and dedicated interface for connecting to other system
- Exponential increasing costs according to enhancement of scale of the hospital:

Complicated each system and number of systems to be connected each other
- Security and privacy: leak of medical information by establishing coordination

To solve these problems, this hospital has established integrating information systems based on XML Web services technology. The basic concept of plan for this integrating information system is:

- Sharing patient's information.
- Promoting the efficiency of business process by establishing coordination of many information systems.
- Aiming at improving services and patient's experience.
- Working with critical path.
- Input of the source of the outbreaks.
- Reducing costs.

Results for the Case: Advantageous Effects of Integration

By adopting the integrating information system based on XML Web services technology, this case demonstrates and proves the advantageous effects of integration (Hori,Ohashi & Suzuki,2005):

- Information sharing of patients.
- Improving documents and forms development and management.
- Accessing data available in 24 hours.
- Improving effectiveness of business process.
- Reducing inquiry by phone call.
- Reducing memory transfer of each doctor's reservation, physical examination, injection.
- Improvement of services for patients.
- Reducing holding time of carte of ambulant patient.
- Abbreviating waiting time.

In addition, as for integration of internal information systems, team medical activities, that is, collaboration with pharmaceutical, nutrition management, radiation ray, physical examination departments have been promoted for patient centric medicine.

The example is presented for realizing clinical management portal with using XML web services, that is, XML data (Figure 2).

The distinctive features are:

• Patient information distributed institutions are to be displayed on each Web parts at regular intervals (via automatically detected by XML Web services)
• Realizing both collaboration in making reports and data sharing
• Various integrated information detection
• Document sharing within medical team
• Realizing communication by creating specific theme based Web site
• Sharing discussion board (questionnaire) both in executives and secretariat

Each block of information is XML Web Service coming out of what may be entirely different applications; yet they are all synchronized and each block will change as the user drills down through the information he or she needs that is specific to a particular patient or problem. Clinicians can enter XML data that are stored on a server or relayed to a legacy clinical information system, and any column on the form can be added automatically (Hori,Ohashi & Suzuki,2005).

TECHNICAL PERSPECTIVE FOR THE MOBILE SECURITY MANAGEMENT

This study can help many organizations and mobile system understand benefits by adopting XML Web services technology. They depend on large amount of information to effectively run their businesses, from tracking customer orders to gauging customer satisfaction. While collecting such information is critical, in many cases capturing necessary information is time consuming and results in inefficient business processes. Such practices vary from completely manual, paper-based systems to semi-automated steps involving standalone desktop applications, e-mail or redundant data entry practices dependent on human follow-through. In order to cope with this issue, the XML Web Services can be implemented to improve and centralize the process of gathering information using rich, dynamic electronic forms.

In general, Mobile system typically experience reduced acquisition cost for ICT solution and implementation, lower training costs, and fewer ongoing costs with implementations in weeks, instead of months, all yielding more immediate customer value. It is necessary to build a flexible foundation for providers to develop their ICT infrastructure. And it is ideal if there were integrating applications within and across hospitals and clinics. Aside from that Mobile Authentication providers concern about integration and messaging as a way to simplify their infrastructure and to reduce cost, they also seek greater flexibility to handle the demanding and changing healthcare field. They also concern about new and innovative components that are easy to use and implement. By reducing implementation and maintenance costs, provider organizations can get the right information at the right place so that they can deliver high-quality and timely care. Therefore, it is critical to create the foundation for integration that connects healthcare providers to information providers and to their systems. By using real-time application integration and efficient messaging across the organization, mobile organizations can support real-time collaboration, manage knowledge more effectively, and deliver personalized information.

Accordingly, development of user interface and framework that developers, business analysts, and administrators can all use to efficiently develop and apply rules and policies is vital for collaboration. Then, the framework needs to be extremely flexible and extensible, so that its functionality has to be fully exposed through public interfaces to allow users to reach higher stage in implementation to meet their business requirements. And, it is also important to construct massively scalable messaging and orchestration-based applications through scale-out architecture as well as to provide direct visibility into transactions to assure the correct and timely access to information for business analysts.

On the other hand, Web Services utilize the text data called XML data for sending and receiving data. This makes interoperability among different OS and programming languages much easier as text data are normally independent of OS and programming languages. Furthermore, as XML data allow users to add new meaning to data with tags, it makes it easier for the receivers to comprehend data. In contrast, Web Services send and receive the XML data via the internet protocols such as HTTP and SMTP for which most of organizations had already configured their firewall setting. Hence, they are not required to re-configure the firewall to pass the communications protocol, which alleviates security issues especially when the number of partner corporation increases.

Systems are applying Web Services as one of linking technologies to integrate systems within an organization and utilizing the existing application systems such as mainframes and client/server systems by wrapping them with Web Services when developing a new application system. Improving development productivity by utilizing ASPs that are developed with component-based approach, and by turning the shared business logic into Web Services therefore can be shared among multiple system.

CONCLUSION

As expressed in the survey of the metropolis of Tokyo, many people recognize the need of improv-

ing the quality and efficiency of mobile healthcare system management. In order to improve the quality of the mobile management system and contribute to community transportation, it is necessary to share information among residents, patients, hospitals, clinics, medical institutes and pharmacies, nursing care, welfare centers and other related organizations. In the Ubiquitous Society, more accurate and prompt healthcare management and quality medical services are expected by utilizing advanced ICT. The system will be needed: effectively make appropriate counseling and educational information more accessible for the people so as to prevent them from suffering mental and/or physical health problems that may affect their work and life. XML Web Services enables many people to contact and stay in close touch with physicians and outside mental health professionals at any moment when necessary through network. Therefore, utilization of XML Web Services would generate innovative ways for the people to maintain and improve their mental and physical health. We believe that our proposal to apply the XML Web Services would make a substantial contribution to the healthcare and medical field to realize the patient-oriented services in the Ubiquitous Society.

HTTP redirect is a convenient scheme to move a Web browser from one web site to another, and is widely used in identity management protocols, including newly emerging Citizen-Centric Identity Management technologies. HTTP redirect, however, can cause a performance bottleneck in the identity management process. Although this problem is already explored partially in OASIS SAML and the Liberty Alliance Project, this paper discusses how the approach used in them can be enhanced from the viewpoint of user centrism. We tested a new model to replace HTTP redirect with server-to-server communication.

As the demand for better services increases, our study reveals important implications to many Internet services. We believe that our study that incorporates the Authentication Roaming Technology and different CAs is truly innovative and meets the urgent need in the Ubiquitous Society. In the future, with this technology, we expect the service to expand so as to enable printing of more official documents such as drivers' licenses. The high speed Internet connections as well as Internet services have become less expensive, and they are widely accessible for the greater part of organizations. The mobile phones, at the same time, have been equipped with multi-functions and become so advanced that they can identify the individuals with biometric authentication technologies. Convenience stores are so essential to people's everyday lives with their easy accessibility at any time of the day and in any part of the cities. In our study, we utilized the multi-copying machine at the Seven-Eleven in a way that it prevents prohibited duplication of the document while it prints out the document and retains its authenticity.

Furthermore, what is highly remarkable is that we provided a secure and protected service by incorporating existing technologies and social infrastructures. User can utilize a various services by registering his or her personal information to the Website with one-stop authentication. Moreover, by utilizing this model, corporations that digitalize their documents for storing and operation purposes can use the convenience stores as document issuance terminals for those corporations. As the service identifies the authenticity of individuals, it can also be incorporated with the Time-Stamp technology to exchange the documents requiring authenticity.

Our study proved the effectiveness of the Authentication Roaming Technology to combine different social infrastructures to create a new service. Though there are still issues to cope with outside of the realm of technology including accountability of each participants and the level of the service, we expect this service to be soon available in the real world.

ACKNOWLEDGMENT

We would like to thank Mr. Shotaro Suzuki, Microsoft Co. Ltd. Tokyo for his help in gathering information in preparing this paper. This paper is mainly based on work in the project funded by NiCT(National Institute of Information and Communications Technology) with contract with TEPCO Systems Corporation and Mitsubishi Electric Corporation. We would like to thank NiCT and the project members for their help in gathering information in preparing this paper.

REFERENCES

Beyerlein, M., Freedmau, S., McGee, C., & Moran, L. (2003). *Beyond Teams Building: The Collaborative Organization*. San Francisco: Jossey-bass/Pfeiffer.

Crounse, B. (2004). Collaborative Health-Better information better care-A special presentation for Microsoft Partners.

Hori, M. (2001). The Development of IT and a New Work Format for Women in Japan . In *Proceedings of t-world 2001, The 8th*. International Assembly on Telework.

Hori, M. (2003). *Society of Telework and Working women*. Tokyo: Chuo University.

Hori, M., & Ohashi, M. (2001). Information Technology and The Possibility of Women's Work: A New Work Format for Women in Japan. In *The 6th International ITF Workshop and Business Conference Working in the New Economy*, Amsterdam.

Hori, M., & Ohashi, M. (2004a). Implementing Adaptive Collaborative Telework in Public Administration . In Cunningham, P., & Cunningham, M. (Eds.), *eAdoption and the Knowledge Economy:Issues, Applications, & Case Studies* (pp. 708–714). Amsterdam: IOS Press.

Hori, M., & Ohashi, M. (2004b). Telework Changes Working Style for Japanese Women. In *Proceedings of AWEEB, International Workshop on Advanced Web Engineering for E-Business*, Frankfurt, Germany.

Hori, M., & Ohashi, M. (2004c). Telework and Mental Health-Collaborative Work to Maintain and Manage Mental Health. In *Proceedings of the the 37th Annual Hawaii International Conference on System Sciences*, Hawaii.

Hori, M., & Ohashi, M. (2005a). Applying XML Web Services into health care management. In *Proceedings of the 38th Annual Hawaii Conference on System Science*, Hawaii.

Hori, M., & Ohashi, M. (2005b). Adaptive Collaboration: The Road Map to Leading Telework to a More Advanced and Professional Working Format. *The Journal of the IPSI BgD Transaction on Advanced Research Issues in Computer and Engineering*, 6-42.

Hori, M., & Ohashi, M. (2006a). The Municipality's Role for Building of the Regional Health & Medical Welfare Information Services System. *Jounal of Policy & Culture, 13.*

Hori, M., & Ohashi, M. (2006b). On the Study of Collaborative Telework in the Infosocionomics Society. *Journal of Policy & Culture, 13.*

Hori, M., & Ohashi, M. (2006c). Citizen-Centric s-Healthcare Management Based on the XML Web Services. In Cunningham, P., & Cunningham, M. (Eds.), *Exploiting the Knowledge Economy: Issues, Applications, & Case Studies* (pp. 957–964). Amsterdam: IOS press.

Hori, M., Ohashi, M., & Ssuzuki, S. (2005). Citizen-Centric Approach and healthcare Management Based on XML Web Services. In *Proceedings of the 12th European Conference on Information Technology Evaluation* (pp. 241).

Microsoft Corporation. (2003). Clinical Systems Integration Reference Implementation for Microsoft [*Guide.*]. *The Office*, 2003.

Microsoft Corporation. (2004). *Path to Profitability reduces Costs and Increase revenues with InfoPath.*

Microsoft Corporation. (2004). *BizTalk Acceleration for HL7.*

Microsoft Corporation. (2009a). *Home: Microsoft's Health Solutions*. Retrieved from http://www.microsoft.com/japan/smallbiz/healthcare/default.mspx

Microsoft Corporation. (2009b). *Cast studies: Medical support and welfare cases*. Retrieved from http://www.microsoft.com/japan/showcase/industry/medical.aspx

Microsoft Corporation. (2009c). *Case Studies: Nihoe Prefectural Hospital*. Retrieved from http://www.microsoft.com/japan/showcase/ninohe_hospital.mspx

Ministry of Health, Labour and Welfare. (2000-2001). *Annual Report on Health, Labour and Welfare*. Tokyo, Japan.

OECD. (2001). *Health at Glance.*

OECD. (2002). *OECD employment outlook.*

Ohashi, M. (2003). *The Report of Society for the Advance Study on e-Society*. The Society of the Basis for e-Community.

Ohashi, M. (2003). *Knowledge-Based Collaborative Work*. The Report of Supplementary Budget Project of the Ministry of Post and Telecommunications.

Ohashi, M. (2003). *Public iDC and c-Society.* Tokyo: Kogaku Tosho.

Ohashi, M. (2003). *Time Business*. Tokyo: NTT Publication.

Ohashi, M. (2004).The Report of the Advanced Studies for the Social Capital of e-Society. *The Society of theBasis for the e-Community.*

Ohashi, M. (2005). *XML Web Services for Next Generation & A view of Citizen Centric*. Tokyo: Kinokuniya Co. Ltd.

Ohashi, M., & Hori, M. (2005). *The Theory of Economics for Network Societ.* Tokyo: Kinokuniya Co.

Ohashi, M., & Nagai, M. (2001). *Internet Data Center Revolution*. Tokyo: Impress.

Ohashi, M., Sasaki, K., & Hori, M. (2004). On the Study of Knowledge Structualization and Adaptive process Based on Project Based Learning. *Journal of Policy Studies, 11*, 55–78.

Takeda, Y., et al. (2006). Avoidance of Performance Bottlenecks Caused By HTTP Redirect in Identity Management Protocols. In *Proceedings of the 2006 ACM Workshop on Digital Identity Management*, Alexandria, Virginia, USA (pp. 5-32).

Web Services Initiative. (2005). *Web Services Application Guideline.*

Web Services Initiative. (2007). *The Report of Web2.0 and Citizen Centric Technology.*

Chapter 6
Perceived Moderating Ability of Relational Interaction vs. Reciprocal Investments in Pursuing Exploitation vs. Exploration in RFID Supply Chains

Rebecca Angeles
University of New Brunswick, Canada

ABSTRACT

This study looks at the perceived ability of two variables, reciprocal investments and relational interaction, to moderate the relationship between the independent variables, components of IT infrastructure integration and supply chain process integration, and two dependent radio frequency identification (RFID) system variables, exploitation and exploration. Using the moderated regression procedure, this study seeks to test the ability of both reciprocal investments and relational interaction to moderate the relationship between the independent and dependent variables using data gathered from 87 firms using an online survey. Results show that relational interaction is an effective moderator between the dependent variable, exploitation, and the following independent variables: data consistency, cross-functional application integration, financial flow integration, physical flow integration, and information flow integration (Table 1). Neither reciprocal investments nor relational interaction effectively moderated the independent variables, IT infrastructure integration and supply chain process integration and the other dependent variable, exploration.

INTRODUCTION

This study looks at the perceived ability of two variables, reciprocal investments and relational

interaction, to moderate the relationship between the independent variables, components of information technology (IT) infrastructure integration and supply chain process integration, and two dependent radio frequency identification (RFID) supply chain system variables, exploitation and

DOI: 10.4018/978-1-61692-020-3.ch006

exploration. Though not at the expected speedy rate of diffusion, RFID system implementation initiatives are still a major consideration in improving supply chains across industries.

The IT infrastructure and business process support that should undergird RFID systems are a great concern considering how supply chains are getting more complex and more international in their geographic scope (Simchi-Levi, Kaminsky, & Simchi-Levi, 2004). Firms that will be using RFID systems to gain exploitation-related goals seek to improve operational efficiencies, streamline activities, and achieve greater control over process execution. On the other hand, those that seek exploration-related outcomes will use RFID systems to find innovative ways of solving problems and meeting challenges. The demands on supply chain partners that will be participating in these RFID initiatives will be significant enough for these firms to consider using either relational interaction routines or reciprocal investments in ensuring the attainment of their goals. Reciprocal investments are transaction-specific investments made by supply chain trading partners in a business exchange intended to cement the relationship beyond what is ordinarily delivered by contractual agreements. Relational interaction routines are a combination of formal and informal mechanisms used to facilitate the exchange of information and knowledge between a focal firm and its trading partners.

This study uses the moderated regression procedure to test the ability of both reciprocal investments and relational interaction to moderate the relationship between the independent and dependent variables using data gathered from 87 firms using an online survey.

BACKGROUND

Literature Review

IT Infrastructure Integration Capability

IT infrastructure integration is defined as the degree to which a focal firm has established IT capabilities for the consistent and high-velocity transfer of supply chain-related information within and across its boundaries. This study closely looks at the IT infrastructure integration requirements needed to support the use of RFID within a supply chain context. The formative construct introduced by Rai, Patnayakuni, and Seth (2006) was adopted in this study and used both conceptually and in the instrumentation as well. They define IT infrastructure integration in terms of two subconstructs, data consistency and cross-functional SCM application systems integration.

The extent to which data has been commonly defined and stored in consistent form in databases linked by supply chain business processes is referred to as data consistency (Rai, Patnayakuni, & Seth, 2006). Data consistency is a key requirement in creating a data architecture that defines the structure of the data and the relationships among data entities that is fundamental in establishing interorganizational data sharing (Van Den Hoven, 2004). Simchi-Levi, Kaminsky, and Simchi-Levi (2004) note that recently, many suppliers and retailers observed that despite the lack of variation in customer demand for products, inventory and back-order levels vary, nevertheless, across many supply chains, oddly enough. This observed variability up and down the supply chain is called the "bullwhip effect" (Moyaux & Chaib-draa, 2007; Simchi-Levi, Kaminsky, & Simchi-Levi, 2004). Sharing consistent data upstream and downstream in the supply chain is one major solution to overcoming the bullwhip effect.

Data from legacy systems of supply chain trading partners need to be accessed to produce useful, integrated data, and to be able to transport this data into various datawarehouse structures. Often, data from diverse sources is inconsistent and unusable for the integration purposes required for supply-chain wide initiatives.

Cross-functional supply chain management applications systems integration is defined by Malhotra, Gosain, and El Sawy (2005) as the level of real-time communication of a hub firm's functional applications that are linked within an SCM context and their exchanges with enterprise resource planning (ERP) and other related inter-enterprise initiatives like customer relationship management (CRM) applications. At the lowest level, an ERP system is essential in enabling the seamless integration of information flows and business process across functional areas of a focal firm --- this is normally referred to as "ERP I" (Law & Ngai, 2007). ERP functionalities are important control and management mechanisms that are connected with the ERP systems of the firm's trading partner --- referred to as "ERP II". ERP implementations are growing more extensive and interconnected among firms in linked value chains. Karimi, Somers, and Bhattacherjee (2007) found that ERP projects with greater functional, organizational, or geographic scope result in higher positive shareholder returns.

To obtain optimum results, supply chain trading partners have to inevitably approach a collaborative posture in their relationships which would rely heavily on cross-functional interenterprise integration. To facilitate the realization of this goal, the Supply Chain Council (SCC), a not-for-profit corporation, has endorsed the Supply Chain Operations Reference Model (SCOR) as the cross-industry standard for supply chain management (Holloway, 2006).

Supply Chain Process Integration

In this study, supply chain process integration is defined following the construct used by Malhotra, Gosain, and El Sawy (2005): the degree to which a hub firm has integrated the flow of

information (Lee, et al., 1997), physical materials (Stevens, 1990), and financial information (Mabert & Venkatraman, 1998) with its value chain trading partners. This formative construct has three subconstruct components: information flow integration, physical flow integration, and financial flow integration (Mangan, Lalwani, & Butcher, 2008).

Information has the potential to reduce variability in the supply chain, enable suppliers to make better forecasts (i.e., more accurately accounting for effects of promotions and market changes, for instance), enable the coordination of manufacturing and distribution strategies, enable lead time reduction, and enable retailers to service their customers better by providing preferred items and avoiding out of stock situations (Simchi-Levi, Kaminsky, & Simchi-Levi, 2004).

This study uses the construct, information flow integration, to mean the degree to which a firm exchanges operational, tactical, and strategic information with its supply chain trading partners (Malhotra, Gosain, & El Sawy, 2005). The instrument used in this study measures the sharing of production and delivery schedules, performance metrics, demand forecasts, actual sales data, and inventory data, for information flow integration.

Malhotra, Gosain, and El Sawy (2005) define physical flow integration as the level to which the hub firm uses global optimization with its value chain partners to manage the flow and stocking of materials and finished goods. Raw materials, subassemblies, and finished goods constitute downstream physical flows, whereas returned products for defects or repairs make up the upstream physical flows. In this study, physical flow integration is measured in terms of multi-echelon optimization of costs, just-in-time deliveries, joint management of inventory with suppliers and logistics partners, and distribution network configuration for optimal staging of inventory (Malhotra, Gosain, & El Sawy, 2005).

Financial flow integration is defined as the level to which a hub firm and its trading partners exchange financial resources in a manner driven by workflow events (Malhotra, Gosain, & El Sawy, 2005). Value chain participants that do not have well-designed business processes often do not have consistent views of important financial downstream flows such as prices, invoices, credit terms and upstream financial flows that could include payments and account payables (Mc-Cormack & Johnson, 2003).

Dependent Variables: Exploitation versus Exploration

Drawing from the theory of learning and action (March, 1991), this study uses the two main categories of IT employed by firms in their value chains: exploitation and exploration. "Exploitation" activities seek to improve operational efficiencies (i.e., through increased standardization, tighter process controls, and reduced manual intervention), streamline activities, and achieve greater control over process execution. "Exploration" activities, on the other hand, involve risk taking, experimentation, and innovation to find novel ways of solving old problems (Pitoura & Bhargava, 1999). Recent literature in management has pursued the idea that "ambidexterity," meaning the ability to pursue both exploitation and exploration activities by a firm and its expected positive effect on firm performance. He, Wong, and Kam (2004) tested this ambidexterity hypothesis by examining how exploration and exploitation can jointly influence firm performance in the context of firms' approach to technological innovation. Using a sample of 206 manufacturing firms, the authors argue for a balanced approach towards both and found that the interaction between explorative and exploitative innovation strategies is positively related to sales growth rate, and that the relative imbalance between explorative and exploitative innovation strategies is negatively related to sales growth rate.

The concepts of exploitation and exploration have been used in a number of studies (Kyriako-poulos & Moorman, 2004; Rothaermel & Deeds, 2004; Holmqvist, 2004; Ozsomer & Gencturk, 2003), but none of them involves RFID within a supply chain context.

Moderator Variables: Reciprocal Investments versus Relational Interaction

Reciprocal investments are transaction-specific investments made by trading partners in a business exchange relationship (Artz, 1999). Williamson (1996) suggested that a mutual reliance relationship develops when both parties invest assets in each other and put them at risk, thus, discouraging the occurrence of opportunistic behaviors on the part of both parties. Thus, reciprocal investments appear to reduce the transaction costs associated with writing, monitoring, and enforcing contractual agreements (Bromiley & Cummings, 1991) and encourage long-term, stable cooperative relationships (Zaheer & Venkatraman, 1995). When a focal firm makes such investments in a small number of business exchange partners, the intention to commit is even more credible (Bakos & Brynjolfsson, 1993).

Relational interaction routines are defined as a combination of both formal and informal mechanisms used to facilitate the exchange of information and knowledge between a focal firm and its trading partners (Patnayakuni, Rai, & Seth, 2006). Organizational routines or a formalized set of procedures put in place so that the firms in the relationship could explore opportunities for improvement by promoting predictable task performance and enabling coordination patterns, process configurations, and communication processes that support the sharing of information and knowledge. One such opportunity lies in planning and coordinating supply chain activities using information flows (Okhuysen & Eisenhardt, 2002). Siemenieniuch, et al. (1999) in fact, found that the integration of information flows between supply chain partners, in fact, resulted when the firms focused on know-how involved in collaborative planning.

MAIN FOCUS OF THE CHAPTER

Hypotheses

This study purports to test the following hypotheses:

H1: The positive relationship between IT infrastructure integration (i.e., data consistency and cross-functional application integration) and exploitation will be moderated by reciprocal investments--- i.e., the higher the level of reciprocal investments, the greater the positive relationship between IT infrastructure integration and exploitation.

H2: The positive relationship between IT infrastructure integration (i.e., data consistency and cross-functional application integration) and exploration will be moderated by reciprocal investments--- i.e., the higher the level of reciprocal investments, the greater the positive relationship between IT infrastructure integration and exploration.

H3: The positive relationship between IT infrastructure integration (i.e., data consistency and cross-functional application integration) and exploitation will be moderated by relational interaction--- i.e., the higher the level of relational interaction, the greater the positive relationship between IT infrastructure integration and exploitation.

H4: The positive relationship between IT infrastructure integration (i.e., data consistency and cross-functional application integration) and exploration will be moderated by relational interaction--- i.e., the higher the level of relational interaction, the greater the positive relationship between IT infrastructure integration and exploration.

H5: The positive relationship between supply chain process integration (i.e., financial flow integration, physical flow integration, and information flow integration) and exploitation will be moderated by reciprocal investments--- i.e., the higher the level of reciprocal investments, the greater the positive relationship between supply chain process integration and exploitation.

H6: The positive relationship between supply chain process integration (i.e., financial flow integration, physical flow integration, and information flow integration) and exploration will be moderated by reciprocal investments--- i.e., the higher the level of reciprocal investments, the greater the positive relationship between supply chain process integration and exploration.

H7: The positive relationship between supply chain process integration (i.e., financial flow integration, physical flow integration, and information flow integration) and exploitation will be moderated by relational interaction--- i.e., the higher the level of relational interaction, the greater the positive relationship between supply chain process integration and exploitation.

H8: The positive relationship between supply chain process integration (i.e., financial flow integration, physical flow integration, and information flow integration) and exploration will be moderated by relational interaction--- i.e., the higher the level of relational interaction, the greater the positive relationship between supply chain process integration and exploration.

Issues, Controversies, Problems

Research Methodology

Data for this pilot research study was collected using a survey questionnaire administered online to members of the Council of Supply Chain Management Professionals (CSCMP). The data analyzed for this paper was drawn from a convenience sample of 87 firms that responded to a certain part of the survey questionnaire --- these are organizations that had not yet implemented RFID but are knowledgeable about it or may be implementing RFID in the future. The specific items used for IT infrastructure integration (i.e., data consistency and cross-functional application integration) and supply chain process integration were borrowed from Rai, Patnayakuni, and Seth (2006); items for exploitation and exploration were borrowed from Subramani (2004); and items for reciprocal investments were drawn from Son, et al. (2005) and the items for relational interaction, from Patnayakuni, et al. (2006).

Since the organizations have not yet implemented RFID, the survey respondent was asked to indicate their perceptions of the importance of the independent, dependent, and moderator variables using multiple items per construct. Seven-point Likert scales were used with minimum-maximum anchoring points appropriate to the construct being measured. The computer program SPSS version 15 was used in conducting a series of simple regression data analyses and their associated moderated regression analysis runs.

Data Measurement Properties

The internal consistency of the items constituting each construct was assessed using Cronbach's alpha and the results are in conformance with Nunnally's (1978) guidelines of getting values of .70 or above. Generally speaking, the items have internal consistency with values beyond the .70 threshold recommended. The different variables used in the study showed the following reliability results: data consistency (Cronbach alpha=.944); cross-functional application integration (Cronbach alpha=.930);

Financial flow integration (Cronbach alpha=.889); physical flow integration (Cronbach alpha=.942); information flow integration (Cronbach alpha=.946); exploitation (Cronbach alpha=.918); exploration (Cronbach alpha=.936); reciprocal investments (Cronbach alpha=.964); and relational interaction (Cronbach alpha=.962).

To establish convergent and divergent validity, the item-to-total correlations of the constructs were examined and, in general, the specific items have a stronger correlation with the construct than with other items (Rai, Patnayakuni, & Seth, 2006).

Sample Profile Description

The convenience sample consists of a total of 87 firms from the membership of the Council of Supply Chain Management Professionals that responded to a certain part of the survey questionnaire --- these were the firms that constitute the convenience sample of organizations that are knowledgeable about RFID or may be implementing RFID in the future. About 51.06 percent of the firms had 1,000 or less employees and 32.62 percent had more than 1,000 employees. The following profile shows the membership of the firms in different industry sectors: service (78.57 percent), manufacturing (21.43 percent).

Moderated Regression Procedure

Moderated regression analysis tests whether the relationship between two variables changes depending on the value of another variable (i.e., interaction effect) (Aguinis, 2004). The moderator variable explains changes in the nature of independent variable to the dependent variable effect, and provides information concerning the conditions under which an effect or relationship is likely to be stronger.

Regression analysis was conducted to test the hypotheses presented in this study. The moderated regression procedure requires testing first order effects, which in this study, will be referred to as "model 1." A model 1 simple regression tests the direct effects of a predictor variable on a dependent variable. Simple regressions, therefore, were ran between each of the independent and the dependent variables. The variance in the dependent variable on account of the independent variable is noted using the R^2 value. Then, the regression procedure testing second order effects is conducted, which will be referred to as "model 2" in this study. A model 2 regression duplicates the model 1 regression equation and adds the product term which includes the hypothesized moderator variable.

It is important to determine how large the change in R^2 should be in order to qualify as "practically significant" or one that should merit serious attention (Aguinis, 2004). After conducting a Monte Carlo simulation, Evans (1985) stipulated that "...a rough rule would be to take 1% variance explained as the criterion as to whether or not a significant interaction exists in the model...." (p. 320). Evans found that in conducting the simulation, when the population scores included a moderating effect, results based on samples consistently demonstrated an R^2 change that was 1 percent or higher. On the other hand, when the population scores did not include a moderating effect, the change in R^2 was usually smaller than 1 percent. In conclusion, empirical and simulation results appear to indicate that a statistically significant R^2 change of about 1 percent to 2 percent demonstrates an effect size worthy of consideration. The results in this study include significant R^2 change values within the range with a maximum value of 5.5 percent and a minimum value of 2.1 percent, which indicate considerable significant moderating effects of one of the proposed moderator variables, relational interaction.

SPSS was used to run the regression equations and model 1 was specified for block 1 and model 2 was specified for block 2. The resulting R^2 values need to be noted for models 1 and 2. If the R^2 value is greater for model 2 than for model 1, then, the moderator variable included in the product term is demonstrating a moderating effect.

Findings

Hypotheses 3 and 7 were supported by the study findings. Results show that relational interaction is an effective moderator between the dependent variable, exploitation, and the following indepen-

dent variables: data consistency, cross-functional application integration, financial flow integration, physical flow integration, and information flow integration (Table 1). Neither reciprocal investments nor relational interaction effectively moderated the independent variables, IT infrastructure integration and supply chain process integration and the other dependent variable, exploration.

Results are shown here in descending order of importance based on the percent R^2 change resulting from the introduction of a product term, RelaInteract3Cat1, in the regression equations. "RelaInteract3Cat1" is the categorical variable that represents the mean of the different items that constitute this construct. Table 1 shows the results of running two regression models: model 1 shows the relationships between the predictor variables and exploitation, without the product term, and model 2, the regression results with the inclusion of the product term. In predicting exploitation, relational interaction appears to be the more powerful moderator variable compared to reciprocal investments in accounting for the variance in the increase in exploitation over and above the variance explained by the independent variables data consistency, cross-functional application integration, financial flow integration, physical flow integration, and information flow integration, as separate independent variables in model 1 equations. As Table 1 shows, with relational interaction as the moderator variable, the percentage increase in variance for exploitation were both considerable and significant for the following independent variables: 1) financial flow integration (5.5 percent, $p<.00$); 2) cross-functional application integration (5.2 percent, $p<.01$); 3) data consistency (3.4 percent, $p<.01$); 4) information flow integration (2.9 percent, $p<.01$); and 5) physical flow integration (2.1 percent, $p<.05$).

The table column labelled "% Variance Explained by Moderator with Product Term" indicates the contribution of the product term --- which is the product of the moderator variable,

Table 1. Moderated regression for exploitation as the dependent variable with relational interaction as moderator (N=87)

Independent Variables: Data consistency and cross-functional application integration (both are components of IT infrastructure integration); financial flow integration, information flow integration, and physical flow integration (all are components of supply chain process integration)					
Dependent Variable: Exploitation					
Moderator Variable: Relational Interaction whose variable name is "RelaInteract3Cat1" (Nominal variable for the mean of the relational interaction items)					
Independent Variable	**Model 1: R² Without Product Term**	**Model 2: R² With Product Term**	**% Variance Explained by Moderator with Product Term**	**F Value of Model 2 (degrees of freedom)**	**Significance of F Change**
Financial flow integration	.614	.669	5.5%	56.023 (3, 83)	p<.000
Cross-functional application integration	.475	.527	5.2%	30.829 (3, 83)	p<.003
Data consistency	.557	.591	3.4%	40.026 (3, 83)	p<.01
Information flow integration	.631	.660	2.9%	53.631 (3, 83)	p<.01
Physical flow integration	.659	.680	2.1%	58.852 (3, 83)	p<.023

in this case, relational interaction and the specific predictor variable. And so, for instance, in the case of financial flow integration, the product term would be the product of coordination information exchanged and IT infrastructure integration (i.e., FinancialFlow3XRelaInteract3Cat1). The next column label shows "F Value of Model 2 (degrees of freedom), which means that the F value of model 2 which includes the product term is shown along with the degrees of freedom for that regression model. The significance of the F change from model 1 to model 2 is indicated by the last column.

The relationships between the predictor variables and exploitation as moderated by relational interaction should be interpreted accordingly. Let's take the case of financial flow integration, the predictor variable whose relationship with exploitation is significantly moderated to the greatest extent by relational interaction (i.e., largest percentage increase in variance of 5.5 percent). About 61.40 percent of the variance in exploitation is explained by financial flow integration and

relational interaction as indicated by model 1 in Table 1. Model 2 is, then, introduced by including the product term (i.e., i.e., FinancialFlow3XRelaInteract3Cat1) which represents the interaction between financial flow integration and relational interaction. As shown on Table 1, the addition of the product term resulted in an R^2 change of .669, $F(3,83) = 56.023$, $p<.000$. This result supports the presence of a moderating effect. In other words, the moderating effect of relation interaction explains 5.5 percent in the increase in exploitation over and above the variance explained by financial flow integration and relational interaction as separate independent variables.

The relationships between the remaining predictor variables and operational exploitation should be conducted accordingly as well: cross-functional application integration, data consistency, information flow integration, and physical flow integration.

Solutions and Recommendations

Discussion of Findings

Relational interaction turned up to be the moderator variable of importance in this study that affects the relationship between the independent variables (i.e., IT infrastructure integration consisting of data consistency and cross-functional application integration and supply chain process integration consisting of financial flow integration, information flow integration, and physical flow integration) and the dependent variable, exploitation.

The descriptive data shows that the reported means for relational interaction items were greater than the means for reciprocal investments: 1) relational interaction (item 1 mean = 4.65; item 2 mean=4.61; item 3 mean=4.84; item 4 mean-4.61; overall mean for relational interaction = 4.6775); reciprocal investments (item 1 mean=3.67; item 2 mean=3.93; item 3 mean = 4.00; overall mean for reciprocal investments = 3.8667). A one sample T test indicates a significant difference between the relational interaction and reciprocal investments means (p<.000). It appears that the relationships between the respondent firms and their trading partners (TP) are in the early stages of development as study respondents are not yet confident that their TPs would make the reciprocal investments needed for education in the use of RFID, initial support in developing RFID linkages, and exchanging business documents using the RFID linkages within a long-term partnership context. Study participants expressed more self-assurance that both their firm and their TPs would have relational interaction routines that would put in place organizational mechanisms that would facilitate information exchange, encourage quality and improvement initiatives, sharing of best practices, and learning about new technologies and markets. It is important to note that it is not necessary to make asset specific and trading partner-specific reciprocal investments in order to put these rela-

tional interaction routines in place. Firms could use digital and electronic linkages that they already have in place in dealing with other supply chain trading partners to support relational interaction coordination mechanisms.

The firms in the sample intend to use the RFID system primarily for exploitation (mean = 4.5160) rather than exploration (mean = 3.7423); once again, t tests indicate a significant difference between the two means (p<.000). This study's major finding that highlights the significant results for exploitation rather than for exploration reconfirm findings of current and past studies. From the Sanders study (2008) involving 241 first-tier suppliers, it was found that majority of the firms used IT mainly for exploitation rather than exploration as IT activities are more conducive for exploitation which mainly involves business process automation to promote task efficiency. The author also surmised that IT may not be as well suited for exploration, which appears to require more face-to-face interaction. In their longitudinal dataset of firms involved in networked alliances active during 1987-96, Gilsing, Beerkens, and Vanharverbeke (forthcoming) found that the optimal number of alliances is larger for those pursuing exploitation as opposed to exploration. This may very well encourage the participation of firms in collaborative exploitation initiatives as well. Even way back in the early nineties, March (1991), one of the major proponents of the exploitation/exploration concepts, observed the preponderance of firms engaging in exploitation rather than exploration due to the fact that exploitation results in immediate positive local feedback.

FUTURE RESEARCH DIRECTIONS

There are a number of suggestions for the future pursuit of this study. It would be more fruitful to replicate the theoretical model in this study but, this time, sampling firms that have actually implemented supply chain systems using RFID.

Another idea would be to introduce the following control variables in the research model: length of relationship between trading partners, volume of business generated with trading partner as a percentage of total revenue, and level of complexity of the product/service delivered. It would be interesting to see if the following conditions encourage firms to make reciprocal investments with their respective trading partners in pursuing exploitation and/or exploration: having a fairly long relationship with the trading partner, dealing with a trading partner that generates a sizable percentage of total sales revenue, and the delivery of a fairly complex product or service. In this study, of course, it was found that relational interaction was the more effective moderator rather than reciprocal investments. It was surmised that, perhaps, the firms in this sample had not experienced the benefits of such investments possibly because the relationship with their respective trading partner is fairly new. However, with the introduction of the control variables, it may be possible to see if reciprocal investments are more frequently made in the relationship and thus, would more effectively moderate the relationships between the independent and dependent variables in this study. A firm may seriously consider making reciprocal investments with a trading partner that accounts for a large percentage of that firm's sales revenues. Similarly, a firm might make such reciprocal investments when the product or service involved in the relationship is complex enough to justify making idiosyncratic operational and/or technological arrangements with the respective trading partner. It would also be instructive to see if the ability of reciprocal investments and relational interaction to moderate the relationships between the independent and dependent variables in RFID supported supply chains would vary by industry.

CONCLUSION

The overall study findings support the importance of relational interaction as a moderator variable between the two elements of IT infrastructure integration, data consistency and cross-functional application integration, and the three elements of supply chain process integration, namely, financial flow integration, information flow integration, and physical flow integration and one of the two dependent variables, exploitation. This study's findings should alert supply chain managers involved in forthcoming RFID implementation initiatives to pay close attention to relational interaction coordination mechanisms to assure the attainment of the RFID system's exploitation goals.

The study has a number of limitations. First of all, study participants that were knowledgeable about RFID or may be implementing RFID in the future were asked to report their perceptions of the importance of the variables used in the study: IT infrastructure integration, supply chain process integration, exploitation, exploration, reciprocal investments, and relational interaction. A future study should capture these perceptions from firms that have actually implemented RFID systems. Second, the data was gleaned from a convenience sample of 87 firms that responded to those items in the survey questionnaire. In the future, a random sample is needed in order to arrive at representative implications and generalizations.

REFERENCES

Aguinis, H. (2004). *Regression Analysis for Categorical Moderators*. New York: The Guilford Press.

Artz, K. W. (1999). Buyer-Supplier Performance: The Role of Asset Specificity, Reciprocal Investments and Relational Exchange. *British Journal of Management, 10*, 113–126. doi:10.1111/1467-8551.00114

Bakos, J. Y., & Brynjolfsson, E. (1993). Information technology, incentives, and the optimal number of suppliers. *Journal of Management Information Systems, 10*(2), 37–53.

Bromiley, P., & Cummings, L. L. (1991). *Transaction Costs in Organizations with Trust*. Working Paper, Department of Strategic Management and Organization, Carlson School of Management, University of Minnesota.

Evans, M. G. (1985). A Monte Carlo study of the effects of correlated method variance in moderated multiple regression analysis. *Organizational Behavior and Human Decision Processes, 36*, 302–323. doi:10.1016/0749-5978(85)90002-0

Gilsing, V., Beerkens, B., & Vanharverbeke, W. (in press). Exploration and exploitation in technology-based alliance networks . In Therin, F. (Ed.), *Handbook of Research on Techno-entrepreneurship*. Northampton, MA: Edward Elgar Publishing.

Greenfield, A., Patel, J., & Fenner, J. (2001, November). Online Invoicing for Business-to-Business Users. *Information Week, 863*, 80–82.

He, Z. L., Wong, P. K., & Kam, P. K. (2004). Exploration vs. Exploitation: An Empirical Test of the Ambidexterity Hypothesis. *Organization Science, 15*(4), 481–494. doi:10.1287/orsc.1040.0078

Holloway, S. (2006). *Potential of RFID in the Supply Chain*. Chicago, IL: Solidsoft Ltd.

Holmqvist, M. (2004). Experiential Learning Processes of Exploitation and Exploration Within And Between Organizations: An Empirical Study of Product Development. *Organization Science, 15*(1), 70–81. doi:10.1287/orsc.1030.0056

Karimi, J., Somers, T. M., & Bhattacherjee, A. (2007). The Impact of ERP Implementation on Business Process Outcomes: A Factor-Based Study. *Journal of Management Information Systems, 24*(1), 101–134. doi:10.2753/MIS0742-1222240103

Kyriakopoulos, K., & Moorman, C. (2004, September). Tradeoffs in marketing exploitation and exploration strategies: The overlooked role of market orientation. *International Journal of Research in Marketing, 21*(3), 219–240. doi:10.1016/j.ijresmar.2004.01.001

Law, C. C. H., & Ngai, E. W. T. (2007). ERP systems adoption: An exploratory study of the organizational factors and impacts of ERP success. *Information & Management, 44*, 418–432. doi:10.1016/j.im.2007.03.004

Lee, H. L., Padmanabhan, V., & Whang, S. (1997). Information Distortion in Supply Chain: The Bullwhip Effect. *Management Science, 43*(4), 546–558. doi:10.1287/mnsc.43.4.546

Lee, Y. W., & Strong, D. M. (2004). Knowing-why about data processing and data quality. *Journal of Management Information Systems, 20*(3), 13–39.

Mabert, V. A., & Venkatraman, M. A. (1998). Special Research Focus on Supply Chain Linkages: Challenges for Design and Management in the 21st Century. *Decision Sciences, 29*(3), 537–550. doi:10.1111/j.1540-5915.1998.tb01353.x

Malhotra, A., Gosain, S., & El Sawy, O. A. (2005, March). Absorptive Capacity Configurations in Supply Chains: Gearing for Partner-Enabled Market Knowledge Creation. *Management Information Systems Quarterly, 29*(1), 145–187.

Mangan, J., Lalwani, C., & Butcher, T. (2008). *Global Logistics and Supply Chain Management*. Hoboken, NJ: John Wiley & Sons, Inc.

March, J. G. (1991, February). Exploration and Exploitation in Organizational Learning. *Organization Science, 2*(1), 71–87. doi:10.1287/orsc.2.1.71

McCormack, K. P., & Johnson, W. C. (2003). *Supply Chain Networks and Business Process Orientation.* Boca Raton, FL: St. Lucie Press.

Moyaux, T., & Chaib-draa, B. (2007, May). Information sharing as a coordination mechanism for reducing the bullwhip effect in supply chain. *IEEE Transactions on Systems, Man, and Cybernetics, 37*(3), 396–409. doi:10.1109/TSMCC.2006.887014

Nunnally, J. C. (1978). *Psychometric Theory.* New York: McGraw-Hill.

Okhuysen, G. A., & Eisenhardt, K. M. (2002). Integrating knowledge in groups: How formal interventions enable flexibility. *Organization Science, 13*(4), 370–386. doi:10.1287/orsc.13.4.370.2947

Ozsomer, A., & Gencturk, E. (2003). A Resource-Based Model of Market Learning in the Subsidiary: The Capabilities of Exploration and Exploitation. *Journal of International Marketing, 11*(3), 1–29. doi:10.1509/jimk.11.3.1.20157

Pagarkar, M., Natesan, M., & Prakash, B. (2005). *RFID in Integrated Order Management Systems.* Chennai, India: Tata Consultancy Services.

Patnayakuni, R., Rai, A., & Seth, N. (2006). Relational Antecedents of Information Flow Integration for Supply Chain Coordination. *Journal of Management Information Systems, 23*(1), 13–49. doi:10.2753/MIS0742-1222230101

Patni Americas, Inc. (2008). *Thought Paper: Global Data Synchronization: A Foundation Block for Realizing RFID Potential.* Cincinnati, OH: Patni Americas, Inc. Retrieved July 24, 2008, from http://www.patni.com/resource-center/collateral/RFID/tp_RFID_Global-Data-Synchronization.html

Pitoura, E., & Bhargava, B. (1999). Data Consistency in Intermittently Distributed Systems. *IEEE Transactions on Knowledge and Data Engineering, 11*(6), 896–915. doi:10.1109/69.824602

Rai, A., Patnayakuni, R., & Seth, N. (2006, June). Firm Performance Impacts of Digitally Enabled Supply Chain Integration Capabilities. *Management Information Systems Quarterly, 30*(2), 225–246.

Rothaermel, F. T., & Deeds, D. L. (2004, March). Exploration and Exploitation Alliances in Biotechnology: A System of New Product Development. *Strategic Management Journal, 25*(3), 201–221. doi:10.1002/smj.376

Sanchez, R. (1995). Strategic Flexibility in Product Competition. *Strategic Management Journal, 16,* 135–159. doi:10.1002/smj.4250160921

Sanders, N. R. (2008). Pattern of information technology use: The impact of buyer-supplier coordination and performance. *Journal of Operations Management, 26,* 349–367. doi:10.1016/j.jom.2007.07.003

Shutzberg, L. (2004). *Radio Frequency Identification (RFID) In The Consumer Goods Supply Chain: Mandated Compliance or Remarkable Innovation?* Norcross, GA: Rock-Tenn Company.

Siemieniuch, C. E., Waddell, F. N., & Sinclair, M. A. (1999). The role of partnership in supply Chain management for fast-moving consumer goods: A case study. *International Journal of Logistics, 2*(1), 87–101. doi:10.1080/13675569908901574

Simchi-Levi, D., Kaminsky, P., & Simchi-Levi, E. (2004). *Managing the Supply Chain: The Definitive Guide for the Business Professional.* New York: McGraw-Hill.

Smith, A. (2009). New framework for enterprise information systems. *International Journal of CENTERIS, 1*(1), 30–36.

Son, J. Y., Narasimhan, S., & Riggins, F. J. (2005). Effects of Relational Factors and Channel Climate on EDI Usage in the Customer-Supplier Relationship. *Journal of Management Information Systems, 22*(1), 321–353.

Stevens, G. C. (1990). Successful Supply Chain Management. *Management Decision, 28*(8), 25–30. doi:10.1108/00251749010140790

Subramani, M. (2004, March). How Do Suppliers Benefit From Information Technology Use in Supply Chain Relationships? *Management Information Systems Quarterly, 28*(1), 45–73.

Van Den Hoven, J. (2004). Data architecture standards for the effective enterprise. *Information Systems Management, 21*(3), 61–64. doi:10.1201/1078/44432.21.3.20040601/82478.9

Williamson, O. E. (1985). *The Economic Institutions of Capitalism.* New York: The Free Press.

Williamson, O. E. (1996). *The Mechanisms of Governance.* New York: Oxford University Press.

Zaheer, A., & Venkatraman, N. (1995). Relational governance as an interorganizational Strategy: An empirical test of the role of trust in economic change. *Strategic Management Journal, 16*(5), 373–392. doi:10.1002/smj.4250160504

Chapter 7
Reverse Engineering of Enterprise Business Processes

Ansem Ben Cheikh
Laboratory of Informatics of Grenoble, France

Agnès Front
Laboratory of Informatics of Grenoble, France

Dominique Rieu
Laboratory of Informatics of Grenoble, France

ABSTRACT

In the current context of globalization and with the increasing need to automate the work, modeling business processes has become essential. Modeling helps not only to understand processes but also to anticipate changes and build a flexible structure. In this chapter the authors adopt from software engineering the concept of reverse-engineering. For organizations with unmodeled BP, reverse-engineering is a way to provide process models ready for improvement or usage in other stages of the business process lifecycle. This chapter proposes a method for business process reverse-engineering fulfilling these requirements. It consists of a multi-view metamodel, covering all perspectives of a process, and a detailed approach to guide the business process modeler. The approach was tested on a web application from the French academic Information Systems.

INTRODUCTION

The Business Process Management (BPM) approach is gaining a lot of success (Trkman, 2009) and technologies supporting BPM are evolving continuously. This is related to the fact that the success of an organization depends on its control of its business processes throughout their lifecycle. But in some cases, business processes are running in the enterprise without being based on formal models. They could be based on out-of-date or unstructured documents and on knowledge of process participants. Then it is essential for these enterprises to reorganize information about processes in order to generate process models useful for the following steps of the lifecycle like automation and monitoring. As a consequence, relevant modeling methods are needed like reverse-engineering which is a solution to model existing business processes. The word

DOI: 10.4018/978-1-61692-020-3.ch007

reverse-engineering has been defined in 1990 by Chikofsky and Cross (Chikofsky & Cross, 1990) as *"the process of analyzing a subject system to: a) identify the system's components and their interrelationships and b) create representations of the system in another form or at a higher level of abstraction"*. Reverse-engineering is only a starting point in the lifecycle. A business process is never stabilized and it will be subjected to continuous improvements that are part of the Business Process Reengineering (BPR) approach. BPR aims to reform and redesign existing systems or applications to reach new ones more efficient and more adapted with the environment (Langer, 2007; Barothy et al, 1995; Tsalgatidou & Junginger, 1995).

The approach of "process mining" defined by Van der Aalst et al (2003) should not be confused with reverse-engineering. The goal of the two approaches is to provide process models from running processes, but process mining uses events triggered during the execution of the process to build a scheduling of the process, while reverse-engineering Reverse-engineering use several types of information to build different perspectives of the business process.

This chapter proposes a method for business process reverse-engineering motivated by the need to collect and reorganize the existing knowledge and to generate models while considering the differences between the strategies of the enterprises and their vision of processes. Goals for modeling business processes may vary from one organization to the other. We summarized these goals in four major points:

Enhancing comprehension and communication. Some organizations need to model their processes to cope with communication problems between the participants in the process. Actually, some processes in organizations are yet considered as black boxes. The distribution of work is not clearly defined between actors who have no knowledge of their real position and the contribution of their work in the scheduling of the business process. The proposed solution is to give structured process models consisting of different levels of details and that are understandable by the participants.

Facilitating process management. The purpose of modeling and particularly our purpose in this chapter are to provide structured processes which are modeled from different viewpoints and which are consequently well documented. Naturally, these processes are easier to maintain than executable processes based on theoretical models that no longer match with the real process. For example, when the different relations and flows between processes are modeled with fine details, it is possible to predict the influence of an eventual modification of a process on the others.

Facilitating process execution. Execution constitutes an essential phase in the lifecycle of a business process. As explained by Muehlen and Ho (2006) this phase may fail as a consequence to a number of risks including the lack of a high implementation view and the lack of a common language between stakeholders. Thus comprehensive models of business process facilitate the implementation and the automation of business processes.

Adapting easily processes with their environment. Other organizations are involved in the current context of globalization which has created a competitive climate. Thus, they are forced to innovate which explains the need for flexible models of business processes ready for improvement. We note also the current tendency to adopt Service Oriented Architecture (SOA). The evolving number of virtual enterprises on the web demonstrates the increasing aim of organizations to exchange their services. Other organizations choose to merge for strategic reasons. Therefore they need to model their internal processes to plan and structure external interactions. For example the purpose of the University of Grenoble is to merge the different administrative processes of the different institutions of university educations working under the authority of the Academy of Grenoble. This example motivates our choice of the case study used in this chapter dealing with a number of business processes used to manage application procedures of students to university formations.

The method of business process reverse engineering proposed in this chapter takes into account these motivations and highlights them to guide the modeling process which represents a strength point for the approach. The method may be considered as an all-purpose method, as it is based on a generic metamodel capturing all the elements involved in a business process. The metamodel consists of 5 complementary views studying the process from different perspectives.

In this chapter, some choices adopted for the proposed reverse-engineering method are described. Then, the multi-view metamodel is presented and the different phases of the proposed reverse-engineering process are described. Each phase is illustrated by examples extracted from the academic web application of University of Grenoble. We give also a brief overview on re-flection tracks that will constitute future trends in research in the field of process modeling.

BACKGROUND

In the literature, the BPM lifecycle consists of three major phases. The first phase is the design phase which consists of two steps: analyzing and modeling business processes. The second phase is the execution phase where some or many of the following technologies should be used: integrating business processes in the information systems, automating business processes and orchestrating operational business processes between them. The third and final phase is the monitoring phase where business processes should be supervised and controlled continuously in order to optimize their functioning. The design phase should provide process models that can be transformed into an executable notation of a workflow engine.

This chapter takes interested in modeling business processes. Although, it does not deal with designing business processes from scratch as we analyze existing ones in order to generate well structured and complete models reflecting the real and the operational scheduling of these processes. The modeling task is a highly skilled task that should be achieved by the business process modeler.

The beginning of the 1990's was marked by an increasing awareness of the importance of business processes. The orientation towards business process was promoted by works like Hammer (1990) and Harrington (1991). Since that, modeling business process was accorded a large interest. In the literature, three areas of interest are identified. First, a large number of works were interested in the study of languages for modeling business process. We cite for example (Wohed et al, 2006; Barn & Oussena, 2009; Engels et al, 2005). Secondly, some works were interested in considering design issues in building process models (Koubarakis & Plexousakis, 2000; Suka-viriya et al, 2007). Finally methods for modeling business process were proposed for reengineering purposes (Damij et al, 2008; Irani et al, 2000). In this chapter we study a novel modeling issue that was not considered before despite the multiple difficulties seen in some organization for abstracting and modeling executable processes.

There are several languages for modeling business processes: OSSAD (Office support System Analysis and Design), EPC (Event driven Process Chain), IDEF (Integration Definition methods), UML (Unified Modeling Language), BPMN (Business Process Modeling Notation). We chose BPMN, a standard of the OMG, which is a specific language for business process modeling. It has the advantage of providing a rich vocabulary to present the process as a flowchart (OMG, 2006). BPMN was proposed in 2002 by IBM and is now standardized by the Object Management Group since 2005. The current version of BPMN is 1.2, while there are still in progress a major revision process for BPMN 2.0.

Each model, in order to be well defined and comprehensive by all parts should respect some constraints and be conformed to a metamodel. BPDM (Business Process Definition Metamodel) is the metamodel for BPMN (a metamodel describes the rules, constraints and theories of a model, in other words, a model should conform to a metamodel). It is an UML profile including BPMN notations (OMG, 2007). The large vocabulary of BPMN makes BPDM supporting a wide variety of business concepts. Moreover, BPDM is considered as a generic metamodel for business processes allowing interoperability of different BPM languages and tools. It provides, also, XML syntax to exchange business process models. BPDM models can be transformed to BPEL (Business Process Execution Language) files.

The use of a metamodel in a modeling process is important to identify the elements that must be considered. The elements are grouped in a definition given by Morley et al (2005) "A business process is a set of activities undertaken for a specific goal. The responsibility of execution of the whole or some of activities by an actor corresponds to a role. The progress of the process uses resources and is conditioned by internal or external events". Therefore, the processes of different types (core, support or monitoring processes) collaborate together to fulfill global goals (WFMC, 1999) in agreement with the strategies of the enterprise. Several works were interested in integrating goals while modeling businesses. In Samavi et al (2008), a framework is proposed to facilitate the representation and analysis of business models and their strategies. Jean (2000) proposes an information system architecture identifying in a matrix the set of business processes resulting from each strategic invariant. Other works (Curtis et al, 1992; List & Korherr, 2006) study business processes from different viewpoints

by proposing multi-view metamodels. Curtis et al (1992) identifies 4 perspectives: functional, behavioral, organizational and informational. List and Korherr (2006) adds the contextual perspective consisting of goals of the enterprise and the business processes and measures for these goals.

However, the metamodels proposed in (Morley et al, 2005; Curtis et al, 1992; List & Korherr, 2006) do not consider some business process concepts and are not related to a modeling language in order to be implemented. Our method uses BPDM because of its advantages listed above. Besides, BPDM presents some drawbacks preventing its use as such. Consequently we propose some modifications on BPDM resumed in three points:

- **Removing details.** BPDM consists of 4 packages and uses an UML infrastructure consisting of 3 packages (OMG, 2007). These packages include 161 interdependant classes. Most of the classes correspond with particular notations of BPMN or aim just to draw links with the UML infrastructure. Our goal is to propose a simple metamodel (i.e a reduced metamodel). These classes and these links detrimental for the generic nature of our method were removed from the metamodel.

- **Enriching the metamodel.** BPDM does not include some meta-information on the process like its objective or its position in the organization. While our method puts forward the importance of considering goals in the all modeling phases of business process. Moreover, BPDM does not take into account the different types of business processes. Thus, we enriched BPDM with classes in order to link the process with its environment and the context in which it operates.

- **Using view mechanism.** BPDM consists of packages built to separate different levels of abstraction or different semantics of the classes. We used these packages to con-

Figure 1. The intentional view

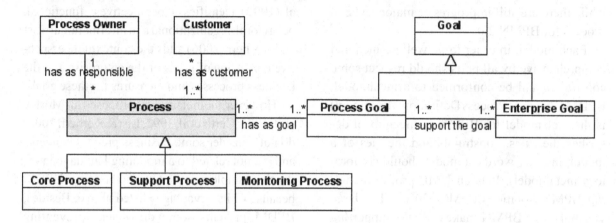

struct views of processes that are weakly coupled between them. Four views are extracted from combining BPDM packages. The fifth view which is the intentional view that is not considered in BPDM was inspired from (List & Korherr, 2006). The different views will be described in the following section.

A MULTI-VIEW BUSINESS PROCESS METAMODEL

The proposed metamodel consists of 5 complementary views which highlight the different elements needed to define a business process. We used the class diagram of UML to represent the different views. The transparent classes are new classes that we used to extend the BPDM metamodel. Grey classes are classes already present in BPDM.

The Intentional View

The intentional view (see figure 1) is not included in BPDM. It was inspired from the contextual perspective proposed in (List & Korherr, 2006) which we simplified. This view specifies the *Process Goal* and its position in the entire set of the *Enterprise Goal*(s). The view determines the type of the process. Core processes are used to characterize the business entities of the organization as they reflect the operational side of the system. Support processes are generic and common processes that may be used by different business processes. Monitoring processes control and supervise the functioning of other processes. The intentional view specifies also the *Customer*(s) of the process which is the external beneficiary of the process and the *Process Owner* which is the organism or the agent owning the process and having the right to modify it.

The Functional View

A process is a set of activities. Each activity may contain several levels of refinement. Some methods and languages require a specific number of levels in the hierarchy of a process, which lays to problems in the case of long and complex processes. The functional view of our metamodel solves this problem since it gives the modeler a certain degree of liberty to choose the number of modeling levels suitable for his issue. This view presented in figure 2, depicts the different functional entities of a process and the links of composition between them. We distinguish between Global Process and Detailed Process. In the

Figure 2. The functional view

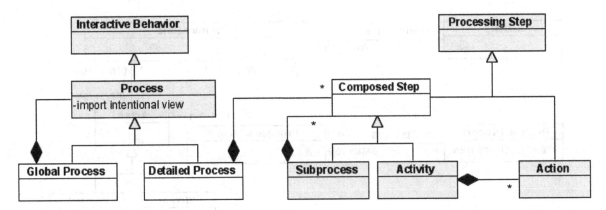

higher level of abstraction the global processes are processes with no internal structure. They are composed with other processes and they are characterized by their goals. On the other hand the detailed processes have an internal structure and are composed with composed steps. A composed step may be an activity or a sub-process. A sub-process is a set of activities and sub-processes from a finer grained level. An activity is a set of Actions. An action is the finest grained functional entity that cannot be composed any more.

The Organizational View

The actors in a business process may be humans or resources of different kinds (software, servers, machine, etc). These actors may be names of persons or resources or just their function in the organizational structure of the enterprise. Modeling processes by using the names of actors could lead the process to a non wished level of details and remove the generic character of the process. Therefore, abstract roles are assigned to the different actors participating in the running of the process. Figure 3 shows the organizational view attributing roles to External and Internal actors. A Performer Role is responsible of some activities in the process. Every detailed process has a

Processor Role that is responsible of the execution of activities and also delegating performer roles assuming these activities.

The Interactional View

Figure 4 depicts the interactional view which captures interactions between elements of a process. The elements of the process that can interact together are called Interactive Part(s). While interacting, these elements may exchange resources of different types. An interaction is a connection between two elements communicating between them. A simple interaction is used to exchange a single resource between two interactive parts, while a compound interaction is a set of interactions (simple or compound). An exchanged resource may be an item of any type. A message flow and an artifact sequence flow are examples of interactions in BPMN. Object flow is an example of interaction in the Activity Diagram of UML.

The Behavioral View

Figure 5 shows the behavioral view which captures the different elements for scheduling the process in time. It highlights the succession between different *Course Parts* of the process. The course parts are:

Figure 3. The organizational view

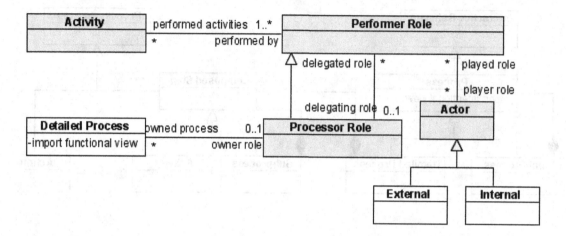

- *Processing Steps:* Sub-processes, activities and actions.
- *Interactions:* exchange of resources between interactive parts (see figure 4).
- *Event Monitor:* a punctual event that triggers in time and influences the flow of the process.

- *Gateways*: the control flows used to express complex specifications to order happening parts in time.

It is essential to specify for a succession the event parts corresponding to its boundaries. In other words, we should specify the state of the

Figure 4. The interactional view

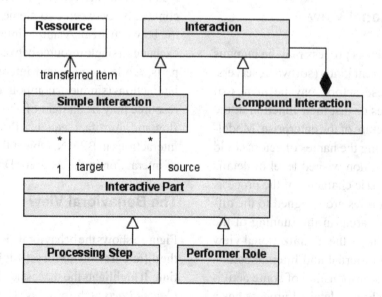

Figure 5. The behavioral view

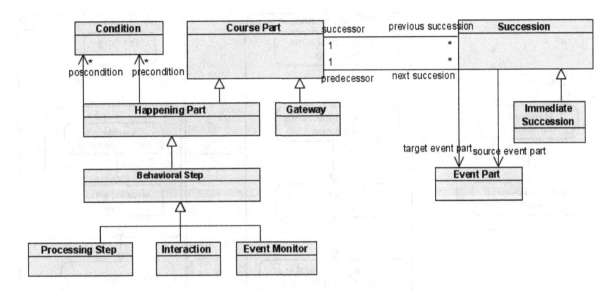

course parts connected by a succession link: if the beginning (or the end) of the predecessor is followed by the beginning (or the end) of the successor. In an Immediate succession, which is a special type of succession, the predecessor follows immediately the successor.

A PROCESS FOR REVERSE-ENGINEERING BUSINESS PROCESSES

For organizations with unmodeled business processes the modeler must perform a hard work to collect the different information needed to reorganize and build efficient models. According to the functional view of the metamodel, several levels of composition must be identified to reach the final structure of the business process. In our approach, these composition levels correspond to abstraction levels as moving from one level to the other will eliminate details and preserve the most important functionalities. While collecting information the modeler should follow a Top-Down approach in order to identify the real vision of the enterprise

about its processes. He will investigate the global processes and discover little by little their structure until meeting the structure of the activities of each process. Then, the modeler will use a Bottom-Up approach by identifying activities and composing them iteratively. The composition of activities should respect the two principles of coupling and cohesion (Papazoglou & Van Den Heuvel, 2007) to construct processes that are highly coherent internally and weakly coupled between them. The definition of the activity granularity and the criteria for coupling and cohesion will perhaps change the organization of the business components to build flexible and efficient models.

The modeling context may also influence the choice of the granularity of activities and the criteria of coupling and cohesion. We propose a reverse-engineering process composed of 3 phases, presented graphically as a BPMN process in the figure 6. The originality of our approach lays in the use of the phase "Restructuring and modeling" used to organize and restructure collected information. Not only BPMN models will be constructed but also process models representing the other views of the business process. Each

Figure 6. The process of reverse-engineering

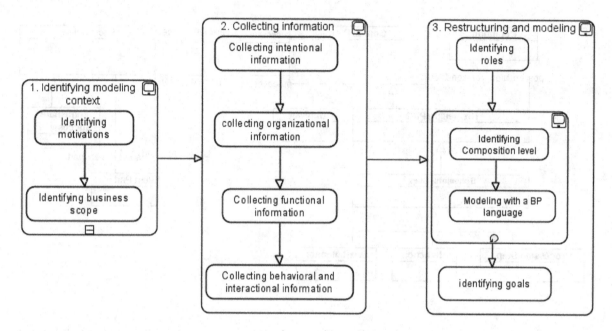

phase consists of several steps detailed below. Each step is illustrated with an example extracted from the academic web application.

Identifying Modeling context

In the first phase *"Identifying modeling context"*, the modeler must specify the modeling context: the motivation for reverse-engineering and its scope, i.e., the set of global processes that must be modeled.

Identifying Motivations

Several motivations may enhance the leaders of organizations to adopt a reverse-engineering approach for their business processes. These reasons result from the need to change or reformulate the vision of the enterprise. Generally reverse engineering is followed by a phase of reengineering. Therefore, considering reverse-engineering motivations should allow flexible models to be constructed. These motivations were described

with details in the introduction and they are classified in 4 categories:

- Enhance process comprehension and communication.
- Facilitate process management.
- Facilitate process execution.
- Adapt easily processes with their environment.

For example the objective of the reverse-engineering of academic the web application is to provide understandable process models by the managers of the application in the university institutions. Thus the objective is to enhance process comprehension and communication.

Identifying The Business Scope

In most cases the modeling scope is determined by the leaders of the organizations that specify the global processes to be studied. But sometimes the scope should be extended to include other processes and other structures of the enterprise that are related to the process models. Then the modeler should take into account the interrelations and the exchange between the business processes. It is also essential to consider the goals of the processes and their position in the enterprise to determine if two processes play the same role or complementary roles. In this case, these processes should be considered in the business scope because modeling one process is affected by the other. Motivations may also affect the business scope since it may highlight some details to be integrated in the process models. For example, modeling business processes for execution purposes can put forward some requirements like considering execution equipments. Modeling business processes for collaboration reasons requires considering collaboration policies.

The identified business scope is a set of global processes if the organization has a primary classification of processes. Elsewhere the business process is a set of organizational parts of the whole organization.

In the case of the academic web application the business scope consists of the candidature procedures for the applicants (students) and the management procedures for the university institutions. On the other side it does not concern the management procedures of the application for the ministry of university education.

Collecting Information

In the second phase "Collecting information", the modeler must collect different types of information (documents, manuals, interviews, organizational hierarchies, process simulation, etc) within the modeling scope. This phase may be hard and complicated if the organization does not possess documents and manuals describing its processes. In this case the modeler should simulate himself the processes if it is possible or conduct interviews with the actors involved in the process. For the academic web application we collected information by simulating the admission procedures as

a student. Then we used documents "applicant's guide" or the information sheets for the academic institutions.

The collecting phase should be organized and planned in order to optimize efforts and time. Then, the modeler could know exactly the information he needs to structure and model the processes of the enterprise. This phase consists of 4 steps used to identify for each view of the metamodel the corresponding information within the business scope. The steps do not contain strict guidelines in order to take into account the differences between information resources within organizations with unmodeled processes. The aim of this phase is to obtain models of information more structured than the existing ones and that can be easily exploited in the following phase.

Collecting Intentional Information

The purpose of this step is to report the vision of the organization of its processes. The modeler should conduct interviews with the leaders of the organizations in order to identify the goals of the different global processes and their contribution in the enterprise goal (see figure 1). Information may be summarized in tables. If there exist any inclusion links between the processes, the links may be represented in functional trees that will be used in the next step. Then it is possible to display goals as hierarchies where nodes are composed goals and leafs are simple goals.

Collecting Organizational Information

In this step the modeler should identify for each global process the different actors involved in. If the global process contains more than one detailed process, there may be more than one processor role (see figure 3). The different actors responsible of the detailed processes should be identified. Later processor roles will be assigned to these actors. The actors participating in the process, as well as their categories (internal or external) should be

Figure 7. Process of the first phase of candidature

Process n°1: first phase of candidature (from January 20th to March 25th)

1. enter n°INE and date of birth
2. fill in the form
3. enter e-mail address
4. receive a confidential code
5. reconnect on the application
6. enter confidential code
7. choose a formation   repeated (maximum 36 choices)
8. validate a formation
9. print formation file

---

identified. They will play performer roles (see figure 3). The delegation links between actors should be identified as well and represented for example with an UML object diagram (not shown here). In this step the hierarchical structure of the organization within the business scope should be retained to be used later in assigning role names to actors.

Collecting Functional Information

In this step, each global process should be studied to identify its components. If there is no available documentation about functional structure, interviews with actors responsible of processes may help to identify the different detailed processes, their sub-processes and activities. A functional tree for each global process should be constructed. These trees highlight the business structure of the enterprise as it is seen by its internal staff. As a consequence, this structure may be incorrect and improper. The restructuring and modeling phase will take in charge the restructuring of the business components.

Collecting Behavioral And Interactional Information

The modeler will go through each functional tree and identify for each functional element (detailed process, sub-process or activity) its scheduling. The scheduling of the processes must be summarized in scenarios like those defined by Cockburn (1998) (see next section for more details about these scenarios). When dealing with a certain process, the modeler should specify all successions and interactional links between elements of the process. The modeler may find also some constraints or some business rules applied on specific elements of the process. These constraints and rules should appear in their appropriate location in the process. The internal structure of these elements should also be summarized in scenarios obtained from documents and manuals or after interviews and simulations.

For example, the "student's guide" of the academic web application describes for the different tasks that must be fulfilled by the student and their deadline. When studying these documents, scenarios can be extracted. Figure 7 presents an example of these scenarios. When simulating the application, we obtained another scenario that was not exactly the same as the one described in the "student's guide".

In the Figure 7, actions are combined with activities. Some rules can be found like "some tasks could not be repeated more than 36 times". Then it is essential to restructure scenarios which will be done in the next phase presented below.

Restructuring and Modeling

This phase constitutes the originality of our reverse-engineering process. The purpose of this phase is to study the global processes one by one in order to restructure the collected information and build process models with business process modeling languages. In our case we will use BPMN but it is possible to use any other language as the metamodel is generic. The process models will be documented with other models to illustrate concepts that are not considered by BPMN. This phase consists of 4 steps detailed below.

Identifying Roles (Organizational View)

The different actors involved in a process were identified in the previous phase. In this step the modeler should assign role names to these actors while distinguishing between processor roles and performer roles. The delegation links between processor roles and performer roles must be highlighted. It is possible to express organizational view with graphical business process modeling languages. For example, with BPMN, processor roles are represented by pools and performer roles delegated by the processor roles are represented by lanes within these pools. For the actor "student" executing the process "candidature in the application" we assigned the role applicant which is more general and can group also non-student persons applying for university education.

Identifying Composition Level (Functional View)

This step and the next one should be repeated several times: each time a composition level should be

identified and modeled until reaching the higher level of abstraction where the detailed processes composing the global process are modeled.

In the first occurrence of this step the modeler should identify the set of activities. An activity is a set of actions performed by a single role. As seen above, the granularity of activities depends on the motivation of the reverse-engineering. For example, an enterprise that models its process to collaborate with external partners does not need to consider the details of operations carried out by the process. It is sufficient to consider the major features that interact with external actors. However to automate a production line, we must model the details considering the activities of finer granularity. In the first occurrence of this step, the modeler must give a clear definition of an activity. This definition may differ from the definition used in the organization and obtained in the collecting phase. Then, all activities must be identified with a name, a number and some characteristic elements like the role, time constraints, preconditions, etc. All these activities with their characteristic elements must be grouped in a table. Table 1 summarizes the activities of the candidature process realized entirely by the applicant. The table contains the elements characterizing these activities.

Modeling with a Bp Language (Behavioral and Interactional Views)

Scenarios obtained in the collecting phase are obtained from the available documents or after interviews with the actors and may be improper or incorrect. Therefore, the user must restructure these scenarios and define a scenario for each activity. A scenario must be written to reorganize the scheduling information collected previously in ordered sentences. The used scenario model is that of use cases defined by Cockburn (1998). A scenario must contain all behavioral and interactional elements of the functional component identified in the previous step. In the first occurrence of the previous step activities was identified. In this

Table 1. Activities of the candidature process

Activity	Role	Temporal constraints	Preconditions	Frequency	Priority
1. register in the application	Applicant	From January, 20th to March, 25th	Valid INE number Web connection	1 time	Mandatory
2. consult a choice	Applicant	From January, 20th to March, 25th	Connected state	indifferent	Optional
3. add a choice	Applicant	From January, 20th to March, 25th	Connected state	From 1 to 36 choice	Mandatory
4. validate a choice	Applicant	From January, 20th to March, 25th	Connected state	From 1 to 36 choice	Mandatory
5. order a choice	Applicant	From January, 20th to March, 25th	Connected state	1 time for a choice	Mandatory
6. delate a choice	Applicant	From January, 20th to March, 25th	Connected state	1 time for a choice	Optional
7. print choice file	Applicant	From January, 20th to March, 25th	Connected state	1 time for a choice	Mandatory
8. prepare and send folders	Applicant	Until April, 4th	Selective choice	1 time for a choice	Mandatory
9. check reception of folders	Applicant	From May, 8th to 12th	Connected state	indifferent	Mandatory
10. send missing pieces	Applicant	Institutions precise dates		1 time for an incomplete folder	Mandatory
11. change choices order	Applicant	From March, 25th to May, 31st	Connected state	indifferent	Optional
12. reply to a poposition	Applicant	3 phases of 72 hours from June, 3rd to 19th	Connected state	1 time for a phase	Mandatory

step we must identify scenarios of activities. The scenario must contain actions composing the activity, events and interactions. Control flows order the elements of the activity in time. Sometimes they do not correspond to a simple succession. Then they must be associated with workflow patterns which are defined by White (2004). These workflow patterns when identified in a process must be assigned to a gateway (see figure 5) and described by a sentence in the main scenario. Below, we present an example of two scenarios constructed from information collected from the academic web application. Figure 8 corresponds to an activity executed by the applicant. Extensions in a scenario correspond to possible exceptions.

After identifying activities and their scenarios, the previous two steps must be repeated to identify sub-processes and their scenarios and

detailed processes and their scenarios (Figure 9). Then the steps must be repeated until defining the complete structure of the studied global process. The structure of every global process may be saved in a functional tree containing all the components of the process (not shown here, but combined with intentional data in the next step in an object diagram represented by the Figure 11). The scenarios should be modeled with a business process modeling language. BPMN models incorporate the behavioral, interactional, functional and organizational views. The different forms of data restructured in this phase (the scenarios, the functional tree, and the roles) must be used to construct business process models. Figure 10 depicts the BPMN diagram of the detailed process described by the Figure 9 and an activity of this process described by the Figure 8.

Figure 8. An activity

Activity n°1: register in the application

Main scenario

1. Action: enter n°INE and date of birth
2. Gateway: exclusive choice
      2a. valid data: jump to 3.

      2b. invalid data: return to 1.

3. Action: fill in the form
4. Action: enter e-mail address
5. Event: receive a confidential code
Extensions

5a. confidential code is not received:
return to 4.

The intentional view cannot be modeled with a BPMN diagram. But, it will be modeled in the next step with an object diagram.

Identifying Goals (Intentional View)

The purpose of this step is to summarize the goals of all processes. After repeating the last two steps for the different composition levels of the global process the modeler can deduce a functional tree representing the different components of

Figure 9. A detailed process

Detailed Process n°1: candidature in the application

Main scenario

1. Activity n°1: Register in the application
2. Sub-process n°1: manage choices
3. Gateway: parallel split
      2a. sub-process n°2: manage folders.

  2b. activity n°9: change choices order.

4. Sub-process n°3: answer propositions

Figure 10. BPMN diagram for the process "candidature in the application"

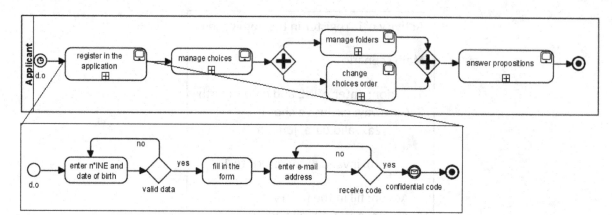

Figure 11. Functional and intentional view combined in an object diagram

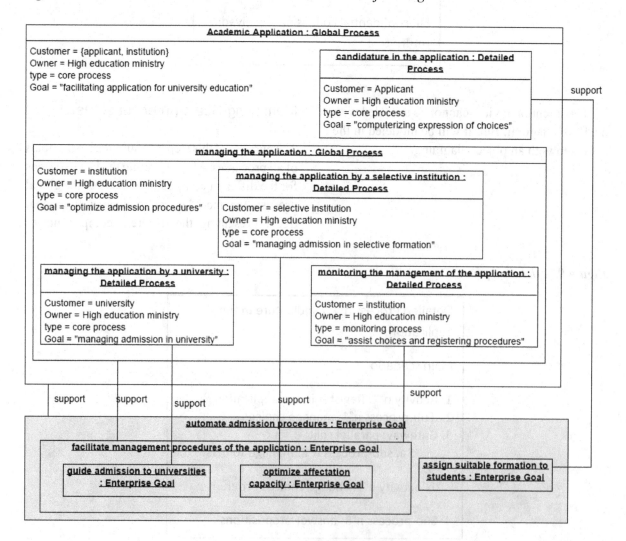

the global process. As the modeler restructured the collecting information, the obtained tree will differ from the functional tree obtained in the last phase. The modeler should use the original functional tree and the table of goals to deduce the goals for the obtained functional components. We propose to model these goals and functional components with an object diagram. Figure 11 depicts the object diagram obtained with the global process of the academic web application PostBac. The object diagram does not represent an instance of the intentional or the functional view of the metamodel as we transformed some classes (Customer, Owner, and Process Goal) related with the Process class by associations to attributes of this class.

In this work we used an object diagram, but intention oriented languages such as Maps defined in (Rolland, 2007), may also be used to represent the intentional relationships between processes.

FUTURE RESEARCH DIRECTIONS

The field of business process modeling has been for two decades an intensive research field. Our method proposes a technique for modeling business processes. This work highlights the need for building first models of business processes that are efficient and flexible. Thus, the models tolerate modifications and changes without affecting the environment of the process. This could lead to a future need to manage variability in business processes to facilitate the use of the same process for different situations or different contexts. The purpose is to obtain adaptable and proactive business processes. Works like Ben Cheikh et al (2009) illustrate the use of variability in business process models. Moreover, an increasing interest is accorded to extending business process models to support techniques like complex event processing or context-awareness. This trend derives from the need to build ubiquitous information systems. Actually, the business layer should sup-

port, as other layers of the IS, adaptivity issues by proposing flexible business processes that could be easily adapted with the execution context and the context of workflow participants. Reactivity should be enhanced as well to guarantee real-time (or near real-time) response to occurring events in the environment. Lot of works handle reactivity and adaptivity paradigms and propose interesting solutions at a technical and application level. However, the business level lacks complete and mature solutions.

A lot of work was done in the BPR approach in order to restructure business process models and integrate innovating techniques. The accent was put especially on the study of different modeling techniques and tools. Some works were interested in the comparison between these tools or on the mapping from one modeling language to one execution language. The future trend is to propose approaches to support model driven process execution in order to build executable process models (usually executable processes are expressed with code) that may be easily modified and discussed by the leaders and the professionals of the organization. A lot of work is done also in computing communities to standardize process tools and enhance existing tools to support a larger set of functionalities or innovating techniques.

Today the increasing tendency is to consider enterprises as service providers. Consequently, business process models should support service oriented aspects. A lot of work was done and there are still needs for mature methodologies in designing service oriented business processes.

Another issue identified by Indulska (2009) as a future challenge in modeling business processes is to establish business value propositions on the process models in order to measure the value of process modeling. This issue was classed number one in a set of future challenges in process modeling by a number of experts: academics vendors and practitioners.

CONCLUSION

Reverse-engineering business processes was proposed as a new paradigm in the modeling of business processes to construct abstract models from existing and running business process that are weakly documented or that are no longer conformed to their models. This technique could also be used in cases of disagreement between participants on the process scheduling or in knowledge extraction to collect participants experience on a particular process. The method proposed in this chapter guides the modeler to better organize the modeling work and take into account several details needed to construct efficient process models. The method is based on a metamodel describing the business process from five perspectives and a detailed approach to construct business process models. The method was applied on a web application extracted from the French academic Information Systems. The reverse-engineering method could be refined in order to be adapted with specific modeling contexts. It is also possible to enhance the usage of metamodel views in order to integrate all of them in the business process diagram, especially the intentional view that is not considered in current modeling languages. Authors aim also to identify links between the views which would be useful in automation or reengineering approach in order to insure a better and easier management of business processes: the results of any modification on a view will be better recognized in other views.

ACKNOWLEDGMENT

This work was done under the project DéSIT (http://projet-desit.imag.fr) which is supported by the cluster TTS of the region Rhône Alpes (France).

REFERENCES

Barn, B. S., & Oussena, S. (2009). BPMN, Toolsets, and Methodology: A Case Study of Business Process Management in Higher Education. In G. A. Papadopoulos et al. (Eds.), *Information System development* (pp. 685-693). Berlin: Springer Science + Business Media. doi. 10.1007/b137171_71

Barothy, T., Peterhans, M., & Bauknecht, K. (1995). Business Process Reengineering: emergence of a new research field. *ACM SIGOIS Bulletin, 16*, 3–10. doi:10.1145/209891.209892

Ben Cheikh, A., Saidi, R., Front, A., & Rieu, D. (2009). Variability integration in multi-view business process design. In *Proceedings of the 13th IBIMA conference on Knowledge management and Innovation in Advancing Economics*, Marrakesh, Morocco.

Chikofsky, E., & Cross, J. I. (1990). Reverse-engineering and design recovery: a taxonomy. *IEEE Software, 7*, 13–17. doi:10.1109/52.43044

Cockburn, A. (1998). Basic use case template. *Humans and technology.* Retrieved from http://members.aol.com/ acockburn/papers/uctempla.htm

Curtis, B., Kellner, M., & Over, J. (1992). Process Modeling. *Communications of the ACM, 35*, 75–90. doi:10.1145/130994.130998

Damij, N., Damij, T., Grad, J., & Jelenc, F. (2008). A methodology for business process improvement and information system development. In *Information and Software Technology.* Amsterdam: Elsevier. doi: 10.1016/j.infsof.2007.11.004

Engels, G., Forster, A., Heckel, R., & Thone, S. (2005). Process Modeling in UML . In Dumas, M., Van der Aalst, S. M. P., & ter Hofstede, M. (Eds.), *Process aware information systems* (pp. 85–117). Hoboken, NJ: John Wiley and Sons. doi:10.1002/0471741442.ch5

Hammer, M. (1990). Reengineering work: don't automate. *Harvard Business Review, 68*, 104–112.

Harrington, J. (1991). *Business process improvement: the breakthrough strategy for total quality, Productivity and Competitiveness*. New York: McGraw Hill.

Indulska, M., Recker, J., Rosemann, M., & Green, P. (2009). Business process modeling: current issues and future challenges. In P. van Eck et al (Eds.), *Advanced Information System Engineering* (LNCS 5565, pp. 501-514). Berlin: Springer Verlag.

Irani, Z., Hlupic, V., & Giaglis, G. (2000). Business Process reengineering: a design perspective. *International Journal of Flexible Manufacturing Systems, 12*, 247–252. doi:10.1023/A:1008103931482

Jean, G. (2000). *L'urbanisation du Business des Systèmes d'Information*. Paris: Hermes Science Publications.

Koubarakis, M., & Plexousakis, D. (2000). A Formal Model for Business Process Modeling and Design. In *Advanced Information System Engineering* (LNCS 1789, pp. 142-156). Berlin: Springer.

Langer, A. M. (2007). Business Process Reengineering . In *Analysis and design of Information Systems* (pp. 268–280). London: Springer.

List, B., & Korherr, B. (2006). An evaluation of conceptual business Process Modeling Languages. In *Proceedings of the 2006 ACM Symposium on Applied Computing* (pp. 1532 - 1539).

Morley, C., Hugues, J., Lebland, B., & Hugues, O. (2005). *Processus métier et Systèmes d'Information*. Paris: Dunod.

Muehlen, M. Z., & Ho, D. T.-Y. (2006). Risk management in the BPM lifecycle. In *Proceedings of The workshop Business Process Design: Past Present and Future* (LNCS 3812, pp. 454-466). Berlin: Springer.

OMG (Object Management Group). (2006). *Business Process Modeling Notation Specification*. Retrieved from http://www.omg.org

OMG (Object Management Group). (2007). *Business Process Definition Metamodel Specification*. Retrieved from http://www.omg.org

Papazoglou, M., & Van Den Heuvel, W. (2007). Business process development life cycle methodology. *Communications of the ACM, 50*, 79–85. doi:10.1145/1290958.1290966

Rolland, C. (2007). Capturing System Intentionality with Maps . In *Conceptual Modeling in Information System Engineering* (pp. 141–158). Berlin: Springer. doi:10.1007/978-3-540-72677-7_9

Samavi, R., Yu, E., & Topaloglu, T. (2008). Strategic reasoning about business models: a conceptual modeling approach. *Information Systems and E-Business management, 7, 171-198*.

Sukaviriya, N., Sinha, V., Ramachandra, T., Mani, S., & Stolze, M. (2007). User-Centered Design and Business Process Modeling: Cross Road in Rapid Prototyping Tools. In C. Baranauskas et al. (Eds.), *Human-Computer Interaction – INTERACT 2007* (LNCS 4662, pp. 165-178). Berlin: Springer.

Trkman, P. (2009). The critical success factors of business process management. *International Journal of Information Management*. doi:. doi:10.1016/j.ijinfomgt.2009.07.003

Tsalgatidou, A., & Junginger, S. (1995). Modeling in the reengineering process. *ACM SIGOIS Bulletin, 16*, 17–24. doi:10.1145/209891.209896

Van der Aalst, W. M. P., van Dongen, B. F., Herbst, J., Maruster, J., Schimm, G., & Weijters, A. J. M. M. (2002). Workflow Mining: A Survey of Issues and Approaches. *Journal of Data and knowledge engineering*, 47, 237-267. doi:10.1016/S0169-023X(03)00066-1

WFMC (The Workflow Management Coalition). (1999). *Terminology and Glossary*. Technical report.

White, S. A. (2004). Process modeling notations and Workflow Patterns . In Fisher, L. (Ed.), *Workflow Handbook* (pp. 265–294). Lighthouse Point, FL: Future Strategies.

Wohed, P., Van der Aalst, W. M. P., Dumas, M., ter Hofstede, A. H. M., & Russell, N. (2006). On the suitability of BPMN for business process modeling. In S. Dustdar, J. L. Fiadeiro, & A. Sheth (Eds.), *Business Process Management* (LNCS 4102, pp. 161-176). Berlin: Springer Verlag.

Section 3
Organizational Knowledge

Chapter 8
Conversation Oriented Decision Support Systems for Organizations

Paulo Garrido
University of Minho, Portugal

ABSTRACT

This chapter proposes concepts for designing and developing decision support systems that acknowledge, explore and exploit the fact that conversations among people are the top-level "supporting device" for decision-making. The goal is to design systems that support, configure and induce increasingly effective and efficient decision-making conversations. This includes allowing and motivating participation in decision-making conversations of any people who may contribute positively to decision-making and to the quality of its outcomes. The proposal sees the sum total of decisions being taken in an organization as the global decision process of the organization. The global decision process of the organization is structured in decision processes corresponding to organizational domains. Each organizational domain has associated a unit decision process. If the organizational domain contains organizational sub-domains, then its compound decision process is the union and composition of its unit decision process and the unit decision processes of its sub-domains. The proposal can be seen as extending, enlarging and integrating group decision support systems into an organization-wide system. The resulting organizational decision support system, by its conversational nature, may become the kernel decision support system of an organization or enterprise. In this way, the global decision process of the organization may be made explicit and monitored. It is believed that this proposal is original.

INTRODUCTION

Information and communication systems substitute and enlarge human capabilities. A striking aspect of such enlargement has been the development of automatic control devices that substitute people in taking decisions that guide machines and other physical systems. Another has been the development of decision support systems (DSSs), information systems for decision support, covering

DOI: 10.4018/978-1-61692-020-3.ch008

several aspects of decision-making in organizations. According to Power (2002), a decision support system (DSS) can be of five types, with respect to the way it assists users:

- Communication-driven
- Data-driven
- Document-driven
- Knowledge-driven
- Model-driven

This classification does not exhaust all possibilities. Turoff and co-workers (2002) introduced the concept of Social Decision Support System (SDSS) as a type of information system with first objective "to facilitate the integration of diverse views into a growing knowledge base." Moreover, its "design embodies the hope that modern human networking technology can be configured and used to allow the emergence of a collective human intelligence by very large groups of individuals." A SDSS is envisaged as a DSS that allows the contributions and cooperation of a large number of people, with no special structuring requisites, to produce useful decisions on problems of wide interest. In the limit, one can formally enlarge the concept of SDSS to include the support of some conceivable decision by some conceivable population.

In such generality of possible applications, one stands out of special interest: *organizational decision*. Organizations are the social tools through which people create and access wealth, in its many forms. Therefore, the efficiency and success of organizations are a necessary condition for the well-being of people and societies. The efficiency and success of an organization depends critically on the quality of its decision processes. Arguments based on collective intelligence (Garrido, 2008) pinpoint the importance of the social dimension in decision-making. Grant (1996) also supports decentralization of decision-making based on the input of relevant knowledge being a critical factor for decision quality. Consequently, the specializa-

tion of the concept of SDSS to fit the characteristics of organizations appears as a promising research avenue. This chapter extends the results of previous research in the subject, which can be found in Garrido and Faria (2008).

When considering the import of the social dimension in organizational decision, one is led to acknowledge *the fundamental role of conversations among people* in decision processes. If conversations do not occur, organizational decisions are taken in an absolute individual fashion, or are taken by automatic devices. These no-conversation modes have their usefulness, but it is hard to deny that, from some level up of decision difficulty, conversations among people are necessary for good decisions, if not only for decisions, and that *people's practice expresses such necessity*.

In fact, people tend to enter in conversations with other people, formally or informally, when they face a decision that appears too difficult to be taken alone or that may have a significant impact on the members of a collective. Therefore, one can see conversations as the "decision support system of last resort" or, better, the "top-level decision support system". It makes sense to ask for a type of information system that supports conversations within processes of decision-making, acknowledging the unique and top-level function of conversation in decision processes. I will call *conversation-oriented decision support system* (CODSS) an information system of such type.

The concept of CODSS intersects the concept of Group Decision Support System (GDSS) but attempts to go further. GDSSs (Gray, 2008) support groups of people in an organization who meet frequently or work together in a project and must take decisions. Their role is to facilitate the decision-making for the group given a number of issues that must be considered. In this way, design of GDSSs has as a goal to make conversations more effective in leading to decisions and, in latest developments, to lift restrictions of same time or same space for the decision process to occur or go on. In this respect, a GDSS also is a CODSS. Yet, the conceptual basis of departure is different. The concept of CODSS sees conversations as a social and ubiquitous resource for decision-making, which leads to a global view of decision support for an organization drawing upon the conversation potential of all its members.

The concept of CODSS also intersects the concept of Organizational Decision Support System (ODSS) and attempts to go further. An ODSS (George, 2008) is a "distributed computer-based system employing advanced communication and collaboration technologies to provide decision support for organization tasks that involve multiple organizational units, cross functional boundaries, and/or cross hierarchical layers". If one integrates this definition with the collective intelligence inspired view of SDSSs and the acknowledgement of conversations as a social and ubiquitous top-level resource for decision-making, then one is led into aiming a type of information system that can act as the *supporting kernel* for the *global decision process* of an organization.

I take the global decision process of an organization as the sum total of activities generating decisions along time in the organization. The global decision process is constituted by decision processes that either run in parallel and do not interact or interact in many ways. Often decisions taken in one decision process trigger other decision processes. The global flow of decision inside an organization appears as a complex structure of bundles, chains, trees or loops.

As referred above, decisions inside the flow can be taken automatically by machines, individually by persons, or socially by groups of people with conversations as mediators. Conversations are the glue that makes the decision flux coherent or incoherent. Even when people take decisions alone, eventually with the support of machines, it is undeniable that they are influenced by conversations. The choice of machines to decide automatically or to support decision is itself conditioned by conversations. Hence, the quality of conversations is a crucial factor for the effectiveness of the global

decision process of an organization, as well as the attention people give to them.

A classical analysis of a decision process shows the importance of conversations if one considers a person x facing the necessity of taking a decision alone. This happens *prima facie* because x perceives a situation S that does not meet a criterion r and by this constitutes an *issue* for decision. To take a decision on the issue, x must perceive a set of available options O that, if realized, conceivably can change S in a situation S' approaching the satisfaction of or satisfying the criterion r. To decide, x must evaluate the options in O and choose the most promising one. Then, x must actually take the decision, which means to assume responsibility for the chosen option. Furthermore, if the decision affects other people, or if its realization depends on other people, it is in the best interest of x that those people understand why the decision was taken and comply with it. For this to happen, x must develop additional effort.

Now, if x has the option of not taking the decision alone, but can resort to conversations with other people, the task faced may be considerably facilitated. First, other people can enlarge the perception x has of the issue leading to validate it as a *de facto* issue – or not. If the last case, x may spare time and energy. Second, other people can enlarge the set of options x perceives to a set O' with a larger number of options. Third, other people can help x to arrive to a more precise evaluation of options. If any of these two things happen, the probability of x taking a better decision augments. Fourth, if people participate in conversations, or are in principle allowed to participate, the probabilities that they understand the why of the decision and that they comply with it – even if not agreeing with it – augment. Fifth, x can diminish its own responsibility in taking the decision by changing it from an individual one to a collective one.

These are potential gains of x in resorting to conversations to take decisions. Surely, there are also potential losses. Conversations require time and effort. The information generated may be irrelevant to decisions' quality. Participating in conversations about a decision to be taken does not guarantee that people will arrive to understand its why better or that they will comply with it faithfully. Turning an individual decision into a collective one may have as consequence to dilute responsibility.

It follows that the design of a CODSS shall have in mind to maximize the potential gains and reduce the potential losses. To maximize gains, the design must keep open the participation, in the limit to all people affected by the decision. It must make available tools for conversations to be effective and efficient in generating relevant contributions to decisions' quality. It must have the capability to register, store and classify issues and related conversations, so that it augments organizational memory and fosters organizational learning.

Simultaneously, the design shall have in mind to minimize the number of interactions needed, limit "conversational noise" and lift restrictions of same time and same space for conversation to occur. Such minimization of losses or decision cost must accompany organizational learning. If a CODSS is successful in fostering organizational learning, the extent of conversations for the same type of issue should decrease along time. In a sense, if the goal of a CODSS is to support conversations for decision, its aim in the long term will be to reduce conversations to the minimum required, to be a positive factor for coordination and collaboration to happen with minimal cost or attrition.

Furthermore, a CODSS must be configurable in order that those in charge of taking decisions can tailor it according to their own understanding of the realities of the organizational domain for which they are taking the responsibility of deciding.

A key question to be answered is which are the structural components of a CODSS? From the viewpoint of conversations being the glue that permeates an organization's global decision process, one is led to require that CODSSs can serve organizational domains of any dimension from small to the whole organization in the limit. This requires independence of scale of the structural components and an architecture enabling recursive connections of them, so that, say, a CODSS may grow up from a given organizational domain, at any level in the hierarchy of responsibilities, to the whole organization.

A CODSS should also be able to connect to other decision support and information systems of the organization in order to ease and speed the flow of information among them. In this way, a CODSS may become a hub organizing decision and the flows of information to and from decision.

Given the posited characteristics above, I think the organizations that can benefit first from this concept of CODSS are those whose leaders, and desirably the decision-makers and all participants:

1. Recognize that conversations among people are a necessary and effective component in a vast class of required or possible decisions (usually the more important ones).
2. Want to explore and exploit the potential benefits of supporting such decisions in an integrated way along the organization based on information systems.
3. Understand the potential risks implicit in the implementation of the concept.

In the following, the reader may find proposals to address several topics on CODSS raised above.

BACKGROUND

Decision support systems are an established field of information systems science. (Power, 2002) is a landmark book on DSSs. (Power, 1995–2002) is also a good source of general information. (Burstein & Holsapple, 2008) gives a recent in-depth treatment of the field. GDSSs are dealt in

(Gray, 2008; Chi, 2008) while (George, 2008; Nunamaker Jr. & Deokar 2008) cover ODSS.

Earlier works on GDSSs and distributed GDSSs are presented in (Turoff & Hiltz, 1982) and (Turoff *et al.*, 1993). These papers already flag concerns leading to the concept of (large-scale) social DSSs introduced in (Turoff *et al.* 2002), as referred above.

SDSSs have received increasing attention, with the explicit or implicit aim to create tools for applying and developing human collective intelligence. (Rodriguez & Steinbock, 2004) analyzes the problems inherent in representative decision-making and sketches a social network-based method for societal-scale decision-making. This work has been refined and extended with the concept of expertise domains in (Rodriguez, 2004). (Rodriguez & Steinbock, 2006) attempts the construction of a unified framework for large-scale collective decision-making as a "weighted semantic network, generated by individual choices, that connects humans, domains of expertise, problems and solutions". As it seems, the concepts developed are at the core of the Smartocracy project described in (Rodriguez *et al.*, 2007).

More recent papers (Watkins & Rodriguez, 2008; Rodriguez & Watkins, 2009) give an overview of web-based collective decision-making systems and a reframing in modern technical terms of ideas of eighteen's century thinkers (Condorcet, Paine and Adam Smith) promoting "inalienable human rights, self-governing republics, and market capitalism".

While Marko Rodriguez and co-workers have been more focused on mathematical oriented analysis of mechanisms leading to decisions in SDSSs, researchers at the Center for Collective Intelligence, Massachussets Institute of Technology (MIT–CCI, 2006), have explored a more conversational approach. (Klein, 2007) explores "some of the issues and design options involved in supporting large-scale on-line argumentation". The main idea is to use technologies that allow visualizing arguments (Kirschner *et al.*, 2003) to

support collaborative decision-making beyond its usual domain at the scale of groups. (Iandoli *et al.*, 2007) presents a "collaboration platform, based on argumentation theory, which is aimed at addressing" the weaknesses of technologies, such as forums, wikis and blogs, as social tools for decision-making, and reports field tests of the platform. From a communication oriented perspective (Takahashi *et al.*, 2009) analyzes "the role of an online community in supporting and sharing the results of informal improvisation among Salespeople and employees in a business development department". The results reported by the paper suggest that "an online community may play an important role both in making visible information needs and in providing information" in a way that outperforms established methods of the formal organization.

While the proposal presented in this chapter had as first guiding idea the specialization of the concept of SDSS to fit the characteristics of organizations, its recognition of conversations' role in decision-making owes to (Stacey, 2003). In this book, Ralph Stacey develops a theory of organizations based on the idea of these being complex responsive processes, a term he coined to distinguish human organizations from 'complex adaptive processes'. The theory sees conversations among people (not limited to decision-making) as the main evolutionary factor of an organization.

STRUCTURING A CODSS: ORGANIZATIONAL DOMAINS AND DECISION PROCESSES

Mathematically speaking, if an organization has a set of m people then it is possible to conceive of organizing them in 2^m subsets of people or sub-organizations. In practice, only a few of all these possible subsets will correspond to actual sub-organizations – the organization itself being one of them and the largest, i.e., the whole set. Let a sub-organization and the set of people in it be identified. Sub-organizations may be disjoint, for example two departments in the same division, or they may have a relation of strict inclusion, for example, a department may be a part of a division; it is also possible that sub-organizations intersect without neither being included in another, for example, a project group with people from several departments. The existence of these possibilities reflects two practices arising from conflicting needs.

The first practice consists in establishing a hierarchical structure of the organization in order to limit inefficacious or useless interactions among people and to define clearly the decisional structure of the organization, determining who holds the power to take decisions and to what extent. A strict hierarchical structure for decision results provided the following conditions be satisfied:

1.   For any sub-organization X included in a sub-organization Y, the decision power of X's head (or heads) is limited to X's members and subordinated (even if indirectly) to Y's head (or heads) decision power;
2.   For any pair of sub-organizations X_1 and X_2 only one of three possibilities arises: X_1 and X_2 are disjoint; X_1 includes X_2; X_2 includes X_1.

A strictly hierarchical structure can have problems to adapt efficiently and even to accomplish its mission. To counteract this, a second practice of forming sub-organizations with people belonging to several sub-organizations of the strict hierarchical structure can be worked out. This negates condition (ii) above. Let us say that a sub-organization (a project group) X_3 is formed with people from sub-organizations (departments) X_1 and X_2. It follows that X_3 intersects both X_1 and X_2 without being included in either. Albeit this practice can result in some tension, it can also make the organization more efficacious and flex-

ible, by lifting restrictions that a strict hierarchical structure imposes on people's coordination and collaboration.

Along this set-theoretical reasoning, usually a person belongs to more than one subset of people or sub-organization. Say that she belongs to sub-organization X. Then she also belongs to any sub-organization Y whose set of people includes the set of people of X, in particular she belongs to the universe of people of the organization. Furthermore, she can belong to other sets for which the relation of X being included in does not hold.

A CODSS must allow mapping the configuration of sub-organizations inside the organization, the association of people to them and must support the conversational decision processes associated to the sub-organizations (and the whole organization).

The abstract conceptual device through which sub-organizations (and the whole organization) are mapped onto a CODSS will be called *organizational domain*. One takes an organizational domain as a well-defined set of people within an organization for which at least one formalized decision process exists. A sub-organization (or the whole organization) is represented inside a CODSS as an organizational domain. An organizational domain includes support for the conversational decision processes whose outputs (decisions) are implemented through actions of people in the domain. Suppose a department's head decides to request an increase of budget to the division's head. He has not the power to decide upon the request but has the power to allocate department's resources to prepare the request. Therefore, from the perspective of a CODSS structure an organizational domain is defined by decision processes closed with respect to the domain.

Let us assume that an organizational domain Y is represented inside a CODSS. The conversational decision processes occurring among people in Y will be mapped on the CODSS structure as:

- The *unit decision process* of the organizational domain
- The *compound decision process* of the organizational domain

The unit decision process (UDP) of Y is the software supporting the top-level conversational decision process ultimately responsible for the conduction of Y. People responsible for Y as a whole are inherently in charge of creating, maintaining and improving this top-level conversational decision process and they will get support for it from the UDP of Y.

Let us assume now that organizational domain Y includes other organizational domains X_1, X_2, ..., X_n. The compound decision process (CDP) of Y is the software structure composed by the UDP of Y, the UDPs of X_1, X_2, ..., X_n and their connections. In the following, more details are given about these concepts.

UNIT DECISION PROCESSES

One assumes now that a CODSS has been implemented and is used in an organization. Under this condition, one will identify a sub-organization with its representation through the concept of organizational domain. Likewise, one will identify conversational decision processes in the sub-organization with the UDP and CDP supporting them. The rationale for this is if a CODSS is implemented and used, the support it provides to conversational decision processes becomes integrated in these. Furthermore, the conversational decision processes will be changed, as many other human interaction processes have been changed by the utilization of computers. It becomes easier to refer to the potentially emerging reality in terms of organizational domains, UDPs and CDPs, as these concepts provide a higher level of abstraction with a consequent wider field of application.

Inside a domain some people will be in charge of taking decisions, some will not. For short, I will

use the acronym DM for someone in charge of taking decisions and responsible for the decisions taken. Irrespectively of being or not DMs, every people are considered potential contributors to the stream of decisions that the UDP outputs. The status of DMs must of course be acknowledged in a UDP as those people who actually take decisions.

A DM may decide alone, in which case he simply declares the decision taken through the UDP. If a DM finds useful to get inputs or contributions from other people in the domain then she raises an *issue*. Raising an issue activates support for conversation upon which the decision is taken. The concept of issues may be applied to both cases: a DM deciding alone, may be considered a special case of an issue having been raised and decided without a conversation process. From this point of view, a UDP is composed by issues leading to decisions.

There is no reason for issues being only raised by DMs. If any person in the organizational domain can raise issues, another potential benefit of a CODSS may arise in that issues that would escape DMs attention are caught by the UDP and adequately dealt with.

Formalism for Supporting Unit Decision Processes

One presents now a formal analysis of the decision process to make more precise the support and advantages that a CODSS can make available to decision processes with conversations. The analysis enlarges and details the sketch given in the introductory section. The formalism is a classical one, with elements from Simon (1976), Newell and Simon (1972). It is presented as a possible example to base implementations.

Let us consider a DM taking a decision alone. To decide, the DM disposes of a set of perceptions P_1. This set encompasses, necessarily, perceptions about the environment or state of affairs S_1 that does not meet some reference criteria R_1. The issue of taking a decision is raised in first place by the perception of the criteria not being satisfied, and the judgment that something should be done with respect to it. This creates a goal g_1 that could be defined as:

- To validate the issue as an actual problem;
- Given that the issue is an actual problem, to assess the relevance or urgency of solving it in the frame of other issues that must be considered;
- Given both above, to select from different courses of action or options, one that expectably will lead to satisfying the criteria.

In any case, the DM will perceive or conceive of a set of available actions A_1, from which a subset must be chosen, forming an option. This formulation allows defining the set of options O_1, as the power set of A_1, i.e., all possible combinations of taking or not taking the actions in A_1.

Using a set of criteria C_1 that includes R_1, the person will valuate the consequences of each option, creating a set of valuations, $V_1 = C_1(O_1)$ from which the decision should follow.

By asking other $n - 1$ people to contribute through conversations, the DM can potentially enlarge the set of perceptions he disposes to a set P_C. Formally, one can view such set as the union of perceptions of each person:

$$P_C = P_1 \cup P_2 \cup \ldots \cup P_n \qquad (1)$$

There will be a potential gain in terms of a better decision for the DM if P_C strictly includes P_1: $P_C \supset P_1$. Otherwise, the DM gets no new inputs and her decision cannot be different from the situation of taking the decision alone. In this case, he (and the organizational domain) may incur effectively a loss by the costs inherent in the conversation that took place. However, a subjective gain may be considered to come from either enlarged confidence on the decision or from a warning on the

decision capabilities of the people entering the conversation.

Enlarging the set of perceptions may be the result of enlarging the set of perceptions of the state of affairs, the set of criteria, and the set of available actions. As with P_C, one can view formally such enlargement as unions:

$$S_C = S_1 \cup S_2 \cup \ldots \cup S_n$$
$$C_C = C_1 \cup C_2 \cup \ldots \cup C_n \qquad (2)$$
$$A_C = A_1 \cup A_2 \cup \ldots \cup A_n$$

One can note that the first two equations in (2) may express a reframing of the issue. The third equation means that the set of options and the set of valuations may grow:

$$O_C = \text{powerset}(A_C)$$
$$V_C = C_C(O_C) \qquad (3)$$

Equations (2) and (3) can base a measure – if only qualitative – of the gains that conversations can carry to decisions. If the CODSS offers facilities for determining such measures and for classifying issues and their complexity, DMs will be in position to tune the use of conversations in the most profitable way.

The analysis and formalism above suggest that a CODSS should support UDPs through collecting and registering contributions in a way that makes evident the statement of the issue or goal for initiating the decision process, the information about the state of affairs, the possible actions and the criteria, consequent options and valuations from each contribution.

Flow of the Decision Process

Let us imagine roughly how a UDP with conversation would go. Say that an issue has been raised. This means that, at least, a description S_1 of a state of affairs and an applied reference criteria R_1 providing some evidence for the necessity of doing something about it (other than what has been done) have been presented through the CODSS. Possibly, actions to take, options and their valuations may have been presented, all through adequate forms. Then, other people can contribute enlarging the first presentation of the issue. After some time the DM finds appropriate, determined by time constraints or because no real enlarging on any of the sets is observed, he takes a decision.

It is recognizable that the decision process, conceived in this way, implies a flow along different states. Therefore, it makes sense to require that a CODSS provides states and transitions between states to formalize the flow. Say that an issue has been raised by a non-DM. It must be recognized as being worth to enter the decision process. If recognized it may also make sense to prioritize it. States of *raised, recognized, prioritized* are possible descriptions. When the decision is taken, the issue enters the state of *decided*. Upon getting confirmation that the decision worked it may be said *closed*. Transitions between states should be the responsibility of the DM in charge. Inherently to her function, a DM can pose an issue in the recognized or prioritized states from the start. Surely, it also makes sense that a DM poses the issue as *decided* if he took the decision alone or without resorting to the CODSS.

Any potential benefit from conversation in decision process comes with the cost of involving more people in the process, which means that they must spend time and energy to think or research about their aspects and the contributions of others, and to transmit to the system the results of their thinking or research. Because of inherent costs, DMs always face the problem of establishing a trade-off in allocating resources to the decision process. Stating an issue as decided (without conversation) may be the best course of action in many cases. The concept of CODSS presented

here targets enlarging behavioral possibilities of people inside an organization, not restricting them.

Polling and Voting Mechanisms

Supporting DMs through conversation, or any other contributions, does not entail that the decision itself should be taken by other people than the DM. If it happens that:

1. A DM consistently arrives to good decisions in the sense that people in the organizational domain perceive that decisions are beneficial to them in the long term.
2. People in the organizational domain understand that their contributions are necessary for good decisions.

It becomes expectable that people contribute without conditioning their contributions to these being accepted or the decision being mandatorily collective – that is being arrived at by some voting process.

However, the existence of polling or voting mechanisms at each organizational domain level in a CODSS is a must or a distinctive advantage at least. On one hand, a DM may want to know the result of a poll on some aspect of an issue or on the whole issue – and eventually decide accordingly. On the other hand, voting may be mandatory for some decisions and it may be useful to have such possibility in the CODSS.

THE COMPOUND DECISION PROCESS

If an organizational domain Y has organizational sub-domains $X_1, X_2, ..., X_n$, it is possible to have an UDP at Y and at each X_i. The compound decision process (CDP) of Y is the union and composition of the UDPs at Y and at each X_i. The decision processes are dependent and, often, strongly interrelated. I envisage the function of a CODSS as giving support to every UDP and to every CDP. If Y corresponds to a whole organization then its CDP becomes the global conversational decision process of the organization.

Here, I consider three issues in conceiving support to CDPs: the address space of each person, relating and linking decision processes, and explicitly mapping decision processes.

The Address Space of Each Person

It is clear that one cannot expect much usefulness from raising issues to people if they are unrelated to their interests – or if the people cannot contribute to deciding on them. Therefore, the following question arises. Should a person be allowed to raise issues to any organizational domain? In other words, as information overload should be minimized, which should be the address space of each person to raise issues? A seemingly natural criterion seems to define such address space as the set of all subsets of people in the organization to which the person belongs. Say that a person belongs to department X of division Y of organization U. Then she can pose decisions to X or to Y or to U. Such arrangement expectably will preserve relevance of raised issues, participation of people, and promote clear thinking about decisions.

Relating and Linking Decision Processes

Relating and linking decision processes in a CDP can be seen to happen along and inside organizational domain levels, for example, from a division to its departments and then up again or from a department to other departments. Two possible relations of decision processes, which give naturally rise to linking, are *sequencing* and *nesting*.

I will say that decision process D_1 will be in sequence with D_2 if D_2 has been triggered by D_1, but the completion or closing of D_1 does not depend on D_2. I will say that decision process D_1

will nest D_2 if D_2 has been triggered by D_1, and the completion or closing of D_1 does depend on the completion of D_2.

If a CODSS allows to tag decision processes in terms of their sequencing and nesting relations (and the associated implementation of decisions) it will be possible to develop visualizations and analysis of the unfolding of CDPs, a most useful possibility.

Other possibilities of relating and linking are of interest. Decision processes can be classified by type. Assuming that a CODSS will keep the records of most decision processes in an organizational domain, such information can be explored to look for similar decision problems, best solutions, or to develop facilitators for people to raise issues.

Explicitly Mapping Decision Processes

The conceptual architecture presented for a CODSS raises the possibility of explicitly mapping the CDPs and their constituent processes in several ways, for example, through textual or graphical visualizations.

I think this is a most advantageous possibility to consider, explore and exploit. Such mapping would allow for a clear conscience among people in any organizational domain of (i) the issues at stake, (ii) their relative importance, (iii) the existence of decision processes, and (iv) how these could be changed and made more efficient.

This view makes more explicit the role CODSSs can have in organizational learning: they will be devices through which people learn to decide better either alone or collectively.

FUTURE RESEARCH DIRECTIONS

Any decision process has a cost in itself, and going for a CODSS as described will have inherent costs, in investment, setting up and operating the system. Profitability will depend on synergistic factors some of them I will indicate as being:

- Improved decisions quality
- Improved motivation and satisfaction of people
- Improved efficiency of the global and the local decisions processes of the organization
- Organizational learning

All these in turn should translate into more value *per persona* produced by the organization. To get estimates of the value's increase is a difficult task, given that a not-yet-tried concept is being proposed and given that unpredictable, relevant gains to expect, may come from non-linear effects of interaction among people that a CODSS may enable. However, logically deriving bounds from a set of reasonable assumptions may give a first map of possibilities.

The following questions to address relate to how one must design a CODSS so that people using it start to produce better decision processes with minimal learning. Design should also aim (i) smooth integration in the culture and established ways of interaction among people and (ii) effective integration in the global information system of the organization. In requiring smooth integration in the culture, one does not mean that this culture will not change because of the organization adopting a CODSS.

A standing question, only pointed above, is how a structure of a CODSS will treat organizational domains that intersect other organizational domains without being included in them. More exactly, how such relation will be reflected in the linking of the UDPs involved.

CONCLUSION

This chapter has developed concepts for Conversation-Oriented Decision Support Systems (CODSSs). Several ideas converge in the concepts

presented. If one considers the ubiquitous role and practice of conversations in many decision processes, and the top-level character of these, then it appears promising to explore the possibility of substantially improving decision quality in organizations through computer support of the social interactions involved in decision-making.

A structure for a CODSS has been presented as mapping in itself the configuration of organizational domains of an organization. Each organizational domain has associated its unit decision process (UDP) and its compound decision process (CDP). It becomes natural that the interface with users be framed through such a map, each user addressing or relating with decision processes occurring in the organizational domains to which he belongs.

A formalism to base the support of interaction among users and the collecting of users' contributions has been presented. Users may have the power to take decisions or not, be DMs or non-DMs, but, in principle, all members of an organizational domain are deemed as potential contributors to decisions. Being a potential contributor includes raising issues to be decided.

To exploit further the potential advantages of a CODSS, this should allow perceiving decision processes as state transition flows, with associated devices to enable polling and voting on issues, linking and classifying decision processes. This raises the possibility of mapping through a CODSS the global decision process of an organization.

Potential Benefits and Pitfalls

At the individual decision level, the basic fact giving a potential gain for DMs is that a CODSS can ease or facilitate:

- To perceive more potential relevant issues for decision as any member can raise an issue.
- To get an enlarged perception about the issue to be decided upon, that may translate

in a better decision under the current frame of thinking. In an even more favorable outcome, it may translate in a better frame of thinking to consider the issue.

One may expect that the greater the diversity or variety (Asbhy, 1956) of contributions, the more probable is the potential gain. In assuring such diversity, preventing groupthink (Wikipedia, 2009) and "organizational silence" (Morrison and Milliken, 2000) are major concerns. CODSSs should support anonymous contributions in a way that people can trust.

On the other hand, some raised issues may be irrelevant; the perception created by the conversation process may not enlarge the perception of the issue; the conversation may not give rise to a better decision than the one a DM would take if deciding without conversation. Human time costs incurred in the decision process would be then unproductive. This problem *in se* can also occur without using a CODSS, but using a CODSS could inflate it. This potential pitfall prompts for three necessary steps of understanding:

- That a CODSS *aims at greater automation* of the decision processes but it *cannot substitute* people thinking and judgment.
- That using a CODSS *entails a period* of individual and organizational learning.
- That the general principles for a CODSS stated above can be *implemented in many flexible ways* desirably matched to the reality of the people in the organization and their current interactions.

In particular, the possibility that all the people contribute to decisions *does not entail* that all the people decide. Additionally, it also *does not entail* that people are obliged to contribute with extra effort for the organization.

At the global decision level, the basic fact giving a potential gain for the people in the organiza-

tion is the possibility of mapping the global decision process of the organization in very flexible ways, triggering a wider and deeper conscience of decision processes as a critical factor to success.

ACKNOWLEDGMENT

I am grateful to Nelson Faria for cooperation and support. The funding of FCT (Fundação para a Ciência e Tecnologia) is gently acknowledged.

REFERENCES

Ashby, W. R. (1956). *An Introduction to Cybernetics*. London: Chapman & Hall.

Burstein, F., & Holsapple, C. (Eds.). (2008). *Handbook on Decision Support Systems*. Berlin: Springer-Verlag.

Chi, L., Hartono, E., Holsapple, C., & Li, X. (2008). Organizational decision support systems: Parameters and benefits . In Burstein, F., & Holsapple, C. (Eds.), *Handbook on Decision Support Systems 1: Basic Themes* (pp. 433–468). Berlin: Springer-Verlag. doi:10.1007/978-3-540-48713-5_22

Garrido, P. (2008). Collective intelligence . In Putnik, G., & Cunha, M. (Eds.), *Encyclopedia of Networked and Virtual Organizations* (pp. 280–287). Hershey, PA: Information Science Reference.

Garrido, P., & Faria, N. (2008). Design of a social decision support system for organizations. In J. Boaventura (Ed.), *Proceedings of Controlo 2008 – Eight Portuguese Conference on Automatic Control* (pp. 802-807). Vila Real, Portugal: UTAD. Retrieved November 26, 2009, from http://hdl.handle.net/1822/9788

George, J. F. (2008). The nature of organizational decision support systems . In Burstein, F., & Holsapple, C. (Eds.), *Handbook on Decision Support Systems 1: Basic Themes* (pp. 415–432). Berlin: Springer-Verlag. doi:10.1007/978-3-540-48713-5_21

Grant, R. M. (1994). Toward a knowledge-based theory of the firm. *Strategic Management Journal, 17*(Special Issue: Knowledge and the Firm), 109–122. Retrieved December 3, 2009, from http://www.jstor.org/stable/2486994

Gray, P. (2008). The nature of group decision support systems . In Burstein, F., & Holsapple, C. (Eds.), *Handbook on Decision Support Systems 1: Basic Themes* (pp. 415–432). Berlin: Springer-Verlag. doi:10.1007/978-3-540-48713-5_19

Iandoli, L., Klein, M., & Zollo, G. (2008). *Can We Exploit Collective Intelligence for Collaborative Deliberation? The case of the Climate Change Collaboratorium*. CCI Working Paper 2008-002. Cambridge, MA: Center for Collective Intelligence, MIT Sloan School of Management. Retrieved from http://papers.ssrn.com/sol3/papers.cfm?abstract_id=1084069

Kirschner, P., Shum, S., & Carr, C. (Eds.). (2003). *Visualizing Argumentation: Software tools for collaborative and educational sense-making*. London: Springer-Verlag.

Klein, M. (2007). *Achieving Collective Intelligence via Large-Scale On-Line Argumentation*. CCI Working Paper No. 2007-001. Cambridge, MA: Center for Collective Intelligence, MIT Sloan School of Management. Retrieved December 14, 2009, from http://papers.ssrn.com/sol3/papers.cfm?abstract_id=1040881

MIT–CCI. (2006). *Home page – MIT Center for Collective Intelligence*. Retrieved December 15, 2009, from http://cci.mit.edu/index.html

Morrison, E., & Milliken, F. (2000). Organizational silence: a barrier to change and development in a pluralistic world. *Academy of Management Review, 25*(4), 706–725. doi:10.2307/259200

Newell, A., & Simon, H. A. (1972). *Human Problem Solving*. Englewood Cliffs, NJ: Prentice-Hall.

Nunamaker, J. F. Jr, & Deokar, A. V. (2008). GDSS parameters and benefits . In Burstein, C., & Holsapple, C. (Eds.), *Handbook on Decision Support Systems 1: Basic Themes* (pp. 392–415). Berlin: Springer-Verlag. doi:10.1007/978-3-540-48713-5_20

Power, D. J. (2002). *Decision Support Systems: Concepts and resources for managers*. Westport, CO: Quorum Books.

Power, D. J. (1995–2009). Decision Support Systems Resources. *DSSResources.COM*. Retrieved December 10, 2009, from http://dssresources.com/

Rodriguez, M. (2004). Advances towards a general-purpose societal-scale human-collective problem-solving engine. In *Proceedings of the International Conference on Systems, Man and Cybernetics* (Vol. 1, pp. 206-211). The Hague, Netherlands: IEEE SMC. Retrieved December 12, 2009, from http://arxiv.org/abs/cs/0501004

Rodriguez, M., & Steinbock, D. (2004). A social network for societal-scale decision-making systems. In *North American Association for Computational Social and Organizational Science Conference Proceedings 2004*. Retrieved November 26, 2009, from http://arxiv.org/abs/cs.CY/0412047

Rodriguez, M., & Steinbock, D. (2006). *The Anatomy of a Large Scale Collective Decision Making System*. Technical Report LA-UR-06-2139. Los Alamos National Laboratory. Retrieved from http://markorodriguez.com/Articles_files/ci-anatomy.pdf

Rodriguez, M., & Watkins, J. (2009). Revisiting the age of enlightenment from a collective decision making systems perspective. *First Monday, 8*(4). Retrieved December 12, 2009, from http://www.uic.edu/htbin/cgiwrap/bin/ojs/index.php/fm/article/view/2584/2250

Rodriguez, M. A., Steinbock, D. J., Watkins, J. H., Gershenson, C., Bollen, J., Grey, V., & deGraf, B. (2007). Smartocracy: social networks for collective decision making. In *Proceedings of HICSS '07 – The 40th Annual Hawaii International Conference on System Sciences*. Washington, DC: IEEE Computer Society.

Simon, H. A. (1976). *Administrative Behavior*. New York: The Free Press.

Stacey, R. (2000). *Strategic Management & Organisational Dynamics – The challenge of complexity* (3rd ed.). Harlow, UK: Pearson Education.

Takahashi, M., Herman, G., Ito, A., Nemoto, K., & Yates, J. (2009). *The Role of Online Community in Relation to Other Communication Channels in a Business Development Case*. CCI Working Paper 2009-002. Cambridge, MA: Center for Collective Intelligence, MIT Sloan School of Management. Retrieved December 14, 2009, from http://cci.mit.edu/publications/CCIwp2009-02.pdf

Turoff, M., & Hiltz, S. (1982). Computer support for group versus individual decisions. *IEEE Transactions on Communications, 30*(1), 82–91. doi:10.1109/TCOM.1982.1095370

Turoff, M., Hiltz, S., Baghat, A., & Rana, A. (1993). Distributed group support systems. *Management Information Systems Quarterly, 17*(4), 399–417. doi:10.2307/249585

Turoff, M., Hiltz, S. R., Cho, H.-K., Li, Z., & Wang, Y. (2002). Social decision support systems (SDSS). In *Proceedings of the 35th Hawaii International Conference on System Sciences*. Retrieved November 26, 2009, from http://www.hicss.hawaii.edu/HICSS_35/HICSSpapers/PDFdocuments/CLCSC03.pdf

Watkins, J., & Rodriguez, M. (2008). A survey of web-based collective decision making systems . In Nayak, R., Ichalkaranje, N., & Jain, L. (Eds.), *Evolution of the Web in Artificial Intelligence Environments* (pp. 245–279). Berlin: Springer-Verlag. doi:10.1007/978-3-540-79140-9_11

Wikipedia. (2009). *Groupthink*. Retrieved November 26, 2009, from http://en.wikipedia.org/wiki/Groupthink

Chapter 9
Representing Organizational Conservation of Information:
A Review of Telemedicine and E-Health in Georgia

Max E. Stachura
Medical College of Georgia, USA

Joseph Wood
Dwight D. Eisenhower Army Medical Center, USA

Fjorentina Angjellari-Dajci
Paine College, USA

James M. Grayson
Augusta State University, USA

Elena V. Astapova
Medical College of Georgia, USA

Hui-Lien Tung
Paine College, USA

Donald Sofge
Naval Research Laboratory, USA

W.F. Lawless
Paine College, USA

ABSTRACT

The authors review a model of the conservation of information (COI) applied to organizations. Following this review, the authors briefly review the mathematics in support of this model and its implications for the development of theory. They apply the model to a review of the status of telemedicine and e-health in Georgia, which they had begun to study last year. After their reviews, the authors discuss future steps and draw conclusions about the model and its benefit to organizational attention and decision-making.

DOI: 10.4018/978-1-61692-020-3.ch009

OVERVIEW

In this paper, we present the background of the problem as we first discovered it. The problem was organizational attention and its impact on decision-making for which both can range in an organization from fragmented to well-focused. We discovered the problem while studying the Department of Energy (DOE) nuclear waste management program. We review the mathematics behind our solution to the problem (conservation of information, or COI) as well as its implications for the development of theory. We review the status of its application to telemedicine and e-health in Georgia as part of a new project for us which we began late last year (Stachura et al., 2009). And we provide a review of future steps and our conclusions as they pertain to the problem, the mathematics, and the particular application to telemedicine and e-health.

BACKGROUND

We have been developing theory over the past decade for a computational model of organizations and decision-making, primarily centered around the idea of the physics of the conservation of information (Lawless et al., 2009). Our conservation of information (COI) model is based on a preliminary theory of a social-psychological harmonic oscillator (SPHO), in which Nash Equilibria act as points of conflict that drive a public's attention back and forth as a conflict is driven across time by self-interests. The oscillations from an SPHO generate fluctuations that produce information characteristic of an organization's stability response, which forms the central part of our model of the conservation of information (COI). Our theory of SPHOs is not yet complete, but the part that is complete appears to be well-grounded and with provocative implications for the advancement of social-psychological and organizational theory.

We began studies of this problem with studies of organizational attention and decision-making in DOE's nuclear waste management (Lawless et al., 2008; Lawless et al., 2005). Since then, the focus of the problem has become more general, shifting from field research with observations of citizen organizations advising the Department of Energy (DOE) on its environmental cleanup and laboratory simulations of DOE field results to analyzing stock market data and working on computational modeling (coupled differential equations, control theory, AI, Gaussian distributions, uncertainty models, Fourier transform pairs, continuous and discrete wavelets). The solutions and evidence we have collected indicate that the results apply to organizational models with agents of any type, including those composed of humans-robots-machines, the combination of which necessarily invokes mathematical models of organizations.

The problem is based on the type of information available to social deciders. It has often been assumed by scientists that this information is "complete" and representative of what a human agent believes at any one point in time (but below see the review by Baumeister et al., 2005 on the failure of self-esteem to predict academic or work behaviors; and Kelley, 1991, on the failure of preferences in game theory to predict the actual choices made by humans playing games against real opponents). However, we have concluded that the information collected from an individual agent is more or less meaningless, since human agents spend their time making decisions under the forces of interdependence.

Interdependence is both simple and complex. Sensory observation limits the field of action responses. As an agent acts on its environment, its sensory observations are impacted, changing future motor responses, and further changing observations with each iteration. More importantly, and disconcerting for social-psychological and organizational theorists, interdependence is a state that collapses during measurement (e.g., surveys, such as for self-esteem, game theory preferences, etc.). Moreover, the lack of a theory of measurement at the individual level is amplified at the group (Levine & Moreland, 1998), organization (Pfeffer & Fong, 2005), and virtual organization levels (Lawless et al., 2008b). How then to represent interdependence among agents and organizations? While this problem is ancient, with threads running from Aristotle on thoughts about objects to the perspective shifts of Copernicus in the study of planetary motion, the mind-body duality of Descartes, and the emotions-thoughts complementarity of William James, our interest is not historical but theoretical.

Traditional social and game theories, known collectively as methodological individualism, have been used to study interdependence for decades. Game theory was one of the first to model interdependence rationally and to solve it in the laboratory for two sets of non-cooperative opponents. These "toy" problem solutions are known as Nash Equilibria, which Luce and Raffa (1967) believed resulted in unfair distributions of a game's resources among its participants. Axlerod (1984) concluded that the unfair distribution from "the pursuit of self-interest" (p.7) in games could be controlled with punishment sufficient to promote "the evolution of cooperation". But Luce and Raiffa (1967) warned that it was unlikely that "any sociology be derived from the single assumption of individual rationality" (p. 196)

Indeed, outside of the laboratory, game theory has not been validated (Safney, 2007) nor it has produced satisfactory solutions (Schweitzer et al., 2009). One problem with Nash Equilibria is that they have been conceived as 2-D solutions of games between opponents that largely overlook their social effect on the population, which would make it a 3-D problem and more realistic. Our conservation of information model offers a new theory for interdependence set in 3-D.

The general strategy of working with interdependence in social science creates confounds (Kenny et al. 1998), which has lead to the need to remove or control the effects of interdependence in the analyses of social data. For example, Dawes et al. (1989) found that actuarial data of human behavior were less immune to the effects of interdependence and thus more reliable and valid than clinical or forensic (expert) diagnoses of human pathology. Our goal is the opposite as we have tried to remove observer independencies to better establish the science of interdependence in organization, system and social processes (Lawless et al., 2009). For example, community oppression under the leadership of an illegal gang and its gang leaders may indicate over time and resources and geospatially the variability in the power expended by the gang to control one community's members versus another's should indicate the costs of control, censorship, and violence.

In this new paper, we focus on interdependence and its application to the Department of Energy (DOE), industry, and telemedicine and e-health. In our field work with DOE, we have found in the past that majority rule decision-making generates more conflict but is faster and produces qualitatively better decisions than does consensus rule decision-making (Lawless et al., 2008a). For industry, we have found that smaller organizations are more unstable than larger ones, a here-to-fore unsuspected reason for mergers and acquisitions (Lawless et al., 2009). And for telemedicine and e-health, we have speculated that these new technologies will revolutionize health care by expanding its reach, by modernizing its delivery, and by holding down the inexorable rise in its costs (Stachura et al., 2009).

While the Hawthorne effect - observing human workers affects their performance – is an old finding (Roethlisberger & Dickson, 1939), the problem was first recognized in social psychology by Allport (1962) who concluded that the shift from an individual to a social perspective was the major remaining unsolved problem in social psychology. Then at the end of his career, Kelley (1992), as one of the first users of game theory in social psychology, concluded that self-reported preferences did not correlate with the actual choices made when games were actually played.

Experiments conducted on the visual perception of graphics have discovered very approximate power laws relating the numerical measure to the reported perceived measure (Tufte, 2001). Because perceptions change with experience and perceptions are context-dependent (Macdonald-Ross, 1977) different people see the same areas somewhat differently. For example, the reported perceived area of a circle grows exponentially more slowly than the actual (physical) measured area.[1]. Even for something as simple as the length of a line Asch (1956) asserted that the reported perception depends not only on the context, but also on what other people have already said about the lines. The above results beg the question of whether we need designs that correct for the visual transformations of the average perceiver participating in the average psychological experiment (Tufte, 2001). While we know that a satisfactory answer to the above question is to use a table of actual physical data, it is the absence of such data that represents the biggest challenge. Even when actual data is available, it is poorly correlated with self-reported (perceived data; reviewed in Lawless et al., 2009). Lawless and his colleagues (2000) found no association in multiple regressions between winners--losers in air-to-air combat and book knowledge of air combat maneuvering. Carley (2002) concluded that collecting data directly from humans changes their responses. And in a meta-analysis of thirty years of data, Baumeister and his colleagues (2005) found only a negligible association between self-esteem and actual academics or work performance. Similarly, a discrepancy exists between the views of managers and the decisions made by their organizations (Bloom et al., 2007). To explain these findings, we have concluded that observational data (self-reports, surveys, and interviews) from agents can be independent of action data (e.g., individuals who are walking, driving a car, or flying an airplane; similarly, organizations during business meetings, during merger and acquisition activities, and during the search for technology partners).

States of interdependence are common in organizations (Smith & Tushman, 2005), probably because individuals multitask poorly (Wickens, 1992), but multitasking is the fundamental reason why organizations exist (Ambrose, 2001). However, organizational theory has failed, per Pfeffer and Fong (2005), possibly because social scientists have not yet accounted for the existence of illusions and incorporated them in social theory.

Adelson (2000) gives us tools to use against the theoretical problem presented by illusions. If human agents construct visual representations of their world with but only a small contribution from sensory data, the rest split between grouping and experience shaping processes, then cognitive and social dissonance processes operate on these representations to form world views independently of a data driven reality, producing the large disconnects between self-reports and actual behaviors. But the result is a profusion of illusions that must be contended with. For example, the illusions known as "risk perceptions" have not only driven the recent "domino-effect" collapse of the financial system in 2008-09 (e.g., the collapse and merger of Countrywide Financial Corporation and Merrill Lynch by Bank of America, J.P. Morgan Chase taking over Bear Sterns, IndyMac collapsing, Fannie and Freddie going into receivership, Lehman Brothers filing for bankruptcy, and American International Group struggling to recapitalize), but they are more likely to occur under certain decision making structures (consensus rules) or during states of high interdependence (e.g., market bubbles, bank runs, and panics) than others which pursue instead risk determinations (scientific methods; majority rules; in Lawless et al., 2008).

Figure 1. The checkerboard illusion (Adelson, 2000). The brain constructs the shadowed area in checker square B as being much lighter than is the darkened square in A. However, both are the same darkness. To confirm, print out a copy and cut out one square and slide it over the other. Alternatively, by joining the squares marked A and B with two vertical stripes of the same shade of gray, it becomes apparent that both squares are the same. Yet, another way to prove this is to use a photometer, which shows that the two squares have exactly the same illuminance

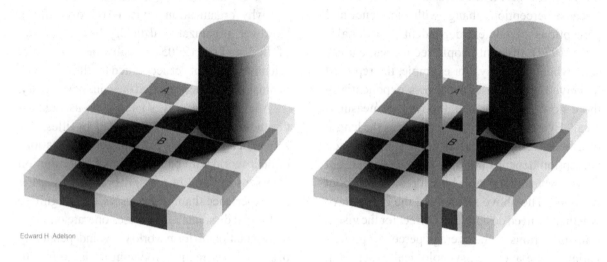

Edward H. Adelson

MATHEMATICS. CONSERVATION OF INFORMATION (COI)

We have written this paper with non-mathematical readers in mind. The more difficult aspects we have moved to footnotes. And wherever mathematics is found, we try to restate in simpler terms when possible.

A Hilbert Space (HS) is an abstract space defined so that vector positions and angles permit the calculations of distance, reflection, rotation and geospatial measurements, or subspaces with local convergences where these measurements can occur. That would allow real-time determinations of the situated, shared situational awareness in localizing the center of a target organization, $\sigma_{x\text{-}COG}$, to represent the shared uncertainty in social-psychological-geospatial terms, and σ_k to similarly represent the spatial frequencies of an organization's patterns displayed across physical space (e.g., the mapping of social-psychological or organizational spaces to physical networks). It would establish an "oscillation" between two socio-psycho-geospatial operators A and B such that:[2]

$$[A,B] = AB - BA = iC \neq [B,A]. \qquad (1)$$

This type of an oscillation defines a social-psychological decision space within an organization. It is called an "oscillator" because decision-making occurs during rapid-fire turn-taking sessions that "rotate" attention for the topic under discussion in the minds of listeners or deciders first in one valence direction (e.g., "endorsing" a proposition) followed by the opposite (e.g., "rejecting" a proposition) to produce a "rocking" or back and forth process, like an organizational or social-psychological harmonic oscillator (SPHO) within an organization, or like the merger and acquisition (M&A) negotiations between a hostile predator organization and its prey target (see the example of a "rocking" oscillation in Figure 2 below, right). But these oscillations may not occur in the minds of the agents who are driving the discussion (e.g., oscillation occurs in the minds of neutral jury

Figure 2. Left: A "stable" outline of the armed USAF Predator UAV (i.e., MQ-1). Right: An "unstable" or "rocking" oscillation of a bistable illusion of two incommensurable images formed with the same 2-D data to produce a sketch of a young woman looking over her right shoulder or of an old woman glancing downward and to her left

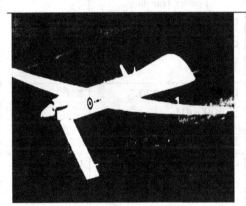

members as first a prosecutor's case is presented to them followed by a defense attorney's case, but specifically not in the partisan minds of the prosecutor or defense attorney, unless they are seeking a compromise; or not in the minds of a predator organization or its prey M&A target organization but more likely in the observers more neutral to the M&A process but while not being neutral to making a profit; in Lawless et al., 2009).

A democratic space could be defined as a space where decisions characterized by SPHOs are made by majority rule (e.g., jury, political, or faculty decisions); the lack of an SPHO identifies decisions made by minority (consensus) or authoritarian rules (e.g., decisions common to military, authoritarian government or CEO business decisions) (Lawless et al., 2007).

The key to building the abstract representations necessary to construct an SPHO may be to locate opposing clusters of the shared interpretations of concepts geospatially across physical space or via a socio-psychological network anchored or mapped to physical network space. SPHOs should generalize to entertainment or stories. Similar to a decision process involving drivers and neutrals, we propose that a story or stage production, as found by Hasson and his colleagues (2004) in

their study of inter-subjectivity among viewers of a Clint Eastwood movie, engages and holds an audience's attention with this rocking process. This insight suggests that the reverse engineering of terrorist organizations may be possible (Lawless et al., 2007).

The operators A and B are community interaction matrices that locate social objects interdependently, ι, in social space (shared conceptual space) that are in turn separately anchored (embeded or situated) in geospatial or physical space. ι states are non-separable and non-classical; disturbances collapse ι states into classical information states. Two agents, one as a President of a Telemedicine firm and the second as the firm's Chief Technology Officer, meet near the President's office, the choice of seating location reflecting the relative social power of the President over the subordinate CTO, but the second holding a skill set prized by the organization and its competitors that permits the two to negotiate while both are aware of their different functions and relative social ranks in the organization (Ambrose, 2001), generating bistable social perspectives that reflect the separate social constituencies that drive compromises (Wood et al., 2009); e.g., in contrast to the gridlock in the Hanford cleanup driven by its consensus-ruled

Table 1. Notional Gaussian distributions with their standard deviations, their Fourier transforms with their standard deviations, and Fourier pairs for both. Notice in all cases that the Fourier pairs are greater than ½

Function	σ_f	Fourier Transform	σ_F	$\sigma_f\sigma_F$
978-1-61692-020-3. ch009.m01	.33	978-1-61692-020-3. ch009.m02	5.01	1.67
978-1-61692-020-3. ch009.m03	.94	978-1-61692-020-3. ch009.m04	2.51	2.36
978-1-61692-020-3. ch009.m05	2.66	978-1-61692-020-3. ch009.m06	1.25	3.33

Citizens Advisory Board (CAB) where compromises can be easily blocked, compromises made by the majority-ruled Savannah River Site (SRS) CAB have accelerated environmental remediation at SRS (Lawless et al., 2008).

Per Bohr (1955), complementarity actors and observers and incommensurable cultures generate conjugate or bistable information couples that he and Heisenberg (1958) suggested paralleled the uncertainty principle at the atomic level. We have built a model to test their speculation and to extend it to role conflicts (Lawless et al., 2009). But even for mundane social interactions, Carley (2002) concluded that humans became social to reduce uncertainty. Thus, the information available to any human is incomplete, producing uncertainty. More importantly, this uncertainty has a minimum irreducibility that promotes the existence of tradeoffs between any two factors in an interaction (uncertainty in worldviews, stories or business models, ΔWV, and their execution, Δv; uncertainty in centers of gravity Δx_{COG} and spatial frequencies, Δk; and uncertainty in energy, ΔE, and time, Δt).

The uncertainty in these oscillations can be reformulated[3] to establish that Fourier pairs, consisting of standard deviations, are equal to:

$$\sigma_A\sigma_B \geq \tfrac{1}{2} \qquad (2)$$

Equation (2) indicates that as variance in factor A broadens, variance in factor B narrows, and vice versa for Fourier pairs. This effect is illustrated using notional data to build three Gaussian distributions with increasing standard deviations as shown in Table 1. Notice that as the standard deviations (σ_f) for the primary functions increase, the standard deviations for their Fourier transforms decrease (σ_F), a simple illustration of COI. Also notice that the relationship for the Fourier pairs ($\sigma_f\sigma_F$) reflected in Equation (2) hold in all of the cases illustrated. And as long as we are dealing with Gaussian distributions, this result must hold (for a proof in signal detection theory, see Cohen, 1995; also, see Rieffel, 2007).

To summarize, a model of interdependence in the interaction of organizations must be able to:

1. Reflect orthogonal perspectives; e.g., between prosecutors and defense attorneys (Busemeyer, 2009); between actions and observations or between multiple cultures

(Bohr, 1955); between USAF combat fighter jet pilots and book-knowledge of air combat maneuvering (Lawless et al., 2000); between game-theory preferences and actual choices made during games (Kelley, 1992); and to capture the discrepancy between the views of managers and the decisions made by their organizations (Bloom et al., 2007).

2. Allow rotation vectors as a function of the direction of rotation. Permit measurements between vectors and rotations.

3. Enable a mathematics of interdependent (i) bistability where measurements disturb or collapse the i states that occur during social-psychological interactions in physical space.

4. Test the proposition that information in organizational interactions can be modeled by the conservation of information.

TELEMEDICINE AND EHEALTH. BACKGROUND AND RATIONALE

Background of Prior Work

From our review (see Stachura et al., 2009), digital technologies are transforming many areas of human endeavor from commerce and entertainment to government and communications. Policymakers are emphasizing Information Technology (IT) for healthcare to improve service delivery, promote efficiency, educate consumers, and increase satisfaction. But other than gathering information from websites, few people are using IT to communicate online with health care personnel or to purchase medical services. This digital divide has impeded e-health's acceptance. Less well educated, lower income individuals in rural areas use the web less often for health care than better educated, higher income urbanites. To gain the benefits of IT for healthcare, it needs to become more widespread and its benefits more evident to consumers of all types across the country.

Medical care depends on physicians to collect and process patient information. But increasing knowledge requirements for patients and doctors, the need to evaluate populations of patients whether treated or not, unmet healthcare expectations, the costliness of fragmented care, and the rising demand for chronic disease care challenge traditional healthcare models that refinements alone may not solve. Healthcare IT is the best option for future medical progress. IT includes computer-aided diagnosis and treatment monitoring; telemedicine; and IT to inform the public and physicians on health and healthcare. But incorrect beliefs about IT pose a deterrent to telemedicine. Even senior healthcare executives hold beliefs inimical to the increased adoption of IT in healthcare.

In our earlier paper (Stachura et al., 2009), we also reviewed applications of Telemedicine and eHealth in Georgia from an organizational perspective. To evaluate the role of COI in organizational effectiveness, we reviewed organizational and system theory along with past applications and field and laboratory results, three case studies using Telemedicine and eHealth, a model using natural selection (machine learning), and a Monte Carlo simulation of return on investments (ROI). Theory provided us with the tools to analyze tradeoffs based on COI in eHealth management decision-making. In the three case studies, we provided an overview of a Telemedicine and eHealth network from the State of Georgia in the United States that was operating in the Southeast Public Health District (SEPHD), East Georgia Health Cooperative (EGHC), and Island Health Care (IHC)/The Healthcare Alternatives (THA) Group. Next, we analyzed the case studies with COI and the weaknesses and strengths of our theory and approach. Finally, we close with a review of Future Trends.

Overall, indicators pointed to good progress, but a lack of uniformity in the organizational metrics exist to clearly indicate where effectiveness has occurred. At this time, not all of the data needed to model the three case studies had been provided. Qualitatively, all three case studies appear to be successful. However, we looked forward to a more in-depth analysis based on tradeoffs (COI). While too early to judge whether this combination will eventually be successful, our companion study of promoting online web-based metrics for MDRCs has been successful beyond all of our expectations as the modest system that we proposed has been picked up by DOD for all of its IRBs (Wood et al., 2008; 2009; and Tung et al., 2008; 2009). COI predicts that fragmentation will significantly reduce organizational performance and outcomes. Although at this time we cannot identify systemic problems and make recommended changes to enhance MCG's programs, that is our ultimate aim.

New Work

Traumatic Brain Injury (TBI) is the "signature wound" of soldiers returning from Iraq and Afghanistan theaters of conflict. Due to the increased use of explosive devices, although improved body armor and helmets save lives, facial exposure during combat results in symptoms of TBI in soldiers who live through trauma that would have otherwise been fatal.

Initial TBI treatment TBI aims to sustain life and prevent further injury. Chronic care requires re-habilitation and use of assistive technologies that will enable victims to live as independently as possible after they have returned to their homes and communities.

TBI victims experience a range of chronic symptoms that may include confusion, headache, fatigue, trouble sleeping, irritability, anger, depression, withdrawal, altered response, and reduced cognition. While the aim of chronic care and rehabilitation is recovery and independent living, short-term achievements that facilitate these outcomes include the ability to socialize, restoration of self-esteem, amelioration of depression and other emotional issues, re-learning to communicate, to walk, and to think functionally. Some patients with mild TBI recover completely, but others require life-long therapy.

While patients with mild traumatic brain injury may fully recover from their impairments, for others, chronic treatment for TBI will be life-long. In many cases, the type and intensity of treatment will decrease over-time as the TBI treatments advance, and as the TBI patient and his or her family learn more about how to care for and cope with traumatic brain injury.

While behavioral TBI symptoms are generally observable, physiological correlations may also be detected such as, for example, changes in pulse rate, blood pressure, and abnormal respiratory rates. Even levels of patient activity throughout the day, or the quality of nightly sleep might provide insightful. Remote monitoring (e-health) to detect these changes could offer an improved and cost-effective means for monitoring and treating TBI sufferers.

In addition, many symptoms attributable to TBI, including neuro-psychiatric symptoms, can be mimicked or modified by abnormal circulating hormone levels. Modulation of peripheral endocrine gland hormone secretion is under the control of the anterior pituitary gland, which in turn, is under the control of neuro-hormones secreted by a portion of the brain – the hypothalamus. The hypothalamus and pituitary gland are connected by a fine stalk, permeated by fragile portal blood vessels through which neuro-hormones travel from the hypothalamus to the pituitary. Thus, there are three sites, individually or in combination, at which TBI could result in abnormal pituitary hormone secretion: hypothalamus (brain), stalk, or anterior pituitary gland itself.

Finally, while initial treatment and stabilization of the TBI patient will likely occur in the controlled setting of the hospital, the true test of success will be the patient's ability to re-insert him/herself into their pre-injury lives. These long-term efforts will occur at home and in communities that may be distant from institutions staffed with the expertise to provide necessary treatment and on-going support for both the patient and the patient's caregivers – family members and significant others. Successful management of TBI victims must include the patients and their caregivers on-going access to expertise and resources to solidify and maintain initial therapeutic gains after the soldiers return home, and in the course of their normal daily activities (domestic life, work, school, and leisure) in their home communities.

Project A: "Returning Soldier Assessment and Adjustment"

Collaborating Agencies:

- General Electric Global Research Division
- US Army/Fort Gordon/Eisenhower Army Medical Center
- Center for Telehealth, Medical College of Georgia

Part A.1: **Remote Monitoring of Patients with Traumatic Brain Injury to Facilitate Diagnosis and Management.**

The key objective of this research proposal is to test the hypothesis that the symptoms of TBI can be quantified using advanced remote, passive sensors and that the data captured can be correlated with medical assessments to enable a clearer understanding of disease incidence and progression in TBI.

The steps to be undertaken in our approach to achieving this key objective include:

1. Identification of the key symptoms and clinical pathways of TBI
2. Mapping disease symptoms to standard, physical and behavioral, clinical models
3. Development of a sensor informatics system that measures relevant activities and behaviors;

4. Deployment and validation of the system in Warrior Transition Battalion (WTB) barracks
5. Testing of the central hypothesis that the system and model can explain the symptoms associated with TBI and that it fits relevant behavioral models
6. Perform additional clinical studies that will explore potential treatment pathways, and allow the development of management recommendations.

Part A.2: **Contribution of Neuro-Endocrine Abnormalities to Manifestations of TBI.**

The key objective of this research will be to screen for pituitary hormone abnormalities in warriors hospitalized for the treatment of TBI.

The pituitary gland is part of a neural/hormonal axis (hypothalamus, hypothalamic-pituitary portal blood system along the pituitary stalk, anterior pituitary gland) responsible for maintaining physiologic metabolic balance. *Brain injury* that damages neural—hypothalamic—ability to exert control over the anterior pituitary gland can disrupt normal hormonal cycles that vary according to the time of day (circadian, diurnal), in month-long cycles (menstrual), or in response to the individual's metabolic status (feedback). Hypothalamic hormones that regulate anterior pituitary hormones travel down the portal blood vessels of the stalk. If the *pituitary stalk* is damaged (as in whiplash injury) and the flow of these brain influences is interrupted, the anterior pituitary loses important regulatory direction. Stalk interruption results in loss of cyclic hormone production, and decreased anterior pituitary hormone production in general, among which the consequences are the inability to respond to stress. Damage to the *pituitary gland* itself results in decreased production of all anterior pituitary hormones, again with the reduced ability to respond to stress or make other metabolic adjustments.

At a critical and specific time of day, we will obtain a single blood sample from each TBI victim and measure the level of a panel of hormones in an attempt to identify hormone levels or patterns of hormone levels that differ from those of individuals not afflicted with TBI.

Project B: "Telehealth Psychological Service Delivery to Patients with TBI"

Collaborating Agencies:

- Center for Telehealth, Medical College of Georgia
- Charlie Norwood VA Medical Center

A growing literature suggests several promising directions for both the assessment of, and treatment for, individuals with mild to moderate TBI during acute and post-acute rehabilitation. For example, cognitive behavioral therapy (CBT) has been shown to be effective for treating the psychological and behavioral consequences of TBI, including depression, anxiety, sleep disturbance, and pain (e.g., Ouellet & Morin, 2004). As the longer-term implications for adjustment to injury and quality of life post-TBI are just now beginning to be realized, it is clear that efficacious, cost-effective, non-stigmatizing and even novel post-acute interventions are needed. It is essential that these new approaches must take into account access to mental health care because definitive treatment is seldom completed in hospital and active duty soldiers and veterans are often discharged to their homes or to other care facilities that have limited access to the healthcare systems most able to provide the required effective interventions.

In the past decade, telehealth technologies have emerged as efficient and effective service delivery tools to bridge geographical barriers. Telehealth service delivery models, especially those incorporating web-based telehealth technologies available in the home, provide a solution to the problem of access by allowing health care professionals to provide mental and behavioral health care to patients living in, and attempting to

reintegrate themselves into, communities where access to provider experts is not readily available.

This research examines the effectiveness of such telehealth service delivery models for veterans and active duty soldiers who have sustained a mild to moderate TBI. We plan to use a three-arm randomized control trial to test the hypothesis that evidenced-based CBT for TBI patients, delivered via videoconferencing technology ("Telehealth") will be at least as effective as traditional ("In-Person") CBT delivery for improving psychological functioning, and that both CBT service delivery modes will be superior to "Usual Medical Rehabilitation Care." Consented participants are assigned randomly to one of the three treatment arms (consented means those subjects who have freely given their consent to participate). Our methods allow the direct comparison of each service delivery mode's effectiveness in terms of two categories of outcome variables: (1) clinical outcomes, including symptom severity and overall psychological functioning as represented by symptoms of depression and anxiety, sleep disturbance, and pain; and (2) process outcomes, such as treatment adherence, session attendance, attrition, patient perception of treatment, and patient acceptance of technology facilitated treatment delivery.

Demonstrated efficacy of telehealth-delivered CBT for patients with mild to moderate TBI will allow for the development of remote service delivery and chronic support programs that do not require patients to travel repeatedly or to travel to distant hospitals for outpatient treatment. Our ultimate goal is telehealth-delivered CBT in the home in order to provide long-term access to high quality treatment by, and support from, trained mental health providers when and where that treatment and support is needed, to reduce stigma associated with mental health treatment by military personnel, and to promote both optimal recovery and successful community reintegration.

Project C: "TBI Caregiver On-Line Needs Assessment and Resource Access"

Collaborating Agencies:

- Charlie Norwood VA Medical Center
- Center for Telehealth, Medical College of Georgia

In 1998, the Family Caregiver Alliance estimated direct and indirect costs of TBI to the US health care system, to patients and to their families at $48.3 billion annually, with survivor costs of $31.7 billion annually. Lifetime costs for one individual can total as much as $4 million. TBI can seriously affect cognitive, physical, and psychological skills. Physical deficits can involve ambulation, balance, coordination, fine motor skills, strength, and endurance. Cognitive deficits of language and communication, information processing, memory, and perceptual skills are common. Psychological status is often altered. And adjustment to disability issues during treatment is frequently an important factor for all concerned.

When a TBI victim returns to the bosom of her/his family and community, she/he has been changed from the person they once knew. She/he has support needs with which they are unfamiliar and inexperienced. Unfortunately, there is not now in place a mechanism for these caregivers to understand and articulate their own needs for developing competence in the support of their damaged loved ones, and there is no systematic way for them to learn of and gain access to the resources required to assist them in that effort

The purpose of the study is to develop an online assessment questionnaire and resource center for caregivers of patients with TBI. The study is based on the Resiliency Model of Family Stress, Adjustment, and Adaptation and the Life Patterns Model to form the conceptual framework for the effort.

In the initial phase of the study a needs assessment questionnaire for lay caregivers of individuals afflicted with TBI will be developed and refined. The subsequent study phase will include placing the questionnaire on a selected website for use by actual caregivers and other interested parties. A series of branching programs will be developed to link questionnaire results to relevant educational and related resources. In addition to resources with general relevance and accessibility, a long range goal will be to include support references and resources that are not only specifically relevant, but also locally available.

FUTURE STEPS

It is too early in the studies we have proposed in this paper to observe oscillations in the laboratory, but their common presence easily observed in the field suggests that we should fully expect to discover them also geospatially between treatment at regional with telemedicine and primary centers without it; between total treatment costs and timeliness without and with e-health; and between worldview self-reports of those who have been treated in large centers and those in family and home-town locations (we will consider 1989Dawes and his colleagues, 1989!, who stressed the importance of demographic data with questionnaires as more reliable and valid data). In the future, we also plan to collect comparative data to test with panels for the existence of social and psychological oscillations. And we plan further progress reports.

CONCLUSION

Social-psychological oscillations (SPHOs) are a natural and common experience for humans. We have built a mathematical model of these oscillations which shows significant promise theoretically and with applications in the field. Regarding its application to telemedicine and e-health, it is too early to draw conclusions or to fully integrate it into theory. But we can state unequivocally that the telemedicine and e-health research agenda proposed in this paper is exciting and, hopefully, promises to uncover more questions that we can possibly answer.

REFERENCES

Adelson, E. H. (2000). *Lightness perceptions and lightness illusions. The new cognitive sciences* (Gazzaniga, M., Ed.). 2nd ed.). Cambridge, MA: MIT Press.

Allport, F. H. (1962). A structuronomic conception of behavior: Individual and collective. *Journal of Abnormal and Social Psychology, 64*, 3–30. doi:10.1037/h0043563

Ambrose, S. H. (2001). Paleolithic technology and human evolution. *Science, 291*, 1748–1753. doi:10.1126/science.1059487

Asch, S. E. (1956). Studies of Independence and Submission to Group Pressure. A Minority of One Against a Unanimous Majority. *Psychological Monographs, 70*.

Baumeister, R. F., Campbell, J. D., Krueger, J. I., & Vohs, K. D. (2005 January). Exploding the self-esteem myth. *Scientific American.*

Bloom, N., Dorgan, S., Dowdy, J., & Van Reenen, J. (2007). Management practice and productivity. *The Quarterly Journal of Economics, 122*(4), 1351–1408. doi:10.1162/qjec.2007.122.4.1351

Bohr, N. (1955). Science and the unity of knowledge . In Leary, L. (Ed.), *The unity of knowledge* (pp. 44–62). New York: Doubleday.

Bradbury, J. A., Branch, K. M., & Malone, E. L. (2003). *An evaluation of DOE-EM Public Participation Programs (PNNL-14200)*. Richland, WA: Pacific Northwest National Laboratory.

Busemeyer, J., & Trueblood, J. (2009). Comparison of quantum and Bayesian inference models. In P. Bruza, D. A. Sofge, W. F. Lawless, K. Van Rijsbergen & M. Klusch (Eds.), *Quantum Interaction. Third International Symposium, QI-2009*. Berlin: Springer-Verlag.

Carley, K. M. (2002). Simulating society: The tension between transparency and veridicality . In *Social Agents: ecology, exchange, and evolution*. Chicago: University of Chicago, Argonne National Laboratory.

Cohen, L. (1995). *Time-frequency analysis: theory and applications*. Upper Saddle River, NJ: Prentice Hall Signal Processing Series.

Dawes, R. M., Faust, D., & Meehl, P. E. (1989). Clinical versus actuarial judgment. *Science, 243*(4899), 1668–1674. doi:10.1126/science.2648573

Gershenfeld, N. (2000). *The physics of information technology*. Cambridge, UK: Cambridge University Press.

Hasson, U., Nir, Y., Levy, I., Fuhrmann, G., & Malach, R. (2004). Intersubject Synchronization of Cortical Activity During Natural Vision. *Science, 303*, 1634–1640. doi:10.1126/science.1089506

Heisenberg, W. (1999). Language and reality in modern physics. In *Physics and philosophy. The revolution in modern science* (pp. 167-186). New York: Prometheus Books. (Original manuscript published in 1958).

Kelley, H. H. (1992). Lewin, situations, and interdependence. *The Journal of Social Issues, 47*, 211–233. doi:10.1111/j.1540-4560.1991.tb00297.x

Kenny, D. A., Kashy, D. A., & Bolger, N. (1998). Data analysis in social psychology . In Gilbert, D. T., Fiske, S. T., & Lindzey, G. (Eds.), *The handbook of Social Psychology (Vol. 1*, pp. 233–268). Boston: McGraw-Hill.

Lawless, W. F., Bergman, M., & Feltovich, N. (2005). Consensus-seeking versus truth-seeking. *Practice Periodical of Hazardous, Toxic, and Radioactive Waste Management*, *9*(1), 59–70. doi:10.1061/(ASCE)1090-025X(2005)9:1(59)

Lawless, W. F., Bergman, M., Louçã, J., Kriegel, N. N., & Feltovich, N. (2007). A quantum metric of organizational performance: Terrorism and counterterrorism. *Computational & Mathematical Organization Theory*, *13*, 241–281. doi:10.1007/s10588-006-9005-4

Lawless, W. F., Castelao, T., & Ballas, J. A. (2000). Virtual knowledge: Bistable reality and the solution of ill-defined problems. *IEEE Systems Man, and Cybernetics*, *30*(1), 119–126. doi:10.1109/5326.827482

Lawless, W. F., Howard, C. R., & Kriegel, N. N. (2008b). A quantum real-time metric for NVO's . In Putnik, G. D., & Cuhna, M. M. (Eds.), *Encyclopedia of Networked and Virtual Organizations*. Hershey, PA: Information Science Reference. doi:10.4018/978-1-59904-885-7.ch083

Lawless, W. F., Sofge, D. A., & Goranson, H. T. (2009). Conservation of Information: A New Approach to Organizing Human-Machine-Robotic Agents Under Uncertainty. In P. Bruza, D. A. Sofge, W. F. Lawless, K. Van Rijsbergen & M. Klusch (Eds.), *Quantum Interaction. Third International Symposium, QI-2009*. Berlin: Springer-Verlag.

Lawless, W. F., Whitton, J., & Poppeliers, C. (2008a). Case studies from the UK and US of stakeholder decision-making on radioactive waste management. *Practice Periodical of Hazardous, Toxic, and Radioactive Waste Management*, *12*(2), 70–78. doi:10.1061/(ASCE)1090-025X(2008)12:2(70)

Levine, J. M., & Moreland, R. L. (1998). Small groups . In Gilbert, D. T., Fiske, S. T., & Lindzey, G. (Eds.), *Handbook of Social Psychology* (Vol. 2, pp. 415–469). Boston, MA: McGraw-Hill.

Macdonald-Ross, M. (1977). How Numbers Are Shown: A Review of Research on the Presentation of Quantitative Data in Texts. *Audio-Visual Communication Review*, *25*, 359–409.

Meihoefer, H. J. (1969). The Utility of the Circle as an Effective Cartographic Symbol. *Canadian Cartographer*, *6*, 105–117.

Meihoefer, H. J. (1973). *The Visual Perception of the Circle in Thematic Maps: Experimental Results*.

Ouellet, M.-C., & Morin, C. M. (2004). Cognitive behavioral therapy for insomnia associated with traumatic brain injury: a single-case study. *Archives of Physical Medicine and Rehabilitation*, *85*, 1298–1302. doi:10.1016/j.apmr.2003.11.036

Pfeffer, J., & Fong, C. T. (2005). Building Organization Theory from First Principles: The Self-Enhancement Motive and Understanding Power and Influence. *Organization Science*, *16*(4), 372–388. doi:10.1287/orsc.1050.0132

Rieffel, E. G. (2007). Certainty and uncertainty in quantum information processing. In *Quantum Interaction: AAAI Spring Symposium*, Stanford University, AAAI Press.

Slovic, P., Flynn, J. H., & Layman, M. (1991). Perceived risk, trust, and the politics of nuclear waste. *Science*, *254*, 1603–1607. doi:10.1126/science.254.5038.1603

Slovic, P., Layman, M., Kraus, N., & Flynn, J. Chalmers, J., & Gesell, G. (2001). Perceived risk, stigma, and potential economic impacts of a high-level nuclear waste repository in Nevada. In J. Flynn, P. Slovic, & H. Kunreuther (Eds.), *Risk, Media and Stigma* (pp. 87-106). London: Earthscan.

Smith, W. K., & Tushman, M. L. (2005). Managing strategic contradictions: A top management model for managing innovation streams. *Organization Science, 16*(5), 522–536. doi:10.1287/orsc.1050.0134

Stachura, M. E., Astapova, E. V., Tung, H. L., Sofge, D. A., Grayson, J., Bergman, M., et al. (2009). Conservation of information (COI), Geospatial and operational developments in e-Health and Telemedicine for virtual and rural communities. In M. Manuela Cunha, Antonio Tavares & Ricardo Simoes (Eds.), *Handbook of Research on Developments in e-Health and Telemedicine.* Hershey, PA: IGI.

Tufte, E. R. (2001). *The Visual Display of Quantitative Information.* Cheshire, CT: Graphics Press.

Tung, H. L., Marshall-Bradley, T., Wood, J., Sofge, D. A., Grayson, J., Bergman, M., & Lawless, W. F. (2009). Enterprise Information Systems: Two Case Studies. In M. Manuela Cunha, Eva F. Oliveira, Antonio J. Tavares, & Luis G. Ferreira (Eds.), *Handbook of Research on Social Dimensions of Semantic Technologies and Web Services.* Hershey, PA: IGI.

Wickens, C. D. (1992). *Engineering psychology and human performance* (2nd ed.). Columbus, OH: Merrill Publishing.

Wood, J., Tung, H. L., Marshall-Bradley, T., Sofge, D. A., Grayson, J., & Lawless, W. F. (2009). Applying an Organizational Uncertainty Principle: Semantic Web-Based Metrics. In M. M. Cunha, Eva Oliveira, Antonio Tavares & Luis Ferreira (Eds.), *Handbook of Research on Social Dimensions of Semantic Technologies and Web Services.* Hershey, PA: IGI.

KEY TERMS AND DEFINITIONS

Conservation of Information (COI): The conservation of information (COI) concept is derived from signal detection theory (SDT) based on duration-bandwidth tradeoffs: The shorter the duration of a signal, the wider becomes its bandwidth and vice versa. To extend COI to organizational performance and to mergers and acquisitions (M&A), an organization can focus its attention (e.g., situational awareness) on a narrow business model to increase its rate of plan execution or the inverse.

eHealth: e-Health is at the intersection of medical informatics, public health and business, health services and information delivered over the web. It characterizes technology, a way of thinking, and a commitment for global healthcare action. eHealth conveys the promises and excitement of bringing e-commerce to health care.

Illusions: Some illusions are considered to be an error in perception such as an optical illusion or auditory illusion; however, more importantly and for our purposes, other illusions are bistable, like the two faces-vase illusion, producing two opposing interpretations of a single data set.

Majority Rule: a decision rule that selects one of two alternatives, based on which has more than half the votes. It is the binary decision rule used most often in influential decision-making.

Nash Equilibria: In game theory, Nash Equilibri:is a solution concept of a game involving two or more players, in which each player is assumed to know the equilibrium strategies of the other players, and no player has anything to gain by changing only his or her own strategy unilaterally.

Organizations: Organizations are social collectives that perform a function that often cannot be done by an individual alone. Organizations do this by amplifying the capabilities of an individual, by assigning independent roles to individuals, and by coordinating the output of individuals (Ambrose, 2001).

Telemedicine: Telemedicine is the use of telecommunication channels to provide medical information and services. The simplest form of Telemedicine is used daily by most health professionals as they discuss a case over the telephone. More sophisticated Telemedicine applications used by the military and some large medical centers include: using satellite technology to broadcast a consultation between providers at facilities in two countries; videoconferencing equipment; and distance-robotic technology. Bandwidth in the telemedicine system determines its constraints. More bandwidth generates higher costs but more capacity for real-time images, video, and higher quality resolution. The qualities of transmission issues of importance to medicine are sound fidelity, image resolution (spatial or contract), range of motion displayed, and transmission speed. The future semantic web could be telemedicine's answer to the need for high-speed transmission of high quality video.

Social Psychological Harmonic Oscillator (SPHO). Theoretically: the oscillations from an SPHO generate fluctuations that produce information characteristic of an organization's stability response that cooperation can consume (Lawless et al., 2008). The physics of this information forms the central part of our model of the conservation of information (COI).

ENDNOTES

[1] Reported perceived area = (actual area)^x, where $x = 0.8 \pm 0.3$ (Meihoefer, 1969, 1973)

[2] There is the real possibility of three or multi-socio-psycho-geospatial operators. That is, bistable social perspectives should be able to be generalized to form multistable social perspectives. The existence of multiple different cultures, and multiple religions indicates a need for such a generalized model.

[3] Given $[A,B] = iC$, and $\delta A = A - <A>$, then $[\delta A, \delta B] = iC$; further, $<\delta A^2><\delta B^2> \geq \frac{1}{4} <C^2>$, giving the Heisenberg uncertainty principle $\Delta A \Delta B \geq 1/2 <C>$ (for details, see Gershenfeld, 2000, p. 256). The uncertainty equation models the expected variance around the expectation value of the operators while the right hand side gives the expectation value of the commutator. In signal detection theory, the uncertainty principle becomes the Fourier pair $\sigma_A \sigma_B \geq \frac{1}{2}$ (see Cohen, 1995; Rieffel, 2007).

Chapter 10
A Conceptual Model of a Knowledge Warehouse

Meira Levy
Ben-Gurion University of the Negev, Israel

ABSTRACT

A firm's capability to transfer its existing knowledge to various stakeholders and translate knowledge into action determines its success in today's volatile global business environment. However, while many firms systematically manage data and information, managing knowledge remains a controversial issue. One of the reasons for this is inconclusiveness about what knowledge is and whether it can be managed. In order to more precisely define knowledge and its management, a knowledge warehouse conceptual model (KW-CM) is proposed for practically and systematically assimilating of knowledge within organizational business processes. This conceptual model integrates aspects of knowledge that encompass business processes, stakeholders and other organizational information systems within the existing data warehouse (DW) conceptual model. In addition, the paper presents a formal architecture, definitions and guidelines that describe the KW components and processes for leveraging data and information into knowledge. The proposed KW-CM is demonstrated with an example of a DW which handles information regarding customer product usage.

INTRODUCTION

Both data warehouse (DW) and knowledge management (KM) facilitate decision-making processes. The DW makes it possible to carry out complex analyses of organizational transactions in order to provide decision makers with analyzed information (Rizzi, 2007) while KM efforts are directed toward solutions that support decision-making processes. In addition, KM can provide organizational resources (Holsapple, 2001) to enhance decision-making processes and facilitate decision-sharing of decentralized strategic decisions taken by autonomous managers. These steps allow the organization to be more responsive to a volatile environment (Nicolas, 2004). In this

DOI: 10.4018/978-1-61692-020-3.ch010

regard, understanding the different aspects of information and knowledge is important, particularly in light of globalization, ubiquitous computing, and prevailing knowledge-centric views of the firm (Prusak, 2001). However, the distinction between knowledge and information is not always clear and frequently both are discussed as if they were one and the same thing.

"Knowledge management has inspired a shift from a transaction to a distributed knowledge management (DKM) perspective on inter-organizational information processing. [...] Each player in the network acquires specific knowledge from other players for decision support." (Pedersen & Larsen, 2001, p. 139).

According to Stenmark (2002), knowledge is considered tacit while information is explicit and tangible. Knowledge practices involve reasoning about information and data for leveraging performance, problem-solving, decision-making, learning and teaching (Adamson & Venerable, 1998). In my proposed DW conceptual model I adopt Newell's argument (1981):

"If a system has (and can use) a data structure which can be said to represent something (an object, a procedure, whatever), then the system itself can also be said to have knowledge, namely the knowledge embodied in that representation about that thing." (p. 2)

Prusak (2001) claims that one of the challenges facing organizations today is managing knowledge that cannot be digitized, codified, or easily distributed. The DW conceptual model that is presented in this paper also deals with a decision-maker interface on a collaborative information technology that might connect various stakeholders during decision-making processes and foster sharing that kind of knowledge, that resemble tacit knowledge of decision makers.

This paper focuses on integrating KM perspectives within existing DW conceptual modeling methodologies, which deal mainly with operational information. Considerable research into DW systems is being carried out and major theories about DW design methodologies are being developed (e.g. Adamson & Venerable, 1998; Giorgini et al., 2005; Guo et al., 2006; Holten, 2003; and Kerschberg, 2001). However, research into KM systems has not yet evolved sufficiently to have developed systematic, sustained design methodologies, particularly in regard to applying knowledge aspects into information systems (IS) (Jongho et al., 2006). In this paper I present a methodology for modeling a KW, encompassing KM in relation to stakeholders, business processes and various organizational IS.

The paper is organized as follows: in section 2 the theoretical background of KM, DW, and the linkage between the disciplines are discussed. In section 3, the KW concept is presented, followed by its conceptual modeling entitled Knowledge Warehouse – Conceptual Modeling (KW-CM) in section 4. Finally, section 5 concludes and discusses future research directions. Throughout the paper the KW-CM concepts are demonstrated with a DW example which handles information regarding customer product usage.

BACKGROUND

The nature of knowledge and its representation have long been studied in the field of Artificial Intelligence (AI). Newell (2002), for example, realized that a structured symbolic form cannot solely represent knowledge; knowledge requires both structure and process representations. In addition, although knowledge is an abstract concept, a particular "piece" or "facet" of knowledge must be coupled with some formal level of representation to create a sufficiently viable view to justify regarding it as belonging to the knowledge level. In this spirit, the proposed KW-CM exhibits the knowledge level as an extended DW concept model with a knowledge perspective tier.

Conceptual Modeling of Data Warehouse (DW)

By aggregating operational transactions that represent events from various organizational databases, DW makes it possible to implement online analytical processing (OLAP) for supporting decision makers. The DW and OLAP are frequently modeled conceptually with multidimensional modeling (Rizzi, 2007), which represents the transaction data in a cubic metaphor where each aggregative transaction is considered a cell. Furthermore, the cubic dimensions represent analysis criteria, which consist of a hierarchy of attributes that further describe them. This conceptual model is often represented with a star schema including a fact table with aggregated data, surrounded by the source tables. In general, conceptual modeling and representation facilitate the design process by abstracting away implementation considerations. Both designers as well as end-users can better understand the higher level of abstraction in describing the DW process and architecture that this approach achieves.

Several approaches and variations have been proposed for conceptually modeling DW systems. For example, there are the entity/relationship (E/R), the unified modeling language (UML) and of the dimensional fact model (DFM) (Malinowski & Zim´anyi, 2006; Rizzi, 2007). In addition, a hierarchy conceptual model, named MultiDimER (Malinowski & Zim´anyi, 2006), allows each dimension to be represented in hierarchy of attributes that represents any organizational, geographic, or other type of structure that is important for analysis. For instance, a spatial dimension might have a hierarchy with levels such as country, region, city and office. Hierarchies are also required for enabling roll-up and drill-down operations needed for DW analysis.

These modeling techniques address operationally-related concepts of the transaction data bases such as facts, dimensions, measures, hierarchies and cross-dimension attributes. While they support the OLAP processes, which provide reports to decision makers, they lack the KM dimensions that may support integrating these passive knowledge objects within the active decision making processes. The DW conceptual modeling which is presented in this study is designed to bridge this gap with a specific KM layer that handles various knowledge resources.

Knowledge Management (KM)

Knowledge is considered as the main competitive asset of an organization, enabling the enterprise to be productive and to deliver competitive products and services (Druker, 1993). The organizational knowledge is embedded in people, systems, procedures and products. Knowledge workers are required to improve their work on a daily basis in a process that culminates in a significant improvement in performance for the entire enterprise. One of the cornerstones of KM is improving productivity by effectively sharing and transferring knowledge, activities which tend to be time-consuming and often impossible (Druker, 1993; Davenport & Prusak, 2000).

Nonaka (1986) distinguishes between tacit and explicit knowledge. Explicit knowledge is stored in textbooks, software products and documents; implicit knowledge resides in the mind in the form of memory, skills, experience, education, imagination and creativity – manifestations of the mind which are difficult to identify and manage. Alavi and Leidner (2001) claim that information is converted to knowledge once it is processed in the mind of individuals and knowledge becomes information once it is articulated and presented in the form of a text, software product or other means. Then, when the receiver cognitively processes the information, it is converted back into tacit knowledge.

One of the greatest challenges facing knowledge organizations is the problem of knowledge transfer, extracting the tacit knowledge that their knowledge employees possess so as to apply the right knowledge at the right place when needed and to encourage innovation (Nonaks, 1986; Holsapple & Joshi, 2003). Barriers to KM initiatives include the separation between the work and KM processes and the focus on meeting deadline requirements that causes KM tasks to be avoided (Davenport & Prusak, 2000).

KM and decision-making are related and effective KM is considered essential for decision making (Bolloju et al., 2002; Nicolas, 2004; Raghu & Vinze, 2007). In this spirit, several decision support systems (DSS) incorporate the knowledge creation model (Nonaks, 1986; Nemati et al., 2002) that occurs through the synergy between tacit and explicit knowledge, based on a four-step process of socialization, articulation, integration, and internalization (Bolloju et al., 2002; Nemati et al., 2002; Raghu & Vinze, 2007).

The proposed KW-CM seeks to embed KM activities within the business process. This could lead to better knowledge transfer and to overcoming identified barriers towards KM initiatives. Furthermore, KW-CM allows decision makers to get a comprehensive view of DW reports and to establish decision-maker networking throughout the organization.

Organizational Knowledge

Organizational knowledge is often referred to as the collective or organization memory (OM). OM can leverage organizational effectiveness and work coordination by providing knowledge processes that acquire, retain, maintain, search and retrieve (Jennex & Olfman, 2003; Nevo & Wand, 2005). OM resides in various IS and in implementing these processes, organization employees are required to retrieve the relevant knowledge needed in their work context. However, Nevo and Wand (2005) claim that there are several barriers that prevent IS from accessing OM. First, while knowledge can be understood in its creation context, it is often misinterpreted when it is de-contextualized. Another problem relates to the difficulty in combining different types of knowledge that reside in diverse locations (e.g. individuals; procedures, and rules; structure and roles; and physical settings of the workplace). Other problems concern management of tacit knowledge, knowledge volatility and reliability. Therefore, instead of a IS layer intended to support the processes involved in using OM, Nevo and Wand (2005) propose a conceptual model for managing and using OM. Their approach is based on examining, via transactive memory system concepts, the processes which support the sharing of collective knowledge assets within small groups that establish communities of practice. Extending this approach to the whole organizational memory context is possible with IS support.

The transactive memory approach is based on the various ways human encode knowledge: internally, in the mind; externally in an external repository of some kind; or through linkage to someone who holds the knowledge. This linkage resembles a meta-memory, hence memory on memory, consisting of a label of the knowledge and a linkage to its location. In addition, the meta-memory is managed with a directory which supports such information operations as updating, allocation, and retrieval. While humans can establish a naturally transactive memory system within small groups, in an organizational context it is impossible. This is because the required meta-memory is too large for the individual's memory capacity and it is not always clear who holds specific information. To overcome these difficulties, Nevo and Wand (2005) suggest using information technology to support an organization-wide transactive memory system. Their concept views the organization as a group of practice-based communities where each community has established a transactive memory system. These various communities can be linked through an organizational system which holds artificial directories containing transactive knowledge.

In order to establish organization-wide memory, knowledge should be formalized to establish a perceptional common ground for sharing. Accordingly, an organizational ontology that defines the domain of organizational knowledge concepts and their relationships should be constructed. By this ontology Nevo and Wand (2005) refer to knowledge, which is represented by generalized concepts (e.g. project plans) and concept instances (e.g. project A plan) as well as knowledge retainers, represented by roles (e.g. project manager) and role instances (e.g. project A's project manager, named "Linda"). In addition, the ontology includes a tacit knowledge representation, entitled meta-knowledge that defines the natural tacit perceptions possessed by members of communities of practice, addressing issues such as expertise, cognitive capabilities and source credibility (Nevo & Wand, 2005).

In this paper, a similar approach for the KW concept is adopted. The KW serves as a transactive memory for organizing the OLAP reports, using an organizational ontology for defining stakeholders, business processes and IS services, but without referring to these concept instances. However, the tacit knowledge dimension is not handled in a formalized manner, but rather through a collaborative environment that fosters naturally shared practices. Moreover, connecting the KW to the business process context may improve knowledge transfer and acquisition.

DW and KM

Current trends in DW (Kerschberg, 2001; Nemati et al., 2002; Ralaivao & Darmont, 2007) indicate that organizations are now becoming e-Enterprises as they move their operations to the Internet. This development is characterized by establishing partnerships with external stakeholders such as customers and suppliers; and handling complex data, both structured (e.g. enterprise resource planning (ERP), customer relationship management (CRM)) and unstructured (e.g. emails, wikis), as well as incorporating collected Web data into their information repositories. Therefore, DW research should address the need for extending the DW role in a broader perspective that relates not only to operational transaction-oriented data, but also, in order to facilitate business decision-making, to knowledge created by knowledge-workers within the enterprise.

Several studies refer to the notion of integrating KM with DW. Kerschberg (2001) discuss the need to aggregate heterogeneous data, including Web information into the data warehouse; Jongho et al. (2003) propose a systematic conversion of knowledge into hypermedia artifacts and data warehouse components; and Nemati et al (2002) argue that there is a need for a new expanded DSS, which incorporates DW concepts as well as a knowledge creation approach, according to Nonaka's knowledge creation theory (1986). These studies, however, deal mainly with architecture and conceptual models for decision support systems (DSS) where DW is included. This paper, on the other hand, discusses an extended practical conceptual modeling of DW that addresses KM aspects and encompasses stakeholders, business processes and IS.

The current literature review has shown that none of the existing approaches for conceptual modeling of DW addresses KM issues as part of the DW model. This paper aims at bridging this gap by introducing a knowledge warehouse conceptual model (KW-CM) that extends the multidimensional modeling methodology (Rizzi, 2007) with a knowledge layer. The purpose of such a conceptual model is to ensure that decision makers will be able to retrieve and transfer comprehensive and appropriate knowledge to relevant stakeholders.

Figure 1. KW: Four-layer architecture

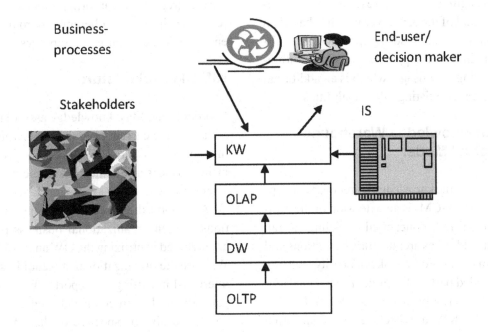

Knowledge Warehouse

While DW aims at facilitating decision-making in organizations, it is not clear whether massive data integration can support decision-making in complex business processes (Tsoukas & Vladimirou, 2001; Holten, 2003; Maddalena, 2004).

"[...] more elaborate techniques are required to extract the hidden knowledge and make these data valuable for decision-makers." (Maddalena, 2004, p. 54)

Several papers addressed this requirement, but they mainly focused on integrating knowledge views such as patterns (Maddalena, 2004), management views (Holten, 2003) and quality factors (Tsoukas & Vladimirou, 2001) to design and implement DW. In my paper, the concept of KW as a central coordinator for DW usage is introduced. KW is part of a four-layer knowledge system (Fig. 1). The first layer consists of the organizational systems that aggregate transactions (on-line transaction processing – OLTP). The second layer is the DW which is constructed based on the OLTP data. Above this layer is the OLAP layer that processes queries on the DW, and produces reports for various stakeholders in the organization. The KW role is to handle these reports while providing the decision maker with a comprehensive organizational view by aggregating related knowledge in the context of a specific business process and pointing to other relevant stakeholders. The benefit of such a component is twofold: first, the decision taken can incorporate other resources of information that may not be part of the DW reports; second, the decision taken becomes part of the current report linkage, available for other stakeholders in current and future decision-making processes.

The main building-blocks of the KW (See Figure 1) are the OLAP reports, business processes, information systems and stakeholders. The first stage in designing KW requires realizing the conceptual model of the KW layer which is based on the DW conceptual modeling approach. The KW approach can further support aggregating information regarding DW usage, which is an additional enhancement to existing DW capabilities.

KW-CM: Knowledge Warehouse Conceptual Model

The concept of the knowledge warehouse conceptual model (KW-CM) is an extension of the multidimensional DW conceptual modeling (Rizzi, 2007) that addresses architecture, definitions and formalism issues. For the sake of brevity, only the new, extended part of the model is described (for a detailed description, see Rizzi, 2007). In what follows, the KW architecture and conceptual modeling issues are explained and demonstrated including formalism of the main concepts. The KW-CM can help decision-making by giving decision makers a comprehensive understanding of the OLAP report, and by contextualizing its content in relation to other organizational information and stakeholders. Hence information is turned into knowledge.

The KW-CM concept is demonstrated through an example of a DW that handles information regarding customer product usage. In this context, consider a scenario in which a manger gets an OLAP report showing insufficient usage of a feature in a new product line. In order to support the manager in making an intelligent decision, more information is needed. For instance, data records in the customer relationship management (CRM) system reveal recurring complaints regarding the feature. Furthermore, the marketing information system provides information about which campaign management processes have been issued regarding this feature. The manager also needs a point of contact in the R&D department

for discussing the problems that were reported. These knowledge resources, possibly more, may be relevant for the specific issue at hand. Therefore, aggregating the information and knowledge resources into one coherent environment may enhance the decision-making process.

KW-CM Architecture

In order to facilitate knowledge assimilation that addresses the current needs of the learning organization, it is essential to discuss knowledge items in the broader sense of their business environment. Therefore, when decision makers discuss the DW OLAP reports, they need to consider several questions: Which organizational business processes are involved in utilizing the DW analysis reports? Who are the organizational stakeholders that are interested in getting the reports? What other organizational IS can contribute to getting a more comprehensive perspective of the DW analysis reports at hand?

In answering these questions there should be a systematic definition of how to connect information regarding business processes, stakeholders and IS with DW analytic reports. Accordingly, the original DW that was constructed (Adamson & Venerable, 1998; Kerschberg, 2001; Giorgini et al., 2005; Guo et al., 2006; Malinowski & Zim'anyi, 2006; Rizzi, 2007) remains unchanged, and is considered a black box. In the new DW, entitled KW, that we are constructing, the facts (events) are the OLAP reports with KW dimensions that consist of business processes, stakeholders and IS (see Fig 2).

The KW dimensions exhibit the reports' metadata, which in this case means data about the report. This metadata is implemented with an organizational ontology which maps the information regarding the reports, business processes, stakeholders and IS into concepts and relations. Further, the organizational ontology concepts are installed in the KW according to the report

Figure 2. A basic fact schema for KW

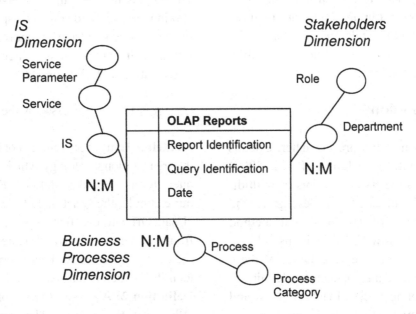

that was issued and serve in the aggregating of knowledge processes (see 4.2).

The KW processes are different from traditional DW processes. While DW processes aggregate data of organizational events into a new database (DB) with OLAP capabilities, KW processes utilize the linkages metadata in the KW for linking IS, stakeholders and business processes to an OLAP report. These processes occur when observing a specific report in a specialized KW environment (see 4.3).

For each DW dimension there is a specialized KW process, entitled KW-Process. The IS KW-Process is implemented by services, which are software components that serve as interfaces to IS, for extracting the needed information. In cases where no IS service is provided, a reference to the IS will be presented to the decision-maker, for self-knowledge extraction. The stakeholders and the KW-Processes present the linkage information to the decision-maker within the KW environment. Having such an organizational ontology can support further development of interfaces to other applications across the organization.

Thinking about the example above, a manager who holds the report regarding the under-used feature can use a service that aggregates all the information about the specific product feature from the CRM and present it to the manager. Since the original OLAP report is based on specific fields, it is reasonable that part of them will be used for aggregating information from other IS systems as well. For example, in the former case, the product and the under-used feature identification numbers are part of the OLAP report and are also the parameters according to which information will be extracted from the CRM.

The three KW dimensions -- IS, business processes and stakeholders -- have N:M relations with the OLAP report facts table. For instance, in the discussed example, the report can be linked to the CRM as well as to the ERP system for aggregating customer information. At the same time, there is a linkage that connects the report to business processes of a new feature development and product bug review. In addition, the stakeholders who relate to the report are the head of the R&D department, the specific product manager, the head of the marketing department and so forth. Therefore, three additional bridge tables are required for implementing these relations, but for brevity and comprehensibility considerations these tables are not presented in Fig. 2.

KW-CM Definitions

The conceptual modeling presented here extends the DW conceptual modeling (Rizzi, 2007) which addresses the basic concepts of multidimensional DW with additional descriptive and cross-dimension attributes. A similar method for expressing the KW-CM definitions is being used, following formal representation of these definitions and guidelines for using the definitions during the modeling process. In what follows, and due to space limits, only a partial ontology will be presented and demonstrated. However, these examples illustrate the basic idea of how to logically link the various KW components.

In order to formalize the KW-CM, the organizational ontology terms are presented by sets. For example, term A is defined as a set: A={x|x is an item in a set which represents a term in the ontology} (e.g. queries). Relation "Re" between terms is represented as a relation: Re(x,y), where x is the first term and y is the second term (e.g. query x has "queryRelatesToReport" relation with report y). A Relational Data Base (RDB) R is defined as a set of attributes: SchR={ati|ati is an attribute in a set which represents RDB R} (e.g. OlapReports).

It should be noted that each organization needs an ontology that is contextualized to its business environment. However, future research might focus on building a general ontology that can serve as a basic organizational ontology to be refined according to specific organizational terms.

Definition 1: A *DW report* is defined according to its query definitions, assuming that each query type has a unique term in the organization ontology and a specific process in the OLAP layer. Therefore,

this term is included in the KW-CM fact table, making it possible to connect a specific report to its query, serving also as a report type identifier.
Formalism 1: Q is the set which represents the organizational OLAP queries:

Q={y|y is a query processed by the OLAP layer}.

Guideline 1: In order to build a coherent KW-CM, the organizational ontology, which holds the report query terms, should be defined. For instance, in our example, the Q set includes a query entitled "UsageOfFeatureX" that aggregates information from the operational DB and creates a report about the usage of feature X. This query has a unique identifier which will be part of the KW fact table.
Definition 2: A *KW-CM fact* table exhibits the DW reports that the OLAP layer produced. Each report is considered a primary event and appears only once with an identification number, the date it was issued and its query term, taken from the organizational ontology.
Formalism 2: KW-CM includes a RDB that is defined as $SchKW\text{-}CM\text{:}=\{at1=Ri,\ at2=Qi,\ at3=Date\}$ where Ri is the report unique identifier, which is the same identifier in the report repository, and serves as the RDB primary key; $Qi \in Q$; and date refers to the day on which the report was issued. Although the date is part of the report data, it is inserted in the KW to enable further KW analysis.
Guideline 2: The KW-CM fact includes a reference to a report which exists in one of the organizational repositories, as well as an ontological term of its query. The KW-CM fact table is updated whenever a new report is produced. For example, the report that was described in guideline 1 above, will have a correspondence record in the RDB with an identifier number; Qi="UsageOfFeatureX"; and the date it was issued.
Definition 3: A *KW-CM service* is a linkage to a service for extracting information from a specific

IS. Having such services is critical for aggregating information which is relevant to the KW-CM facts.

Formalism 3: IS is the set which represents the organizational information systems (IS); S is the set which represents the organizational IS services; and P is a set which defines the service parameters.

IS={x|x is an organizational IS}. S={y|y is a service provided by organizational IS}. P={z|z is a parameter of one or more services). The relation IS-S(x,y) indicates that service y is related to IS x. The relation SP(z,y) indicates that parameter z relates to service y. If q $\in$ Q, then the relation SQ(y,q) indicates that service y relates to query q.

Guideline 3: Each IS component of the KW-CM should have a service and service parameters that will serve as a gate through which information can be extracted. Following the example of the under-used feature, there is a need to aggregate information regarding the management campaigns that relate to this specific feature. The IS set will include ISi="CampaignManagementSystem", assuming that there is an organizational system IS that aggregates information about campaign management; the P set will include Pi="Feature" and Si="FindManagementCampai gnsOfFeature". In addition, there will be a relation of IS-S("CampaignManagementSystem", "FindManagementCampaignsOfFeature") a relation of SP("Feature", FindManagement-CampaignsOfFeature") and for the former Qi="UsageOfFeatureX", there will be a relation SQ("FindManagementCampaignsOfFeature", "UsageOfFeatureX").

Definition 4: A *KW-CM ontology* handles the KW-CM stakeholders and business process terms. As explained above, since only a partial ontology is defined, stakeholder roles and department- related terms as well as terms that define business process categories will not be described.

Formalism 4: ST is the set which represents the stakeholders and BP is a set which defines the business processes.

ST={x|x is a stakeholder in the organization} and BP={y|y is an organizational business process. If z $\in$ Q, then the relation ST-Q(x,z) defines a stakeholder x that relates to query z, and the relation BP-Q(y,z) defines a business process y that relates to query z.

Guideline 4: Each one of the KW-CM stakeholders and business processes components should have a representation in the KW-CM ontology. For example, if a stakeholder of a specific query is the R&D department, the KW-CM ontology should include such a stakeholder definition. The same is applicable for presenting the various organizational processes in such ontology. Such an ontology can serve us further when extracting information from the KW-CM, such as finding all the business processes that relate to a specific query. By way of demonstration, in the context of the former example, STi="headOfTheR&Ddepartment" and BPi="ProductSatisfectionReview", and for the Qi="UsageOfFeatureX" there will be relations of ST-Q("headOfTheR&Ddepartment", "UsageOfFeatureX ") and BP-Q("ProductSatisfectionReview", "UsageOfFeatureX ").

Definition 5: The *KW-CM ontology* will hold for each query regarding its input and output parameters. This will make it possible to connect the query parameters with the required services parameters.

Formalism 5: QIP is the set which represents the query input parameters and QOP is the set which represent the query output parameters.

QIP={x|x is a query input parameter} and QOP={y|y is a query output parameter). If z $\in$ Q, then the relation QIP-Q(x,z) indicates that parameter y is an input parameter of query z, and the relation QOP-Q(y,z) indicates that parameter y is an output parameter of query z.

Guideline 5: The organizational ontology should define for each query its input and output parameters, assuming that these parameters are aligned with the service parameters. Therefore, the terms of the service parameters and the query input and output parameters should share the same terminology. For example, if a DW report aggregates information regarding the usage of a specific feature, based on specific user age attribute, the ontology will include Qi="UsageByAge" which creates the report with QIPi="user-age", as the query input parameter, followed a relation of QIP-Q("user-age", "UsageByAge"), as well as QOPi="customer-name" as the query output parameter, and a relation of QOP-Q("customer-name", "UsageByAge"). In addition, the ontology may include a service entitled "CustomersByAge" that has an input parameter of "user-age" that collects information from the ERP. Therefore, the ontology will also include the relation SQ("CustomersByAge", "UsageByAge") that connects the service "CustomersByAge" to its related "UsageByAge" query.

KW-CM Environment

A *KW-CM environment* is part of the KW-CM which defines the interface where the KW-CM gathered information will be presented to its decision-makers. In addition to the architecture of the KW-CM, its functionality should also be defined, including its search and information gathering capabilities. The design of such an environment is beyond the scope of the current paper but there is a need to explicitly define its requirements.

The KW-CM aggregating information should be presented via a collaborative environment rather than in a DW report. This environment includes a linkage to the specific DW report; the aggregative information, hence the relevant records which were found via the IS services as a result of searching the required fields; the report's relevant stakeholders; and the business processes for which the report is applicable. In case the linked IS does not provide service for extracting information, there will be an option to present the decision-maker a link to that system for further usage. Moreover, the KW-CM environment should include additional place for unstructured information where the stakeholders can express insights or share experience while discussing issues concerning a specific DW report.

In addition, the decisions taken following the analysis of the DW report can also be managed in such environment, including interfacing organizational decision support systems, if such exist. The benefit of such environment is obvious when tracking previous DW report activities within the organization.

The KW-CM defined above serves as an organizational transactive memory, which links knowledge items, represented by OLAP reports, with other information items that exist in other IS, while connecting them to relevant stakeholders in the context of a business processes.

CONCLUSION AND FUTURE RESEARCH

The requirement of facilitating the usage of IS and DW, in particular, during decision-making processes is well acknowledged (Tsoukas, H., Vladimirou, 2001; Stenmark, 2002; Holten, 2003; Maddalena, 2004). This paper presents an enhancement to using a DW by embedding a knowledge layer on top of existing DW and OLAP applications. The rationale behind this stems from the need for embedding knowledge processes within business processes in a context which is relevant for their stakeholders. The KW-CM approach addresses both needs, managing the structured knowledge that come from the organizational IS, business processes and stakeholders ontology, as well as organizing unstructured information to be shared in a collaborative environment.

Nevu and Wade (2007) claim that there is a need to align system performance with stakeholder expectations. Therefore, encompassing the stakeholder view in the KW-CM, starting from the conceptual modeling, can enhance the usability and satisfaction from DW. Furthermore, the suggested environment can help in analyzing DW usage and improvements. Since the KW-CM architecture defines a separate layer for the KW it is applicable for existing DW without the need to redesign them.

The presented KW concept modeling opens a new direction in DW research and implementation. Further work will address designing and implementing issues concerning KW-CM application and use. This involves various aspects of IS such as IS services, organizational ontology-related issues as well as KW processes and KW analytic processes, human-computer interactions (HCI) and computer supported collaborative work (CSCW).

REFERENCES

Adamson, C., & Venerable, M. (1998). *Data Warehouse Design Solutions*. Danvers, MA: John Wiley & Sons.

Alavi, M., & Leidner, D. E. (2001). Review: Knowledge management and knowledge management systems: Conceptual foundations and research issues. *Management Information Systems Quarterly, 25*(1), 107–136. doi:10.2307/3250961

Bolloju, N., Khalifa, M., & Turban, E. (2002). Integrating knowledge management into enterprise environments for the next generation decision support. *Decision Support Systems, 33*, 163–176. doi:10.1016/S0167-9236(01)00142-7

Davenport, T. H., & Prusak, L. (2000). *Working Knowledge*. Boston, MA: Harvard Business School Press.

Druker, P. (1993). *Post-Capitalism Society*. Oxford, UK: Butherworth-Heinemann.

Giorgini, P., Rizzi, S., & Garzetti, M. (2005). Goal-oriented requirement analysis for data warehouse design. In *Proc. DOLAP* (pp. 47-56).

Guo, Y., Tang, S., Tong, Y., & Yang, D. (2006). Triple-Driven Data Modeling Methodology in Data Warehousing: A Case Study. In *Proc. of ACM 9th International Workshop on Data Warehousing and OLAP (DOLAP)*, Arlington, Virginia, USA (pp. 59-66).

Holsapple, C. W., & Joshi, K. D. (2001). Organizational knowledge resources. *Decision Support Systems, 31*, 39–54. doi:10.1016/S0167-9236(00)00118-4

Holsapple, C. W., & Joshi, K. D. (2003). A Knowledge Management Ontology . In Holsapple, C. W. (Ed.), *Handbook on Knowledge Management* (*Vol. 1*, pp. 89–124). Lexington, KY: Springer.

Holsapple, C. W., & Singh, M. (2003). The Knowledge Chain Model: Activities for Competitiveness . In Holsapple, C. W. (Ed.), *Handbook on Knowledge Management* (*Vol. 2*, pp. 215–251). Lexington, KY: Springer.

Holten, R. (2003). Specification of management views in information warehouse projects. *Information Systems, 12*, 709–751. doi:10.1016/S0306-4379(02)00080-7

Jennex, M. E., & Olfman, L. (2003). Organizational Memory . In Holsapple, C. W. (Ed.), *Handbook on Knowledge Management* (*Vol. 1*, pp. 207–234). Lexington, KY: Springer.

Jongho, K., Woojong, S., & Heeseok, L. (2003). Hypermedia modeling for linking knowledge to data warehousing system. *Expert Systems with Applications, 24*, 103–114. doi:10.1016/S0957-4174(02)00088-X

Kerschberg, L. (2001). Knowledge Management in Heterogeneous Data Warehouse Environments. In *3rd International Conference on Data Warehousing and Knowledge Discovery (DaWaK 01)*, Munich, Germany (LNCS 2114, pp. 1–10). Berlin: Springer.

Maddalena, A. (2004). Pattern Based Management: Data Models and Architectural Aspects. In W. Lindner et al. (Eds.), *EDBT 2004Workshops* (LNCS 3268, pp. 54–65).

Malinowski, E., & Zimányi, E. (2006). Hierarchies in a multidimensional model: From conceptual modeling to logical representation. *Data & Knowledge Engineering*, *59*, 348–377. doi:10.1016/j.datak.2005.08.003

Nemati, H. R., Steiger, D. M., Iyer, L. S., & Herschel, R. T. (2002). Knowledge Warehouse: An Architectural Integration of Knowledge Management, Decision Support, Artificial Intelligence and Data Warehousing. *Decision Support Systems*, *33*(2), 143–161. doi:10.1016/S0167-9236(01)00141-5

Nevo, D., & Wand, Y. (2005). Organizational memory information systems: a transactive memory approach. *Decision Support Systems*, *39*, 549–562. doi:10.1016/j.dss.2004.03.002

Nevu, D., & Wade, M. R. (2007). How to avoid Disappointment by Design. *Communications of the ACM*, *50*(4).

Newell, A. (1981). *The Knowledge Level*. AI Magazine.

Nicolas, R. (2004). Knowledge management impacts on decision making process. *Journal of Knowledge Management*, *8*(1), 20–31. doi:10.1108/13673270410523880

Nonaka, I. (1986). A Dynamic Theory of Organizational Knowledge Creation. *Organization Science*, *5*(1), 14–37. doi:10.1287/orsc.5.1.14

O'Dell, C., & Grayson, J. C. (2003). Identifying and Transferring Internal Best Practices . In Holsapple, C. W. (Ed.), *Handbook on Knowledge Management* (pp. 601–622). Lexington, KY: Springer.

Pedersen, M. K., & Larsen, M. H. (2001). Distributed knowledge management based on product state models - the case of decision support in health care administration. *Decision Support Systems*, *31*(1), 139–158. doi:10.1016/S0167-9236(00)00124-X

Prusak, L. (2001). Where did knowledge management come from? *IBM Systems Journal*, *40*(4), 1002–1007. doi:10.1147/sj.404.01002

Raghu, T. S., & Vinze, A. (2007). A business process context for Knowledge Management. *Decision Support Systems*, *43*, 1062–1079. doi:10.1016/j.dss.2005.05.031

Ralaivao, J., & Darmont, J. (2007). Knowledge and Metadata Integration for Warehousing Complex Data. In *6th International Conference on Information Systems Technology and its Applications (ISTA 07)*, Kharkiv, Ukraine.

Rizzi, S. (2003). Open problems in data warehousing: 8 years later. In *Proc. DMDW*.

Rizzi, S. (2007). Conceptual Modeling Solutions for the Data Warehouse . In Wrembel, R., & Koncilia, C. (Eds.), *Data Warehouses and OLAP: Concepts, Architectures and Solutions*. Hershey, PA: IRM Press.

Schreiber, G., Akkermans, H., Anjewierden, A., de Hoog, R., Shadbolt, N., van de Velde, W., & Wielinga, B. (2000). *Knowledge Engineering and Management - the CommonKADS Methodology*. Cambridge, MA: MIT Press.

Song, I.-Y., Rowen, W., Medsker, C., & Ewen, E. (2001). An analysis of many-to-many relationships between fact and dimension tables in dimensional modeling. In *Proceedings of the Third International Workshop on Design and Management of Data Warehouses (DMDW'2001),* Interlaken, Switzerland.

Stenmark, D. (2002). Information vs. Knowledge: The Role of intranets in Knowledge Management. In *Proceedings of the 35th Hawaii International Conference on System Sciences.*

Tsoukas, H., & Vladimirou, E. (2001). What is organizational knowledge? *Journal of Management Studies, 38*(7), 972–993. doi:10.1111/1467-6486.00268

Chapter 11
BI-FIT:
Aligning Business Intelligence End-Users, Tasks and Technologies

Rick Tijsen
Utrecht University, The Netherlands

Marco Spruit
Utrecht University, The Netherlands

Martijn van de Ridder
Capgemini Nederland, The Netherlands

Bas van Raaij
Capgemini Nederland, The Netherlands

ABSTRACT

Over the years many organizations have invested in Business Intelligence (BI) systems. While BI-software enables organization-wide decision support, problems are encountered in the "fit" between systems' provision and changing requirements of a growing amount of BI (end-) users. This chapter aims at investigating the factors that influence the "fit" between Business Intelligence (BI) end-users, tasks and technologies (BI-FIT). Based on an extensive literature study on the elements of BI-FIT, in this research the BI-FIT Framework is developed that shows the most relevant factors and the interrelationships between BI end-users, tasks and technologies. The framework can be used to help organizations to identify and fulfill the needs of BI end-users, thereby improving adoption and increasing satisfaction of the BI end-user base.

INTRODUCTION

In today's globalized economy, especially during times of recession, the uncertainty that organizations are facing when taking decisions has become bigger. In order to deal with this uncertainty, or-ganizations process information (Daft & Lengel, 1986). According to Galbraith (1974, p. 28) "the principle of a managerial task is to reduce uncertainty by processing information." The demand for profits, increasing (global) competition, and demanding customers all require organizations to take the best decisions as fast as possible (Vitt,

DOI: 10.4018/978-1-61692-020-3.ch011

Luckevich, & Misner, 2002). Therefore, the ability to quickly take advantage of the exponential growing amount of information has become an extremely critical component for the success of the modern organization (Barlow & Burke, 1999; Huber, 2003). The need for fast decision making on the one hand, and the longer time needed to acquire the right information on the other hand causes a so-called "information gap" (den Hamer, 2005; van Beek, 2006). Business Intelligence (BI) is implemented in order to narrow down this information gap.

Background

Over the years BI has increasingly been moving into the mainstream of knowledge worker computing (Negash & Gray, 2003). No longer are BI solutions solely being used by information specialists or analysts. This is reflected in the population of BI-end users, which is becoming increasingly more heterogeneous in both the skills that end-users bring to BI-systems as well as in the demands they place on them (Gile, 2003). Unfortunately, according to several authors many BI projects fall short of their promise to deliver value. According to Raden (2004, p. 10), "business intelligence applications have low adoption rates within organizations". Furthermore, Biere (2003, p. 8) states that "too many organizations take the easy technology-driven route by selecting some tools, hoping the end users will "magically" emerge with what they want." Finally, Ferguson (1996, p. 13) states that "less attention is devoted to actual BI usage on the problem of getting data out of the system. This approach has diminished the potential benefit of BI systems since it assumes that all users are capable of finding their way around in this 'ocean' of information." In other words, an implementation from a technology-driven perspective does not ensure the adoption and usage of end-users, which constrains organizations to benefit from the potential of their BI investments.

Looking from an end-users perspective, end-users simply want a better way to solve data-related business problems. The end-user's perception of the benefits received from a BI solution is dependent on the degree of productivity increase or the amount of positive results that they receive. If a BI solution helps them look better, and lets them do their job better, they will be more likely to use it (Turban et al., 2007). While BI-software enables organization-wide decision support, problems are encountered in the fit between systems' provision and changing requirements of a growing amount of (end-) users (Dekkers, Versendaal & Batenburg, 2007). The main reason why this "fit" (hereafter referred to as BI-FIT) is missing is that when BI-solutions are implemented in practice, end-users are usually considered (if considered at all) to be equal in their adoption and usage of the system (Biere, 2003), which is not always the case (Borgman, 1989). If end-users get provided with a BI-solution that does not fit their capabilities or tasks, they will most likely not use it, or use it in the wrong manner, or even become negative about the BI-solution, which obviously does not contribute to a positive result. However, if end-users are equipped with a BI-system that fits their needs, they will produce better intelligence to support their decisions, and in the end reduce uncertainty. In order to establish this fit, in this chapter the BI-FIT framework is proposed, which provides an answer to the following research question:

"What are the major factors influencing the fit between Business Intelligence end-users and Business Intelligence solutions?"

Research Motivation and Methodology

Although BI is widely applied in practice, scientific research in the field is limited. Several authors state that BI research "seems to have flown under the radar of academics" (Negash & Gray, 2003; Pirttimäki, Lönnqvist, & Karjaluoto, 2006). Most available literature focuses on BI technology such as data-warehousing (Barbara, Wixom, & Watson, 2001; Kimball, 2008), OLAP (online analytical processing) (Chaudhuri & Dayal, 1997; Tremblay et al., 2007) and data-mining (Fayyad & Uthurusamy, 1996; Han & Kamber, 2006). Unfortunately, considerably less attention is given to the organizational side of BI, investigating BI processes and BI organization (Philips & Vriens, 1999; Pirttimäki & Hannula, 2003; Zeng, Xu, Shi, Wang, & Wu, 2006a). By investigating BI-FIT, this chapter provides new insights into research on the organizational aspects of BI as well as a better understanding of BI end-user adoption.

In general, the goal of Information Systems (IS) research is to produce knowledge that enables the application of information technology for managerial and organizational purposes (Hevner, et al., 2004). The main goal of this research is to develop a model that depicts the major factors influencing BI-FIT, which can be used to assist organizations in identifying and defining differing BI end-user groups and their needs, in order to provide end-users with a BI solution that fits. For this purpose, a design research approach is used. By means of constructing an artifact, new scientific knowledge can be generated (Hevner et al., 2004; Vaishnavi & Kuechler, 2007). In this research the artifact is the BI-FIT Framework, which is developed according to the steps (problem awareness, suggestion and development, evaluation & conclusion) in developing design research artifacts as described by Vaishnavi et. al. (2007). Awareness of the problem area was raised in discussions with BI practitioners from the field, BI literature reporting BI success and failure, and in articles in BI professional magazines and blogs. A detailed problem description was provided in the previous section.

Based on the problems as described in the background section of this chapter it has become clear that when implementing BI, more time and attention needs to be devoted to the actual end-users of the BI solution, instead of purely focusing on technology. However, because limited knowledge on BI end-user adoption is available, it was decided to investigate the main factors influencing BI usage from an end-users perspective. Furthermore, the factors identified are used to develop the BI-FIT Framework which can be used to assist organizations in providing their end-users with a BI-solution that fits their needs. The BI-FIT Framework has been validated by carrying out a case study within six organizations, following Yin (2008; 2003). Hevner et al. (2004) also suggest case studies as an appropriate evaluation method in design research. After analyzing and discussing the data gathered during the case studies, conclusions are drawn and recommendations for further research will be provided.

END-USER FIT

The relationship between investment in information technology (IT) and its effect (IT-impact) on organizational performance is a major area of interest for (IS) researchers and practitioners. It must be clear that it is not the investment in technology that is the driver for IT impact, but the actual usage of the technology (Devaraj & Kohli, 2003). Persuading end-users to adopt information technologies persists as a major challenge confronting those responsible for implementation. An important question in this context is: What causes individual end-users to adopt new information technologies, and in particular BI-systems? The term "individual" is used explicitly because this research starts from the observation that the growing amount of BI end-users are heterogeneous, both in the skills they bring to BI-systems and the demands they place on them (Gile, 2003). The same IT-system can be seen as successful by one individual end-user or group but as a failure or at least problematic by another end-user or group

Table 1. Overview of IS acceptance models

Authors	Model	Factors influencing adoption
Delone & Mclean (1992)	Information Success Model	System and information quality.
Davis (1993)	Technology Acceptance Model	Individual end-users "perceived usefulness, and perceived ease of use."
Goodhue & Thompson (1995)	Task – Technology–Fit Model	Fit between Indivdual -, Task- & Technology characteristics.

(Agarwal & Prasad, 1999). Several interconnected factors seem to influence this.

In literature several models have been proposed that intend to explain the factors that influence end-users IT adoption and utilization and therefore explain IT success or failure. The Information Success Model (ISM) developed by Delone and Mclean (1992) was a breakthrough because they proposed a model to asses IS from the end-users' perspective. Basically, the ISM suggests that system quality and information quality determine IT success. However, among others Davis (1993) criticizes the ISM model by stating that quality is not the only factor determining success, and has developed the Technology Acceptance Model (TAM). The TAM has been proposed to explain the factors that influence an end-users decision to utilize a system or not, and is a widely cited model in IS research. Basically, the TAM defines the constructs "perceived ease of use" and "perceived usefulness" to predict an end-user's attitude towards using and actual system use (Davis, 1993). Both factors themselves are influenced by so-called "external factors" like for example individual characteristics of end-users or IT-system characteristics. Although the TAM is a widely cited model, it is criticized concerning its "lack of task focus", because it does not take into account that end-users use IT even if they do not like it, simply because it improves their job performance (Goodhue & Thompson, 1995). Furthermore, one of the main properties of the TAM, is that it is designed for voluntary use of IS systems (Davis, 1993), which is not always applicable.

In response to the critique on existing IT acceptance models, Goodhue & Thompson (1995) developed the Task-Technology-Fit model (TTF). The 'fit' is explained as "the extent to which technology functionality matches task requirements and individual abilities" (Goodhue & Thompson, 1995, p. 216). In other words, "the TTF posits that IT systems will be used if, and only if, the functions available to the user support (fit) the activities and individual capabilities of the user" (Dishaw & Strong, 1999, p. 11). Furthermore, the TTF model has proven that not only the individual factors (individual characteristics, task characteristics, technology characteristics) are important, but also the quality of the "fit" between them. To conclude, the discussion of IS acceptance models has learned us that several interrelated factors influence BI adoption and usage. An overview is depicted in Table 1.

Based on the TTF model, the BI-FIT model is proposed, which depicts the main factors that influence the fit between BI end-user and solutions. The BI-FIT model is included in Figure 1. Adopted from the TTF model, the BI-FIT model assumes that a high degree of "BI-FIT" has a positive effect on adoption, which positively influences performance and a low degree of "BI-FIT" has the opposite effect. Since the BI-FIT is considered to be dynamic, and therefore should be monitored because of changes over time in individual, task or technology characteristics. This research does not employ the TTF model as an instrument to measure constructs, but rather to contribute to a better understanding of the interrelationships be-

Figure 1. BI-FIT model, based on the TTF model

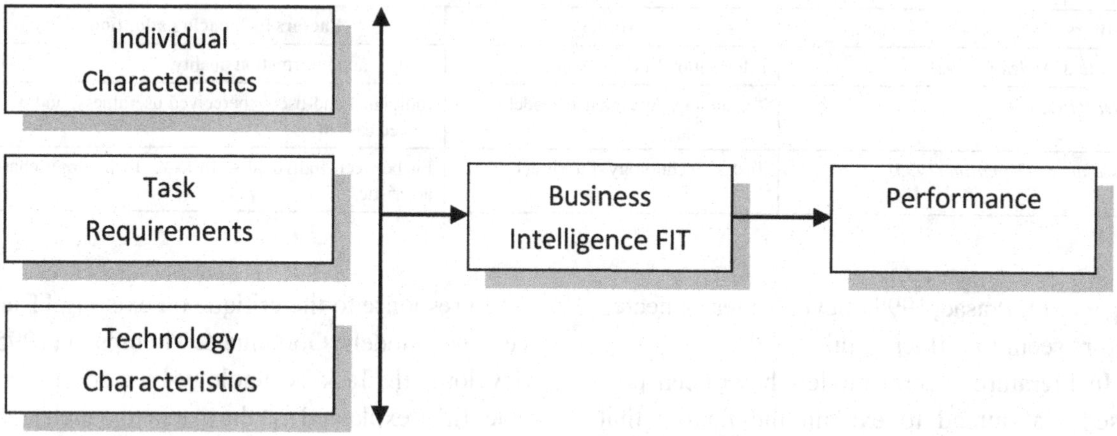

tween and consequences of BI-specific individual, task and technology characteristics.

BI-FIT FRAMEWORK

One of the main objectives of any BI-implementation is to meet the diverse needs of a diverse set of end-users. Therefore, the first requirement is to understand "who" the end-users are in order to determine "what" they need (Gile, 2003). As discussed above, end-users are not equal, and therefore have different requirements. Unfortunately, in most cases it is not possible to develop a customized solution for each individual end-user. Therefore, there is a need for end-user segmentation, in order to understand the needs of the different user constituencies within the BI end-user community, since each has a different set of requirements and preferences. Based on the factors that influence the BI-FIT which were discussed above, a BI end-user segmentation model is developed which is described in the remainder of this chapter.

Individual Characteristics

Individuals within an organization need the ability to perform their task efficiently by applying information technologies and systems to their work, also defined as end-user computing competency (Yoon, 2008, p. 415). Several studies have examined acceptance and usage of BI or related systems (DSS, EIS, ESS, MIS etcetera) focusing among others at individual characteristics, and have identified computer proficiency (also named IT know-how, computer experience, IT skills) and analytical capabilities as influencing factors (Agarwal & Prasad, 1999; Dixon, 1999; Hung, 2003; Pijpers et al., 2001; Seeley & Targett, 1999; Taylor & Todd, 1995). A BI end-user with a high computer proficiency is more likely to successfully use advanced BI-tool functionalities and contrariwise. The same applies for analytical capabilities. For example, the degree of computer proficiency and analytical abilities required to understand and draw conclusions based upon a simple report is quite different from the capabilities necessary to create a customized report.

Therefore, computer proficiency and analytical capabilities are used to classify BI end-users focusing on their individual characteristics, by dividing them into three groups: Novice, Power and Expert end-users, as depicted in Figure 2. In addition, end-users are divided based upon whether they solely consume or also produce information. The reasoning behind this is that some end-users will take a hands-on approach to tools and data,

Figure 2. BI-FIT framework (before validation)

End-user				Task				Technology		
Definition	Computer proficiency	Analytical capabilities	# Users	**Definition**	Distribution mechanism	Data-demand	Analytical complexity	**Definition**	Techn. complexity	BI- Tool Functionality
Novice Users (information consumer)	Low ↑	Low ↑	High ↑	Routine Analysis	Push ↑	Static ↑	Simple ↑	Basic Analytics	Simple ↑	Preformatted reporting, Parameter-driven reporting, Scorecards, Dashboards
Power Users (information producer)				Ad-Hoc Analysis				Root-cause Analytics		Ad-Hoc reporting, Online analytical processing (OLAP)
Expert Users (information producer)	↓ High	↓ High	↓ Low	Advanced Analysis	↓ Pull	↓ Dynamic	↓ Complex	Advanced Analytics	↓ Complex	Data-mining, Advanced statistics

while others wait for finished analysis and reports. One is oriented to the analytics, while the other just wants the resulting information (Biere, 2003). Therefore, novice users are classified as information consumers, and power and expert users are as information producers.

Task Requirements

In addition to individual characteristics, as discussed above, an end-users decision to adopt and use a system also depends on whether it enhances or "fits" the end-users' task. Tasks have been broadly defined as the action(s) carried out by an individual for turning inputs into outputs (Tremblay et al., 2007). End-users use BI-systems to get relevant information which helps them to reduce uncertainty when taking decisions, and enables them to make decisions based on a solid foundation of facts (Nemati et al, 2002). Since the details of business decisions are quite different for each organization, level (i.e. operational, tactical, or strategic), process and user-task context, it is not possible to investigate task requirements for every specific decision task to be supported within an organization.

However, it is possible to examine what BI end-users expect to get out of BI applications, not specifically looking at the content but by examining how and in what way end-users want to interact with information. According to several authors (Haller, Jenichl, & Küng, 1998; Nemati et al., 2002; Wong et al., 2002), the various ways of processing information can separated into two "modes": Verification mode and Discovery mode. In verification mode the user proposes a hypothesis (e.g. business questions) and uses the information to either confirm or reject it, whereas in the discovery mode the end-user does not use a predefined hypothesis, but desires to discover new information, without preconceived notes of what the results would indicate (Fayyad & Uthurusamy, 1996). According to Azvine et al. (2006), the analytical needs of business end-users all come down to answering the following three questions, sorted by ascending complexity:

- What has happened?
- Why did it happen?
- What will happen?

Simple or routine analysis is conducted to answer the often recurring "what happened" question (verification mode) and if exceptions are found, less frequent occurring ad-hoc analysis is conducted to try to answer the more complex "why" question (verification mode). Future oriented analysis aims to figure out "what will happen" (discovery mode) is considered to be the most advanced type of analysis. In addition, data usage and distribution seem to be influenced by the complexity of the analytical question. For example:

Routine analysis is often recurring daily, weekly or monthly, usually presented in standardized preformatted reports which are often "pushed" to end-users by e-mail or other electronic distribution means whereas when carrying out less regular ad-hoc analysis or advanced analysis, end-users actively use the system to fetch or "pull" their required data for analysis, which varies along the nature of the analytical question. As depicted in Figure 2, analytical tasks are divided into routine, ad-hoc and advanced analysis tasks, based on their analytical complexity, data distribution, and variation in data usage.

Technology Characteristics

As discussed earlier, organizations have huge amounts of detailed operational data, usually spread across many departments in the organization or locked into a sluggish operational IT environment, which keeps business decision makers from getting the right information in time (Zeng et al., 2006b). This is demonstrated by the following statement: "I know the answer to my problem is hidden in my data… But I cannot dig it up!!" (Michalewicz et al.,2007, p. 1). Therefore, the most important aspect of most BI projects, is "to provide the best possible mechanism for information delivery to business end-users". To make this happen, organizations can choose from a broad spectrum of BI front-end functionality (also referred to as analytics) ranging from (simple) pre-defined reporting to (advanced) data-mining tools to fulfill their analytical needs (Breitner, 1997).

According to den Hamer (2005), the selection of the appropriate BI instrument strongly depends on the type of question that needs to be answered varying from simple 'what' to complex 'why' questions. This is supported by Azvine et al. (2005) who states that data-analysis tools can be categorized looking at their ability to support end-users in fulfilling their analytical needs (as defined in section 4.2). Furthermore, as the

analysis becomes more complex, the required BI functionality also places a higher demand on end-users' abilities. Based on their purpose and complexity, BI tool functionality can be classified into three categories: Basic, Root-cause and Advanced analytics, as depicted in Figure 2.

BI-FIT Framework

Multiple groups of business end-users, within different skills, preferences and tasks throughout the organization spread among various organizational levels use BI tools to facilitate their decision making processes. Unfortunately, business end-users —while being experts in their area— do not necessary possess expert skills in data analysis (Kohavi, Rothleder, & Simoudis, 2002; Nauck, Spott, & Azvine, 2003). Therefore, the BI end-user segmentation model, as depicted in Figure 2 has been developed in order to assist organizations fulfilling their end-users needs. It is important to note that there may not be a relationship between the end-users" skills (abilities) and organizational position (i.e. operational, tactical, strategic). Obviously, there is no doubt whether an expert end-user is able to deliver added value, but it is not necessarily the case that an end-user with a better ability to use BI systems will have a bigger impact on business (Biere, 2003).

The BI end-user segmentation model, depicted in Figure 2, shows a "fit" between end-users' individual capabilities, tasks and technologies on the horizontal rows of the model. For example, a novice user carries out routine analyses, using basic analytical tool-functionalities. A "fit" can also exist when a power user carries out a routine analysis, using basic tool functionality, but only if the power user is also provided with root-cause analytics to conduct further analysis if exceptions are found. However, this is not possible the other way around. An important question in this context is: What happens if a novice user finds an exception and is required to do further analysis? This is an example of a "misfit" between end-users individual capabilities and task. According to the model the novice user does not possess the required capabilities to do so, therefore no "fit" exists. In this case two options are possible. The first option is that the novice user contacts a power user, and asks the power user to do the extended analysis. The second option is to educate the novice user, in order to become a power user, if the novice user has a regular need for further analysis.

A "misfit" can also exist between task and technology. Consider an expert end-user who needs to conduct an advanced analysis, like e.g. data-mining, but is not provided with the required tools. In this case the user will feel limited in his or her possibilities, and will not adopt the BI-solution, and probably start searching or developing alternative solutions. To conclude, the BI segmentation model is the result of an extensive literature study on the elements of BI-FIT. It shows the most relevant factors and the interrelationships between BI end-users, tasks and technologies. Having discussed the problem awareness and suggestion and development phase of the research approach, the next step in the research is to evaluate and validate the theory in practice. The validation of the BI-FIT framework is discussed the following section of this chapter.

VALIDATION OF THE BI-FIT FRAMEWORK: MULTIPLE CASE STUDIES

Focusing on the problem area of this research, use cases are an appropriate choice of research method, because case study research is well suited for organizational issues rather than technical issues (Yin, 2008). This also applies to this research, which investigates problems of organizational nature. The case study research method is applied in this research to capture the knowledge of practitioners and to validate the theories created.

In order to enrich and validate the theory created with experiences from practice, it is investigated how organizations deal with differing BI end-users and the factors influencing of BI-FIT. This is done by identifying and comparing the end-users' constituencies and their BI usage in the case organizations with the BI-Fit Framework. In addition, the elements of the framework are validated by discussing the relevant segmentation criteria used to distinguish BI end-users. Despite the fact that all individual cases are interesting, this chapter focuses on the overall results.

Case Organizations

The case studies have been conducted at relatively large organizations of differing sizes, operating in several types of industries, and offering a wide variety of products and services. The main criterion in our search for suitable organizations was that all approached organizations have a professionally implemented BI system in place. Important criteria for selecting respondents per case were that the cooperating respondents had an overall view of BI usage in their organization and that they had been actively involved during the implementation of the BI solution. To increase the validity of the results, triangulation is applied because multiple respondents have been interviewed per case and in addition to interviews also documentation was studied. An overview of the case study organizations and respondents is provided in Table 2&3 respectively.

Validation of the Segmentation Criteria

After introducing the research topic, all interviewees responded to have recognized the problem area, and stressed the importance of end-user adoption. Furthermore, there was consensus about the fact that especially when a high amount of end-users needs to be addressed, end-users cannot be satis-

Table 2. Case overview

Organizations	A	B	C	D	E	F
Type / Branch	Electronics	Transport	Food & Beverages	Non -Profit	Telecom-munications	Transport
Market	B2B & B2C	B2B	B2B & B2C	G2C	B2B & B2C	B2B
Revenue € (million)	26.385	3.5	485	112	14.602	1.330
# Employees	+/ - 120.000	+/ - 100	+/ - 2.900	+/ - 550	+/ - 40.000	+/ - 2.750
BI front-end tool	SAP BW	Microsoft Reporting	SAP BW	Business Objects	Cognos	Webfocus
# BI End-users	+/ - 250	+/- 20	+/- 700	+/ - 250	+/- 1500	+/- 100

(figures taken from 2008 annual reports)

fied with a 'one size fits all solution'. Next, after discussing the main assumptions and elements of the BI-FIT model, respondents were asked to identify the relevant individual characteristics applicable for BI. It appeared that in addition the above discussed computer proficiency and analytical abilities, most respondents consider process knowledge, as an important capability of BI end-users. So basically when conducting analysis using BI tooling, an end-user must know how-to analyze (analytical capabilities), how-to use the tool (computer proficiency), and must also posses knowledge of the business process that is analyzed, in order interpret the outcome of the analysis, and to be able to understand the impact on the business. Furthermore, as the complexity of the analysis goes up, a more profound business knowledge is required. Therefore, business knowledge seems like a plausible contribution to

the model. The redefined framework is depicted in Figure 3.

Findings: BI Usage in Practice

While investigating the case organizations' end-user communities it appeared that in some organizations an explicit end-user segmentation model had been developed, while others had not explicitly done so. In the case of organizations A and C, end-users are explicitly divided into groups, and it appears that next to the purpose of segmenting end-users, as discussed in Section 3, such as establishment of the end-user fit, other purposes of end-user segmentation are to ensure a flexible reporting process (because of the responsibility of the "power" user, as discussed below), and to select the appropriate form of training, as e.g. novice users require different training than expert users.

Table 3. Respondent overview

Organizations	A	B	C	D	E	F
Respondent 1 Function	Project manager	BI consultant	BI consultant	BI consultant	BI manager	BI manager
Respondent 1 project –role	BI project manager	Project manager / analyst	Developer / analyst	BI project manager	BI manager	BI manager
Respondent 2 Function	Key-user F&A	BI Consultant	BI manager	BI support	NA	BI support
Respondent 2 project-role	Key-user	BI Developer	BI manager	Functional support	NA	Functional/technical support

Figure 3. BI-FIT framework (After validation)

End-user					Task				Technology		
Definition	Computer proficiency	Analytical capabilities	Business Knowledge	# Users	Definition	Distribution mechanism	Data-demand	Analytical complexity	Definition	Techn. complexity	BI- Tool Functionality
Receivers (information consumer)	Low	Low	Low	High		Push	Static	Simple		Simple	Preformatted reporting, Parameter-driven reporting, Scorecards, Dashboards
Novice Users (information consumer)					Routine Analysis				Basic Analytics		
Power Users (information producer)					Ad-Hoc Analysis				Root-cause Analytics		Ad-Hoc reporting, Online analytical processing (OLAP)
Expert Users (information producer)	High	High	High	Low	Advanced Analysis	Pull	Dynamic	Complex	Advanced Analytics	Complex	Data-mining, Advanced statistics

It appears that in each organization explicitly or implicitly —after some time of BI usage—end-user groups are formed, which in general can be compared to the end-user types as defined in the model, although using different terminology. An overview of the used terminology is depicted in Table 4. In addition to terminology differences in practice an additional level of BI usage exists, as found in organization A, C and E. These end-users are defined as "receivers" or "consumers", conducting solely routine analysis, using predefined reports, in most cases send out by e-mail. The main difference between receivers and novice users is that they are not required to have any BI tool/computer proficiency, do not require tool training, and tool license (or a cheaper license, depending on the BI-tooling). In the segmentation model these end-users belong to the group of information consumers, and are placed above the novice user, as entry level BI users.

Furthermore, an interesting finding is that the power user has an important role, which is to support the novice user. In most organizations novice users are by far the largest amount of end-users. While conducting their standard analysis, it often happens that the novice user is in need for further analysis or has a request for change. As explained earlier, in this case the novice user can obviously consult an analyst of the BI department or competency centre (BICC) in place. However, as in most cases BI support is integrated into the generic IT departments, usually it takes a long time for change requests to be handled (as IT departments are often optimized for supporting operational systems). If this happens more often, the novice user will lose his or her trust in the system, and stop using it and start developing his or her own solution in e.g. Excel. Or maybe even try to adapt the reports themselves, if they have access to the required tooling. Either way, ad-hoc development is not efficient in general, and abandoning of the BI system does not positively influence organizational results.

However, as one of the respondents stated "a change in today's business, needs to be reflected in tomorrow's reports". This basically means that

Table 4. Terminology overview

User Segments	Terminology
Novice User	Information consumer, Knowledge worker, Manager, Receiver.
Power User	Power user, Analyst, Business user, Tactical user, Builder.
Expert User	Expert user, Data-miner.

Figure 4. Division of end-users

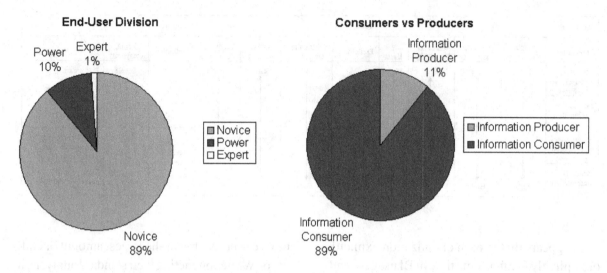

BI requires a flexible and quick requirements process. Therefore, it is important to have a substantial amount of power users in each process that can assist novice users. Especially, because in addition to the required tool and analytical skills, power users also possess the required business knowledge (in contrast to organization wide BI support) in order to support the novice users in their process. Therefore, power users play an important role to ensure the required flexibility of the BI process. In addition to the above findings, it was also investigated how many end-users are present in each segment. Figure 4 shows that the focus is largely on novice usage (i.e. information consumers) with considerably less power users and hardly any expert users. Although it was expected to have less power and expert users than novice users, because of the higher demands placed on their individual capabilities, especially the power user group was expected to be bigger. Furthermore, following Negash and Gray (2003) most BI tooling focuses on the power user. In addition, Gile (2003, p. 2) states that "more than 75 percent of the costs associated with BI are for technology that addresses the needs of information producers". Perhaps this is a signal for BI vendors to start developing tooling that aim at

bringing more analytical functions to novice users. However, obviously we must be aware that not only the ability to use a tool can help to make an end-user a good analyst, also the analytical abilities and business knowledge are important.

Investigating the relationship between information producers and consumers, in general two opinions prevail. In short, 40% of the respondents stressed that end-users should not be limited in their possibilities, and therefore should get complete tool access, offering the end-user as much flexibility as possible. The latter 60% stress that end-users only be provided with ad-hoc and or advanced analytics, when it is required for their task. The first approach offers maximum flexibility to end-users. However, on the other hand often most end-users are hardly using ad-hoc and or advanced analytics, and if it is used occasionally, time and money is lost because end users are not experienced, which results in inefficient usage. In addition, taking into account the risk for errors, definition usage, (full) license costs and training, it seems like the benefits outweigh the advantage of flexibility.

Last but not least, it is interesting to see that hardly any expert users were around. Because of the absence of expert users, it seems like the added value of expert analysis is underestimated, and most probably organizations are not making use of the full potential of BI-technologies. Furthermore, it must not be forgotten that although only relatively few end-users are capable of conducting advanced analysis, results can be shared with many. To conclude, in order to benefit from the potential of the available data in an organization, and to ensure a flexible BI process it is important to be able to include a substantial amount of power users in each process, and relatively few expert users to fully take advantage of the possibilities that BI has to offer.

CONCLUSION

This research has been triggered by the observation that BI applications have low adoption rates within organizations and many BI projects fall short of their promise to deliver value. After investigating the problem area, it appeared that this is caused by among others the technology-driven approach that prevails at BI implementations, focusing largely on BI-automation. Unfortunately, because of this approach little attention is spent to the actual (business) end-users of BI, which does not assure that a "fit" is established between BI end-users, tasks and technologies, which is crucial for the adoption of BI by individual end-users. Therefore, one of the most important requirements of any BI project should be to understand "who" the end-users are, in order to determine "what" they need, which is extremely important for achieving BI success. However, it appears from the case investigations that in practice, BI projects constrained by a limited amount of time and budget often focus on the technical realization of the system, which is a very concrete thing, and seems to be more important than making sure the actual end-users are provided with an appropriate solution.

For an end-user to adopt BI, it is important that a "fit" is established between the BI end-user and the BI solution. The end-user fit can be established by making sure that end-users are provided with a solution that matches their individual characteristics, and provides added value in task execution. The main deliverable or in the design science approach referred to as 'artifact' developed in this research, is the so-called "BI-FIT Framework", which has been developed to support organizations in establishing this "fit". It can be used to help organizations to identify and fulfill the needs of end-users, thereby improving adoption and increasing satisfaction of the BI end-user base, which is not only applicable for new BI implementations, but can also be useful to "assess" existing BI implementations, from the end-user perspective. Another way of utilizing the BI-FIT Framework is to investigate whether a "fit" exists between the organization and BI. If, for example it appears that hardly any "power" or "expert" users exist within an organization, it could be concluded that the potential of BI-technologies is insufficiently utilized. Or contrariwise if only "power" or "expert" users exist, this could mean that time and money is wasted, because of decentralized development, continuous reinvention of the wheel, license and/or training costs.

Limitations and Further Research

Focusing on the objectivity of the research, it is important to note the limitations identified. First of all, it is important to note that qualitative research proposes a risk for the objectivity of the research, because when conducting case study research, a certain influence of the experiences, opinions and feelings of the researcher on the analysis is possible. Furthermore, the investigation of the case organizations end-user constituencies has been based on respondents' knowledge of BI usage in their organizations. Therefore, the position of the respondents in the organization and their viewpoints might have biased the validation. No quantitative methods have been applied to investigate the end-users communities for the specific cases. For further research, it would be interesting to validate the model using quantitative research methods. Using i.e. a questionnaire to identify end-users constituencies, by investigating their BI specific individual, task and technology characteristics and relevant situational factors (if applicable), in order to improve the objectivity of the validation. In addition, the questionnaire used to investigate end-user constituencies, could be used to comprehend the BI-FIT Framework with an assessment tool, allowing organizations and BI practitioners to investigate BI usage within their organizations, and afterwards use the results to improve the BI-FIT within their organizations.

Another recommendation for further research, would be to extend the BI-FIT Framework by focusing on specific types of organizations and their characteristics, the influence of organization size and to determine the "optimal" division and/or mix of end-user types. For example in this research organizations from different industries (i.e. transport, telecommunications, food and beverages, electronics, environmental protection) operating in differing markets (B2C, B2B, G2C, G2B) have been investigated. However, it could be beneficial to concentrate on specific types of organizations, and/or industries and their characteristics. For each industry most probably an "ideal BI situation" exists, dependent on several factors like i.e. information intensity, dynamics of the environment and strategy in use which can be compared to the current situation in practice. For example taking organizational strategy, it would be interesting to explore the differences in strategy approach, taking for example Treacy and Wiersema's (1993) product leadership, customer intimacy or operational excellence. Considering these factors, most probably a certain division of end-user types is required. In other words, it is interesting to discover the "optimal" division of end-users types that is needed within an organization. For example, you might conclude that BI usage is inadequate considering the fact that an organization is following a customer intimacy strategy, operating in a dynamic environment that requires fast decisions making, but does not have sufficient power or expert users present to make this happen. In addition, it would be interesting to investigate the influence of organization size on its BI end-user community. As it was discussed in section 4.3, a larger organization is more likely to have "expert" users than a small organization.

REFERENCES

Agarwal, R., & Prasad, J. (1999). Are Individual Differences Germane to the Acceptance of New Information Technologies? *Decision Sciences, 30*(2), 361–391. doi:10.1111/j.1540-5915.1999. tb01614.x

Azvine, B., Cui, Z., & Nauck, D. D. (2005). Towards real-time business intelligence. *BT Technology Journal, 23*(3), 214–225. doi:10.1007/s10550-005-0043-0

Azvine, B., Cui, Z., Nauck, D. D., & Majeed, B. (2006). *Real Time Business Intelligence for the Adaptive Enterprise*.

Barbara, Wixom, & Watson. (2001). An Empirical Investigation of the Factors Affecting Data Warehousing Success. *Management Information Systems Quarterly, 25*(1), 17–41. doi:10.2307/3250957

Barlow, H. A., & Burke, M. E. (1999). The organization as an information system: Signposts for new investigations. *East European Quarterly, 4*, 549–556.

Biere, M. (2003). *Business Intelligence for the Enterprise*. New York: IBM Press.

Borgman, C. L. (1989). All users of information retrieval systems are not created equal: an exploration into individual differences. *Information Processing and Management: an International Journal, 25*(3), 237–251. doi:10.1016/0306-4573(89)90042-3

Breitner, C. A. (1997). *Data Warehousing and OLAP: Delivering Just-In-Time Information for Decision Support.*

Chaudhuri, S., & Dayal, U. (1997). An overview of data warehousing and OLAP technology. *SIGMOD Record, 26*(1), 65–74. doi:10.1145/248603.248616

Daft, R. L., & Lengel, R. H. (1986). Organizational information requirements, media richness and structural design. *Management Science, 32*(5), 554–571. doi:10.1287/mnsc.32.5.554

Davis. (1993). User acceptance of information technology: system characteristics, user perceptions and behavioral impacts. *International Journal of Man - Machine Studies, 38*, 475-487.

Dekkers, J., Versendaal, J., & Batenburg, R. (2007). *Organizing for Business intelligence: A Framework for aligning the use and development of information.* Paper presented at the Merging and Emerging Technologies, Processes and Institutions.

DeLone, W. H., & McLean, E. R. (1992). Information Systems Success: The Quest for the Dependent Variable. *Information Systems Research, 3*(1), 60–95. doi:10.1287/isre.3.1.60

den Hamer, P. (2005). *De organisatie van Business Intelligence.* Den Haag, Nederland: SDU Publishers.

Devaraj, S., & Kohli, R. (2003). Performance Impacts of Information Technology: Is Actual Usage the Missing Link? *Management Science, 49*, 273–289. doi:10.1287/mnsc.49.3.273.12736

Dishaw, M. T., & Strong, D. M. (1999). Extending the technology acceptance model with task–technology fit constructs. *Information & Management, 36*(1), 9–21. doi:10.1016/S0378-7206(98)00101-3

Dixon, D. R. (1999). The behavioral side of information technology. *International Journal of Medical Informatics, 56*(1-3), 117–123. doi:10.1016/S1386-5056(99)00037-4

Fayyad, U., & Uthurusamy, R. (1996). Data mining and knowledge discovery in databases. *Communications of the ACM, 39*(11), 24–26. doi:10.1145/240455.240463

Ferguson, M. (1996). Tools and Techniques for Analyzing and Mining Warehouse Data. *InfoDB, 9*(3), 13–18.

Galbraith, J. R. (1974). Organization design: An information processing view. *Interfaces,*28–36. doi:10.1287/inte.4.3.28

Gile, K. (2003). *Business intelligence and redefining the analytic end user.* Forrester Research.

Goodhue, D. L., & Thompson, R. L. (1995). Task-technology fit and individual performance. *Management Information Systems Quarterly, 19*(2), 213–236. doi:10.2307/249689

Haller, M., Jenichl, G., & Küng, J. (1998). *Data Mining, Multidimensional Databases and the Web for a Better Interpretation of Data.* Paper presented at the 5th International Conference IDG'98

Han, J., & Kamber, M. (2006). *Data Mining: Concepts and Techniques.* Morgan Kaufmann.

Hevner, A. R., March, S. T., Park, J., & Ram, S. (2004). Design science in information systems research. *Management Information Systems Quarterly, 28*(1), 75–106.

Huber, G. P. (2003). *The necessary nature of future firms: Attributes of Survivors in a changing World.* San Francisco: Sage.

Hung, S. Y. (2003). Expert versus novice use of the executive support systems: an empirical study. *Information & Management, 40*(3), 177–189. doi:10.1016/S0378-7206(02)00003-4

Kimball, R. (2008). *The Data Warehouse Lifecycle Toolkit* (2nd ed.). New York: John Wiley & Sons.

Michalewicz, Z., Schmidt, M., Michalewicz, M., & Chiriac, C. (2007). *Adaptive Business Intelligence*. Berlin: Springer.

Nauck, D., Spott, M., & Azvine, B. (2003). SPIDA—A Novel Data Analysis Tool. *BT Technology Journal, 21*(4), 104–112. doi:10.1023/A:1027339722343

Negash, S., & Gray, P. (2003). *Business Intelligence*. Paper presented at the Ninth Americas Conference on Information Systems.

Nemati, H. R., Steiger, D. M., Iyer, L. S., & Herschel, R. T. (2002). Knowledge warehouse: an architectural integration of knowledge management, decision support, artificial intelligence and data warehousing. *Decision Support Systems, 33*(2), 143–161. doi:10.1016/S0167-9236(01)00141-5

Philips, E., & Vriens, D. (1999). *Business Intelligence, Marketing Wijzer*. Amsterdam: Kluwer Bedrijfsinformatie B.V.

Pijpers, G., Bemelmans, T., Heemstra, F., & Montfort, K. v. (2001). Senior executives ' use of information technology. *Journal of Information and Software Technology, 43*, 959–971. doi:10.1016/S0950-5849(01)00197-5

Pirttimäki, V., & Hannula, M. (2003). Process models of business intelligence. *Frontiers of e-business research*, 250-259.

Pirttimäki, V., Lönnqvist, A., & Karjaluoto, A. (2006). Measurement of Business Intelligence in a Finnish Telecommunications Company. *Electronic Journal of Knowledge Management, 4*(1), 83–90.

Raden, N. (2004). Dashboarding ourselves. *Intelligent Enterprise, 7*(8).

Seeley, M., & Targett, D. (1999). Patterns of senior executives' personal use of computers. *Information & Management, 35*(6), 315–330. doi:10.1016/S0378-7206(99)00002-6

Taylor, S., & Todd, P. (1995). Assessing IT Usage: The Role of Prior Experience. *Management Information Systems Quarterly, 19*(1), 25.

Tracy, M., & Wiersema, F. (1993). Customer intimacy and other value principles. *Harvard Business Review, 71*(1), 84–93.

Tremblay, M. C., Fuller, R., Berndt, D., & Studnicki, J. (2007). Doing more with more information: Changing healthcare planning with OLAP tools. *Decision Support Systems, 43*(4), 1305–1320. doi:10.1016/j.dss.2006.02.008

Turban, E., Aronson, J. E., Liang, T. P., & Sharda, R. (2007). *Decision Support and Business Intelligence Systems*. Englewood Cliffs, NJ: Pearson Education International.

Vaishnavi, V. K., & Kuechler, W. (2007). *Design Science Research Methods and Patterns: Improving and Innovating Information & Communication Technology*. Retrieved from http://home.aisnet.org/displaycommon.cfm?an=1&subarticlenbr=279

van Beek, D. (2006). *De Intelligente Organisatie, prestatieverbetering en organisatieontwikkeling met Business Intelligence*. Amsterdam: Tuteint Nolthenius.

Vitt, E., Luckevich, M., & Misner, S. (2002). *Making Better Business Intelligence Decisions Faster*. Redmond, WA: Microsoft Press.

Wong, S. T. C., Hoo, K. S., Knowlton, R. C., Laxer, K. D., Cao, X., & Hawkins, R. A. (2002). Design and Applications of a Multimodality Image Data Warehouse Framework. *Journal of the American Medical Informatics Association, 9*, 239–254. doi:10.1197/jamia.M0988

Yin, R. (2008). *Case study research: Design and methods*. San Francisco: Sage Pub.

Yoon, C. Y. (2008). *A structural model of end-user computing competency and user performance*. Knowledge-Based Systems.

Zeng, L., Xu, L., Shi, Z., Wang, M., & Wu, W. (2006a). *Techniques, Process, and Enterprise Solutions of Business Intelligence*. Paper presented at the Conference on Systems, Man, and Cybernetics Taipei, Taiwan.

Chapter 12
Information Management Process in Continuous Improvement Area at Worldwide Steel Company

Gabriela Alves
FEAD, Brazil

Jorge Neves
UFMG, Brazil

ABSTRACT

This chapter aims to present specific features concerning information management in the Continuous Improvement area of the Americas Long Carbon sector in ArcelorMittal. The aim is also to learn what the informational resources related to continuous improvement area are and describe how the process of managing information actually happens. The study was based on theoretical models of Davenport (1998) and Choo (2006) and tried to understand how the efficient management of information can aid in decision making at organizations. The result of the documentary research revealed the existence of initiatives throughout the different units in the Americas and also revealed corporate tools for information management. The field research results indicate the need for a structured and formalized model of information management that responds to users in adequate time, while alert to the need for policies that encourage the sharing of information related to the improvement of processes, products and services.

INTRODUCTION

To say we are in an economy based on knowledge or information has become a habit. However, until today just a few organizations integrate knowledge and strategies. There are several possible explanations for this phenomenon. The more likely one might be related to the fact that the use of the information strategies is much harder than to simply talk about it. (McGee & Prusak, 1994 p.17) According to Drucker (2000, p.10), companies have no choice but to become a company based on information.

Prahalad (1997) believes that a company actually controls its destiny when it has the ability

DOI: 10.4018/978-1-61692-020-3.ch012

to predict, uniqueness related to its business and ability to share. The companies that have flexibility to react to market changes are more likely to last. However, having access of information is not enough; it is necessary to know how and when to use it.

It seems to be growing the feeling that world events are rapidly converging to shape a world that is unique, integrated and which influences economic, cultural or any other traditional cross borders very easily. The implications of these changes are significant and affect all spheres of life, providing new challenges for all organizations (Parker, 1998, p.400).

An example of such change that is impacting the whole economy is the steel industry, which has been growing and, according to Lopes (2007), would grow even more.

In this optimistic scenario, in October 2006, Mittal Steel took over the majority of the shares of Arcelor and the company became ArcelorMittal, the largest steel group in the world.

It is necessary to emphasize that this study was conducted in an environment of growth and optimism in the steel market. Nevertheless, as of September 2008 the world economic scene changed dramatically and all sectors of the economy were affected. The economic crisis caused a drop in steel prices worldwide, reduction of new applications and more factories stopped production for a few weeks to reduce inventories. In this scenario, the year of 2009 will be crucial to redesign the way not only of the steel industry, but the world economy.

The main objective of this paper is to find out the characteristics of the appropriate model for the information management exclusively for the continuous improvement area in ArcelorMittal Long Carbon Americas.

REFERENCIAL THEORY

The theoretical framework was divided into five major groups:

1. Continuous Improvement
2. Information and Knowledge
3. The Intelligent Organization
4. Information Environment
5. Information Management

Continuous Improvement

We must return to the concept of quality to speak about continuous improvement within the organization and the context of this research.

For some authors, quality can mean the fit for use. For audit process it means meeting the requirements of standards. In the business environment, the concept is tied to meeting the specifications of the products required by customers. According to Garvin (1992) (apud Cruz, Rodrigues and Nagano 2007), it can be defined in four stages of quality:

1. Phase of inspection (reactive): Focus on the verification of compliance with the specifications of the pre-defined product;
2. Phase of the statistical process control (preventive): Focus on ensuring the uniformity of the product;
3. Phase of quality control (preventive): Focus comprises the tasks and the process beyond the products;
4. Phase of Total Quality Management: At this stage, the focus is on the overview of the organization, seeking to integrate different technical processes, operational and administrative, to the continuous improvement of management in the organization.

Campos (1992) was one of the main advisers of the cycle of PDCA (Deming Cycle), which stands for Plan, Do, Check and Action (PDCA). According to him, continuous improvement is

Table 1. Data, information and knowledge

Data	Information	Knowledge
Simple observations about the world state	Data endowed with relevancy and purpose.	Valuable information from human mind
Easily structure	Requires unit analysis	Hard to structure
Easily obtained by machines	Requires agreement of the meaning	Hard to capture from machines
Often quantified	Requires necessarily human measurement	Often tacit
Easily transferable		Hard to transfer

Source: Davenport, 1998, p.18

related to two types of management: maintenance and improvements. Further, for the same author, are obtained through the PDCA and are maintained through the cycle of SDCA: Standard, Do, Check, Action.

ArcelorMittal has started the quality movement in different ways in each country. In Brazil for example, it started in 1989 with Prof. Vicente Falconi Campos and it is being developed nowadays. In this country, almost all units have a department of quality which is responsible for maintaining management model.

Within the company management model the improvements can come from a chronic problem or from an organization guideline through the strategic deployment.

Information and Knowledge

It is very difficult to delimit the borders amongst the meanings given to data, information and knowledge. Davenport (1998, p.18) presents some characteristics of the three terms in order to make the distinction between them clearer.

According to Nonaka and Takeuchi (1997, p. 64), information is a stream of messages, being the organizational knowledge created from the flow of this information and anchored in believes of the knowledge owner.

For authors such as Drucker (2000, p.13), information is any data given with relevance and purpose. Data conversion into information

requires knowledge. According to McGee and Prusak (1994), information is a key strategy in the organization, a strategic resource equivalent to labor, technology or capital.

The Intelligent Organization

Why do we speak so much about smart organizations? How could we determine whether an organization is smarter than another? Could we perhaps classify them according to its profitability?

According to Gregory *apud* Choo (2002, p.11), there are two meanings for intelligence: having the knowledge and create it.

Moreover, Garvin (2000 P.54-72) believes that successful organizations manage efficiently their process of learning. According to the author, a smart organization is an organization that learns and is able to create, acquire and transfer knowledge.

According to Edmondson (2008), most executives believe that efficient execution of their processes by production at the right time and in time delivery of products and services is the best way to achieve customer satisfaction and financial results. The reality is a little different; even the most perfect performance can not assure enduring success in the knowledge economy.

The author proposes four stages for execution with a focus on learning: to provide guidance to the process, to provide tools that allow employees

Figure 1. An ecological model for information management. Source: Davenport, 1998, p. 51

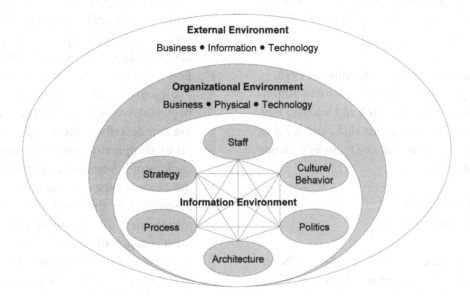

to collaborate in real time, to collect data and to establish a process of disciplined reflection.

According to Leonard-Barton (1998, p. 20), the key point for a company to manage its knowledge is to understand its strategic skills, which represent a competitive advantage that is not easily imitated. They can provide a permanent advantage over competitors.

Choo suggests that the survival of businesses depends on their ability to process information about the environment and transform them into knowledge that enables them to adapt to change. This skill to adapt is a smart organizational characteristic and it is the key to have an intelligent organizational behavior in an environment of rapid changes. (Choo, 2002).

Information Environment

The barrier to the sharing of ideas is no longer on the stack of information and tacit knowledge which is difficult to be explained or stored. These days the biggest barrier is the organization environment. To promote information sharing, the emergence of ideas, innovations and problem

solving through collaborative practices, organizations must provide an environment conducive to such exchanges or encourage the development of an appropriate context.

Davenport used the term ecology to name the holistic way to treat and manage information. Coined by the author, the term information ecology means the interfaces between the various environments of information (Davenport 1998, p. 43-64).

Davenport (1997) uses the metaphor of information ecology to examine the attributes and the key dynamics to characterize an effective and healthy organizational environment of information. (CHOO 2002, p. 48)

Information ecology is a multidisciplinary and holistic approach to treating information and its relationship with the external environments, organizational and informational, as shown in *Figure 1*.

"We must keep in mind that the relationship between the organizational context and its information environment is a two-way street, that is, the environment can guide and motivate a specific

information environment, as well as the latter can enable or restrict company". (DAVENPORT, 1998, p. 224).

However, according to Davenport (1998, p. 44), this approach requires an extensive administrative competence. Working and learning how to manage the best of various skills and areas of science is not a simple task and requires patience and perseverance.

Key Attributes of the Ecology of Information

According to Davenport (1998, p.44-50) the information ecology requires a vision of the whole and has four key attributes:

a) Integration of several types of information - the information ecologies thrive on information diversity. We must integrate the diverse types of information: the computer and not computerized, the informal and formal, structured and unstructured, and integrate the various types of media available in the organization, such as video, audio and text. The party information should not direct the User Information to any particular type. It should combine the various sources of information and offer the most comprehensive "menu" of options.

b) Recognition of evolutionary change - the information ecology is constantly changing over time, which means that information systems, whether computerized or not, have to be flexible at the same rate of evolution of information. The information environment, as well as the physical environment is unstable and often unpredictable. It is difficult to find a way to deal with the progressive needs of the information, and this path varies from business to business. How to predict what will happen in a determined type of market in three to five years? What is the

balance between the informational structures durable and mutable? Answers are hard to find, but the first step is to recognize that evolution is a reality of any organization.

c) Emphasis on observation and description - Biologists and environmentalists have begun their work, perhaps by simply observing and describing the world around us in all its complexity and particularity. In the ecology of information, we must never lose the characteristics of observers to be more descriptive in the process of information management. As the information environment changes all the time, there are always new discoveries to make. How to efficiently manage the information without knowing in detail all or at least most of the components of this complex process? In the ecology of information, an important or essential step is to recognize and describe the various types and formats of information and how it is used in the organization's processes. How is the information collected, shared and used? This is the main question to be answered in the process of information management.

d) Focus on people and informational behavior - In the ecology of the physical world any initiative needs the participation of human beings. Locally, to avoid pollution in a river town or globally to reduce CO_2 emissions in the atmosphere. In the information ecology, the whole initiative also depends on the participation of people involved in the process. These are the people who will ensure the quality and reliability of the information. Ten years ago, Davenport said that information providers are much more concentrated in the production and distribution of information than their users. Nowadays, it is still a reality in most organizations. Thousands of reports are produced and sent to many people who sometimes do not even know what to do with them. People often receive a lot of information. Most of the times it is not important for the development of their work. They do not know how and where to find what they need, nor how to share what they know. We need a total change in the information culture of a company if you want to manage their information. Any initiative towards information management should be about changing people's behavior.

Model for Information Ecology

In the ecological model of information management proposed by Davenport (1998 p.50-64), there is the integration of the various environments of the organization as well as the ecology of the physical world. The three environments described by the author not only relate to each other, but there is no clear definition of where one begins and another ends. They are always connected.

The External Environment

Organizations are affected by external agents, which in most cases, can not be controlled, so you need information about what happens in the external environment to assist in decision making. The author (1998, p. 248) suggests three possible answers to the external environment:

a) Adjustment - simply adjust to the outside world;

b) Research - to investigate the external environment in search of changes that the company should respond;

c) Adequacy - shaping the products and services of the company to external conditions, seeking a competitive advantage.

Following the metaphor of ecology, the external environment itself constitutes an enormous ecology, with countless interactions and inter-relationships. What makes your scanning by any organization for more than it is. In Davenport's

book "Information Ecology" (1998, p. 249), the foreign market is broken down in three types of markets:

a) **Business Markets:** This is the sector in which the organizations operate, what creates general business conditions, regulatory standards to which the company is subject. Anything that impacts the business. For any company, it is important to know and understand what happens in the sphere of consumers, suppliers, government ministries and competition.

b) **Technology Markets**: It is necessary to know the technologies available in the market so you can safely decide if and how a technology will be useful to the organization. This refers not only to products, but the information services available in the external environment. Markets and outsourcing of information technology provide a range of facilities for the management of information. However, it is important to remember that in the process of information management, technology is just the middle. A company can acquire the most modern system of information management in the world. However, if the company does not share the information, the modern system will become a white elephant, with no effective result. Behind every machine full of information, it is necessary that people not only feed the machine with useful information, but use and share them.

c) **Information Markets**: The firms must be attentive to the identification of external sources of information available that match their interests. In information markets, there is a variety of sources and formats combined, like published writings, opinions of experts and consultants for industry, database, and even rumors of recent business events. The organizations enter the market to buy or sell information. The information is so malleable that it can be structured and restructured, sold and bought in several different ways.

The Organizational Environment

The company organizational context and its information environment are closely linked, since the organizational environment can direct or motivate the information environment of a company. The direction and intensity of this connection varies from organization to organization, but is never one-way street. In the ecological approach, it is necessary to take into account the organizational environment as a whole. As in the external environment, Davenport broke down the organizational environment in three main components:

a) **Business Situation**: Davenport does not include the financial conditions of the organization, although they can decisively affect the process of managing information. Attention should be paid to business strategies, administrative procedures, organizational structure and human resources policy, since these components will affect the strategy and the use of information.

  i.   Business Strategy –it is generally the direction chosen by an organization with regards to markets, products and services. After the chosen strategy, defined goals, which usually do not mention the means of implementation or the use of information? Whatever the strategy is, it will have implications for the information environment. For example, one strategy in rapidly changing markets, implies an information environment that includes: focusing on information from competitors, information quality and insufficient quantity on the development of new products, willingness to change management strategies, information, meetings

and frequent reviews on the cost and quality, time and know-how, strength and amount of funds available. The information environment, depending on their maturity in the organization, can also impact the business strategies.

  ii. Business Processes – The way work is done is connected to the accessibility and quality of data, which implies the sharing of information between departments and managers. Just when companies restructure their administrative procedures, they realize that they must first modify elements of the information environment. The converse is also true: information environments may lead to new requirements of work processes.

  iii. Organizational Structure and Culture – It is not enough to have a lean organizational structure and say that this is sufficient for the flow of information. The organizational structure should facilitate traffic of quality information for those who need it, but only the structure is not sufficient. Often, even with fewer layers of management, one employee has access to a director because of the company culture. As already stated, the culture of the organization must first facilitate the flow of information or the best informational system will be ineffective.

  iv. Human Resources – It might be the most important point of the ecology approach, because there is no ecology of information without knowing who acts and works in the environment. These are the people who acquire, share and use the information. Thus the profile of those involved must meet the information strategies of the company. Some companies find it important that all employees are kept up to date on what happens in the industry, not only regarding competitors but also about what the theory has progressed in relation to its business. An employee who does not like reading or who does not want to study is not appropriate for the company's strategies. The hiring of people willing to live in this reality is the first step for an efficient information environment.

b) **Technology investments**: Great technology does not mean good and useful information. Technology should facilitate the access to it. Although it is not the most important component of the information environment, technology is essential to improve the use of information. It does not necessarily have to be the most complicated, powerful or more expensive, but more suitable for the organization. An ArcelorMittal Continuous Improvement general manager said that a process, product or service must be on adequate quality to use or will not be competitive. What good is enriching a product or a service with attributes that will never be used? According to Davenport, using the most appropriate technology can bring countless benefits to information oriented organizations. For example, instead of investing in a technology that will never be used, you can apply its financial resources by empowering people. In addition, more familiar technologies facilitate and encourage access - the User spends his time with the content of information and not on how to operate the system. A company needs to assess how the investment in technology help or hinder the strategy and the informational environment of information. The author lists some points that should be observed when investing in new information technologies:

i. A high degree of network interconnectedness facilitates the exchange of information in organizations.

ii. Knowledge and information workers require personal computers or workstations on each desktop.

iii. Effective information management increasingly involves providing network access to internal information repository.

iv. An increasing number of sophisticated software packages could help manage and distribute qualitative or document-based information in organizations.

c) **Physical Arrangement**: The provision of physical space can contribute to the sharing of information or hinder it. However, the nature of work and culture of the organization must be respected. A physical space that facilitates the flow of information in a software company may be completely inappropriate for a research center, for example. According to the author, we exchange information with people we keep in touch frequently, especially staff. A communication barrier is overcome when we know the caller. Davenport has some arguments to justify our preference for face-to-face communicating:

i. Facility - a personal communication is easy if it does not require any writing - not even a phone number.

ii. Likely Unplanned - the contact is visual, there is no need to remember anything.

iii. "Wealth" - the non-verbal communication and body language enrich communication.

iv. Trust - the personal contact creates more confidence for the exchange of information, due to the fact that it is easier to exchange information with someone else, but also because sign language is important and people can build trust based on the context, on the experience of life and on the behavior of the person you are talking to. Several companies have altered their physical structure in order to facilitate the process of information management. This does not mean that physically distant people can not exchange best practices and experiences, but it is more difficult and requires much more communication devices than people who know each other personally. Despite its importance, the personal contact is not the only factor generating confidence and enriching communication. The possession of knowledge can also act as a facilitator of information exchange. When there is a respected expert in a particular area, this exchange flows due to the respect that exists for him. In spite of being personally distant, they have knowledge in common. The exchange of information is much more fruitful when people are in the same wavelength.

The information environment is the center of the ecology approach. To manage the information in a holistic manner, it is necessary to understand the whole scenario in which the information is used. The author broke down the environment in six critical components:

a) **Information Strategy:** The strategies of information should involve senior management and be clear about the purpose of information. Knowing why it is important to the organization. With no information strategy, the organization can be seen buried in an "information world" without the expected efficiency.

b) **Information Policy:** Business strategies should be aligned with the policies of management information. This is a critical component because it involves the power provided by information.

c) **Information Behavior and Culture**: Positive or negative behavior in relation to

information sharing builds the information culture and that defines whether or not the exchange of information and ideas take place.

d) **Information Staff**: A good informational team should be multidisciplinary with diverse skills. People are the best means to identify, filter and integrate information.

e) **Information Process:** The process shows how the work is done. The organization must have a large vision, defining the informational processes as all the activities carried out by those who work with information.

f) **Information Architecture**: It is a guide to design and locate the information within the organization. In an information environment the facility to understand and clear communication are important factors to have the information flowing in a correct way.

The firms must be able to interpret the environment, collect information and treat it. This process of knowledge creation is what will subsidize it for strategic decision making and its market positioning. If knowledge is power, the companies must know to use it in their favor.

Information Management

Only when the information management is done knowingly and seen as a natural process, the organization will actually be based on information (McGee & Prusak, 1994). For these authors, information must be mapped, identified, categorized, and finally released. Firstly it must be identified what to be collected.

There is no right or wrong style, but the style most appropriate for the time the organization is experiencing. In one organization, several types of information management can co-exist.

Davenport (1998) describes a generic process of managing information. According to him, each organization can set its process in a different way, with different stages.

1. Determination of requirements: The determination of the information requirements is a difficult problem, since it involves the perception of managers or employees involved in the process.
2. Capture: The acquisition of information is a system of continuous acquisition. It has four different activities: Exploration of the environment - the required information is located and collected. Classification of information - the information must be categorized using criteria previously established. Format - the structure and format of information must be pleasant to the user. Distribution- It is necessary to define which and to whom information will be sent and choose the most efficient way for distribution.
3. Use: The use is the final step in the information management .It has no meaning until it is used. It is like a very efficient medicine in the closet or used inappropriately: it does not make the desired effect.

According to Davenport (1998) in order to improve the management of informational processes, we must emphasize the need for constant improvement of people and inter-related processes.

Choo (2006, p. 403-404) sees the process of managing information as a continuous cycle of six related cases. According to Choo (2006), information management should be viewed as the administration of a network of processes that acquires, creates, organizes, and distributes the information.

The efficient use of information is what Choo (2006, p.404) calls adaptive behavior: a selection of actions directed to specific objectives.

Choo (2006) analyses each case from the perspective of the information administrator whose responsibility is to plan, develop systems, services, processes and information resources.

1. Information needs identification: information is needed to reduce the ambiguities that indicate changes in the environment.
2. Information acquisition: it requires a plan to collect and share information by the organization sources.
3. Storage and information organization: it reflects how the organization notices and represents its environment.
4. Products and services information: it must meet the need of information of the organization members.
5. Information Distribution: the way information is disseminated and how it will be in the right place, right time and right hands.
6. Information Use: it is a result from the sense building, knowledge creation and decisions. In each case, the use of information is a social fluid and reciprocal process.
7. Adaptive behavior: the company's reactions interact with other company's actions and thus, generate new signs and messages, keeping new cycles of information use.

The organization needs not just to interpret the environments, in which it is inserted, but to create, acquire and transfer new knowledge, changing the behavior before the decision-making process. "The key to understanding the organizations as information systems is to recognize the two anomalies that face all organizational activity: uncertainty and ambiguity" (CHOO, 2006, p. 417).

RESEARCH METHODOLOGY

The research was conducted by a quantitative approach. It was applied and descriptive. Descriptive is proposed for further description of the real company area by studying the information management products and processes in this area. Applied is proposed to study a specific problem, the information management in the continuous improvement area in ArcelorMittal Americas.

To conduct this research, aware of the high geographical dispersion of the target population and the wide availability of information concerning key personnel of each unit in relation to information management, it was decided to hold a non-probabilistic sample. Thus, the search for this sampling plan was as follows:

Population: CEOs (Chief Executive Officer), Coos (Chief Operating Officer), VPs (Vice Presidents), Managers and Continuous Improvement professionals involved

Sampling framework: Continuous improvement and development area's employees of the Americas Long Carbon units.

In addition, it was adopted in this research: survey method, documentary research and bibliography search as data collection techniques.

The research instrument selected was the self-administered questionnaire and the questions were arranged to ensure no induction of certain patterns of response.

To ensure reliability of data, the questionnaires were made available through an internet site created specifically for this study. There was no identification of the interviewee whatsoever and the data were treated in total confidentiality.

After data collection, data were coded, categorized, classified, tabulated and had distribution of frequency defined. After entering data in the software and tabulation of these, descriptive analysis is followed by tables. We used unvaried analysis, by variable and analysis of associations between the variables.

Company Characterization

With strategically located plants, ArcelorMittal is present in 60 countries with over 330 thousand employees, an annual production capacity of 130 million tons of flat, long and stainless steel, which represents more than 10% of total steel manufactured in the world. In 2007, sales were over 30 billion euros and leadership in main markets: automotive, construction, appliances, packaging

and industry in general, especially in the research, development and technology.

The research focused in the study of information management at the Americas ArcelorMittal long steel segment (LCA Long Carbon Americas) continuous improvement area.

The main objective of this area is to diagnose process, product and services' opportunities as well as to develop projects targeting on production increase or cost reduction.

RESULTS

During the documentary research, several management information initiatives among Long Carbon Americas units were detected. Each plant is looking for the best way to manage its information using the tools available or creating new tools.

One of these initiatives is the Corporate Information System Management ArcelorMittal Long Carbon Americas (SIGA). It is the management information system used by the LCA that allows the monitoring of companies performance within LCA in Brazil, Argentina, Costa Rica, Mexico, in Trinidad and Tobago, Canada and the United States from its monthly management reports.

Worldwide the company uses BPM software (Business Performance Management), but for some specific reasons LCA works with the information in the SIGA before sending it to BPM. With SIGA system deployment there was an integration of all the information tools and systems, before dispersed in different systems and reports (*Figure 2*). The software now works as the main information repository on LCA management and it is used by all LCA units.

Other initiatives are the Global Cost Benchmark (GCB) and Global Technical Benchmark (GTB). The objective of both databases is to standardize, collect, analyze and distribute comparable information across all units in the company. The first is focused on costs and the second on technical indicators.

Figure 2. Scenario of the management information after SIGA deployment. Source: provided by LCA Performance and reporting manager

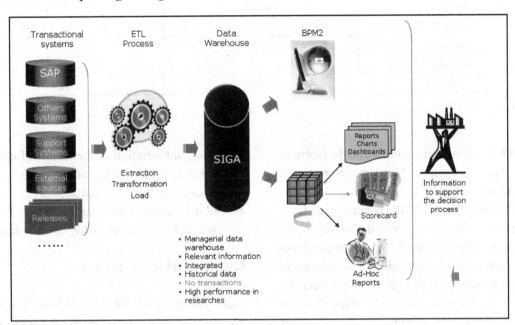

The GTB uses the same kind of platform the GCB does, but besides the GCB tools, the GTB team developed SHARE, a problem solving software. SHARE, unlike the SIGA and the BPM, is oriented to the monitoring of technical indicators.

When SHARE was created, various analysis tools were introduced in the program. They made the software automatically inform the user what project would cause the greatest impact on the desired outcome. At the same time the software indicates which benchmarking companies are available for contact. The SHARE analysis function allows studying the indicators interdependence so the user can best discern the problem.

SHARE's main function is to support the units to carry out technical benchmark, identifying the indicators that have greater process impact. Data from SHARE respect the same taxonomy, measure units and calculation methods. The units are encouraged not only to feed their data into the system, but to use the software for procedure analysis, and use the data as a platform for planning their performance improvement.

SHARE relies on an assistant program that analyzes the data and presents a Pareto graphic with a descriptive statistic summary. The software is a technical information repository whereas SIGA is a management data repository.

Another initiative is a corporate community called KMP: Knowledge Performance Management, which acts as practice community or as large groups to exchange best practices. There are groups or KMP communities formed to discuss the various metallurgical processes. These groups have representatives from all ArcelorMittal units and they have meetings periodically. The papers presented during these meetings are published in the KMP SharePoint. The SharePoint concept is that knowledge is only valid when it is available. SharePoint, GTB and other information repositories are concentrated in a single portal called Global Knowledge Management Program.

The survey was conducted from September 11th to October 7th 2008 with professionals linked to product, process and service improvement from LCA. Ninety invitation letters were sent out by e-

Table 2. Process of determining needs of information

Process	Frequency	%
None	2	3.92
Informal	24	47.07
Structured	25	49.01
Total	51	100.00

Source: Research data

mail with a link to a questionnaire on the Internet. The response rate was 57% (51 questionnaires). This rate was satisfactory considering the motivational efforts made and the occupational level of the people selected to enroll the survey.

Regarding the spot check, 61% of respondents are between 36 and 45 years old, 90% are male and 63% have an academic background in engineering.

The perception of 65% of the respondents is that the company has a formalized process as far as strategical information management. However, the answers point that the information management process is emerging and has some improvement opportunities.

This study adopted the Davenport (1998) generic information management model; it was used as a basis for the formulation of questions and the grouping of responses.

Determination of the Information Requirements

The data indicate a difficulty in defining the demands of the information clients. About 51% of respondents characterized the process of de-

termining information demand as informal or nonexistent. 49% of respondents characterized this process as structured and 60% of respondents agreed that people who generate the information are aware of their target audience and objective.

Capture of Information

After you have set what the information needs are, the next step is to get them. The information obtaining process requires time, skill, insight and continuity. The research results show that in LCA, the search for information related to processes, products and services improvement is conducted in an unsuitable manner. Approximately 57% of respondents rated as inappropriate for the time spent collecting information.

The result of the research shows that 83% of respondents are aware of whom to look for when information is needed. However 55% do not recognize the existence of organized file information. Therefore, we can infer that a large proportion of the information files related to improving production processes and services are scattered in the personal files. 75% of respondents rated as high

Table 3. Information recovery

Difficulty Degree	Frequency	%
Reduced	12	23.53
Middle	31	60.78
High	8	15.69
Total	51	100.00

Source: Research data

Table 4. Employees' opinion about how the knowledge should be shared

Sharing	Frequency	%
Only within the unit	2	3.92
Among units	5	9.80
Within the unit and between units;	44	86.28
Total	51	100.00

Source: Research data

or medium the level of difficulty for information recovery. The existence of an organized file is a variable that impacts the evaluation of efficiency of information management.

To learn where to find the information is very important although not enough to get it. A process for efficient search and retrieval of information begins by defining the terms of taxonomy, classification and archiving to enable rapid and efficient consultation for users. At the junction of the variables only receive the necessary information and the awareness of search for information, statistics were not significant. 70% of respondents disagreed with the statement that they only receive useful information.

Distribution of Information

After setting, finding, sorting and formatting the information, you must deliver it to its destination. Getting the right information, at the appropriate time and the user who needs it are the steps to optimize the use of information. Well-prepared information in the hands of those who do not need it is a waste of time and effort.

Approximately 86% of respondents do not recognize a policy direction for the distribution of information. Data from research show that the management information efficiency is linked to the existence of management information practices.

According to Choo (2002) the ultimate goal of distribution and dissemination of information is to facilitate its sharing. Data from research show that the respondents recognize the need

to share information within the unit and among units, but 75% of respondents have from very small to medium degree of willingness to share information ranging. The data research however, does not allow us to identify the cause of this phenomenon, but it suggests that some factors may contribute to the low interviewee's availability to share information, such as low efficiency in the provision process, products or services improvements in the unit, lack of encouragement policies to information-sharing and no lay-out to promote exchange of information.

It is even interesting that respondents with medium or high availability to share information tend to agree that the company is using the knowledge already existed in the group. Thus, we are led to infer that even those with a willingness to share information, would only do it if it was internally.

Use of Information

Even the complete and efficient information is inert if not analyzed and used by the user. It is at this stage that the information comes alive, or rather, it gains sense and helps those who use it in the decision making process.

Although 82% of people agreed that there is the formal implementation of actions to improve the use of information, 70% of respondents identified personal contact as the main way to get the information necessary for these process improvements. The data do not allow us to conclude the reason why they prefer the personal contact. Meanwhile, another data revealed that 94% of respondents

Table 5. Employees' availability for sharing technical information

Sharing availability	Frequency	%
Very little	2	3.92
Reduced	13	25.49
Middle	23	45.10
High	13	25.49
Total	51	100.00

Source: Research data.

Table 6. Information Capture

Capture ways	Frequency	%
Partnership with another professional	36	70.59
Software	21	41.18
By yourself	10	19.61
Partnership with consulting firms	3	5.88

Source: Research data

agreed that a centralized system for the exchange of best practices would facilitate the work of all.

With a centralized system or not, the company needs to make the information flow and find the best path to an effective use. The data showed statistical significance of the research associated to the variables efficiency of information management and the existence of procedures for the managing information process. What allows us to conclude that an important step in LCA information management process is to define procedures for its operation? The system will only be characterized and noticed by users as structured and formal once the process of standardizing the

management and dissemination of new procedures to its users is finished.

From the correlation analysis, four new variables combined were generated. However, it appears that the two most important variables combined carry about 64% of the information of the original system. This indicates that the relationship could reasonably be translated through these two new variables, reducing the size of the original system from four to two.

According to the analysis it was found that the characteristics associated with higher overall efficiency of a managing information system for

Table 7. If there were a centralized local system to exchange best practices, it would facilitate the work of all

Agreement	Frequency	%
Completely agree	22	43.14
Agree	26	50.98
Disagree	3	5.88
Total	51	100.00

Source: Research data

the interviewees are the speed of response and formalization of the structure.

The use of knowledge and the file organization appear as issues related to both standards, efficient and inefficient, however were not decisive for the classification system of information management.

CONCLUSION

The research's main goal was to set out what the features of the appropriate model for the management information at the continuous improvement area in ArcelorMittal Long Carbon Americas are.

The research data showed that management information to processes, products and services improvement efficient in LCA has two main features: it is a formalized process and it must have quick response in information search.

Despite several initiatives towards the information management nowadays, most respondents do not have a clear vision of where to get the necessary information; they recognize the rework and have medium level of willingness to share information. Data from research show that although the respondents still prefer to share information internally, they are willing to share information as long as the system is structured and formalized.

SharePoint is the initiative with the greatest potential to become a global ArcelorMittal tool for official information management activities. For the SharePoint to become something more than an information repository, research data allow us to conclude that there must be a structured process of information management as a whole. The process must be formalized, standardized and official with clear procedures which should be disseminated throughout the company.

Research data also showed that respondents use personal contact as main source of research and information exchange, having e-mail as their most used tool.

These figures lead us to conclude that for technical information to be disseminated, personal contact is very important. A tool that can help the dissemination and sharing of information is the practice community where members can meet regularly in person or through video conference.

To lay out all the information available for improvements that are being or will be developed is still an idea that may not please people involved in the development of new products, for instance. Thus, the community members should be accepted by the responsible member, and his stay may be subject to its contribution for the group.

FUTURE RESEARCH DIRECTIONS

Having presented and analysed the results of this research, we became aware of its limitations. For further research, some suggestions can be given, including:

a)   Evaluate the impact of individual behavior in the process of information management.
b)   Investigate how the process of information management is in a multicultural company.
c)   Study the feasibility of deploying world model suitable for ArcelorMittal Americas.

REFERENCES

Alves-Mazzotti, A. J., & Gewandsznajder, F. (1999). *O método nas ciências naturais e sociais: pesquisa quantitativa e qualitativa*. São Paulo, Brasil: Thomson.

American Psychological Association. (2001). *Publication Manual of the American Psychological Association* (5th ed.). Washington, DC: Author.

Argyris, C. (1977 September). Double Loops Learning in Organizations. *Harvard Business Review*.

Auster, E., & Choo, W. (1994). How Senior Managers Acquire and Use Information in Environmental Scanning. *Information Processing & Management, 30*(5), 607–618. doi:10.1016/0306-4573(94)90073-6

Barbosa, R. (2002). Inteligência Empresarial: uma avaliação de fontes de informação sobre o ambiente organizacional externo. *DataGrama-Zero, Revista de Ciência da Informação, 3*(6). Retrieved October 2007, from http://www.dgz.org.br/dez02/F_I_art.htm

Benzecri, J. P. (1979). Sur le calcul des taux d'inertie dans l'analyse d'un questionnaire. *Les Cahiers de l'Analyse des Donnees, 3*, 377–384.

Campos, V. (1992). *TQC: Controle da qualidade total (no estilo Japonês)*. Rio de Janeiro, Brasil: Block.

Campos, V. (2002). *Gerenciamento pelas Diretrizes (Hoshin Kanri)*. Belo Horizonte, Brasil: Editora de Desenvolvimento Gerencial.

Choo, W. (2002). *Information management for the intelligent organization: the art of scanning the environment*. Medford, NJ: Information Today, Inc.

Choo, W. (2006). *A Organização do conhecimento: como as organizações usam a informação para criar significado, construir conhecimento e tomar decisões*. São Paulo, Brasil: Editora Senac São Paulo.

Cruz, C., Rodrigues, E., & Nagano, M. (2007) Análise do relacionamento da gestão do conhecimento e as práticas para melhoria da qualidade: Estudo de caso em uma empresa de alta tecnologia. *Revista Gestão Industrial, 3*(2), 45-56. Retrieved Febraury 2008, from http://www.pg.cefetpr.br/ppgep/revista/revista2007/vol2/artigo/V3N2B4.pdf

Davenport, T. (1998). *Ecologia da Informação: por que só a tecnologia não basta para o sucesso na era da informação*. São Paulo, Brasil: Futura.

Davenport, T., & Prusak, L. (1998). *Conhecimento Empresarial: como as organizações gerenciam o seu capital intelectual*. Rio de Janeiro, Brasil: Campus.

Drucker, P. (2000). O advento da Nova Organização . In *Gestão do Conhecimento. Harvard Business Review. (A. C. da Cunha Serra, Trad.)*. Rio de Janeiro, Brasil: Campus.

Edmondson, A. (2008, July). The competitive Imperative of Learning. *Harvard Business Review, 86*(7/8).

França, J., & Vasconcellos, A. (2007). *Manual para Normalização de Publicações técnico-científicas*. Belo Horizonte, Brasil: UFMG.

Garvin, D. (2000). Construindo a Organização que Aprende . In *Gestão do Conhecimento. Harvard Business Review. (A. C. da Cunha Serra, Trad.)*. Rio de Janeiro, Brasil: Campus.

Garvin, D., Edmondson, A., & Gino, F. (2008 March). Is Yours a Learning Organization? *Harvard Business Review*.

Goulart, I. (2002). Estudos exploratórios em psicologia organizacional e do trabalho . In Goulart, I. (Ed.), *Psicologia organizacional e do trabalho, teoria, pesquisa e temas correlatos*. São Paulo, Brasil: Casa do Psicólogo.

Greenacre, M. (1984). *Theory and applications of correspondence analysis*. London: Academic Press.

Lebart, L., Morineau, A., & Warwick, K. M. (1984). *Multivariate Descriptive Statistical Analysis: Correspondence Analysis and Related Techniques for Large Matrices*. New York: J. Wiley & Sons.

Leonard-Barton, D. (1998). *Nascentes do Saber*. Rio de Janeiro, Brasil: Fundação Getúlio Vargas.

Lopes, M. (2007). *Panorama do Desenvolvimento da Siderurgia Brasileira*. Instituto Brasileiro de Siderurgia. Retrieved November 2007, from http://www.abmbrasil.com.br

Ludke, M., & Andre, M. (1986). *Pesquisa em educação: abordagens qualitativas*. São Paulo, Brasil: EPU.

Marconi. M & Lakatos, E. (1988). *Técnicas de Pesquisa*. São Paulo, Brasil: Editora Atlas.

McGee, J., & Prusak, L. (1994). *Gerenciamento estratégico da informação*. Rio de Janeiro, Brasil: Campus.

Nonaka, I. (2000). A empresa criadora de conhecimento . In *Gestão do Conhecimento. Harvard Business Review. (A. C. da Cunha Serra, Trad.)*. Rio de Janeiro, Brasil: Campus.

Nonaka, I., & Takeuchi, H. (1997). *Criação de Conhecimento na Empresa: como as empresas japonesas geram a dinâmica da inovação*. Rio de Janeiro, Brasil: Campus.

Parker, B. (1998). Evolução e Revolução: Da Internacionalização à globalização . In Caldas, M., Fachin, R., & Fischer, T. (Eds.), *Handbook de Estudos Organizacionais. Modelos de Análise e Novas Questões em Estudos Organizacionais (Vol. 1)*. São Paulo, Brasil: Atlas.

Prahalad, C. (1997). A Organização Reestruturável . In *A Organização do Futuro: como preparar as empresas de amanhã*. São Paulo, Brasil: Futura.

Prahalad, C., & Hamel, G. (1998). A Competência Essencial da Corporação . In Montgomery, C. A., & Porter, M. E. (Eds.), *Estratégia A Busca da Vantagem Competitiva*. Rio de Janeiro, Brasil: Elsevier Editora.

Sunstein, C. (2006). *Infotopia: How many minds produce knowledge?* New York: Oxford University Press.

Trivinos, A. (1987). *Introdução à pesquisa em ciências sociais: a pesquisa qualitativa em educação*. São Paulo, Brasil: Atlas.

Vergara, S. (2007). *Projetos e relatórios de pesquisa em administração* (8ª ed.). São Paulo, Brasil: Atlas Editora.

Vieira, M. (2004). Por uma boa pesquisa (qualitativa) em administração . In Vieira, M., & Zouain, M. (Eds.), *Pesquisa qualitativa em administração*. Rio de Janeiro, Brasil: Editora FGV.

Yin, R. (2001). *Estudo de caso: planejamento e métodos*. Porto Alegre, Brasil: Bookman.

Section 4
EIS Design, Application, Implementation and Impact

Chapter 13
The Needed Adaptability for ERP Systems

Ricardo Almeida
Universidade do Porto, Portugal

Américo Azevedo
Universidade do Porto, Portugal

ABSTRACT

The new market trends are forcing companies to constantly reorganize their business processes so that they can react quickly to the new economic challenges. Although not always, enterprise information systems provide an appropriate response to these situations due to several reasons, such as technology failure, lack of adaptable configuration tools or even the financial investment required, which makes it unaffordable to companies. This article presents a functional model for ERP Systems (called FME) that would guarantee a baseline structure to build solutions which would provide a complete configuration and, therefore, a timely reaction to market fluctuations. This model also summarizes some of the most used functionalities of the available ERP Systems.

INTRODUCTION

The last decades have been characterized by constant market fluctuations in the global economy stability, causing companies to face a pressing need to restructure their strategic business processes. These changes usually require tactical decisions for quick and accurate responses over companies working processes, heading for short-term adaptation actions to face the new market needs. However, this constant (and ill) adaptation

DOI: 10.4018/978-1-61692-020-3.ch013

is often considered a veritable Babel Tower since its maintenance is performed without a completely "thought and organized" process. A simple change in a process may lead to organizational restructuring and, therefore, it requires for changes and new configurations on the existing information systems.

This new trend requires enterprise information systems to be provided with tools for rapid customization (and management) in order to enable an effective and timely response to these needs. In this context, there are several Enterprise Resource Planning (ERP) systems in the market capable of providing an answer to these requirements, such as SAP, Microsoft Dynamics, JD Edwards, Priority, PHC Software, Manufactor Software, Primavera Software, and others. However, they present different solutions and framework concepts for the same functions, and none of them presents a complete solution.

This work presents an "adaptive" functional model that could be assumed as the "baseline" for ERPs systems. This model aims primarily to provide the necessary conceptual architecture so that it is possible to build software solutions that guarantee a complete parameterization and configuration, as well as an effective response to organization's needs.

MAJOR PROBLEMS FOUND

Implementing and managing ERP Systems may be a complex process due to several causes, such as human inadaptability, for instance. According to Lin (2002), about half of ERP implementations fail to meet expectations. Most of them suffered from over-budget, over-time, user dissatisfaction, threatened lawsuit, besides having failed to introduce all planned modules; or the big and horizontal ERP Systems pulling back into beta testing.

The following topics summarize some of the most common features in this business, according to the experience of the authors.

Market Awareness

Software companies develop ERP Systems, taking into consideration the roadmap's interests on time and cost restrictions, somewhat "forgetting" to study the actual needs of the market. According to Davenport (1998), software houses try to structure the systems in order to reflect best practices (series of assumptions about the way companies operate in general), but it is the vendor, not the customer, that is defining what "best" means. In many cases, the system will enable a company to operate more efficiently than it did before. In some cases, though, the system's assumptions will run counter to a company's best interests.

Most of the time, software companies are aware of the companies' major difficulties when regarding their software distribution policies (leaving the responsibility of consulting and analyzing the market to smaller companies, named partners, who sometimes aren't prepared for such a difficult task). According to Bingi (1999), because the ERP market has grown so much and so fast, there has been a shortage of competent consultants. Finding the right people and keeping them through the implementation is a major challenge, since ERP implementation demands multiple skills – functional, technical and interpersonal skills. Although this strategy (high number of partners) might increase software house's sales, it keeps them away from the companies' "real need" analysis.

Mandal (2003) has defended that software vendors should apply for an "iterative evolutionary method" to develop enterprise-wide information systems since that would enable system developers and their customers to communicate effectively with each other in order to make the system evolve towards a defined objective. Such a strategy would help them analyze the impact of the software implementation on the organization. Unfortunately, such kinds of strategies (although, sometimes promised) were never "really" taken into consideration.

Factors Preventing Decision-Making

According to Holland (1999), a new ERP platform forms a critical infrastructure in any company for, at least, the next decade. This sentence enhances the importance of a consistent decision of an ERP system for an organization.

However, the implementation of an ERP system is often a complex process in the sense that it requires internal restructuring, both in terms of work procedures and human resources. The growth of Project Management, such as science common practice, proves the importance and complexity of these processes in guaranteeing a complete control of tasks, resources and associated costs. Even at a stage of "cruising speed" (in which, finally, the company begins to truly enjoy the usage of an integrated system), any change is considered (by company managers) a cost for the organization, even when ranked as essential to answer to a new market adversity. According to Oliveira (2004), the impact that Information Systems and Technologies have in the lifecycle of organizations is such that a simple study on their information systems is enough to classify them (as innovative) in the market.

These "pessimistic" thoughts have been growing since managers realized that they invest continuously (and highly) on technical and human factors for an ERP system that responds, only partially, to the expectations that have been set. According to Davenport (1998), the growing number of horror stories about failed or out-of-control projects certainly gives managers a pause. Nowadays, any change becomes subject of a "deep" financial analysis and hard consideration by managers.

The following topics summarize some of the factors influencing the decision of managers, concerning the change or customization of an ERP system in their organization:

Organizational Changes (Human)

As already mentioned, an ERP system can "force" changes on organization's structures, and therefore, user's adaption to new functions and work procedures. According to Davenport (1998), an enterprise system imposes its own logic on a company's strategy, culture and organization. Umble (2003) described that even the most flexible ERP system imposes its own logic on a company's strategy, organization, and culture. Thus, implementing an ERP system may force the reengineering of key business processes and/or the development of new business processes to

support the organization's goal. Such an approach might cause some workers to refuse to change to the new system!

Another author enhances the human factor (Courtois, 2006), defending that the success of a system depends on the people's motivation regarding the implementation project, in the sense that they need to know exactly which are their expectations and to follow organization's interests.

Besides that, the period in which two applications run "in parallel" should also be considered to ensure a continuous and "untailored" process. Although this scenario seems to be the most secure, in fact, it promote fatigue on users. Yusuf (2004) has identified some risks related to human concerns when implementing ERP Systems, such as resistance to change to new process methods by management and supervision; possible failure to cut over to the new system through an inability to load data; possible failure to cut over to the new system through the inappropriate system testing of volume, stress and data conversion.

Implementation Costs (Finance)

According to Bingi (1999), the total cost of implementation could be three to five times the purchase price of the ERP system. The implementation costs increase as the degree of customization increases. The cost of hiring consultants and all that goes with it can consume up to 30 percent of the overall budget for the implementation, thus making this stage one of the most expensive. Besides that, it's one of the stages that is most "affected" when a reengineering decision is applied or when a wrong analysis is made, since it gathers the business rules definition and customization procedures.

Supplier Dependency

When an organization buys an ERP system, it becomes, in a certain way, dependent of its software supplier/partner to configure and parameterize the system. After the implementation stage, high-cost maintenance contracts to ensure the ERP system evolution to the organization's needs may be required. These types of scenarios are normally predicted by managers and may become a constraint when deciding for an ERP system.

This "dependency" can be reduced if internal teams constantly follow all phases of the implementation stage and ask for a high degree of participation. This will give some autonomy for companies to manage their maintenance costs.

Implementation Times

According to Bingi (1999), the problem with ERP packages is that they are very general and need to be configured to a specific type of business that takes a long time, depending on the specific requirements of the business. For example, SAP is so complex and general that there are nearly 8000 switches that need to be set properly so that it is possible to handle the business processes the way a company needs. The extent of customization determines the length of the implementation. The more customization needed, the longer it will take to roll the software out and the more it will cost to keep it up-to-date.

Tchokohué (2003) mentioned a study made by the Standish Group, which found that 90% of ERP implementations end up late or over budget. And, in some cases, the implementation time is extended indefinitely, which has negative consequences for both the companies and the morale of their employees.

An additional factor can be added if the implementation process is carried out by less competent partners/implementers, which will increase implementation times, risks and costs.

Upgrade Process (New Versions)

Other handicaps detected on these kinds of systems (even the "most advanced" ERP Systems that include many configuration features) are that they become a "nightmare" when an upgrade is needed. This is due to the fact that it is very hard to maintain the same performance when a new release is available to market. Besides these problems, a technological restriction can also be pointed: some of the ERP Systems are developed based on two layers (Presentation and Data layers), which turn the upgrade operations into a difficult task. This type of architecture does not provide the desired scalability for such a complex and multi-department system.

These scenarios also "spread" the feeling that is necessary to buy the first ERP versions to avoid the first errors of the so-called the Beta versions. This became a usual procedure on software markets, with customers preferring to wait for "mature" versions to reduce implementation problems.

As a first conclusion, it can be assumed that all these indicators are considered by company managers to analyze the impact on their organization. Companies deal daily with the evaluation of alternative scenarios to support the decision process, comparing all the benefits and weaknesses of each option (internally, regarding process modification; externally, the market reaction that can be provided).

TRADITIONAL ERP SYSTEMS' ARCHITECTURE

The actual ERP Systems already include solutions for quick customizations. However, all of them present some advantages and disadvantages among each other, thus making it difficult to find a "standard meaning". This chapter presents the traditional functional structure of these kinds of systems.

Figure 1 presents a scheme, which represents the existing functional structure for ERP Systems, divided into 3 parameterization levels. A first level for ERP internal business development can be defined that includes all the business rules developed by the software house as standard operation routines. The second level is defined as

Figure 1. Parameterization's level of ERP Systems

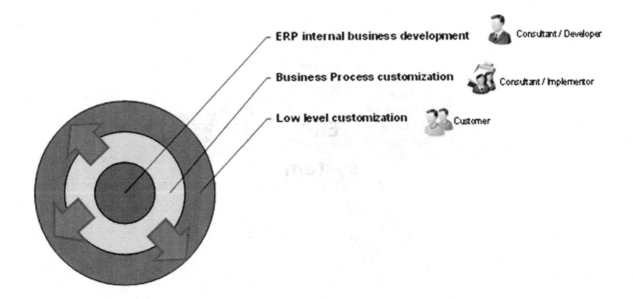

the Business Process customization level, which has to do with the entire advanced configuration promoted by consultants and implementers in order to guarantee the system's adaptation to the company requirements. Finally, the third level is dedicated to Low level customization, which includes the entire parameterization available for ERP users.

1st Level: ERP Internal Business Development

This level includes all the standard routines developed by the software house for the ERP system. On an implementation process, this level is never applied unless a "software bug" is detected or the customer argues for a specific need that even the "Business Process implementation" level cannot handle.

This level is assumed to be the "heart" of an ERP! Built on a complex structure (data and programming code), it is responsible for guaranteeing the perfect integration between processes and data so that it is possible to achieve complete and coherent amount of information. Changes at this

level are always avoided by the software houses in order to prevent major problems. Normally, it's only changed when mandatory developments are required caused, for instance, by changes in financial/government legislations.

2nd Level: Business Process Customizations

This level includes all the available configuration tools to be used by consultants. Since the major ERP Systems work on a three-tier development application scheme, it may include several changes to the ERP business rules regarding advanced customizations requested by customers.

Since the most part of the processes is already standardized (financial and commercial, for instance), this level assumes a high level of importance since it reveals the major differences between the ERP Systems. This means that the major difference on buying/choosing an ERP is the ability to customize/parameterize this second level.

Figure 2. FME-Functional model for ERP Systems

3rd Level: Low Level Customizations

This level includes the entire "local" customizations available for users, in order to enable single tasks like choosing colours, configuring columns orders, sending e-mails by a condition, etc. Although not assuming a major importance as in the previous level, in fact, it promotes some flexibility on internal processes, making it possible for users to (easily) enhance their daily procedures.

The ERP Systems on the market have different approaches to answer to these three levels. Some of these software solutions seem to forget that the 2nd and 3rd levels need special attention so that it is possible to answer effectively to company requirements.

The ideal scenario would be an ERP system that could promote a user-friendly configuration tool (for simple tasks and, when needed, for highly advanced tasks concerning the parameterization ability) to conveniently "explore" all capacities of the 2nd and 3rd levels. Therefore, in Figure 1, the arrows represent the desired tendency to expand configuration capabilities.

(DESIRED) FUNCTIONAL MODEL FOR ERP SYSTEMS

It is extremely important that ERP Systems provide an internal reactive model, regarding the availability of configuration and parameterization tools, in order to promote the user's interaction with the software. The next image (Figure 2) presents a functional model (called FME) that could be applied in order to design a complete innovative and integrated system, with a high level of adaptability and interactivity.

The presented model includes an internal user-friendly **Event and alert sub-system** to be used by the "common" user (without technical knowledge). Some examples of this kind of sub-system are as follows: the parameterization to include validations and alert messages so that it is possible to ensure that the mandatory fields presented on the screen are filled up; the configuration of the system so that it is possible to send e-mails after a certain action or condition is detected. This sub-system enhances the "local" flexibility for customers, investing in the user's motivation by solving simple needs. At the same time, it promotes a high level of attention from consultants/implementers on the second level (presented on the previous topic).

Regarding the principle that "ERP Systems must be adapted to companies and not the opposite", surely the systems' interfaces must be changed to add or hide the data required by users. For this aspect, the FME model presents a sub-system called **Interface framework**, which allows the complete design of interfaces (forms) of the ERP system in order to answer to customers' needs. This sub-system allows functionalities such as adding new or hiding existing fields, and even controlling their appearance by user's privileges. A typical example is hiding monetary fields from users that do not belong to the financial user's group.

Looking at an ERP system as a living creature, its blood would certainly be data! ERP Systems need to "grow" in order to follow the lifecycle of organizations, safely keeping information and providing the desired scalability. This sub-system is named **Database framework**, and includes the advanced management of information systems database, for instance, adding user fields to standard tables, creating new tables, creating triggers and indexes, procedures, etc. These types of functionalities should only be performed by specialized teams (consulting/implementers) since its wrong use may affect the global performance of the entire application. On the other hand, a "well-know use" can provide a higher performance on the global system.

As previously mentioned, an ERP system must ensure scalability to the company. It must guarantee that its updates or new versions do not negatively affect the existing data, reducing impacts on the system. Usually, the software houses apply these kinds of operations updating single DLLs or Web-Services to ensure the global application on the system and reducing the need to update the client's software. The sub-system responsible for these procedures is called **Update system.**

The business rules parameterization approach completes the FME model! In this sub-system (called **Business Process framework**), all the configuration tools that allow processes adaptation are included in order to ensure a continuous and accurate information flow in the entire company.

Although dedicated to consultants/implementers, this sub-system should provide a graphical tool for business process representation to achieve a better visualization and configuration. At a high complex stage, the FME model would also recommend allowing the programming code on processes' rules to be edited for a complete customization (but always controlling the correct execution and their dependences with other sub-systems).

The FME model would support any ERP system to achieve integrated functionalities, totally dedicated to organizations' needs. However, like any model, it asks for an additional requirement: documentation! When an ERP system's implementation presents high levels of customization, it demands that his stages be reported to share information for future projects. Although not represented in Figure 2, it is seen as an essential topic in any of the sub-systems presented.

The FME model is easily "inserted" on the actual parameterization levels of the ERP Systems, which enhances the idea of a practice application for a future work. The next image (Figure 3) presents the relation of the FME model's sub-systems with the parameterization levels mentioned on the last topic. The sub-system Event and alert has been basically classified on the "Low level customization", ensuring an easy use for the common users. Furthermore, it also has been included on the "Business Process" level to considerer the required advanced parameterizations made by implementers.

Figure 3. FME model and their parameterization levels

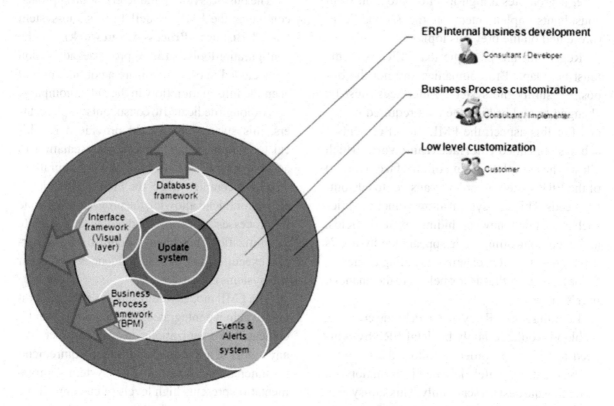

IMPLEMENTATION OF THE FME MODEL

One of the major challenges of our work was to promote a practical application of our model. To achieve such a milestone, 3 sub-systems (Event and alert sub-system, Interface and Database frameworks) of our 5 sub-systems have been implemented on the Portuguese software called Manufactor. This software is a vertical product developed by the company Manufactor Solutions (www.manufactor.pt) and it has been developed on an object-oriented programming approach (in this case, Microsoft Visual FoxPro, version 9.0; named as VFP, from now on), which is highly important for our model.

Implementation of Event and Alert Sub-System

Our model aims to promote "local" flexibility with users to fully provide answers to the usual and daily needs. To achieve such goal, the FME model makes it possible to define rules that will trigger an action. These rules can go from a simple comparison of fields to complex programming code (at Manufactor software, XBase code), for instance, checking data on another server or gathering information from several tables. If the rule is violated, the software will perform an action (that can be triggered as an e-mail, XBase code, data exportation task, external application execution or internal message sending). The next image (Figure 4) presents the available scenarios for this sub-system, for both implementers and users.

A simple example of the XBase code used to trigger an action is presented next to validate if

Figure 4. Event and alert sub-system process

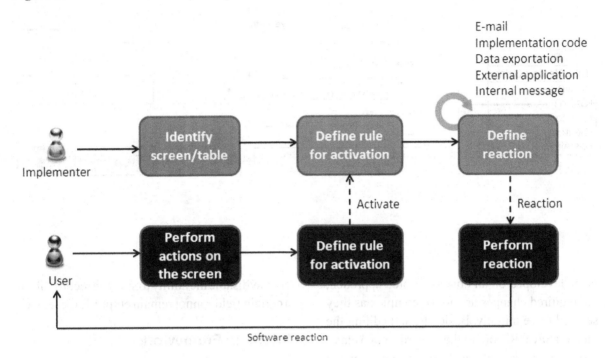

a certain product ("abc") is being purchased on quantities above 1000:

```
IF product_code = "abc" AND
quantity > 1000
THEN
        RETURN .f.
ELSE
        RETURN .t.
ENDIF
```

If the product code is equal to "abc" and quantity is higher than 1000, the rule returns a false value (.f.), which means that the action will be triggered. For harder implementations, the code can achieve a higher complexity, using internal software personal instructions; for instance:

```
u_sqlExec("SELECT SUM(quantity)
AS soma FROM orders " + ;
```

```
" WHERE product_code = '" +
product_code + "'", ;
"result_cursor")
IF RECCOUNT("result_cursor") > 0
        IF result_cursor.soma >
12000
        ...
        ENDIF
ENDIF
...
```

This example uses an internal software functional called "**u_sqlExec**", which sends a string variable (containing a Transact-SQL instruction) to the database layer, and return the retrieved data to a cursor/dataset called "result_cursor".

The FME model defined the trigger execution before (named "User Rules") or after (named "User Events") saving records on the screen. To implement such functionalities, it is necessary to make programming adjustments on Manufactor's main classes. However, since this software has

Figure 5. Changes performed on the Record's main class

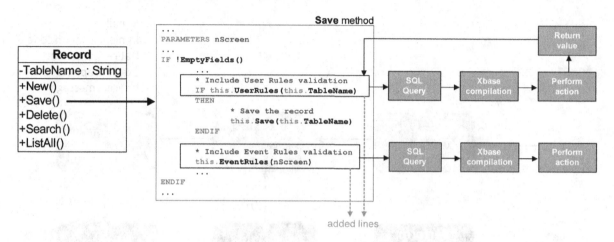

been developed on an object-oriented approach, the required changes are not so complex as they seemed to be initially. Basically, and editing the method Save_Record of the Records' main class, 2 new methods that check the existence of the User Rules and User Events have been included. In case of existence, the XBase code is compiled (in run-time) and executed on the user's desktop. These changes are presented in the next image (Figure 5).

The new methods UserRules and EventRules validate the existence of any configured rules (performing SQL Queries on the database). Since user rules are "associated" to tables, it's necessary to send the table name as a parameter (which is an attribute from the Records' main class); in the case of user events, the association is made by a current screen's internal identifier.

If any rule is detected, the XBase code field is compiled in run-time (to check if the action should be performed or not). If the returned value of the compiled Xbase code field is False, the action is triggered.

User rules have an additional functionality! Since they are executed before the Save routine, they make it possible for a returned value from the performed action to be validated. This means that the XBase code can validate a condition and enable/disable the ability to save the record (like if a certain field cannot remain empty, for instance).

Interface Framework

Sharing information is essential for any organization, as long as it is completely controlled! This means that information should be available to users, but only the data related to their professional role. This is always a major concern in organizations since interfaces are standard and (normally) display all information related to a business process.

Our model allows a complete configuration of user interfaces, associated to their role in the company. For instance, the Product screen may have important information on industrial costs that should be only available to managers, and not for the operational staff. This need has created the term **Customization** in our model, which refers to the availability to create different views of an interface, which can be associated to users or groups.

To achieve our aims, an option called "*Create customization*" has been created on every screen, available to implementers. When this option is activated, all the screen objects are loaded (in run-time) and a new interface is created (for editing),

Figure 6. Interface framework

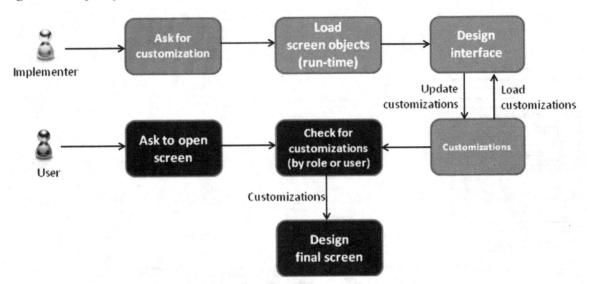

which acts like a copy of the current screen, yet on a design interface (similar to Visual Basic), as shown in Figure 6. This screen is totally managed by the VFP's base events: *MouseDown*, *MouseUp* and *Click* events.

This design interface makes it possible to hide the standard objects (textbox, combo box, buttons, grids, etc) and to add new objects (which will present data, perform standard actions or even XBase code), as shown in the toolbars (Figure 7).

When the design phase is finished, only the changes (left, top, width, height and visible properties) will be saved on the database for the standard objects and the new objects created. Figure 8 presents the new tables created to support this new functionality.

The implementer can also define if a customization is associated to a specific user or professional role in the company. When the user opens a screen/interface, the software validates if there is any customization associated to his name or professional role. If so, it loads the related customizations, it opens the standard screen and applies the changes (modifications on standard objects and new custom objects).

Such functionality allows organizations that will only present the information they wish to their collaborators. It also promotes scalability, since it makes it possible for new user fields and user tables to be added and made available on the Database framework.

As a final note, the "Load Screen Objects (run-time)" task has revealed a lower performance for complex forms (with a high number of objects). The major causes are the recursive routines developed to analyze all the existing objects on container objects (such as page frames and grids). An effective solution to reduce the overall time of loading objects in run-time is that all information should be summarized locally (inside the executable file)!

Routines have been developed to analyze all forms/screens during the compilation time; this action was possible since VFP keeps all programming components (forms, programs, reports, etc) as local tables. So, before compilation, all programming components are "open" and objects are retrieved to a local table; this operation takes almost 30 minutes more to read than 150 screens, which drastically decreases the compilation time.

Figure 7. Designing interfaces

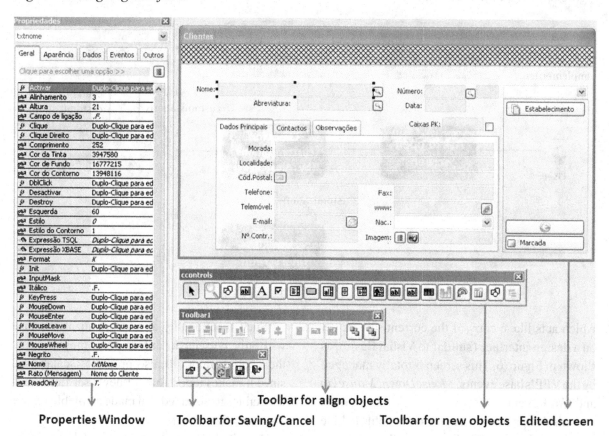

Properties Window   Toolbar for Saving/Cancel   **Toolbar for align objects**   Toolbar for new objects   Edited screen

However, it increases in more than 3 seconds the time that is needed to present objects in run-time (achieving the desired results).

Database Framework

The aim with our model is to allow systems to grow within the organizations. To achieve such

Figure 8. Interface framework's database tables

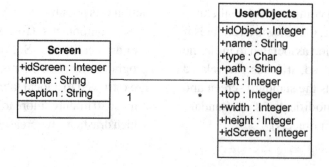

Figure 9. Database framework

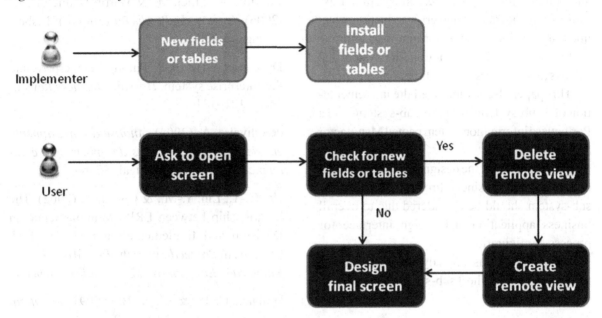

goal, one has to consider the possibility of "creating" (adding new) data on the information system database.

Our approach to the Manufactor software had to do with managing operations like adding new fields to the standard tables. We've called it "User fields". Higher demands require a new complete table, called "User tables", allowing the definition of a new and complete table that can be applied to a grid object, for instance using the Interface Framework described at the previous topic.

Every time a user opens a screen, an internal validation is provided to check if the local VFP remote view is updated with the information's table scheme presented on the server. If not, the local remote view is deleted and a new one is created (with the updated data). This procedure is summarized in the next image (Figure 9).

All the database maintenance related with these user fields and user tables are kept in the application's database, providing an extreme portability (anytime it's needed to change the data server, for instance) and abstraction to the user (since it doesn't need to know the SQL instructions to create fields and tables).

CONCLUSION

According to Davenport (1999), if a company accepts all re-engineering suggestions (when implementing an ERP system), it may see the dream of information integration turns into a nightmare. This enhances the importance of an ERP system on a company and, therefore, the responsibility of a manager when choosing a system.

This paper summarized some of the main restrictions found by companies when configuring ERP Systems, guaranteeing constant adaptations so that it is possible to provide an accurate answer to the market. For several times, financial and time restrictions have blocked the decision to change an ERP system; on other occasions, the systems do not provide the "reaction capacity" that is required in order to face this reality.

To achieve a complete solution, a new functional model (called FME) has been designed to be applied to any ERP system. Using brief descriptions and simple diagrams, this complex model has been summarized and divided into five sub-systems that would ensure a dynamic lifecycle for these kinds of enterprise systems. It promotes and searches for a high process integration, flexibility on the local user and error reduction when updating versions. The major aim is to improve customer satisfaction by using an ERP system that follows (and answers) his needs for longer periods.

This paper also summarized the implementation of 3 sub-systems (of the 5 sub-systems) on a Portuguese information system named Manufactor Software.

For future work, the design of an architectural model for the Business Process Management sub-system should be considered due to overall business application and design interface for process configuration.

Some limitations (already detected) by the implementation of the 3 sub-systems should also be considered:

- The Local VFP remote view only accepts the maximum of 255 fields, which (in upgrade processes) may cause conflicts when updating standard tables with several user fields;
- Customizations can be "override" (by updating processes, when adding new fields to the standard screens or when changing the layout from the previous version).

As a final comment, we would like to state that these 3 sub-systems were included on the Manufactor's framework and it has been actively used in more than 120 industrial companies.

REFERENCES

Bingi, P., Sharma, M. K., & Godla, J. K. (1999). Critical issues affecting an ERP implementation. *Information Systems Management, 16*(3), 7. doi: 1907155

Courtois, A., Pillet, M., & Martin-Bonnefous, C. (2006). *Gestão da Produção* (5th ed.). Lisboa, Portugal: Lidel.

Davenport, T. H. (1998). Putting the enterprise into the enterprise system. *Harvard Business Review, 76*(4), 121–131.

de Oliveira, A. (2004). *Análise do investimento em sistemas e tecnologias da informação e comunicação*. Lisboa, Portugal: Sílabo.

Ho, C.-Y., Lin, Y.-M., & City, J.-L. (2002). The Relationship between ERP Pre-implementation Decision and Implementation Risks on ERP Projects. In *Proceedings of the First Workshop on Knowledge Economy and Electronic Commerce*.

Holland, C. P., & Light, B. (1999). *A critical success factors model for ERP implementation*. IEEE Software.

Mandal, P., & Gunasekaran, A. (2002). Issues in implementing ERP: A case study. *European Journal of Operational Research*, 274–283.

Silva, M. (2005). *Microsoft Project 2003*. FCA.

Tchokogué, A., Bareil, C., & Duguay, C. R. (n.d.). Key lessons from the implementation of an ERP at Pratt & Whitney Canada. *Int. J. Production Economics*. doi: 10.1016

Umble, E. J., Haft, R. R., & Umble, M. M. (n.d.). Enterprise resource planning: Implementation procedures and critical success factors (pp.). *European Journal of Operational Research, 146*, 241–257.

Yusuf, Y., Gunasekaran, A., & Abthorpe, M. S. (2004). Enterprise information systems project implementation: A case study of ERP in Rolls-Royce. *International Journal of Production Economics, 87*, 251–266. doi:10.1016/j.ijpe.2003.10.004

Chapter 14
Multicriteria Flow Shop Scheduling Problem

Ethel Mokotoff
Alcalá University, Spain

ABSTRACT

Quality is, in real-life, a multidimensional notion. A schedule is described and valued on the basis of a number of criteria, for example: makespan, work-in-process inventories, idle times, observance of due dates, etc. An appropriate schedule cannot be obtained unless one observes the whole set of important criteria. The multidimensional nature of the scheduling problems leads us to the area of Multicriteria Optmization. Thus considering combinatorial problems with more than one criterion is more relevant in the context of real-life scheduling problems. Research in this important field has been scarce when compared to research in single-criterion scheduling. Until the late 1980's, only one criterion was considered in scheduling problems. Furthermore, until the 1990's, most work in the area of multiple criteria scheduling consists of bi-criteria studies of the single machine case. The proliferation of metaheuristic techniques has encouraged researchers to apply them to combinatorial optimization problems. The aim of this chapter is to present a review regarding multicriteria flow-shop scheduling problem, focusing on Multi-Objective Combinatorial Optimization theory, including recent developments considering more than one optimization criterion, followed by a summary discussion on research directions.

INTRODUCTION

In this chapter, we consider a scheduling problem for which, after more than 50 years of scientific research, there is an important gap between theory and practice. Flow-shop problem results in several

contexts, where machines are used to represent the resources and different operations must be carried out with them. So, the aim is to find the schedule that optimizes certain performance measures. To the complexity that naturally arises in these problems, considering only one criterion (Garey & Johnson, 1979), we have to add the additional complexity that comes from the mul-

DOI: 10.4018/978-1-61692-020-3.ch014

tivariant condition of corresponding alternative schedules. In fact the description and valuation of alternative decisions are not naturally accomplished by only one criterion, but by several (*e.g.* makespan, flow-time, completion-time, tardiness, inventory, utilization, etc.). This is certainly the natural framework of the Multicriteria Decision Making discipline (MDM). A solution which is optimal with respect to a given criterion might be a poor candidate for another. The trade-offs involved in considering several different criteria provide useful insights for the decision-maker. Thus considering Combinatorial Optimization (CO) problems with more than one criterion is more relevant in the context of real-life scheduling problems.

Most of the multicriterion approaches applied to scheduling problems are based on Multi-Objective Optimization (MOO) models. Of course, to expect to find the "Optimum" schedule must usually be discarded. We would be satisfied to find the set of non-dominated, also called Pareto optimal, alternatives. At this point, we have to let some subjective considerations intervene, such as the decision-maker preferences. It is actually an MDM problem, and at the present time, there is no other rational tool to apply to discard alternatives. MOO was originally conceived to find a set of Pareto optimal alternative solutions. Only with the breakthrough of metaheursitcs in solving CO problems, did researchers begin to adapt them to solve Multi-Objective Combinatorial Optimization problems. Then, the acronym MOCO started to appear in the scientific literature together with the techniques developed to deal with them. Research in this important field has been scarce when compared to research in single-criterion scheduling. Until the late 1980's, only one criterion was considered in scheduling problems. Furthermore, until the 1990's, most work in the area of multiple criteria scheduling consists of bi-criteria studies of the single machine case (Hoogeveen, 1992).

In this paper, an effort has been made to review the publications concerning Multicriteria Permutation Flow-Shop Scheduling problems, from the late eighties to the most recent papers, giving attention to the results that have not been surveyed until now and suggesting directions for future research (the detailed theorems and proofs have been omitted to avoid a huge paper). In the next section, the classical flow-shop scheduling problem statement is presented. We will briefly introduce MOO theory, general Multicriteria Optimization methods and evaluating metrics (section 3), followed by a survey on multicriteria algorithms devoted to the scheduling problem we are dealing with (section 4). We conclude, in section 5, with a summary discussion on research directions.

PERMUTATION FLOW-SHOP SCHEDULING PROBLEM

In the classical permutation flow-shop scheduling problem, there are n jobs and m machines, or stages. Each job needs to complete one operation on each of the machines during a fixed processing time. So, the aim is to find the schedule, or job sequence, that optimizes certain performance measures. In this paper, we focus attention on the permutation flow-shop situation, where all jobs must pass through all machines in the same order. Potts et al. (1991) presents a comparative study of permutation versus non-permutation flow-shop scheduling problems.

The scheduling process involves just finding the optimal job sequencing. Nevertheless, the computational complexity usually grows exponentially with the number of machines, m, making the problem intractable. This problem, like almost all deterministic scheduling problems, belongs to the wide class of CO problems, many of which are known to be NP-hard (Garey & Johnson, 1979). What it means is that it is unlikely that efficient exact optimization algorithms exist to solve them. Only a few scheduling problems have been shown to be tractable, in the sense that they are solvable in polynomial time. For the remaining ones, the only way to secure optimal solutions is usually by enumerative methods, requiring exponential time. The investigation has focused on two approaches: developing approximation algorithms, and optimally solving restricted, more tractable, cases. Thus, heuristic methods have been developed, some of them showing an acceptable performance.

Many real life problems can be modeled as permutation flow-shop scheduling ones. On production lines, it is common to find multi-purpose machines carrying out different products. Our experience has been with the ceramic tile manufacturing sector, however many problems could be mentioned when we speak about scarce resources, or machines, dedicated to the production of some goods, or jobs.

Notation

We will use the notation that follows:

- J: set of n jobs J_i ($i=1,...,n$)
- M: set of m machines M_j ($j=1,...,m$)
- p_{ij}: processing time of job J_i on machine M_j
- d_i: due date of job J_i, time limit by which J_i should be completed
- r_i: time at which the job J_i is ready to be processed
- w_i: priority or weight of job J_i
- C_i: completion time of job J_i
- C_{max}: the maximum completion time of all jobs J_i (this is the schedule length, which is also called *makespan*)
- F_i: flow time of job J_i, $F_i = C_i - r_i$, if $r_i = 0$, then $F_i = C_i$
- L_i: lateness of job J_i, $L_i = C_i - d_i$
- T_i: tardiness of job J_i, $T_{max} = \max\{L_i, 0\}$
- E_i: earliness of job J_i, $E_{max} = \max\{-L_i, 0\}$

The optimal value of any criterion is denoted with an asterisk, *e.g.* C^*_{max} denotes the optimal makespan value.

We will use the three-parameter notation, $\alpha / \beta / \gamma$, introduced by Graham et al. (1979), and extended by T'kindt & Billaut (2006) to multicriteria scheduling problems. The first field specifies the machine environment (F represents general permutation flow-shop); the second, job characteristics; and the third refers to the chosen optimality criterion for single criteria models, and it extends to cover multicriteria as well as methodology.

Definitions

Consider a set of n independent jobs J_i ($i=1,...,n$) to be processed, each of them on a set of m machines M_j ($j=1,...,m$), that represent the m stages of the production process. Every job requires a known, deterministic and non-negative processing time, denoted as p_{ij}, for completion at each machine. Each machine processes the jobs in the same order, thus knowing the order of jobs the resulting schedule is entirely fixed. Any feasible solution is then called a *permutation schedule* or a *sequence*.

In a single-criterion problem, we look for the permutation of jobs from set J that would optimize the performance criterion while for more than one criterion the objective is to find out the set of Pareto optimal solutions. French (1982) presents the following classification:

Criteria based upon completion time measures:
- $F_{max} = \max\{F_1, F_2,..., F_n\}$, the maximum flow time
- $C_{max} = \max\{C_1, C_2,..., C_n\}$, the maximum completion time
- $\sum F_i / n$ or $\sum F_i$ mean flow time or total flow time, respectively
- $\sum C_i / n$ or $\sum C_i$ mean completion time or total completion time, respectively

○ $\sum w_i C_i$ weighted completion time

○ $\sum w_i F_i$ weighted flow time

Flow time is applied as a criterion when the cost function is related to the job standing time. Completion time reflects a criterion where the cost depends on the finish time. In the event of all ready times being zero, $r_i=0$, $\forall i$, completion time and flow time functions are identical. Maximum criteria should be used when interest is focused on the whole system. When some jobs are more important than others, weighted measures could be considered.

Criteria based upon due date measures:

○ $L_{max} = \max\{L_1, L_2,..., L_n\}$, maximum lateness

○ $T_{max} = \max\{T_1, T_2,..., T_n\}$, maximum tardiness

○ $\sum L_i / n$ or $\sum L_i$ mean lateness or total lateness, respectively

○ $\sum T_i / n$ or $\sum T_i$ mean tardiness or total tardiness, respectively

○ $\sum w_i L_i$ weighted lateness

○ $\sum w_i T_i$ weighted tardiness

○ $\sum U_i$ total tardy jobs. The indicator function U_i denotes whether the job J_i is tardy, then $U_i = 1$, or on time, then $U_i = 0$.

When maintaining customer satisfaction by observing due dates, or any other *just in time* concept has to be considered, measures related to the notion of how much is lost by not meeting the due dates are applied. If the penalty is applied only to the delays, tardiness measures are used. When there is a positive reward, or penalization, for completing a job early and that reward/penalization is larger the earlier a job is

completed, lateness measures are appropriate. In the case where all the due dates are zero, $d_i=0$, $\forall i$, tardiness or lateness are identical to completion time functions.

All of the above mentioned criteria are regular in the sense that they are non-decreasing functions of job completion times. French's classification includes some non-regular criteria, such as measures based upon the inventory and utilization costs. For example, to measure the idle time of a machine, the following criterion is used:

• $I_j = C_{max} - \sum_{i=1}^{n} p_{ij}$ total time during which machine M_j is waiting for a job or has finished processing jobs, but the total process of jobs has not finished jet.

In the literature, the most common criterion is the makespan. Only a relative few published works are devoted to flow time and tardiness measures.

Computational Complexity

Since the early algorithm presented by Johnson (1954), which solves $F2//C_{max}$ in polynomial time, only a few restricted cases have been shown to be efficiently solvable. Minimizing the sum of completion times is still NP-complete for two machines (Garey & Johnson, 1979).

The following cases have been shown to be NP-hard:

• $F/p_{ij}=1$, *intree*, r_i/C_{max}
• $F/p_{ij}=1$, *prec*/C_{max}
• $F2/chains/C_{max}$
• $F2/chains, pmtn/C_{max}$
• $F2/r_i/C_{max}$
• $F2/r_i, pmtn/C_{max}$
• $F3//C_{max}$
• $F3/pmtn/C_{max}$
• $F/p_{ij}=1$, *outtree*/L_{max}
• $F2//L_{max}$

- $F2/pmtn/L_{max}$
- $F2//\sum C_i$
- $F2/pmtn/\sum C_i$
- $Fm/p_{ij}=1, chains/\sum w_i C_i$
- $Fm/p_{ij}=1, chains/\sum U_i$ for each $m\geq 2$
- $Fm/p_{ij}=1, chains/\sum T_i$ for each $m\geq 2$

Assumptions

Unless explicitly indicated, in the text that follows we assume that:

- Each job is an entity, composed of m operations, which cannot be processed on more than one machine simultaneously.
- At every machine, there are no precedence constraints among operations of different jobs.
- No preemption is allowed. That is to say, once an operation has started, it must be completed before another operation may initiate on the same machine.
- No cancellation. Each job must be finished.
- Processing times are independent of sequencing.
- Job accumulation is allowed. Jobs can be waiting for a free machine.
- Machine idle time is allowed. The machines can be waiting for jobs or for the end of the total process.
- No machine can process more than one job simultaneously.
- Machines never break down and are available throughout the scheduling period.
- Ready times are zero for all jobs.
- There is no randomness:
- the number of jobs, n, is known and fixed;
- the number of machines, m, is known and fixed;
- the processing times, p_{ij} ($i=1,...,n; j=1,...,m$), are known and fixed;

- all other specifications, needed to define a particular problem, are known and fixed.

The assumptions listed above characterize the classical permutation flow-shop models. However, it is possible to find in the literature variants of permutation flow-shop problems which do not accomplish these features.

Review of Permutation Flow-Shop Scheduling Algorithms, Considering Only a Single-Criterion

Despite the large amount of papers dealing with flow-shop problems, most of the research has been devoted to the permutation problem. From the pioneer paper by Johnson (1954) until the present day, a lot of papers devoted to permutation flow-shop problem have been published. The majority of them consider the problem of minimizing the makespan.

The rule of Johnson to minimize the makespan states that job i must precede job k in a sequence if

$$\min\{p_{i1}, p_{k2}\} < \min\{p_{k1}, p_{i2}\}.$$

Thus, jobs with shorter processing time in the first machine are set to be processed before, and jobs with shorter processing time in the second machine are set to be processed after. The algorithm that applies this rule is optimal for $m=2$, and can approximate solutions for $m>2$ (Campbell et al., 1970).

For the problem restricted to $n=2$ and general m, the graphical method due to Akers (1956) gets the minimum makespan (Brucker, 1988).

Ignall & Schrage (1965) and Lomnicki (1965) propose the earliest Branch and Bound (B&B) algorithms applied to permutation flow-shop. Lageweg et al. (1978) presents a general bounding scheme for permutation flow-shop problem, considering makespan. Though the original intention was to improve B&B techniques (in vogue at the time of its publication), their contributions are still useful in saving computational effort when looking for non-dominated solutions (Mokotoff, 2009). Potts (1980) presents a branching rule. Selen & Hott (1986) proposes a Goal Programming formulation. Taillard (1993) presents, besides a set of very useful benchmarks, a lower bound for the makespan. Carlier & Rebaï (1996) presents two B&B algorithms.

Heuristics and metaheuristics have been mainly developed for CO problems. In contrast to exact methods that guarantee optimality, heuristic methods seek near optimal solutions in a reasonably bounded time. Metaheuristics are more general than heuristics, in the sense that they are applicable to different problems, while heuristics are usually problem-dependent.

A constructive algorithm builds a solution, starting from the input data (without it being necessary to know a previous feasible solution), following a set of rules. There is a class of algorithms which share a similar way of making a schedule: a sorting list with all the jobs is made. The accuracy of any *list scheduling* algorithm is intimately related to the priority rule applied. There are more than one hundred dispatching rules, as can be seen in Panwalkar & Iskander (1977) and Haupt (1989).

The most important constructive algorithms dedicated to the *F//Cmax* problem can be classified by their design as a list scheduling algorithm. In order to minimize the makespan, the list of jobs must be made in such a way as to give higher priority to the jobs consuming more total processing time. That is to say, the jobs with the longest total processing time should not be placed at the last positions of the list. Based on this premise, a simple algorithm is presented by Nawaz et al. (1983) (NEH algorithm, in the following). NEH algorithm produces very good sequences in comparison with heuristics existing even up to the present. The results of the proposed algorithm show that it performs especially well on large flow-shop problems, in both the static and dynamic sequencing environments. Taillard (1990) presents an important improvement in saving computational effort for the NEH algorithm.

Gupta (1972) presents three algorithms to deal with total flow time and maximum flow time (not simultaneously). Laha & Chakraborty (2009) and Rajendran (1993) present constructive algorithms for the $F//\Sigma C_i$ problem. The first one is based on the principle of job insertion, and the second one could be thought as an extension of the NEH algorithm and performs very well.

Improvement algorithms need a feasible solution as starting-point and are intended to improve it by iterative small changes. This iterative improvement can be achieved by means of many different processes.

Threshold algorithms are designed according to three techniques: Iterative Improvement, Threshold Accepting and Simulated Annealing (SA), the most popular one.

Considering $F//C_{max}$, Osman & Potts (1989) presents four SA algorithms varying the neighbouring generating method. Their results show that insertion performs better than swapping. The SA algorithms presented by Nowicki & Zdrzałka (1990) have similar performance than Osman & Potts (1989). Only the algorithm presented in Ishibuchi et al. (1995) seems to perform better for large instances. Laha & Chakraborty (2007) introduces SA in the NEH algorithm and Wodecki & Bozejko (2002) presents a parallel SA.

Parthasarathy & Rajendran (1997) presents an application of SA to the $F//\Sigma w_i T_i$. In this paper, the authors introduced the Random Insertion Perturbation Scheme that is employed in some later papers.

In Laha & Chakraborty (2008) SA is applied to solve the $F//\Sigma C_i$ problem. Liu & Reeves (2001) and Rajendran & Ziegler (2004 and 2005) consider also this problem, Liu & Reeves (2001) using pairwise exchange and Rajendran & Ziegler (2004 and 2005) using Ant Colony Optimization (ACO). Rajendran & Ziegler (1997) presents heuristics dealing with the total weighted flow time.

Based on Johnson's rule, Koulamas (1998) proposes an improvement heuristic which uses job passing.

Tabu Search (TS) is probably the most tested local search concerned with scheduling problems. Some applications to the flow-shop scheduling problem have been presented in: Taillard (1990) and Reeves (1993) and, more recently, in Grabowski & Wodecki (2004).

Unlike the previously-mentioned techniques, Genetic and Evolutionary Algorithms (GA and EA, respectively, in the following) start with a set of solutions instead of only one: Reeves (1995) applies GA to the flow-shop scheduling problem. Differential evolutionary optimization is applied to permutation flow-shop scheduling problem for minimizing makespan, mean flow time and total tardiness, individually considered, in Onwubolu & Davendra (2006).

Research on metaheuristics is quite extensive. Ruiz & Maroto (2005) and Dorn et al. (1996) survey this field.

Real-life scheduling problems require more than one criterion. Nevertheless, the complex nature of flow-shop scheduling has prevented the development of models with multiple criteria. In the following, we will consider the Multicriterion Flow-Shop Scheduling problems.

For further information about deterministic scheduling and flow-shop, considering only single-criterion problems, we refer the reader to the books and PhD thesis of: Blazewicz et al. (2007); Brucker (2004); Ruiz (2003); Pinedo (2002); Andrés (2001); Schulz (1996) and Parker (1995); or the survey papers of: Lawler et al. (1993); Dudek et al. (1992); Monma & Rinnooy Kan (1983) and the earliest Baker (1975).

MULTICRITERIA ANALYSIS FOR COMBINATORIAL OPTIMIZATION PROBLEMS

Quality is, in real-life, a multidimensional notion. A schedule is valued on the basis of a number of criteria, for example: makespan, work-in-process inventories, idle times, observance of due dates, etc. If only one criterion is taken into account, no matter what criterion is considered, some aspect of the quality of the schedule will result regardless. An appropriate schedule can not be obtained unless one observes the whole set of important criteria. The multidimensional nature of the problem at hand leads us to the area of Multicriteria Optimization (see Ehrgott & Wiecek, 2005, for a state of the art).

When a problem appears as a multicriteria case, it is necessary to take into account different objective functions. The solution may vary according to the criterion considered individually. If the criteria are not conflicting, it is possible to obtain a global optimal solution. In the vast majority of cases, they are conflicting and thus the knowledge of the decision-maker preferences is necessary to solve the problem.

Considering only one regular criterion, general scheduling problems belong to the CO field and they have been shown to be NP-hard (except for restricted special cases).

Even though MDM, as well as CO, have been intensively studied by many researchers for many years, it is surprising that a combination of both, *i.e.* MOCO, was not widely studied until the last decade, as it is not long since interest in this field has been shown. The proliferation of metaheuristic techniques has encouraged researchers to apply them to this highly complex problem.

In this section, we will present a brief introduction to MOCO problems, including a general problem formulation, the most important theoretical properties, the existing methods for dealing with them, and the analysis of performance.

Formulation of a MOCO Problem

A MOCO problem is a discrete optimization problem, where each feasible solution X has n variables, x_i, constrained by a specific structure, and there are K objective functions, z_k, to be optimized. Without loss of generality we can formulate the problem as follows:

$$\underset{X \in D}{Min}\ z_k(X),\ k = 1, ..., K$$

where functions z_k are the objectives, X is the vector that represents a feasible solution (a sequence for the flow-shop scheduling problem), and D is the set of feasible solutions, a discrete set.

The criteria (reviewed in section 2.2) are of two different kinds:

- sum function: $\sum f_i$
- bottleneck function: $f_{max} = \max\{f_1, f_2, ..., f_n\}$

We call a feasible solution $X^{(e)} \in D$ efficient, non-dominated, or Pareto optimal, if there is no other feasible solution $X \in D$ such that,

$$z_k(X) \leq z_k(X^{(e)}),\ \forall k$$

with at least one strict inequality.

The corresponding vector of objective values,

$$z\left(X^{(e)}\right) = \left\{ z_1\left(X^{(e)}\right), z_2\left(X^{(e)}\right), ..., z_K\left(X^{(e)}\right) \right\}$$

is called non-dominated vector.

The set of feasible Efficient solutions, $X^{(e)}$, is denoted by E, and the set of non-dominated vectors by ND.

Some Theoretical Concepts

A general result for Multi-Objective Linear Programming (MLP) problems is that the set of efficient solutions to

$$\min\{\mathbf{c}X: AX = \mathbf{b}, X \geq 0\}$$

is exactly the set of solutions to

$$\min\{ \sum_{j=1,...K} \lambda_j c_j X : AX = \mathbf{b}, X \geq 0\} \qquad,$$

where

$$\sum_{j=1,...K} \lambda_j = 1,\ \lambda_j > 0, j = 1, ...K \qquad.$$

It is important to point out that we are dealing with a CO problem, which means that the transformation of the objective functions into a linear function (aggregating into weighted sums) does not transform the problem into a Linear Programming (LP) one. Except in some special cases, *e.g.* preemption allowance, or where idle time insertion is advantageous, for which LP can be applied, the discrete structure of a MOCO problem persists. An important consequence is the fact that the previous result for MLP is not valid, so there could be some efficient solutions not optimal for any weighted sum of the objectives (Ehrgott & Gandibleux, 2002). The set of these solutions are named Non-supported Efficient (NE) solutions, whereas the set of the remaining ones are called Supported Efficient (SE) solutions.

The cardinality of the NE set depends on the number of sum objective functions. For a problem with more than one sum objective function, NE has many more solutions than SE.

Despite these results which constitute the essence of the difficulty of MOCO problems, many published works ignore the existence of NE.

Concerning computational complexity, in obtaining the set of efficient solutions MOCO problems are in general NP-complete. Results are presented by Ehrgott (2000). The cardinality of E for a MOCO problem may be exponential in the problem size (Emelichev & Perepelista, 1992), therefore algorithms could determine just an approximation of E in many cases. Thus, methods may be exact or approximate, and metaheuristics and hyperheuristics are nowadays being applied intensively to MOCO problems.

Multicriteria Optimization Methods

The minimization concept in the above formulation is not restricted to one meaning. Besides the typical classification of optimization methods into exact or approximate, multicriteria optimization methods can be classified by different characteristics.

The MDM always assumes that subjective considerations, such as the decision-maker preferences, have to intervene. Thus, it is usual to distinguish the MDM methods according to when the decision-maker intervenes in the resolution process, as follows:

- *a priori*: All the preferences are known at the beginning of the decision-making process. The search for the solution is carried out on the basis of the known information.
- *interactive*: The decision-maker intervenes during the search process. Computing steps alternate with dialogue steps. At each step a satisfying compromise determination is achieved. It requires the intensive participation of the decision-maker.
- *a posteriori*: The set of efficient solutions (the complete set or an approximation of it) is generated. This set can be analyzed according to the decision-maker prefer-

ences. The choice of a solution from the set of efficient solutions is an *a posteriori* approach.

If the problem criteria show a hierarchical structure, more important criteria should be minimized before less important ones. Thus, optimization methods can be classified as hierarchical or simultaneous.

In bi-criteria models, if z_1 is more important than z_2, then it seem to be natural to minimize with respect to z_1 first, and choose, from among these optimal solutions, the optimum with respect to z_2. This hierarchical approach is called *lexicographic* optimization, and is denoted by $\alpha/\beta/Lex(z_1, z_2)$.

In a general case, lexicographic minimization consists in comparing the objective values of a feasible solution X, with respect to another Y, in a lexicographical order, denoted by $<_{lex}$. Objective functions are ranked according to their importance. We say $X <_{lex} Y$, if, and only if, there is a j such that $z_j(X) <_j z_j(Y)$, and there is not any $h < j$, such that $z_h(Y) <_h z_h(X)$. This means that the first objective function index, $i \in \{1,...,K\}$, for which $z_i(X)$, is not equal to $z_i(Y)$, $z_i(X) < z_i(Y)$.

Simultaneous optimization has to be applied when there is no dominant relation among the criteria. Optimizing with respect to one criterion at a time leads to unbalanced results. It is common, in a case such as this, to use a composite objective function with the original criteria. It gives rise to another classification, because we can generate solutions by means of scalarization and non-scalarizing methods.

Scalarization is made by means of a real-valued scalarizing on the objective functions of the original problem (Wierzbicki, 1980). Well-known examples of scalarization methods are commented in the following.

The *weighted sum* approach consists in building a new objective criterion with the original ones (Isermann, 1977). This composite function can be linear (in the majority of cases), where the scalar coefficients represent the relative importance of every criterion, or it may present a more complex composition. Despite the apparent simplicity of the methods, it conceals two difficulties:

1. The difficulty of expressing the decision-maker preferences by means of a function. Interactive approaches overcome this drawback, *e.g. Analytic Hierarchy Process* could be useful (Saaty, 1980).
2. The computational complexity of minimizing the function in a direct manner.

The set of all SE solutions can be found considering a wide diversified set of weights (Parametric Programming may be used to solve this problem). Selen & Hott (1986) and Wilson (1989) apply this technique to the $F//f(\Sigma C_i, C_{max})$, where f is a linear combination. Shmoys & Tardos (1993) proposes a linear combination of the makespan and a total cost function, for unrelated parallel machine models.

The *distance to the ideal point* approach (Horsky & Rao, 1984) consists in minimizing the distance to an ideal solution. The ideal point is settled according to the optimum of each individual single-criterion. It is also known as the *compromise solution* method.

The *ε-constraint* (Chankong & Haimes, 1983) and the *Target-Vector* approaches are scalarization as well as hierarchical methods. A constraint system representing levels ε_i of satisfaction, for some criteria, is established, and the objective is to find a solution, which provides a value, as close as possible, to the pre-defined goal for each objective. A single-objective minimization subject to constraints of levels ε_i for the other objective functions is formulated. The formulation is solved for different levels ε_i, to generate the entire Pareto optimal set. Some authors consider that the main criteria must be fixed by constraints, others put the main criteria in the objective of the formulation by turn. It would depend on the mathematical programs to solve. Leung & Young (1989) and Eck & Pinedo (1993) present algorithms to minimize the makespan, subject to a determined flow time level (the first one is devoted to preemptive job models). González & Johnson (1980) proposes minimizing the makespan, subject to a bound on the number of preemptions. Sin (1989) considers the problem of minimizing the makespan and the number of preemptions, for a set of jobs, constrained to due dates.

When a set of goals for each criterion is known, the target vector approaches are appropriate. The most popular is *Goal Programming* (introduced by Charnes & Cooper, 1961), for which the minimization of the deviation from the specified goals is the aim.

Non-scalarizing approaches do not explicitly use this kind of scalarizing function. For example, *Lexicographic* and *Max-ordering* are non-scalarizing approaches.

Max-ordering chooses the alternative with the minimum value of the worst values. After a normalization process, z_j is the worst value of X, if and only if,

$$z_j\left(X\right) = \max\left\{z_1\left(X\right), z_2\left(X\right), ..., z_K\left(X\right)\right\}$$

Then, X is the best alternative, if, and only if, there is not Y such that $z_{j(y)}(Y) < z_{j(x)}(X)$.

The *two phases* method by Ulungu (1993) consists in determining the set of SE solutions by means of a weighted sum scalarization algorithm, and then, in the second phase, searching for the NE solutions, following a specific problem-dependent method.

Only a few algorithms have been developed based on B&B techniques for MOCO problems (Ehrgott & Gandibleux, 2001). On the other hand, approximation for MOO is a research area which has gained increasing interest in recent years. Multi-objective metaheuristics seek an approximate set of Pareto optimal solutions. The main question is how to ensure that the obtained non-dominated set covers the Pareto front as widely as possible. In the beginning, methods were adaptations of single-objective optimization. Nowadays they have their own entity. They are initially inspired by EA or neighbourhood search. Furthermore, recent developments are more hybridized, given rise to Multi-Objective Hyperheuristic (MOH) methods. A MOH can be thought as a heuristic method, which iteratively selects the most suitable heuristic amongst many (Burke et al., 2003).

The problem of obtaining a uniformly distributed set of non-dominated solutions is of great concern in Pareto optimization. The specification of the search direction, by tuning weights, is the method that directly attempts to drive the current solution towards the desired region of the trade-off frontier. Hyperheuristic approaches attempt to do it by applying the neighbourhood search heuristic that is more likely to drive the solution in the desired direction. This technique can be applied to single-solution and population-based algorithms.

A priori methods assume that the decision-maker preferences can be expressed. The hierarchical approach penalizes too much the less important criteria, while setting a criterion as the most important one. In reality, the decision-maker preferences are usually smooth, giving less importance to the main criterion and more to the less important criteria. Considering a composite function of the criteria involved in the problem, it is implicitly assumed that the decision-maker preferences are accurately reflected in this objective function. The decision-maker knows the preferable schedule, but it is not easy to express this preference in a function. In general, *a priori* approaches give a solution to the problem that cannot usually be trusted to be the most preferred solution.

To be confident with a particular solution to a problem with multiple objectives, the decision-maker active involvement is required. In interactive methods, she indicates their preferences during the process of solution, guiding the search direction. Agrawal et al. (2008) proposes an interactive

particle-swarm metaheuristic for MOO. The approach presented by Jaszkiewicz & Ferhat (1999) can be placed between the *a priori* and interactive procedures. They present a method that includes some interaction with the decision-maker, but is based on the assumption that decision-maker preferences are already relatively well defined at the beginning of the solution process.

For methods that should offer an approximation of the complete set of efficient solutions, it is guaranteed that no potential preferable solution has been eliminated, but the number of efficient solutions can be overwhelmingly high to warrant proper examination by the decision-maker (*a posteriori* approaches).

In this chapter, we focus on the flow-shop problem. We refer he reader to the following papers for further information on MOCO:

- Ulungu & Teghem (1994) and Ehrgott & Gandibleux (2002), for general MOCO theory.
- Landa-Silva et al. (2004) and Jones et al. (2002), for overviews on metaheuristics.
- Jaszkiewicz (2004), for a comparison of metaheuristics for bi-criteria optimization.
- Aickelin (1999) and Jaszkiewicz (2004), for Multi-Objective Genetic Algorithms (MOGA). For general Multi-Objective Evolutionary Algorithms (MOEA), to Zitzler (1999), Coello & Mariano (2002) and Geiger (2007).
- Serafini (1992), Ulungu (1993), Hapke et al. (1998) and Loukil et al. (2005), for Multi-Objective Simulated Annealing (MOSA).
- Gandibleux et al. (1997), for Multi-Objective TS.

Evaluation of Multi-Objective Pareto Methods

For the MOO algorithms, the analysis of performance is more complex than for single-objective ones. The goal of multiple objective Pareto procedures is to find a good approximation of the set of efficient solutions. It is unlikely that the whole set of Efficient solutions (E) is fully known. While the outcomes from compared algorithms are different, they can still be all equally Pareto efficient.

Usually, the three following conditions are considered as desirable for a good multi-objective algorithm:

- The distance of the obtained set of Potentially Efficient solutions (PE) to the E should be minimized.
- The distribution of the solutions in PE should be uniform.
- The larger the number of obtained solutions, *i.e.* [PE], the better the algorithm.

The last two conditions present more weaknesses than strengths. If E does not present a uniform distribution, or [E]=1, the algorithm that obtains the proper E will not fulfil these conditions. Furthermore, an algorithm that just reports a huge number of solutions does not ensure their quality (in terms of efficiency). To have an idea of quality, a reference set of E (R, in the following) should be considered. The ideal R is the set E. However, for MOCO problems it is unlikely that the whole E is known (except for small size instances, with non-practical application). A useful practice is having a set R as close to E as possible, then filtering the PE output with R, to obtain a net set of non-dominated solutions

N={X is Pareto efficient in $\left(PE \cup R \right)$}

N will be at least as good as R. One can measure the quality of the output as the percentage of solutions in PE that survive the filtering process with R:

$$Q_1(PE) = \frac{\left[PE \cap N \right]}{\left[PE \right]} 100\%$$

Czyzak & Jaszkiewicz (1998) presents a quality measure of the percentage of reference solutions found by the algorithm:

$$Q_2(PE) = \frac{\left[PE \cap R \right]}{\left[R \right]} 100\%$$

Both of the above metrics are cardinal.

In the case of real-life MOCO problems, it may be impossible to obtain, in a reasonable time, a significant percentage of efficient solutions. In this case, obtaining near-efficient solutions would also be highly appreciated. Following Knowles & Corne (2002), a more general and economic criterion may be to concentrate on evaluating the distance of solutions to the efficient frontier. The *Dist1R* and *Dist2R* metrics by Czyzak & Jaszkiewicz (1998), can serve this purpose. We suggest using them because they are not difficult to compute, and they seem to be complementary to the C metric by Zitzler (1999), when compared according to the properties analyzed by Knowles & Corne (2002).

The C metric, also a cardinal measure, compares two sets of PE, A and B. A reference set, R, is not required and it is really easy to compute as:

$$C(A,B) = \frac{\left[b \in B \, / \, \exists a \in A : a \prec b \right]}{\left[B \right]}$$

The following statements can aid the understanding of $C(A,B)$:

- If $C(A,B)$=1, all solutions in B are weakly dominated by A.
- If $C(A,B)$=0, none of the solutions in B are weakly dominated by A.

When two algorithms are compared, $C(A,B)$ and $C(B,A)$ must be computed, because they are not necessary complementary. Unless $C(A,B)=1$ and $C(B,A)<1$, it is not possible to establish that A weakly outperfoms B.

The non-cardinal measures $Dist1R$ and $Dist2R$ require R to be obtained. Their computations, although more complicated than C, do not imply a high complexity. They are based on an achievement scalarizing function:

$$d(X,Y) = \max_{k=1,\dots K} \left\{ 0, \lambda_k (z_k(Y) - z_k(X)) \right\}$$

where $X \in R$, $Y \in PE$, and

$$\lambda_k = \frac{1}{\left(\max_{X \in R} z_k(X) - \min_{X \in R} z_k(X) \right)}$$

$Dist1R$ is defined as:

$$Dist1_R (PE) = \frac{1}{[R]} \sum_{x \in R} \left\{ \min_{Y \in PE} \left\{ d(X,Y) \right\} \right\}$$

While $Dist1R$ measures the mean distance, over the points in R, of the nearest point in PE, $Dist2R$ gives the worst case distance, thus it is defined as:

$$Dist2_R (PE) = \max_{X \in R} \left\{ \min_{Y \in PE} \left\{ d(X,Y) \right\} \right\}$$

The lower the values the better PE approximates R. Moreover, the lower the ratio $Dist2R/Dist1R$ the more uniform the distribution of solutions from PE over R. $Dist1R$ induces a complete ordering and let to weak outperformance relations.

Combining PE yielded by different algorithms for an instance problem, a net set of non-dominated solutions, N, is obtained. The N set is very useful as R for the evaluation of the new developments. An important contribution is updating the published N set obtained for benchmark instances.

SURVEY OF MULTICRITERIA FLOW-SHOP SCHEDULING ALGORITHMS

In this section we will focus on published algorithms devoted to multicriteria flow-shop scheduling problems. For further information on general multicriteria scheduling algorithms, we refer to the following papers:

- Nowicki & Zdrzałka (1990) presents a survey of the field of scheduling with controllable processing times.
- Gordon et al. (2002) focuses on due date assignment models.
- Hoogeveen (2005) includes an overview of the bi-criteria worst-case analysis.
- Landa-Silva et al. (2004) reviews meta-heuristics for general multi-objective problems and presents the application of these techniques to scheduling problems.

For exhaustive surveys of multicriteria scheduling problems, see:

- Ruiz-Díaz & French (1983)
- Nagar et al. (1995a)
- T'kindt & Billaut (2001)

The book of T'kindt & Billaut (2006) can be useful as a good comprehensive reference work on multicriteria scheduling.

Permutation flow-shop scheduling research has been mostly restricted to the treatment of one objective at a time. Furthermore, attention focused on the makespan criterion. However, the total flow time performance measure has also received some attention. These two measures, each of which is a regular performance measure, constitute a conflicting pair of objectives (Rinnooy Kan, 1976). Specifically, the total flow time criterion is a work in process inventory performance measure whereas the makespan criterion is equivalent to the mean utilization performance measure. While total flow time is a customer-oriented performance measure, the makespan criterion is a firm-oriented performance measure. Therefore, the set of efficient solutions to a bi-criteria model that seeks to optimize both measures simultaneously would contain valuable trade-off information, crucial to the decision-maker, who has to identify the most preferable solution, according to her preferences.

Solving a bi-criteria model for a general number of machines implies heavy computational requirements, since both criteria makespan and total flow time, lead to NP-hard problems even when they are treated individually ($F3//C_{max}$ and $F2//\Sigma C_i$ are NP-hard in the strong sense). The majority of initial research on bi-criteria flow-shop problems concerns the two-machine case, in which some combination of ΣC_i and C_{max} has to be minimized. Because any lexicographic approach including ΣC_i will be NP-hard, research effort is being concentrated on approximate algorithms.

In the following, we summarize the published results for each case problem.

$F2//\Sigma C_i, C_{max}$

Rajendran (1992), Neppalli et al. (1996), Gupta et al. (2001) and T'kindt et al. (2003), present lexicographical approaches, where the total flow time has to be minimized among the schedules that minimize the makespan.

Local search algorithms based on ACO have been proposed by T'kindt et al (2002).

Huang & Lim (2003) presents a technique named Local Dynamic Programming.

T'kindt et al. (2003) presents a B&B algorithm, which can solve problem instances of up to 35 jobs to optimality.

Sayin & Karabati (1999) presents an *a posteriori* approach based on B&B.

$F2//f(\Sigma C_i, C_{max})$

Nagar et al. (1995b) and Sivrikaya-Serifoglu & Ulusoy (1998), present heuristics and B&B algorithms.

$F2//f(C_{max}, T_{max})$

Daniels & Chambers (1990) presents an exact B&B.

$F2//f(C_{max}, \Sigma U_i)$ and $F2//f(C_{max}, \Sigma T_i)$

Liao et al. (1997) presents B&B algorithms.

$F//f(\Sigma C_i, C_{max})$

Selen & Hott (1986) and Wilson (1989), present a Mixed Integer Formulation considering a linear combination of makespan and flow time.

Chang et al. (2002) proposes a MOGA algorithm based on the concept of *gradual priority weighting*. The search process starts along the direction of the first selected objective function, and progresses such that the weight for the first objective function decreases gradually, and the weight for the second objective function increases gradually.

$F//\Sigma C_i, C_{max}$

Bagchi (1999) presents a MOGA that improves a previous MOGA presented by Srinivas & Deb (1995). Pasupathy et al. (2006) presents a MOGA based on ranks that are computed by means of crowding distances.

Varadharajan & Rajendran (2005) and Mokotoff (2009), present MOSA algorithms. The first one is based on a similar idea than Chang et al. (2002), whereas the second one is based on the concept of Pareto dominance.

Framinan et al. (2002) investigates *a priori* and *a posteriori* heuristics. The *a posteriori* heuristic uncovers non-dominated solutions by varying the weight criteria in an effective way.

Rajendran & Ziegler (2009) applies ACO techniques.

$F//C_{max}, \Sigma T_i$

Talbi et al. (2001) and Arroyo & Armentano (2005), propose Multi-Objective Local Search (MOLS) based on the concept of Pareto dominance. The first one applies MOLS when a simplification of Genetic Local Search stops. The last one includes preservation of dispersion in the population, elitism, and use of a parallel bi-objective local search so as intensify the search in distinct regions.

$F//C_{max}, T_{max}$

Arroyo & Armentano (2005) applies their MOLS algorithm to this problem.

$F//f(C_{max}, T_{max})$

Daniels & Chambers (1990) present an approximate B&B.

$F//\Sigma C_i, C_{max}, \Sigma I_j$

Ho & Chang (1991) and Rajendran (1995), propose heuristic procedures based on the idea of minimizing the gaps between the completion times of jobs on adjacent machines (one of the improvement techniques used by Mokotoff, 2009, was inspired by this mechanism).

Yagmahan & Yenisey (2008) applies ACO.

$F//$many Criteria

Dorn et al. (1996) presents a comparison of four iterative improvement techniques for flow-shop scheduling problems that differ in local search methodology. These techniques are iterative deepening, random search, TS and GA. The evaluation function is defined according to the gradual satisfaction of explicitly represented domain constraints and optimization functions. The problem is constrained by a greater variety of antagonistic criteria that are partly contradictory.

$F//f(\Sigma C_i, C_{max}, \Sigma T_i)$

Murata et al. (1996) presents a MOGA based on a weighted sum of objective functions with variable weights. This algorithm belongs to the class of MOEA and it has been improved in Ishibuchi & Murata (1998) by adding a local search procedure to the offspring.

Chang et al. (2007) applies subpopulation GA. Artificial chromosomes are created and introduced into the evolution process to improve the efficiency and the quality of the solution.

$F//$inventory cost function of: earliness, tardiness and work in process

Bülbül et al. (2003) applies Dantzig-Wolfe reformulation and Lagrangian relaxation to an Integer Programming formulation.

Comparison and Study

Geiger (2007) presents a study of the problem structure and the effectiveness of local search neighbourhoods within an evolutionary search framework.

Minella et al. (2007) and Zitzler & Thiele (1999) are previous surveys focusing on MOEA that include computational comparison for the Pareto approach.

CONCLUSION

In this paper, we have attempted to present a survey encompassing Multicriteria Flow-Shop Scheduling problems. Because they have important applications in Management Science, these models have been intensively studied during the last years. Considerable progress has been made toward presenting effective solutions to practical problems, especially with the proliferation of metaheuristic approaches. Some variants, *e.g.* setup depending on the sequence, have been investigated and well solved by means of *meta* and, more recently, *hyper* heuristic techniques.

However, to obtain the exact set of *PE* solutions for these problems efficiently is not a plausible accomplishment since the single criterion problems are NP-hard in itself.

Therefore, it is necessary to distinguish between two different questions: the first one is to efficiently solving real problems, whose complexity is ever increasing; the second one is focusing on the rigorous mathematical approaches to find an analytically satisfactory answer to each problem structure.

About the first question, we think that recent published results give support to the hypothesis which states that more hybridized approaches, *i.e.* hyperheuristics, perform better than traditional metaheuristics. MOH combine different heuristic techniques that are selected according to their suitability, at each iteration. It is not realistic to hope for general meta-optimization methods that solve MOCO problems efficiently. Hyperheuristic approaches constitute a fruitful line of research.

With respect to the second question, the exhaustive theoretical study of the structure and properties of each problem may be one of the most challenging goals of MOCO.

Due to the complexity of evaluating the quality of different algorithms, we include in this paper a revision of different metrics. In this sense, we want to emphasize the importance of the useful practice of reporting a Net set of *PE* solution obtained for the benchmark problems of Taillard (1993) by the algorithms proposed in the corresponding paper. Moreover, we suggest reporting the following metrics: Q_1, Q_2, C, *Dist1R* and *Dist2R* to evaluate the different attributes of the proposed methods (see section 3.4.)

ACKNOWLEDGMENT

This research was in part supported by the Research Projects ECO2008-05895-C02-02, Ministerio de Ciencia e Innovación, Spain.

REFERENCES

Agrawal, S., Dashora, Y., Tiwari, M. K., & Son, Y. J. (2008). Interactive Particle Swarm: A Pareto-Adaptive Metaheuristic to Multiobjective Optimization. *IEEE Transactions on Systems, Man and Cybernetics – Part A, 38*(2), 258-277.

Aickelin, U. (1999). *Genetic Algorithms for Multiple-Choice Problems*. Unpublished doctoral dissertation, University of Wales, Swansea.

Akers, S. B. (1956). A graphical approach to production scheduling problems. *Operations Research, 4*, 244–245. doi:10.1287/opre.4.2.244

Andrés, C. (2001) *Programación de la Producción en Talleres de Flujo Híbridos con Tiempos de Cambio de Partida Dependientes de la Secuencia: Modelos, Métodos y Algoritmos de Resolución: Aplicación a Empresas del Sector Cerámico.* Unpublished doctoral dissertation, Universidad Politécnica de Valencia, Valencia.

Arroyo, J., & Armentano, V. (2005). Genetic local search for multi-objective flowshop scheduling problems. *European Journal of Operational Research, 167*, 717–738. doi:10.1016/j.ejor.2004.07.017

Bagchi, T. P. (1999). *Multiobjective Scheduling by Genetic Algorithms*. Dordrecht, The Netherlands: Kluwer Academic Publishers.

Baker, K. R. (1975). A comparative study of flow shop algorithms. *Operations Research, 23*, 62–73. doi:10.1287/opre.23.1.62

Blazewicz, J., Ecker, K., Pesch, E., Schmidt, G., & Weglarz, J. (2007). *Handbook on Scheduling*. Berlin: Springer.

Brucker, P. (1988). An efficient algorithm for the job-shop problem with two jobs. *Computing, 40*, 353–359. doi:10.1007/BF02276919

Brucker, P. (2004). *Scheduling Algorithms*. Berlin: Springer.

Bülbül, K., Kaminsky, P., & Yano, C. (2004). Flow shop scheduling with earliness, tardiness, and intermediate inventory holding costs. *Naval Research Logistics, 51*, 407–445. doi:10.1002/nav.20000

Burke, E. K., Landa-Silva, J. D., & Soubeiga, E. (2003). Hyperheuristic Approaches for Multiobjective Optimization. In *The Fifth Metaheuristics International Conference* (pp. 052.1-052.6). Kyoto: The University of Tokyo.

Campbell, H. G., Dudek, R. A., & Smith, M. L. (1970). A Heuristic Algorithm for the n Job, m Machine Sequencing Problem. *Management Science, 16*(10), 630–637. doi:10.1287/mnsc.16.10.B630

Carlier, J., & Rebaï, I. (1996). Two branch and bound algorithms for the permutation flow shop problem. *European Journal of Operational Research, 90*, 238–251. doi:10.1016/0377-2217(95)00352-5

Chang, P. C., Chen, S. H., & Liu, C. H. (2007). Sub-population genetic algorithm with mining gene structures for multiobjective flowshop scheduling problems. *Expert Systems with Applications, 33*, 762–777. doi:10.1016/j.eswa.2006.06.019

Chang, P. C., Hsieh, J.-C., & Lin, S. G. (2002). The development of gradual priority weighting approach for the multi-objective flowshop scheduling problem. *International Journal of Production Economics, 79*, 171–183. doi:10.1016/S0925-5273(02)00141-X

Chankong, V., & Haimes, Y. Y. (1983). *Multiobjective Decision Making Theory and Methodology*. New York: Elsevier Science.

Charnes, A., & Cooper, W. (1961). *Management Models and Industrial Applications of Linear Programming*. New York: John Wiley and Sons.

Coello, C., & Mariano, C. (2002). Algorithms and Multiple Objective. In Ehrgott, M., & Gandibleux, X. (Eds.), *Multiple Criteria Optimization. State of the Art Annotated Bibliographic Surveys* (pp. 277–331). Boston: Kluwer Academic Publishers.

Czyzak, P., & Jaszkiewicz, A. (1998). Pareto Simulated Annealing – A meta-heuristic technique for multiple objective combinatorial optimization. *Journal on Multi-Criteria Decision Analysis, 7*, 34–47. doi:10.1002/(SICI)1099-1360(199801)7:1<34::AID-MCDA161>3.0.CO;2-6

Daniels, R. L., & Chambers, R. J. (1990). Multiobjective flow-shop scheduling. *Naval Research Logistics, 37*, 981–995. doi:10.1002/1520-6750(199012)37:6<981::AID-NAV3220370617>3.0.CO;2-H

Dorn, J., Girsch, M., Skele, G., & Slany, W. (1996). Comparison of iterative improvement techniques for schedule optimization. *European Journal of Operational Research, 94*, 349–361. doi:10.1016/0377-2217(95)00162-X

Dudek, R. A., Panwalkar, S. S., & Smith, M. L. (1992). The lessons of flowshop scheduling research. *Operations Research, 40*, 7–13. doi:10.1287/opre.40.1.7

Eck, B. T., & Pinedo, M. (1993). On the minimization of the makespan subject to flowtime optimality. *Operations Research, 41*, 797–801. doi:10.1287/opre.41.4.797

Ehrgott, M. (2000). Approximation algorithms for combinatorial multicriteria optimization problems. *International Transactions in Operational Research, 7*, 5–31. doi:10.1111/j.1475-3995.2000.tb00182.x

Ehrgott, M., & Gandibleux, X. (2001). Bounds and bound sets for biobjective Combinatorial Optimization problems . In Köksalan, M., & Zionts, S. (Eds.), *Multiple Criteria Decision Making in the New Millennium (5ᵗʰ ICMCDM), LNEMS 507* (pp. 241–253). Berlin: Springer.

Ehrgott, M., & Gandibleux, X. (2002). Multiobjective Combinatorial Optimization: Theory, Methodology, and Applications . In Ehrgott, M., & Gandibleux, X. (Eds.), *Multiple Criteria Optimization: State of the Art Annotated Bibliographic Surveys* (pp. 369–444). Boston: Kluwer Academic Publishers.

Ehrgott, M., & Wiecek, M. (2005). Multiobjective Programming . In Figueira, J., Greco, S., & Ehrgott, M. (Eds.), *Multiple Criteria Decision Analysis* (pp. 667–722). New York: Springer.

Emelichev, V. A., & Perepelista, V. A. (1992). On cardinality of the set of alternatives in discrete many-criterion problems. *Discrete Mathematics and Applications, 2*(5), 461–471. doi:10.1515/dma.1992.2.5.461

Framinan, J. M., Leisten, R., & Ruiz-Usano, R. (2002). Efficient heuristics for flowshop sequencing with the objectives of makespan and flowtime minimisation. *European Journal of Operational Research, 141,* 559–569. doi:10.1016/S0377-2217(01)00278-8

French, S. (1982). *Sequencing and Scheduling: An Introduction to the Mathematics of the Job Shop*. Chichester, UK: Ellis Horwood.

Gandibleux, X., Mezdaoui, N., & Fréville, A. (1997). A tabu search procedure to solve multiobjective combinatorial optimization problems. *Lecture Notes in Economics and Mathematical Systems, 455,* 291–300.

Garey, M. R., & Johnson, D. S. (1979). *Computers and Intractability: A Guide to the Theory of NP-Completeness*. San Francisco: Freeman.

Geiger, M. (2007). On operators and search space topology in multi-objective flow shop scheduling. *European Journal of Operational Research, 181,* 195–206. doi:10.1016/j.ejor.2006.06.010

González, T., & Johnson, D. B. (1980). A new algorithm for preemptive scheduling of trees. *Journal of the Association for Computing Machinery, 27,* 287–312.

Gordon, V., Proth, J. M., & Chu, C. (2002). A survey of the state of the art of common due date assignment and scheduling research. *European Journal of Operational Research, 139,* 1–25. doi:10.1016/S0377-2217(01)00181-3

Grabowski, J., & Wodecki, M. (2004). Some local search algorithms for no-wait flow-shop problem with makespan criterion. *Computers & Operations Research, 32,* 2197–2212. doi:10.1016/j.cor.2004.02.009

Graham, R. L., Lawler, E. L., Lenstra, J. K., & Rinnooy Kan, A. H. G. (1979). Optimization and approximation in deterministic sequencing and scheduling: A survey. *Annals of Discrete Mathematics, 5,* 287–326. doi:10.1016/S0167-5060(08)70356-X

Gupta, J. N. D. (1972). Heuristic Algorithms for Multistage Flowshop Scheduling Problem. *AIIE Transactions, 4*(1), 11–18.

Gupta, J. N. D., Neppalli, V. R., & Werner, F. (2001). Minimizing total flow time in a two-machine flowshop problem with minimum makespan. *International Journal of Production Economics, 69*(3), 323–338. doi:10.1016/S0925-5273(00)00039-6

Hapke, M., Jaszkiewicz, A., & Slowinski, R. (1998). Interactive Analysis of multiple-criteria project scheduling problems. *European Journal of Operational Research, 107*(2), 315–324. doi:10.1016/S0377-2217(97)00336-6

Haupt, R. (1989). A survey of priority rule-based scheduling. *Operational Research Spektrum, 11*, 3–16. doi:10.1007/BF01721162

Ho, J. C., & Chang, Y.-L. (1991). A new heuristic for the n-job, m-machine flowshop problem. *European Journal of Operational Research, 52*, 194–202. doi:10.1016/0377-2217(91)90080-F

Hoogeveen, H. (2005). Multicriteria Scheduling. *European Journal of Operational Research, 167*, 592–623. doi:10.1016/j.ejor.2004.07.011

Hoogeveen, J. A. (1992). *Single-Machine Bicriteria Scheduling*. Unpublished doctoral dissertation, CWI, The Netherlands Technology, Amsterdam.

Horsky, D., & Rao, M. R. (1984). Estimation of attribute weights from preference comparison. *Management Science, 30*(7), 801–822. doi:10.1287/mnsc.30.7.801

Huang, G., & Lim, A. (2003). Fragmental Optimization on the 2-Machine Bicriteria Flowshop Scheduling Problem. In B. Werner (Ed.), *Proceedings: 15th IEEE International Conference on Tools with Artificial Intelligence* (pp. 194-198). Sacramento: IEEE Computer Society.

Ignall, E., & Schrage, L. E. (1965). Application of the branch-and-bound technique to some flowshop scheduling problems. *Operations Research, 13*, 400–412. doi:10.1287/opre.13.3.400

Isermann, H. (1977). The enumeration of the set of all efficient solutions for a linear multiple objective program. *Operational Research Quarterly, 28*(3), 711–725.

Ishibuchi, H., Misaki, S., & Tanaka, H. (1995). Modified simulated annealing algorithms for the flow shop sequencing problem. *European Journal of Operational Research, 81*, 388–398. doi:10.1016/0377-2217(93)E0235-P

Ishibuchi, H., & Murata, T. (1998). A multi-objective genetic local search algorithm and its application to flowshop scheduling. *IEEE Transactions on Systems, Man and Cybernetics – Part C, 28*(3), 392-403.

Jaszkiewicz, A. (2004). A Comparative Study of Multiple-Objective Metaheuristics on the Bi-Objective Set Covering Problem and the Pareto Memetic Algorithm. *Annals of Operations Research, 13*, 135–158. doi:10.1023/B:ANOR.0000039516.50069.5b

Jaszkiewicz, A., & Ferhat, A. B. (1999). Solving multiple criteria choice problems by interactive trichotomy segmentation. *European Journal of Operational Research, 113*(2), 271–280. doi:10.1016/S0377-2217(98)00216-1

Johnson, S. M. (1954). Optimal two- and three-stage production schedules with setup times included. *Naval Research Logistics, 1*, 61–68. doi:10.1002/nav.3800010110

Jones, D. F., Mirrazavi, S. K., & Tamiz, M. (2002). Multi-objective meta-heuristics: An overview of the current state of the art. *European Journal of Operational Research, 137*, 1–9. doi:10.1016/S0377-2217(01)00123-0

Knowles, J., & Corne, D. (2002). On Metrics Comparing Nondominated Sets. In IEEE (Ed.), *Proceedings of the 2002 Congress on Evolutionary Computation* (pp. 711-716). New York: IEEE.

Koulamas, C. (1998). A new constructive heuristic for the flowshop scheduling problem. *European Journal of Operational Research, 105*, 66–71. doi:10.1016/S0377-2217(97)00027-1

Lageweg, B. J., Ixnstra, J. K., & Rinnooy Kan, A. H. G. (1978). A general bounding to minimize makespan/total flowtime of jobs. *European Journal of Operational Research, 155*, 426–438.

Laha, D., & Chakraborty, U. K. (2007). An efficient stochastic hybrid heuristic for flowshop scheduling. *Engineering Applications of Artificial Intelligence, 20*, 851–856. doi:10.1016/j.engappai.2006.10.003

Laha, D., & Chakraborty, U. K. (2008). An efficient heuristic approach to flowtime minimization in permutation flowshop scheduling. *International Journal of Advanced Manufacturing Technology, 38*, 1018–1025. doi:10.1007/s00170-007-1156-z

Laha, D., & Chakraborty, U. K. (2009). A constructive heuristic for minimizing makespan in no-wait flowshop scheduling. *International Journal of Advanced Manufacturing Technology, 41*, 97–109. doi:10.1007/s00170-008-1454-0

Landa-Silva, J. D., Burke, E. K., & Petrovic, S. (2004). An Introduction to Multiobjective Metaheuristics for Scheduling and Timetabling. *Lecture Notes in Economics and Mathematical Systems, 535*, 91–129.

Lawler, E. L., Lenstra, J. K., & Rinnooy Kan, A. H. G. (1993). Sequencing and scheduling: Algorithms and complexity . In Graves, S. C., Rinnooy Kan, A. H. G., & Zipkin, P. H. (Eds.), *Handbooks in Operations Research and Management Science, 4, Logistics of Production and Inventory* (pp. 445–524). Amsterdam: Elsevier. doi:10.1016/S0927-0507(05)80189-6

Leung, J. Y.-T., & Young, G. H. (1989). Minimizing schedule length subject to minimum flow time. *SIAM Journal on Computing, 18*, 314–326. doi:10.1137/0218022

Liao, C. J., Yu, W. C., & Joe, C. B. (1997). Bicriterion scheduling in the two-machine flowshop. *The Journal of the Operational Research Society, 48*, 929–935.

Liu, J., & Reeves, C. R. (2001). Constructive and composite heuristic solutions to the $P//\Sigma C_i$ scheduling problem. *European Journal of Operational Research, 132*, 439–452. doi:10.1016/S0377-2217(00)00137-5

Lomnicki, A. (1965). Branch-and-bound algorithm for the exact solution of the three-machine scheduling problem. *Operational Research Quarterly, 16*, 89–100. doi:10.1057/jors.1965.7

Loukil, T., Teghem, J., & Tuyttens, D. (2005). Solving multi-objective production scheduling problems using metaheuristics. *European Journal of Operational Research, 161*, 42–61. doi:10.1016/j.ejor.2003.08.029

Minella, G., Ruiz, R., & Ciavotta, M. (2007). A review and evaluation of multi-objective algorithms for the flowshop scheduling problem. *INFORMS Journal on Computing, 20*, 451–471. doi:10.1287/ijoc.1070.0258

Mokotoff, E. (2009). Minimizing the Makespan and Total Flow Time on the Permutation Flow Shop Scheduling Problem. In J. Blazewicz, M. Drozdowski, G. Kendall & B. McCollum (Eds.), *Proceedings of the 4th Multidisciplinary International Conference on Scheduling: Theory and Applications* (pp. 479-506). Dublin: The University of Nottingham.

Monma, C. L., & Rinnooy Kan, A. H. G. (1983). A concise survey of efficiently solvable special cases of the permutation flow-shop problem. *RAIRO Recherche Opérationelle, 17*, 105–119.

Murata, T., Ishibuchi, H., & Tanaka, H. (1996). Multi-Objective Genetic Algorithm and its Applications to Flowshop Scheduling. *Computers & Industrial Engineering, 30*(4), 957–968. doi:10.1016/0360-8352(96)00045-9

Nagar, A., Heragu, S. S., & Haddock, J. (1995b). A Branch and Bound approach for a two machine flowshop scheduling problem. *The Journal of the Operational Research Society, 46*, 721–734.

Nagar, J., Haddock, J., & Heragu, S. S. (1995a). Multiple and bicriteria scheduling: A literature survey. *European Journal of Operational Research, 81*, 88–104. doi:10.1016/0377-2217(93)E0140-S

Nawaz, M., Enscore, E. E. Jr, & Ham, I. (1983). A heuristic algorithm for the m machine, n job flowshop sequencing problem. *OMEGA . The International Journal of Management Science, 11*, 91–95.

Neppalli, V. R., Chen, C. L., & Gupta, J. N. D. (1996). Genetic algorithms for the two-stage bicriteria flowshop problem. *European Journal of Operational Research, 95*, 356–373. doi:10.1016/0377-2217(95)00275-8

Nowicki, E., & Zdrzałka, S. (1990). A survey of results for sequencing problems with controllable processing times. *Discrete Applied Mathematics, 26*, 271–287. doi:10.1016/0166-218X(90)90105-L

Onwubolu, G., & Davendra, D. (2006). Scheduling flow shops using differential evolution algorithm. *European Journal of Operational Research, 171*, 674–692. doi:10.1016/j.ejor.2004.08.043

Osman, I. H., & Potts, C. N. (1989). Simulated Annealing for Permutation Flowshop Scheduling. *OMEGA . The International Journal of Management Science, 17*(6), 551–557.

Panwalkar, S. S., & Iskander, W. (1977). A survey of scheduling rules. *Operations Research, 25*, 45–61. doi:10.1287/opre.25.1.45

Parker, R. G. (1995). *Deterministic Scheduling Theory*. New York: Chapman & Hall.

Parthasarathy, S., & Rajendran, C. (1997). An experimental evaluation of heuristics for scheduling in a real-life flowshop with sequence-dependent setup times of jobs. *International Journal of Production Economics, 49*, 255–263. doi:10.1016/S0925-5273(97)00017-0

Pasupathy, T., Rajendran, C., & Suresh, R. K. (2006). A multi-objective genetic algorithm for scheduling in flow shops to minimize the makespan and total flow time of jobs. *International Journal of Advanced Manufacturing Technology, 27*, 804–815. doi:10.1007/s00170-004-2249-6

Pinedo, M. L. (2002). *Scheduling: Theory, Algorithms, and Systems*. New Jersey: Prentice Hall.

Potts, C. N. (1980). An adaptive branching rule for the permutation flow-shop problem. *European Journal of Operational Research, 5*, 19–25. doi:10.1016/0377-2217(80)90069-7

Potts, C. N., Shmoys, D. B., & Williamson, D. P. (1991). Permutation vs. non-permutation flow shop schedules. *Operations Research Letters, 10*, 281–284. doi:10.1016/0167-6377(91)90014-G

Rajendran, C. (1992). Two-stage flowshop scheduling problem with bicriteria. *The Journal of the Operational Research Society, 43*(9), 879–884.

Rajendran, C. (1993). Heuristic algorithm for scheduling in a flowshop to minimize total flowtime. *International Journal of Production Economics, 29*, 65–73. doi:10.1016/0925-5273(93)90024-F

Rajendran, C. (1995). Heuristics for scheduling in flowshop with multiple objectives. *European Journal of Operational Research, 82*, 540–555. doi:10.1016/0377-2217(93)E0212-G

Rajendran, C., & Ziegler, H. (1997). An efficient heuristic for scheduling in a flowshop to minimize total weighted flowtime of jobs. *European Journal of Operational Research, 103*, 129–138. doi:10.1016/S0377-2217(96)00273-1

Rajendran, C., & Ziegler, H. (2004). Ant-colony algorithms for permutation: flowshop scheduling. *European Journal of Operational Research, 155*, 426–438. doi:10.1016/S0377-2217(02)00908-6

Rajendran, C., & Ziegler, H. (2005). Two ant-colony algorithms for minimizing total flowtime in permutation flowshops. *Computers & Industrial Engineering, 48*, 789–797. doi:10.1016/j.cie.2004.12.009

Rajendran, C., & Ziegler, H. (2009). A Multi-Objective Ant-Colony Algorithm for Permutation Flowshop Scheduling to Minimize the Makespan and Total Flowtime of Jobs . In Chakraborty, U. K. (Ed.), *Computational Intelligence in Flow Shop and Job Shop Scheduling* (pp. 53–99). Berlin: Springer-Verlag. doi:10.1007/978-3-642-02836-6_3

Reeves, C. R. (1993). Improving the Efficiency of Tabu Search for Machine Scheduling Problems. *The Journal of the Operational Research Society*, *44*(4), 375–382.

Reeves, C. R. (1995). A Genetic Algorithm for Flowshop Sequencing. *Computers & Operations Research*, *22*, 5–13. doi:10.1016/0305-0548(93) E0014-K

Rinnooy Kan, A. H. G. (1976). *Machine Scheduling problems: Classification, Complexity and Computations*. The Hague: Martinus Nijhoff.

Ruiz, R. (2003). *Técnicas Metaheurísticas para la Programación Flexible de la Producción*. Unpublished doctoral dissertation, Universidad Politécnica de Valencia, Valencia.

Ruiz, R., & Maroto, C. (2005). A comprehensive review and evaluation of permutation flowshop heuristics. *European Journal of Operational Research*, *165*, 479–494. doi:10.1016/j.ejor.2004.04.017

Ruiz-Díaz, F., & French, S. (1983). A survey of multi-objective combinatorial scheduling . In French, S., Hartley, R., Thomas, L. C., & White, D. J. (Eds.), *Multi-Objective Decision Making* (pp. 59–77). New York: Academic Press.

Saaty, T. L. (1980). *The Analytic Hierarchy Process*. New York: McGrawHill.

Sayin, S., & Karabati, S. (1999). A bicriteria approach to the two-machine flow shop scheduling problem. *European Journal of Operational Research*, *113*, 435–449. doi:10.1016/S0377-2217(98)00009-5

Schulz, A. (1996). *Scheduling and Polytopes*. Unpublished doctoral dissertation, Technical University of Berlin, Berlin.

Selen, W. J., & Hott, D. D. (1986). A mixed-integer goal-programming formulation of the standard flow-shop scheduling problem. *The Journal of the Operational Research Society*, *12*(37), 1121–1128.

Serafini, P. (1992). Simulated annealing for multiple objective optimization problems. In *Proceedings of the Tenth International Conference on Multiple Criteria Decision Making, vol. 1* (pp. 87-96). Taipei.

Shmoys, D. B., & Tardos, É. (1993). An approximation algorithm for the generalized assignment problem. *Mathematical Programming*, *62*, 461–474. doi:10.1007/BF01585178

Sin, C. C. S. (1989). *Some topics of parallel-machine scheduling theory*. Unpublished doctoral dissertation, University of Manitoba, Winnipeg.

Sivrikaya-Serifoglu, F. S., & Ulusoy, G. (1998). A bicriteria two machine permutation flowshop problem. *European Journal of Operational Research*, *107*, 414–430. doi:10.1016/S0377-2217(97)00338-X

Srinivas, N., & Deb, K. (1995). Multiobjective function optimization using nondominated sorting genetic algorithms. *Evolutionary Computation*, *2*(3), 221–248. doi:10.1162/evco.1994.2.3.221

T'kindt, V., & Billaut, J.-C. (2001). Multicriteria scheduling problems: a survey. RAIRO- . *Operations Research*, *35*, 143–163. doi:10.1051/ro:2001109

T'kindt, V., & Billaut, J.-C. (2006). *Multicriteria scheduling: Theory, Models and Algorithms* (2nd ed.). Berlin: Springer.

T'kindt, V., Gupta, J. N. D., & Billaut, J.-C. (2003). Two machine flowshop scheduling problem with a secondary criterion. *Computers & Operations Research, 30*(4), 505–526. doi:10.1016/S0305-0548(02)00021-7

T'kindt, V., Monmarche, N., Tercinet, F., & Laugt, D. (2002). An ant colony optimization algorithm to solve a 2-machine bicriteria flowshop scheduling problem. *European Journal of Operational Research, 142*(2), 250–257. doi:10.1016/S0377-2217(02)00265-5

Taillard, E. (1990). Some efficient heuristic methods for the flor shop sequencing problem. *European Journal of Operational Research, 47,* 67–74. doi:10.1016/0377-2217(90)90090-X

Taillard, E. (1993). Benchmark for basic scheduling problems. *European Journal of Operational Research, 64,* 278–285. doi:10.1016/0377-2217(93)90182-M

Talbi, E.-G., Rahoual, M., Mabed, M. H., & Dhaenens, C. (2001). A Hybrid Evolutionary Approach for Multicriteria Optimization Problme: Application to the Flow Shop . In Zitzler, E., Deb, K., Thiele, L., Coello, C. A. C., & Corne, D. (Eds.), *Evolutionary Multi-Criterion Optimization (EMO 2001), LNCS 1993* (pp. 416–428). Berlin: Springer. doi:10.1007/3-540-44719-9_29

Ulungu, E. L. (1993). *Optimisation Combinatoire MultiCritère: Détermination de l'ensemble des solutions efficaces et méthodes interactives.* Unpublished doctoral dissertation, Université de Mons-Hainaut, Mons.

Ulungu, E. L., & Teghem, J. (1994). Multiobjective Combinatorial Optimization problems: A survey. *Journal of Multi-Criteria Decision Analysis, 3,* 83–104. doi:10.1002/mcda.4020030204

Varadharajan, T. K., & Rajendran, C. (2005). A multi-objective simulated-annealing algorithm for scheduling in flowshops to minimize the makespan and total flowtime of jobs. *European Journal of Operational Research, 167,* 772–795. doi:10.1016/j.ejor.2004.07.020

Wierzbicki, A. P. (1980). A methodological guide to the multiobjective optimization. In K. Iracki, K. Malanowski, & S. Walukiewicz (Eds.), *Optimization Techniques (9th IFIP COT 1979)* (LNCS 22, pp. 99-123). Berlin: Springer.

Wilson, J. M. (1989). Alternative formulation of a flow shop scheduling problem. *The Journal of the Operational Research Society, 40*(4), 395–399.

Wodecki, M., & Bozejko, W. (2002). Solving the Flow Shop Problem by Parallel Simulated Annealing . In Goos, G., Hartmanis, J., & van Leeuwen, J. (Eds.), *Parallel Processing and Applied mathematics (PPAM 2001), LNCS 2328* (pp. 236–244). Berlin: Springer.

Yagmahan, B., & Yenisey, M. M. (2008). Ant colony optimization for multi-objective flow shop scheduling problem. *Computers & Industrial Engineering, 54,* 411–420. doi:10.1016/j.cie.2007.08.003

Zitzler, E. (1999). *Evolutionary Algorithms for Multiobjective Optimization: Methods and Applications.* Unpublished doctoral dissertation, Swiss Federal Institute of Technology, Zurich.

Zitzler, E., & Thiele, L. (1999). Multiobjective evolutionary algorithms: A comparative case study and the strength pareto approach. *IEEE Transactions on Evolutionary Computation, 3,* 257–271. doi:10.1109/4235.797969

Chapter 15
Beyond ERP Implementation:
An Integrative Framework for Higher Success

Rafa Kouki
Université Laval, Canada

Robert Pellerin
École Polytechnique de Montréal, Canada

Diane Poulin
Université Laval, Canada

ABSTRACT

Research about ERP post-implementation and ERP assimilation is very limited. Similarly, scant research investigated ERP experiences in developing countries. Based on a qualitative research methodology grounded in the diffusion of innovations theory, the present study aims at investigating the determining contextual factors for ERP assimilation. A cross-case study analysis of four firms in a developed and a developing country suggests that in both contexts, the primary factor for encouraging a successful ERP assimilation is top management support. Other factors such as post-implementation training and education, IT support, organizational culture, managers and users involvement, strategic alignment, external pressures and consultant effectiveness are also identified as factors that influence ERP assimilation. Several assimilation impediments that should be watched are also specified.

INTRODUCTION

ERP systems are software packages that embed, in their basic architecture, business knowledge and business process reference models as well as the knowledge and expertise of implementation partners (Srivardhanaa & Pawlowski, 2007). Lured by the numerous advantages of ERP systems and their ability to provide a competitive advantage, companies worldwide have substantially invested in ERP applications. Despite the large investments in ERP, the relatively long experience of companies with this system and the accumulated knowledge about ERP projects, few firms are efficiently using their system (Yu, 2005). Similarly, there have been studies reporting cases of initial implementation failure that transformed into suc-

DOI: 10.4018/978-1-61692-020-3.ch015

cess, yielding significant benefits for the business (Jasperson et al., 2005).

Completing the system's implementation is, in fact, not the end of the ERP journey. Like other complex information technologies, once the system is installed, the adopting organization must ensure the effective assimilation of the ERP in order to be able to reap its benefits (Chatterjee et al., 2002). Effective assimilation is achieved when employees' sense of ownership of the system is high, when it becomes institutionalized in the organization's work processes, and when it is efficiently deployed at the various levels of managerial activities (Botta-Genoulaz & Millet, 2005; Cooper & Zmud, 1990). A primary objective of this research is therefore to investigate the factors that could explain why some firms are more successful in assimilating their systems than others.

Moreover, prior ERP research predominantly focused on the North American context (the United States in particular) and, to a lesser extent, the western European context. Scant studies dealt with developing countries (Ngai et al., 2008), despite the valuable lessons that could be learned from their experiences. Huang and Palvia (2001) argue that in developing countries, ERP technology confronts extra challenges which are intrinsically connected to several contextual reasons such as culture, economic conditions, government regulations, management style, and labor skills. Nevertheless, studies about ERP experiences in developing countries are scarce. Additional efforts are therefore required to fill this research gap. For our research, we chose to study two sets of companies: one operating in a developed country which is Canada, the second operating in Tunisia; a developing country from the unexplored North African region.

This chapter is organized as follows. First, we provide an account of the theoretical foundations of the concept of assimilation. Next, we describe the theoretical framework and the methodology that guided our empirical research. In section 4, the cases' analyses and research findings are presented

followed by a discussion of the findings. Lastly, we offer some concluding thoughts.

THEORETICAL FOUNDATIONS

The diffusion of innovation theory represents our primary approach in studying the assimilation process. Roger's diffusion of innovation theory posits that both the perceived attributes of the innovation and the firm's characteristics influence the adoption and use of an innovation (Rogers, 1983). Although it seems to be quite appropriate for studying innovation use, Roger's model has been criticized for being mainly applicable to simple technological innovations requiring individual decision-making. More research has therefore been made, based on Roger's theory, to better explain the diffusion of complex technological innovations. For instance, Tornatzky & Feleischer's (1990) model considers three aspects of the firm's context (technology, organization, environment (TOE)) that influence a complex innovation's adoption and assimilation process. In their diffusion stage model, Cooper and Zmud (1990) identify six stages for IT projects, three of which denote the post-implementation phase: acceptance, routinization, and infusion. During the infusion stage, the system becomes deeply and comprehensively embedded in the organization's work system and value chain. At this stage, the firm further integrates the system and extends its functionalities by adding new modules or applications to support new activities and reach external partners (Muscatello & Parente, 2006).

RESEARCH FRAMEWORK

Drawing on ERP implementation and IS assimilation literature, we focused on factors within the three main contexts that could influence the ERP assimilation process: technological context factors, organizational context factors, and en-

Figure 1. Research framework

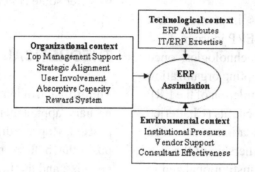

vironmental context factors. The technological context includes the ERP attributes such as ease of use and reliability which may have an impact on the system's assimilation (Hsieh & Wang, 2007) and the IT/ERP expertise. The organizational context comprises top management support, strategic alignment, user involvement, absorptive capacity and reward system. The environmental context includes the institutional pressures, the post-implementation vendor support and the consultants' effectiveness.

The following figure illustrates the research framework that guided our empirical investigation. Since our research was primarily exploratory, we chose not to specify any formal hypothesis that could act as an impediment to discovering important insights and new dimensions during our research.

METHODOLOGY

In order to realize the research objectives and answer the corresponding research questions, we opted for an interpretive and exploratory approach. We also followed the in-depth multiple case study strategy to have an in-depth understanding of the experiences of the firms and the interviewees with the system and to shed light on the particularities of each ERP experience (Yin, 2003). Indeed, there are several advantages to using the case study

research method, such as studying a phenomenon in its natural setting, directly observing causality relationships, asking follow-up questions for more extensive, valid and rigorous findings and insights, and combining evidence and logic to build, develop or support theories that are not available using other research methods (Muscatello & Parente, 2006). ERP systems projects represent a major undertaking in a firm, often involving all company departments and processes, requiring heavy investments of both time and money, and which could extend over periods ranging from months to years. All of these factors contribute to the complexity of the ERP systems initiative. Consequently, a quantitative methodology would not allow for an in-depth understanding of the firm's and the respondents' experiences with the system.

Four manufacturing companies were chosen: two in Canada and two in Tunisia. Although this is a relatively small sample, this is consistent with other qualitative research samples which have even used a single (Yin, 2003). Indeed, according to Patton (2002) "the validity, meaningfulness, and insights generated from qualitative inquiry have more to do with the information richness of the cases selected and the observational/analytical capabilities of the researcher than with sample size"(p.245).

In spite of its small size, Tunisia has transformed itself into a newly industrialized and open

Table 1. Profiles of companies A, B, C and D

Charecteristics	Canada Tunisia			
	Company A	Company B	Company C	Company D
Industry	Agrifood	Plastic products	Agrifood	Petrochemical
Employees	~ 500	~ 1000	~ 700	~400
Sales (Mln US)	> $160	> $160	> $90	> $100
Vendor	SAP	JDE	JDE	JDE
Go-live date	1997	2004	2000	1996 then 2006
Implementation approach	Big-Bang at the headquarters and one plant then phased by site	Big-Bang at the headquarters and 2 plants then 3rd plant	By module	Big-Bang
Motivations for ERP adoption	Y2K problem; clients' pressures; need for a system that evolves with the firm's requirements	Integration of financial data; old system is outdated	Data centralization; insuring tracking and transparency	Part of a wider (pan African) project for business process standardization; intermediate stage towards a higher performance system

economy and has, in parallel, been dynamically developing its information technology (IT) infrastructure (FIPA-Tunisia, 2007). Since signing the free trade agreement with the European Union in 1995 to remove tariffs and other trade barriers on the majority of consumer goods by 2008, manufacturing firms carried the burden of improving their products and services, in terms of quality, flexibility, reliability, and speed, in order to be able to compete with firms in more advanced countries (Yagoubi, 2004). Among other things, these firms had to modernize their technologies and upgrade their management and production methods and practices. In order to improve their effectiveness and flexibility, several Tunisian firms both large and small and medium enterprises (SME) adopted ERP systems.

Table 1 provides a brief description of the characteristics of these companies

The primary source of data was the in-depth interviews with at least five managers in each company. The interviews aimed at probing the interviewees about their firm's implementation project, and their experience with the ERP system and the ERP project. The bulk of the interview then focused on the importance and the impact of the suggested variables and on the identification of new variables that the interviewees perceived as necessary for a successful ERP assimilation. The researcher and a research assistant, with good knowledge of ERP and other IT systems, conducted all the interviews. This allowed the cases to be viewed from different perspectives. Each interview lasted between 60 and 90 minutes, and was recorded and transcribed prior to analysis. The information obtained through the interviews was supplemented by information from internal and external organizational documents. The transcription reports were reviewed with the interviewees and the research assistant to verify the convergence of the collected data. The data was then reduced to codes in categories that corresponded to the set of new and originally identified themes.

CASE ANALYSIS

ERP Attributes

Innovation attributes such as ease of use, relative advantage, and compatibility are strongly acknowledged in innovation literature to have an impact on the technology's diffusion and the level of use of the system (Wu & Wang, 2006; Hsieh & Wang, 2007).

All respondents agreed that the level of complexity decreases over time as users get more and more accustomed to the system. Also, according to several respondents in companies B and C, early post- implementation output quality issues such as data accuracy, timeliness, integrity, and reliability negatively impacted the level of users' involvement and deployment of the system and, in many cases, encouraged the use of parallel systems. In spite of the frequent interventions of the IT/ERP experts, many of these issues persisted. The causes were attributed not to the system, as several respondents asserted, but rather to the human factor such as employees' resistance and managers' lack of commitment.

IT/ERP Expertise

Once the implementation process is over, the IT department would be responsible for debugging and trouble shooting the system, continuously refining and adjusting it to the evolving business needs and retraining users (Stratman & Roth, 2002 ; Kumar et al., 2003).All the companies we studied, except for Company D, had an internal ERP team. The major problem which was identified by respondents in companies B and C was the high turnover rate of ERP experts. This issue was justified by the high demand for ERP experts, the heavy workload and the external competitive wages of such experts. Evening and night shifts represented a different type of problem for Company A. Most of the evening and night workers received less support and training than their day colleagues. Efforts were made to provide appropriate support for evening and night shifts, but it was insufficient. Another critical point that can hinder ERP assimilation, as noted by respondents at companies B and C, is an organizational culture that values product innovations over IT innovations. They argued that the system's acceptance and assimilation would have been much easier

if their organization's culture assigned a higher value to IT innovations, the IT department, and IT objectives and strategies.

Top Management Support

Top management support refers to the extent that top management supports, directly and indirectly, and commits to the continuous use of the ERP. Top management involvement and their sustained support throughout all the phases of the project help ensuring a smooth change management and mobilizing commitment of other stakeholders (Somers & Nelson, 2004). Their commitment is crucial for the post-implementation stage especially when it comes to providing the essential resources for maintenance and upgrades and implementation in other units and departments. Likewise, top management's perceptions of and attitudes towards the system could shape the norms and values of the organization to facilitate (or impede) system assimilation (Chatterjee et al., 2002).

All the companies reported that they were receiving adequate financial support for upgrades and system requirements from senior management. However, the financial support does not necessarily reflect the real perceptions of top management about the system's value. In Company A, for instance, the CEO was consistently involved in the ERP steering committee, and the system was always among the firm's top priorities. On the other hand, top management at Company C lacked interest and trust in the system due to the frequent delays and problems experienced after the implementation of each module. Furthermore, priority was always given to projects with quicker and more tangible returns than those of the ERP system. As a respondent at Company B put it, *"Culturally speaking, priority is given to investments in products and not in IT."* Indeed, respondents at companies B, and C stressed the importance of the role of top management in supporting the prevalence of an ERP culture, *"a culture of openness, information sharing, doing work on time, real-time, and transparency*." Moreover, imposing the system's use, strict control of users to prevent them from using parallel systems, and the relocation of employees who produce parallel reports were examples of policies that respondents suggested top management could apply in order to improve system assimilation.

Strategic Alignment

Researchers seem to agree that major gains are realized when the IT supports, stimulates, and enables the firm's strategy (Tallon, 2008). Evaluating the system's strategic alignment involves not only the system's support of the firm's strategy but also the IT's support of the business processes, the IT's reporting relationship with top management (IT-top management distance) and involvement in business strategy formulation, and the management practices that impact alignment (Tallon, 2008; Rathman, et al., 2005).

Companies A and D exhibited the highest level of strategic alignment. The system was highly valued in these firms by both senior and middle managers, and was always considered to be an institutional tool for the firm's operational effectiveness. The situation was in the process of improving in Company B with the arrival of the new CEO and the new managers, all of whom had experience with ERP systems. One interesting factor that was highlighted by respondents at companies B and D is the reporting relationship between the IT manager and the CEO on the one hand, and the IT manager and other department managers on the other hand. A respondent at Company D argued that the fact that the IT manager was at the same reporting level as the other departments' managers compromised the execution of his recommendations. In fact, these recommendations were seen as emanating from a mere peer rather than serious orders from senior management. Moreover, the fact that at Company B the IT service was supervised by the finance department reinforced a general perception in the

company that the function of the ERP system was to primarily serve the finance department and to tighten control over the other departments' operations. These perceptions negatively impacted the system assimilation level in the company.

User Involvement

Wagner and Newell (2007) argue that unlike other IS projects, ERP user involvement has is more beneficial during the post-implementation stage than earlier stages. Indeed, as users gradually learn about the system by experiencing it (experiential learning), they start to understand the system's functionalities and to explore its possibilities and limits. They can therefore better describe their requirements and ask for adjustments to satisfy their needs (Musaji, 2005). The more they are satisfied with the system, the more they are engaged with it and the higher their level of assimilation (Wagner & Newell, 2007).

The ERP steering committee at Company A presented users with a valuable tool to get their voices heard. During the committee's regular meetings, users' suggestions were evaluated and classified by priority for possible implementation. IT respondents at companies B and C stressed that users' seniority, computer literacy, and ability to express their needs were elements that had a significant impact on the level of involvement with and commitment to the system.

One important factor that was highlighted by respondents in all of the four companies was the level of involvement of managers and its impact on their subordinates' commitment to and involvement with the system. At Company C, the reluctance of middle managers to commit to the system was a result of their *"fear of becoming unnecessary for the firm's functioning."* For those who had more trust in the system, their limited involvement was attributed to the heavy workload of the daily tasks. At the other extreme of the spectrum, managers at companies A and D had a very high level of system ownership and commitment to the system. Moreover, brainstorming sessions and meetings to discuss changes and exchange experiences were common rituals in the company, including its plants.

Absorptive Capacity

Being a complex technology, ERP imposes a heavy learning burden on novel users in terms of understanding the system, and learning how to use it (Ke & Wei, 2006). Cohen and Levinthal (1990) define the absorptive capacity as the firm's ability to appreciate an innovation, to assimilate and to apply it to new ends. They stress that the firm's absorptive capacity is, in fact, largely a result of the firm's pre-existing knowledge in areas related to the focal innovation. Hence, the more a firm possesses prior ERP related knowledge, the less arduous the assimilation process is (Ke & Wei, 2006).

Among the four companies, only Company D had previous experience with an ERP system, which explains its smooth transition towards developing a high-level ERP system and a high level of assimilation of the system. In addition to their high-quality help desk, the fact that the system permitted interaction with a bigger population of users (pan African) allowed Company D's users to benefit from a wide pool of rich system knowledge. Due to their accumulated learning and long experience with the system, most of Company A's modules were deployed nearly to their maximum potential. Consultants were the major source of knowledge for the four companies when new modules were to be implemented or assistance was needed concerning the interaction between modules.

The issue of the absence of a knowledge management system that captures and stores the acquired knowledge and experience was highlighted by several interviewees when discussing ERP knowledge resources.

One other major missing element, according to most respondents, is a formal post-implementation training program. Companies B and C were in fact suffering from varying levels of redundancy and parallel systems, which significantly lowered their system assimilation efficiency. This redundancy was essentially attributed to the lack of training and proper communication during both the implementation and the post-implementation stage. Newcomers, in the case of all the studied companies, were informally trained on the job by their colleagues, learning only the very basic actions needed to do their work. Some respondents highlighted the negative impact of such informal training on the level of understanding and assimilation of the system; this explains the heavy and recurrent need of new system users for IT support, especially when faced with unexpected problems.

Reward System

It has been argued in previous studies that reward strategies, such as rewarding the acquisition of new skills and linking compensation to company profits, promote learning and the institutionalization of favorable behaviors (Jerez-Gómez et al., 2005).In a study evaluating the importance of critical success factors across ERP project phases, Nah and Delgado (2006) found that ERP team skills and compensation were the most important factors for the post-implementation stage.

None of the studied firms, however, changed their reward system to encourage and reward ERP system use or to retain ERP experts and trained superusers. Companies B and C suffered from a general high turnover rate. According to one respondent *"people find big opportunities somewhere else... ERP opens doors. We're talking about significant increases of advantages for the employee who leaves to work with a consulting company versus being an employee in the company."* On the other hand, Companies A and D were proud of the high level of loyalty of their employees, especially the IT/ERP team of Company A, which they attributed to the "family-like" ambiance that prevailed in the company and the "good" wages compared to other companies in the industry.

Institutional Pressures

DiMaggio and Powell (1983) argue that due to the companies' need to legitimize themselves in their external environment, mimetic, coercive, and normative pressures influence organizations to become more and more similar to each other, or to a phenomenon called institutional isomorphism. In the context of ERP systems, Liang et al. (2007) concluded that these forces, mediated by top management, have an important influence on ERP assimilation during the post-implementation stage.

In all the companies studied, the desire to improve internal efficiency and performance and to preserve a leading position in the market was among the main drivers towards better deployment of the system. There were, however, other external pressures that pushed some firms to use the system effectively. After most of its competitors adopted ERP systems, Company A felt a strong need to surpass its competitors not only by further deploying the system's functionalities, but also by innovating with the system. At Company D, the requirements of the firm's headquarters to master the system and to comply with the work norms of other regions' divisions for further global integration represented a major pressure driving the firm to use the system efficiently. It was mentioned by several members of the ERP teams/units that taking part in ERP conferences, on-line forums, and training sessions motivated them to improve their system deployment. This is in fact a form of normative pressures.

Vendor Support

With the rapid technological development of ERPs and the desire of companies to extend and enhance their systems, continuous investments are required (upgrades, new modules, etc.). Maintaining a strategic relationship with the vendor is therefore believed to be vital for the ERP adopting firm (Wang et al., 2008; Somers & Nelson, 2004; Chang, 2004).Given that the original vendors are knowledgeable about their customers' businesses, processes, and requirements, they are well-equipped to serve the firms' needs. Therefore, vendor support, which can include technical assistance, software updates, emergency maintenance, user training, and other support services, is judged to be very important for the ERP's success and efficient deployment (Wang et al., 2008; Chang, 2004; Somers & Nelson, 2004).

None of the three companies A, B and C maintained a strategic relationship with the original vendor. In the case of the subsidiary Company D, there was no direct contact with the vendor because the system was implemented by an internal team of the multinational group, who assisted the subsidiaries in installing the system.

Consultant Effectiveness

Consultant effectiveness designates the competence and expertise of consultants in providing various types of assistance to firms, such as knowledge, training, maintenance, technical support, and any other type of help the organization needs (Wang et al., 2008). Although the use of consultants has been commonly considered as essential for the ERP implementation stage, it has been found that this factor is of great importance for the post-implementation stage as well (Nah & Delgado, 2006).

Companies A, B, and D needed external expertise intervention when implementing a new module. Respondents from Company A stressed the *"extreme importance"* of the high expertise of the consultant even during the post-implementation stage, because as in the case of the other implemented modules, the company needed to properly learn about the module and its different functionalities. In Company D, respondents opined that even though the virtual help desk was very competent, the presence of the consulting team was essential during the system's stabilization. Unfortunately, this was not possible because the consulting team was responsible for implementing the system at other subsidiaries in Africa.

EVALUATION OF ASSIMILATION LEVELS AT THE STUDIED COMPANIES

The assimilation level varied widely across organizations and within the same country. Company A had the oldest experience with the ERP system. The core system capacity was deployed to over 85%. According to Company A's respondents, the system was deeply embedded in the firm's work routines and provided almost all of the required information to make decisions. Strategic and planning decisions, however, were made outside the ERP system, but using data from the ERP system. Efforts to improve the system's effectiveness have not stopped since its introduction in 1997, especially after the widespread adoption of the system in the industry. These improvements included both deepening the functionality deployment of the already-installed modules and extending the system with new modules.

At Company B, the system was at a stabilization stage. Two of the plants were integrated and a project to integrate the third plant was under way. System deployment was limited to the basic functionalities. However, parallel system use, redundancy dissatisfaction among users and managers, and lack of trust in the reliability of the system's outputs were prevailing in the company. Efforts to improve system deployment were being made, especially after the arrival of the new

CEO and managers. Despite the challenges experienced, the system represented a main source of data for the company. The system was satisfying most of the finance department's needs, but was only responding to 30 to 40% of the operations department's requirements.

At Company C, several modules were implemented, but they lacked complete cross-functional integration, which hindered the traceability of the products' costs. The system was considered to be a basic source of data for several departments and was believed to serve about 50% of the company's needs. In spite of the numerous problems surrounding the ERP initiative, as discussed in the sections above, significant efforts were being made by the IT department to stabilize the system, integrate the modules, and to improve its deployment.

At Company D, the system was also at a stabilization stage. The transition to the new system was smooth and assimilation was rapidly taking place. The system was diffused across almost all of the company's units and all of the implemented modules were integrated, therefore providing the managers with an enterprise-wide visibility. As the system becomes more stabilized and its outputs more reliable, it will be used for managerial control besides operational control. However, planning and strategic decisions were being made outside the system using less complicated software.

It is worth noting that several managers praised the fact that ERP decreased the time needed to gather critical information for all levels of decision-making. However, they stressed the importance of the human being's role in making decisions and solving problems compared to a system that produces automated decisions. In fact, most of the interviewed managers thought of the system as being mostly transactional and as being unsuitable for strategic and planning decisions.

The following figure illustrates the assessment of the assimilation level of the four companies based on the three dimensions of assimilation, namely: the degree of institutionalization of the system in the work processes, the degree of sys-

Figure 2. Assessment of the assimilation level in companies A, B, C and D

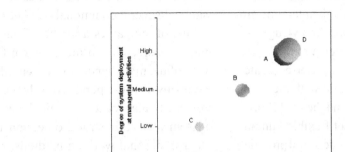

DISCUSSION

The primary objective of this study was to explore the determinants of a successful ERP assimilation. A relative commonality exists across the studied companies regarding the determining and constraining factors for achieving a high level of ERP assimilation. First, this study affirms that regardless of national differences, top management financial and moral support is strongly related to effective ERP assimilation. Top management's knowledge about the system, its potential for the company, and its requirements should be regularly reviewed and updated. Clear and effective communication is also necessary between the ERP/IT manager and top management in order to dispel any resistance, lack of trust in the system, or confusion resulting from the challenges of the post-installation stage. A main task of top management is ensuring the continuous alignment of the system with the business vision and strategy, and communicating the latter clearly in the firm. In order to reinforce the effective deployment of the system across the organization, top management could reinforce the policies prohibiting parallel

tem deployment at managerial activities and the degree of employees' ownership of the system.

systems and redundant data, and a strict control of system use could eliminate deficiencies and force system deployment for at least basic user tasks.

Another lesson learned from this research is that middle managers' involvement and ownership of the system is crucial to encouraging system assimilation in their departments (Yu, 2005). Also, users' involvement during the post-implementation stage is a valuable ingredient for system acceptance and assimilation. With their situated practice, users learn more about the system limitations and start suggesting changes and modifications to satisfy their needs. Elements such as education level, seniority, IT proficiency, and openness to change are factors that could moderate the impact of users' involvement.

Our analysis highlights the organizational culture, as an important factor for promoting assimilation and system success (Ifinedo, 2007). ERP assimilation would be greater and easier if the organizational culture values IT and IT strategies and objectives. Our data analysis also showed that open cultures that promote learning, transparency, knowledge and information sharing, innovation and cooperation are more likely to assimilate the system well than those that lack these characteristics.

Another important insight is that a skilled and competent internal IT/ERP team is a significant success factor for facilitating the system assimilation process (Yu, 2005). The advantage of an internal ERP team is their good knowledge of the organization's processes, their proximity to workers, which enables them to better evaluate the problem and its consequences. With the high turnover rate of ERP expertise and the skill shortage, top management should set flexible human resource policies on pay and contracts, and provide opportunities for career development (Willcocks & Sykes, 2000).

Our data analysis showed the critical value of a formal post-implementation training program (Nah & Delgado, 2006), especially if this activity was overlooked during implementation. Furthermore, in order to cope with the high turnover rate of ERP experts and with the constantly increasing knowledge of the system (from external parties, workers' experiences with the system, etc.), the use of an ERP knowledge management system was considered to be a highly effective tool to encourage learning as well as knowledge sharing and creation. Unlike previous researches, our findings showed that maintaining a strategic relationship with the system vendor was not essential. Services such as updates and maintenance could be obtained from other vendors. Consultant effectiveness, however, remained an important factor for assimilation.

Institutional forces vary across companies depending on their industries and markets. The strongest forces are government regulations and the pressures from headquarters and external partners to properly assimilate the system in order to be able to provide integrated, detailed, and real-time information. The economic motivation remains, however, the main incentive for properly assimilating the system, deploying its functionalities to the maximum, and continuously optimizing its value in order to fully benefit from its advantages.

The second objective of this study was to investigate the differences between the two groups of companies. It is important to say from the outset that if our findings, as we saw earlier, showed several commonalities between the two groups of companies, a number of constraints were more conspicuous in the Tunisian Company C. One of the main handicaps to assimilation in that company was the persistent reluctance amongst several managers to commit themselves to the system and their strong objection to changing their traditional working methods. No doubt by being so, they caused, among other things, the ongoing lack of integration (and aggregation) of the organization's data and they limited the constructive sharing of information between the different units of their firms. The managers' lack of commitment can be attributed to two main factors. Firstly, for many managers, information is not considered a corporate asset. It is rather, a personal asset which should be shared selectively with other employees in the firm. Additionally, there is the rejection of the plant workers to spend extra time entering data and their perception of the system as merely adding extra load to their duties, controlling their actions and even tracking their mistakes. No doubt, this had badly impacted the quality of the system's data and outputs (i.e. their reliability, accuracy, completeness and precision) which, in turn, had frustrated the managers and discouraged them from using the system.

The lack of users' and managers' commitment and the fear of the loss of power were also problematic in the Canadian company B. It was easier and relatively faster for its IT/ERP unit to limit these problems than in the Tunisian company C. Indeed, the high power distance, in-group loyalty, and competitiveness amongst Tunisian managers discouraged many of them from accepting the IT manager's leadership and dissuaded them from following his/her instructions. Needless to say, such a competitiveness between managers and the resulting fear of appearing incompetent in terms of mastering the system further hampered system assimilation by discouraging inexperienced managers and novice users from benefiting from the experiences of other managers working in another

Table 2. Summarizes our findings for each of the four companies A, B, C and D

	Canada		Tunisia	
	Company A	**Company B**	**Company C**	**Company D**
Assimilation success factors				
Middle managers involvement	+ +	+	- -	-
Institutional forces	+ +	+	+	+
Reward system	Unchanged	Unchanged	Unchanged	Unchanged
Knowledge management system	Inexistent	Inexistent	Inexistent	Inexistent
Vendor's support	No long term relationship	No long term relationship	No long term relationship	No long term relationship
ERP attributes	Flexibility, user friendliness, reliability	Flexibility, user friendliness, reliability	Flexibility, user friendliness, reliability	Flexibility, user friendliness, reliability
Organizational culture	+ +	-	-	-
TPM support	+ +	+	+ +	+
Strategic alignment	+ +	+	-	-
Users' involvement	+ +	+	-	-
Absorptive capacity	+	-	-	-
IT/ERP expertise	+	+ -	+ -	+ -
Consultants' effectiveness	+	+	+	+
Assimilation challenging factors				
High turnover rate of ERP expertise and superusers	-	+	+ +	+ + +
Small IT team/ work overload	+	+ +	+ +	+ +
Heavy work load for employees	-	+	+ +	+
Information overload	+	+	+	+
Heritage of problems from previous project stages		+ +	+	+ +
Personal traits (level of IT curiosity, computer literacy, personal innovativeness with IT, age, seniority)	+	+	+	+
Legacy thinking	-	+ +	+ +	+ +
On job training risks (transfer of inefficient methods of work)	+	+	+	+
Redundancy/ parallel systems	-	+ +	+ +	+ +

"sister" company and who were more advanced in the system deployment. Therefore, it is incumbent upon the Tunisian IT manager to strive to build strong relationships based on collaboration, trust, mutual understanding and clear communication in order to ensure the involvement and commitment of managers and users to promote the assimilation of the system in the company. These efforts

need to be buttressed up by the reduction of the reporting relationship distance between the IT manager and top management. This would put the IT manager at a senior position which would allow him/her to enjoy a higher level of authority in the organization.

Compared to companies C, Company D was in a much better position and exhibited a

Figure 3. ERP assimilation framework

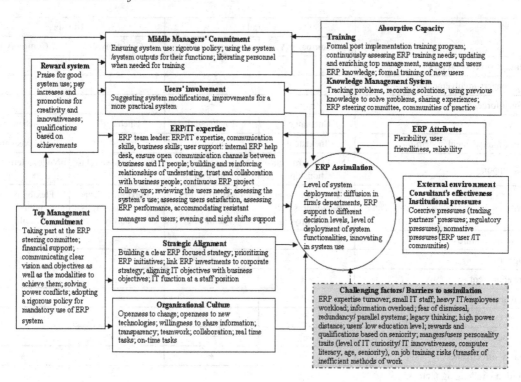

high level of system assimilation even though its system was still at a stabilization stage. This wide difference in assimilation level can be attributed to several factors. First, Company D had a lengthy, successful prior experience with ERP systems. Second, this company is a subsidiary of a European multinational company that has been established in Tunisia for more than 80 years. Therefore, the values and culture of the European company, including information sharing, open communication, participation, encouraging learning and motivation, were deeply rooted and clearly manifested in its subsidiary.

Figure 3 illustrates the new framework of ERP assimilation and the influencing organizational, technological and environmental factors based on our findings. The figure shows the direct and important impact of top management support on the other organizational factors. Similarly, the figure suggests that amending the reward system and increasing the benefits for employees and

mainly for the IT/ERP expertise, the retention rate of these experts would increase. A knowledge management system would also be a valuable source of information for both the existing users and the new comers, as well as for the IT/ERP expertise. Likewise, the users' training needs should be continuously assessed and a formal training program should be considered in order to ensure the users' satisfaction with the system and in order to upgrade and update their ERP knowledge. For the external environment, the consultants' effectiveness as well as, the coercive and normative forces are the main factors that impact the assimilation process. Finally, firms adopting ERP systems should watch for the various challenging factors that could hamper the effective assimilation process. Compared to the initial research framework, the organizational culture, the knowledge management system and the middle managers' involvement in addition to the challenging factors emerged as additional factors to the ERP assimilation framework. The vendor's support, on the other hand, disappeared from the framework as it was not considered to be an essential factor for ERP assimilation success.

CONCLUSION

While organizations' objectives to implement an enterprise-wide IS may greatly differ, ultimately a joint objective can be seen when their system is effectively assimilated in a given firm for an eventual achievement of the aspired benefits which motivated the initial adoption of the system. As a matter of fact, the increasing worldwide implementation of ERP systems, along with the high rates of ineffectively deployed systems, and the high risks of failure in sustaining long term success, had all necessitated the investigation of post-implementation issues and the monitoring of the effectiveness of how these systems are assimilated. By mainly providing a deeper understanding of ERP assimilation, this research positions itself in the emerging stream of research of ERP systems and its post-implementation stage in particular.

Based on the results of the case study analysis of four manufacturing companies in two different geographical contexts (a developed country (Canada) and a developing country (Tunisia)), we proposed an integrative framework of the facilitating factors and discussed the impediments of an effective ERP assimilation.

Our results demonstrate these main findings. Firstly, one must not ignore the fact that the post-implementation stage is a tight ring in the ERP lifecycle. In other words, not only does the degree of success of the post-implementation process depend heavily on the quality of the implementation process, but also it has a significant influence on the degree of efforts required to promote ERP assimilation during the post-implementation stage. This concerns mainly the degree of top management commitment and support to the system,

training and education efforts, and the managers' and users' perceived usefulness of the system.

Secondly, with time (i.e. time span since the system was installed), the impact of the human factor on the degree and effectiveness of ERP assimilation supersedes the technological factors. This is chiefly suggestive of the support of top management which is the key factor behind the promotion, directly and indirectly, of the pace and depth of ERP assimilation across the organization. Suffice it to say that this is very critical especially during the early post-go-live stage, called also the shakedown or stabilization stage. Indeed, the top management's good understanding of the risks and possible hurdles and complications of the shakedown down phase—like the possible performance dip, the low system performance, the increased requirements for extra expenditures on overtime labor, consultant services and additional IT resources— is of capital importance in helping the organization and its employees overcome that risky period and in setting the grounds for a successful system assimilation.

This stage is very fragile and its success is essential for the system's survival and the subsequent progressing in the assimilation levels. There is no question that top management's views of the system's usefulness and its potential for the organization, despite the possible (short-term) difficulties, contribute, for instance, in shaping the perceptions of both middle management and users in operational positions and the embedded organizational culture of the company. These could be reflected, for example, in their participation or follow-up of the ERP project's evolvements and upgrades, their providing of adequate financial support for system developments, maintenance and extensions, their alignment of ERP unit objectives with business objectives. In addition, there are the clear and focused ERP organization's strategy, the changing of the reward system and investing in high quality ERP expertise and in continuous training and education.

Similarly, a closer and direct reporting relationship between top management and the IT manager who would rank the IT manager (and the IT function) at a senior position can provide him/her with more authority and influence in the organization (Law and Ngai, 2007). By being at a senior position, the IT manager may be seen by other managers as a senior executive. This can facilitate the execution of the IT manager's recommendations about the system. Correspondingly, as a senior executive, the IT manager can participate at the firm's strategic planning, thus improving the strategic alignment between the organization's strategy and the system. Equally, the close and direct relationship with the top management cannot only help the IT manager influence the top management perceptions about the system, but it can also make him/her gain their support for an active intervention and promotion of the system assimilation. Successfully handling top management perceptions about the system are, however, highly dependent on the IT manager's persuasion skills and personal appeal (Law and Ngai, 2007).

Furthermore, our study stresses the importance of the personal traits of managers and users, such as level of curiosity, computer literacy, personal innovativeness with IT, age, seniority, education level, etc., in promoting or hindering system assimilation. Therefore, organizations should invest heavily in time and effort to manage carefully and properly the human factor. This can be realized through several initiatives such as effective post-implementation training, communication and education, appropriate user support and reward systems, ERP communities of practice which allow users to exchange experiences and improve the existing system.

As far as the impact of the environmental context is concerned, regulatory pressures, trading partners' pressures, and consultants' effectiveness were the main external factors identified in this research as factors influencing ERP assimilation.

Comparing the two groups of companies in the two contexts showed several commonalities in success factors and issues which, by and large, were related to the stabilization periods almost all companies were going through with the exception of Company A which exhibited a higher level of assimilation than all other companies. This is true of all success factors which were identified, as well as the great majority of ERP assimilation impediments. Yet, there are some issues which were more apparent in the Tunisian company C than in the other companies. These include the persistent reluctance of several mangers to commit themselves to the system, power and interests conflicts between middle managers and the IT manager, the tendency to use seniority more than skills as an indicator of qualification, and the high competitiveness between managers. Conversely, these problems were inexistent in the medium sized subsidiary of the multinational company, which was also at a stabilization stage but of a second ERP project. Indeed, similar to company A, this subsidiary enjoyed an organizational culture based on consultation and openness to innovations in general and technological ones in particular.

Major Contributions

Given the relatively limited research on post-implementation issues and ERP assimilation, we used an exploratory qualitative approach. Drawing on information and insights we gained from the qualitative study during which we interviewed managers with varied responsibilities in six manufacturing organizations, we added to ERP research namely by identifying the facilitators of a successful ERP assimilation. Another major contribution is the discovery of several impediments which may slow or even hamper the effective assimilation process in both contexts. Similarly, we contributed to research by proposing an integrative framework which illustrates the relationships between the different factors we had identified. Needless to say, this framework can be instrumental to future investigations of the assimilation process of other complex IT and enterprise systems.

By applying the TOE framework for ERP assimilation, one major theoretical contribution is the fact that we stressed the solid theoretical basis of the TOE framework and showed that it is useful not only for the early stages of an innovation adoption, but also for later stages that come after the adoption of an innovation and namely the crucial post-implementation stage. No wonder then the TOE framework proved to be very useful in identifying the facilitators and the inhibitors of the assimilation of ERP systems.

Moreover, to our best knowledge, this research is the first on ERP assimilation that searched the effects of two different contexts: a developing and a developed country (that is Tunisia and Canada). In spite of the escalating investments in enterprise systems application in North Africa, our present research adds enormously to our knowledge of ERP experiences in a region that is still neglected in the overall ERP research. By investigating the similarities and the differences between companies located in the two countries, this study also contributes to the relatively scarce research on the impact of national environments on ERP practices.

Hence, there is little doubt that practitioners not only in the above studied countries but also in countries with similar contexts can benefit from our research in several ways. Firstly, the integrative framework we suggested, along with the lessons learned throughout the research, can guide practitioners (particularly ERP project managers, top management, and other managers) in firms willing to adopt an ERP system. In fact, our work can tell them much on how to promote ERP assimilation and what to watch for during their ERP implementation stage. It can also inspire them in handling their post-implementation assimilation efforts. Similarly, practitioners who are experiencing low assimilation levels and

struggling with post-implementation predicaments can have a much better understanding of underlying causes and possible remedies. In addition, practitioners can benefit from the determinants and the handicaps which we identified if they seek to develop the appropriate interventions that will improve assimilation and limit its pitfalls. In doing so, organizations can accelerate the value creation of the ERP system and the achievement of its benefits.

Future Research

Our study sets the foundation for several future research areas which we do feel are extremely important and need to be better explored.

The main objective of this research was to explore the determinants of ERP assimilation rather than to test relationships. Several relationships figured in our integrative framework were observed and need to be tested using confirmatory factor analysis to validate our findings and to determine whether they are generalizable or typical of the studied cases.

Secondly, different implementation approaches were adopted by the companies we studied. Further ERP assimilation research could investigate the impact of the implementation approach on the level of assimilation. Furthermore, our research used companies with different sizes and ERP brands, and they belonged to different industrial sectors. We recommend that cases with comparative characteristic be used to improve the results validity. In addition to providing more understanding to managers, sector specific, or brand specific or size specific findings would allow the refinement of the framework according to the studied specificities. Similarly, our research demonstrated that ERP systems need time to stabilize and to progress towards higher levels of assimilation. Since the early stages of ERP post-implementation are known to be very problematic and frustrating for all the organizations, revisiting the firms and assessing their advancement and improvements in their assimilation process could update the developed framework and enhance our understanding of these systems.

As a result, another rewarding research would be to investigate ERP assimilation success factors and to carry out cross-case studies in other national contexts, either in other countries in the studied regions or in totally different regions. Similarly, prior research indicated that several national/environmental characteristics impact ERP practices. That is what future research could consider factors which we did not consider in our research. This is true, for example, of a country's economic status, language, political environment, and its government's efforts to promote the IT infrastructure, etc. The findings of these two research avenues could certainly validate our findings and could result in a framework that is adapted specifically to some particular regions.

Another important remark is the fact that in spite of the pervasiveness of these systems, firms are still reluctant to be open to share information. Furthermore, several areas of ERP research still need to be explored. This means that case study research methodology will unquestionably remain one of the most important methodologies of choice for the investigation of unexplored areas of ERP research.

REFERENCES

Botta-Genoulaz, V., & Millet, P. A. (2005). A Classification for Better Use of ERP Systems. *Computers in Industry, 56*(6), 537–587.

Chang, S. (2004). ERP life cycle implementation, management and support: implications for practice and research. In *Proceedings of the 37th Annual Hawaii International Conference on System Sciences (HICCS 04)*, Big Island, Hawaii (pp. 80227-80237).

Chatterjee, D., Grewal, R., & Sambamurthy, V. (2002). Shaping up for ecommerce: Institutional enablers of the organizational assimilation of Web Technologies. *Management Information Systems Quarterly, 26*(2), 65–89. doi:10.2307/4132321

Cohen, W., & Levinthal, D. (1990). Absorptive Capacity: A new perspective on learning and innovation. *Administrative Science Quarterly, 35*(1), 128–152. doi:10.2307/2393553

Cooper, R. B., & Zmud, R. W. (1990). Information Technology Implementation Research: A Technological Diffusion Approach. *Management Science, 36*(2), 123–139. doi:10.1287/mnsc.36.2.123

DiMaggio, P. J., & Powell, W. W. (1983). The Iron Cage Revisited: Institutional Isomorphism and Collective Rationality in Organizational Fields. *American Sociological Review, 48*(2), 147–160. doi:10.2307/2095101

FIPA-Tunisia (The Foreign Investment Promotion Agency). (2007). Key figures: Economic Data: GNP/GDP. Retrieved October, 16, 2008, from http://www.investintunisia.tn/site/en/article.php?id_article=846

Hsieh, J. J. P., & Wang, W. (2007). Explaining Employees' Extended Use of Complex Information Systems. *European Journal of Information Systems, 16*(3), 216–227. doi:10.1057/palgrave.ejis.3000663

Huang, Z., & Palvia, P. (2001). ERP implementation issues in advanced and developing countries. *Business Process Management, 7*(3), 276–284. doi:10.1108/14637150110392773

Ifinedo, P. (2007). Interactions between organizational size, culture, and structure and some IT factors in the context of ERP success assessment: an exploration investigation. *Journal of Computer Information Systems, 27*(4), 28–44.

Jasperson, J. S., Carter, P. E., & Zmud, R. W. (2005). A Comprehensive Conceptualization of Post-Adoptive Behaviors Associated with Information Technology Enabled Work Systems. *Management Information Systems Quarterly, 2*(3), 525–557.

Jerez-Gómez, P., Céspedes-Lorente, J., & Valle-Cabrera, R. (2005). Organizational Learning and Compensation Strategies: Evidence from the Spanish Chemical Industry. *Human Resource Management, 44*(3), 279–299. doi:10.1002/hrm.20071

Ke, W., & Wei, K. K. (2006). Organizational Learning Process: Its Antecedents and Consequences in Enterprise System Implementation. *Journal of Global Information Management, 14*(1), 1–22.

Kumar, V., Maheshwari, B., & Kumar, U. (2003). An investigation of critical management issues in ERP implementation: empirical evidence from Canadian organizations. *Technovation, 23*(10), 793–807. doi:10.1016/S0166-4972(02)00015-9

Liang, H., Saraf, N., Hu, Q., & Xu, W. (2007). Assimilation of Enterprise Systems: The Effect of Institutional Pressures and the Mediating Role of Top Management. *Management Information Systems Quarterly, 31*(1), 59–87.

Musaji, Y. (2005). ERP Post-implementation Problems. *Information Systems Control Journal, 4*. Retrieved September 21, 2008 from http://www.isaca.org/Template.cfm?Section=Home&Template=/ContentManagement/ContentDisplay.cfm&ContentID=26149

Muscatello, J., & Parente, D. (2006). Enterprise Resource Planning (ERP), A Post--Implementation Cross-Case Analysis. *Information Resources Management Journal, 19*(3), 61–80.

Nah, F., & Delgado, S. (2006). Critical Success Factors for ERP Implementation and Upgrade. *Journal of Computer Information Systems, 46*(5), 99–113.

Ngai, E. W. T., Law, C. C. H., & Wat, F. K. T. (2008). Examining the critical success factors in the adoption of enterprise resource planning. *Computers in Industry, 59*(6), 548–564. doi:10.1016/j.compind.2007.12.001

Patton, M. Q. (2002). *Qualitative Research and Evaluation Methods*. Thousand Oaks, CA: Sage Publications.

Rathman, R. G., Johnsen, J., & Wen, H. J. (2005). Alignment of business Strategy and IT Strategy: A Case Study of A Fortune 50 Financial Services Company. *Journal of Computer Information Systems, 45*(2), 1–8.

Rogers, E. M. (1983). *Diffusion of Innovation* (3rd ed.). New York: Free Press.

Somers, T. M., & Nelson, K. G. (2004). A Taxonomy of Players and Activities across the ERP Project Life Cycle. *Information & Management, 41*(3), 257–278. doi:10.1016/S0378-7206(03)00023-5

Srivardhanaa, T., & Pawlowski, S. D. (2007). ERP systems as an enabler of sustained business process innovation: A knowledge-based view. *The Journal of Strategic Information Systems, 16*(1), 51–69. doi:10.1016/j.jsis.2007.01.003

Stratman, J. K., & Roth, A. V. (2002). Enterprise resource planning (ERP) competence constructs: two-stage multi-item scale development and validation. *Decision Sciences, 33*(4), 601–628. doi:10.1111/j.1540-5915.2002.tb01658.x

Tallon, P. (2008). A process-oriented perspective on the alignment of information technology and business strategy. *Journal of Management Information Systems, 24*(3), 227–268. doi:10.2753/MIS0742-1222240308

Tornatzky, L. G., & Fleischer, M. (1990). *The processes of technological innovation*. Lexington, MA: Lexington Books.

Wagner, E., & Newell, S. (2007). Exploring the Importance of Participation in the Post-Implementation Period of an ES Project: A Neglected Area. *Journal of the Association for Information Systems, 8*(10), 508–524.

Wang, E., Shih, S. P., Jiang, J. J., & Klein, G. (2008). The consistency among facilitating factors and ERP implementation success: A holistic view of fit. *Journal of Systems and Software, 81*(9), 1609–1621. doi:10.1016/j.jss.2007.11.722

Willcocks, L. P., & Sykes, R. (2000). Enterprise resource planning: the role of the CIO and it function in ERP. *Communications of the ACM, 43*(4), 32–38. doi:10.1145/332051.332065

Wu, J., & Wang, Y. (2006). Measuring ERP Success: The Ultimate Users' View. *International Journal of Operations & Production Management, 26*(8), 882–903. doi:10.1108/01443570610678657

Yagoubi, M. (2004). HRM in Tunisia . In Kamoche, K., Debrah, Y., Horwitz, F., & Muuka, G. N. (Eds.), *Managing Human Resources in Africa*. London: Routledge.

Yin, R. K. (2003). *Case study Research: Design and Methods*. London: Sage Publications.

Yu, C. S. (2005). Causes influencing the effectiveness of the post-implementation ERP system. *Industrial Management & Data Systems, 105*(1), 115–132. doi:10.1108/02635570510575225

Chapter 16
An Exploratory Analysis for ERPS Value Creation

Carmen De Pablos Heredero
Rey Juan Carlos University, Spain

Monica De Pablos Heredero
In Situ Group and Rey Juan Carlos University, Spain

ABSTRACT

A great number of firms worldwide have invested a lot in the application of ERP systems to modify their business model and be able to offer better processes. When firms implement ERP systems they try to integrate and optimize their processes in what they consider their key areas. The present chapter tries to offer a view centered on the main reasons why Spanish firms have implemented ERP systems in the last ten years and what have been their main critical success factors and their main failure factors too. For that, the authors apply a model that they have previously developed based in 5 main groups of variables. The authors ask firms about their perceptions and final results provided by the variables affecting their change processes in the ERP implementation. The authors try to offer a realistic view of what has been taking place in the Spanish market.

INTRODUCTION

Firms have great invested in ERP systems in the last fifteen years (Wang et al., 2008).

Summer (1999) admits that ERP systems can provide lots of benefits in firms. They allow, for example to compete in a global context, to reduce the warehousing material and the costs of production and the increase in the level of service offered to the customer (Ang et al., 2002).

DOI: 10.4018/978-1-61692-020-3.ch016

Akkermans and Van Helden (2002:35) recognise that the ERP implementation demands a great effort and compromise from all the organisational levels. The problems that the firms face when trying a successful implementation have long been explained in the literature review (Holland and Light, 1999, Rosario, 2000, Esteves and Pastor, 2001, Wang et al., 2008).

Trying to find solutions to the problems that due to the implementation of ERP systems can appear, different academics and consultants have done research on the process of implementation and more specifically, about the determination of the factors that contribute to the success in the implementation, best known as critical success factors (Summer, 1999, Umble et al, 2003, Fui-Hoon et al., 2003, Finney and Corbett, 2007).

In this chapter we ask firms about their perceptions and the final results they achieve as a consequence of the ERP implementation processes occurred in the last 10 years. For that we apply the model of critical success factors we have designed (De Pablos and De Pablos, 2008) based in the analysis of five main groups of variables affecting to the final results in ERP implementations.

1. The decision-making policy of the firm in the ERP selection, implementation and use
2. The training characteristics of the people involved in the ERP implementation and final use
3. The organisational inertia in the firm
4. The final internal user satisfaction
5. The final external user satisfaction

CRITICAL SUCCESS FACTORS AFFECTING TO THE FINAL RESULTS IN ERP IMPLEMENTATIONS

The Decision-Making Policy of the Firm in the ERP Selection, Implementation and Use

We include as the main variables explaining this factor the decision-making policy of the firm in the ERP selection, implementation and use, the existence of managerial support, the existence of clear procedures established for the required reengineering of business processes in the firm, the effectiveness of the project management and the existence of a wide commitment in the different stakeholders taking part in the implementation process (vendor support, external services, etc.)

The Existence of Managerial Support

Finney and Corbett (2007) stresses in their study how this aspect is one of the most cited in the literature review. Besides in our recent interview with consultants specialised in ERP implementation in the Spanish market this aspect is highly stressed as one of the most important CSFs.

Top management support in ERP implementations offer two main aspects,

*   It provides leadership
*   It provides de necessary resources to successfully implementing an ERP system, firms need spend time with people and provide them with the needed resources. The implementation could fail in case that the critical resources are not available when needed.

For achieving success in a project of ERP implementation it is important to involve the managers in the organisation. Managers must involve to the rest of the people in the organisation in the collaboration and support with the project.

For that reason, periodical committees headed by the main managers in the firm must be held. The organisation must be kept informed about the evolution of the project and about the problems arisen.

The Existence of Clear Procedures Established For the Required Re-Engineering Of Business Processes in the Firm

It has mainly to do with managing the cultural change, identified by Al-Mashari et al. (2003), Fui-Hoon et al (2003) and Finney and Corbett (2007).

Implementing ERP systems requires the redesign of the existent business processes. Many times the ERP implementations fail because some firms underestimate the extent to which they have to change processes. Motwani et al. (2002) suggested that the organisations should be prepared for fundamental change to ensure the success of the business process reengineering.

The companies must profit from the ERP implementation to optimise their business processes by promoting the change in the management system and the experience in the consultancy teams that take part in the implementation of the new system. Therefore, it is critical the process of change that accompanies to the project. The focus in the change of the management allows surpass the state of uncertainty that appears in the people working in this kind of projects.

In the management of the change in a project for the implementation of an ERP system, the firm must work on three different aspects: information, training and involvement.

The Effectiveness of the Project Management

It has to do with the aspects of the change management (Falkowski et al., 1998;: Holland and Light, 1999; Rosario, 2000; Sommers and Nelson, 2003), and project cost planning and management (Holland and Light, 1999; Somers and Nelson, 2003).

Project management plans, co-ordinates and controls the complex and diverse activities of modern, industrial and commercial projects. The implementation of ERP systems implies the working of different activities, all involving business functions and requiring a long time effort. There are five main parts to consider in project management

1.   Having a formal implementation plan
2.   Offering a realistic time frame
3.   Celebrating periodic status meetings
4.   Having an effective project leader
5.   Including project team members that, at the same time, are stakeholders

The Existence of a Wide Commitment in the Different Areas of the Firm

It refers to the existence of a communication plan (Falkowski et al., 1998; Holland et al., 1999; Summer, 1999; Rosario 2000; Mabert et al. 2003) empowered decision makers, and team morale and motivation

Taking into consideration that the ERP systems are enterprise wide information systems that attempt to integrate information across all functional areas in an organisation, it is important to get the needed support from all functional areas in the organisation. Everyone in the organisation must be responsible for the whole system and key users from different departments must have cleared the project implementation phases.

When realising the implementation of an ERP, a previous methodology must be established, where clearly the steps in the project and the involvement of each of the key-users and the consultancy team that takes part in the implementation are specified.

The Existence of a Wide Commitment in the Different Stakeholders in the Implementations (Vendor Support, External Services)

It is close referred to the selection of the ERP (Sommers and Nelson, 2003; Al-Mashari et al., 2003) and the consultant selection and relationship (Al-Mashari et al., 2003; Motwani et al., 2002.

It is very important for the customer that decides to implement an ERP system in his/her organisation and for the providers, to align the implementation services with the achieving of the objectives fixed for the project. Those objectives must be defined in the design document elaborated once that the analysis and requirements feeding phases have been finished. The design document must contain the situation of the business processes before the implementation and the future situation, once that the business process reengineering effort to implement the ERP systems, has taken place.

The Training Characteristics of the People Involved in the ERP Implementation and Final Use

It is related to the aspects of training and job re-design, data conversion and integrity (Umble et al., 2003; Sommers and Nelson, 2001, 2004), and system testing Nah et al. (2001). The interviews with the consultants offer us a similar criterion when they refer to the need of establishing training programs for the users.

As we know by the nature of an ERP system, it includes all the material and human resources related to the management of the information in the firms. In this sense, a first vision distinguishes between both types of human resources in the information system of a firm: the final users and the personal working on them.

Final users are all those persons that take part in the information system of a firm to get the final product, as defined by Garcia Bravo (2000). We can consider that all the members in an organisation are potential final users of the system, since all of them are going to use and modify information.

The role of final users has more relevance in the last years due to the decentralization of these systems. This way, a greater proportion of the people in the organisation are involved not only in the processing of information and the obtaining of a result, but in some other activities as can be the development of the systems.

The personal of the information systems include all the workers in charge of the ERP development, management and maintaining. Traditionally it has been considered that these system technicians are specialised in the information system.

The change in the role of the information systems in the organisations has evolved along time. This way, by considering the ERP strategic role, it has been assumed that the responsibilities

in the ERP are not just technical ones but they necessarily include some other functions related to the strategic management or the firm's policy. Additionally, part of these workers must have specific skills in the management of human resources.

For that, we must also consider the differentiation between managerial and ethical skills widely spread.

It is also typical the division of people working on information systems according to the hierarchical order of responsibility assumed. We can consider this way, that the system always includes a top executive of the company, the Chief Information Officer, CIO, directly reporting to the President or the Chief Executive Officer in the firm (CEO); a certain number of intermediate managers, with limited responsibilities, the technical personal, specialised in some tasks and the operations personal, in charge of the performance of structured tasks.

Functions of the Workers in ERP Systems

Monforte Moreno (1995) refers to the organisation of the ERP systems as a series of functions, independent from the firm's dimension, which we can sum up in the following ones,

Development of the systems, programming and processes of exploitation: it includes the tasks related with the analysis, design, development and implementation of the ERP systems in the firm, together with the programming and maintaining of applications.

Security of the ERP systems, it includes the needed operations to avoid the loss of information, the prevention of physical and logical attacks to the system or the insurance of the buildings facing human or natural errors.

The administration of the ERP information, related with the management of the use of the resources of information systems and the "internal payment" of these services to the departments requiring them.

Figure 1. The phases for the project

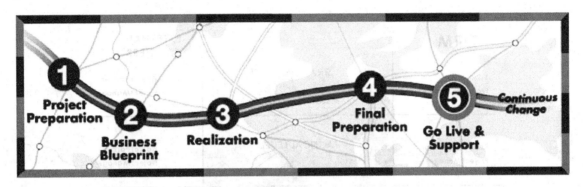

Standards and system techniques, it refers to the planning in the acquiring of new technologies and their implementation in the firm. One of the main tasks for these aims it is the constant seeking of the technological environment, to analyse the new availabilities of resources for acquisition.

In a similar way, McLeod (2000) propose a scheme of the organisation adapted to the model of the life cycle, reflected in figure 1. The main character is the CIO with a wide group of responsibilities and functions. In the middle level, the author situates a group of supervisors of the different areas of the system, under his/her control. And reporting to these last ones, we can find the technical people and the operators working in each of the functions.

Human Efforts of the ERP Implementation and Rewards

The strategic management in the human resource area refers to a group of policies that define the strategy of human resources in a firm, this means, the main decisions related to this area. They can have a significant influence over the organisation and the results.

Some of the main human resources policies widely studied have been the following ones,

Recruitment policy: it deals with integrating in the organisation people having the required skills for the development of a group of activities and firm's functions in relation with the ERP system. In this sense, one of the decisions more studied is "to do instead of buying", that faces the internal formation of the new personnel with the search in the market of the human resources containing the proper profile in competencies. It also belongs to this ambient the decision about the factors that must be taken into account when searching new human resources.

Training and development policies, they have to do with the increase of stock of individual skills coming from the human resources in the firm, that can besides contribute to the improvement of collective skills. Inside this ambit, we can consider the decisions around the quantity of training that must be offered on the ERP system.

Policies on the design of the work profile, they mainly refer to the variety of functions and tasks included inside a work profile around the ERP system. Inside this part, policies for job enrichment and level of the desired specialisation are included.

Rewarding policies, related with the rewards that the workers receive from their work. In this sense, we must consider included here all the decisions dealing with rewards, shares offered, holiday programs and any other extra rewards.

These policies will be the main part in the strategy with ERP workers.

Most analysis consider five different configurations in the human resources policy in a firm,

Figure 2. The organization of teams

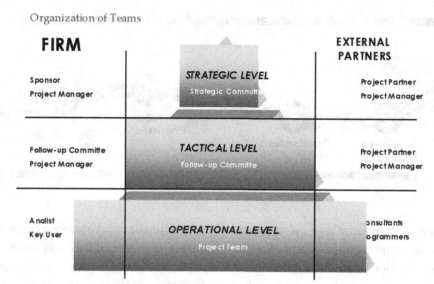

policies oriented to the human capital, policies oriented to the tasks (technical people rewarded, work assured and work utility)

It seems clear that the human resources policies of the information system can be varied, especially by having into account the wide number of available tools in this area.

The Ethics and the ERP System

The CIO must be the highest responsible for the computer ethics in the ERP system, and must then supervise and pay attention to the influence of the ERP over society and consider the policies that can be adopted for a correct use of the technology. This preoccupation for the ethics is immediately perceived by people working with the ERP systems, especially for those in charge of the more invisible part of them.

Parker (1988) proposes ten actions to promote the ethical conduct in the employees in the information system of a firm that could be extended to the ERP cases,

- To formulate a conduct code
- To establish the clear acting rules in situations of ethic conflict
- To clearly specify the sanctions applied in non ethic conducts
- To public recognise the ethical conducts
- To develop programs, meetings and recommend readings
- To inform, promote the knowledge of the Acts implied with the proper use of IS and IT at Organisations
- To delimitate the ethical responsibilities if each worker according to their tasks.
- To promote the use of "restructuring programs" for people avoiding ethical norms.
- To promote the integration of workers in the professional associations
- To offer example with the own acts

The Organization Inertia in the Firm

It is referred to the aspects of visioning and planning (Falkowski et al., 1998; Holland et al., 1999;

Figure 3. The steps in the process of change

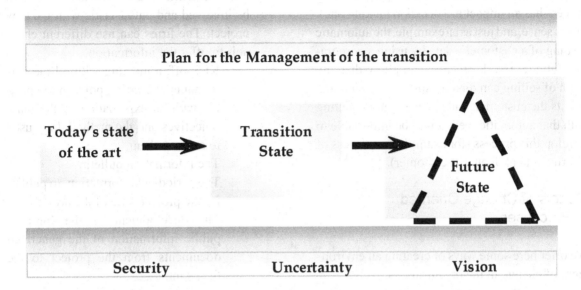

Rosario, 2000; Al-Mashari et al., 2003). It is in relation with the need of establishing a responsible for the software implementation referred by the consultants in the interviews.

The organisational inertia has to do with aspects in relation to culture, values and ways of group expression in the organization. Organizational change implies the leaving of some structures, procedures and behaviours and the adoption of other ones, with the main objective of improving the final performance. The management of the change implies the application of concepts, techniques and methodologies that are going to make it possible the complex migration from an initial not desired status to another final desired one.

The management of change must start with the challenge of determining what is going to be changed. We have to distinguish between people; they must make decisions in relation to what it is going to be changed since they have responsibilities in the organisations, and those who are directly related in the process, people who are asked in an informal way and those others who are not even asked for. Once the change has been implemented, there will be people informed and trained in the process and people who have just

been informed. These circumstances logically are going to have an impact in the change, in a positive or negative way.

The Process: The Main Axis for the Change

Organisations develop their objectives through processes. A process is a group of tasks allocated in different firm areas and that develops a group of functionalities or specialisations. In this sense, we can say that a process is trans-functional. A process has a point of start and end and around it many different functions are working in different periods of time, in a parallel or sequential way.

The concept of trans-functionality in the process and the consideration of the co-living of different kind of processes in the organisations are very important when considering the organisational change. In the first place, because the effort in the change it is going to promote impact in the whole process, because any of the firm's task is part of a whole business process, and, in the second place, because a change in any part of a process, it does not matter its nature, will have an impact in a process connected with the previous one but of different nature (for example a working process has an impact in a decision making one). In this sense, and just as an example, the automatic feeding of a customer's data by using a corporative Intranet (work process) can allow that any point of selling can directly solve a decision that affects the customer, and in case of not counting with that automatic feed, it will be impossible to develop this process (for example the process of offering a bank loan to a customer).

Models of Change Oriented to Processes

We offer here some ways of creating an environment of change in the organisations,

- To create a dissatisfaction: by showing lack of skills in the status quo, by communicating relevant variations in the internal profile and the external situation, that show the need of change. For example, the globalisations of the markets have made appeared the need of marketing the products in new geographical areas. For that reason, it is important for the system and the people in the company to be able to work in different languages and currency.
- To reduce the fear for the change: by establishing open discussions, based on the experience of other companies and other parts in the organisation. For example, the resistance to change can be a decisive cause for the failure of a project of ERP implementation. For that reason, most companies apply for the collaboration of external consultancy firms experienced in the same industry, to be informed before starting any project.
- To create energy in the company around the benefits of the change in people from an individual and collective perspective. For this reason the information must be properly managed. It must reach to every-

one in the firm and it must help people to be involved and enthusiastic with the new project. The firms can use different channels to offer the information

- ○ Kick-off: a meeting with all the participants. A starting point in the project with an explanation of the main objectives and the methodology used to achieve them.
- ○ The information bulletin
- ○ The periodical information, to publicity the project state of the art
- ○ The development of the Intranet: public information of the generated documents from the project to the firm's intranet.

To build support for the change: by identifying the persons in charge of the change efforts and work with them. Before starting a project, it is important to define who are responsible of it in the firm that it is implementing the system and in the external collaboration groups too.

- To define specific objectives for the change: in detail and that can be measured in clear deadlines. Work teams are usually established to fix the objectives associated to the different business areas implied in the project and measure the persecution of the objectives and typical deviations.
- To define awards and punishments in the change and their impact in the profiles and work places. In the contracts of collaboration with external providers, it is important to include mechanisms of punishment by both parts (provider and customer). They can be activated in case there are deviations in the final ERP functionality or in the initial agreed deadlines.
- To plan the adequate training and synchronised with change. In the various phases of the project, different training plans are established according to the different users

Figure 4. The management of change: Tools

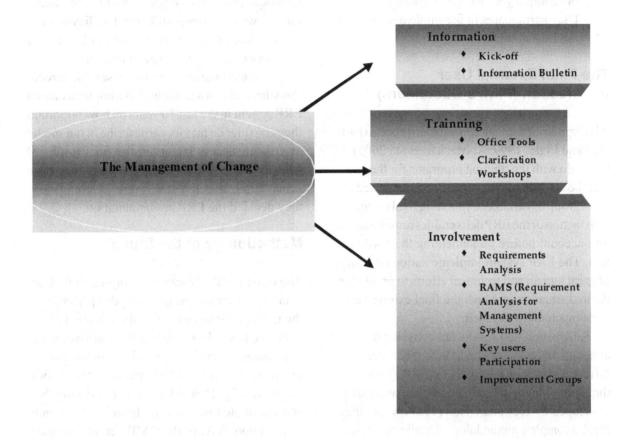

implied on them. As we descend in the organisational levels, the training required is more specific and specialised.

- To communicate the efforts for the change and make participate to the employees in them, etc. Communication matrixes must be defined where the different people's profiles and the related information with the project are informed in each of the project steps.

The Final Internal User Satisfaction

It is based in the system testing (Nah et al., 2001; Al-Mashari et al., 2003), and pos-implementation evaluation (Holland and Light, 1999, Nah et al., 2001; Al-Mashari et al., 2003; Umble et al., 2003). It is highly related with the feedback we have obtained from the consulting firms operating in the Spanish market since they stress that it is very important to check that the software meets the needs of the whole company.

It refers to the participation in the system development and implementation by different representatives of the target groups. System implementation means a threat to users perceptions of control over their work and a period of transition in which users must cope with differences between old and new work systems. User involvement is effective because it offers perceived control by taking part in the whole plan.

Users can be involved twice when implementing an ERP system:

- User involvement at a stage of definition of the company's ERP system needs,
- User participates in the implementation of the ERP system.

The Final External User Satisfaction (Firm's Customers)

It is inspired in the client consultation process (Holland and Light, 1999; Al-Mashari et al., 2003). It has to do with the training programs for the users that the consultants surveyed have mentioned us.

A group of variables explaining final customer satisfaction of the ERP deliverables must be taken into account before implementing the ERP system. The ERP system implementation demands of great human and technical efforts to promote a desired situation in which the final external user feels much more satisfied.

Satisfaction and results are considered, variables of the greatest importance when defining different styles of internalising ERP systems in the firms. Maybe the most complete analysis is developed by Ives and Olson (1983) where they reach a complete methodology that allows measuring the user satisfaction in IT use. This approach has been mentioned in various analyses that study the impact of information and communication technologies in firms of different nature. It seems to be a useful tool to be applied to the case or ERP implementations due to the difficulty in measuring such abstract term as satisfaction.

THE EMPIRICAL ANALYSIS

The present work is part of a wider study supported and financed by The Spanish Innovation Ministry, where we try to analyze the impact of information and communication technologies in different firm's innovation policies. The general model analyses different entrepreneurial and institutional factors that promote the performance of open innovation practices in firms.

In the general study we are developing different techniques of analysis, revision of the literature, interviews with groups of interest, policymakers, and academics, consultancy firms and final user firms operating in the Spanish market.

In this exploratory work we present the perceptions that a group of firms that have implemented an ERP system in the last 10 years on how important they consider de factors we describe in our model as critical success factors in the final results of EPR implementations and if in reality they have achieved the objectives they were searching when they decided the ERP implementation.

Methodology of the Study

The design in the research attempted to find out data about firm's expectations and experiences in the use of ERP systems. For the selection of the firms we have chosen the SABI database. SABI is a financial database showing information of the main Spanish and Portuguese companies, elaborated by Dijk Electronic Publishing S.A and distributed in Spain by Informa, Economic Information, S.A. In the SABI version we have used for the analysis (December 2007), there are 982.410 firms. We have selected all kinds of firms differentiating them by the criteria of size and age. The first part of the work consisted in deciding the questions for the analysis. This part has taken place from February till April 2008.

According to the model we have presented, we have decided to ask about these characteristics,

A. Characteristics dealing with the decision-making policy of the firm in the ERP selection, implementation and use
   1. Why did the firm decided to implement an ERP?
   2. Did the project have full managerial support?
   3. Did the firm establish clear procedures for the re-engineering of business processes in the firm?

4. Did the firm offer quantitive or qualitative measures to deeply know about the effectiveness of the project management?

5. Did the firm perform a formal implementation plan?

6. Was the firm offering a realistic time frame?

7. Did the firm held periodic status meeting to know about the evolution of the project?

8. Has the firm included in the project team member, firm's stakeholders?

9. Did the project count on with a wide commitment in the different areas?

10. Did the project count on with a wide commitment coming from the different stakeholders in the implementation (vendor support, external services)?

B. Characteristics dealing with the training of the people involved in the ERP implementation and final use

1. Did the firm establish functions in the equipment responsible for the ERP implementation?

2. Did the firm establish group responsibilities?

3. Did the firm establish individual responsibilities?

4. Did the firm train employees in the ERP implementation?

5. Did the firm train external collaborators in ERP main objectives for the organization?

6. Did the firm communicate potential users about the ERP implementation?

7. Did the firm establish a rewarding policy for the workers taking part in the ERP implementation process?

8. Did the firm formulate a conduct code for the ERP implementation?

9. Did the firm establish the clear acting rules in situations of ethic conflict?

10. Has the firm clearly specified the sanctions applied in non ethic conducts?

11. Has the firm developed programs, meetings and recommend readings in the new ERP system?

12. Has the firm informed, promoted the knowledge of the Acts implied with the proper use of IS and IT at Organisations?

13. Has the firm delimitated the ethical responsibilities if each worker according to their tasks?

14. Has the firm promoted the use of "restructuring programs" for people avoiding ethical norms?

15. Has the firm promoted the integration of workers in the professional associations?

C. Characteristics dealing with the organizational inertia of the firm

1. Has the firm created positive energy in the workers about the change final results?

2. Has the firm used any mechanism to reduce fear for the change?

3. Has the firm identified people in charge of the change efforts?

4. Has the firm defined specific objectives for the change process?

5. Has the firm establish clear deadlines for the change process?

6. Has the firm used a proper methodology for the ERP implementation?

7. Has the firm discussed with final users about the desired improvements in the change process?

D. Characteristics dealing with the final internal user satisfaction

1. Has the internal user been involved at any stage of the definition of the company's ERP system needs?

2. Has the internal user participated in the implementation of the ERP system?

Figure 5. Level of responses by different industries

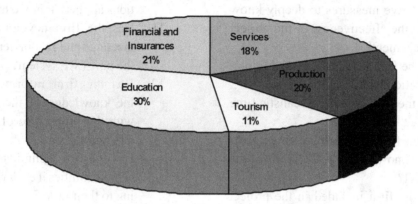

E. Characteristics dealing with the final external user satisfaction
   1. Is there any mechanism in the firm that allows taking information from final external user's satisfaction?
   2. Is the final user satisfied with the new system?
   3. Is the firm using any tool to incorporate the feedback received from the final external user into the system?

A questionnaire was elaborated for the firms. It was offered via the web page of the Social Science Faculty, by previously informing to the interested firms via email in the period from May 15th till July 15th, 2008.

As we have just presented, most of the questions we have applied concerning to this analysis, have been suggested by the literature review in some cases, and in others, they have been obtained directly from firms that have directly experienced an ERP implementation in the last 10 years

The greatest part of the questions are waiting for a response in the typical 1 to 5 Likert scale with degrees ranking from 5 "completely agree" to 1 "completely disagree", and yes/no responses. The SPSS software has been used for the statistical analysis of the obtained data.

We have received a 32% of final responses from the chosen sample. The firms are localized in five different industries: services to firms (22%), production (12%), tourism (34%), education (8%), financial and insurance services (24%). A 36,6% of firms are older than 15 years, and a 54,3% are small and medium size firms.

THE RESULTS

Now we show the percentages of the perceptions that we have collected from the answers received.

If we compare the obtained responses with the different critical success factors mainly stressed in the literature review (we must remember that Fui-Hoon et al. (2003) and Finney and Corbett (2007) make a complete revision of the authors offering publications in journals of reference), we see that there is a clear fit between what the theory explains to us and what in reality the firms realities show.

According to the answers we have obtained from firms up to know, we can admit that they consider as most important critical success factors affecting ERP implementations the following ones.

According to the answers we have obtained from firms up to know, we can admit that they consider as less important critical success factors affecting ERP implementations the following ones.

Table 1. What are the perceptions of firms that have implemented ERP systems in the last 10 years on different critical success factors

Scale (5 completely agree..........1 completely disagree)	5	4	3	2	1
1.	82,6%	12%	4,4%	1%	0%
2.	94,4%	4,6%	1%	0%	0%
3.	57,6%	25,7%	7,9%	4,8%	4%
4.	75,6%	31,5%	6,1%	0%	0%
5.	68,4%	26,7%	4,9%	0%	0%
6.	56,8%	31%	6,7%	3,7%	1,8%
7.	26,8%	29,8%	15,6%	13,6%	14,2%
8.	76,3%	15,6%	8,1%	0%	0%
9.	83,4%	11,1%	5,5%	0%	0%
10.	23,4%	21,6%	36,3%	12,8%	5,9%
11.	16,7%	14,8%	14,3%	31,1%	23,1%
12.	37,8%	26,4%	25%	14,6%	13,2%
13.	30,8%	26,4%	15%	14,6%	13,2%
14.	56,8%	31%	6,7%	3,7%	1,8%
15.	26,8%	29,8%	15,6%	13,6%	14,2%
16.	77%	14,6%	7,1%	1%	0%
17.	85%	9,2%	6,5%	2%	0.5%
18.	23,4%	21,6%	36,3%	12,8%	5,9%
19.	12,8%	11,7%	16,3%	35,1%	24,1%
20.	37,8%	26,4%	25%	14,6%	13,2%
21.	26,8%	29,8%	15,6%	13,6%	14,2%
22.	76,3%	15,6%	8,1%	0%	0%
23.	78,4%	10,1%	4,5%	2,1%	1,5%
24.	37,8%	26,4%	25%	14,6%	13,2%
25.	30,8%	26,4%	15%	14,6%	13,2%
26.	56,8%	31%	6,7%	3,7%	1,8%
27.	26,8%	29,8%	15,6%	13,6%	14,2%
28.	76,3%	15,6%	8,1%	0%	0%
29.	56,8%	31%	6,7%	3,7%	1,8%
30.	26,8%	29,8%	15,6%	13,6%	14,2%
31.	75,4%	16,3%	6,6%	3,2%	0%
32.	73,4%	12,1%	8,5%	4,1%	2,8%
33.	23,4%	21,6%	36,3%	12,8%	5,9%
34.	11,7%	18,8%	12,3%	38,1%	26,1%
35.	23,4%	21,6%	36,3%	12,8%	5,9%
36.	10,7%	12,8%	13,3%	34,1%	26,1%
37.	37,8%	26,4%	25%	14,6%	13,2%

Table 2. What firms consider most important CSF in the ERP implementation process

Number of the factor	Most important critical success factor
1	The reason why the firm decides to implement an ERP system
2	The managerial support in the project
4	The existence of quantitative and qualitative measures to know about the final effectiveness of the project
9	The commitment to the project offered by different areas
16	The communication of the ERP implementation to potential users
17	The existence of a rewarding policy for the workers taking part in the ERP implementation process
23	The establishment of ethical responsibilities of workers according to their tasks
31	The use of a proper methodology for the ERP implementation
32	The discussion with final users about the desired improvements in the change process

CONCLUSION

Firms are each time more involved with the implementation of ERP projects These projects imply a great effort in planning strategies for managing the change of the business processes and the motivation and training of the employees taking part in the project and final users. There are many risks associated to an ERP implementation process.

In this chapter we have performed a first exploratory analysis by taking into consideration a model that we have recently proposed in a previous publication that can help firms to make the best of the ERP implementation and exploitation according to the objectives of the firm. The model is composed by five different aspects, the decision-making policy of the firm in the ERP selection, implementation and use, the training characteristics of the people involved in the ERP implementation and final use, the organizational

Figure 6. Most important critical success factor

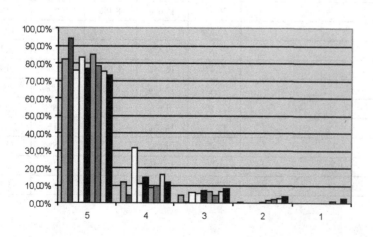
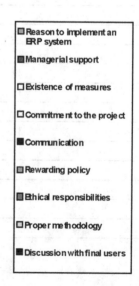

Table 3. What firms consider less important CSF in the ERP implementation process

Number of the factor	Less important critical success factor
7	If the firm offers periodic status meetings to know about the evolution of the project
11	If the firm has defined functions in the equipment responsible for the ERP implementation
19	If the firm has established the clear acting rules in situations of ethic conflict?
34	If the internal user has participated in the implementation of the ERP system
36	Degree of final user satisfaction with the new system?

inertia in the firm, the final internal user satisfaction, the final external user satisfaction-

We have asked a group of firms of different size and age operating in the Spanish market in a variety group of industries about how they have experienced the critical success factors in their own ERP implementation experiences. Amongst the critical success factors that the firms consider most important ones, we can cite, the reason why the firm decides to implement an ERP system, the managerial support in the project, the existence of quantitative and qualitative measures to know about the final effectiveness of the project, the

commitment to the project offered by different areas, the communication of the ERP implementation to potential users, the existence of a rewarding policy for the workers taking part in the ERP implementation process, the establishment of ethical responsibilities of workers according to their tasks, the use of a proper methodology for the ERP implementation, the discussion with final users about the desired improvements in the change process.

We have just developed a very preliminary and exploratory analysis, and it implies a great barrier for extrapolating the results of the analysis at this

Figure 7. Less important critical success factor

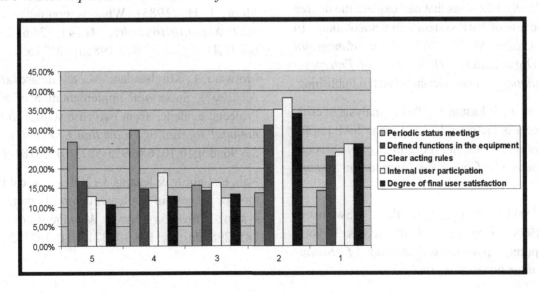

moment. Now we are in the process of obtaining more rich information from the data collected and see if we can find differences according to firm sizes and ages, the industry where the firm is located, the use they are making of the ERP system, the degree of access of different business partners into their ERP system, etc.

REFERENCES

Akkermans, H., & Van Helden, K. (2002). Vicious and virtuous cycles in ERP implementation: a case study of interrelations between critical success factors. *European Journal of Information Systems, 11*(1), 35–46. doi:10.1057/palgrave/ejis/3000418

Al-Mashari, M., Al-Mudimigh, A., & Zairi, M. (2003). Enterprise Resource Planning: a taxonomy of critical factors. *European Journal of Operational Research, 146*, 352–364. doi:10.1016/S0377-2217(02)00554-4

Ang, J. S. K., Sum, C. C., & Yeo, L. N. (2002). A multiple-case design methodology for studying MRP success and CSFs. *Information & Management, 39*(4), 271–281. doi:10.1016/S0378-7206(01)00096-9

De Pablos Heredero, C., & De Pablos Heredero, M. (2008). Elements that can explain the degree of success of ERP systems implementation . In Cruz-Cunha, M. M. (Ed.), *Social, Managerial and Organizational Dimensions of Enterprise Information Systems*. Hershey, PA: IGI Publishing.

Esteves, J., & Pastor, J. (2001). Analysis of critical success factors relevance along SAP implementation phases. In *Proceedings of the Seventh Americas Conference on Information Systems* (pp. 1019-1025).

Falkowski, G., Pedigo, P., Smith, B., & Swamson, D. (1998). A recipe for ERP success. Beyond Computing. *International Journal of Human-Computer Interaction, 16*(1), 5–22.

Finney, S., & Corbett, M. (2007). ERP implementation: a compilation and analysis of critical success factors. *Business Process Management Journal, 13*(3), 329–347. doi:10.1108/14637150710752272

Fui-Hoon, F., Zuckweiler, K. M., & Lee-Shang, J. (2003). ERP implementation: Chief Information Officers' Perceptions on Critical Success Factors. *International Journal of Human-Computer Interaction, 16*(1), 5–22. doi:10.1207/S15327590IJHC1601_2

García Bravo, D. (2000). *Sistemas de información en la empresa. Conceptos y aplicaciones*. Madrid: Pirámide.

Holland, C. P., & Light, B. (1999, May). A critical success factors model for ERP implementation. *IEEE Software*, 30–36. doi:10.1109/52.765784

Mabert, V., Soni, A., & Venkatamara, M. (2003). Enterprise Resource Planning: managing implementation process. *European Journal of Operational Research, 146*(2), 302–314. doi:10.1016/S0377-2217(02)00551-9

McLeod, R. (2000). *Management information systems*. Mexico City: Prentice Hall.

Monforte Moreno, M. (1995). *Sistemas de información para la dirección*. Madrid: Pirámide.

Moor, J. H. (1985). What is computer ethics? *Metaphilosophy, 16*(4), 266–275. doi:10.1111/j.1467-9973.1985.tb00173.x

Motwani, J., Mirchandani, M., & Gunasekaran, A. (2002). Successful implementation of ERP Projects: evidence from two case studies. *International Journal of Production Economics, 75*, 83–96. doi:10.1016/S0925-5273(01)00183-9

Nah, F., Lau, J., & Kuang, J. (2001). Critical factors for successful implementation of enterprise systems. *Business Process Management, 7*(3), 285–296. doi:10.1108/14637150110392782

Parker, D. (1988). Ethics for Information Systems Personnel. *Journal of Information Systems Management, 5*, 44–48. doi:10.1080/07399018808962925

Rosario, J. G. (2000 May). On the leading edge: critical success factors in ERP implementation projects. *Business World*, 21-27.

Smith, A. (2009). New framework for enterprise information systems. *International Journal of CENTERIS, 1*(1), 30–36.

Sommers, G., & Nelson, C. (2003). A taxonomy of players and activities across the ERP project life cycle. *Information & Management, 41*(3), 257–278. doi:10.1016/S0378-7206(03)00023-5

Summer, M. (1999). Critical success factors in enterprise wide information management systems projects. In *Proceedings of 5ᵗʰ Americas Conference on Information Systems* (pp. 232-234).

Umble, E. J., Haft, R. R., & Umble, M. M. (2003). Enterprise Resource Planning: implementation procedures and critical success factors. *European Journal of Operational Research, 146*, 241–257. doi:10.1016/S0377-2217(02)00547-7

Chapter 17
Production Information Systems Usability in Jordan

Emad Abu-Shanab
Yarmouk University, Jordan

Heyam Al-Tarawneh
Ministry of Education, Jordan

ABSTRACT

Enterprise systems are becoming more important as they support the efficiency and effectiveness of operations and reduce cost. In this chapter we explored the literature related to production information systems (PIS), enterprise systems, and other applications and their influence in an industrial zone in Jordan. Constructs from the Innovation Diffusion Theory were used, where results indicated that the adoption rate is acceptable and all variables have high means with respect to their evaluation by managers, but only two variable significantly predicted intention to use. In a second study that explored the status of IT usage in manufacturing firms using a different sample, results indicated that accounting information systems were widely used and distribution systems and manufacturing aiding systems were the least used. Other findings, conclusions and future work are stated at the end of the chapter.

INTRODUCTION

The industrial sector in Jordan is one of the main dimensions in the economic life of the country and is a major contributor in local production figures. Statistics indicate a contribution of 21.5% of the local production in the year 2006, which concluded 90% of the national size of exportation (Jordan Industrial Chamber Website, 2008). Thus, the attention paid to this sector is one of

the factors that lead to improving this sector's efficiency and productivity. Statistics also indicated that this sector employs 15% of The Jordanian workforce, which is a high percentage compared to other sectors (same source).

Research defined innovation as an intellectual performance that leads individuals to problem solving, or the intellectual effort that leads to non-repetitive or ordinary results (Trairy, 2008). Gnaim (2005) used another definition of innovation but in the higher education quality area, where he claimed that innovation is doing something good and not

DOI: 10.4018/978-1-61692-020-3.ch017

bad. Finally, Smadi (2001) stated that employee innovation in the manufacturing area in Jordan was more prevalent in small-size businesses than in larger ones, where he explored 870 employees and studied their inclination to adopt the Kaizen model in improving work environment.

One of the most important tools that help in improving this sector is information technology (IT), where its role in this sector ranges from supporting operations to a major role in automation and control of operations. The important role of information technology in manufacturing especially in reducing cost and pushing operations forward, and adding value to the manufacturing process, which satisfies firms' objectives. The importance of production information systems (PIS) is becoming vital to all manufacturing firms to gain and sustain competitive advantage. The adoption of PIS is becoming a priority to firms in this sector especially those who work in alliance with foreign (global) firms.

The word adoption is not a secret one, firms need to convince their employees and managers to effectively use and utilize information systems in a way that achieves firms' objectives. What makes this adoption more important, is that when we deal with complex systems (like EIS or PIS) users need more attention and involvement to guarantee their acceptance and thus the full benefit from such systems (Wang, Hsieh, Butler & Hsu, 2008). Research indicates the importance of users' adoption when dealing with new technology. Users are cautious to use new technology unless they believe it will bring to them some advantage, and would be easy to use. Also, they need to make sure it is compatible with systems they used before and many other factors that influence their perception of technology. This study reviewed the literature related to the technology acceptance area and adopted the innovation diffusion theory (IDT) proposed by Rogers in early 1983 (Rogers, 1995; Moore and Benbasat, 1991). This study reviewed also the literature in the area of production systems explored the factors predicting the rate of adoption

of such systems through the reported opinions of managers in this sector. Finally, conclusions and future work are stated at the end.

BACKGROUND

Many theories tackled the adoption of new technology concepts and proposed a variety of theories and models that exceeded hundreds of propositions and variables. The argument in this domain emphasizes finding the suitable set of "factors" that can predict users' behavior with respect to using new technology. Most theories and research utilized the users' "intention to use" the technology as a surrogate to actual usage of the technology. Thus, many theories used "Intention to Use" (ITU) as the dependent variable, and proposed many predictors ranging from two variables to more than ten in some cases. The following section will explore the literature related to the IDT and other theories in the technology acceptance domain, then literature related to production information systems and enterprise resources planning systems usage.

Production Information Systems

Enterprise Information Systems (EIS) control all major business processes with a single software architecture in real time (Turban, Leidner, McLean & Wetherbe, 2008). Under the EIS category, the same authors list production information systems (PIS), Supply Chain Management Systems (SCM systems), Customer relationship Management Systems (CRM systems), Product lifecycle management systems (PLM systems), and Enterprise Resource Planning systems (ERP Systems). EIS account for 54% of licensing revenues, and expected to have the highest growth rates (expected to be $55 billion in 2012) (McCrea, 2008). Our focus in this study is more towards PIS and ERP as they relate to manufacturing and industrial applications.

Production Information Systems (PIS) are defined as systems that work with production and operations information. PIS collect information from end terminals (like point of sale terminals - POS, shop floor machines, and operation and factory sensors) and store in transaction processing machines and then feed some management information systems (MIS) or other types of functional systems like: decision support systems (DSS), and enterprise resource planning systems (ERP) (Turban, Leidner, McLean & Wetherbe, 2008). The output of PIS is used to support managers in the process of decision making and to improve the managerial functions in the firm. The described architecture is not a unique one, as many disputes are related to the difference between functional systems and management information systems, as an example, PIS can get input data from transaction processing systems (TPS) and generate reports and output that can be used in the managerial decision making process. Some academicians describe all these systems as MIS, even enterprise resource planning systems (ERP).

Many definitions were reported in the literature for PIS like the definition used by Ciurana, Garcia-Romeu, Ferrer and Casadesus (2008) which indicates that PIS are systems that are related to transferring raw material into products with special specifications.

PIS are defined as data processing network systems (Hssain, Djeraba & Descotes-Genon, 1993, pp. 1). It seems that it is a simple definition but, the authors add further that it includes other components like the input data from process devices (sensors and terminals). On the other hand, the output is meaningful information used in decision-making. The authors report three methodological requirements related to design of PIS: managing the large volume of data and knowledge compounding the core of the network, coping with high complexity of operations, and providing reliable and available data and knowledge inputs to the PIS. Hsu and Rattner (1990) conclude that to meet these requirements, design

of PIS should be a part of a global design approach within total-system architecture.

PIS aim at planning and scheduling and organizing for operations with related issue of work orders to shop floors and production (Ciurana, Garcia-Romeu, Ferrer & Casadesus, 2008). The importance of PIS comes from the role that it plays in facilitating the process of design and production of products, and forwarding it to customers (the distribution function). Research related to PIS focused on the applications related to the theory of planning and production control, where the main objective is reducing costs and risks, this is applied in more than one industry and type (Wang & Hu, 2008). On the other hand, research stressed the importance of providing the correct and timely information through the installation of sensors on the production line, or the use of web-based systems. Research emphasized the importance of synchronization of information systems to guarantee the required reduction of cost and the needed customer satisfaction (Mourtiz et al., 2008).

PIS can aid in the reduction of cost and facilitation (smoothing) of the flow of material in the manufacturing process. Also, the flow of information and material is becoming more vital to the production process when considering the global perspective or the supply chain management concept (SCM). A study that explored mobile communication technology importance in the integration process when transferring information and material between suppliers and customers, concluded that it is very important to utilize the benefits of PIS to reduce cost and gain integration between partners (Ende, Jaspers & Gerwin, 2008). In another study that explored the application of fuzzy logic concepts within a smart agent, solutions were provided for production problems utilizing previous solutions to previous problems (Lu & Sy, 2008). Authors concluded that it is useful in the industrial environment to provide decision makers with information residing in PIS to make accurate and timely decisions.

Finally, a group of Greek researchers studied the manufacturing strategies and the influence of IT on financial performance, where cluster analysis method with VACOR algorithm was used. Results indicated that the usage of information technology in industrial sector would have a significant effect on financial measures especially in organizations utilizing flexible manufacturing and with medium cost. The influence of using IT was higher in organizations that concentrate less on innovation and quality (Theodorou & Florou, 2008).

ERP Systems Research

The American Production and Inventory Control Society (APICS, 1998) defines ERP as *"an accounting-oriented computer information system that assists enterprises to define and plan on the resources required during the operation process of purchase, production, distribution and strategic planning to satisfy customers'orders"* (Lo, Tsai & Li, 2005, pp. 13). Deloitte Consulting (1999) refers to ERP systems as a packaged business solution that is designed to automate and integrate business processes, share common data and practices across the enterprise and provide access to information in a real time environment.

The previous definitions present a link between PIS and ERP systems, where the operation and production are closely linked through both types of systems. Thus, this study will visit literature related to ERP systems that might built a better picture of users' adoption of these systems.

ERP developers claim that their systems are claimed to increase firms' productivity, improve operational efficiency, improve communication and collaboration, grant better control on processes, enhance scalability and performance, leverage IT infrastructure, and reduce cost (SSA Report, 2006). ERP systems expand the processes of operations to reach external partners as well as internal firm constituents (Microsoft, 2003) and increase the level of automation and the value of business (SAP, 2006). Oracle proposed an enterprise manufacturing intelligence (EMI) tool that adds contextual dimension to shop floor data then synchronizes with ERP systems. Such addition provides real time intelligence to operations and move manufacturing and resource planning to another level (Smith, 2008).

When looking at research work, Carton and Adam (2008) concluded that ERP systems improved management decision making process. The authors did a case study in the pharmaceutical sector and concluded to the fact that implementing and utilizing ERP systems faces many barriers that prevent firms from benefiting from the rich information like: the lack of skills needed and the lack of access to data. Also they emphasized the incompatibility of transaction data with aggregate management queries.

Research work related to the perceptions of users towards ERP systems implementation explored different factors that make ERP systems more acceptable. Fan and Fang (2006) tested empirically the DeLone and McLean model. Their main findings were the significant relationship between system quality and system use; system quality and perceived usefulness; information quality and user satisfaction; perceived usefulness and system use; perceived usefulness and user satisfaction; system use and individual impact; user satisfaction and individual impact; and finally, individual impact and organizational impact. The major conclusion of the study was that user perceptions of IS success plays a critical role in ERP implementation. Similar to their study, Singla (2005) explored ERP performance and found that adopters consistently outperformed non-adopters across a wide variety of measures. The study used tangible and intangible benefits of ERP and a set of business performance measures.

Some research explored the resistance to change when applying and ERP systems. The study utilized an empirical test using a sample of Dunlop C&F employees (30 responses). Results indicated that firms need to work towards improving the user's attitude towards the ERP system.

Again attitude is affected by users' self-efficacy and perceived usefulness. Other issues that can inflect failure into the implementation process might be employee education and vendors' support (Tsai & Hung, 2008). ERP systems integrate resources to enhance the overall performance and reduce costs (Lo, Tsai & Li, 2005). In a try to differentiate between ERP adopters' performance and non-adopters' performance, Hunton, Lippincout and Reck (2003) reported a decline in performance over time for non-adopters, while adopters enjoyed a steady performance.

We conclude that it is crucial to benefit from the capabilities of PIS, ERP and other IS in the industrial sector to gain competitive advantage in the market through the reduction of cost and the smoothing of material and information flow, and better utilization of resources.

Innovation Diffusion Theory

Rogers's diffusion of innovation (DOI) model appeared to be one of the most widely accepted models by researchers in identifying the "perceived" critical characteristics for innovation in information systems research and technology adoption research.

Rogers (1995) defines the "innovation diffusion process" as the spread of new ideas from its source of invention or creators to its ultimate users or adopters. Innovation is 'an idea, practice or object that is perceived as new by an individual or other unit of adoption (Rogers 1995, p.11). Diffusion is the 'process by which an innovation is communicated through certain channels over time among the members of a social system (Rogers 1995, p. 5).

Rogers classified people into categories according to their innovativeness; where individuals who are relatively earlier in adopting new ideas than other members of their social system are considered to be more innovative. The categories are the following arranged from adopters to non-adopters: innovators, early adopters, early majority, late majority, and laggards.

According to Rogers' theory, people start to adopt innovations slowly, and then the increased number of adoptions will continue until it reaches a peak, after that it diminishes leaving few individuals as non-adopters (laggards). Innovators are willing to try new ideas and venturesome. Early adopters are the opinion leaders in their community and carefully adopt new ideas. Individuals in the "early majority" category adopt new ideas before the average person and rarely seen as a leaders. On the other hand, individuals in the "late majority" category adopt an innovation only after a majority of people have tried it. At the end come the laggards who adopt the innovation only when it is a common and traditional aspect of their life or work. People in this category are suspicious of change, and resist such initiatives.

The Innovation Diffusion Theory (IDT) is a well accepted model in social sciences as it investigates the environment of adopting new innovations (the technology or information systems in this case) in organizations. The IDT was first proposed by Rogers (1983) and then modified by many researchers who modified the model and proposed different set of variables (Moore & Benbasat, 1991). Rogers (1983) proposed his theory as a model that includes the factors influencing the usage and adoption of innovation.

Rogers proposes five important factors that influence the adoption decision: the first is *relative advantage*: the degree to which the innovation perceived as being better than its precursor/supersedes. Second, *compatibility*: the degree to which an innovation is perceived as being consistent with existing system of values, past experiences and needs. The third is *complexity*: the degree to which an innovation perceived as being difficult to understand and use. Fourth, is *triability*: the degree to which an innovation can be tried and experimented with a limited basis. Finally, *observability*: the degree to which the

Figure 1. The IDT model proposed by Moore and Benbasat (1991)

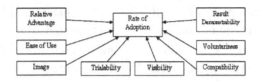

beneficial results of use are observable and visible to users. Rogers addressed that innovation was more likely to succeed and be more readily adopted if the relative advantage as a consequence of its introduction was evident; if it was compatible with the adopter, its operations and its view of the world; if it was not 'too' complex; and if it was trialable and results can be observed prior to adoption.

The theory measures three major areas: the adoption rate of technology related to time, where the theory is a suitable tool for measuring the diffusion of innovation in organizations (Brancheau & Wetherbe, 1990). Later, some researchers utilized this theory in studying the gap in technology accommodation (Fichman & Kemerer, 1999). Second, the work of Brancheau and Wetherbe (1990) included demographic factors related to the innovator characteristics that were explored in addition to the original factors proposed in the original theory. Brancheau and Wetherbe concluded that younger individuals were more receptive to technology adoption earlier in the process. Also, better educated individuals (subjects with higher degrees of education) were more open to interacting with the technology and thus were the ones with initiatives and opinion. Finally, the same authors explored the adoption of technology, where they anticipated that adopting a technology would go through four stages: awareness, persuasion, decision and implementation. The work of Brancheau & Wetherbe, coincides with the work of Agarwal (2000) with respect to the four adoption stages reported. Agarwal proclaimed that the IDT provides a better explanation of the adoption process and its interaction with time.

The work done by Moore and Benbasat (1991) is considered one of the important milestones in the life of this theory, where they used Rogers' work to develop a well validated instrument to measure the factors involved in predicting the rate of adoption. Moore and Benbasat built an instrument that explains the rate of adoption with reliable level of measurement. They added at the first stage of their study two major constructs and found them to be distinctive from the five proposed ones in Rogers' work. The first was *Image*; defined as "the degree to which use of an innovation is perceived to enhance one's image or status in one's social system". The second is *voluntariness of use*; defined as "the degree to which use of the innovation is perceived as being voluntary or of free will" (Moore & Benbasat, 1991, pp. 195).

The constructs' formulation took a multi-stage process and resulted in an eight construct model predicting the rate of adoption. Researchers focused their efforts on the time extension of the adoption process, where they used a longitudinal perspective instead of the snapshot view (cross-sectional snapshot of the data). The model utilized in their work is depicted in Figure 1.

Moore and Benbasat built their results on the responses of 540 employees from more than one organization, where the personal work-station was the technology under consideration. The major objective of the study was to build a highly reliable instrument to measure the set of factors used in the IDT. The study included four stages; the first was to review all the literature and the instruments available and used at that time. The second stage, researchers reviewed the items used for each variable in the instrument using a panel of experts. The third stage performed a pilot test on 20 subjects, followed by a test on 66 subjects to improve the instrument and increase its validity and reliability. Finally, the instrument was used on a large scale, where 34 items were the results of this study that measured the variables of the study.

In later studies, Agarwal and Parasad (1998) used part of the variables of the IDT like relative advantage, ease of use and compatibility, to study personal innovativeness influence on the rate of adoption of new technology. The results of the study indicated that personal innovativeness will be a significant moderator in the relationships influencing the rate of adoption of new technology. On the other hand, other studies that depicted the set of factors used in the IDT showed that this theory is stronger in predicting the rate of adoption than one of the widely used models in the area; the technology acceptance model-TAM (Davis, 1989). Results indicated that the IDT explained 45% of the variability in the rate of adoption, where the TAM explained only 32.7% of the variability of the same construct (Plouffe, Hulland & Vandenbosch, 2001).

Other studies that adopted some of the variables listed in the IDT and proposed by Moore and Benbasat (1991) went and tested the tendency to purchase on the Internet (Fitzgerald & Kiel, 2002). Using a snowball sampling method, 128 respondents were recruited to complete a survey that included measures from three domains: perceived attributes of use (included six constructs from the IDT and perceived risk), traditional normative beliefs (partner, family, friends, and near peers), and Internet normative beliefs (e-mail, discussion groups, virtual communities, and chat rooms). The mediators in the model were attitude, and motivation to comply with normative beliefs, and the dependent variable was future use intent. The results indicated that attitude was a strong factor explaining the intent to use for both adopters and non-adopters. Also, the major constructs explaining attitude were result demonstrability

and risk for adopters, and risk for non adopters.

Mirchandani and Motwani (2001) performed a study related to the usage of e-commerce activities and focused on the relative advantage and compatibility, but added few constructs like: enthusiasm of top manger, compatibility with the company, relative advantage, and knowledge within the firm. Speier and Venkatesh (2002) proposed a comprehensive model to explore the perceptions of salespeople that affected their decision to reject a technology. The study analyzed the responses at two points of time utilizing 454 salespeople across two firms that implemented sales force automation tools. The model tested the interactions between individual characteristics, role perceptions, organization's characteristics, individual perceptions of the technology, professional state, person-fit technology, objective outcomes, and subjective outcomes. Relative advantage was the only significant factor from the set of individual perceptions of the technology that affected job-fit (at both time measures). Voluntariness had a low effect on the individual perception factors. Finally, the study reported a failure of the sales force automation technology based on the rejection of the salespeople as a result of negative job-related perceptions.

In an integration of multiple models in the technology acceptance area, Hardgrave, Davis, and Riemenschneider (2003) integrated the TAM/TAM2, IDT, and TPB/TRA to come up with a model that consisted of perceived usefulness, complexity, compatibility, social pressure and organizational mandate (voluntariness) as predictors of intention to follow a methodology. The results confirmed the effect of all factors except complexity (ease of use). The authors redefined the model to account for the indirect effects and proposed another model that linked complexity to usefulness, which yielded a significant result. Also, social influence and compatibility kept their significant relations with intention and usefulness.

Finally, in Saudi Arabia, Al-Gahtani (2003) tested a subset of the IDT constructs in a study

Table 1. Information related to the factories studied

Number of factories according to number of employees			Number of factories according to sales size (in 1000JD)			Number of factories according to number of computers	
Employees	Factories		Sales	Factories		Computers	Factories
1-50	31		Less than 100	10		Less than 10	36
51-100	7		100-1000	16		10-100	22
101-200	7		1000-10000	13		> 100	10
201-1000	20		> 10000	8		No Info.	6
>1000	9		No Info.	27		**Total**	**74**
Total	**74**		**Total**	**74**			

aimed at computer technology adoption by Saudi workers in 136 organizations. The usable responses were 1190, and the dependent variable was adoption of computer technology. The results confirmed the five proposed constructs adapted from the IDT (relative advantage, complexity, compatibility, trialability, and observability).

JORDANIAN MANUFACTURING FIRMS ADOPTION OF PIS

This paper investigated the extent that manufacturing firms in Jordan are adopting IT as one of the innovation tools that help in the production and operation processes. PIS are considered, for the purpose of this research, the innovation under consideration. This research consists of two tests, where a group of surveys were distributed on factories mainly in the Northern region of the country (mainly in Al-Hasan Industrial Zone). The total collected surveys were 74 surveys that included a number of questions related to the information technology and applications content of the firm and some information about the organization itself and their information systems usability. On the other hand, another survey was distributed in Al-Hasan Industrial Zone and only to general managers, information managers and heads of departments. The second survey focused

on managers' perceptions about adopting this type of systems and how well they accepted such technology. Total number of surveys collected was 91 usable surveys. The two studies were not addressing the same sample, and results of both studies are not closely related.

Jordanian PIS Usability

Table 1 shows the demographic details of the sample distributed, where 100 surveys were distributed and 74 were collected (response rate 74%). The survey aimed at collecting data related to managers' opinions on the usage and availability of PIS and other related systems. The main objective was to measure the adoption of PIS in the manufacturing sector in Jordan. When asking managers about using IT in their operations, 66 factories out of 74 reported that they used one or more of the systems listed in Table 2. Also, 8 factories only reported that they did not use any type of IT or systems in their operations. Table 2 lists different types of systems and the users among Jordanian factories.

Managers were asked about the relationship between supply chain management systems (SCM) and the employment of PIS, and how these systems are related to suppliers' capabilities also. Results indicated that 39 factories employ central systems, 13 factories employ distributed systems,

Table 2. Detailed type of information systems used in Jordanian factories

#	Item (question asked)	Number of factories
1	Do you use any type of Information Technology	66
2	Do you use accounting information systems	60
3	Do you use special sales systems	42
4	Do you use production information systems	45
5	Do you use inventory and warehousing systems	47
6	Do you use computer-aided design systems	23
7	Do you use human resource and salary systems	52
8	Do you use quality assurance/control systems	36
9	Do you use Distribution systems	25
10	Do you use procurement information systems	37
11	Do you use manufacturing aiding systems	25

but integrated together. Also, results indicated that 20 factories employed enterprise systems that are utilized in many functions and tasks. Finally, only 8 factories have extended systems that reach suppliers, distributors and customers (SCMS or ERP).

The second part of the survey included items related to the systems used in these factories. 47 managers indicated that they are interested in extending and using part or all of the systems listed in Table 2. Also, the distribution of the source and type of these systems were as follows: 32 factories used locally designed systems, and 33 factories used ready-made exported systems (off-shelf systems).

One of the objectives of this study was to see the relationships between variables like computer diffusion, sales and employee size. This was done through the correlations between those variables to test if any relationship exists between those. Also, to relate demographics with the main objective of this work, we estimated a new construct based on the count of the number of systems employed by the firm (example: manager of firm XYZ checked yes for using three systems (accounting information systems, HR systems and sales systems), so the total number of systems employed were three). This number (or set of data) was correlated against each of the variables mentioned. The correlations matrix is depicted in Table 3.

The results indicated significant correlations between the three variables and the total number of systems deployed. Also, it is shown that significant correlations existed between all three variables.

Table 3. Correlations matrix of the demographics against the number of systems employed

	Number of employees	Sales size	Number of computers
Number of employees	1		
Sales size	0.551**	1	
Number of computers	0.636**	0.810**	1
Total number of systems	0.437**	0.394**	0.398**

** Correlation is significant at the 0.001 level

Table 4. Descriptive statistics related to constructs in the IDT model

Variable	Number of Surveys	Min	Max	Mean	Standard Deviation
Rate of adoption	91	1	7	4.762	1.775
Relative advantage	91	2	7	5.777	1.123
Ease of use	91	1	7	5.409	1.334
Image	91	1	7	4.538	1.505
Compatibility	91	2	7	4.597	1.362
Result demonstrability	91	1	7	4.797	1.517
Visibility	91	1	7	4.637	1.540
Trialability	91	1	7	5.588	1.303
Voluntariness	91	1	7	4.654	1.615

The Intentions of Managers to Adopt PIS

The second major objective of this study was to explore managers' intentions to adopt or continue using PIS systems utilizing Rogers' IDT model. In a separate study, the researcher employed a survey that introduced a description of PIS and asked questions related to the different constructs of the model. The main source for the items used in the study was Moore and Benbasat (1991) work. The items were translated to Arabic language and tested using 10 experts for language. The nature of this exploratory study makes it convenient to use such method and the size of data allows for such test. Data used a seven point Likert scale, where 1 indicates a high disagreement to the statement and 7 indicates a high approval to the statement. The total number of surveys collected was 91 surveys from factories in Al-Hasan Industrial Zone (total number distributed = 100).

The survey included 3 items for measuring rate of adopting, 5 items for measuring relative advantage, 3 items for measuring compatibility, 3 items for measuring image, 2 items for measuring voluntariness, 2 items for measuring trialability, 2 items for measuring visibility, 4 items for measuring results demonstrability, and 4 items for measuring ease of use. Table 4 shows some descriptive statistics related to constructs.

On the other hand, correlations between all variable depicted in the IDT model were calculated and they are shown in Table 5. All correlations were significant except two and as shown in the matrix (with different levels of significance). Also, all variables were entered to calculate the regression coefficients between the rate of adoption and all variables. Results indicated that a significant correlation exists between the variables and the rate of adoption, where the coefficient of determination $R^2 = 27.6\%$, with a p value less than 0.001 ($F_{8,82} = 5.285$, $p < 0,001$). Results are shown in Table 6.

DISCUSSION OF RESULTS

This exploratory work tried to answer two major questions using multiple studies and methods. The first objective was to explore the extent to which PIS are used and adopted in manufacturing companies in Jordan. Through a descriptive survey, opinions were collected from managers of 74 factories in an industrial zone in Jordan. Results indicated that 66 factories (89%) used at least one system related to production and operations. The most popular systems used in Jordan were accounting information systems (60 factories, 81%), and the least used systems were computer aided design systems (23 factories, 31%). Results indicated also that PIS were used in 45 factories (61%), and

Table 5. Correlation matrix showing the IDT variables

	RoA	RA	EoU	I	C	RD	V	T	V
Rate of adoption (RoA)	1								
Relative advantage (RA)	.271**	1							
Ease of use (EoU)	.030	.332**	1						
Image (I)	.386**	.397**	.481**	1					
Compatibility (C)	.351**	.269*	.419**	.637**	1				
Result demonstrability (RD)	.440**	.281**	.489**	.579**	.598**	1			
Visibility (V)	.310**	.256*	.367**	.465**	.578**	.495**	1		
Trialability (T)	.289**	.244*	.301**	.292**	.460**	.337**	.635**	1	
Voluntariness (V)	.207**	.156	.390**	.274**	.455**	.422**	.526**	.453**	1

**. Correlation is significant at the 0.01 level (2-tailed).
*. Correlation is significant at the 0.05 level (2-tailed).

inventory and warehousing systems were used in 47 factories (63.5%). The results indicated a fair adoption rate for such systems. Part of the reason for that is the influence of partnership with global firms and international organizations that outsource part of their production within Al-Hasan Industrial Zone. It also seems that accounting and human resources systems were more popular as it is a major function for any firm regardless of their size of operations. This conclusion might be as a result of another test we did on the size of firms with respect to their sales and number of employees.

Using supply chain management systems (SCMS) was not that popular as only 8 firms used an extended system (11%), and the reason for that are the distinctiveness of the sample, as the sample in the first study came from an industrial zone, where international contracts are more common and a closed system from the local market is forced in this free zone. Such situation might be in a lesser need to an extended integrated system

Table 6. Coefficients table for the multiple regression test

Variable	Beta	Std Error	Std Beta	t	Sig
Constant	1.334	1.026		1.301	0.197
Relative advantage	0.246	0.158	0.156	1.556	0.124
Ease of use	**-0.506**	**0.148**	**-0.380**	**-3.411**	**0.001**
Image	0.269	0.156	0.228	1.720	0.089
Compatibility	0.016	0.178	0.013	0.092	0.927
Result demonstrability	**0.444**	**0.146**	**0.380**	**3.038**	**0.003**
Visibility	-0.010	0.156	-0.009	-0.067	0.947
Trialability	0.210	0.164	0.154	1.283	0.203
Voluntariness	0.041	0.125	0.037	0.329	0.743

Dependent variable: Rate of adoption, method: enter

(SCMS). Finally, enterprise systems were not that popular as only 20 factories indicated using such integrated type of systems (27%)

When trying to explain the results of the correlations between the total number of systems (a measure of usability in this study) and the number of computers and employees and the total sales, it seems obvious that the size of the firm is a direct influencer (predictor) of the usability of IT. The larger firms will have higher numbers of employees and larger sales and thus they tend to utilize technology to improve operations and gain competitive advantage in the market. Also, it is logical to conclude that the firm size is directly correlated to complexity of operations and thus firms adopt IT to better control operations and improve flow of material and information. Finally, we can conclude that firms with higher sales will have larger tendency to invest in IT and thus buy more computers and adopt more types of systems.

The second objective was to explore managers' intention to adopt such systems. Results indicated a high intention to adopt PIS because of two main reasons: The first was the high mean values of predictors, which indicates the high perceptions of managers towards the adoption process. All means were above 4.5 out of 7, which indicate a high acceptance rates with respect to all variables used. The second reason for this conclusion is the high significant bivariate correlations with the rate of adoption, and this indicates that the method used and the large number of predictors was a limitation. The only variable with none significant correlation is ease of use and this supports the limitation of the method used. The highest correlation was between rate of adoption and results demonstrability (0.440**).

On the other hand, when summed together, the set of variables competed on the variance and only two variables showed significant prediction of rate of adoption. The two variables are: results demonstrability; the ability to see tangible results out of the system, and ease of use; where the complexity of the system is a huge obstacle to using it.

The IDT model explained 27.6% of the variance in the rate of adoption. Results might have some limitations as the IDT have 8 predictors competing on the variance in the rate of adoption and this might limit the ability to explain the dependent variable well. The regression method used was to enter all variables forcefully and this might be the reason behind this surprising result. As this study is an exploratory one, we can conclude that a larger sample size and a thorough conceptual analysis of the predictors will lead to better utilization of variables and better and accurate results.

CONCLUSION

This paper aimed at exploring the status of using IT and specifically PIS in the area of production and manufacturing in Jordan. The study utilized two samples for two separate studies; the first was a sample of managers mainly related to IT in a group of factories in Al-Hasan Industrial Zone and other areas mainly in the Northern part of Jordan to explore the usage of PIS and other types of systems in the industrial area. The second study utilized another sample (after four months and from a different set of factories), from the same area and from the Northern part of the country to test the IDT using an instrument translated from Moore and Benbasat work (1991). Results indicated that systems like accounting information systems and HR and payroll systems were the mostly used among firms and distribution and manufacturing aiding systems were the least used among the sample used. The role of IS in production area was highly appreciated and a major conclusion is that the size of firm indicates the high computer usage and the diversity of systems used.

The second study resulted in high and significant indicators in predicting the adoption rate, and most of the constructs used in the IDT were significantly correlated to rate of adoption. But when regressing all indicators on rate of adoption, only two competed on the variance and yielded significant explanation of the variability of the dependent variable and they were results demonstrability and ease of use.

One of the limitations of this research, which makes its generalizability limited, is the usage of two separate samples. This research utilized two different samples, and to relate the real usage of PIS to the adoption rate, the same sample would have been used. Still the inferred results of this work are valid, but researchers are encouraged to use one sample and extend the size to improve the statistical generalizability. The second limitation of this study is the instrument used; this study used a translated instrument from the original one used in Moore and Benbasat (1991) in English, and thus researchers are encouraged to use the instrument in Arabic to improve the language and improve content and face validity of the instrument. Finally, research related to PIS and the factors influencing the adoption of such systems is not highly popular, which resulted in high competition between variables. The IDT needs a larger sample or dropping some of the variables based on conceptual bases. When exploring systems like ERP or PIS systems, as they are considered complicated and comprehensive systems, one needs to keep relative advantage and ease of use for sure, but further exploration needs to be done to try to deduct the scale size and improve predictability of the model.

FUTURE RESEARCH DIRECTIONS

This research is needed in this area and considered a first step in validating the instrument and testing factors influencing the rate of adoption. It is highly important to continue such research using longitudinal settings to explore the adoption and check the validity of results.

Future research is needed to validate the instrument and apply it to more settings and environments. Another direction that is needed is the multi-stage process applied by Moore and

Benbasat (1991), where the adoption rate is investigated with time and also, a better conceptual perspective is reached through the reduction of variable. One idea is to compare other models predictability with the IDT like the Technology Acceptance Model (TAM), the theory of Reasoned Action (TRA), the Theory of Planned Behavior (TPB) and its extension the Decomposed Theory of Planned Behavior (DTPB).

As we now know the situation of PIS usability in industrial zones, would that knowledge facilitate better research in other environments like local industrial areas and other major factories in Jordan? Also, would it result in a different conclusion if we explored other types of systems? Finally, results indicated a weakness in utilizing computer aided design systems, future research can explore the reasons behind such phenomenon and would that be related to the industrial development of the sector in general or because of this global partnership with local factories specifically in the industrial zone.

REFERENCES

Agarwal, R. (2000). Individual acceptance of information technologies . In Zmud, R. (Ed.), *Framing the domains of IT management* (pp. 85–104). Cincinnati, OH: Pinnaflex Education Resources, Inc.

Agarwal, R., & Prasad, J. (1998). A conceptual and operational definition of personal innovativeness in the domain of information technology. *Information Systems Research*, *9*(2), 204–215. doi:10.1287/isre.9.2.204

Brancheau, J. C., & Wetherbe, J. C. (1990). The adoption of spreadsheet software: testing innovation diffusion theory in the context of end-user computing. *Information Systems Research*, *1*(2), 115–143. doi:10.1287/isre.1.2.115

Carton, F., & Adam, F. (2008). ERP and Functional Fit: How Integrated Systems Fail to Provide Improved Control. *The Electronic Journal Information Systems Evaluation, 11*(2), 51 – 60. Retrieved from http://www.ejise.com

Ciurana, J., Garcia-Romeu, M., Ferrer, I., & Casadesus, M. (2008). A Model for Integrating Process Planning and Production Planning and Control in Machining Processes. *Robotics and Computer-integrated Manufacturing, 24,* 532–544. doi:10.1016/j.rcim.2007.07.013

Davis, F. D. (1989). Perceived usefulness perceived ease of use, and user acceptance of information technology. *Management Information Systems Quarterly, 13*(3), 319–340. doi:10.2307/249008

Deloitte Consulting. (1999). *ERPs Second Wave* [Report]. Deloitte Consulting. Retrieved from http://www.deloitte.com

DeLone, W., & McLean, E. (1992). Information Systems Success: The Quest for the Dependent Variable. *Information Systems Research, 3*(1), 60–95. doi:10.1287/isre.3.1.60

Department of Statistics. Jordan. (2008). *Statistics related to the Jordanian Industrial Sector.* Retrieved from http://www.dos.gov.jo/dos_home_a/gpd.htm

Ende, J., Jaspers, F., & Gerwin, D. (2008). *Involvement of system firms in development of complementary products: The influence of novelty.* Technovation.

Fan, J., & Fang, K. (2006). ERP Implementation and Information Systems Success: A Test of DeLone and McLean's Model. In *PICMET2006 Conference proceedings,* July 2006, Turkey (pp. 9-13).

Fichman, R. G., & Kemerer, C. F. (1999). The illusory diffusion of innovation: an examination of the assimilation gaps. *Information Systems Research, 10*(3), 255–275. doi:10.1287/isre.10.3.255

Fitzgerald, L., & Kiel, G. (2001). *Applying a consumer acceptance of technology model to examine adoption of online purchasing.* Retrieved February 2004, from http://130.195.95.71:8081/WWW/ANZMAC2001/anzmac/AUTHORS/pdfs/Fitzgerald1

Gnaim, K. (2005). Innovation is one of Quality aspects. *Quality in Higher Education, 1*(2).

Gupta, S., & Keswani, B. (2008). *Exploring the Factors That Influence User Resistance to the Implementation of ERP.* Hyderabad, India: The ICFAI University Press.

Hardgrave, B. C., Davis, F. D., & Riemenschneider, C. K. (2003). Investigating determinants of software developers to follow methodologies. *Journal of Management Information Systems, 20*(1), 123–151.

Hssain, A., Djeraba, C., & Descotes-Genon, B. (1993). Production Information Systems Design. In *Proceedings of Int Conference on Industrial Engineering and Production Management (IEPM-33),* Mons, Belgium, June 1993.

Hsu, C., & Rattner, L. (1990). Information Modeling for Computerized Manufacturing. *IEEE Transactions on Systems, 20*(4).

Hunton, J., Lippincott, B., & Reck, J. (2003). Enterprise Resource Planning Systems: Comparing Firm Performance of Adopters and Nonadopters. *Accounting Information Systems, 4,* 165–184. doi:10.1016/S1467-0895(03)00008-3

Jordan Industrial Cities. (2008). *Statistics from the website of the JIC.* Retrieved from http://www.jci.org.jo

Lo, C., Tsai, C., & Li, R. (2005, January). A Case Study of ERP Implementation for Opto-Electronics Industry. *International Journal of The Computer . The Internet and Management, 13*(1), 13–30.

Lu, K., & Sy, C. (2008). *A real-time decision-making of maintenance using fuzzy agent*. Expert Systems with Applications.

McCrea, B. (2008). ERP: Gaining Momentum. *Logistic Management,* November 2008, pp. 44-46.

Microsoft. (2003). *Microsoft Business Solutions.* Retrieved from http://www.microsoft.com/business solutions

Mirchandani, D. A., & Motwani, J. (2001). Understanding small business electronic commerce adoption: an empirical analysis. *Journal of Computer Information Systems, 41*(3), 70–73.

Moore, G., & Benbasat, I. (1991). Development of an instrument to measure the perceptions of adopting an information technology innovation. *Information Systems Research, 2*(3), 192–222. doi:10.1287/isre.2.3.192

Mourtzis, D., Papakostas, N., Makris, S., Xanthakis, V., & Chryssolouris. (2008). Supply chain modeling and control for producing highly customized products. *Manufacturing Technology Journal.*

Plouffe, C., Hulland, J., & Vandenbosch, M. (2001). Research report: richness versus parsimony in modeling technology adoption decisions-understanding merchant adoption of a smart card-based payment system. *Information Systems Research, 12*(2), 208–222. doi:10.1287/isre.12.2.208.9697

Report, S. S. A. (2006). *SSA ERP on SOA Platform.* SSA Global and IBM. Retrieved from http://www.ssaglobal.com

Rogers, E. M. (1983). *The diffusion of innovations.* New York: Free Press.

Rogers, E. M. (1995). *The Diffusion of Innovation* (4th ed.). New York: Free Press.

SAP. (2006). *SAP Customer Success Story.* Retrieved from http://www.sap.com

Singla, A. (2005). Impact of ERP Systems on Small and Mid Sized Public Sector Enterprises. *Journal of Theoretical and Applied Information Technology,* 119-131.

Smadi, S. (2001). Employees' Attitudes Towards the Implementation of the Japanese Model Kaisen for Performance Improvement and Meeting Competitive Challenges in The Third Millennium: The Jordanian Private Industrial Sector. *Abhath Al-Yarmouk,* 313-335.

Smith, F. O. (2008 May). Oracle Says It Will Leapfrog Competitors in Manufacturing Intelligence. *Manufacturing Business Technology,* 26-29.

Speier, C., & Venkatesh, V. (2002). The hidden minefields in the adoption of sales force automation technologies. *Journal of Marketing, 65,* 98–111. doi:10.1509/jmkg.66.3.98.18510

Theodorou, P., & Giannoula, F. (2008). Manufacturing strategies and financial performance-The effect of advanced information technology: CAD/CAM systems. *The International Journal of Management Science, 36,* 107–121.

Trari, A. (2008). مكتبة جامعة اليرموك. Retrieved from http://library.yu.edu.jo/

Tsai, W., & Hung, S. (2008). E-Commerce Implementation: An Empirical Study of the Performance of Enterprise Resource Planning Systems Using the Organizational Learning Model. *International Journal Of Management, 25*(2).

Turban, E., Leidner, D., McLean, E., & Wetherbe, J. (2008). *Information Technology for Management* (6th ed.). Hoboken, NJ: John Wiley.

Wang, T., & Hu, J. (2008). An Inventory control systems for product with optional components under service level and budget constraints. *European Journal of Operational Research, 189,* 41–58. doi:10.1016/j.ejor.2007.05.025

Wang, W., Hsieh, J., Butler, J., & Hsu, S. (2008). Innovative Complex Information Technologies: A Theoretical Model And Empirical Examination. *Journal of Computer Information Systems*, (Fall): 27–36.

Section 5
EIS Adoption

Chapter 18
Measuring Utilization of ERP Systems Usage in SMEs

Hedman Jonas
Copenhagen Business School, Denmark

Johansson Björn
Lund University, Sweden

ABSTRACT

Since deployment of Enterprise Systems (ES) such as Enterprise Resource Planning systems (ERPs) within enterprises, both Large Enterprises (LEs) as well as Small and Medium-sized Enterprises (SMEs) have increased and continue to increase, making it increasingly desirable to measure the degree of utilization of ERP systems in enterprises. One reason for this interest is that no benefits are realized if the systems are not used; since ERPs are massive investments, they need to show benefits, or at least be able to measure the benefits. However, to be able to do so, there is a need to explain ERP systems utilization and the factors that influence ERP utilization. This chapter provides an explanation of factors influencing ERP systems utilization by testing a research model building on four dimensions: volume, breadth, diversity, and depth. The contributions of the research are: First, it provides support for the notion of diffusion found in the theory of network externalities where a critical mass is necessary to achieve benefits. This can be used to better understand failures in ERP projects. Second, the use of volume, breadth and depth provide insights for use as a construct and the need to treat it more rigorously. Third, the study contributes to our understanding of the many aspects of use of IT, such as ERPs, and potentially contributes to value and firm performance from ERP utilization.

INTRODUCTION

Enterprise Resource Planning (ERPs) systems have constituted one of the most important developments in corporate information systems (IS)

during the last decade (Davenport, 1998; Hitt et al., 2002; Upton & McAfee, 2000). The business interest in **ERP Systems** can be explained from descriptions of benefits associated with implementation and utilization of ERPs (Robey et al., 2002), of which there are several studies on inspiring success (Davenport, 2000). There are,

DOI: 10.4018/978-1-61692-020-3.ch018

however, also considerable failures (Larsen & Myers, 1998; Scott & Vessey, 2000). Benefits of ERPs are only partly related to technology, most of these stemming from organizational changes such as new business processes, organizational structure, work procedures, integration of administrative and operative activities, and global standardization of work practices, all of which lead to organizational improvements which the technology supports (Hedman & Borell, 2003). It can definitely be said that implementation of ERP systems is a difficult and costly organizational experiment (Robey et al., 2002; Santhanam et al., 2009). Davenport (1996) describes the implementation of ERP systems as "perhaps the world's largest experiment in business change" and for most organizations "the largest change project in cost and time that they have undertaken in their history." The implementation is a necessary but insufficient prerequisite for benefits and value, and business value can only be derived from an efficient and effective utilization of information technology resources. (Agarwal et al., 2000). The management of ERP system utilization is thus of critical importance, and involves development and implementation, as well as **usage** of resources (Balakrishnan & Das, 2009; Kalling, 1999).

Although many benefits of ERP systems have been identified and studied (Shang & Seddon, 2002), past research has focused on defining success factors (Robey et al., 2002), such as top management involvement and support, rather than investigating how **ERP systems utilization** relates to benefits. One possible explanation for this is that in previous ERP research on benefits and success, the state of go-alive in the implementation of ERPs is often equivalent to use, i.e., that benefits are directly and causally related to the first day of use. The predominant view of utilization is "**use**" in different forms e.g., intention of use, or user satisfaction, etc. (DeLone & McLean, 1992). DeLone and McLean (2003) claim that there are deficiencies related to the 'use' construct, emphasizing that 'use' as a construct

is too simplistic and needs to be developed. A potential elaboration which this paper takes is that ERP systems utilization should be explored from an organizational perspective as well as from a system perspective. To this end, we introduce **utilization** of ERP systems as a **measure of use**, and develop a model of **ERP utilization** which we relate to and describe as internal **diffusion** of ERP systems in organizations. The underlying hypotheses for using diffusion of ERP as a measure is that it is not until ERP is diffused and integrated with a large part of an organization that benefits will be received, i.e., a critical mass is reached. This also means that internal diffusion of the ERP is necessary before ERP utilization in an organization is a fact.

The purpose of this research is to increase knowledge of the relationship between **utilization** of ERP system and benefits. This will be done through a theoretical and empirical investigation of ERP utilization. In addition, the paper provides input into the complex matter of the dependent variable "use." It does so by providing an alternative way of investigating the "**use**" concept which goes beyond use and user satisfaction or intention to use.

This chapter is structured as follows. In the next section we present previous research useful for developing a model for measurement of ERP utilization, focusing on measuring use of ERPs in small and medium-sized enterprises (**SME**s). Thereafter, we introduce our methodological approach and the survey context. We then present and discuss our **measurement** tool of ERP utilization. Finally, we address the usefulness of the measurement tool, both from a practical and a theoretical perspective.

MEASURING USE OF ERP SYSTEMS IN SMES

In order to do research on ERP utilization, there is a need to define concepts such as: ERPs, **SME**s,

Measurement, and Use. Starting with defining ERPs, it can be said that relatively often ERPs are strongly connected to the system that SAP AG has developed and then starts to deliver it labeled as SAP R/3. However, it is noteworthy that ERPs consist of many more software packages, not only SAP R/3. In order to explain and define ERPs, it is necessary to give some kind of historical overview. According to Møller (2005), ERPs emerged in the 1950s and 1960s, when computers were introduced into organizations; today, however, these systems are seen as legacy systems, and not many would describe them as ERPs. Alternatively, ERPs as a software package were probably invented in the 1990s, with the introduction of, for instance, SAP R/3. This type of software is often defined as standardized packaged software (Xu & Brinkkemper, 2007) designed with the aim of integrating the entire value chain in an organization. (Lengnick-Hall et al., 2004; Rolland & Prakash, 2000). Wier et al. (2007) argue that ERPs aim to integrate business processes and ICT into a synchronized suite of procedures, applications and metrics, which goes over firms' boundaries. Kumar and van Hillegersberg (2000) purport ERPs originated in the manufacturing industry, where the first generation of ERPs was introduced. According to these authors, development of the first generation ERPs was an inside-out process, going from standard inventory control (IC) packages, to material requirements planning (MRP), to material resources planning (MRP II) and then expanding it to a software package with the aim of supporting the entire organization and all its business processes (second generation ERPs). This evolved software package is then described as the next generation ERP, labeled as ERP II (Møller, 2005).

This development has increased the complexity both for when it comes to usage and for development of ERPs. The complexity comes from the fact that ERPs are systems that are supposed to be integrated into the organization (both inter-organizational as well as intra-organizational) and its business process in a one suite package (Koch, 2001). From an historical overview, ERPs and the way in which organizations use ERPs have changed a lot. The fact that the ERP market continually changes also influences how ERPs are developed and sold, which impacts not only the stakeholders that are in an ERP value-chain (Ifinedo & Nahar, 2007; Somers & Nelson, 2004), but also the work tasks that respective stakeholders have in the value-chain (Johansson & Newman, 2009). Summing up the ERP definition, we can say that ERPs are a standard software package that aims at coordinating and integrating the information flow in the adopting organization (Hedman, 2003). ERPs also include what could be called "best practices" and therefore have a high impact on adopting organizations' business processes (Hedman & Borell, 2004). This high impact makes it very interesting to investigate and measure utilization of ERPs in organizations. Another area of interest when it comes to diffusion of ERPs is the organizational size. It is clear that for ERP vendors, SMEs are the focus for their future sales of ERPs. This adds to the motivation to focus on ERP systems utilization in SMEs.

When discussing IS diffusion in SMEs the definition of SMEs is fundamental. In this paper, we adopt the definition of SMEs delivered by the European Commission: "A small enterprise is an enterprise with fewer than 50 employees and a medium-sized enterprise is an enterprise with more than 49 and fewer than 250 employees."

There are two more concepts that need to be defined, namely: **measurement** and **use**, which are the main focus of this chapter. We aim to present a method for measuring use by describing min relation to ERP systems utilization. However, we will first discuss the use of IS in SMEs and existing knowledge on measuring use of IS.

Measuring Use of Information Systems (IS) in SMEs

When it come to **usage** and **diffusion** of IS in SMEs, there is a great deal of research studying e-commerce or e-business diffusion; examples of studies are Eriksson and Hultman's (2005) and Zhu and Kraemer's (2005). Results from this research are often accompanied with a discussion of usage from a maturity model (Hedman & Borell, 2004), such as the Gibson and Nolan's growth model (1974). Most often these studies do not consider internal diffusion in a specific organization, nor do they aim at measuring **use** and value of the adopted system. Zhu and Kraemer (2005) present a conceptual model that aims at measuring use and value of e-business in organizations. The authors claim that it is necessary to develop and test a model for measuring IS use due to the paucity of research on post-adoption of IS. According to Zhu and Kraemer, existing research has focused on adoption decisions and on measures, such as intent to adopt and factors focusing on adoption versus non-adoption. They conclude with a call for more research on post-adoption in the form of actual usage. Thus, there is a clear connection to value, which is confirmed by Zhu and Kraemer positing that actual **usage** is an important link to IT value. The authors suggest a model that builds on the technology-organization-environment (TOE) framework.

The TOE framework combines three aspects on adoption, implementation, and use of technological innovations: 1) the context of the technology, focusing on existing as well as new technologies, 2) organizational context referring to descriptive measures, such as scope, size, etc., and 3) the arena seen as the environmental context in which the organization conducts its business.

Straub et al.(1995) claim that system usage has been the most frequently used measure when it comes to measuring IS success. They describe it as two different forms of measuring system usage: subjective or objective. The subjective **measure-** **ment** means that the users state the extent to which they use the system – in the form of self-reporting. The objective **measurement** means that the system is used when doing the measurement – in the form of computer-recorded measures. It soon becomes apparent that both these methods create some problems: if self-reporting – the outcome builds on the specific users' thoughts regarding the extent to which they use the system; if computer-recoded, the data are purportedly more correct, albeit measuring **usage** in this way raises some ethical issues.

Sedera and Tan (2007) describe the problems related to usage and research made on IS success. One of the problems is that usage is defined in several different ways, with at least three contrasting meanings. First, IS **usage** is described as a variable for deciding on benefits from use of IS. This is exemplified by Sedera and Tan as IS for decision making. The second definition emphasizes **usage** as a dependent variable which influences future IS **usage**, and is described as IS acceptance or successful implementation of IS. The third meaning is that **usage** is seen as a process which leads to an impact on individuals as well as organizations. In this case, **usage** is exemplified by IS success. The measurement model that we present aims at combining the three different definitions on IS **usage**, described by Sedera and Tan.

Measuring Utilization of ERP Systems Usage in SMEs

In summary, there is considerable work on the use of IT/IS, in which a collective use is described (Burton-Jones & Gallivan, 2007). The authors question whether it is really possible to use IT/IS collectively, and claim that there is a need to increase the understanding of use from a multi perspective level. We agree with Burton-Jones and Gallivan that there is a general need for this multi perspective understanding,; however, we also submit that in specific ERP cases there is an increasing need for research on use also from an individual level. The reason for this may be found in the basic definition of ERPs, namely, that ERPs are software that aims at integrating the entire organization's business processes into a standard software package. This suggests that if the implementation is to be successful, it requires that more or less all employees adopt the system. Thus, it is not whether an organization adopts an ERP that makes it come into **usage**; instead, it could be claimed that it is whether the individuals in the organization start to use the ERP that decides whether the ERP comes into usage or not.

Bernroider and Lesuere (2005) used the definition on **SME**s described above when they investigated differences between SMEs and LEs regarding diffusion of ERPs. They report that from an investigation of one thousand enterprises in Austria, 67.6% of all LEs implemented ERPs, while only 15.5% of SMEs did the same. However, what they also found was that SMEs implemented other specific software applications, such as customer relationship management (CRM) and supply chain management (SCM), to a greater extent than LEs. One possible reason for this is that SMEs are more specialized than LEs. Another reason could be the lack of resources available in SMEs for implementing a full-size ERP system.

Morabito et al., (2005) posit that ERPs have raised high attention in practice, academic, and media, and that research around ERPs primarily focuses on two aspects: 1) the organizational and economic impact of ERP adoption, and 2) how to best manage adoption. However, the issue remains as to which unit of analysis should be used when researching diffusion of ERPs. It could be that there is a need to combine different units of analysis to be able to deliver in-depth answers to questions related to diffusion of ERP systems. In this chapter, we look into the diffusion of ERPs in SMEs. When doing that, an obvious unit is the organization, as such, and whether they have adopted an ERP or not; however, it is probably

also necessary to say something about individuals' adoption of the ERP. Even when doing so, it must be taken into consideration that it only gives a partial explanation as to the extent to which the ERPs are diffused and adopted. To be able to give a full explanation, we also need to consider the extent to which a specific user uses the specific ERP in a specific business process. Thus, we have at least three different units of analysis: organizations, individuals, and business processes (or work tasks).

This is in line with what Sedera and Tan (2007) suggest as necessary to have in order to get a "very rich" measure of usage. However, Sedera and Tan also suggest that the IS, as such, should be measured, which differs from what we would suggest. What we suggest is that there is a need to further define the construct usage. This is confirmed by Burton-Jones and Gallivan (2004), that usage is not well defined in the IS literature. They report four reasons for researchers calling for a renewed focus on the usage construct. First, there is a lack of studies that see usage as an independent variable for systems consequences, and in these studies usage is assumed to be unproblematic. Second, in the studies of consequences of systems usage, the results have been mixed, and the result of increased usage could be either increased, decreased, or have no effect on performance. Third, the appropriate way of measuring usage has not been questioned to the extent it needs to be; as described by Delone and McLean (2003), the problem is that usage as a complex variable has not been defined in the way it needs to be defined. Fourth, the studies of usage have been made from either an individual level or an organizational level, and there has been little integration between these levels. However, there is still the question of how to measure utilization of ERP systems usage in organizations. In the next section, we suggest a relevant model based on four dimensions, as suggested by Massetti and Zmud (1996).

RESEARCH MODEL

The vast functionality and organizational coverage of an ERP requires a comprehensive way to measure utilization (Hedman, 2003). In our literature survey, no operationalization of measurement on **ERP systems utilization** was found. The closest models were those of Grover et al. (1998) and Teng et al. (2002); however, they both measured diffusion through a single measurement. Another model is presented in the work by Massetti and Zmud (1996) which develops an instrument of measuring extent of EDI usage in organizations. Their **measurement** instrument includes the following four dimensions: volume, breadth, diversity, and depth. From Massetti and Zmud's description, we transform: volume, breadth, diversity, and depth from an EDI context to an ERP context. We now describe in greater detail our interpretation of Massetti and Zmud's concepts in an ERP context.

Volume represents the extent to which a firm's business processes and users are supported through ERP. The volume of ERP in business processes is determined by mapping the extent to which the ERP supports the core and support processes. The volume of users is determined by comparing the number of employees that could benefit from the ERP with the number of current ERP users in the organization. Also, for the total number of IS in the organization, the percentage of IS defined as ERP is determined. The ERP volume shows if the organization is willing to support a large part of the users and processes with ERP. Volume is measured by four items: 1) degree of ERP users (number of current ERP users / maximum number of potential ERP users, 2) ERP share of all computer based IS, 3) ERP support of primary business processes (sales/marketing/production/service), and 4) ERP support of secondary business processes (procurement, R&D, HR, and finance).

ERP breadth, the second dimension, represents the extent to which a firm has integrated ERP connections with each of its business processes. This shows to what degree the ERP is used as an integrated system within the organization, thereby making use of master data. The ERP breadth gives us an idea about whether the organization is trying to get rid of bottlenecks in the information flow, or whether the ERP is thought of as an exclusive functional support for a certain type of business process, such as production. ERP breadth is measured by three items: 1) share of business processes that use master data, 2) degree of internal business processes integrated through the ERP, and 3) degree of business processes integrated with external partners.

The third dimension, ERP diversity, represents the extent to which different types of business processes are supported through ERP. The diversity of ERP in business processes is measured by mapping the number of core and support processes that are supported by ERP. This measurement is connected to the many different types of functionality that ERP should support. Diversity is measured by eight items indicating that the business processes are supported by ERP: 1) Sales, 2) Marketing, 3) Production, 4) Service, 5) Procurement, 6) R&D, 7) HR, and 8) Finance.

ERP depth represents the extent to which a firm's business processes are supported by ERP on different hierarchical levels. This also points to the integrated system and the **use** of master data. The ERP depth informs us whether the organization believes that an ERP can be useful in all hierarchical parts of the organization and for all processes. The final dimension is measured by three items used at the hierarchical levels: 1) Strategic, 2) Tactical, and 3) Operational.

Table 1 summarizes the four dimensions and the associated items. From the discussion thus far, a model for measuring ERP systems utilization impact on benefits is depicted in Figure 1.

The model suggests that if organizations increase the use of ERP described as **ERP systems utilization**, then perceived **net benefits** increase. ERP systems utilization is measured by the four dimensions proposed by Massetti and Zmud (1996): volume, breadth, diversity and depth.

Table 1. The four dimensions and items used to measure each dimension

Dimensions	Items	Type of scale
Volume (four items)	Degree of ERP users (Number of current ERP users / Maximum number of potential ERP users.	%
	ERP share of all computer based information system	%
	ERP support of primary business processes (sales/marketing/production/service)	%
	ERP support of secondary business processes (procurement, R&D, HR, finance)	%
Breadth (two items)	Share of business processes that uses master data	%
	Degree of internal business processes integrated through the ERP	%
	Degree of business processes integrated with external partners	%
Diversity (eight items)	To the extent the following processes are supported (Sales, Marketing, Production, Service, Procurement, R&D, HR, Finance) by the ERP	Likert
Depth (three items)	To what extent is ERP used at the following hierarchical levels: (Strategic-, Tactical-, Operational level)	Likert
Benefits (five items)	Operational benefits, managerial benefits, strategic benefits, IT infrastructural benefits, and organizational benefits	Likert

Figure 1. Research model

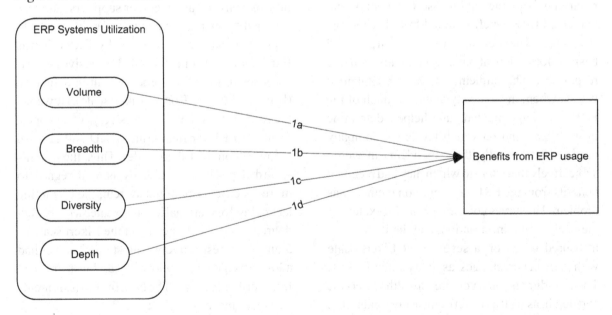

From this, the following propositions are given:

- Proposition 1a: Increase measured as Volume related to ERP systems utilization means an increase in "Perceived Net Benefits" from ERP usage.

- Proposition 1b: Increase measured as Breadth related to ERP systems utilization means an increase in "Perceived Net Benefits" from ERP usage.

- Proposition 1c: Increase measured as Diversity related to ERP systems utilization means an increase in "Perceived Net Benefits" from ERP usage.

- Proposition 1d: Increase measured as Depth related to ERP systems utilization means an increase in "Perceived Net Benefits" from ERP usage.

METHODOLOGY

To test the ERP utilization model, we collected data through a survey of 77 Swedish firms using the ERP system Movex (Movex is now re-named to M3 and owned by Lawson). In the data collection process, we collaborated with the Swedish Movex User Association who invited Movex to use firms to participate in the study (cf. Hitt et al.'s (2002) study). The questionnaire consisted of four parts – background information, questions regarding implementation, use (17 items), and perceived ERP benefits gained from ERP **usage** (five items). The background information provided basic information about the company and the respondent. The implementation part explained which, when, in what way and how much of the ERP was implemented; use helped determine in what way and on which levels the company used the ERP; finally, the respondents answered subjectively the extent to which they had received benefits from the ERP, i.e., common method bias problem. The survey contained 28 items, excluding the background information, and the items were measured based on a seven-point Likert scale with parts in percentages, as indicated in Table 1. The four dimensions: volume, breadth, diversity, and depth, as well as benefits measurements were operationalized, as is evident in Table 1.

Perceived **net benefits** were measured in relation to the following five categories of benefits: operational benefits, managerial benefits, strategic benefits, IT infrastructural benefits, and organizational benefits (Shang & Seddon, 2002).

The results of the demographic data collected in the survey revealed that 32% of the respondents were IT executives, 31% financial executives, and 30% ERP responsible. They had an average of 15.7 years of experience in ERP systems, and they came from a broad spectrum of industries, with a strong focus in manufacturing (61%). Most of the companies had finalized their ERP implementation, and were constantly adding new functionalities and upgrades to the ERP they had implemented.

The number of ERP users was 72% of the total number of potential users. **ERP Systems** are an important part (63%) of the overall information processing. The ERP systems were mainly used in primary business processes (85%), but were also used (71%) in secondary business processes. 75% of business processes used master data and 76% of business processes were integrated through the ERP system. ERP system was, to a lesser extent, used for integrating business processes residing in subsidiaries, customers, or suppliers, and was dropped from further analysis. With respect to support of business processes by ERPs, it was found that most companies had extensive support for sales, production, procurement and finance (between 4.6 and 5.9 on the Likert scale). However, the results show that there was very little support from the ERP for marketing, R&D and HR (all below 3.0 on the Likert scale). Thus, these items were dropped in the final analysis. With regards to more specific users of the system, the hierarchic tactical and operational levels revealed a fairly high degree of use, with means on the Likert scale of 5 and 5.88, respectively. The strategic level had a lower usage level, below 3.0, and was dropped from further analysis. The benefits measurements exhibited means of 3.35 to 5.19.

The rest of the paper describes the results and conclusions from the testing of the model. Before proceeding, there is one limitation that needs to be reflected upon, namely, the organizational size. The ambition was to develop a model aimed at measuring the extent of ERP's utilization in SMEs. However, the organizational size of our sample is not coherent with our definition of SMEs, from

Table 2. Diffusion indexes correlated with benefit measurement

Index	Pearson's R	Adjusted R²	Std. Error of Estimate	F-test	Sig.	t-test*
Volume	.446	.155	.919	4.447	.003	.000
Breadth	.426	.160	.916	8.221	.001	.000
Diversity	.546	.259	.861	7.656	.000	.000
Depth	.542	.274	.852	15.357	.000	.000

which follows that the results from the test do not describe the situation in SMEs. However, this was a test of the model, and our ambition is to do further research which then could provide additional knowledge when comparing results from the perspective of organizational size. Additionally, this limitation will make it possible to generalize future research results to a higher grade. Further, the underlying theory might not be as promising as we had hoped for, since Massetti and Zmud's (1996) dimensions might not work in the context of ERP system.

RESULTS

We used multivariate linear regression to measure the association of ERP utilization (volume, breadth, diversity, and depth) and perceived net benefits (operational benefits). Prior to the linear regression analysis on the scores of the items in the questionnaire, all items were standardized. This was done since we used different scales (percentage and Likert). The four dimensions or latent constructs (volume, breadth, diversity, and depth) of ERP utilization were tested against the dependent variable (**net benefits**, which was measured through the item operational benefits). For the actual analysis, we ran four separate linear regression analysis. A more advanced statistical analysis could be considered, but since this research was in its early stage, we explored the underlying construct prior to testing the relationships among constructs. We used SPSS version 17

for our analysis. Table 2 summarizes the results of the four regression analysis. Returning to the propositions, we can conclude that volume and breadth received low support in this test, whereas diversity and depth received support.

DISCUSSION AND CONCLUSION

The purpose of this paper was to develop and test a model describing the connection between diffusion of ERP and Perceived Net Benefits. **Diffusion** of ERP was measured as the extent of ERP systems' utilization from the four dimensions: volume, breadth, diversity, and depth. These four latent constructs were measured through two to eight individual items. However, only two of the four dimensions were found to be statistically verified. One conclusion that can be drawn from the fact that we did not get significant results on the dimensions, volume and breadth, could be that ERP systems historically are systems that are used to a higher extent at the operational level, and therefore could be seen as a commodity – necessary to have but not providing any perceived benefits from the respondents' views. Another potential explanation is our interpretation of the underlying model/theory, i.e., Massetti and Zmud's EDI usage **measurement**, which was either incorrectly interpreted, or it could be that the model was not applicable to the ERP context. A third possible explanation is the operationalization of Massetti and Zmud's four dimensions. Hence, the measurement model needs to be further developed so that it more clearly measures benefits. It can also be said that the model needs to be further developed so that it better considers the huge complexity that ERP systems cover, which means that it has to consider qualitative benefits in the form of non-monetary benefits to a greater extent. However, our model and the results presented thus far are definitely a first attempt at measuring qualitative ERP systems benefits and exploring how ERP systems are internally diffused in an organization. It can also be concluded that the results thus far contribute new knowledge on ERP systems diffusion, and increase our understanding of use as a concept, since it expands the usage of the construct beyond the level of **use** as a go-live measurement. However, more research on post-adoption with respect to ERP systems **usage** is necessary in order to fully understand how benefits gained from ERP systems can be influenced. Thus, here is an explicit call for theories that can explain the utilization of ERP systems and the linkage to benefits.

The four dimensions all showed different results. We had expected the dimension of volume to show strong support, but received contradictory results. The idea with this dimension was to cover **ERP Systems**' ability to support the organization and its users, as well as business processes. Previous research used the quota of users that could benefit from ERPs, compared to current users of a specific ERP, as the sole measurement for diffusion.

The dimension, breadth, did not provide us with the expected results, that is, the extent to which the business processes had ERP support, whether that support crossed the borders of the functional areas and integrated them, and to what extent it was valid for integration in the organization. In future research, these three factors need to be studied in depth, preferably using a case study technique. The performance of the breadth dimension indicates that the factors of organization and functionality are not significant to the ERP diffusion. It also shows that ERP diffusion in combination with these factors has a low impact on benefits.

In comparison with the dimensions of volume and breadth, the performance of the diversity dimension was strong. This points to the fact that organizations need support for many different kinds of business processes; hence, there is a need for versatile ERP. The need for diversity is, in other words, an important initial characteristic that, in time, should be substituted with, for instance, ERP's ability to mirror and support the processes that can benefit from the ERP.

The performance of the depth dimension provided us with a result similar to diversity; as indicated above, this could be due to **ERP Systems** needing to be used at different hierarchical levels, resulting from the fact that ERP systems support both the operational and managerial level. Further research related to the depth dimension is needed to shed light on the relation between ERP systems depth and benefits distribution in organizations.

The contributions of the paper are the following: First, it provides some support for the notion of diffusion found in the theory of network externalities, and shows that a critical mass is necessary to achieve benefits. This can be used to better understand failures in ERP projects. Second, the use of the model and its dimensions (volume, breadth, diversity and depth) provide insights to the use construct and point to the need to treat it more rigorously. Third, the study contributes to our understanding of the many aspects of use of IT, and to the potential contribution to value and firm performance from IT utilization, especially in relation to utilization of ERP systems **usage** in SMEs.

REFERENCES

Agarwal, R., Raha, A. R., & Ghosh, B. (2000). Our experience and learning in ERP implementation. *ACM SIGSOFT Software Engineering Notes, 25*(2).

Balakrishnan, V., & Das, A. (2009). Analysis of critical problems in ERP implementation to enhance SOA for energy and utilities - a case study. In *SEFBIS Professional Journal of the Scientific and Educational Forum on Business Information Systems* (pp. 18-29).

Bernroider, E. W. N., & Leseure, M. J. 2005. Enterprise resource planning (ERP) diffusion and characteristics according to the system's lifecycle: A comparative view of small-to-medium sized and large enterprises. *Working Papers on Information Processing and Information Management*, 32.

Burton-Jones, A., & Gallivan, M. J. (2004). *Towards a deeper understanding of system usage in organizations: a multilevel perspective*. Working paper, Computer Information Systems Department J. Mack Robinson College of Business Georgia State University.

Burton-Jones, A., & Gallivan, M. J. (2007). Toward a deeper understanding of system usage in organizations: A multilevel perspective. *Management Information Systems Quarterly*, *31*(4), 657–679.

Davenport, T. (1996). *Holistic management of mega-package change: The case of SAP*. Boston: Center of Business Innovation, Ernest & Young LLP.

Davenport, T. (1998). Putting the Enterprise into the Enterprise System. *Harvard Business Review*, *76*(4), 121–131.

Davenport, T. (2000). *Mission Critical: Realizing the Promise of Enterprise Systems*. Boston: Harvard Business School Press.

DeLone, W. H., & McLean, E. R. (1992). Information systems success: The quest for the dependent variable. *Information Systems Research*, *3*(1), 60–95. doi:10.1287/isre.3.1.60

DeLone, W. H., & McLean, E. R. (2003). The DeLone and McLean model of information systems success: A ten-year update. *Journal of Management Information Systems*, *19*(4), 9–30.

Eriksson, L. T., & Hultman, J. (2005). One digital leap or a step-by-step approach? - An empirical study of e-commerce development among Swedish SMEs. *International Journal of Electronic Business*, *3*(5), 447–460. doi:10.1504/IJEB.2005.008519

Gibson, C. F., & Nolan, R. L. (1974). Managing the four stages of EDP growth. *Harvard Business Review*, *52*(1), 76–88.

Grover, G., Teng, J., Segars, A. H., & Fiedler, K. (1998). The influence of information technology diffusion and business process change on perceived productivity: The IS executive's Perspective. *Information & Management*, *34*, 14–159. doi:10.1016/S0378-7206(98)00054-8

Hedman, J. (2003). *On Enterprise Systems Artifacts: Changes in Information Systems Development and Evaluation. Lund Studies in Informatics, No. 2*. Lund, Sweden: Department of Informatics.

Hedman, J., & Borell, A. (2003). ERP systems impact on organizations. In Grant, G. (Ed.), *ERP & Data Warehousing in organizations: issues and challenges* (pp. 1–21). Hershey, PA: Idea Group Publishing.

Hedman, J., & Borell, A. (2004). Narratives in ERP systems evaluation. *Journal of Enterprise Information Management*, *17*(4), 283–290. doi:10.1108/17410390410548698

Hitt, L. M., Wu, D. J., & Xiaoge, Z. (2002). Investment in Enterprise Resource Planning: Business Impact and Productivity Measures. *Journal of Management Information Systems*, *19*(1), 71–98.

Ifinedo, P., & Nahar, N. (2007). ERP systems success: an empirical analysis of how two organizational stakeholder groups prioritize and evaluate relevant measures. *Enterprise Information Systems, 1*(1), 25–48. doi:10.1080/17517570601088539

Johansson, B., & Newman, M. (2009). Competitive Advantage and Enterprise Resource Planning (ERP) Systems: Some Conflicts in the Value-Chain. In *Americas Conference on Information Systems (AMCIS) 2009*, San Francisco.

Kalling, T. (1999). *Gaining competitive advantage through information technology: a resource-based approach to the creation and employment of strategic IT resources*. Lund, Germany: Lund Business Press.

Koch, C. (2001). *ERP-systemer: erfaringer, ressourcer, forandringer*. København, Danmark: Ingeniøren-bøger.

Kumar, K., & Van Hillegersberg, J. (2000). ERP experiences and evolution. *Communications of the ACM, 43*(4), 22–26. doi:10.1145/332051.332063

Larsen, M., & Myers, M. D. (1998). When Success Turns into Failure: A Package-Driven Business Process Re-engineering project in the Financial Services Industry. *The Journal of Strategic Information Systems, 8*, 395–417. doi:10.1016/S0963-8687(00)00025-1

Lengnick-Hall, C. A., Lengnick-Hall, M. L., & Abdinnour-Helm, S. (2004). The role of social and intellectual capital in achieving competitive advantage through enterprise resource planning (ERP) systems. *Journal of Engineering and Technology Management, 21*(4), 307–330. doi:10.1016/j.jengtecman.2004.09.005

Massetti, B., & Zmud, R. W. (1996). Measuring the extent of EDI usage in complex organizations: Strategies and illustrative examples. *Management Information Systems Quarterly, 20*(3), 331. doi:10.2307/249659

Møller, C. (2005). ERP II: a conceptual framework for next-generation enterprise systems? *Journal of Enterprise Information Management, 18*(4), 483–497. doi:10.1108/17410390510609626

Morabito, V., Pace, S., & Previtali, P. (2005). ERP Marketing and Italian SMEs. *European Management Journal, 23*(5), 590–598. doi:10.1016/j.emj.2005.09.014

Robey, D., Ross, J. W., & Boudreau, M.-C. (2002). Learning to Implement Enterprise Systems: An Exploratory Study of the Dialectics of Change. *Journal of Management Information Systems, 19*(1), 17–46.

Rolland, C., & Prakash, N. (2000). Bridging the Gap Between Organisational Needs and ERP Functionality. *Requirements Engineering, 5*(3), 180–193. doi:10.1007/PL00010350

Santhanam, R., Sasidharan, S., Meharia, P., Brass, D., & Sambamurthy, V. (2009). Improving the success of enterprise information system implementation - current findings and future research. In *SEFBIS Professional Journal of the Scientific and Educational Forum on Business Information Systems* (pp. 29-42).

Scott, J. E., & Vessey, I. (2000). Implementing Enterprise Resource Planning Systems: The Role of Learning from Failure. *Information Systems Frontiers, 2*(2), 213. doi:10.1023/A:1026504325010

Sedera, D., & Tan, T. C. F. (2007). Reconceptualizing Usage for Contemporary Information Systems Success. In *European Conference of Information Systems (ECIS)*.

Shang, S., & Seddon, P. B. (2002). Assessing and managing the benefits of enterprise systems: the business manager's perspective. *Information Systems Journal, 12*(4), 271–299. doi:10.1046/j.1365-2575.2002.00132.x

Somers, T. M., & Nelson, K. G. (2004). A taxonomy of players and activities across the ERP project life cycle. *Information & Management, 41*(3), 257–278. doi:10.1016/S0378-7206(03)00023-5

Straub, D., Limayem, M., & Karahanna-Evaristo, E. (1995). measuring systems usage: Implications for IS theory testing. *Management Science, 41*(8), 1328–1342. doi:10.1287/mnsc.41.8.1328

Teng, J. T. C., Grover, V., & Guttler, W. (2002). Information technology innovations: General diffusion patterns and its relationships to innovation characteristics. *IEEE Transactions on Engineering Management, 49*(1), 13–27. doi:10.1109/17.985744

Upton, D. M., & McAfee, M. M. (2000). A path-based approach to information technology in manufacturing. *International Journal of Technology Management, 20*(3/4), 354–372. doi:10.1504/IJTM.2000.002876

Wier, B., Hunton, J., & Hassab Elnaby, H. R. (2007). Enterprise resource planning systems and non-financial performance incentives: The joint impact on corporate performance. *International Journal of Accounting Information Systems, 8*(3), 165–190. doi:10.1016/j.accinf.2007.05.001

Xu, L., & Brinkkemper, S. (2007). Concepts of product software. *European Journal of Information Systems, 16*(5), 531–541. doi:10.1057/palgrave.ejis.3000703

Zhu, K., & Kraemer, K. L. (2005). Post-Adoption Variations in Usage and Value of E-Business by Organizations: Cross-Country Evidence from the Retail Industry. *Information Systems Research, 16*(1), 61–84. doi:10.1287/isre.1050.0045

Chapter 19
Factors Influencing Users' Intention to Continue Using ERP Systems

Ahmed Elragal
German University in Cairo, Egypt

Dalia Birry
Alexandria University, Egypt

ABSTRACT

There has been an increasing interest in ERP systems in both research and practice in the last decade. But unfortunately in many occasions a lot of companies have stopped using these systems after they went-live with the implementation. This study is an attempt to reveal the factors influencing users' intention to continue using the ERP system. A survey was sent to respondent gaining a number of 223 responses. A hypothesized model was developed based on three theories; TAM, ECT, and TPB. The model was tested using regression analysis of the collected responses. Results showed that users' intension to continue using the ERP systems are affected by: perceived usefulness, satisfaction, subjective norm, and perceived behavior control. Meanwhile, perceived usefulness is affected by confirmation and subjective norm while

INTRODUCTION

In the last decades business relied more on information and communication technologies (ICT) to handle their day-to-day operations in an efficient manner. So management and business organizations spend a great amount of resources on information technology (IT) with expectation of increasing productivity, efficiency and long term benefits (Alshare et al., 2004) to adapt such

substantial growth. This huge investment made IT puts increasing pressure on management to justify the outlay by quantifying the business value of information technology.

To cope with such changes, organizations paid attention to the importance of using IT to gain advantage in competitive market. Enterprise Resource Planning systems (ERP) are one of the highly complex information systems (IS) which have been adopted by a lot of organizations worldwide (Elsawah et al., 2008).

DOI: 10.4018/978-1-61692-020-3.ch019

ERP may well count as one of the most significant developments in the corporate use of IT since the 90's (Davenport, 1998). A typical ERP system may combine inventory data with financial, sales and human data, allowing organizations to achieve many work activities like pricing products, producing financial statements and managing human, material and financial resources effectively (Markus et al., 2000). This means that the ERP system is integrated and enterprise-wide which automates core corporate activities. It helps organizations to replace the present IS's which aren't integrated to an integrated system.

ERP implementations are very complex and expensive, but once they are implemented successfully, significant improvement in business processes, communication and interaction between users and customers will eventually occur. In addition to better production scheduling and reduction in manufacturing costs. Also management can observe reduction of cycle times of documents and elimination of redundant data and operations (Zhang et al., 2003).

It was reported that 75% of the ERP projects are classified as failures and many ERP projects ended catastrophically (Griffith et al., 1999). Of course failure rates differ from country to country based on many factors. For instance, in Egypt the failure rate of implementation problems is extremely higher than that in the western companies because of the challenging Egyptian culture which is entirely different from where these systems were developed (Elsawah et al., 2008; Rasmy et al. 2005).

Accordingly the objective of this chapter is studying the factors that influence the formation of users' intention to continue using ERP systems. Therefore, the research questions are as follows:

1. What are the salient factors underlying ERP users' intention to continue using ERP systems after its initial acceptance?

2. How do these factors influence continuance intention?

This chapter is structured as follows: we will first introduce the background of similar studies and then describing the relevant theories which will help us to build our research model. Then we will introduce our research model and its hypotheses. Survey and statistical analysis will then follow and finally ideas for future research are presented.

BACKGROUND

During the last two decades the investment in IT has been increasing to reach almost about half of all capital investments on a global basis (Mahmood et al., 2000). In addition, growing numbers of strategic information systems that shape or critically support organizational processes have also been reported (Mahmood et al., 2000). This has led to the growing body of academic research examining the determinants of information acceptance and utilization among users.

Information Systems (IS) are general concepts. Since IS has different functions, so different industries and different organizations use different information systems (Yeh, 2007). Davenport (1998; 2000) has defined ERP systems as systems that aim at providing integrated software to handle multiple corporate functions e.g. finance, human resources, manufacturing, materials management, and sales and distribution. This means they incorporate information and information-based processes in and across organizational functions areas in the organization. This is important to point out that ERP systems are different from the others systems as:

- The integrated nature of ERP systems causes dramatic changes in the procedures and processes of the business (reengineering);
- As ERP systems are not built but adopted, this involves the need to introduce customizations to the users (Wu & Wang, 2006);

- The user becomes dependent on the ERP vendor for assistance and updates (Wu & Wang, 2006).

In addition, ERP implementation includes changes in technological, operational, strategic, managerial and organizational related components (Ifinedo, 2007).

ERP implementation is risky and the cost of the technology is expensive. In addition, the implementation environment is affected by a large number of software, complexity of the requirements from those systems and the need to adopt any existing or future software to the core ERP technology (Gyampah, 2007). But once it is successfully implemented, it allows organizations to:

- Integrate all their activities together with supply chain and customer services;
- Facilitate information flows;
- Consolidation sources of data and data entries to eliminate multiple sources of data;
- Communicate different organizational units to help meeting the requirements of employees and customers alike.

Thus, researchers have devoted more efforts at identifying factors that might be important to avoid ERP failures. Specially, it was reported that only one quarter of ERP projects are successful and the other three quarters are considered as failures projects (Rasmy et al., 2005). A number of explanations for ERP implementation failures have been offered in different research. Yeh (2007) summarized them as technical (e.g. lack of technically knowledge staff and problems in software customization and testing), economic (e.g. lack of economic resource, underestimated the economic resources needed and lack of planning and justification), and finally human/organizational (e.g. lack of strong and committed leadership).

The most important and common reason in most ERP project failures is human resources (Nah et al., 2004). The main and the common problem is resistance to change. This seems the main obstacle the organizations are facing. Employees are often reluctant to learn new technology or the IT department is reluctant to change to due their involvement to the existing product.

This raises the question "which factors influence the decision to accept ERP systems and to continue using them in the post-acceptance phase?" In the acceptance phase, the initial adoption of ERP is an organizational decision although employees are the ones who are going to use it (Tan & Siau, 2006). Prior studies (Orlikowski, 1991; 1992) suggested that employees sometimes decide not to use ERP system, although the organizational decision is to adopt it. In other words, the long-term viability of an ERP system and its radical success depend on its continued and extensive use by individual. That's because if the individual are unwilling to use ERP, their work would be worsted which in turn would affect the productivity (Frey, 1993). In similar lines, Jasperson et al. (2005) advice that more research should focus on the post acceptance usage and continues phenomenon.

Recker & Rosemann (2007) suggest a theoretical model studying factors that influence the formation of an intention to continue using a process modeling technique. Their suggestion has been a motivation for us to develop a model studying the factors influence users' intention to continue using IS (ERP in our study).

MAIN FOCUS OF THE CHAPTER

A number of models have been proposed to explain users' intention to accept new IS provided by their companies. Most of the existing studies on users' intention focus on the phenomenon of first-time use of IS, IS Continuance, herein referred to as an individual's continued use of a particular technology product, have received relatively less attention within the IS community (Bhattacherjee, 2001). Although the initial acceptance and use are necessary but they are not sufficient conditions for IS Continuance, so this study attempts to understand and explains the factors that influence users' intention to continue using IS for long time especially ERP systems.

DESCRIPTION OF RELEVANT THEORIES AND CONCEPTS

Investment in information systems is a real value to organizations if the information systems are used by a manner achieving the strategic objectives. Thus the acceptance of the user of IS is a key factor for the success of the investment in IS. Although the initial acceptance of IS is the first step and important to the success of IS, but the continuous use of those systems for a long period of time depends on the continuous use and not the first use only. So when implementing an information technology, the ultimate goal of the manager is the technology intended level of usage is achieved. As the system can't be considered successful if the technology is not used or the intended level is not achieved (Gyampah, 2007).

As stated by Markus & Keil (1994: pp.11-12), "because use is not build in, these systems never achieve their true potential for improving organizational performance". They also noted if the system is technically successful but it is unused or under used, it will cost the organization too much. Davis et al. (1989: p.982) reported "computer systems can't improve organizational performance if they are not used". On the same sequence Yi & Davis (2001: p.522) noted "Organizations will not realize desired returns on their investments in information technology designed to improve decision-making unless users are able to use them". Lastly Gyamah (2007: p.1234) noted "An implementation project can achieve technical, budgetary and schedule success, but if the users of the technology do not use it, the intended benefits for implementation that technology are not likely to be obtained".

In this section, we introduce three complementary theoretical model on the acceptance and continues decision in the IS discipline. These theories will be the base of our model of process ERP continuance.

We focus in our study on the three models. First, Technology Acceptance Model (TAM) which shows the determinants of formation of users' intention to accept IS. Second, the expectation confirmation theory (ECT) which explains post-adoption behavior with respect to the match with preadoption belief and expectation. Third, Theory of Planned Behavior (TPB) which explains user intention and behavior through the added factor perceived behavior control (PBC).

Technology Acceptance Model

The primary underlying model for this research is the technology acceptance model (TAM). TAM is specifically meant to explain behavior of computer usage. "The goal of TAM is to be capable of explaining user behavior across a broad range of end-user computing technologies and user populations, while at the same time being both parsimonious and theoretically justified" (Davis et al., 1989: p.985).

Although TAM was introduced in 1986 by Davis -from nearly twenty three years- and was tested by Davis et al. (1989) it continues to be the "most applied theoretical model in the IS discipline" (Lee et al, 2003). It is derived from Theory of Reasoned Action (TRA) by Fishbein & Ajzen (1975). While TRA is a general theory of human behavior, TAM is a model specific to IS usage. It explains technology acceptance quite well (Wang, 2005). As note by Venkatesh & Davis (2000: p.186), "TAM consistently explains a substantial proportion of the variance (typically about 40%) in usage intentions and behavior and that TAM compares favorably with alternative models such as the Theory of Reasoned Action and the Theory of Planned Behavior".

The model suggests that users' decisions to accept new IS are influenced by two core constructs. These two constructs are Perceived Usefulness and Ease of Use. *Perceived usefulness (PU)* is defined as "the degree to which a person believes that using a particular system would enhance his/her performance" (Davis et al., 1989, p. 985). *Ease of use* is "the degree to which user expects the target system to be free of effort" (Davis et al., 1989, p.985). Related studies have reported in the post-acceptance stage, perceived usefulness directly influence users' intention to reuse (continue using) system provided. On the other hand perceived ease of use has significant influence on intention in pre-acceptance stage but once user begin actually use the system, it rationally becomes less important in formation his intention (Szajna, 1996).

TAM has been identified as a very commonly employed theoretical framework for studying IS acceptance (Lee et al., 2003). There are great amount of research related to TAM has reportedly made it one of the most influencer IS theories overall. In short, if the central goal to predict IS usage, it can be argued that TAM is preferable (Taylor & Todd, 1995).

Some current research on ERP implementation has used TAM or various factors from it in trying to understand user acceptance and continues use to ERP system. It is also used in some many researches to examine the successful story of ERP implementation in the organization (Gyampah & Salam, 2004).

Expectation Confirmation Theory

Expectation Confirmation Theory (ECT) is widely used in consumer behavior literature to study consumer satisfaction, post-purchase behavior (e.g. complaining, repurchase) and service marketing in general (Andserson & Sullivan, 1993; Dabholkar et al., 2000). The ECT framework works as follows. First, consumers form an initial expectation of a specific product or service prior to purchase. Second, users accept and use that product or service. Following a period of initial consumption, they form perceptions about its performance. Third, they assess the difference between its perceived performance and their original expectations, and determine the extent of the confirmation. Fourth, users then form a satisfaction based on their confirmation level and expectation on which confirmation was based. Finally, satisfaction leads to a repurchase intention, on the other hand, dissatisfaction tends to discontinue users' subsequent use.

In Sum, ECT posits that initial pre-usage *expectations* coupled with *perceived performance*; lead to post-adoption satisfaction which in turn forms the user intention to continue using IS system. Satisfaction is mediated through positive or negative confirmation which formed by comparing expectation and perceived performance (Oliver, 1980). Perceived performance is often conceptualized as perceived usefulness of using IS (Bhattacherjee, 2001). In our research model, we are going to assess the impact of confirmation on perceived usefulness and satisfaction.

Theory of Planned Behavior

Theory of Planned Behavior (TPB) was introduced by Ajzen (1991). It extends the Theory of Reasoned Action. A key purpose of TPB is to provide a basis of tracing the impact of two primary factors on user intention. These factors are Subjective Norm and Perceived Behavior Control. TPB posits that user's intention is formed due to attitude toward the system, subjective norm and perceived behavior control. *Attitude (A)* defined as the user's evaluation of the desirability of his or her using the system (Mathieson, 1991, p.175). *Subjective Norm (SN)* reflects perceptions that significant desire the individual to perform or not perform a behavior (Taylor & Todd, 1995; Matheison, 1991). Lastly *Perceived behavior Control (PBC)* refers to the individuals' perceptions of the presence or absence of requisite resources and opportunities

(Ajzen et al., 1986, p. 457) necessary to perform the behavior. In our research model, we are going to assess the impact of subjective norm and perceived behavior control on users' intention to continue using the ERP.

THE RESEARCH MODEL AND HYPOTHESES

From the above discussions of the three theoretical perspectives upon the continuance decision we will introduce in the following section our hypotheses:

Confirmation of users' expectation of using IS can indirectly influence IS continuance use mediated by satisfaction or perceived usefulness.

Just as in IS acceptance contexts perceived ease of use can affect perceived usefulness. Confirmation can also influence perceived usefulness in the post-acceptance contexts. The users in the acceptance phase are unsure of what to expect as they do not have enough information about the system. This leads to low initial usefulness perceptions of new IS (Bhattacherjee, 2001; Bhattacherjee & Premkumar, 2004) which are easily confirmed. Such perceptions may be adjusted higher as they know more about the system. In summary, users often adjust their perceptions to be consistent with reality. This means confirmation can elevate perceived usefulness.

Expectation confirmation theory posits that user satisfaction is determined by two factors: expectation of IS and confirmation of the expectation which will lead to reusing the IS. As noted by Bhattacherjee, "Confirmation is positively related to satisfaction with IS use because it implies realization of the expected benefits of IS use while disconfirmation denotes failure to achieve expectation" (Bhattacherjee, 2001, pp.355-356). Also Wang & Hsieh (2006) confirmed in the results of their study that confirmation of expectation is positively associated with satisfaction. Based on the above discussion the following hypotheses are proposed:

H1a: In an ERP implementation environment Confirmation of Expectation has a positive effect on Perceived Usefulness.

H1b: In an ERP implementation environment Confirmation of Expectation has a positive effect on Satisfaction.

Satisfaction is a key variable to measure the extent of the continuing use of the IS or repurchase a product/ services. It is considered as the basis of building and strengthening the users' loyalty to long-term using IS or product/services. Cheung & Limayem (2005) presented a study on students using Blackboard as a course management system (CMS). His objective is to gain a better understanding of the factors influencing students' continued usage of a news technology. Their results present strong support for the direct impact of satisfaction on users continues intention and they noted in their research that satisfaction is the strongest factor to continue system usage. Satisfaction has been widely adopted as an important determiner of IS success. Danaher & Rust (1996) found that a customer (user) who is more satisfied with a service (system) will have higher subsequent usage levels. Also Chou & Chen (2009) found in their study that satisfaction with IS use is the strongest predicator of users' continuance intention. Satisfaction lead to using the system but using the system can not lead to satisfaction (Baroudi et al., 1986). This leads to the following hypothesis:

H2: In an ERP implementation environment Satisfaction has a positive effect on Users' Intention to continue using ERP system.

Subjective Norm is one direct determinant of theory of Planned Behavior (Ajzen,1991) which is defined as the degree to which an individual believes that people who are important to him/her think he/she should perform the behavior in questions. Thus, employees are likely to be influences when deciding to continue use ERP by both what their peers think, due to the competitive nature with organization; and what their supervisors and mangers may think, due to possible affect on their work performance. In addition, they are affected by the need of team work with other employees.

According to previous researches, Subjective Norm has a significant effect on users' intention, either directly or indirectly through perceived usefulness (Taylor & Todd, 1995; Karahanna et al., 1999; Venkatesh & Morris, 2000; Venkatesh & Davis, 2000). Also (Lai et al., 2005) confirm that Subjective Norm had the second largest total effect on user intention to use a system, suggesting that employee are likely to be influenced by their managers, supervisors, friends and peers when deciding whether to use the system provided or not. As subjective Norm shape the potential adopters' beliefs about when and why to adopt an innovation. When a supervisor or peers suggest the usefulness of a particular system in the post acceptance stage, the individual would accept the idea even if they realize this during the acceptance stage. Premkumar et al. (2008) confirmed that Subjective Norm has a significant effect on users' intention to use internet messaging (IM). According to the above discussion, the following hypotheses are presented:

H3a: In an ERP implementation environment Subjective Norm has a positive effect on Users' Intention to continue using ERP system
H3b: In an ERP implementation environment Subjective Norm has a positive effect on Perceive Usefulness.

Perceived Behavior Control was added into the theory of planned Behavior to answer the limitation of theory of Reasoned Action, to deal with individuals that may lack complete volitional control over behavior (Ajzen, 2002). So according to Ajzen (1991), the more resources (money; computer, time, network) and opportunities individuals think they possess, the greater would be their perceived control over their behavior,

and therefore, the greater the likelihood for these individuals to behave accordingly, in this study is ERP system. Perceived Behavior Control is based partly on past experience and partly from the second hand information, through the exchange of information by family, friends and factors that may control the level of perceived difficulty of performing the behavior of interest (Ajzen, 1991). Many studies have shown common results regarding Perceived Behavior Control as a predictor of intention. According to Wang et al (2007), Perceived Behavior Control influence users' intention to shop line. Also Gopi & Ramayah (2007) noted in their research that Perceived Behavior Control influences investors' intention (users' intention in our study) toward internet stock trading (ERP in our study). Hence, the hypothesis formulated is:

H4: In an ERP implementation environment Perceived Behavior Control has a positive effect on Users' Intention to continue using ERP system.

Technology acceptance research has shown that perceived usefulness is the salient belief influencing individuals to accept an IS. Also IS Continuous Model (Bhattacherjee, 2001) has shown that perceived usefulness is an important variable impact individual intention to continue using IS. Prior studies found that perceived usefulness influences an individual intention during both acceptance and post-acceptance stage of IS use (Davis et al, 1989; Karahanna et al., 1999). Also Szajna (1996) reported that, there are two factors influence users' intention in the acceptance stage -Perceived Usefulness and Perceived Easy of Use- but in the post-acceptance stage Perceived Usefulness is the only variable affect users' intention. Attitude is a pre-acceptance affect, while satisfaction is a post-acceptance affect. It is confirmed that perceived usefulness can directly impact attitude in the acceptance stage. Like wise, perceived usefulness is expected to be the most salient ex post expectation influence users' post–acceptance affect (satisfaction) Bhattacherjee

(2001). It is noted by Bhattacherjee (2001) that perceived usefulness is based on others' opinions or information proposed through mass media in the acceptance stage, while perceived usefulness in post-acceptance stage is formed through users first-hand experience and is, therefore, more reliable. As such, Perceived Usefulness is the key factor that motivates users' intention to continue using a system in the future (Bhattacherjee & Sanford, 2006). When users believe that ERP can enhance the productivity and efficiency of their work, they tend to develop positive attitude toward the system and consider the use of ERP as a beneficial and useful (Chen & Chien, 2009). Based on the above discussion, the following hypothesis is proposed:

H5a: In an ERP implementation environment Perceived Usefulness has a positive effect on Users' Intention to continue using ERP system.
H5b: In an ERP implementation environment Perceived Usefulness has a positive effect on satisfaction of using ERP system.

We summarize the proposed relationship to be tested in this research in (Figure 1).

RESEARCH METHODOLOGY

Survey

Data was collected through online questionnaire from Egyptian companies using ERP systems. Online survey has the advantages of speeding up large amount of data collection and allowing for electronic data entry (Parasuraman & Zinkhan, 2002). The unit of analysis is end-users of an ERP system within organizations. Participation in this study was voluntary.

All used instruments had been validated by prior studies. These instruments were modified for the adaptation to ERP usage. The scales of confirmation and users' intention to continue using

ERP were measured using three items derived from Bhattacherjee (2001). While perceived usefulness and satisfaction derived from Zvirian et al. (2005). Subjective norm and perceived behavior control derived from Taylor and Todd (1995). All scales used five-point Likert scales anchored between "strongly disagree" (1) to "strongly agree" (5) with "uncertain" (3) except satisfaction anchored from "almost never" (1) to "almost always" (5) with "about half of the time" (3). Please refer to the appendix of this chapter for a full version of the instrument.

The demographic and other data included information about the respondent's gender, age and years of using ERP system in his/her current organization. In addition to his/her current position, the kind of industry and the kind of ERP system he/she is using.

The data was collected through online questionnaire on Survey Monkey website. We collected the data for a whole month by forwarding the link of the questionnaire to the companies implemented any kind of ERP, either international ERP (Oracle, SAP, Microsoft, and Focus) or local ERP (ALMOTAKAMEL). The companies, we have chosen, implemented ERP at least for one year.

Results

A total of 223 responses were obtained from the companies in Egypt. Some demographics were collected and the analysis of which is presented in the following figures. (Figure 2), gender distribution is presented showing great percentage of male users of ERP.

(Figure 3) presents the ERP systems surveyed in our research study. The results show that the majority of users are using Oracle ERP with next level using SAP and Microsoft while the group of users utilizing local (ALMOTAKAMEL) and emerging Indian ERP (Focus) is still in its infancy.

The industries represented in the study are reasonably versatile reflecting different interests

Figure 1. The research model

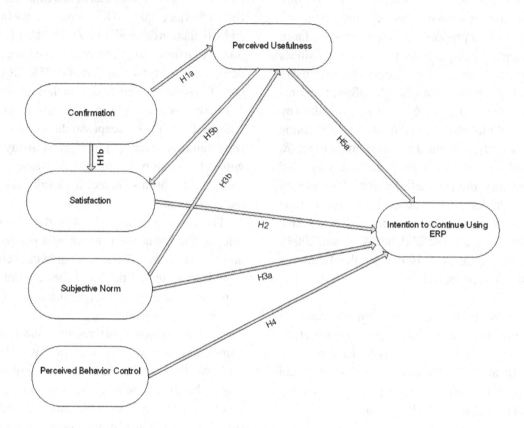

Figure 2. Gender distribution

Gender	Frequency	Percent
Male	177	79%
Female	46	21%

Figure 3. ERP systems

Vendor	Frequency	Percent
ALMOTAKAMEL	5	2.5%
FOCUS	1	0.5%
SAP	39	17%
MICROSOFT	19	9%
ORACLE	157	70%
UNKNOWN	2	1%

and backgrounds. Results indicating industry and its frequency are presented in (Figure 4).

In (Figure 5), respondents function is presented together with its frequency and percentage of occurrence. Again, the respondents belong to quite different backgrounds.

Survey Validation

To test the research instrument reliability Cronbach Alpha was used. The overall reliability of

the instrument is 0.89. All measures show acceptable reliability exceeding the cutoff value of 0.7 (Elsawah et al., 2008). Acronyms used to refer to survey measures as follows: (CONF: confirmation, P_USEF: perceived usefulness, SN: subjective norm, PBC: perceived behavior

Figure 4. Profile of industry

Industry	Frequency	Percent
Oil and Gas	25	11%
Manufacturing	30	13%
ICT	37	17%
Audit firm	5	2.5%
Call Centre	32	14%
Pharmaceutical	12	5%
Food & Beverage	28	12%
Travel & Airlines	2	1%
Courier	1	0.5%
Banking	15	7%
Telecom	22	10%
Cement	5	2.5%
Others	9	4%

Figure 5. Profile of respondents' position

Users' function	Frequency	Percent
Finance	35	16%
ERP	8	4%
IT	9	4%
GM	13	6%
HR	15	7%
Logistics	19	9%
Marketing	5	2%
Production	5	2%
Customer Service	14	6%
Systems Admin	5	2%
Other user categories	95	43%

Figure 6. Reliability of the constructs

Measures	Items	Cronbach's Alpha	Cronbach's Alpha if Item Deleted
CONF	3	0.835	0.916
P_USEF	8	0.876	0.866
SN	2	0.954	0.881
PBC	3	0.832	0.869
INTEN	3	0.845	0.852
SATISF	12	0.964	0.843

Figure 7. Correlation between constructs

	Mean	S.D.	CONF	P_USEF	SN	PBC	INTEN	SATISF
CONF	3.88	0.59						
P_USEF	4.28	0.59	0.40**					
SN	4.24	0.92	0.30**	0.59**				
PBC	3.76	0.89	0.18**	0.69**	0.55**			
INTEN	4.21	0.88	0.34**	0.79**	0.64**	0.75**		
SATISF	3.96	0.82	0.42**	0.79**	0.69**	0.78**	0.80**	

**. Correlation is significant at the 0.01 level (2-tailed).

control, INTEN: intention to continue using ERP, SATISF: satisfaction). (Figure 6) has the details.

DISCUSSION AND CONCLUSION

Significant correlations found between all constructs. Significant correlation coefficient scores support the study hypotheses because it tells that there is a significant relationship between the constructs. To explain, for H1a the correlation between CONF and P_USEF is found to be 0.40 which indicates the significant relationship between CONF and P_USEF. However, the cor-

relation coefficient does not explain the effect of a variable on another but rather it measures the strength and direction of the relationship. So, regression analysis will be used to measure the effect. Same logic applies to H1b (0.42), H2 (0.80), H3a (0.64), H3b (0.59), H4 (0.75), H5a (0.79), H5b (0.79). (Figure 7) shows correlation coefficients between survey constructs.

Here in this section, we have seen that the variables included in a certain hypotheses retained a significant positive relationship its strengths ranges from 0.40 to 0.80.

Now the next step is to investigate the impact of a variable on another, for which we will use regression analysis. In the following section, we are going to test all study hypotheses in terms of whether they are supported or not.

We tested the hypothesized relationship using regression analysis. The first model to test is the one representing H2, H3a, H4, and H5a. In which we assume that INTEN is affected by P_USEF, SN, PBC and SATISF. Regression results show an R2 of 74%; which means that the predictor variables are able to explain 74% of the changes in the dependent variable. The ANOVA results show that the model is significant at 0.00 meaning that the changes in INTEN are not due to chance and the entire model is significant. Finally, the coefficients table shows the following equation where all predictor variables are significant: INTEN = -0.49+ 0.53 P_USEF+ 0.13 SN+ 0.23 PBC+ 0.27 SATISF. To summarize, the following hypotheses are supported by the regression results:

H2: In an ERP implementation environment Satisfaction has a positive effect on Users' Intention to continue using ERP system (Supported).

H3a: In an ERP implementation environment Subjective Norm has a positive effect on Users' Intention to continue using ERP system (Supported).

H4: In an ERP implementation environment Perceived Behavior Control has a positive effect on Users' Intention to continue using ERP system (Supported).

H5a: In an ERP implementation environment Perceived Usefulness has a positive effect on Users' Intention to continue using ERP system (Supported).

In the second model we test H1a and H3b. The model assumes that SN and CONF affect P_USEF. Regression results show an R2 of 41%; meaning that both SN and CONF are able to explain 41% of the changes in P_USEF. According to the results of ANOVA the model is significant at 0.00 meaning that the changes in P_USEF are not due to chance and the entire model is significant. The coefficients table shows the following equation where all predictor variables are significant: *P_USEF = 1.88+ 0.34 SN+ 025 CONF.* This shows that SN and CONF are significant to P_USEF. The following hypotheses are supported by the regression results:

H1a: In an ERP implementation environment Confirmation of Expectation has a positive effect on Perceived Usefulness (Supported).

H3b: In an ERP implementation environment Subjective Norm has a positive effect on Perceive Usefulness (Supported).

The final model to test is the one testing H1b and H5b in which we assume that CONF and P_USEF affect SATISF. Regression results show an R2 of 63% which means that CONF and P_USEF are able to explain 63% of the changes in SATISF. The ANOVA results show that the model is significant at 0.00 which means that changes in SATISF are not due to chance. The entire model is significant. The model equation is: *SATISF= -1.06+ 0.16 CONF+ 1.02 P_USEF.* And as per the coefficients table both predictor variables are significant which lead to the conclusion that hypotheses tested are both supported by the regression results:

H1b: In an ERP implementation environment Confirmation of Expectation has a positive effect on Satisfaction (Supported).

H5b: In an ERP implementation environment Perceived Usefulness has a positive effect on satisfaction of using ERP system (Supported).

FUTURE RESEARCH

Future research, with various sample (different industry, type of ERP) and longitudinal studies are required. In addition to, future research is needed to investigate the success of the system from the view point of IT managers and Users.

Also, future research is required to discuss the success factors of ERP from the viewpoint of the companies responsible for the implementation of ERP system.

REFERENCES

Ajzen, I. (1991). The theory of planned behavior. *Organizational Behavior and Human Decision Processes, 50*, 179–211. doi:10.1016/0749-5978(91)90020-T

Ajzen, I. (2002). Perceived behavioral control, self-efficacy, locus of control and the theory of planned behavior. *Journal of Applied Social Psychology, 32*, 1–20. doi:10.1111/j.1559-1816.2002.tb00236.x

Ajzen, I., & Madden, T. J. (1986). Prediction of good-directed behavior: attitudes, intentions and perceived behavioral control. *Journal of Experimental Social Psychology, 22*, 453–474. doi:10.1016/0022-1031(86)90045-4

Alshare, K., Grandon, E., & Miller, D. (2004). Antecedents of computer technology usage: considerations of the technology acceptance model in the academic environment. *Journal of Circuits . Systems and Computers, 19*(4), 164–180.

Anderson, E. W., & Sullivan, M. W. (1993). The antecedents and consequences of customer satisfaction for firms. *Marketing Science, 12*, 125–143. doi:10.1287/mksc.12.2.125

Baroudi, J. J., Olson, M. H., & Ives, B. (1986). An empirical study of the impact of user involvement on system usage and information satisfaction. *Communications of the ACM, 29*, 232–238. doi:10.1145/5666.5669

Bhattacherjee, A. (2001). Understanding information systems continuance: an expectation–confirmation model. *Management Information Systems Quarterly, 25*, 351–370. doi:10.2307/3250921

Bhattacherjee, A., & Premkumar, G. (2004). Understanding changes in belief and attitude toward information technology usage: A theoretical model and longitudinal test. *Management Information Systems Quarterly, 28*(2), 229–254.

Bhattacherjee, A., & Sanford, C. (2006). Influence process for information acceptance: An elaboration likelihood model. *Management Information Systems Quarterly, 28*(4), 805–825.

Chen, Y., & Chien, S. (2009). Investigating factors influencing the use of E-Government service. In *Proceedings of the Americas Conference on Information Systems* (pp. 695).

Cheung, C., & Limayem, M. (2005). Understanding continuance of advanced internet-based learning technologies: the role of satisfaction, prior behavior, and habit. In *Proceeding of Pacific Asia Conference on Information Systems* (pp. 1323-1332).

Chou, S. W., & Chen, Pi-Yu, (2009). The influence of individual difference on continuance intentions of enterprise resource planning (ERP). *Int. J. Human-Computer Studies,* 1-31.

Dabholkar, P. A., Shepard, C. D., & Thorpe, D. I. (2000). A comprehensive framework for service quality: An investigation of critical conceptual and measurement issues through a longitudinal study. *Journal of Retailing, 76*, 139–173. doi:10.1016/S0022-4359(00)00029-4

Danaher, P. J., & Rust, R. T. (1996). Indirect financial benefits from service quality. *Quality Management Journal, 3*(2), 63–75.

Davenport, T. (1998). Putting the Enterprise into the Enterprise System. *Harvard Business Review, 76*(4), 121–131.

Davenport, T. (2000). *Mission Critical*. Boston: Harvard Business School Press.

Davis, F. D. (1989). Perceived usefulness, perceived ease of use, and user acceptance of information technology. *Management Information Systems Quarterly, 13*(3), 319–340. doi:10.2307/249008

Davis, F. D., Bagozzi, R. P., & Warshaw, P. R. (1989). User acceptance of computer technology: a comparison of two theoretical models. *Management Science, 35*, 982–1003. doi:10.1287/mnsc.35.8.982

Elsawah, S., Abdelfattah, A., & Rasmy, M. H. (2008). A quantitative model to predict the Egyptian ERP Implementation Success Index. *Business Process Management, 14*(3), 288–306. doi:10.1108/14637150810876643

Fishbein, M., & Ajzen, I. (1975). *Belief, attitude, intention and behavior: An introduction to theory and research*. Reading, MA: Addison-Wesley Publishing Company.

Frey, B. S. (1993). Shirking or work morale? The impact of regulating. *European Economic Review, 37*(8), 1523–1532. doi:10.1016/0014-2921(93)90120-Y

Gopi, M., & Ramayah, T. (2007). Applicability of theory of planned behavior in predicting intention to trade online some evidence from developing country. *International Journal of Emerging Markets, 2*(4), 348–360. doi:10.1108/17468800710824509

Griffith, T. L., Zummato, R. F., & Ayman, L. (1999). Why new technologies fail? *Industrial Management (Des Plaines), 41*(3), 29–34.

Gyampah, A. K. (2007). Perceived usefulness, user involvement and behavioral intention: An empirical study of ERP implementation. *Computers in Human Behavior, 23*, 1232–1248. doi:10.1016/j.chb.2004.12.002

Gyampah, A. K., & Salam, A. M. (2004). An extension of the technology acceptance model in an erp implementation Environment. *Information & Management, 41*, 731–745. doi:10.1016/j.im.2003.08.010

Ifinedo, P. (2007). An empirical study of ERP success evaluations by business and IT mangers. *Information Management & Computer Security, 15*(4), 270–282. doi:10.1108/09685220710817798

Jasperson, J., Carter, P. E., & Zumd, R. W. (2005). A comprehensive conceptualization of post-adoptive behaviors associated with information technology enabled work systems. *Management Information Systems Quarterly, 29*(3), 525–557.

Karahanna, E., Straub, D. W., & Chervany, N. I. (1999). Information Technology Adoption Across Time: Across-Sectional Comparison Of Pre-Adoption and Post-Adoption Beliefs. *Management Information Systems Quarterly, 23*, 183–213. doi:10.2307/249751

Lai, J., Ong, Ch., Yang, Ch., & Tang, W. (2005). Factors influencing employees' usage behavior of KMS in e-business. In *Proceedings of the Pacific Asia Conference on Information Systems* (pp. 126-137).

Lee, Y., Kozar, K. A., & Larsen, K. R. T. (2003). The technology acceptance model: past, present, and future. *Communications of the AIS, 12*(50), 752–280.

Mahmood, M. A., Burn, J. M., Gemoets, L. A., & Jacquez, C. (2000). Variables affecting information technology end-user satisfaction: a meta-analysis of the empirical literature. *International Journal of Human-Computer Studies, 52*, 751–771. doi:10.1006/ijhc.1999.0353

Markus, M. L., & Keil, M. (1994). If we build it, they will come: designing information systems that people want to use. *Sloan Management Review, 35*(4), 11–25.

Markus, M. L., Tanis, C., & Fenema, P. C. V. (2000). Multisite ERP implementations. *Communications of the ACM, 43*(4), 42–46. doi:10.1145/332051.332068

Mathieson, K. (1991). Predicting user intentions: comparing the technology acceptance model with the theory of planned behavior. *Information Systems Research, 2,* 173–191. doi:10.1287/isre.2.3.173

Nah, F. F., Tan, X., & The, S. H. (2004). An empirical investigation on end-users' acceptance of enterprise systems. *Information Resources Management Journal, 17*(3), 32–53.

Oliver, R. L. (1980). A cognitive model for the antecedents and consequences of satisfaction. *JMR, Journal of Marketing Research, 17,* 460–430. doi:10.2307/3150499

Orlikowski, W. J. (1992). The duality of technology: rethinking the concept of technology in organization. *Organization Science, 3*(3), 398–427. doi:10.1287/orsc.3.3.398

Orlikowski, W. J., & Baroudi, J. J. (1991). Studying information technology in organizations: research approaches and assumptions. *Information Systems Research, 2,* 1–28. doi:10.1287/isre.2.1.1

Parasuraman, A., & Zinkhan, G. M. (2002). Marketing to and serving customers through the internet: an overview and research agenda. *Journal of the Academy of Marketing Science, 30*(4), 286–295. doi:10.1177/009207002236906

Premkumar, G., Ramamurthy, K., & Liu, H. (2008). Internet messaging: An examination of the impact of attitudinal, normative, and control belief systems. *Information & Management, 45,* 451–457. doi:10.1016/j.im.2008.06.008

Rasmy, M. H., Tharwat, A., & Ashraf, S. (2005). Enterprise resource planning (ERP) implementation in the Egyptian organizational. *BNET Business Network,* 1-13.

Recker, J., & Rosemann, M. (2007). Integration of models for understandinding continuance of process modeling techniques. In . *Proceedings of the Americas Conference on Information Systems, 14,* 1–11.

Szajna, B. (1996). Empirical evaluation of the revised technology acceptance model. *Management Science, 42*(1), 85–92. doi:10.1287/mnsc.42.1.85

Tan, X., & Siau, K. (2006). Understanding modeling method by IS developers: a theoretical model and an empirical test. In *Twenty-Seventh International Conference on Information Systems* (pp. 937-947).

Taylor, S., & Todd, P. A. (1995). Understanding information technology usage: a test of competing models. *Information Systems Research, 6,* 144–179. doi:10.1287/isre.6.2.144

Venkatesh, V., & Davis, F. D. (2000). A theoretical extension of the technology acceptance model: four longitudinal field studies. *Management Science, 45*(2), 188–204.

Venkatesh, V., & Morris, M. G. (2000). Why don't men stop to ask for directions? Gender, social influence, and their role in technology acceptance and usage behavior. *Management Information Systems Quarterly, 24,* 115–137. doi:10.2307/3250981

Wang, M., Chan, C., Chang, S., & Yang, Y. (2007). Effects of online shopping attitudes, subjective norms and control beliefs on online shopping intentions: a test of the theory of planned behavior. *International Journal of Management, 24*(2), 296–302.

Wang, W. (2005). Factors influencing employees' deep usage of information systems. In *Proceedings of the Pacific Asia Conference on Information Systems* (pp. 30-43).

Wang, W., & Hsieh, P.-A. (2006). Beyond routine: Symbolic adoption, extended use, and emergent use of complex information systems in the mandatory organizational context. In *Proceedings of the Twenty- Seventh Conference on Information Systems*, Milwaukee, 2006 (pp. 732-750).

Wu, J., & Wang, Y. (2006). Measuring ERP Success: The Ultimate Users' View. *International Journal of Operations & Production Management, 26*(8), 882–903. doi:10.1108/01443570610678657

Yeh, J. (2007). How the organizations change in ERP implementation. In *Proceedings of the Americas conference*.

Yi, M. Y., & Davis, F. D. (2001). Improving computer training effectiveness for decision technologies behavior modeling and retention enhancement. *Decision Sciences, 32*(3), 521–544. doi:10.1111/j.1540-5915.2001.tb00970.x

Zhang, L., & Matthew, K. O. Lee, Zhang, Z., & Banerjee, P. (2003). Critical success factors of enterprise resource planning systems implementation success in china. In *Proceedings of the 36th Hawaii International Conference on System Sciences*.

Zviran, M., Pliskin, N., & Levin, R. (2005). Measuring user satisfaction and perceived usefulness in the ERP context. *Journal of Computer Information Systems*, 43–52.

APPENDIX

Survey Instrument

- Please mark the most appropriate number of each statement which corresponds most closely to your desired response:

- Please Mark the number that corresponds to your satisfaction with your ERP system:

- **Demographics**
  1. Position:
  2. Industry:
  3. ERP system:
  4. Years using the ERP system in your current organization:
  5. Gender:
  6. Age:

Figure 8.

Variables	Strongly Disagree	Disagree	Uncertain	Agree	Strongly Agree
	1	2	3	4	5
Confirmation:					
My expectation with using the ERP is better than what I expected					
The data items provided by the ERP are better than what I expected					
Overall, most of my expectations from the ERP are confirmed					
Perceived Usefulness:					
Using the ERP improved the quality of some task of my work					
Using the ERP gave me greater control over my work					
Using the ERP enabled me to accomplish some tasks more quickly					
Using the ERP increased my productivity while working					
Using the ERP improved my job performance in some tasks of my work					
Using the ERP enhanced my effectiveness on some task of my work					
Using the ERP made it easier to do some tasks of my work					
Overall, I found using the ERP to be advantageous in various tasks of my work					
Subjective Norm:					
Those people who influence my intention would support me using the ERP than my traditional way for my work					
Those people who are important to me think that I should use the ERP rather than my traditional way for my work					
Perceived Behavior Control:					
I would be able to use the ERP in my work					
Using the ERP is entirely within my control					
I have the resources and the knowledge and the ability to make use of ERP					
Intention:					
I intend to continue using the ERP rather than discontinue its use to contribute to my work					
My intention is to continue using the ERP than use any alternative means (Traditional ways)					
I planned to adjust my work processes to better fit the best practices of the ERP					

Figure 9.

Variables	Almost Never	Some of the time	About half of the time	Most of the time	Almost always
	1	2	3	4	5
Satisfaction:					
Does the ERP system provide the precise information you need?					
Are you satisfied with the accuracy of the ERP system?					
Does the ERP system provide up-to-date information?					
Does the information content of the ERP system meet your needs?					
Is the ERP system user friendly?					
Does the ERP system provide sufficient information?					
Do you think the output is presented in a useful format?					
Does the ERP system provide reports that seem to be just about exactly what you need?					
Do you get the information you need in time?					
Is the information clear?					
Is the ERP system easy to use?					
Is the ERP system accurate?					

Chapter 20
ERP System Selection Criteria:
The Case of Companies in Slovenia

Andreja Pucihar
University of Maribor, Slovenia

Gregor Lenart
University of Maribor, Slovenia

Frantisek Sudzina
Copenhagen Business School, Denmark

ABSTRACT

The chapter proposes a possible model of criteria for ERP system selection. The proposed model consists of four groups of ERP system selection criteria: the ERP systems benefits criteria, the system quality criteria, the vendor related criteria and the ERP system package criteria. The data was collected in companies in Slovenia. Research results have confirmed internal consistency of ERP selection criteria in each group. For each criterion the importance is evaluated by small, medium-sized and large companies. Beside that also company size, implemented information strategy, representation of the IT department on the board level in the company and turnover impact on importance of each criterion is evaluated and presented. The model presented in this chapter could be useful for ERP system providers to better understand companies' needs and to provide systems tailored for individual needs of the company. The model could also be useful for companies considering ERP system implementation to avoid high costs of failed implementations.

INTRODUCTION

Nowadays, companies face a rapidly changing business environment with increased competition and raised customer expectations in expanded markets. This situation increases the pressure on companies to change their existing business practices and procedures to achieve lower total costs of operation in the entire supply chain. It is crucial that companies shorten throughput times, drastically reduce inventories, expand product choice, provide more reliable delivery dates and better customer service, improve quality, and efficiently coordinate global demand, supply, and production (Umble et al., 2003; Jafari et al., 2006). All this is not possible without usage of information technology.

DOI: 10.4018/978-1-61692-020-3.ch020

From the information technology and information systems perspective, coordination of the individual elements of the overall set of business processes in the company could be supported by enterprise resource planning (ERP) systems. ERP systems also referred to as enterprise-wide systems due to their enterprise-wide scope, provide seamless integration of all the information flows and business processes across functional areas within a company such as finance, human resources, manufacturing, logistics, sales, distribution and purchasing (Davenport, 1998; Markus & Tanis, 2000; Law & Ngai, 2007; Bernroider, 2008). Thus ERP systems aim to integrate business processes and ICT into a synchronized suite of procedures, applications and metrics which goes over firms' boundaries (Wier et al., 2007).

ERP systems can be considered as the most important development in the corporate use of information technology and are beginning to become the backbone of any organization. ERP systems have gained major prominence by enabling companies to streamline their operations, leverage and integrate business data process (Karsak & Ozogul, 2009).

In spite of added value promised to be gained from ERP system adoption there are still many companies – mostly small and medium sized, which are only in a phase of consideration and acquisition of ERP system. Due to their nature (complexity and high implementation costs), ERP systems used to be mostly implemented in large companies. However, for the past few years, ERP vendors also intensively face challenges in providing ERP systems, especially tailored for the needs of small and medium sized companies (Malie et al., 2008).

The reasons for this trend lie in a saturation of the market, as many large organizations have already implemented an ERP system. There are also increasing possibilities and need for the integration of systems between organizations (pressures of large organizations). The other reason also lies in the availability of relatively inexpensive hardware (Gable and Stewart, 1999).

The ERP systems' market consists of many different products, services and methodologies, not all of them applicable to different organizations (Malie et al., 2008). We acknowledge importance of ERP system readiness assessment addressed by Razmi, Sangari and Ghodsi (2009), and importance of training in the actual implementation process investigated by Plaza and Rohlf (2008). During the ERP system selection process, organizations need to consider different criteria related to ERP systems. Knowing the importance of these criteria could help companies to select more suitable ERP system and to avoid mistakes and large costs of failed implementations.

In this chapter, the importance of ERP selection criteria, which were investigated in companies in Slovenia are presented. The research was done in 131 companies in 2007. Altogether 28 ERP selection criteria were identified and investigated. The investigated criteria are grouped into the 4 groups: ERP benefits criteria, system quality criteria, vendor related criteria and ERP package criteria. Beside the criteria importance also companies characteristics - company size, implemented information strategy in the company, representation of the IT department at the board level and growth of the company - impact on importance of ERP selection criteria is presented.

The findings of this chapter are useful for organizations considering the ERP system implementation to avoid possible large costs of failed implementations and for ERP system providers to better understand different customers' needs and expectations. On the other hand, the chapter does not focus on project management issues. These were investigated by e.g. Soja (2006).

The rest of the chapter is organized as follows: the next section provides review of ERP system selection criteria. In the following section, data

Figure 1. Groups of criteria impacting on ERP system selection

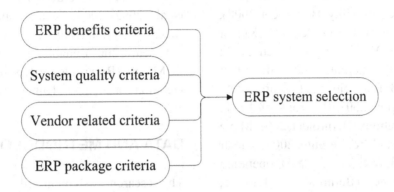

and methodology are described. The penultimate section discusses research findings. The final section summarizes conclusions.

LITERATURE REVIEW

ERP selection criteria investigated in this research were mainly adopted from Bernroider and Koch (2001) and supported by other research results and data from the field of ERP implementation and usage. Although the evaluation of information systems investments began already in 1960's (Frielink, 1061; Joslin 1968), very little had been written recently about packaged software selection criteria in academic journals (Keil & Tiwana, 2006). As Cebeci (2009) stresses, it is a critical issue to select the suitable ERP system which meets all the business strategies and the goals of the company. Karaarslan and Gundogar (2009) point out, ERP system selection is getting increasingly difficult because of a large variety of ERP software solutions available. ERP criteria identified from prior research can be divided into four groups: ERP benefits criteria, system quality criteria, vendor related criteria and ERP package criteria (Figure 1).

ERP benefits criteria are related to benefits, which are promised to be gained by ERP implementation. This group include the following criteria: enhanced decision making (Bernroider,

2008; Nah & Delgado, 2004), reduced cycle times (Bernroider, 2008); Bernroider & Leseure, 2005), business process improvement (Bernroider, 2008); Bernroider & Leseure, 2005; Kumar et al., 2002, 2003; Nah & Delgado, 2004; Bernroider & Koch, 2001), improved service levels and/or quality (Bernroider, 2008; Bernroider & Leseure, 2005; Wei et al., 2005); enablement of desired business processes (Bernroider, 2008; Bernroider & Leseure, 2005; Kumar et al., 2002, 2003), integrated and better quality of information (Bernroider, 2008; Bernroider & Leseure, 2005; Nah & Delgado, 2004), increased organizational flexibility (Bernroider, 2008; Umble et al., 2003; Bernroider & Koch, 2001), increased customer satisfaction (Bernroider & Koch, 2001; Bernroider & Leseure, 2005) and improved innovation capabilities (Bernroider, 2008; Bernroider & Leseure, 2005; Bernroider & Koch, 2001).

System quality criteria consist of ERP systems characteristics related to its usability, flexibility and functionality. This group consists of the following criteria: system flexibility (Bernroider, 2008; Malie et al., 2008; Bernroider & Leseure, 2005; Kumar et al., 2002, 2003; Wei, et al., 2005; Verville & Halingten, 2003; Bernroider & Koch, 2001; Bernroider, 2008), system functionality (Bernroider, 2008; Malie et al., 2008; Bernroider & Leseure, 2005; Botta-Genoulaz et al., 2005; Kumar et al., 2002, 2003; Wei, et al., 2005, Han, 2004; Liao et al., 2007; Lall & Teyarachakul,

2006; Verville & Halingten, 2003; Bernroider & Koch, 2001), system usability (Bernroider, 2008), system interoperability (Bernroider, 2008; Kumar et al., 2002, 2003; Verville & Halingten, 2003; Bernroider, 2008), internationality of system (Bernroider, 2008; Bernroider & Leseure, 2005; Verville & Halingten, 2003; Bernroider & Koch, 2001), system reliability (Bernroider, 2008; Malie et al., 2008; Bernroider & Leseure, 2005; Kumar et al., 2002, 2003; Wei, et al., 2005), operating system independency (Bernroider & Leseure, 2005; Bernroider & Koch, 2001).

Vendor related criteria include vendor support (Malie et al, 2008; Bernroider & Leseure, 2005; Kumar et al., 2002, 2003, Wei, et al. 2005; Liao, et al., 2007; Ubmle et al., 2003; Rao, 2000; Fisher et al., 2004; Lall & Teyarachakul, 2006; Verville & Halingten, 2003), vendor reputation and market position of vendor (Malie et al, 2008; Kumar et al., 2002, 2003; Wei et al., 2005; Han, 2004; Liao, et al., 2007; Lall & Teyarachakul, 2006; Verville & Halingten, 2003; Bernroider & Koch, 2001).

ERP package criteria are related to characteristics of the system itself from implementation time and costs to the system functionality from the technical point of view. The group consist of the following criteria: short implementation time (Malie et al., 2008; Wei et al., 2005; Umble et al., 2003; Fisher et al., 2004; Lall & Teyarachakul, 2006; Verville & Halingten, 2003; Bernroider & Koch, 2001), software costs, such as licenses, maintenance (Bernroider, 2008; Bernroider & Leseure, 2005; Kumar, et al., 2002, 2003; Wei, et al., 2005; Umble et al., 2003; Fisher et al., 2004; Lall & Teyarachakul, 2006), e-business enablement (Bernroider & Leseure, 2005), organizational fit of system (Malie et al., 2008; Botta-Genoulaz et al., 2005; Kumar et al., 2002, 2003; Nah & Delgado, 2006; Umble et al., 2003; Lall & Teyarachakul, 2006), connectivity, such as intra/extranet, mobile computers (Bernroider & Leseure, 2005), advanced technology (Bernroider & Leseure, 2005; Kumar et al., 2002, 2003; Liao et al., 2007; Rao, 2000), incorporation of business

best practice (Bernroider & Leseure, 2005; Kumar et al., 2002, 2003), availability of an industry focused solution (Malie et al., 2008; Bernroider & Leseure, 2005), enabling technology for CRM, SCM, etc. (Bernroider & Leseure, 2005; Botta-Genoulaz et al., 2005; Kumar et al., 2002, 2003).

DATA AND METHODOLOGY

The research was conducted in 2007/2008. The questionnaires with introduction letters were sent to 300 large companies, 300 medium sized companies and 600 small companies. The number of questionnaires mailed to small companies was double the number of medium-sized and large companies because small companies constitute the highest proportion of companies and based on experience, they are less likely to respond. Lists of addresses and information about the number of employees and turnover were retrieved from National Statistical Bureau.

The questionnaire survey is mainly based on criteria identified by Bernroider and Koch (2001) and supported from other data in the field. Criteria used in the research were grouped into four groups: ERP benefits criteria (enhanced decision making, improved service levels/quality, reduced cycle times, business process improvement, enabler for desired business processes, integrated and better quality of information, increased organizational flexibility, increased customer satisfaction, improved innovation capabilities), system quality criteria (system flexibility, system functionality, system usability, system interoperability, internationality of system, system reliability and operating system independence), vendor related criteria (vendor support, vendor reputation and market position of vendor) and ERP package criteria (short implementation time, software costs (licenses, maintenance), e-business enablement, organizational fit of system, connectivity (intra/extranet, mobile, etc.), advanced technology, incorporation of business best practice, availability of an industry focused solution and enabling technology for CRM, SCM, etc.).

These dependent variables were measured on five point Likert scale, where 1 is of very little importance and 5 is of very high importance.

Compared to (Sudzina, 2007), besides company size, representation of the IT department on the board level (CIO) and information strategy, also turnover growth was used as independent variables. Companies with 10 to 49 employees are considered to be small, with 50 to 249 employees are considered to be medium sized, and with 250+ employees are considered to be large companies. This definition is consistent with European Commission's definitions (European Commission 2003) and National Statistical Bureau.

Although SMEs are generally considered to be flexible, adaptive and innovative (Rao, et al., 2003), and thus have more ability to respond to the new opportunities and innovations than larger enterprises (Lomerson et al., 2004), various studies have reported that SMEs are generally lagging behind large organizations with regards to the adoption and usage of new ICT (Eleftheriadou, 2008; Kartiwi & MacGregor, 2007; Levy et. al., 2005; Levenburg, 2005; Chitura, 2008; Riquelme, 2002). Considering this situation, one of the purposes of this study was also to investigate, if there are any significant differences between opinion of small, medium-sized and large companies regarding the importance of ERP selection criteria.

"Information strategy" refers to the formal information strategy adopted on the company level. Possible impact of alignment of business and information strategy was identified by Oh and Pinsonneault (2007). "Presentation of the IT department on the board level" means that there is a CIO (Chief information officer) or similar director-level position for IT in the company. Companies with adopted information strategy and with a formal position of IT or CIO director were expected to be more advanced in their understanding of the impact of ICT on business performance. Thus, the purpose of the study was to discover if there

are some significant differences in ERP selection criteria importance between those companies and companies without an implemented information strategy and represented CIO on the board level.

Growth of the company was measured with achieved turnover in the previous year (2006) and was divided into (1) reduction in turnover, (2) stable turnover, (3) growth of turnover from 0-5%, (4) growth of turnover from 5-10% and (5) growth of turnover higher than 10%. The purpose of the study was to identify if there are some significant differences in ERP selection criteria importance between companies with different levels of turnover.

Number of respondents rating a particular criterion, alongside the mean and the standard deviation, are provided in tables 1, 3, 5, and 7. Correlation matrices for the groups of criteria are provided in tables 2, 4, 6, and 8. Pearson product-moment correlation coefficient was used. Pair-wise deletion was used to deal with missing data in the correlation calculation.

Analysis of variance (ANOVA) was used to analyze impact of independent variables on ERP system selection criteria. A multivariate approach is used and results are commented on the confidence level $\alpha = 0.05$. Tukey-Kramer multiple-comparison test was used to identify between what instances of an independent variable there are significant differences. Presented are only ANOVA tables, in which significant impact was identified. Internal consistency of criteria groups was tested using Cronbach's alpha (Nunnally, 1967). Usually the value of 0.7 and above is acceptable (Nunnally, 1978). This cut-off is used in this book chapter as well.

RESEARCH FINDINGS

Companies Profile Data

Altogether 68 (22.6%) large companies, 36 (12%) medium-sized companies and 27 (4.5%) small

Table 1. Companies' characteristics

Company characteristics / data per company size	Small-sized companies	Medium-sized companies	Large companies
Percentage of respondents	4.5%	12%	22.6%
Industry sector (total)	100%	100%	100%
- Manufacturing	14.8%	41.7%	57.4%
- Trade	22.2%	22.2%	14.7%
- IT services	18.5%	2.8%	1.5%
- Services	18.5%	8.3%	5.9%
- Construction	11.1%	8.3%	1.5%
- Transport	7.4%	5.6%	4.4%
- Food	0%	2.8%	4.4%
- Other	7.4%	8.4%	10.3%
Revenue			
- higher than 10%	7.7%	5.9%	9.7%
- growth from 5 – 10%	30.8%	8.8%	12.9%
- growth from 0 – 5%	11.5%	29.4%	12.9%
- stable revenue	26.9%	26.5%	27.4%
- reduction of revenue	23.1%	29.4%	37.1%
CIO represented on the board level	33.3%	50%	29.9%
Implemented IT strategy	14.8%	48.6%	54.4%
ERP users	37%	66.7%	75%
ERP vendors			
- SAP	0%	12.5%	29.4%
- Navision	30%	12.5%	13.7%
- Perftech Largo	0%	16.7%	9.8%
- Baan	0%	0%	5.9%
- Kopa	0%	0%	3.9%
- S21	0%	0%	3.9%
- Pantheon	20%	8.3%	2%
- Adempiere	10%	0%	0%
- FRAPIS	10%	0%	0%
- Own development	20%	4.2%	7.8%
Current stage of ERP usage			
- ERP system is being considered	32.0%	11.4%	13.2%
- ERP system is being evaluated for the selection of a specific solution	4.0%	8.6%	8.8%
- ERP system is being configured and implemented	8.0%	5.7%	8.8%
- An ERP system was recently implemented and is now being stabilized	40.0%	48.6%	23.5%
- An ERP system is being used and maintained for some time	8.0%	25.7%	33.8%
- We have now substituted our first ERP system with a new one	8.0%	0%	11.8%

Table 2. Importance of ERP benefits criteria

ERP benefits criteria	N	Mean	Std. Deviation
Integrated and better quality of information	109	4.59	0.641
Business process improvement	109	4.25	0.683
Improved Service Levels/Quality	109	4.21	0.746
Enhanced decision making	109	4.11	0.885
Reduced cycle times	109	4.07	0.836
Increased customer satisfaction	109	4.03	0.967
Increased organisational flexibility	109	3.90	0.781
Enabler for desired business processes	109	3.80	0.869
Improved innovation capabilities	109	3.26	0.976

companies responded to the questionnaires. Altogether 47 chief information officers, 27 chief executive officers, 15 IT managers, 6 accounting officers, 6 managers, 4 chief financial officers and 26 other employees have participated in this research.

From the company sector perspective, the most respondents from large companies are from manufacturing sector (57.4%), followed by trade (14.7%) and by services sector (5.9%). The most respondents from medium-sized companies came from manufacturing (41.7%), trade (22.2%), services (8.3%) and building and construction (8.3%). In case of small companies, most respondents came from trade (22.2%), IT services and services (each of 18.5%), manufacturing (14.8%), building and construction (11.1%), and transport (7.4%).

9,7% of large companies had higher revenue growth than 10%, 12,9% had revenue growth from 5-10%, 12.9% from 0-5% of growth, 27,4% had stable revenue and 37,1% had reduction of turnover in the previous year of the research study. 5,9% of medium sized companies had higher revenue growth than 10%, 8,8% had revenue growth from 5-10%, 29.4% from 0-5% of growth, 26,5% had stable revenue and 29,4% had reduction of turnover in the previous year of the research study. 7,7% of small companies had higher revenue growth than 10%, 8,8% had revenue growth from 5-10%, 29,4% from 0-5%

of growth, 26,9% had stable revenue and 23,1% had reduction of turnover in the previous year of the research study.

29,9% of large organizations indicated that they have CIO represented at the board level in the company, while CIO is represented only in half of the medium sized companies and only in 33% of small sized companies. Half of the large and medium-sized companies and only 15% of small companies reported that they have formal IS/IT strategy implemented in the companies.

From all participated companies 85 (64.8%) indicated that they already use ERP system in the company (75% of large companies, 66.7% of medium-sized companies and 37% of small companies). Due to the small number of respondents from small companies, using ERP systems, the data for small companies are not representative. The data from National Statistical Bureau for the year 2008 indicates that 78% of large companies, 34% of medium-sized companies, 12% of small companies and only 3% of micro companies (5-9 employees) already use ERP system. We may notice that the proportion of large companies, which are using ERP solution, is very similar. However there is a much higher proportion of medium-sized and small companies, which participated in our research, who already use ERP solution. This might be a result of smaller number of respondents from small companies and also by

Table 3. Correlation matrix for ERP benefits criteria

	Improved Service Levels/Quality	Reduced cycle times	Enhanced decision making	Business process improvement	Integrated and better quality of information	Increased organizational flexibility	Increased customer satisfaction	Improved innovation capabilities	Enabler for desired business processes
Improved Service Levels/Quality	1	0.336	0.284	0.151	0.242	0.311	0.460	0.186	0.234
Reduced cycle times	0.336	1	0.287	0.215	0.206	0.277	0.268	0.224	0.174
Enhanced decision making	0.284	0.287	1	0.176	0.191	0.233	0.250	0.276	0.273
Business process improvement	0.151	0.215	0.176	1	0.269	0.425	0.315	0.207	0.280
Integrated and better quality of information	0.242	0.206	0.191	0.269	1	0.213	0.198	0.198	0.217
Increased organizational flexibility	0.311	0.277	0.233	0.425	0.213	1	0.414	0.394	0.357
Increased customer satisfaction	0.460	0.268	0.250	0.315	0.198	0.414	1	0.507	0.228
Improved innovation capabilities	0.186	0.224	0.276	0.207	0.198	0.394	0.507	1	0.435
Enabler for desired business processes	0.234	0.174	0.273	0.280	0.217	0.357	0.228	0.435	1

Table 4. Importance of system quality criteria

System quality criteria	N	Mean	Std. Deviation
Systems reliability	109	4.61	0.624
System functionality	109	4.37	0.689
System usability	109	4.31	0.836
System flexibility	109	4.22	0.821
System interoperability	109	4.09	0.967
Internationality of Software	109	3.70	1.182
Operating system independency	109	3.36	1.126

the reason that companies with highest revenue (in the year 2006) participated in the research.

In large companies most frequently used ERP system is SAP (29,4%), MS Dynamics NAV (13,7%) and Perftech Largo (9,8%) from local ERP system provider. In most of medium-sized companies use Slovene providers's Perftech Largo system (16,7%), followed by SAP and MS Dynamics NAV (both 12%). This is followed by usage of ERP systems from Slovene provider Datalab Pantheon (8,3%). Only 7,8% of large and 4,2% of medium-sized companies reported to use in-house developed ERP systems. In small companies the most commonly used ERP system is MS Dynamics NAV (30%), followed by Datalab Pantheon and in-house developed ERP systems (both 20%).

In 33.8% of large companies have stable use of ERP system for some years. ERP system has just been recently implemented in 23.5% of large companies. Medium-sized companies in most cases have recently implemented ERP systems (48.6%). In 25.7% of medium-sized companies have stable use of ERP system for some years. Most of small companies have only recently implemented ERP system (40%). 32% of small companies are in the stage of considering ERP system implementation.

Detail representation of characteristics of participated companies in the research is presented in the table 1.

ERP Selection Criteria Importance

In the Tables 2, 4, 6, and 8, the importance of ERP selection criteria is presented by mean values, ordered from very high importance to very little. The importance of ERP selection criteria was investigated by 5 point Likert scale, where 1 is of very little importance and 5 is of very high importance. The data are analyzed and presented for all companies together as the company size impact on importance of ERP criteria was separately investigated by ANOVA multivariate approach. ANOVA analysis results are presented in the section 3.3. Correlation matrices for the groups of criteria are provided in tables 3, 5, 7, and 9.

Table 2 presents the importance of ERP benefits criteria. The most important ERP benefits criteria are integrated and better quality of information (4,59), business process improvement (4,25), improved service levels and quality (4,21), enhanced decision making (4,11), reduced cycle times and increased customer satisfaction (4,03).

Table 3 presents correlation matrix for ERP benefits criteria. The results of Cronbach alpha test show that ERP benefits criteria are internally consistent (Cronbach's alpha is 0.774118, standardized Cronbach's alpha is 0.773752).

Table 4 presents importance of system quality criteria. The most important criteria in this group are system reliability (4,61), system functionality (4,37), system usability (4,31), system flexibility (4,22) and system interoperability (4,09).

Table 5. Correlation matrix for system quality criteria

	System functionality	System flexibility	System usability	Operating system independency	System interoperability	Internationality of system	System reliability
System functionality	1	0.559	0.520	0.161	0.327	0.290	0.531
System flexibility	0.559	1	0.392	0.327	0.188	0.091	0.377
System usability	0.520	0.392	1	0.147	0.399	0.192	0.469
Operating system independency	0.161	0.327	0.147	1	0.313	0.081	0.099
System interoperability	0.327	0.188	0.399	0.313	1	0.489	0.389
Internationality of system	0.290	0.091	0.192	0.081	0.489	1	0.290
System reliability	0.531	0.377	0.469	0.099	0.389	0.290	1

Table 6. Importance of vendor related criteria

Vendor related criteria	N	Mean	Std. Deviation
Vendor support	109	4.39	0.805
Vendor reputation	109	3.50	1.051
Market position of vendor	109	3.44	1.049

Table 7. Correlation matrix for vendor related criteria

	Vendor reputation	Vendor support	Market position of vendor
Vendor reputation	1	0.202	0.697
Vendor support	0.202	1	0.300
Market position of vendor	0.697	0.300	1

Table 8. Importance of ERP package criteria

ERP package criteria	N	Mean	Std. Deviation
Organizational fit of system	109	4.16	0.945
E-business enablement	109	4.15	0.803
Software costs (licenses, maintenance, etc.)	109	3.92	0.818
Short implementation time	109	3.90	0.793
Incorporation of business best practices	109	3.87	0.747
Advanced technology	109	3.84	0.796
Connectivity (Intra/Extranet, Mobile Comp., ...)	109	3.83	0.948
Availability of a industry focused solution	109	3.79	0.872
Enabling technology for CRM, SCM, etc.	109	3.53	1.175

Table 5 presents the correlation matrix for system quality criteria. The results of Cronbach alpha test show that system quality criteria are internally consistent (Cronbach's alpha is 0.726115, standardized Cronbach's alpha is 0.763553).

Table 6 presents importance of vendor related criteria. The most important criterion in this group is vendor support (4,39). Vendor reputation and market position of vendor seems to be less important during the ERP selection process.

Table 7 presents the correlation matrix for vendor related criteria. Although vendor related criteria do not achieve 0.7 threshold (Cronbach's alpha is 0.682800, standardized Cronbach's alpha is 0.666446), they should be considered internally consistent because they measure similar items seen from a qualitative point of view.

Table 8 presents the importance of ERP package criteria. The most important criteria in this group are organizational fit (4,16) of the system and e-business enablement (4,15).

Table 9 presents the correlation matrix for ERP package criteria. The results of Cronbach alpha test show that ERP package criteria are internally consistent (Cronbach's alpha is 0.757510, standardized Cronbach's alpha is 0.758011).

Table 9. Correlation matrix for ERP package criteria

	Incorporation of business best practice	E-business enablement	Organizational fit of system	Software costs (licenses, maintenance, etc...)	Advanced technology	Availability of an industry focused solution	Short implementation time	Enabling technology for CRM, SCM, etc...	Connectivity (Intra/Extranet, Mobile computers, ...)
Incorporation of business best practice	1	0.022	0.198	0.103	0.171	0.371	0.178	0.217	0.086
E-business enablement	0.022	1	0.161	0.268	0.175	0.141	0.295	0.241	0.377
Organizational fit of system	0.198	0.161	1	0.285	0.154	0.337	0.302	0.113	0.343
Software costs (licenses, maintenance, etc...)	0.103	0.268	0.285	1	0.220	0.324	0.222	0.099	0.332
Advanced technology	0.171	0.175	0.154	0.220	1	0.368	0.254	0.313	0.467
Availability of an industry focused solution	0.371	0.141	0.337	0.324	0.368	1	0.274	0.405	0.335
Short implementation time	0.178	0.295	0.302	0.222	0.254	0.274	1	0.308	0.414
Enabling technology for CRM, SCM, etc...	0.217	0.241	0.113	0.099	0.313	0.405	0.308	1	0.422
Connectivity (Intra/Extranet, Mobile computers, ...)	0.086	0.377	0.343	0.332	0.467	0.335	0.414	0.422	1

Figure 2. Companies' factors impacting on ERP selection criteria

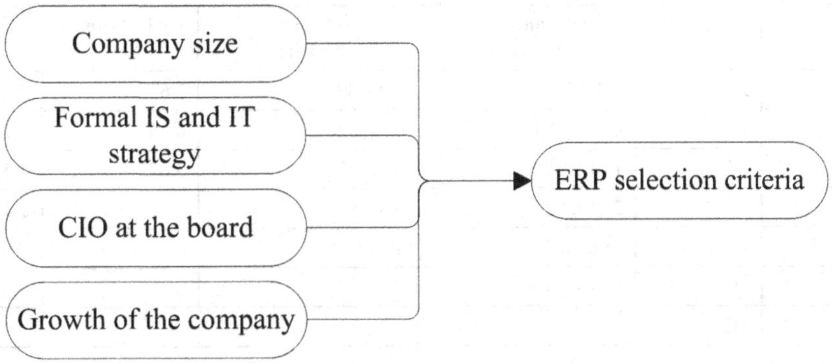

Table 10. Business process improvement

Factor	DF	Sum of Squares	Mean Square	F-Ratio	P-value
Company size	2	0.06367563	0.03183782	0.08	0.925988
Information strategy	1	2.192879	2.192879	5.30	0.023335*
CIO	1	0.06323607	0.06323607	0.15	0.696643
Growth	4	5.2559	1.313975	3.18	0.016668*
S	103	42.61518	0.4137397		
Total (Adjusted)	111	51			
Total	112				

* Term significant at alpha = 0.05

Companies' Factors Impacting on ERP Selection Criteria

With ANOVA multivariate analysis we investigated company size, representation of the IT department on the board level (CIO), implemented information strategy and turnover impact on ERP selection criteria (Figure 1). Growth was divided in to (1) reduction in turnover, (2) stable, (3) growth of 0-5%, (4) growth of 5-10% and (5) higher growth than 10%. In tables 5 – 11 we present the ANOVA multivariate analysis results. The results (tables) are presented only for selection criteria, where the impact of one or more companies' factors was identified. These selection criteria are: business process improvement, e-business enablement, increased organizational flexibility, systems reliability, advanced technology, operating system independency, and system interoperability.

Business Process Improvement

The analysis of the impact of company size, information strategy, representation of the IT department on the board level (CIO), and growth on importance of business process improvement have shown that importance of business process improvement depends on information strategy (Table 10). Importance is higher in companies with information strategy (4.34) than in companies without one (4.05). Importance is lower in companies with stable turnover (3.77) than in companies with growth of 5-10% (4.45), 10%+ (4.30).

Table 11. E-business enablement

Factor	DF	Sum of Squares	Mean Square	F-Ratio	P-value
Company size	2	3.841785	1.920892	3.63	0.029926*
Information strategy	1	0.3438284	0.3438284	0.65	0.422035
CIO	1	1.612522	1.612522	3.05	0.083822
Growth	4	2.267272	0.5668181	1.07	0.374646
S	104	55.03207	0.5291545		
Total (Adjusted)	112	65.13274			
Total	113				

* Term significant at alpha = 0.05

Table 12. Increased organizational flexibility

Factor	DF	Sum of Squares	Mean Square	F-Ratio	P-value
Company size	2	6.306276	3.153138	5.39	0.005915*
Information strategy	1	0.02746195	0.02746195	0.05	0.828866
CIO	1	0.7661105	0.7661105	1.31	0.255016
Growth	4	4.00039	1.000098	1.71	0.153319
S	104	60.81945	0.5848024		
Total (Adjusted)	112	72.28319			
Total	113				

* Term significant at alpha = 0.05

E-Business Enablement

The analysis of the impact of company size, information strategy, representation of the IT department on the board level (CIO), and growth on importance of e-business enablement have shown that importance of e-business enablement depends on company size (Table 11). The importance is lower in large (4.04) than in small companies (4.51).

Increased Organizational Flexibility

The analysis of the impact of company size, information strategy, representation of the IT department on the board level (CIO), and growth on importance of increased organizational flex-ibility have shown that importance of increased organizational flexibility depends on company size (Table 12). The importance is lower in large (3.71) than in midsized companies (4.29).

Systems Reliability

The analysis of the impact of company size, information strategy, representation of the IT department on the board level (CIO), and growth on importance of systems reliability have shown that importance of systems reliability depends on company size (Table 13). Impact is lower in small companies (4.33) than in large companies (4.71).

Table 13. Systems reliability

Factor	DF	Sum of Squares	Mean Square	F-Ratio	P-value
Company size	2	2.20308	1.10154	3.39	0.037501*
Information strategy	1	0.732296	0.732296	2.25	0.136372
CIO	1	0.04068135	0.04068135	0.13	0.724210
S	104	33.8009	0.3250087		
Total (Adjusted)	112	39.84071			
Total	113				

* Term significant at alpha = 0.05

Table 14. Advanced technology

Factor	DF	Sum of Squares	Mean Square	F-Ratio	P-value
Company size	2	0.6338901	0.316945	0.57	0.568595
Information strategy	1	2.736629	2.736629	4.90	0.029035*
CIO	1	4.679244	4.679244	8.38	0.004629*
Growth	4	4.418611	1.104653	1.98	0.103279
S	103	57.50521	0.558303		
Total (Adjusted)	111	71.49107			
Total	112				

* Term significant at alpha = 0.05

Advanced Technology

The analysis of the impact of company size, information strategy, representation of the IT department on the board level (CIO), and growth on importance of advanced technology have shown that importance of advanced technology depends on representation of the IT department on the board level (it is lower in companies without a CIO or alike (3.73) than in companies with one (4.17)) and on information strategy (it is lower in companies without a formal information strategy (3.79) than in companies with one (4.11)) (Table 14).

Operating System Independency

The analysis of the impact of company size, information strategy, representation of the IT department on the board level (CIO), and growth on importance of operating system independency is presented have shown that importance of operating system independency depends on company size (Table 15). The importance is lower in large (2.99) than in small companies (3.84).

System Interoperability

The analysis of the impact of company size, information strategy, representation of the IT department on the board level (CIO), and growth on importance of system interoperability is presented have shown that importance of system interoperability depends on information strategy (Table 16). The importance is lower in companies without implemented formal information strategy (3.85) than in companies with one (4.24).

Table 15. Operating system independency

Factor	DF	Sum of Squares	Mean Square	F-Ratio	P-value
Company size	2	11.35308	5.676538	4.67	0.011444*
Information strategy	1	2.361447	2.361447	1.94	0.166369
CIO	1	0.3809693	0.3809693	0.31	0.576803
Growth	4	3.902208	0.9755521	0.80	0.526257
S	103	125.1977	1.215511		
Total (Adjusted)	111	140.7768			
Total	112				

* Term significant at alpha = 0.05

Table 16. System interoperability

Factor	DF	Sum of Squares	Mean Square	F-Ratio	P-value
Company size	2	0.4142835	0.2071417	0.23	0.795753
Information strategy	1	3.893648	3.893648	4.30	0.040493*
CIO	1	0.1628703	0.1628703	0.18	0.672221
Growth	4	0.3771625	0.09429064	0.10	0.980802
S	104	94.08573	0.9046705		
Total (Adjusted)	112	99.68142			
Total	113				

* Term significant at alpha = 0.05

DISCUSSION

This chapter examines the importance of ERP system selection criteria also studied by Bernroider & Koch (2001) and Bernroider & Leseure (2005). Altogether, 28 ERP selection criteria were identified and investigated in the research. The investigated criteria were grouped into the ERP benefits criteria, the ERP system quality criteria, the ERP vendor-related criteria and the ERP package criteria. All the groups have been found internally consistent.

Out of 28 investigated selection criteria, 17 are the most important in a means of expectations of companies in Slovenia from ERP system selection. These criteria are the following:

- The most expected benefits gained from ERP system adoption perceived by companies are integrated and better quality of information (4,59), business process improvement (4,25), improved service levels and quality (4,21), enhanced decision making (4,11), reduced cycle times and increased customer satisfaction (4,03). These are the ERP selection criteria that were ranked as of highest importance in the group of ERP benefits criteria.
- The highest expectations of companies regarding the ERP system quality criteria are system reliability (4,61), system functionality (4,37), system usability (4,31), system flexibility (4,22) and system interoperability (4,09).

- The most important expectation of companies from ERP vendors is vendor support (4,39). Vendor reputation and market position of the vendor were less important criteria for the companies.
- Companies' most important expectations from the ERP package criteria are the organizational fit of the ERP system (4,16) and e-business enablement (4,15).

All of these criteria are the most sensitive for companies in the phase of ERP system selection and its usage. ERP vendors are strongly recommended considering these criteria to meet companies' expectations in a most efficient way.

In addition to the importance of ERP selection criteria for companies, also the impact of companies' factors (company size, implemented information strategy in the company, representation of the IT department on the board level in the company (CIO) and growth of the company, measured by turnover growth in 2006) on importance of ERP system criteria was also investigated.

The analysis of companies' factors impacting ERP selection criteria has shown that company size has an impact on e-business enablement criterion. Large companies perceived lower importance (4,04) of e-business criterion as small companies (4,51). This could be explained by the fact, that the percentage of large companies, who implemented ERP systems and are already using e-business with their business partners, is much higher than in small companies. Most of small companies are still considering ERP implementation and are considering the most suitable solutions for e-business implementation. Small companies are under pressure from large companies, which are expecting their e-business integration in supply chain. The role of Slovene ICT providers is very important in this case. Local providers offer ERP systems focused and tailored especially for SMEs' needs. These ERP systems integrate standardized operations, based on national business practices, law and regulations, including automated calcula-

tion for taxations, customs, payments procedures, salaries calculation, etc. Most of the ERP systems from local providers also integrate XML schemes for basic business documents (order, order confirmation, dispatch advice and invoice) based on the eSLOG national standard. This enables SMEs to adopt not just an ERP system but also e-business, which is the only way to equal participate in local and global markets.

The importance of increased organizational flexibility criterion depends on the company size. The importance of this criterion is significantly higher in medium-sized companies (4,29) than in large companies (3,71). Data from National Statistical Bureau indicates that 75% of large companies and only 34% of medium-sized already implemented ERP system. Medium-sized companies might perceive this criterion as more important as they still have to improve their internal business processes to be prepared for e-business integration with their partners in the supply chain.

Another criterion depended on company size is operating system independence. The importance of this criterion is significantly higher for small companies (3.48) than for large companies (2.9). This is related to fewer resources being available for ICT investments in small companies. Small companies are most likely to use less complex, cheaper, affordable solutions, including open source solutions. In a phase of ERP system acquisition, small companies will be more sensitive regarding the ERP system independence from operating system.

Company size also has an impact on the system reliability of the ERP system selection criterion, where importance is higher for large companies (4.71) than for small companies (4.33). The higher importance of this factor in large companies could be explained by the complexity of business processes, which are more complex in large companies, where more people are cooperating in the same business processes and thus greater system reliability is needed. It is expected that in the ERP system acquisition phase the large companies will have higher expectations regarding the reliability of ERP system than in small companies.

The importance of business process improvement criterion depends on implemented information strategy in the company and turnover growth. Importance is higher in companies with implemented information strategy (4.34) than in companies without one (4.05). Companies with implemented information strategy seem to pay more attention to business process improvement in the company, especially enabled by ERP system implementation. Importance of business process improvement criterion also depends on growth of the company. Importance is lower in companies with stable turnover (3.77) than in companies with growth of 5-10% (4.45) and with growth of more than 10 percent (4.30). It seems that companies with higher growth are more aware about the need of business process improvement to achieve higher efficiency.

The importance of the advanced technology criterion depends on the representation of the IT department on the board level. The importance is lower in companies without a CIO or similar (3.73) than in companies with one (4.17). The advanced technology criterion also depends on implemented formal information strategy. The importance is lower in companies without a formal information strategy (3.79) than in companies with one (4.11). It seems that companies with a CIO represented on the board level and an implemented formal information strategy have greater understandings at a higher management level of the importance of advanced technology usage for achieving lower costs of business operation and higher efficiency.

The importance of system interoperability criterion depends on implemented information strategy in the company. The importance is lower in companies without implemented formal information strategy (3.85) than in companies with implemented information strategy (4.24). Formal information strategy defines the role and importance of information systems and technologies in the company. The information is also better com-

municated and accepted in the whole company.

Compared to other research (Bernroider & Koch, 2001; Bernroider & Leseure, 2005) examined criteria confirms importance of the following ERP criteria: system reliability, vendor support, functionality of the system, business process improvement, improved service levels, and integrated and better quality of information. These criteria are perceived as most important ERP system selection criteria in companies of all size.

According to the study of Bernroider & Leseure (2005), we have also identified some differences of the importance of e-business enablement of ERP selection criteria, which was in our case more important ERP selection criterion than in the previously mentioned research study. E-business enablement is becoming an increasing important ERP system selection criterion as the need for better business integration, supported by ICT of all partners in supply chain is urgent to achieve competitive advantage in the market.

CONCLUSION

This chapter provides a possible model for ERP system selection. The model consists of four groups of criteria: the ERP systems benefits criteria, the system quality criteria, the vendor related criteria and the ERP system package criteria. Research results have confirmed internal consistency of ERP selection criteria in each group. For each criterion the importance is evaluated by small, medium-sized and large companies. Beside that also company size, implemented information strategy, position of CIO or similar position on the board level in the company and company revenue impact on importance of each criterion is evaluated and presented.

The results have shown sensitivity of some criteria. Company size significantly impact on importance of e-business enablement, increased organizational flexibility, system reliability and operating system independency criteria. Implemented information strategy in the company significantly impact on business process improvement, advanced technology and system interoperability selection criteria. Importance of business process improvement selection criterion depends on the company growth. Importance of advanced technology depends on position of CIO on the board level.

Market analysis have shown that ERP systems are mostly implemented in large companies, while many of medium-sized and small companies are still considering implementation of ERP systems.

It is expected that most of small and medium-sized companies will implement ERP systems in next years. The small and medium-sized companies become a challenging market for IT providers, who already provide ERP systems focused and tailored especially for small and medium-sized companies' needs. The model presented in this chapter could be useful for them to provide ERP systems tailored for individual needs of the company. The model could also be useful for companies considering ERP system implementation to avoid high costs of failed implementations.

REFERENCES

Bernroider, E. (2008). IT governance for enterprise resource planning supported by the DeLone-McLean model of information system success. *Information & Management, 45*(5), 257–269. doi:10.1016/j.im.2007.11.004

Bernroider, E., & Koch, S. (2001). ERP selection process in midsize and large organizations. *Business Process Management Journal, 7*(3), 251–257. doi:10.1108/14637150110392746

Bernroider, E. W. N., & Leseure, M. J. (2005). *Enterprise resource planning (ERP) diffusion and characteristics according to the system's lifecycle: A comparative view of small-to-medium sized and large enterprises.* Working papers on information processing and Information Management. Institute of information processing and information management. Vienna University of Economics and Business Administration.

Botta-Genoulaz, V., Millet, P.-A., & Grabot, B. (2005). A survey on the recent reserach literature on ERP systems. *Computers in Industry, 56*(6), 510–522. doi:10.1016/j.compind.2005.02.004

Cebeci, U. (2009). Fuzzy AHP-based Decision Support System for Selecting ERP Systems in Textile Industry by Using Balanced Scorecard. *Expert Systems with Applications, 36*(5), 8900–8909. doi:10.1016/j.eswa.2008.11.046

Chitura, T., Mupemhi, S., Dube, T., & Bolongkikit, J. (2008). Barriers to Electronic Commerce Adoption in Small and Medium Enterprises: A Critical Literature Review. *Journal of Internet Banking and Commerce, 13*(2), 1–13.

Davenport, T. (1998). Putting the Enterprise into the Enterprise System. *Harvard Business Review, 76*(4), 121–131.

Eleftheriadou, D. (2008). Small - and Medium-Sized Enterprises Hold the Key to European Competitiveness: How to Help Them Innovate through ICT and E-business. *The Global Information Technology Report 2007-2008.* World Economic Forum European Commission. (2003). *SME Definition: Recommendation 2003/361/EC Regarding the SME Definition.*

Fisher, D. M., Fisher, S. A., & Kiang, M. Y. (2004). Evaluating mid-level ERP software. *Journal of Computer Information Systems, 45*(1), 38–46.

Frielink, A. B. (1961). *Auditing automatic data processing.* Amsterdam: Elsevier.

Gable, G., & Stewart, G. (1999). SAP R/3 implementation issues for small to medium enterprises. In *Americas Conference on Information Systems*, Milwaukee, WI (pp. 779-781).

Han, S. W. (2004). ERP - Enterprise resource planning: A cost-based business case and implementation assessment. *Human Factors and Ergonomics in Manufacturing, 14*(3), 239–256. doi:10.1002/hfm.10066

Jafari, S. M., Osman, M. R., Yusuff, R. M., & Tang, S. H. (2006). ERP Systems Implementation In Malaysia: The Importance Of Critical Success Factors. *International Journal of Engineering and Technology, 3*(1), 125–131.

Joslin, E. O. (1968). *Computer selection*. London: Addison-Wesley.

Karaarslan, N., & Gundogar, E. (2009). An Application for Modular Capability-based ERP Software Selection Using AHP Method. *International Journal of Advanced Manufacturing Technology, 42*(9-10), 1025–1033. doi:10.1007/s00170-008-1522-5

Karsak, E. E., & Ozogul, C. O. (2009). An Integrated Decision Making Approach for ERP System Selection. *Expert Systems with Applications, 36*(1), 660–667. doi:10.1016/j.eswa.2007.09.016

Kartiwi, M., & MacGregor, R. C. (2007). Electronic Commerce Adoption Barriers in Small to Medium-Sized Enterprises (SMEs) in Developed and Developing Countries: A Cross-Country Comparison. *Journal of Electronic Commerce in Organizations, 5*(3), 35–51.

Keil, M., & Tiwana, A. (2006). Relative importance of evaluation criteria for enterprise systems: a conjoint study. *Information Systems Journal, 16*(3), 237–262. doi:10.1111/j.1365-2575.2006.00218.x

Kumar, V., Maheshwari, B., & Kumar, U. (2002). Enterprise resource planning systems adoption process: a survey of Canadian organizations. *International Journal of Production Research, 40*(3), 509–523. doi:10.1080/00207540110092414

Kumar, V., Maheshwari, B., & Kumar, U. (2003). An investigation of critical management issues in ERP implementation: emperical evidence from Canadian organizations. *Technovation, 23*(10), 793–807. doi:10.1016/S0166-4972(02)00015-9

Lall, V., & Teyarachakul, S. (2006). Enterprise Resource Planning (ERP) System selection: A Data Envelopment Anaysis (DEA) approach. *Journal of Computer Information Systems, 47*(1), 123–127.

Law, C. C. H., & Ngai, E. W. T. (2007). ERP system adoption: An exploratory study of the organizational factors and impacts of ERP success. *Information & Management, 444*(4), 418–432. doi:10.1016/j.im.2007.03.004

Levenburg, N. M., Schwarz, T. V., & Motwani, J. (2005). Understanding adoption of internet technologies among SMEs. *Journal of Small Business Strategy, 16*(1), 51–69.

Levy, M., Powell, P., & Worrall, L. (2005). Strategic Intent and E-Business in SMEs: Enablers and Inhibitors. *Information Resources Management Journal, 18*(4), 1–20.

Liao, X. W., Li, Y., & Lu, B. (2007). A model for selecting an ERP system based on linguistic information processing . *Information Systems, 32*(7), 1005–1017. doi:10.1016/j.is.2006.10.005

Malie, M., Duffy, N., & van Rensburg, A. C. J. (2008). Enterprise resource planning solution selection criteria in medium-sized South African companies. *South African Journal of Industrial Engineering, 19*(1), 17–41.

Markus, M. L., & Tanis, C. (2000). The Enterprise System Experience: From Adoption to Success . In Zmud, R. W. (Ed.), *Framing the Domains of IT Management: Projecting the Future through the Past* (pp. 173–207). Cincinnati: Pinnaflex, Educational Resources Inc.

Nah, F. F. H., & Delgado, S. (2006). Critical success factors for enterprise resource planning implementation and upgrade. *Journal of Computer Information Systems, 46*(SI), 99-113.

Nunnally, J. C. (1967). *Psychometric Theory.* New York: McGraw-Hill.

Nunnally, J. C. (1978). *Psychometric Theory* (2nd ed.). New York: McGraw-Hill.

Oh, W., & Pinsonneault, A. (2007). On the Assessment of the Strategic Value of Information Technologies: Conceptual and Analytical Approaches. *Management Information Systems Quarterly, 31*(2), 239–265.

Plaza, M., & Rohlf, K. (2008). Learning and Performance in ERP Implementation Projects: A Learning-curve Model for Analyzing and Managing Consulting Costs. *International Journal of Production Economics, 115*(1), 72–85. doi:10.1016/j.ijpe.2008.05.005

Rao, S. S. (2000). Enterprise resource planning: business needs and technologies. *Industrial Management & Data Systems, 100*(1-2), 81–88. doi:10.1108/02635570010286078

Razmi, J., Sangari, M. S., & Ghodsi, R. (2009). Developing a Practical Framework for ERP Readiness Assessment Using Fuzzy Analytic Network Process. *Advances in Engineering Software, 40*(11), 1168–1178. doi:10.1016/j.advengsoft.2009.05.002

Riquelme, H. (2002). Commercial Internet Adoption in China: Comparing the experiences of small, medium and large businesses. *Internet Research: Electronic Networking Applications and Policy, 12*(3), 276–286. doi:10.1108/10662240210430946

Soja, P. (2006). Success Factors in ERP Systems Implementations: Lessons From Practice. *Journal of Enterprise Information Management, 19*(6), 646–661. doi:10.1108/17410390610708517

Sudzina, F. (2007). Importance of EPR selection criteria in Slovak companies. *Manažment v teórii a praxi, 3*(4), 4-20.

Umble, E. J., Haft, R. R., & Umble, M. M. (2003). Enterprise resource planning: implementation procedures and critical success factors. *European Journal of Operational Research, 146*(2), 241–257. doi:10.1016/S0377-2217(02)00547-7

Verville, J., & Halingten, A. (2003). A six-stage model of the buying process for ERP software. *Industrial Marketing Management, 32*(7), 585–594. doi:10.1016/S0019-8501(03)00007-5

Wei, C. C., Chien, C. F., & Wang, M. J. J. (2005). An AHP-based approach to ERP system selection. *International Journal of Production Economics, 96*(1), 47–62. doi:10.1016/j.ijpe.2004.03.004

Wier, B., Hunton, J., & Hassab Elnaby, H. R. (2007). Enterprise resource planning systems and non-financial performance incentives: The joint impact on corporate performance. *International Journal of Accounting Information Systems, 8*(3), 165–190. doi:10.1016/j.accinf.2007.05.001

Chapter 21
INOVA Framework:
A Case Study of the Use of Web Technologies for the Integration of Consulting Techniques and Procedures

L. Borrajo-Enríquez
University of Santiago de Compostela, Spain

P. Saco
University of Santiago de Compostela, Spain

Jose M. Cotos
University of Santiago de Compostela, Spain

Alberto Casal
INOVA, Spain

Christian Larsson
INOVA, Spain

ABSTRACT

Nowadays, the WWW is playing a vital role in the business world. Most enterprises are becoming digital. Content management systems provide an effective method to improve the development of web applications and make the maintainer's job easier. The purpose of this work is to study the benefits that the use of web technologies can suppose for a SME company when they are applied to integrate their work techniques and procedures. The authors have also tried to use it to provide their customers with several services, and to make easier the company expansion process. The framework developed includes a security system for the access to the contents based on the RBAC model. The use of the INOVA framework has provided a benefit as much for INOVA itself, as for its customers, by including in a centralized way document resources and toolkits that can be accessed remotely.

DOI: 10.4018/978-1-61692-020-3.ch021

INTRODUCTION

Due to the great number of consulting companies in the market, a consulting company has to offer some innovative products if it wants to stand out. To do so, INOVA specialized in the Innovation, Optimization and Valorization of the projects that their customers carry out.

The growth of the Internet, the rise of telecommunication, and advances in computer technology have provided businesses with new opportunities. At the same time, it poses new communication challenges. In order to operate efficiently, a business needs a way for its employees to share information. No matter the size of the business, an effective, easy to use information sharing solution is critical to success.

This project was created with the idea of developing a framework (Figure 1) to improve and increase the services INOVA offers to the general public, to their customers, and to their own staff. To do so, we pretended to computerize several applications and utilities that the INOVA staff had developed trough time, both to the general public, and to their internal use.

INOVA staff realized that some of the applications they had developed through time as internal utilities to be used by them, could be useful for their clients and for the general public. In the market did not exist any products that would give those services to the users, or at least not in the specific field they work with.

As a result, we created a web portal that would give the INOVA employees and users in general access to this application from anywhere (http://www.inovaportal.com). We have followed the standards to develop the portal, putting a special care in maintaining a clear, simple and intuitive user interface. As a result, it is accessible via different navigators, even using text navigators such as lynx.

In this paper we are describing the goals we pursued, the solution adopted to achieve them, the problems encountered during the development of the system, and the solutions adopted to deal with those problems.

The reminder of this paper is outlined as follows: In the Background section we explain which the situation in the market is and we provide some examples of some of the existing features and what is innovative about our solution. The Main section of the chapter has been divided in several parts. First, we offer a description of the project, giving also a list of web portal requirements. After that, we explain the system architecture. Another important part of the main section will be the web portal software description, where we explain the most important modules that we have developed in our system to meet our objectives. Next, we give our perspective about the problems we have encountered and the solutions we found to deal with them. At the end we explain the directions we plan to follow in future research, and a conclusion about this project.

BACKGROUND

There exist an extensive number of cases in which an enterprise or an institution has decided to improve the services they offer to the public by developing a web portal. Internet offers a way to distribute knowledge and share information. To do so, a big part of them rely on a Web Content Management System to use as a base to the development of their web portal. A web content management system provides some tools that are very useful.

They provide tools that allow manage the content in the web portal easily, without the need of extensive computer knowledge. They usually utilize templates to display the content, and allow the separation of the content from the web portal design.

In my opinion one of the most important reasons to use a WCMS is that they usually provide a granular permission system, which allows a big

Figure 1. INOVA framework

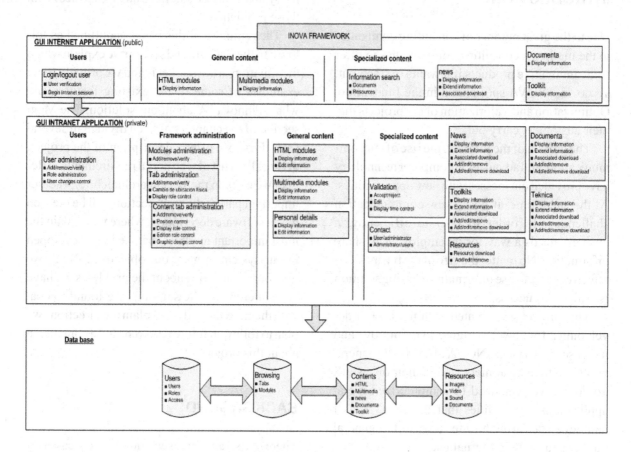

flexibility and facilitates enormously the security in the web portal and the management of users.

There are several papers that talk about the use of web content management systems. Some of them emphasize in specific parts of the development of a complex web portal, such as the management of roles and security (Pastore, 2006), the web accessibility (Rainville-Pitt, 2007), the use of templates to facilitate the design of web pages (Salazar, 2006), the user-friendly characteristic that apports a CMS (Yang, 2008)

Others propose how to analyze and design the development of a CMS based web application (Soure, 2007), (Souer, 2008), or how to make a quick prototype of digital enterprises (Aktunc, 2008).

Our intention is to use the CMS to help us develop tools for users in the field of consulting. Although there are already some CMS applied in other fields (Yen, 2008) there are not any tools in the market that provides what we are trying to achieve.

In our chapter we try to go one step further than other papers related with content management systems, explaining not only the different types of roles or the separation of content from design, but also some of the innovative tools we are trying to offer to the enterprises that visit the web portal, and to general public, in the consulting fields of innovation, optimization and valorization.

MAIN FOCUS OF THE CHAPTER

Project Description

We can distinguish two main goals in this project, which can be explained in a brief description as:

- To offer support services to the companies to perform improvement operation processes, innovation processes, and to help them obtain funding for their projects.
- To improve the internal processes of INOVA, allowing the INOVA staff to access a database with potential customers and to have and use standardized protocols for improvement and innovation processes.

These main goals were divided in several subtasks, allowing us to see in more detail the specific objectives we had to meet in this project:

- To update the old INOVA web portal, the contents as much as the design, and to offer the general public open access to the corporative company web portal, information about relevant publications in the areas of innovation, optimization and valorization, interesting links and innovation related news and INOVA news.
- To create an internet based platform with integrated extranet & intranet systems that allows:
- To create a database with information about potential customers, in such a way that they were able to access, previous registration, to software applications such as online forms that allow them to test in an approximated way the capacity and the needs of innovation, optimization and valorization of their companies, information about existing funding that the users and their businesses could apply for carrying out R&D and optimization projects, or management techniques.

- To offer the current customers of INOVA, via extranet, access to applications that would help in the tracking and management of their projects, give information about technological agents, and show a detailed list of techniques to implement innovation, optimization and valorization processes in their company.
- To establish an intranet system for the INOVA staff assigned to projects that allows them to access to applications related to innovation, optimization, and valorization processes.

By completing the goals explained above, INOVA intends to achieve some milestones:

- To increase significantly the number of projects in the companies which lead to innovative products highly valued in the market.
- To integrate the management of the innovation as an additional element in the day-to-day management of the companies, guaranteeing their sustainability in the environment of high competitiveness and globalization in which we are living.
- To contribute to the development of the Information Society.
- To contribute, specifically, in the improvement of the Information Technology and Communication infrastructures involved in the business management.
- To enhance the participation level of the small to medium-sized Spanish enterprises in R&D European programs, increasing the outputs obtained from these participations.

Web Portal Requirements

- *Robustness and flexibility.* The system must use and integrate existing and open source solutions and combine the modules and applications developed in the framework among them.

- *Scalability*. The web portal had to be structured by modules, so it could grow in size and capacity based on the demand. There must exist also the possibility of migrate the web portal to more powerful platforms in a small amount of time and price in case the demand or the new technological advances suggest to do so.
- *Efficiency*. The web portal applications must be able to grow quickly and efficiently. This must be done with a small amount of time and at the lowest cost possible.
- *Friendliness and quality*. It must be intuitive and attractive for enterprises, and integrate simple and error-free functionalities.
- *Computing power*. The framework must support data processing algorithms, and calculate complex recommendations. The portal must be able to support several work sessions of users using the system at the same time. It must also acknowledge previous work sessions of the users and customize the interface of the portal to that user.

System Architecture

The mentioned requirements must be met in an architecture based on open software. After analyzing which were our needs, we decided to use the following architecture:

- OS platform: CentOS 5.2. It is an Enterprise-class Linux Distribution, totally free, which allows us to have the functionality we need, and ensures us a certain amount of stability.
- HTTP Server: Apache 2.0. This open-source HTTP server provides HTTP services in a secure and efficient server that follows the current HTTP standards.

- Database: MySQL 5.1 (Welling & Thomson, 2005). We chose this database because of its characteristics of open source software, its reliability and its high performance. Because of the amount of data we are going to store in our database is not projected to grow to high levels, we considered MySQL was an adequate solution. Although we had started working with version 4.1, the fact that the 5.1 version allows to execute triggers and procedures decided us to upgrade to that version.
- Programming languages: HTML, PHP 5.2.5, CSS, Javascript.
- Web based Content Management System. We decided to use a CMS to help us match the efficiency requirement, develop the web portal and simplify the publication of new web content, allowing content creators to submit content without requiring technical knowledge of HTML. Besides, it helps in the implementation of a model view controller pattern (MVC) (Gamma et al, 1993), which facilitates the task of administering and managing the web portal.

Chosen CMS: Xaraya

After comparing several CMS, we finally decided to use Xaraya. Some of the reasons to do so, are the following:

- Xaraya is an open source framework based on PostNuke which gives programmers and designers considerable flexibility.
- Its modular design allows separating function from form and content from design (Yu, 2005). Because of the use of modules, the scalability of the system is extensive.
- It uses robust permissions, data management, and multilingual systems to dynamically integrate and manage content.
- It follows the WWW standards.

- Its development and support community is extensive, and users are constantly creating new modules that improve the functionality of the framework.
- Xaraya integrates perfectly with Apache and makes use of the PHP functions.
- The privileges are managed in a modular way, allowing different types of access depending on the user, the page visited, or the content of that page. As a result, the interface can be simpler or more sophisticated depending on the type of user.
- It allows setting the content to approval before updating the webpage.
- It is compatible with Secure Socket Layer (SSL) among other protocols, such as LDAP. The system can be switched to SSL mode to login, or to access certain pages or sections.
- The edition of contents can be made using a WYSIWYG editor, allowing publishers to create formatted content without having knowledge of HTML, CSS or XML.
- It supports a huge amount of types of data, which makes the edition of contents even simpler.
- It has a powerful templating system (called BlockLayout), which helps to maintain a consistent design throughout the site. Although the code in general resides in the PHP files, the markup that is actually displayed to the browser is stored in the templates that the code calls. These templates can be dynamic thanks to the BlockLayout system: the page displayed changes depending on the data it receives and processes.

Web Portal Software Description

The INOVA web portal is a modular system. This means that each part of the portal is clearly defined, and it carries out a specific function that may be used alone or combined with other modules of the same program. The modules can interact between them, sharing data and results. Through this interaction, they produce a complex system. In the following subsections we describe some of the modules we consider that have a bigger relevance in the INOVA framework.

Roles Management System

The roles module manages users, groups and roles in Xaraya. We call users to registered individuals on a web portal.

Several types of users were defined in our framework. We could separate them in two main branches: common users and administrators. A scheme with the main type of users can be seen in figure 2.

Due to the amount of types of users in the web portal, we decided to use a role-based access control (RBAC) model (Al-Kahtani & Sandhu, 2002) (Chandramouli, 2001). Using this system, the security administration consists in that the roles must be correctly assigned to the different types of users, based on the capacities and the responsibilities that they have. The security administration is much more accessible, due to the roles assignation to organize access privileges.

The users are categorized in groups. A group usually gives the users in it common privileges and properties.

In the common users we could distinguish four main groups:

- Anonymous users.
- Registered users.
- Customers.
- INOVA staff.

For the administrator's branch, the division is slightly more complicated. We could define the following general groups of administrators:

- *Editors*. Those who can edit partially or totally the web portal, add new content,

345

Figure 2. INOVA web portal roles

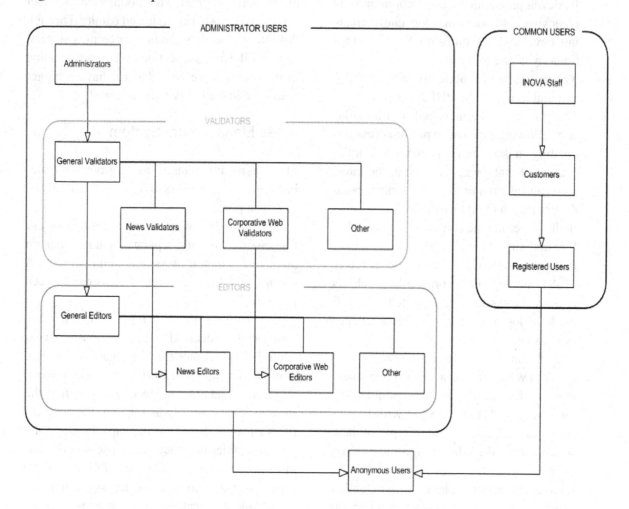

but not delete it. Besides, the modified or added data must be validated before being published in the web page.

- The editors can have editing privileges over the entire web portal, or only over a small part. For instance, there are news editors (those who can add or edit news), or public web editors (those who can modify the corporative pages).

- The reason to have those partial editors can be explained easily with an example. INOVA has appointed another company the task of looking for interesting news in the fields they consider of interest for their clients. Having the news editor role, they

can give to them one of these accounts, so they can add or edit news. Before being published in the web page, a validator (usually a member of INOVA) will check if the information is valid, and decide if it must be shown in the web portal.

- *Validators.* As we explained in the previous point, a validator checks if the information given by an editor is valid. In addition, they can add, delete or edit data from the web portal.

- As in the case of the editors, they could use their privileges over the entire web portal, or only over a part of it, depending on the type of validators they are.

- *Administrators*. They have several tasks: administering users, checking the links in the web portal are valid, managing the database, etcetera.

The users in a higher level inherit the privileges of the user in a lower level. For instance, a registered user, as well as their own privileges, will inherit the privileges of the anonymous users.

The reason the two branches are divided, is that administrator users could be not members of the INOVA staff, and vice versa.

One important feature is that a user can be of more than one type of role. For instance, a user could be a validator and an INOVA member. This is very useful in some cases, where a user can be, for instance, a corporative web validator, and a news editor.

The list of roles is open, allowing the creation of new roles in the future if we consider it necessary, with specific permissions for these new roles.

By the moment, a user can be created only if an administrator does so, assigning it to a group. In the future, any user could register as a "registered user" using a registering form that will be accessible in the main page of the web portal.

Privileges Management System

The privileges are responsible for the security of the web portal. The idea we follow is that anything that is not explicitly permitted is denied. This means that the access to the system or to part of the system is only available where is explicitly granted. Since is a important part of the system, we wanted to include it in this document.

The privileges are assigned to the roles. A role given a privilege has the access that the privilege represents. Privileges can be defined very narrowly. Thus, a privilege could be limited only to a type of content, to a specific module, or to a component within a module. They also can be assigned to a certain part of the web portal.

Privileges, as we explained in the previous section, are inherited. A role's privileges consist of those directly applied, and those assigned to any of its ancestors.

The system supports eight levels of access:

- No access.
- Overview: The user can read content, although also a "weak" type of read. It allows, for instance, to see a summary of published content, but not the whole content.
- Read. The user can read content.
- Comment: Users can submit content, such as a document, or a comment.
- Moderate: The user can manage someone else's content.
- Edit: The user can change existing content but not add or delete.
- Add: The user can add or edit content.
- Delete. The user can delete content.
- Admin: The user has unrestricted access.

The levels are cumulative. That means that a user having a given access also has the access right of levels below it. For example, "edit" access also implies "read" access.

Information Management System

The system has several types of information management systems to treat with different type of data. In the following subsections we explain what we consider some of the more relevant systems. By the combination of these systems and other applications we are going to develop in the future, we intend to create a web portal of reference in the fields of innovation, optimization, and valorization of private companies.

News Management System

This system allows administrators with enough privileges to add, to edit or to modify existing news. If these administrators have validation privileges, then they can change the status of the news to public, which will make them visible in the web portal. In the case the user does not have validation permissions, the news will be added, but they will not be visible by the non-administrator users until somebody validates the data.

Besides the usual information concerning the new, news editors have the option to put the starting date and the final date of the new. When this data is filled, the framework will automatically show or hide this new for the usual users, although editors will be able to see it.

While a typical user will see the logo of the new, the title, date of the new and description, an administrator will be also able to see the date of beginning and end of the new, its status, and a link to modify it.

With this system, INOVA intends to provide users with an easy way to access to relevant news in the fields of innovation, optimization, and valorization.

In the system appear two type of news:

- INOVA news. Data that are related with the INOVA work and with the company, in one way or another.
- Interesting news. News that could be of interest for the general public, in the fields in which INOVA work.

Publications Management System

INOVA wanted to store documents and links to articles published in different formats and types of publications. To do so, we created a database which stored a wide range of metadata about these articles.

The quantity of publications is quite extensive. Therefore, we have developed a search engine to look for that data, based on the type of sources of those documents, and the keywords related with them (Figure 3).

This search engine is accessible to any user, but just partially: an anonymous user can have access to the search engine, and receive a list of results, with a small amount of information. If the users

are registered, they would also be able to access to more information about the specific document they are interested in, included information about the source and the original document, either linked, or downloadable in PDF format. Besides, an administrator user with edition privileges over documents, could also access to the edition page of the document directly from it.

With this system, users have access to a high quantity of data related with specific themes in a centralized way. This facilitates considerably the search of these publications, without having to look for the source of them, and saving a lot of time.

Financing Management System

As a complementary application, it was decided to create a software solution to provide the INOVA clients and users in general a way of efficiently searching for financial funding of their interest in the fields of R&D and optimization.

The software application provides a search engine to look for the exact needs of the enterprise, and provides a list of possible financing solutions. Following the same idea than the publication management system, it provides different level of access depending on the type of user using the search application. In the case of anonymous users, they could see the list of possible financing subventions. A registered user could see the detailed information of the subventions, while editors could edit this information in case they consider it necessary.

Like in the publications system, this application saves huge amounts of time, since a user just has to use the search engine to access to a list of all the possible financial funding they can apply for.

Technological Agents Management System

Another software utility we try to provide our customers is a technological agents management system. We call technological agents to companies who can offer some product or solutions in a specific field.

Figure 3. Example of a search engine for the publications management system

The public programs of financial subventions to the R&D require or highly value that the companies asking for these subventions cooperate with another agents of the science – technology – business system.

The creation of consortiums for the cooperation in R&D projects is not trivial and requires a series of contacts and information that most SMEs are not used to know in most of the cases, mainly when they do not have previous experience asking for these subventions.

What we offer in our web portal is a search engine for users. A user may be in need of finding a technological agent to make some collaboration with them. For instance, to develop a specific project in the future, they could need a technological agent in the field of telecommunication. With this search engine, they could define the fields that could be interesting for them, and also the geographical area in which they are looking for this agent. With this they will have a list of possible technological agents, a brief description about them, the fields in which they work, and contact information about the agent.

Another part of this system gives information about the future perspectives of different technologies. It provides a list of innovative areas related with those technologies, and a description about them. It also supplies a list of technological agents working in those areas, if available.

This utility is proven to be quite useful for users, helping them to find agents that could have interest in collaborate with them in their projects.

Work Procedures Standardization System

To define the level of innovation of a company, INOVA must do a with set of actions (or groups of tasks) that can be grouped in a catalog of Innovation procedures. Depending of the type of company they are analyzing and the type of results they are looking for, they use some toolkits or another (Figure 4). The importance of these toolkits is variable for each project, provoking that some of them are priority over the others.

Before developing this framework, they did not have these toolkits in an electronic way. When they wanted to use one of those toolkits, they could not access to a centralized database with the information about them, or the way they had to use them. That caused in some cases that these tools were not applied in a standard or even correct way.

To fix this problem, it was decided to develop a software application, as a part of the web portal, with information about these toolkits. It includes a description of the toolkit, when it must be ap-

plied, a guide about how to use it, recommendations, links, etc. This information is public for any member of the INOVA staff. Some information is also public for everybody, such as the description or the time estimated to obtain results.

This catalog of toolkits improves the characteristics of existing ones because of two main reasons it is structured so it can cover or the steps and actions that integrate the innovation processes (the generation of ideas, the study of the viability of the projects, etc.).

This improves significantly the efficiency of the company, since the consult about how to proceed in each situation is available wherever they are, and they can look up the guidelines they must follow using a friendly and easy-to-use interface.

Projects Workflow Management System

This system was thought to help the INOVA staff with the projects they work in. It provides several workflows that help them now which are the next step they must follow in order to continue with their job. Taking on account the specific characteristics they have to deal with, the system gives the INOVA members a set of roadmaps, so they know exactly what they have to do at any time with the processes related to the innovation, optimization and valorization of the companies they work for.

This improves the efficiency of the INOVA staff, since by the use of this system; they have a way to establish the situation of each project at any time, and to know which are the future steps they must follow.

Evaluation Toolkits

A very important part of our system was formed by a set of evaluation toolkits.

These toolkits were deployed to help to establish the benchmarking of the businesses of their customers, based on the levels of innovation, optimization, and valorization they had.

Figure 4. Example of some of the available toolkits

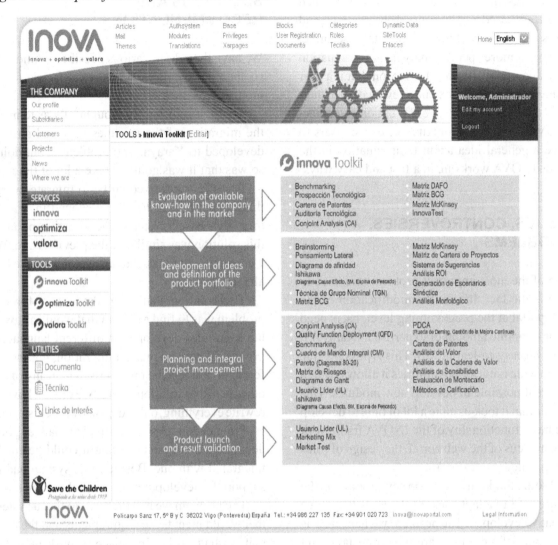

The goal of these toolkits was to provide the INOVA staff a set of tool that would help them give a consistent report of the needs of their customers, based on these results as much as in their own experience.

These toolkits were not thought only as tools for the internal staff. Nowadays there are not any tools in the market that can give a user a general approach to the levels of innovation, optimization and valorization that their company have without paying a pretty high amount of money. Because of this reason, we decided to give partial access to these tools to any user. By answering a set of questions related with their businesses, they can partially establish what their needs are. The responses received to these questions are processed internally by the system. After it, a conclusion is given to the user, showing some graphic results that will tell them the status of their companies in five important points, and if its situation in the fields of innovation and optimization is acceptable, or if otherwise, they need to take special care in improving the problems they have. Besides these graphics, the users will receive some suggestions about which are the weak points they have, and the steps they should follow to improve that situation.

We must highlight that of course, the obtained results are based in some general observations, and users can not expect them to be totally accurate, without a more specific analysis of the situation of the company. It is for this reason that if a user is interested in a more extended evaluation of their needs, they will also have the option to contact INOVA. With these toolkits, we expect users to have a general idea about their situation in the fields INOVA works in, in a fast and easy way.

ISSUES, CONTROVERSIES, PROBLEMS

One of the most important problems we have to face is the fact that for the modification of the web portal at the programming level, users need a considerable amount of expertise in Xaraya. It is not an easy-to-learn CMS. This is possibly due to the wide range of possibilities it allows, which makes it possible to develop new modules. This causes that it took us quite a lot of time to develop the basic functionality of the INOVA framework (the nucleus of the web portal, the design of roles and privileges, etcetera).

We are thinking in develop new modules in the future, and to adapt some of the tools they have already developed. The problem we have now is that some of these tools are written in Java, and the migration to PHP is quite tedious.

They also want to migrate their documentation system to an improved one. For this, they want to use a commercial solution that has not a good integration with Xaraya.

Beside this, another problem we are facing right now is that INOVA intends to implement some e-collaboration tools. These types of tools are not easy to implement in Xaraya, since it does not exist any module that can give the functionality we are looking for.

SOLUTIONS AND RECOMMENDATIONS

We have thought in various possible solutions to fix these problems we will have to face in future months.

The first solution we thought of was to make the migration of the modules they had already developed to Xaraya. The problem about doing so was that it was going to take a lot of time.

Another solution could be to migrate everything that we had already developed in Xaraya to a Java based system. The negative point in this solution was similar to the previous one. We were not going to take advantage of what we had already develop.

The solution that seemed the best for our problem was to find a system that would allow to have modules developed in different languages. We would have to make a migration, but the effort to do it would be much less than in any of the other possible solutions, since we did not have to rewrite everything, only adapt it to the new system.

We needed that system also had a good documentation system or that it could be easily integrated with one. Besides, this system had to support the development of e-collaboration tools.

The problem we had then was to find a system that would meet these requirements and the ones that we had in the first place (robust, modular, open-source, flexible, a good permissions system…).

After analyzing different possibilities, we finally opted for Liferay. Nowadays, this is one of the leader open source portals in the marketplace. Liferay provides a unified web interface to integrate data and sources scattered around many sources. It can be defined as a built-in content management system as well as a built-in collaboration suite. Its portal interface is composed of a number of portlets. A portlet is user interface software that is managed and displayed inside a web portal. It produces fragments of markup code that are aggregated into a portal page, processing requests and generation dynamic content. The portlets must follow a standard, which is intended to allow the creation of portlets that can be plugged to any portal supporting the standards. This can be useful if in the future we decide to change our system to another web portal, since we could reuse this portlets.

Liferay has a wide list of portlets already available (currently there are defined more than 60). It also provides integration with Alfresco, which would be useful for the documentation module we want to develop. Besides, it is a good portal for small team collaboration. This is interesting to share contents in different levels. For instance, between the members of the same project, between the members of INOVA, between different groups inside INOVA, etc.

It also has a fine grained permissions system, which is a very important characteristic, since part of the information we work with is quite sensible.

The web portal is developed in Java, J2EE and Web 2.0 technologies. Besides these technologies, Liferay offers the possibility of developing portlets in PHP, Javascript and many other languages. This is one of the main reasons to choose this web portal, since we could adapt the PHP modules that we developed in Xaraya to a module in Liferay, allowing a better integration.

To sum up, we think that the best solution for the problems we will have to face in the following months is to use the Liferay Portal to develop our web system.

We are not sure yet if we will migrate the portal we have already developed in Xaraya, or if on the other hand, we will create a different web portal to develop the new tools, maintaining two different portals (Xaraya, for the tools we have already develop), and Liferay for the new tools, which are thought to be used as internal tools by INOVA staff.

FUTURE RESEARCH DIRECTIONS

In the future we plan to include new applications into the INOVA web portal, almost continuously, since we have a lot of ideas to develop that we think would be beneficial for users and staff, and that would contribute to improve the quality of private companies and of their projects. In the following months, we pretend to add a funding management system based on the profile and the financing level of the customer's company. Also, we are including a private section for customers, to allow INOVA to share files and relevant information with them, and a collaborative system that allows the INOVA members to work online and together in their projects.

Another module we want to develop is called INOVA Project. This module will consist in a planner module, to be used as an internal application by the INOVA staff. With this module, they will have the possibility to add the projects they are working on and define the original planning for those projects and apply resources to them. While they develop those projects, they will be able to see the current situation of it, if they are delayed or not, if a task is taking too much time, or if the resources applied are enough. To see it in a graphical mode, they will have access to a Gantt graph. Besides, the users will have access to multiple reports, providing information related with a project, with the staff workload, etc.

Other future work closely related with this one will be a documentation module. The users related to a project would have access to documentation that could be relevant for them. Depending on the type of user, they will have access to a certain type of documentation. For instance, the customer could have access to reports.

Another feature will be an alerts module. This module is thought to send to administrators or people with certain responsibilities e-mails with information about different types of notifications. For instance, problems in the web portal, information about new documents, notification that a certain task of a project (in the INOVA Project module) is out of date, and so on.

Another future features will be a contacts module, or a shared agenda, among others.

We are thinking about the possibility of developing our future modules in another technology. Although the technology we are using right now gives us enough functionality by the moment, and for most of the modules we want to develop, we are thinking about produce some utilities that would not be easily supported by our current system.

For instance, we think about develop some e-collaboration utilities that are fully supported and easily integrated with some Java based software.

CONCLUSION

The purpose of this work is to study the benefits that the use of web technologies can suppose for a company when they are applied to integrate their work techniques and procedures. We have also tried to use it to provide their customers with several services, and to make easier the expansion process of the company.

The use of a CMS as a starting point has allowed:

- The quick development of prototypes.
- The fast adjustment of the users to the tasks of creation, edition and publication of contents in the framework since they do not need to have previous specialized computing knowledge.
- A secure system for the contents, because of the effective management of the roles that it makes for the access and publication to the framework.
- The access of multiple authors, editors, and customers from different locations and with a controlled access to the information.
- The modular structure of the framework has allowed evolving and improving the prototyping. The evolution process of the

system has maintained its functionality and has been transparent for the users, since it did not interfere with the previous developed modules.

The use of the INOVA framework has led the company to improve in the management of their documents, their sources of information and their customers, since they have at their disposal a centralized system with search engines and a management system, having the possibility of accessing remotely.

It has also supposed a benefit for the customers, since the framework provides them with valuable sources of information and an approach to the use of control and evaluation tools to find out the state of innovation of their companies.

Although each result obtained is not totally innovative by itself, the fact that users can have access to a wide range of tools related with the fields of innovation, optimization and valorization of private companies, is something totally new.

We are constantly increasing these features, with the idea of offering more and more applications for the general public, the INOVA customers, and INOVA staff.

ACKNOWLEDGMENT

The authors wish to thank the Ministerio de Industria, Turismo y Comercio (FIT-350100-2007-88) and the Dirección Xeral de Investigación, Desenvolvemento e Innovación (08SIN036E) for financial support.

REFERENCES

Aktunc, O., Dronavallli, S., & Tanik, M. (2008). Rapid prototyping of digital enterprises using content management systems. In *IEEE 2008 Southeastcon* (pp. 231-235).

Al-Kahtani, M. A., & Sandhu, R. (2002). A model for attribute-based user-role assignment. In *Computer Security Applications Conference 2002* (pp. 353–362).

Chandramouli, R. (2001). A framework for multiple authorization types in a healthcare application system. In *17th Annual Computer Security Applications Conference (ACSAC)* (pp. 137-148).

Gamma, E., Helm, R., Vlissides, J., & Johnson, R. E. (1993). Design Patterns: Abstraction and Reuse of Object-Oriented Design. In *Proceedings of the 7th European Conference on Object-Oriented Programming* (LNCS 707, 406-431).

Pastore, S. (2006). Web Content Management Systems: using Plone open source software to build a website for research institute needs. In *Digital Telecommunications, ICDT '06. International Conference* (pp. 24-29).

Rainville-Pitt, S., & D'Amour, J. (2007). Using a CMS to create fully accessible websites. In *Proceedings of the 2007 international Cross-Disciplinary Conference on Web Accessibility (W4a)* (Vol. 225).

Salazar, E. (2006). Content Management for the Virtual Library. *Information Technology and Libraries*, 25(3), 170–175.

Souer, J., Honders, P., Versendaal, J., & Brinkkemper, S. (2007). Defining operations and maintenance in web engineering: a framework for cms-based web applications. In *Digital Information Management, 2007. ICDIM '07. 2nd International Conference* (Vol. 1, pp. 430-435).

Souer, J., Luinenburg, L., Versendaal, J., van de Weerd, I., & Brinkkemper, S. (2008). Engineering a design method for web content management implementations. In *Proceedings of the 10th international Conference on information integration and Web-Based Applications & Services (iiWAS '08)* (pp. 351-358).

Welling, L., & Thompson, L. (2005). *PHP and MySQL Web development* (3rd ed.). Indianapolis, IN: Sams Publishing.

Yang, M., Chang, W., Yarnk, K., Cheng, T., Luo, W., Hsu, S., & Yang, P. (2008). *Proceedings of the 2008 3rd international Conference on innovative Computing information and Control.*

Yen, Ch., Yen, Ch., & Hsu, J. (2008). An implementation of Web Based PDM with Open Source CMS. In *Virtual Environments, Human-Computer Interfaces and Measurement Systems, VECIMS 2008. IEEE Conference* (pp. 162-165).

Yu, H. (2005). *Content and Workflow Management for Library Web Sites: Case Studies*. Hershey, PA: Information Science Publishing.

Section 6
EIS Social Aspects

Chapter 22
Crucial Consequences of Un–Holistic Business Information

Vojko Potocan
University of Maribor, Slovenia

Matjaz Mulej
University of Maribor, Slovenia

ABSTRACT

Modern business environments require innovated business concepts. Meeting them in enterprises' functioning depends also on creation and implementation of appropriate information support. In terms of contents, information support and information must be reliable to not be misinformation; information and communication technology is not enough for it because information means impact. Potential errors on the long path from data to information must hence be prevented. A one-sided approach, which belongs to the practices of professionals as narrow specialists, can prevent errors and misinformation rarely – when rather one-sided information is enough. More complex situation and processes require a more holistic approach that, in its turn, requires interdisciplinary creative co-operation of specialists of various interdependent professions. The authors try to contribute to discussion about reliability of information by thinking how can one tackle the data-to-information-to-decision process in order to diminish dangers of poor reliability of information/decision.

INTRODUCTION

For centuries, handicraft and agricultural producers used to prevail and to basically know who their expectable customers (= market) are (Collins, 2001; Florida, 2002; Daft, 2003; Potocan, 2003; etc.). Their technology did not change much either. Thus, their **information** requirement was limited

DOI: 10.4018/978-1-61692-020-3.ch022

to finance. This old habit is still around – finance and accountancy still tend to be one department; controlling tends to be a little bit more holistic only. There is hardly any "Information Department" making all kind of **data** and **messages** into requisitely holistic **information** for business operation management (Afuah, 1998; Laudon et al., 2005; Potocan, 2005; Kelley, 2009).

It must serve a much innovated business management concept, which most authors briefs: from

Table 1. The selected level of holism and realism of consideration of the selected topic between the fictitious, requisite, and total holism and realism of approach and wholeness of insights, actions, and other outcomes

←--→		
Fictitious holism/realism (inside a single viewpoint)	Requisite holism/realism (a dialectical system of all essential viewpoints)	Total = real holism/realism (a system of all viewpoints)
Dangerous due to causing one-sided oversights along with partial insights based on specialization	Attainable, but depending on human choice of the essential viewpoints/professions from all possible, and their synergies	Ideal, but impossible to attain due to huge complexity of reality reaching beyond human capability

"make-and-sell", to "sense-and-respond", toward "anticipate-and-learn" (Afuah, 1998; Cohen, 2002; Barabba, 2004; Bernson, Standing, 2008). The new situation requires a new approach – "state of mind" that balances creativity and intuition with analytics and science (Afuah, 1998; Gunton, 1998; Brown, Duguid, 2000; Verma, Kapur, 2006; Curtis, Cobham, 2008).

Information management innovation is needed, and (requisitely) holistic thinking must be its background. The problem of the theory and practice of business informatics has lied in the target orientation aimed at requisite **business information** (Gunton, 1998; Anderson, 2000; Harmon, 2003; Laudon et al., 2007; Potocan, 2008). And in attempts to increase **holism** of information, we are facing two basic problems of data suitability, e.g. what is adequately target-oriented **information**; and how to create (and define) a suitable level of generalization of information, resulting from **data** and **messages**, in order to avoid **errors**.

We hence try to research more deeply **errors** in **information** systems and add to discussion about reliability three pointed-out topics: reality and captured data are not the same, decision-making takes place within a context, and only selected data are processed. We also try to contribute to discussion by thinking how can one tackle the data-to-information-to-decision process in order to diminish the number and weight of errors. Data recording errors follow earlier errors – data selection, and data selection basis and errors in it.

WHOLENESS OF INFORMATION SUPPORT FOR BUSINESS OPERATIONS

The Concept of Requisite Holism and Wholeness

Holism of human behavior has never been attainable, neither is wholeness of its outcomes if the word is taken completely literally like it is put in dictionaries: in them it includes every attribute, all attributes, and nothing (!) is left aside. All (!) professions (which tend to be several thousand) would have to be included. And this cannot be done. That's why Mulej and Kajzer introduced the law of requisite holism (Mulej, 1974; Mulej, Kajzer, 1998; Mulej et al, 2000; Mulej et al., 2003; Mulej et al., 2005; Mulej, 2007) to make the Mulej's concept of the Dialectical System (DS) clear and acceptable. It expresses the experience that one has the unavoidable habit to select the DS as a synergetic network of all crucial viewpoints to be considered, and to leave the others aside, or to reduce even more. Reductionism is both unavoidable and dangerous. See Table 1.

Selection of the crucial viewpoints and neglecting of other viewpoints of consideration is due to the decision-makers and their attributes as their subjective starting points that include—in synergy—both knowledge and emotions. The latter are expressed as values and may become culture, ethics, and norms.

Table 2. Circular interdependence of values, culture, ethics, and norms (VCEN)

Individual values (interdependent with knowledge)	↔	Culture = values shared by many, habits making them a round-off social group
↕		↕
Norms = prescribed values on right and wrong in a social group	↔	Ethics = prevailing values on right and wrong in a social group

Values, Culture, Ethics, and Norms and Their Impact over the Wholeness of Information Support for Business Operation

We mentioned dilemma about a requisitely holistic, dialectically systemic consideration of a synergetic entity made of norms, values, culture and ethics and their impact over the wholeness of information support for business operation (see Table 2) (See: Mulej, 1974; Mulej, Kajzer, 1998; Potocan, 1997; Mulej et al., 2000; Potocan, 2003; Mulej, 2007; Potocan, 2008; etc.).

How do we understand this synergetic entity? From business practice, we are persuaded that ethics is more a feeling than a part of the left-brain rationality/knowledge/skill. It enables us to distinguish right from wrong (Ulrich, 1997; Jennings, 2005; Shaw, 2007; etc.). Empirical researchers consider ethics a synergy of behaviors, which tend to be preferred in a society or community, as a social group, for long enough periods of time to become codified. Moral rules result, as a formal next step (Ulrich, 1997; Jennings, 2005; Shaw, 2007; etc.).

Rules co-create a culture, be it the one of social sub-groups, of organizational units, of organizations as wholes, or the one of regions, nations, social classes, professions (Mulej et al., 2003; Potocan, 2003; Mulej et al., 2005; Potocan, Kuralt, 2007; etc.). Thus, something, which is originally an individual attribute, comes to be objectified as a component of the objective conditions (i.e. outside the impact of tackled individuals). It becomes a part of broader requirements imposed over the individuals, and tends to return, in this

way, back to individuals as a part of their (socially obligatory!) values, i.e. their emotional perception of the objective needs or requirements and possibilities they face.

Thus it enters (or re-enters) the individual's starting points, which influence perception, definition of preferences, their realization in the form of goals, later on of tasks, of procedures of realizing the tasks, and achievements etc. It means that for any human activity ethics is equally essential as professional knowledge and skills, creativity and co-operatively. We have even found all of them mutually interdependent.

Thus, the prescribed norms result from values of the influential people, such as opinion leaders in the society at large, market, business organizations (or another organization all way from family to United Nations), and influence the less influential people, if the latter accept them. This acceptance or refusing or circumventing results from the influenced people's emotions, such as trust to the influential people, and/or knowledge causes their capability to comprehend the norms.

VCEN influence the selection of the Dialectical systems, including the content of the information support to decision and actions.

The Contents of Information Support, Its Holism and Wholeness

Globalization of the world economy puts competitive pressure over the businesses, requiring their high quality business operation, which can be significantly improved by management **innovation** providing a more holistic managerial and operational behavior. Management, be it innovated or outdated, determines the quality of the entire business. Business management uses **information** presenting important characteristics of the field dealt with, and its own and co-workers' knowledge, i.e. long-term information (from both the content and methodological aspects) (Potocan, 1997; Harmon, 2003; McLeod, Schell, 2003; Potocan, 2005; Baltzan, Phillips, 2008).

Information differs from **data**. Available **data** tend to be too many to become informative (= influential). Selection of data enables informing, which cannot attain full wholeness, but the requisite wholeness, hopefully. This requires an **information management innovation** (Potocan, 1997; Schultheis, Sumner, 1998; Anderson, 2000; Tichy, Cohen, 2002; Moss, 2004; Potocan, 2005; Bernson, Standing, 2008; Potocan, 2008). It results in the requisite wholeness of **information**. In business, it surfaces in and influences the basic business and other processes supporting the entire business.

Both non-economic and general economic **information** on business operation dealt with are needed in the business managers' economics-oriented decision making, and can be quantitative and/or qualitative. To run one's business operation well one, namely, needs all / requisite various **information** with which quantity, value, and quality (or any other important) characteristics of business are presented. Making and using **information** opens a variety of content, VCEN and methodology issues making it adequate (= providing requisite, wholeness, realism, applicability, and influence).

The business operation can be found adequate, when it is successful (efficient and effective in economic terms), respected (from the aspect of business behavior), and ethical (morally adequate from the aspect of a responsible attitude towards the social and natural environment). To make it so, the business operation managers need general information, too.

The majority of general information can have a direct or indirect impact on economics of business operation. For this reason, this **information** can be also a part of the economic information in the broadest sense of the word. Beside, there is also **information** that can be called non-economic information for business (such as law, technology, sociology, political trends, local, national, professional, and other cultures, values, ethics, norms, education, demographic trend, etc.). These include **messages**, **data**, or **information** that is not directly related to the business operation, or is not included in the management of the business operation dealt with, but of its environment. Because of its impact over economics of business operation this "non-economic" information can be called indirect economic information. Especially, under an open-system approach to business management it is included in requisite information and knowledge.

With all the briefed diversity, the problem of the theory and practice of business informatics, since its beginning, has lied in the target orientation aimed at requisite wholeness of economic information. In the past, information support to management was very often limited to the financial aspect of the economics business operation alone. Financial information does present an important subsystem of information and nothing more. The modern **business information** focuses on providing more / requisitely holistic information necessary for the business operation management. This is an important trend in **information management innovation**.

Herein we find the increased importance of the indirect economic information. It is difficult to treat because its definition is problematic. Its content can be objective and subjective: defined by processes events as well as by observers and decision makers.

The **information** is called objective, if it can be well defined and, therefore, well investigated on the basis of different quantitative units (e.g.: quantity, weight, value). Under equal conditions it is repeatable. But conditions can be subjectively selected, depending on the selected system of viewpoints (per professions, interests, etc.), and so can "objective" information. It tends to lack wholeness, which is precondition of total objectivity, for natural reasons:

- Nature has enormously many more attributes than humans can capture,
- There is no **information** without perception by observer/s, and
- Humans are neither able to know everything, nor to think of everything at the same time.

Reductionism is consequence of this limited human capacity, and it allows for depth and hinders **holism** of behavior and wholeness of insight and other outcomes. Therefore objectivity of reality is not limited, but objectivity of **data** and **information** is.

On the other hand, **information** that cannot be exactly defined is called subjective. As a rule, it is collected and examined by the application of various qualitative units, or even by application of descriptive criteria only, which cannot be measured in quantitative units. Reductionism results again, allowing for depth and hindering **holism** and wholeness. But now its presence is clear and admitted.

Thus, the **information** capacity of collected data and **messages** depends of the level of **holism** of the selected system of viewpoints of both the data providers and data collectors and processors. If their holism lacks, misinformation and / or disinformation can results from lack of wholeness of insight.

Therefore, in attempts to increase wholeness of information, we face two aspects of data suitability, i.e.:

- An adequately target-oriented information, and
- A suitable/requisite level of generalization of information, resulting from **data** and **messages**.

For the needs of the individual business operation (different kinds, types, and forms) and business operation in the individual areas of work (e.g. per business functions, or per projects), we need the **information** that is suitably conceived and created in accordance with the set goals of our work. On the other hand, we need different general information for each business operation, both for business participants to set goals and to realize them.

Information can be created on different levels of generalization resulting from requirements of the business management. The level of generalization can be in the interval between entirely general information and completely specific information. This fact brings us again to the issue of background of attainment of a selected level of **holism**/wholeness. It is essential for **information** to be reliable rather than misinformation or disinformation.

Creation of requisite wholeness of information provides content, which serves as a basis for the consideration of the informational support to business. Though, such **information** provides only for the basic, but not for the sufficient precondition for the informational support to business to attain requisite wholeness. The other basic precondition of understanding and application of **information** consists of creation and use of a suitable information infrastructure as a component of wholeness of business intelligence.

All these and similar issues allow for the conclusion that the attainment of wholeness of information faces entanglement.

Entanglement of Provision of Requisite Wholeness of Information Support for Business

Let us now spend a few minutes with the issue of entanglement (Mulej et al., 2000; Potocan, 2003; Mulej et al., 2005; Potocan, 2005; Mulej, 2007; Potocan, 2008; etc.).

The concepts of entanglement are not always precisely defined, on one hand. On the other hand, there also appears the question how to manage/ master entangled phenomena as economically as possible and, at the same time, successfully - effectively and efficiently.

What are both theoretical and practical issues of entanglement? We are more interested in the process than in the structure and in **holism** of consideration than in its partiality (one-sidedness).

The entanglement has been increasing since the existence of life on earth. However, one also knows of the need for a more detailed consideration of entanglement. If one does not consider both synergies and details, one risks oversimplification and important oversights, as a result, which may cause entangled consequences.

We can hardly choose between levels of entanglement of reality. The choice we have is rather between the entanglement of consideration / investigation / management of reality and the entanglement of their consequences. It is probably logical to find it more beneficial to devote most of our attention to the phenomena of entanglement in order to avoid complicated and/or complex consequences:

- When we discuss the details concerning an individual component of an entity under investigation, then we can talk about the entanglement of the type complicatedness. It can also be defined as the entanglement based of the characteristics of the components and present a part of the real characteristics of phenomena, which have different components / parts. The greater is the variety of components, the higher is also the level of complicatedness and vice versa. Synergies do not count.

- With concentration on the characteristics, which result from mutual influences between the components of an entity (and their background - basically their interdependence) we deal with the entanglement called complexity. It shows the characteristics of phenomena, which differ in struc-

tures and synergies from their components alone. Their structure is formed by a number of different types, varieties and forms of relations between the components inside the systems and with their environment. The greater is the variety of relations, the higher is also the level of complexity and vice versa. Synergies are central and critical. Attributes of components are found less important.

Both entanglements exist in reality, of course. There can, therefore, be a number of their various contents. A similar conclusion holds of the variants concerning the level of entanglement of both types which is, very often, bigger in reality than in a usual consideration (also in a scientific one). When examining the phenomena, the following can be achieved, hence: (in one extreme) totality, (in the other extreme) zero-level, or (between both extremes) a requisite level, of consideration of characteristics of phenomena. It all depends on our selection of a viewpoint / viewpoints / system or network of viewpoints / dialectical system of all essential and only essential viewpoints.

In our consideration of entanglement, we additionally encounter the problems of how to define a requisite entanglement of our examination. But this issue exceeds frames of this contribution.

How do discussed characteristics impact consideration of **reliability of information** in the case of business information?

RELIABILITY OF INFORMATION

Failure to inform depends on more entangled processes than the ones offered as their first and, of course, simplified approximation quoted by Eli B. Cohen, and aimed at provoking our thinking (Cohen, 2002; see also Tichy, Cohen, 2002; McLeod, Schell, 2003; Laudon et al., 2007) in his book. We used Cohen's book as a base for our discussion, but his cognitions are very similar to cognitions of other authors on reliability of **business information** in last 30 years (See also: Schultheis, Sumner, 1998; Verma, Kapur, 2006; Laudon et al., 2007; Kelley, 2009; etc.). Two tables adapted from Cohen's book (Cohen, 2002) (3 and 4 below) say so:

We see an essential part of entanglement to be added in the following facts, at least (Mulej et al., 2003; Potocan, 2003; Potocan, 2005; Mulej, 2007; Potocan, 2008):

- Which part of attributes of reality does one consider? In a business case, the same business reality can provide basis for different pictures of reality, if it is watched from the viewpoints of e.g. book keeping, marketing, sales, supplies, technology for the daily routine, technology research, development, **innovation** (which can be of many kinds – from technology to culture and management style etc.), human resources, organizational culture, private relations along with the official ones inside the company or with its business, social or natural environments, legal situation (which again can be of many kinds – from business and employment contracts to punishable actions), etc.

- Which part of possible data does one record? In a business case, they can have to do with all the above realities or some of them; they can depict their past, present, or future situations, their local, regional, national, or international situation, their situation in terms of the stage in their process of unfolding, their situation in terms of availability and eligibility of qualitative and/or quantitative data, their situation in terms of computer support to recording or another technology, etc.

- Which contents can the processing of selected data have? In a business case, they can have to do with all the above realities and possible recording types, and add to

them very different levels of e.g. depth and/or breadth of insight; further routine processing or creative processing can be added, all the way to **innovation**, or perhaps to manipulation leading to misinformation or des-information, which can tackle co-workers, managers, owners, or competitors, government, etc.

- Who is the decision-maker? In a business case, these may be managers and/or owners. But it is not realistic enough, if one thinks of them only: everybody makes his or her decision every moment (including decisions such as: »I am going to have a cigarette now / later«, or »I am going to toilet now / later«, »It is time to go home«, »It is time to work harder«, »I will read / not read this message / I may read it later«, »I will make a / no suggestion«, »I will be passive / active about the company problems«, etc.).

- Do decision-makers acknowledge that complexity of business has grown and most attributes of the life reality in business have changed, while the need to make good decisions has not changed? A simplified, e.g. quantified, model of reality can hardly be realistic enough for good, i.e. requisitely holistic and realistic decisions, and resulting actions.

- Do decision-makers admit that problems are to reality what atoms are to tables, and we experience tables, not atoms? Problems are abstracted from experience by analysis. We do not experience individual problems, but complete systems (= complex entities) of those that are strongly interacting. Most authors call them messes. Defining them is the first step of real problem solving.

- How do decision-makers deal with the old proverb "What you see depends on where you sit in an organization", i.e. the multiple and diverse viewpoints and resulting insights into the same fact, causing (very)

Table 3. The simple three-stage framework of information delivery

Data → Processing of data → Information

Table 4. Expanded framework on information delivery

Reality → Data recording → Processing of selected data → Decision maker ← context Error types: I. Data recording, II. Process Stage, III. Decision Making

different assessments of fact resulting in (very) different conclusions? ("Everyone's eyes have their own painter", an old proverb says.)

- How do decision-makers deal with the experience that the "information asymmetry" makes you know a part of reality better than your counterparts do, while making you blind for another part / many other parts (your business partners, including your staff, may distrust you and fail to disclose their **information** to you).

- How do decision-makers perceive, understand and assess context of their decision-making / thinking / action? All the above varieties may enter the scene, and make a long set of very different synergies. Very different **information** may result.

- How do decision-makers consider the fact that totally holistic information (i.e. knowing everything) is impossible, and they must base their decisions on assumption about reality and its future? How do they use imagination to make realistic strategies? How do they select the essential from the less essential data / viewpoints / **information** / insights / knowledge?

- How do decision-makers tackle the fact that managing today includes a lot of **innovation** / transformation of e.g. way of interaction with customers, way of formulation of problems internally, way of imaging the future – in order to make a

difference, hence to survive in globalize competition? How is informing adapted to this rather new fact?

We do not say that Cohen's Tables 3 and 4 are not O.K (Cohen, 2002). We are just following his suggestion to think more deeply about **errors** in informing systems to add to his quoted three pointed-out topics:

- Reality and captured data are not the same,
- Decision-making takes place within a context, and
- Only selected data are processed.

He is right: »decision-making is only indirectly influenced by reality; there are many steps that separate reality from the decision-making process«. On this basis he wants to apply »this framework as a means to organize the types of **errors** that lead (information) systems to misinform their clients«.

We want to contribute by thinking in another direction: how can one tackle the data-to-information-to-decision-to-action process in order to diminish the number and weight of errors. Data recording errors follow earlier **errors** in data selection, and in data selection basis.

We will follow the concept depicted in Table 5 (Mulej et al., 2003; Mulej et al., 2005; Potocan, 2008; etc.).

For decision makers to use a requisitely holistic approach and thus to attain requisite wholeness

Table 5. Dependence of the errors on the decision-makers' approach

Errors to be detected, classified, and prevented or removed	
Non-Essential errors (with no-critical consequences)	Essential errors (with important consequences)
↓↑	↓↑
No over-biased / too one-sided / too partial / too poorly holistic approach, but requisite holism reaching sufficient holism of decision makers in any step of the entire process from setting criteria for watching reality and collecting data all way to the final (business) decision and action – caused by no crucial lack of specialists' interdisciplinary co-operation	Biased / one-sided / too partial / too poorly holistic approach reaching insufficient holism of decision makers in any step of the entire process from setting criteria for watching reality and collecting data all way to the final (business) decision and action – caused by a crucial lack of specialists' interdisciplinary co-operation
↑↓	↑↓
Selection and application of subjective starting points following the Dialectical Systems Theory and Standardized Decision-Making Model	Selection and application of subjective starting points not following the Dialectical Systems Theory and Standardized Decision-Making Model, but a one-sided / single-disciplinary approach

of their decisions and actions, knowledge of one single profession and use of one single viewpoint can suffice only exceptionally. The given reality is too entangled. Thus, creative interdisciplinary cooperation is often unavoidable. Though, specialists tend to learn to be specialists rather than to intentionally and carefully listen to humans who disagree with them and thus tend to help them attain requisite wholeness.

SOME CRUCIAL CONSEQUENCES OF ERROS IN INFORMATION

A rather overseen cause of errors in **information** has to do with one-sidedness resulting from ownership. Many talk about ownership/property without defining it. We hear that, by definition, private ownership/property is more efficient and effective than the state/social/public one, but we do not hear on which criteria this opinion is based. Is the ancient Rom ownership/property from slavery times at stake? Or is the definition from the management literature and practice calling sometimes the subordinates 'process owners' and it means they are responsible for the process they are in charge to run? If they are responsible, to whom and on which criteria they are responsible and working well? Etc.

Now the 2008- crisis has provided to humankind the **information** that we have been working, as humankind, in so very wrong ways that we are making the mere existence of the current civilization of our-selves questionable. Hence, the question of ownership/property and its definition is no longer a simple academic one. Owners decide. »What is good for the big companies is good for the country in which they reside and are owned«. Thus, they decide also about the country and its measure of good and bad, right and wrong, which are in principle common to all humans.

The often overseen data that should become **information** include the real, broader, more systemic meaning of **data** called GDP (Gross Domestic Product). It is the most applied information about economic success and has been so over the two centuries of the industrial phase of humankind's existence. It is supposed to provide **information** about the economic basis of human well-being, i.e. success. This used to make sense, because before the industrialization phase the wealth of humankind had been growing at the rate of three percent (3%) per millennium until 1820, while it grew for 5500% in the industrial two centuries after 1820; (Targowsky, 2009). This enormous growth has crucial ecological consequences, but there is no ecological information system (Gomes, 2009; Abu-Shanab, and Al-Tarawneh, 2009). This, perhaps, has not been a serious error in **information** system two centuries ago, but it is so today.

Over the recent decades, after the 2nd world war, the human population has grown 2,5 times and the production, including the exploitation of the planet Earth and its natural resources and preconditions of humankind survival, has grown 7 (seven) times (Plut, 2009). In one single year around 2000 the addition GDP of the world was bigger than the entire GDP of 1900 (Brown, 2008; Korten, 2009; Taylor, 2008; etc.). But the planet Earth did not grow bigger, but depleted – actually, our own natural preconditions of life got depleted. Many researchers are warning: this can last no longer, so do the above cited ones. The industrial paradigm of the socio-economic life has helped humankind over the recent two centuries, but it is ruining humankind now, and has done so for several recent decades. It must change into another paradigm, with which humankind will be able to survive. **Innovation** may no longer be only technological for the same socio-economic paradigm, which needs **innovation** of its own essence.

This is possible. Science has created means of engineering and social technologies for humans to enjoy a new paradigm and survive, once they decide to change/innovate their own habits. This tackles the influential ones, first of all, of course. The big majority is adaptive to them anyway. Thus, the point is: are the influential ones free-riders of cooperative? Under the power of free-riders, the exploitation of the nature and related humans in processes of so far will go on and ruin humankind, leaving a dying-out planet Earth to our children and grandchildren, not to some distant-time generations to come.

The right information, thus, exist, but it is blocked off from application by a wrong information.

Over the same recent decades the world has accepted the dictatorship of the Chicago school of neo-liberal economics (Toth, 2008; etc.). Hence, the liberalistic economic theory of Adam Smith was out of scene. Market stopped being a competition-place and became the power-place of monopolistic owners replacing the real competitors allowing for a full insight into their business that was local and included personal responsibility of the owners, having no share-holding or limited-liability companies dividing rights from obligations and obscuring the business. One speaks about an un-complete competition, officially.

Humankind has three options to choose from:

1. To go on like over the industrial period, although the practiced model has been introduced when the amount of humans and exploitation of the planet Earth used to be equal to a tiny fragment of the amount of today. This practice will ruin the natural preconditions of human survival of the current civilization in a few years, a few decades at best.

2. To undertake measures like those in 2008- and 2009-, when governments and companies have been moving chairs around the deck of the Titanic vessel facing the iceberg, rather than radical shifting their direction to avoid the iceberg. The consequences will be the same as with the option one, perhaps a few years later. Our children and grandchildren will receive a dying planet Earth rather than a life of well-being.

3. To radically innovate the practices of so far to add sufficiency to efficiency, including replacing the official measures like GDP and alike with the one of human happiness. How can this be done?

Over the same recent decades, tacitly and step-by-step in literature and political documents of United Nations, European Union and some international businesses' unions, social responsibility was added to owners' responsibility. If the ownership/property concept of the ancient Roman law's definition that ownership means the owner's right to use and abuse the owned property (including the dependent humans such as employees etc.) was still up-to-date rather than obsolete and dangerous for humankind, such documents would not exist and be popular (Google shows on the website 'social responsibility' several millions of contributions.). Neither these documents nor the concept of social responsibility would be necessary. They basically require the end of abuse of power of the owners/companies over their subordinates/employees/co-workers, business partners, broader society, and natural preconditions of humankind's survival. Obviously, the concept of sustainability is integrated into the social responsibility. The latter is very much integrated into criteria of the European Award for Business excellence. There are also authors viewing social responsibility as the humankind's way to the world peace. Thus, social responsibility reaches very far beyond charity to which it used to be confined in the older perceptions, which are still very much around and making sense, but only as a small part of the concept.

The ancient Roman law's concept of ownership is being innovated in line with the management's concept of 'process owners' providing for the right to use with no right to abuse one's property, if this causes damage to people directly or via nature. Its point is the humankind's survival.

On the other hand, if the monopolistic companies and societies' owners liked social responsibility and its revolutionary enlargement of 'process owners' concept to all owners and humans, the definition of social responsibility would, e.g. in the European Union's document of 2001 not be limited to companies and to their free will. Social responsibility is namely said to include responsible behavior beyond legislation, rather than being included in law.

Thus, the need for social responsibility is enormous, and so are obstacles to it. For the first time in human history, the entire humankind, rather than some local small groups of people, is in danger of extinction. And for the first time in history, owners are no longer permitted any abuse, but must require from them-selves what

they require from their subordinates. Horizons are growing broader.

Hopefully, the process of **innovation** of the values, culture, ethics, and norms of the most influential part of humankind will not take too long.

On the other hand, the industrial period has produced knowledge for humans to avoid the briefly annotated problems, once the power-holding owners of the world innovate their habits from greed to needs only, reducing wants to real needs. If USA e.g. invested the money in their domestic production of solar and wind energy instead of investing in the war for oil from the Middle East, USA could export energy, along with covering all their own needs for energy for housing, production, transportation etc.

If the world power-owners agreed that the national and international law do not cover and solve all humankind's problems, but a supra-national world-wide law, constitution, and government is also necessary, but limited to the most general needs of humankind and made of honest and holistic thinker and decision-makers rather than bureaucrats, the current problems would also be solvable.

In other words, the information about the 2008- crisis is an error with crucial consequences. The 2008- crisis is no banking and real-estate crisis only, but a deep crisis of the industrial socio-economic concept that used to be very helpful over three decades and has become very detrimental over the recent decades. It is a crisis of ownership/property being defined as the 'right to use and abuse', which means that it is a crisis of one-sided rather than holistic, or requisitely holistic, at least, behavior (made of monitoring, reflecting, thinking, emotional and spiritual life, decision making, communication, and action). It is a crisis of using so one-side measures of success that people causing accidents and sending people to hospital are statistically found more beneficial to humankind than people producing their own salad in their own garden with their own seeds and buying nothing in the market. This one-sidedness causes humankind to subsidize making of our own air, water and found poisonous for a tiny minority of humans to earn big money, while 85% of humankind live on less than six US$ a day (in India the poverty line is even at ten US$ a month per person).

The right of irresponsibility and the right of abuse are so dangerous, that a socio-economic innovation must take place to make human behavior more holistic by adding broad and long-term criteria to narrow-minded and short-term criteria of behavior, especially of the most influential humans. In other words: social responsibility may not remain a free-will option, neither may the right of irresponsibility and abuse survive for humankind to survive.

The rights of irresponsibility and abuse have been too dangerous for millennia to be allowed to survive any longer. They destroyed the slavery and feudal times, but not they brought comparable socio-economic relations back. For selfish reasons, humans must become less selfish and stop hating their fellow-humans, them-selves and their children and grandchildren in need of a healthy nature and life style.

Humankind needs a new economic and legal paradigm aimed at **holism** rather than one-sidedness of behavior. This includes new criteria of economic success exposing efficiency and sufficiency, real need rather than greed, wellbeing and happiness, humans as part of nature rather than unlimited masters over nature, sustainable future, not only sustainable development, including a sustainable present time. The revolution is made of **innovation** of values, culture, ethics, and norms, while the revolution in producing and social technology is around and provides all we need to become happy rather than desperate – once the decisive power-holding owners are willing to accept that the new paradigm of requisite holism under the name of social responsibility must unavoidable replace the obsolete industrial paradigm. Otherwise, humankind has a very black future very close in time to come.

SOME CONCLUSIONS

Modern business environments require innovated business concepts. Meeting new requirements concerning enterprises' functioning depends also on creation and implementation of appropriate information support. For centuries information requirements of enterprises were primarily limited to finance. In modern environment enterprises need **information management innovation**; holistic thinking must be its background for action to attain requisite wholeness.

Information support and **information** must be reliable to not be misinformation. Reliability of both is crucial for quality of business. Over the recent decades technological innovations improved acquisition, distribution and application of business information. Less has been done for assurance of quality of contents of business **information**, aimed at requisitely holistic behavior and resulting requisite wholeness of attainment of business goals definition and realization. The available technological solutions concerning informatics technology (hardware, software, communications, or data bases) must hence be completed up with non-technological **innovation**s (e.g. Creation of Requisitely Holistic Management Information). They can enable more **reliability of information**'s contents.

Reliability of **business information** can be improved, if one understands, considers and realizes business process requisitely holistically, because information serves it. Requisite holism and wholeness can essentially contribute to its reliability. Hence at matters one tackles the data-to-information-to-decision process in order to diminish the number and weight of **errors**. Data recording errors follow earlier errors – data selection, data collection and errors in their backgrounds.

A requisite contents' reliability of **business information** depends on (dialectical) systems thinking and business cybernetics, which have been to poorly apply so far in this context.

REFERENCES

Abu-Shanab, E., & Al-Tarawneh, H. (2009). Production Information Systems Usability. In Martins do Amaral, A. (Ed.), *M. Cruz-Cunha, E. Qintela Varajào* (pp. 43–53). Ofir, Portugal: CENTERIS.

Afuah, A. (1998). *Innovation Management*. Oxford, UK: Oxford University Press.

Anderson, D. (2000). *Managing Information Systems*. New York: Prentice Hall.

Baltzan, P., & Phillips, A. (2008). *Business Driven Information Systems*. New York: McGraw-Hill/Irwin.

Barabba, V. (2004). *Surviving Transformation: Lessons from GM's Surprising Turnaround*. Oxford, UK: Oxford University Press.

Bernson, S., & Standing, C. (2008). *Information Systems: A Business Approach*. New York: John Wiley and Sons.

Brown, J., & Duguid, P. (2000). *The Social Life of Information*. Boston: Harvard Business Press.

Brown, R. (2008). *Plan B 3.0, Mobilizing to Save Civilization*. New York: Earth Policy Institute.

Cohen, E. (Ed.). (2002). *Challenges of Information Technology Education in the 21st Century*. Hershey, PA: Idea Group Publishing.

Collins, J. (2001). *Why some companies make the leap... and others don't*. Sydney, Australia: Random House.

Curtis, G., & Cobham, D. (2008). *Business Information Systems: Analysis, Design, and Practice*. New York: Financial Times Management.

Daft, R. (2003). *Management*. New York: Dryden Press.

Florida, R. (2002). *The Rise of the Creative Class*. New York: Basic Books.

Gomez, M. (2009). Corporate Environmental Management Information Systems - The next Generation . In *Abu-Shanab, unpublished introductory talk with power-point transparencies*. Ofir, Portugal: CENTERIS.

Gunton, T. (1998). *Infrastructure: Building a Framework for Corporate Information Handling*. New York: Prentice Hall.

Harmon, P. (2003). *Business Process Change*. San Francisco: Morgan Kaufmann.

Jennings, M. (2005). *Business: Its Legal, Ethical and Global Environment*. Brentford: South-Western.

Kelley, G. (Ed.). (2009). *Selected Readings on Information Technology Management*. Hershey, PA: IGI Global.

Korten, S. (2009). *Agenda for a New Economy*. San Francisco: Berrett-Koehler.

Laudon, K., Laudon, J., & Laudon, K. (2005). *Management Information Systems*. New York: Prentice Hall.

Laudon, K., Laudon, J., & Laudon, K. (2007). *Essentials of Management Information Systems*. New York: Prentice Hall.

McLeod, R., & Schell, G. (2003). *Management Information Systems*. New York: Prentice Hall.

Moss, T. (2004). *Reliability Data Handbook*. New York: ASME.

Mulej, M. (1974). The Dialectical Theory . In *Slovene*. Ljubljana, Slovenia: University of Ljubljana.

Mulej, M. (et al.) (2000). *Basic of Systems Theory*. Maribor, Slovenia: FEB.

Mulej, M. (at al.). (2003). Informal systems thinking or systems theory. *Cybernetics and Systems*, 34(2), 71–92. doi:10.1080/01969720302868

Mulej, M. (2007). Systems theory: A worldview and/or a methodology aimed at requisite holism/realism of humans' thinking, decisions and action. *SRBS*, *24*(3), 347–357.

Mulej, M., & Kajzer, S. (1998). Ethics of Interdependence and the Law of Requisite Holism . In Rebernik, M., & Mulej, M. (Eds.), *STIQE '98* (pp. 56–67). Maribor, Slovenia: ISR.

Mulej, M., Likar, B., & Potocan, V. (2005). Increasing the capacity of companies to absorb inventions from research organizations and encouraging people to innovate. *Cybernetics and Systems*, *36*(5), 491–512. doi:10.1080/01969720590944276

Plut, D. (2009). *Planet in Slovenija pred izzivi globalizacije in sonaravnega razvoja*. Ljubljana, Slovenia: University of Ljubljana.

Potocan, V. (1997). A New Perspectives on Business Decision Making. *Management*, *2*(1), 13–24.

Potocan, V. (2003). *Business Organization*. Maribor, Slovenia: DOBA.

Potocan, V. (2005). Holistic information support for virtual business organization. *Journal of business and economics research*, *3*(11), 25-36.

Potocan, V. (2008). Reliability of information . In Engemann, K., & Lasker, G. (Eds.), *Advances in decision technology and intelligent information systems* (*Vol. 9*, pp. 21–25). Windsor, Ontario: IIAS.

Potocan, V., & Kuralt, B. (2007). Synergy in business: Some new suggestions. *The Journal of American Academy of Business*, *12*(11), 199–204.

Schultheis, R., & Sumner, M. (1998). *Management Information System*. Boston: McGraw Hill.

Shaw, W. (2007). *Business Ethics*. New York: Wadsworth Publishing.

Targowsky, A. (2009). *How to Transform the Information Infrastructure of Enterprises into Sustainable, Global-oriented and to Monitor and Predict the Sustainability of Civilization. Unpublished introductory talk with power-point transparencies, CENTERIS 2009*. Portugal: Ofir.

Taylor, G. (2008). *Evolution's Edge: The Coming Collapse and Transformation of our World*. Gabriola Island: New Society Publishers.

Tichy, N., & Cohen, E. (2002). *Leadership Engine*. New York: Harper.

Toth, G. (2008). *Resnično odgovorno podjetje (in Slovene)*. Ljubljana: GV.

Ulrich, P. (1997). *Integrative Wirtschaftsethik*. Berlin: Paul Haupt.

Verma, A., & Kapur, P. (Eds.). (2006). *Quality, Reliability and Information Technology*. Oxford, UK: Alpha Science.

Chapter 23
The Social Cost of Social Value Creation:
An Exploratory Inquiry into the Ambivalent Nature of Complex Information Technology Intensive Firms

Jonatan Jelen
Parsons the New School for Design, USA

Marko Kolakovic
University of Zagreb, Croatia

ABSTRACT

Google, eBay, Amazon, Facebook, Myspace, Craig's List and their foreign equivalents, such as the Chinese QQ and Baidu, for example, are ostensibly complex, and – more troublesome - their attitudes are becoming increasingly contradictory, controversial, and conflicted: For one, Tom Malone's decade-old predictions of a decentralized network of a multitude of small, cooperating firms did not materialize; to the contrary and counter to the spirit of the democratic nature of information and information technology, these e-giants are defining their own industries and defying regulation, submitting the participants in their respective markets to proprietary rules via three central tenets: regulatory capture, regulatory arbitrage, and regulatory opportunism. In the present critical chapter the authors explore these traits of the Complex Information Technology-Intensive firms and formulate elements of a framework for their ambiguous nature that may lead to social cost exceeding their initially glorified social value creation.

INTRODUCTION

Our object of inquiry are information technology-intensive firms that are also 'complex' system, serving multiple constituencies with multiple objectives, their existence as networks is virtual, they are modular or even incomplete firms with mostly only fractional functionalities compared to the traditional Porterian value-chain model, their user constituencies are fragmented and mostly not the paying clients, the metrics to measure the attainment of their goals are based on unobservables and rather difficult if not impossible to quantify and capture. They are community-based, social

DOI: 10.4018/978-1-61692-020-3.ch023

value-oriented, and network-centric models. Of an entirely new character, they do not merely represent a form of speciation or evolution from previous models. In order to configure and sustainably maintain such volatile and inherently unstable social networking models tremendous amounts of intentional and deliberate intelligent design is required. This is especially true when – as is the case with those types of firms - the variables strategy, structure, scale, scope, and social position have been radically deconstructed, reconfigured, and reconstructed in truly Schumpeterian spirit of creative destruction. Indeed those firms are not merely some adaptive evolution with a change in degree from some previous state but represent a radical departure from the original design of firms with a new nature altogether.

Insofar our perspective is different from previous treatments of the subject: While much of the literature concerned with this aspect of IT since the mid 1990s deals with the pragmatic impact of information technology on organizational design, and primarily remains concerned with epistemic problems and transactional aspects: their focus is on structuration issues, harnessing the potential of information technology through optimization, and the impact of IT on firms' activities, decision making processes and management effectiveness (see for example Brynjolfsson & Hitt 1997, and Brynjolfsson, et al. 1994), on one hand, and the necessary attributes to function under the new environmental conditions brought about by IT on the other (see Huber, 2003). Others have been concerned with the fragmented, partial, fractional, and modular nature of firms morphing into network structures (see Brusoni & Tronchetti-Provera, 2005). And yet an entirely separate issue was the effect of IT on markets (e.g. Varian, 2001, and Varian et al., 2004). Our concern, however, is ontological and explores the very reason for existence of such firms, their new nature, their fundamentally redefined character as productive elements of the economic complex. Indeed, they

are a new breed of firms that represent a paradigmatic change but with paradoxical consequences.

They are designed sui generis, ex nihilo, ex ante, and de novo: The design variables strategy, structure, scale, scope and social position are used at the opposed and of the spectrum of their initial meaning. For example strategy is not competitive but cooperative; structure is not bureaucratic-hierarchical but network-flat, scope is not driven by transaction cost, but by transaction profits; size is not a quantified measure, but a qualitative result of dominance; finally, the social position of the firm is not across the table of its users, consumers, and clients, but implicates them as partners in a collaborative way to co-produce and co-generate the products, experiences, and content. The resulting entirely new business models of social networks, transmutability (Arakji & Lang 2007; Hughes & Lang 2005), and community models, do not evolve organically, however. Unlike traditional industrial firms that coalesced around different technologies by carefully designing the management control structures as the integrative mechanisms, the new firms require an a priori conceptual design and configuration of the above five variables much like the blueprint for an architecture.

This paradigmatic distinctiveness, however, comes with a series of paradoxes: strategy and structure of these firms are becoming increasingly controversial as is the anecdotal ambition of Google for 'organizing the world's knowledge'. The scaling and scoping of their activities to monopoly status and single-firm dominant industry position increasingly contradicts the original aspirations for an atomized and consequently democratized network of equal participants. And since pursuing social goals with economic means was never straight forward they seem increasingly conflicted with their for-profit model for social value generation; unlike taxation, Google's redistribution of income and revenue between different constituencies is devoid of formal authority.

And a further combination of these three paradoxes could result in social cost outweighing the social benefits of the paradigm shift towards a new nature of those firms. And while their existence is certainly a result of creative destruction, their actions would prove contradicting the Schumpeterian spirit of increased competitiveness for the benefit of productive capacity and efficacy.

METHODOLOGY

In the present exploratory paper we propose elements of a framework that captures three important components responsible for the resulting ambivalent nature of these firms. Methodologically our approach is a composite of (a) an empirical (grounded-theory) approach based on several dozens of semi-structured interviews with high-profile professional and practitioners in the larger New York metropolitan business community in the context of a larger inquiry into "the new nature of the firm" that we have been conducting since early 2007; (b) an exploratory inquiry based on observable behaviors of these firms as publicly traded entities followed by Wall Street analysts; and (c) a critical conceptual study exposing the unobservable context and suggesting new theoretical developments with regards to the unanticipated consequences of such ambivalent nature of the said Complex Information Technology-Intensive firms.

The Contradiction in Scale and Scope

Originally, at the advent of the digital age, we may have expected the notion of size to lose its importance. Size as a protection against environmental turbulence and contested market share became overrated. The nature of IT was utterly different form the previous technologies of transformation, transportation, energy-generation, energy-distribution, coordination, and communication. Unlike information that simply exists (in its own right), previous technologies only existed when

they manifested themselves, when they were practiced; and the more they were practiced the more credible their existence, i.e. economics of scale were important. A notable property of information is, however, is that it is in fact independent of its practice. Information doesn't have to be practical to exist.

Yet, the prominent forms of our newly proposed category are all but indifferent to size and scale. While traditionally firms were either part of the problem, or part of the solution, or part of the landscape, they can now be either

- the entire landscape or
- move the landscape altogether. So, Amazon, Google, and eBay did not content themselves to being yet another player in their respective industries; they became the entire market respectively, inviting everyone else to join and participate. Apple single-handedly changed the way music will be enjoyed in the future.

The organic logic of the network has thus been undone. Similar to the notion of market makers, several firms realized the advantage of actually themselves becoming and being networks. The network effect has thus become captive of individual firms quickly stepping up and internalizing network effects. And they didn't do it by chance or accidental evolution, they did it by intelligent design to do just that. Amazon had over-engineered their capacity from the early beginning in order to not have to struggle and incur risks with incremental adaptation later.

Ronald Coase informed institutional economics in 1937 of the true substance of the firm: it's ability to arbiter transaction *costs* which markets couldn't. (See also the subsequent work by Williamson, 1981, and Williamson & Winter, 1991, ultimately resulting in what is called New Institutionalism). The CITI firms have not only substituted this concepts with transaction *profits* (e.g. eBay), but moreover expanded it to a level where scope becomes an instantaneous decision, not a deliberate, incremental process.

The CITI firms

- have demonstrated their ability to morph from single company models to markets in their own right at will and nearly instantaneously, all the while passing through stages of intermediary, infomediary, and aggregator, to name just a few prominent e-business and e-commerce positions (e.g. Amazon as a bookseller and as a business enabler for a myriad of smaller booksellers and individuals who want to recycle their used books but can't afford the fixed cost in marketing expenditure for their e-commerce presence);
- can hop from industry to industry and between industries at will and almost instantaneously (e.g. Google's search engine activities, yet also the G1 phone, and the recently reported aspirations to generate green electricity; Facebook is a platform for users to produce themselves with other users but quickly become an essential tool for job seekers, employers, and recruiters for various purposes with respect to sourcing and hiring issues);
- escape definitions and notions that tie them to a particular industry and thus potentially avoid the associated regulations and constraints (e.g. Craig's List that only recently and under only under political and ethical pressure accorded to policing their immorally solicitive personal ads).

Such radical redefinitions with respect to scale and scope are worrisome for several reasons:

- The all-fixed-cost-zero-variable-cost characteristic of digital production that so easily results in a near-natural monopoly argument for single-firm digital industries dangerously justifies conglomerates of un-

precedented levels of power and control. While their size may not be easily quantifiable in accounting and financial terms their impact on our everyday lives is profound. And while many aspects of their activities and their existence enrich our lives tremendously, it remains that their sole existence and the lack of market space for alternative options predicate our lives in unpredictable ways as well.

- The ease to morph from market forms to intermediary model to single integrated company can preempt many an attempt at innovation and improvement by new entrants. The barrier to entry can be raised indefinitely and to insurmountable heights, and potentially more effective and efficient solutions can be kept form the public discretionarily.
- Finally, the intensity of competition is raised beyond rivalry. All that counts is to occupy enough of a market space that includes the tipping point; such competition in the early stages before the merit of any technology is identifiable is highly skewed and can result in entirely unjustified early technological choices with uncertain and unpredictable consequences.

The Controversy With Regards To Strategy and Structure

Much is being written and analyzed with regards to CITI firms' strategic and structural ambitions. They appear grounded in cooperation or co-opetition at the least, their structures are open and accommodative, they are engaging and integrative with respect to their fellow market participants. Yet, of less prominent nature is the agenda of their strategies and structures vis-à-vis the regulator. In there lies the real value of analysis.

CITI firms spend a disproportionate amount of energy dedicated to influencing and manipulating their legal and regulatory environment. They do so in three particular ways:

- At the most intense level, they exhibit a rightout hostile attitude translating in so called regulatory capture, a term first introduced by Joseph Stigler (1971):
  - As the CITI firms assure to grow intensely and extensively so as to become their own industry they concomitantly refocus much of the regulatory energy onto them. But the novelty, velocity, and ingenuity of their activities overwhelms even the most imaginative regulators quickly as was evidenced by the recent Craig's List scandal and the associated belated reaction on the part of authorities to curtail the immoral and rightout illegal soliciting prostitution.
  - With their particular version of market dominance they have distorted the construct of monopolistic competitions by taking it to an entirely unprecedented level, even more extreme than monopoly. At least in the traditional model, the monopolist's freedom to make discretionary decisions was counterbalanced by the demand decisions of consumers. The monopolist's decision therefore was still limited to Marginal Supply = Marginal Revenue. With their controlling position over the entire network, however, the CITI firms are not bound by this limitation. They can ultimately sidestep it by proposing their own currency, such as in the famous Amazon gift certificate cases. While competition is certainly not the panacea to many of the traditional lack of capacity to innovation, so neutralized regulatory efforts, concentration of market power, and control of creative

initiative (such as Amazon's Kindle and the associated proprietary system software and enhanced Digital Rights Management, for example) nevertheless reduce competitiveness bar beyond what might be considered beneficial competition. This may result in social cost by what was prevented from being created or what was created suboptimally without there being appropriate oversight or stimulating competing activity.

- Of lesser nominal intensity, but nevertheless heightened level of aggression are the CITI firms' efforts with regards to regulatory arbitrage. These represent a veritable assault on established institutional legal standards through either aggressive expansion of the law (such as the intellectual property protection mechanisms to patent business methods, preventing many transactions in e-commerce) or sheer sidestepping of the law (such as in contractual disputes, ignoring the rule of *due process*).
  - We define regulatory arbitrage as the exploit as yet unrealized opportunities resulting from some information-technological asymmetry.
  - One such example is the accelerated enforcement of contractual obligations and the punitive character of contractual terminations with so called shrinkwrap or clickwrap contracts in the interest of expedience and efficiency. The age old rule of *due process* requiring court-based proceedings for breach of contract is rendered ineffective and firms self-manage contract issues.
  - Another example is the restrictions on fair use by digital rights management practices lobbied into law through the Digital Copyright Millenium Act

(signed into law by President Bill Clinton on October 28, 1998).

° Finally the most telling example is ironically also the most ambivalent, and near inconclusive:

° Important impact was exerted by CITI firms through a less noticed market-institutional by-product, the regulatory framework for intellectual property rights. In an initial wave, it was a defying P2P movement symbolized by Napster that tried to neutralize copyright.

° In an offsetting movement the extension of patent law proved even more controversial. While it seemed a benign idea initially, the framework's extension to include business method patents in the 1998 State Street Bank v. Signature Financial group decision (*ibid.*) was nothing short of a true quantum leap in terms of legitimizing monopoly and chilling competitiveness. The lobbying for this integrative approach to patents paid off handsomely: Amazon leaped ahead with a series of controversial patents such as the One-Click-Stop-Shop, Google patented its method of assessing relevancy, and eBay snapped up the repackaging of trust with its seller rating application. In fact the U.S. PTO saw rapid rise in patent applications from 1998 to 1999 and had to change the durational terms of patents from 17 years (as of grant) to 20 years (as of filing) (see Alter 1999).

° While the recent Bilski decision (*in re* Bilski, 545 F.3d 943, 88 U.S.P.Q.2d 1385, Fed. Cir. 2008) may have effectively put an end to this period of protective excess for intellectual property right, it remains that the then unthoughtful complacency and convenience of the regulator may have caused irreversible damage. For many information technology-industrial categories the monopolies are in place and are exerting control over ideas, resources, and commercialization. While large amounts of value were generated, much value creation may also have been prevented.

° The described situation seems rather antithetical to the spirit of information and information technology. While intellectual property rights were intended to allow information creators to secure benefits from their innovation creation they were not intended to allow for a comprehensive position of monopoly. Granting such a position was bestowed on the legislator. Yet the framework for IP is admittedly antiquated and rather inadequately adapted from an industrial world where scarce resources necessitated allocational efficiency and economies of scale. By judicious, selective, and discretionary manipulation of a framework that has long overwhelmed its regulators, these firms are taking the law in their own hand creating *de facto* situations often stronger than authoritative law or legitimate governance: In the name of freedom of the Internet these organizations are increasingly restricting the functioning of industry participants and preventing new entrants by creating monopolies and forging ever-faster consolidation. They are outmaneuvering legitimate legal governance through regulatory arbitrage waging standard wars and sidestepping due process.

° These actions rival in fact the position of the legislator in this respect.

They have assumed the position of the legislator through clever combinations and synergies among several intellectual property rights patents, combining them to an effective weapon against other industry participants, securing their own position and not limited to securing the profits and benefits from their creations. Such behavior, primarily anti-competitive and only secondarily profit-motivated had already previously been an issue in Microsoft securing its own position beyond what had been solely possible through marketing. (For a comprehensive treatment of this particular attitude on the part of CITI firms see the work of Lawrence Lessig, 1999, 2001 as well as Van Waarden, 2001)

○ This last example also demonstrates the ingenuity of the CITI firm to increase effectiveness of their quasi-regulatory ambitions through a layered approach, synergistically leveraging a composite of all three regulatory strategies including the one of regulatory opportunism (c below).

• Finally, it its least intense form, the posture of firms is that of regulatory opportunism, i.e. the deliberate, intentional and preemptive occupation of yet unregulated space via the creation of *de facto* regulation and near-binding proprietary standards. With regulatory opportunism we are addressing the proclivity of CITI firms to fill regulatory vacuum resulting from intentional and explicit regulatory forbearance. Analogous to the construct of technological opportunism (Srinivasan et al., 2002), we propose that in a more benign and docile posture these CITI firms hone their law-sensing and law-response capabilities in the light of changes and turbulence in their legal environment and are likely to create pressures to make the legal environment gravitate towards them. We suggest that regulatory opportunism prompts those firms to perceive regulatory vacuum as legally turbulent and therefore as a potential source of growth for the firm responding affirmatively to absorb the inefficacies as a result of absent regulation.

The Conflict With Respect To Social Position

Complex Information Technology-Intensive firms initially campaigned on a platform of social value creation. Their purpose and reason for existence was the disproportionate generation of social value far above and beyond the residual private profit that they would also generate. They conveniently deemphasized the fact that their legal configuration was very much for-profit. They claimed to be able to meet an even exceed not-for-profit aspirations with formal for-profit structures.

In the financially constrained pos-recessionary world for patient capital formation this is a particularly tempting and attractive model because of its sustainability and capacity. Compared to the difficult and discretionary and opaque charity, donor, and public funding model, and the restrictive earned income strategy, in the for-profit mode, the private sector can be tapped consistently for its wealth and transparency is easier to come by through equity positions of funders.

But while this may seem very compelling from the point of view of financing it is questionable if not objectionable in terms of the redistributive effects between the different constituencies involved. Such models indeed equate to a form of taxation: make the marketers pay for the home users' benefits of a search engine, for example. The critique here is not with respect to the ingenious model itself, it is with respect to its unchecked consequences. These activities, while undoubtedly beneficial to all parties involved sidestep the original authority for such redistribution, the taxing fiscal entity. The self-imposed and self-regulated responsibilities may prove inadequate in the long run. They may reveal discriminatory in yet unanticipated ways. They may be yield yet unrecognized exposure and ultimately discredit the model. And they may macroeconomically suboptimally allocate the proceeds of the redistribution. In all they are merely subject to the biased control of one single of the involved entities, the shareholder constituency, but otherwise escape responsibility on the part of the other stakeholders and sidestep public scrutiny.

CONCLUSION

The empirical data of our more than two year's inquiry into 'the new nature of the firm' has been increasingly inconclusive as to the social efficacy of the major and most prominent Complex Information Technology-Intensive firms. While at first we expected to be able to simply identify some elements and substantial components of a paradigmatically motivated new framework for the CITI firm, we are increasingly concerned with the paradoxical effects of the existence of these firms. In the above we have attempted to capture these paradoxical effects as they affect the nature of these firms and render its contributions in terms of social value creation more and more questionable. Not only are CITI defined by an entirely different understanding of each one of the constitutive design variables strategy, structure, scale, scope, and social position, they indeed have also to some extend skewed their definition and their application resulting in an ambivalent nature of the firm with ambiguous outcomes.

LIMITATIONS AND FURTHER RESEARCH

The present was a exploratory paper, outlining the contours of what we labeled the "ambivalent nature" of CITI firms based on a composite of empirical data and critical theory. The alleged activities of CITI firms are to a large extent unobservable and don't lend themselves easily to direct empirical investigation. They could, however, be captured via proxy metrics, such as market share, regulatory disputes, and public action. A necessary next step is to juxtapose the results of such quantifiable and qualifiable data with the ones already available for positive feedback effects, accelerated innovation, lock-in and switching cost principles of networked and digital goods. Next steps would proceed to collect and evaluate such evidence. And in a further step yet, via abandoned projects or firm failures in the industry, assessing for example the number of firms or innovations that never reach their tipping point, one may be able to quantify social costs and potential losses of social value.

REFERENCES

Alter, S. (1999). The effects of State Street on electronic commerce and the Internet: The year in review. *Wilmer Hale*. Retrieved July 25, 2009, from http://www.wilmerhale.com/publications/whPubsDetail.aspx?publication=618

Arakji, R. Y., & Lang, K.-R. (2007). Digital consumer networks and producer-consumer collaboration: innovation and product development in the digital entertainment industry. In *Proceedings of the 40th Annual Hawaii International Conference on System Sciences (HICSS'07)* (pp. 211c-211c). doi: 10.1109/HICSS.2007.173

Brusoni, S., & Tronchetti-Provera, S. (2005). The limits to specialization: Problem solving and coordination in 'Modular Networks.' [Retrieved from ABI database.]. *Organization Studies*, *26*(12), 1885–1907. doi:10.1177/0170840605059161

Brynjolfsson, E., & Hitt, L. M. (1997). Information technology and internal firm organization: an exploratory analysis. [Retrieved from ABI database.]. *Journal of Management Information Systems, 14*(2), 81–101.

Brynjolfsson, E., Malone, T. W., Gurbaxani, V., & Kambil, A. (1994). Does information technology lead to smaller firms? [Retrieved from JSTOR database.]. *Management Science, 40*(12), 1628–1650. doi:10.1287/mnsc.40.12.1628

Coase, R. H. (1937). The Nature of the Firm. [Retrieved from ABI database.]. *Economica, 4*, 386–405. doi:10.1111/j.1468-0335.1937.tb00002.x

Huber, G. P. (2003). *The necessary nature of future firms: Attributes of survivors in a changing world.* Thousand Oaks, CA: Sage.

Hughes, J., & Lang, K.-R. (2006). Transmutability: Digital decontextualization, manipulation, and recontextualization as a new source of value in the production and consumption of culture products. In *Proceedings of the 39th Annual Hawaii International Conference on System Sciences (HICSS '06)* (pp. 165a-165a). doi: 10.1109/HICSS.2006.511

Lessig, L. (1999). *Code and other laws of cyberspace.* New York: Basic Books.

Lessig, L. (2001). *The future of ideas, The fate of the commons in a connected world.* New York: Random House.

Srinivasan, R., Lilien, G. L., & Rangaswamy, A. (2002). Technological opportunism and radical technology adoption: An application to e-business. [Retrieved from ABI database.]. *Journal of Marketing, 66*(3), 47–60. doi:10.1509/jmkg.66.3.47.18508

Stigler, G. (1971). The theory of economic regulation. [Retrieved from ABI database.]. *The Bell Journal of Economics and Management Science, 2*, 3–21. doi:10.2307/3003160

Van Waarden, F. (2001). Institutions and innovation: The legal environment of innovating firms. [Retrieved from ABI database.]. *Organization Studies, 22*(5), 765–795. doi:10.1177/0170840601225002

Varian, H. R. (2001). High-technology industries and market structure. In *Proceedings of Federal Reserve Bank of Kansas City* (pp. 65-101). Retrieved from ABI database.

Varian, H. R., Farrell, J. V., & Shapiro, C. (2004). *The economics of information technology: An introduction.* Boston: Cambridge University Press.

Williamson, O., & Winter, S. (Eds.). (1991). *The nature of the firm: origins, evolution and development.* New York: Oxford University Press.

Williamson, O. E. (1981). The economics of organization: The transaction cost approach. [Retrieved from ABI database.]. *American Journal of Sociology, 87*(3), 548–577. doi:10.1086/227496

Section 7
IT/IS Management

Chapter 24
Information Systems Projects in Contact Centers

Rui Rijo
Institute for Systems and Computers Engineering at Coimbra, Portugal

João Varajão
Universidade de Trás-os-Montes e Alto Douro, Portugal

Ramiro Gonçalves
Universidade de Trás-os-Montes e Alto Douro, Portugal

ABSTRACT

Over the past decade, Contact Centers have experienced exceptional growth. In UK and USA Contact Centers employ about three percent of the working population. Contact Center's projects are complex because occur in a multidisciplinary area with multiple actors and constraints. Information systems play a decisive role in these projects. However, several studies indicate a low success level of information and communications technology projects leading to research opportunities for their improvement. In their previous research the authors have identified a framework with the key factors to be considered in these projects. Due to the highly dynamic reality of the Contact Centers, the framework must evolve in order to maintain its usefulness for project managers and other center professionals. Focus groups are interactive discussion groups used for generating knowledge and hypotheses, exploring opinions, attitudes and attributes. In this way, the study presented in this chapter aims to verify, expand and actualize the existent framework, using a focus group with professionals in the area.

INTRODUCTION

Over the past decade, Contact Centers have experienced phenomenal growth in several countries around the world. Fuelled by advances in Information and Communication Technology (ICT) and the plummeting costs of data transmission, orga-

nizations have found it cost effective to provide service and sales to users (of the Contact Center) through remote technology-mediated centres (Holman, Batt, & Holtgrewe, 2007).

Contact Centers' users gain from new or lower cost services, while governments view them as a source of jobs and economic development. Organizations reduce costs, increase productivity and gather information about their users that

DOI: 10.4018/978-1-61692-020-3.ch024

enable either the identification of new business opportunities either the personalization of the services/products generating more business and better services.

A multi-disciplinary approach is called for in order to balance service quality, efficiency and profitability from the likely conflicting perspectives of users, service-providers, managers and society (Gans, Koole, & Mandelbaum, 2003; Mandelbaum & Zeltyn, 2007). Research crosses a significant number of disciplines from Operational Research, Statistics, Human Resources Management, Psychology and Sociology to Marketing and Information Systems (Gans et al., 2003).

ICT plays an important role in the Contact Centers, supporting the operations and data mining user's information. However, Standish Group studies indicate low success rates in the ICT projects (Standish Group, 2006). This situation represents research opportunities in order to contribute to improve the success level of the projects.

In our research we focus on Contact Centers Information Systems (CCIS) project management. In order to increase success rate, identify best practices, create decision processes and, in the future, prepare standards, it is fundamental to identify and systematize the concepts used and the key issues to consider in CCIS project management. In this way, a framework with the key factors to be considered in a CCIS project and the characterization made by project managers specialists in this area was proposed in our previous work.

Because of its growth and development, Contact Centers' reality is dynamic leading to the evolution of the framework. To verify framework's actuality, adapt and expand it in order to keep its usefulness, the present research study was conducted.

Focus groups are an important approach to create knowledge. They permit time efficiencies and to take advantage of possible synergies that the combined effort of a group will provide.

Taking the characteristics of the reality to study and our access to it, focus group was choose as the suitable method to gather empirical data in the present research.

The result is an expanded and actualized tool for CCIS project management.

This chapter is organized as follows: the background section introduces key Contact Center's concepts; the following section presents the existent framework; the research objectives and design section explains in detail the objectives of this work. Research design is presented and justified; data collection and analysis describes how empirical data was gathered and analyzed; the reviewed framework, the main contribution of this paper, presents the resulting framework for CCIS project management; finally, a summary of the results is given in last section. Future research directions are also discussed.

BACKGROUND

Call centres appeared in the middle of eighties (Cardoso, 2000; Cohen, 1980; Gaballa & Pearce, 1979; Hawkins, Meier, Nainis, & James, 2001) and they are the predecessors of contact centers. A call center constitutes a set of resources that enable the delivery of services via the telephone. Resources are typically people, the agents that handle calls, also known as customer service representatives (CSR), which interact with the users of the services provided by an organization.

An interaction is a contact between a user (customer or citizen) and the organization. Call centers may handle inbound and outbound interactions. Inbound interactions are those initiated by users requesting some service to the center. Outbound interactions are those initiated from within a center.

Call centers use Interactive Voice Response (IVR), Computer Telephony Integration (CTI) and Skills Based Routing (SBR) and present three main architectural possibilities.

IVR consists of computer automats that allow users to "self-serve" while communicating their needs. Users interacting with an IVR use their telephone keypads or, with speech-recognition technology, voice commands to provide information, such as account numbers or indications of the desired type of service. IVR uses synthesized voice to report information, such as bank balances or departure times of planes. IVR can also be used to provide simple services, such as the transfer of funds among bank accounts.

CTI technology is used to integrate more closely the telephone and information systems. CTI allows a binding between a telephone call and the context associated to that call, including user's personal data, desired service and the transactions done during the call (Cardoso, 2000). CTI can be used to automatically display the caller's user record on the agent's workstation screen. It eliminates the need for the agent to ask the caller personal information saving, in this way, agent's time and reducing calls' duration. It can also reduce variability among service times, thus improving the standardization of call handling procedures.

Agents' skills can be used to route calls. This routing, based on agents' skills is called skills based routing (Avramidis & L'Ecuyer, 2005; Koole & Mandelbaum, 2002). Agents can be organized upon their skills, for instance the ability to speak languages. If one call arrives and the system detects its origin, then it can be delivered to agents speaking the right language, providing a better service to the user.

CTI are IVR help to integrate a special information system into a call center's operations, the Customer Relationship Management system (CRM). CRM systems track user's records and allow them to be used in operating decisions. CRM allows an efficient and personalized relationship between the organization and each user, independently of the number of the users (Cardoso, 2000; Gans & Zhou, 2003). "Call centers" became "Contact Centers" with the use of interaction channels like e-mail, fax, sms, chat or web. With these new channels

and business approaches, complexity increased and, agent's skills had to improve to do the work with new technologies and services.

Three main possible architectures and associated technologies can be identified. These architectures, centralized, distributed, and hosted may be used in conjugation generating hybrid ones suiting the organization's specific requirements. Furthermore, several different technologies may be used in the architectures. There is any specific match between architecture and technology.

A centralized Contact Centre, has a technological infrastructure based on a single server or multiple servers, from the physical point of view, but a single one from the logical point of view, and is usually supported on a local network. The interactions, when they reach the Contact Centre, are placed in one single queue regardless of the channel (Demaria, 2005). The system handles each interaction according to a configurable priority. For example, it is usual to treat synchronous interactions like voice and Web collaboration in real time. E-mail and fax interactions, for example, are asynchronous interactions, and may be handled offline (Koole & Mandelbaum, 2002).

Distributed Contact Centre represents an evolution of centralized contact centre, enabling to overcome the geographical and time zone barriers. With the Distributed Contact Centre an organization may operate in multiple geographical distinct places, sometimes with very different time zones, and thus offering a service 24 hours over 24 hours. It also makes possible the load balancing (Whitt, 2005). The basic idea of distributed contact centre is to have a set of centralized contact centres communicating and working as if they are a single one. For example, if a user tries to access the contact centre in her/his geographical area and if the centre is already closed or not responding due to an overload, then the interaction is routed to another contact centre that is available. With this architecture, the interaction can be processed by the agent with all the necessary information (Whitt, 2005). In the end, the original Contact

Centre is updated with the results of the interaction thus ensuring information consistency.

The hosted contact centre is composed of a central system responsible for the overall management of an interaction, since its entry into the system and its routing to the operator with the appropriate profile until its finish and record of the information. This information regards the business component and the interaction component. This central system can respond to multiple contact centres of various organizations. Thus, organizations need only to install the agents' workstations on their side. All the processing is performed from the central system (Demaria, 2005). The control of the interactions is achieved by using session initiation protocol (SIP) and real time transport protocol (RTP). The hosted model works on an software as a service (SaaS) basis, where the computer-based service is provided to customers over a network. The organization pays a fee (usually a monthly fee) for the use of each workstation and the communications. This model allows the organizations to overcome the problem of the initial investment, which is one of the greatest barriers to the adoption of a centre. In this way, the risk of investing in a contact centre is minimized. This model also allows the adjustment of the number of agents, according to the amount of work.

More recently, contact centre technology is based on Voice over IP (VoIP) gateways. With VoIP and an SaaS model, the agent only needs a computer, a network connection, and a microphone to work. VoIP enables the realization of voice calls, with or without video, depending on the option. In this way the initial investment and the total cost of ownership (TCO) is reduced.

With this background information it is possible the understanding of the supporting framework for contact center information systems projects presented in the next section.

FRAMEWORK FOR CONTACT CENTERS INFORMATION SYSTEMS PROJECT MANAGEMENT

In this section we present the framework for CCIS project management resulting from our previous work. Our goal was to identify the key factors in CCIS project management and the characterization of those factors. We recurred to semi-structured interviews and to a set of highly specialized individuals in the area.

The framework considers twelve key factors: flow, channels, technology, service type, integration, geography, dimensioning, way to obtain the service, user and agent focus, legislation, business sector and relevant actors.

A brief overview of the framework will be presented with the characterization of each factor.

The twelve key factors are the following:

- Flow. The concept of flow can be applied to the interaction, to the service provided, to the agent and to the complete flow. In this last case all the relationship between user and the organization is considered. The complete flow can have inbound and outbound parts and include one or more services. From the point of view of an IS, the inbound is considered more complex, demanding a higher level of systems integration and more skilled agents. However outbound services like debt collection are an exception. The dichotomy outbound/inbound should be used to facilitate the organization of the services and not as a rigid division in the services. The use of these concepts must be done carefully in order to preserve the valuable asset of the relation among users and organizations;
- Channels. Interaction channels can be classified logically as self-serviced or assisted. Assisted channels demand agents to process the interaction, self-serviced ones no. Interactions have two main com-

ponents, the relational component and the transactional component. It is necessary to analyze both components when deciding if an interaction can be automatic (e.g. using a self-service channel). Pure transactional interactions tend to be supported by automatic channels. Relational transactions demand human interaction. Channel selection must take into account some factors, among others: organization strategy and image; how usually organization interacts with it's user; target public profile: age, sex, culture, technological skills; product and service characteristics like service level;

- Technology. Contact Centers have technological solutions related with relational marketing (among others, business intelligence, customer relationship management and workflow) and operations. It is possible to distinguish two components in the operations: planning and on-line systems. Planning is related with volume estimation (forecasting), estimation of how many agents are needed based on volume estimation (staffing) and the creation of the appropriated work schedule (scheduling). Operations on-line systems like Computer Telephony Integration (CTI), Automatic Call Distributor (ACD) or quality monitoring and reporting tools are related with interactions' distribution, monitoring and reporting as well as business continuity systems. Today, with high reliability and reduced cost of dedicated lines, operations tend to be centralized in a datacenter with remote agents geographically distributed. This solution facilitates systems administration, increases system reliability, and it is not an obstacle for geographical distribution. Actually, organizations where contact centers are critical to the business are splitting their operations into just two sites. This increases security from the viewpoint

of business continuity (for example, if there is a fire, operations continue) and enables load transfer when burst situations occur;

- Service type. Service type depends of the strategy and on the business area. It is possible to distinguish the following main inbound services types: customer service (refers to information about billing and provisioning), claims, generic information about services or products and technical support. Outbound main services types are debt collection, welcome calls (for first-time service users), churn reduction, sales and inquiries. Specialists believe that it is possible to identify best practices for each type of service;
- Business sector. Knowledge, best practices and experiences of CCIS projects done in a certain business sector, tend to be applied to other organizations operating in the same business sector and in similar markets. Business sectors with a large number of residential users and without an high level of market fragmentation have, naturally, contact centers. Nevertheless, many organizations have the account manager or power user function. Account managers (or power users) are persons that manage a set of customers. They do debt collection, up-selling, cross-selling, and process requests. They aren't pure contact center agents, but they use similar procedures, tools and technologies. So, whenever there are a significant number of interactions, contact center technology and expertise can be applied. Market maturity level and competition influence also the investment in a contact center;
- Integration. The purpose of integration is to make information available to agents and other actors. There are three main strategies: use existing back-end applications if their complexity and response capacity allow; develop a new front-end in-

tegrated with the back-end through a set of transactions; and built a new system from scratch. The evaluation of the integration complexity must consider, among others factors the number, the diversity and the integration level of existing systems; technology details of each system (proprietary systems, standard, open source, others); performance of the systems; interface complexity; decision about synchronous or asynchronous integration; number of transactions to support. Inbound services require, most of the times, a high level of integration;

- Geography. Technology, net capacity and cost have evolved in ways that allow geography to become "transparent". From the information system viewpoint, geographic dispersion is no longer a problem. Yet the design of the information system must take into account geography issues as culture, maturity of the markets, legislation and distributed project management;

- Dimensioning. Correct dimensioning is critical because the workforce represents about seventy percent of the operational cost of a contact center (Gans et al., 2003). Well-designed CCIS reduce the number of necessary agents. On the other hand, the number of agents influences technology, system architecture, processes, among other relevant aspects. Inbound dimensioning requires the estimation of expected volume (number of expected interactions), expected interaction durations, expected distribution by day/month/year, and target service level. This data allows the use of Erlang statistical distributions to calculate the number of necessary agents (Gans et al., 2003). Outbound dimensioning requires definition of target volume, forecast of average interaction duration, and a goal for the percentage of successful contacts. Either in inbound, outbound, or both, growth forecast for the contact center is important for dimensioning;

- Way to obtain the service. An organization has four main ways to set up a contact center service: fully in-house; first line outsourcing, second line in-house; first line outsourcing, second line insourcing (organization owns systems and infrastructure, workforce come from a third party); everything outsourced. The outsourcer solution transforms the initial infrastructure investment (usually high) into operational costs, reduces setup-time and avoids a long learning curve. An outsourcer adds experience but also adds the complexity of managing a third party. Confidentiality, control, and operation of internal resources are main reasons to implement in-house operations. An interesting solution is the mixed model, in-house and outsourcing at the same time. With this solution, it is possible to have the best of both worlds. The organization uses its business knowledge, experience and processes, and gets know-how from the contact center from the outsourcer. All these solutions have impact in the architectural design of the project;

- Actors. The number and the functions of the actors in a contact center vary from one organization to another. Two main functions can be distinguished: production line functions and support functions. Agents, supervisors, and service project management in production line functions are decisive to success of contact center service projects. Each supervisor works with ten or fifteen agents. A service project manager is the person that has the global vision of the project. She/he understands the needs and expectations of the customer, the organization that requires the service. At the level of support functions, there is an axis connecting marketing with operational abilities. Marketing abilities involve front-end creation, from a perspective of what message to transmit, how to relate with users, and what information to provide to the agent, among others. In turn, operational abilities include planning, forecasting, dimensioning, training, quality monitoring, among others; or, in other words, everything related to the industrial component of the project. Another function is system analysis. All the processes have to be thought concerning the way information flows and how they should interact with existent processes, demanding a global perspective of the operations. Human resources department support functions like selection, recruiting, training and administrative tasks. Finally, in-house operations may have a Contact Center Manager, responsible for the entire contact center department;

- User and agent focus. One of the guidelines in a CCIS project is users and agents focus. Usually, users' needs are the main reason for the existence of one organization. When organizations create a contact center or a new service for a contact center – in-house or outsourced – all the solution (marketing and operational components) are conceived to satisfy users' needs to strengthen user-organization relationship. This generates continuous (and probably growing) purchases and consequently continuous profits. Agents are organizations' face to users, so keeping and increasing the relationship is one of the most important goals of the contact center. One of the most frequent approaches in contact center service design is the straightforward adoption of existing processes. The idea is to do the same things in the same way but using telephone, e-mail, or any other channel. This approach may lead to a set of independent, non-related and confusing services, damaging the relationship between the user and the organization. Thus, processes must

be carefully designed to facilitate users' life and agents must have a support system with tools that allow them to efficiently satisfy present and future users' needs. These tools belong to CCIS;

- Legislation. Labour and contact center legislation varies from country to country, conditioning centers activities and consequently CCIS projects. The Global Contact Center Report 2007 (Holman et al., 2007), states substantial differences in the organization of work and human resource practices in Contact Centers across countries. In general national labour market institutions influence management strategies. Another example is the Do Not Call legislation. In some countries like US, people can register their telephone number in a Do Not Call database in order to avoid telemarketers. UK legislation is even more restricting. Labour legislation, work organization and Do Not Call laws, among others, must be considered in the process and project design.

After the framework presentation, our next step is to introduce the objectives and the methodology of the research.

Which Are The Relevant Factors To Consider In A CCIS Project?

This section introduces several research questions that triggered the present study and the research method followed.

Research questions in this work arise from literature revision, empirical experience gathered all along almost ten years of fieldwork in the area and from the observation of the diversity of CCIS projects.

In the contact center literature, Gans, Koole and Mandelbaum (Gans & Zhou, 2003) consider that processes and systems design are one of the most important and strategic decisions to make in a contact center. Aksin and Harker (Aksin & Harker, 2003) explain the importance of information systems in the capacity planning of a contact center.

Regarding project management, several studies (Demarco, 1997; Ewusi-Mensah, 2003; Standish Group, 1996, 1998; Yetton, Martin, Sharma, & Johnston, 2000) indicate misspecifications and poor requisites decomposition and vision as some of the main reasons for project failure. Chaos Reports (Standish Group, 2006) indicate a lower level of success for information system projects, despite the positive evolution in the latest years.

CCIS projects exhibit many particularities. For example, an inbound information service is totally different of an inbound emergency service like 911. Processes, agent's skills, response time, liability, are some of the main differences.

The characteristics of an in-house contact center are also different from one outsourced at a Service Bureau where, among other issues, it's necessary to negotiate project results, service levels, know-how transfer and confidentiality.

For the Service Bureau, it is substantially different whether the project needs integration with client's systems or the project doesn't need any kind of integration.

A distributed contact center communications, data infrastructure and project approaches may be substantially different from one with a centralized architecture.

Finally, contact centers vary from few agents to hundreds or thousands agents.

In short, information systems play an important role in a contact center and there are different approaches to design and manage CCIS projects leading to the following research questions: which are the relevant factors to consider in a CCIS project? How do project managers further characterize those factors?

These reasons justified our previous study in order to identify and characterize concepts and the organizational, social and technological context of the contact centers project management area.

The result was the framework presented in the previous section.

Due to contact centers' growth and changing environment, our goal in this work was to verify, expand and actualize the existent framework. Contact center is a multidisciplinary area that crosses marketing, operational research, psychology, sociology and information systems, among others, so CCIS projects are complex, involving a multiple kind of actors and interests.

All research is based on some underlying philosophical assumptions about what constitutes valid research and which research methods are appropriate (Myers, 1997). To accomplish our present goal, an interpretative approach was followed because of the multidisciplinary and complex reality of the contact centers and the relation between the observer team and the object of study.

In recent years, interpretive research has emerged as an important strand in information systems research (Walsham, 1995). Interpretive research can help information systems researchers to understand human thought and action in social and organizational contexts; it has the potential to produce deep insights into information systems phenomena including the management of information systems and information systems development (Klein & Myers, 1999).

After choosing a proper approach, next step was to choose the research method. There has been a general shift in information systems research away from technological to managerial and organizational issues, hence an increasing interest in the application of qualitative research methods (Myers, 1997). The goal of this study was to verify, actualize and expand the framework with the relevant factors to consider in the CCIS project and their characterization. It was therefore crucial to identify contact center specialists who have the necessary experience and knowledge to provide a characterization of the phenomena involved.

The need to capture such knowledge suggests looking for people with a wide experience in the area, ten years, say. The goal was to find professionals with experience as consultants and project management in CCIS and experience in the development of software for contact centers. Another issue is to have worked in several business areas and diverse geographic areas with markets of different maturities and dimensions. By last, the specialists should have skills beyond computer science.

The observer team has almost ten years of effective work in the area. Their projects cross several geographies, among others, Tokyo (Japan), São Paulo (Brazil), Hong-Kong (China), Macau (China), Kuala Lumpur (Malaysia), Madrid (Spain), Amsterdam (Holland) and Lisbon (Portugal). Projects business areas range from finance and insurance to travel agencies and retail.

Frequently used in exploratory-descriptive studies, as well as in other types of research, focus groups, as data gathering technique, seemed particularly useful in this context, as explained in the next section.

DATA COLLECTION AND ANALYSIS

This section presents the procedures and tools used to gather, organize and analyze data. Many qualitative researchers prefer the term "empirical material" to the word "data" since most qualitative data is non-numeric (Myers, 1997).

Focus groups are interactive discussion groups used to generate knowledge, hypothesis, explore opinions, attitudes and attributes (Fern, 1982). To MacDonald (1992), a focus group is seen as "… [a group] discussion of a particular topic under the direction of a moderator who promotes group participation and interaction and manages the discussion through a series of topics".

Focus groups seek to maximize search time and to take advantage of the synergies that arise from group effort.

Stewart e Shamdasani (1990) point the advantages of focus groups over other methods like individual interviews and Delphi groups from the point of view of the researchers and participants. To participants, focus groups offer synergy, momentum, stimulus, security and spontaneity. To researchers offer collective wisdom, innovative ideas, structure, speed and specialization.

This required preparing a list of subjects to cover. This list of subjects evolved into a sequence of questions and sentences for comment. This tool was reviewed and tuned in order to reach the defined goals.

A letter requesting the participation and explaining the goals, the focus group process, and the use of data gathered was sent to the interviewees.

Focus group was realized in the physical presence of the participants, had the duration of about two hours, and was tape-recorded (with explicit concordance of the participants). Curriculum Vitae of the participants were also requested.

Focus group record was transcribed verbatim and the resulting document was sent to participants for revision and acceptance. Confidentiality was always assured.

Before analysis of content, verbatim documents and notes were organized. That material was processed through content analysis based on emergent thematic categories. Data analysis, in qualitative research, is a phase of the research process that occurs every time the researcher collects new data. In the analysis, researcher must continually use what has already emerged (Deslauriers, 1991). One of the key elements in qualitative data analysis is the systematic coding of text (Miles & Huberman, 1994; Strauss & Corbin, 1990). Codes are the building blocks for model building and the foundation on which the analyst's arguments rest. Codes embody the assumptions underlying the analysis.

The first coding step consisted of organizing all the contents in major topics. As they had been identified, these new topics were also considered in the organization of the information. The second step was to iteratively look for similarities, differences, common denominators, models and

Figure 1. Resulting framework for contact center's information systems project management

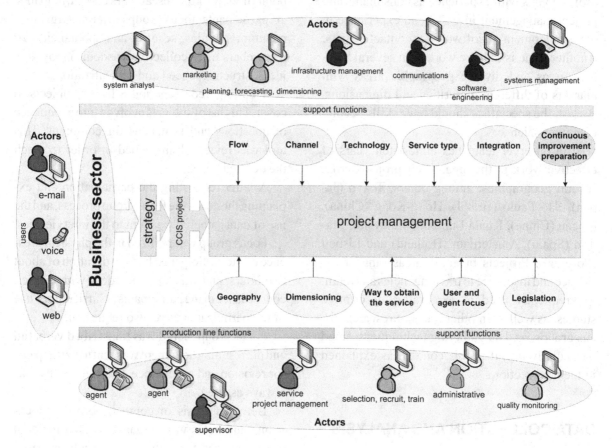

other relevant aspects. Through this process, the different categories began to emerge.

Several memos and diagrams were built along the analysis based either on the verbatim descriptions either on the notes registered during the focus group. Memos and diagrams help put on paper the preliminary products of the iterative analysis (Fortin, 1999).

With the research questions and the data collection and analysis techniques used, it is time to present the results achieved.

REVIEWED FRAMEWORK

This section presents the results of the research.

Figure 1 shows the identified factors and their relationship. Following we discuss the rationale of the framework.

A contact center project must be aligned and included in the strategy of the organization. Business sector, geography environment and users' needs influence strategy definition. Many organizations decide to implement a contact center to improve their performance and competitiveness. Others, having already a contact center, decide to create or reformulate services provided by the center. Any of the previous situations has a CCIS project associated.

Each project may affect several or all contact centers' actors. Any affected actor is a participant in the project.

A CCIS project can consider several or all factors presented, depending on the requisites. Other factors may also be considered. The importance of each factor in a specific project may also vary and that must be decided by the project team.

In every project, organizational aspects are decisive and must be analyzed. Project management literature refers the importance to understand organizational culture and internal forces.

Taking into account strategy, objectives, organizational culture and internal forces, among other organizational issues, choices must be done regarding: the services to provide to users; the appropriated interaction channels; the flows that must exist in order to provide the best services for users; the information/actions to obtain/provide/generate from/to/into existent systems (integration); the best integration approaches; the number of agents and supervisors needed and how must be organized to support the services (dimensioning); the skills they must have; the way to obtain the service (in-house or outsourced; the suitable technology architecture; and the applicable legislation.

All the process must consider the relation between user and agents. This relation is the key link that enables a long-term relationship between user and organization. Those long-term relationships generate profits.

Another issue is the reengineering needed not only at the process level but also at the hierarchy and structure level. Finally, the project must have the top management commitment.

The analysis of the results confirms, generally, the factors and the characterization of the existent framework. Still, there are some new and interesting aspects that expand the framework.

Regarding flow, participants were unanimous considering inbound projects different from outbound ones. They confirm that inbound services usually need to provide more information for the agents.

When a user calls (inbound interaction), the agent only knows the reason why she/he is calling when they start talking. There are some few exceptions, namely when there is an IVR and the user must choose one option indicating the motif of the request. Even in this situation, most users choose randomly an option just to talk to an agent. With this uncertainty, agents must have

access to more information, provided by CCIS, in real-time than in the outbound interaction. In the outbound situation, the interaction is previously prepared in detail so it is possible to determine, for the majority of cases, the information needed and the flow of the interaction.

Another conclusion is that inbound projects usually are longer than outbound ones. Participants stressed that inbound design is done more carefully because inbound services, most of the times, will work for several years. On the other hand, outbound services, most of the times, are prepared to work for a few days or weeks. Examples of these situations are a customer care inbound service in a bank and a promotion outbound service. Customer care is a service designed and implemented to work for long-term because bank customers will use it over years. Some main reasons can be typified, but there is always a degree of uncertainty that must be overcame with agents' experience and capable CCIS. The outbound service, will work for some days or weeks and the target public is previously choose as well as all the details of the interaction flow.

The conclusion is that inbound CCIS services projects are longer than outbound CCIS service projects and demand more experienced analyst and careful design. Focus group confirms our previous research in the way that the dichotomy inbound/outbound represents a logically abstraction facilitating the comprehension and should be used in a proper manner. Actually, the main focus should be the user, her/his needs and the relation between user and the agent (the face of the organization). Inbound and outbound services have relations among them that must be reflected in the CCIS.

Another issue is the automatic blending between inbound and outbound. From the point of view of the CCIS it is possible to implement automatic blending, but from the operational point of view this context switch doesn't work so well. What centers usually do is to make some switch, but manually.

Regarding the channel factor, focus group participants consider that the use of web collaboration to help users to change from assisted to self channels has a moderate success. Video call is a recent new channel. Results present it is as a trend pushed by communications operators in order to create the need for this kind of service.

Concerning technology, VoIP utilization is growing. It allows just one infrastructure to voice and data and more flexibility. It allows the "anytime, anywhere" contact center. With VoIP architecture, agents just need an Internet connection and a headphone–microphone to work. This powerful flexibility however demands an elaborated communications design, considering security, quality of service, liability and load balancing.

Participants consider that service can be grouped in several types like customer service, technical support, debt collection or welcome calls. Know-how re-utilization is extremely important and can be used among service types of similar businesses areas.

Another contribute to expand the framework is related with a new factor that emerged from the focus group: continuous improvement. All participants refer it has an important issue in CCIS design. Each second improved in each interaction in a large contact center has a huge impact in the human and material resources needed for the operations. When a service starts its operation there are always details to improve, new small situations to consider and some flows to adapt. To improve is necessary to measure. Different business sectors have different measures and benchmarking indicators. It is fundamental to identify which ones the organization wants to consider and they must be integrated in the CCIS design in an earlier stage of the project development.

DISCUSSION OF FINDINGS

The results of the study support many of the findings of previous research. Consistent with previous research the key factors in CCIS project management are flow, channel, technology, service type, integration, improvement, geography, dimensioning, way to obtain the service, user and agent focus and legislation.

A new factor emerged: the preparation for continuous improvement. This idea expands the existent framework a step ahead. In the present research, participants indicate that the success of CCIS depend on the continuous improvement of operations after the end of the project. In order to prepare the after-project phase it is necessary to identify what to compare along the time. After the identification of useful key performance indicators, which vary from business sector to business sector, it is necessary to include them in the design of the contact center. The Global Contact Center Benchmarking Report (Merchants, 2007) presents key performance indicators for the contact centers. All of these indicators depend on the existent information system. Most of the conclusions of the resulting framework are supported by other research studies. If the flow is inbound, then the need of integration with the existing systems is usually greater with some exceptions like debt collection. Aksin and Harker (2003) show that in a system with a high level of integration, the increase of the number of the agents has an impact in the system performance.

Dimensioning is a major issue because of the impact in costs (Gans et al., 2003). All identified studies analyze inbound dimensioning. Almost no academic outbound studies were identified (Gans et al., 2003), the exception being Samuelson (1999). Actually, the present study confirms that the division between inbound, outbound and blended useful but, in order to provide a better service to the user, the complete flow should be analyzed. Inbound projects usually are longer and demand a more careful design. Service quality, capture and retention of users should also be used when analyzing performance and dimensioning.

This study also confirms that voice is still the most important channel followed by e-mail, which is growing in use and importance. Video calls appear pushed by communication operators.

The possibilities of obtaining the service are becoming more mixed between in-house, outsource and insource solutions. Actual research considers the outsource possibilities (Aksin, Véricourt, & Karaesmen, 2008; Gans & Zhou, 2007). In either case this decision has an impact in solution design (security issues, performance and distribution, among others) and must be considered in the project.

CONCLUSION

Contact centers' economic role is significant and is growing. Technology, processes and procedures are key issues to ensure productivity in the centers, so CCIS projects assume a central role.

The present research validates, expands and actualizes the existent framework for supporting the activity of CCIS project managers, result of previous research. The framework gathers the relevant factors to consider in a CCIS project and their characterization.

This study was influenced by an interpretative approach. In order to capture specialists' knowledge, a focus group was developed. The participant's specialists have a wide experience of work in the area as consultants, project managers and product developers. They worked in contact centers projects of several businesses, in different geographies, with markets of different maturities and dimensions. A framework with twelve key factors and their characterization was created.

Results expand the framework that was previously proposed and are generally supported by other studies. This brings aspects regarding CCIS projects like considering the complete flow of interactions and not the traditional approach dividing interactions between inbound, outbound and blended. The relation between users and agents is considered the key link for a long-term relationship between users and organizations. Thus, it is

considered a critical issue in the CCIS design. A new factor was included in the framework, the continuous improvement preparation. Any smaller improve may have a huge impact in either in the user's satisfaction either in the cost of the resources. To improve is necessary to measure. Measures come from records in the information systems. Contact centers must define their own key performance indicators, and they must be include in the service's design in an early stage.

The use of an adequate framework for CCIS projects will enable: the development of a systematic and structured research in knowledge areas related with CCIS; the identification of the critical factors and the specific characteristics of the different types of projects; the identification and development of project management approaches, best practices, tools and techniques; organizations to have a framework to build decisions processes based on their needs, choose the best alternatives in order to reach their strategic goals; the creation of standards and norms; the increase of the success in CCIS projects.

This is a dynamic and growing area. Contact centers' research represents a dynamic work that must evolve with the changes in the area. In this way, much work has to be done in the future. New questions arise like: Are traditional information systems project methodologies adequate for contact center projects? How to consider these identified key factors in the project phases?

REFERENCES

Aksin, O. Z., & Harker, P. T. (2003). Capacity sizing in the presence of a common shared resource: Dimensioning an inbound call center. *European Journal of Operational Research, 147*(3), 464–483. doi:10.1016/S0377-2217(02)00274-6

Aksin, O. Z., Véricourt, F., & Karaesmen, F. (2008). Call center outsourcing contract design and choice. *Management Science, 54*(2), 354–368. doi:10.1287/mnsc.1070.0823

Avramidis, A. N., & L'Ecuyer, P. (2005). *Modeling and simulation of call centers.* Paper presented at the Proceedings of the 2005 Winter Simulation Conference.

Cardoso, J. (2000). *Unified Customer Interaction™: Gestão do Relacionamento num Ambiente Misto de Interacção Self e Assistida.* Lisboa: Centro Atlântico.

Cohen, H. S. (1980). *Measuring and modeling user satisfaction with telephone switching and transmission performance.* Paper presented at the 9th International Symposium on Human Factors in Telecommunications, Red Bank, New Jersey.

Demarco, T. (1997). *The Deadline.* New York: Dorset House Publishing.

Deslauriers, J. P. (1991). *Recherce qualitative: Guide Pratique.* New York: McGraw-Hill.

Ewusi-Mensah, K. (2003). *Software Development Failures.* Cambridge, MA: MIT Press.

Fern, E. F. (1982). Why do focus groups work: a review and integration of small group process theories. In Mitchell, A. (Ed.), *Advances in Consumer Research* (*Vol. 9*, pp. 444–451). St. Louis, MO: Association for Consumer Research.

Fortin, M.-F. (1999). *O Processo de Investigação: Da concepção à realização.* Porto, Portugal: Lusociência - Edições Técnicas e Científicas, Lda.

Gaballa, A., & Pearce, W. (1979). Telephone sales manpower planning at Qantas. *Interfaces, 9*(3), 1–9. doi:10.1287/inte.9.3.1

Gans, N., Koole, G., & Mandelbaum, A. (2003). Telephone call centers: tutorial, review and research prospects. *Manufacturing & Service Operations Management, 5*(2), 79–141. doi:10.1287/msom.5.2.79.16071

Gans, N., & Zhou, Y.-P. (2003). A call-routing problem with service-level constraints. *Operations Research, 51*(2), 255–271. doi:10.1287/opre.51.2.255.12787

Gans, N., & Zhou, Y.-P. (2007). Call-Routing Schemes for Call-Center Outsourcing. *Manufacturing & Service Operations Management, 9*(1), 33–50. doi:10.1287/msom.1060.0119

Hawkins, L., Meier, T., Nainis, W. S., & James, H. M. (2001). *The evolution of the call center to customer contact center: ITSC - Information Technology Support Center.*

Holman, D., Batt, R., & Holtgrewe, U. (2007). *The Global Contact Center Report: International Perspectives on Management and Employment.*

Klein, H., & Myers, M. (1999). A set of principles for conducting and evaluating interpretive field studies in information systems. *Management Information Systems Quarterly, 23*(1), 67–93. doi:10.2307/249410

Koole, G., & Mandelbaum, A. (2002). Queuing models of call centers: an introduction. *Annals of Operations Research, 113*, 41–59. doi:10.1023/A:1020949626017

Mandelbaum, A., & Zeltyn, S. (2007). *Service Engineering of Call Centers: Research, Teaching, Practice.* Haifa, Israel: Faculty of Industrial Engineering and Management, Technion.

McDonald, W. J. (1992). The influence of moderator philosophy on the content of focus group sessions: a multivariate analysis of group session content. In Kumar, V. (Ed.), *Enhancing Knowledge Development in Marketing* (*Vol. 3*, pp. 540–545). Chicago, IL: American Marketing Association.

McDonald, W. J. (1994). Provider perceptions of focus group research use: a multicountry perspective. *Journal of the Academy of Marketing Science, 22*(3), 265–273. doi:10.1177/0092070394223007

Merchants. (2007). *Global Contact Centre Benchmarking Report*. New York: Dimension Data Group.

Miles, M. B., & Huberman, A. M. (1994). *Qualitative Data Analysis* (2nd ed.). Thousand Oaks, CA: Sage Publications.

Myers, M. D. (1997). Qualitative Research in Information Systems. *Management Information Systems Quarterly, 21*(2), 241–242. doi:10.2307/249422

Samuelson, D. A. (1999). Predictive dialing for outbound telephone call centers. *Interfaces, 29*(5), 66–94. doi:10.1287/inte.29.5.66

Standish Group. (1996). *Unfinished Voyages*. Retrieved July 20, 2008, from http://www. standishgroup.com/sample_research/unfinished_voyages_1.php

Standish Group. (1998). *Chaos: A recipe for success*. Retrieved July 20, 2008, from http://www. standishgroup.com/sample_research/PDFpages/chaos1998.pdf

Standish Group. (2006). *Projects success rate*. Retrieved December 20, 2008, from http://www. standishgroup.com/quarterly_reports/pdf_copy/q1_2007_sample.pdf

Stewart, D. W., & Shamdasani, P. N. (1990). *Focus Group: Theory and Pratice*. Newbury Park, CA: Sage Publications.

Strauss, A., & Corbin, J. (1990). *Basics of Qualitative Research: Grounded Theory Procedures and Techniques*. Newbury Park, CA: Sage Publications.

Walsham, G. (1995). The Emergence of Interpretivism in IS Research. *Information Systems Research, 6*(4), 376–394. doi:10.1287/isre.6.4.376

Yetton, P., Martin, A., Sharma, R., & Johnston, K. (2000). A model of information systems development project performance. *Information Systems Journal, 10*(4), 263–289. doi:10.1046/j.1365-2575.2000.00088.x

Chapter 25
A Process for Estimating the Value of ITIL Implementations

Pedro Oliveira
Technical University of Lisbon, Portugal

Nuno Furtado da Silva
Accenture Consultancy, Portugal

Miguel Mira da Silva
Technical University of Lisbon, Portugal

ABSTRACT

As World economy lingers it is increasingly more important to justify any investment so that available corporate funds are spent wisely. However, estimating the value of ITIL investments is not an easy task, which means that most CIOs do not invest in large-scale ITIL projects as much as it would be desirable. Instead, CIOs prefer to embark on quick win implementations (e.g. solely implement the incident management process). In this chapter t propose an ITIL Value Estimator. This estimator is based on an estimation process that quantifies the project's total cost, along with each process' benefits. The outcome of the ITIL Value Estimator is a Monte Carlo simulation whose result provides CIOs with a justification of the value of large-scale ITIL implementations, which can be used to gain the upper hand during the decision-making process.

INTRODUCTION

Today's competitive and turbulent economy forces organizations to struggle in order to remain competitive. Organizations can only grow by cutting costs as well as optimizing resources. Having this in mind, a growing number of organizations has become increasingly dependent on Informa-

tion Technology (IT) to manage and grow their businesses.

A five-leg wheel chair is a good analogy to understand how organizations are structured these days. Each leg symbolizes a business function within the organization – for example: sales, marketing, manufacturing, product development and human resources; and, representing the chair's spinal column is the IT department which links and integrates the information that drives the business (Harvard Business Review, 1999).

DOI: 10.4018/978-1-61692-020-3.ch025

If all the wheels (business functions) are aligned, as a result of having a common direction (strategy), then all of them will roll towards the same pathway (business goal). However, this wheel synchrony is only possible because the chair's column (IT department) supports the chair (organization) by connecting all the wheels. This simple analogy pictures the fact that organizations are intrinsically dependent on IT.

In the past, this IT dependency meant a growing IT budget, despite the fact that there was no evidence if IT investments would bring benefits to the organization (Ross & Weill, 2002). However, disproportionate budgets are no longer allowed by the executive board, as Chief Information Officers (CIO) must justify their IT budget, and must prove that IT projects are indeed necessary for the organization to maintain its competitive level.

CIOs who have negotiation skills are able to understand the power division in the board, pinpoint who has decision rights and who is accountable in the decision-making process, and then successfully use relationships with key stakeholders to influence their stance (Broadbent & Kitzis, 2004).

Another essential skill CIOs should have is a broader understanding of the organizations' structure. Organizations are gradually becoming flat instead of having a vertical structure. This transition leads to the establishment of horizontal processes in detriment of vertical silos, which made it possible to align IT and business. And, CIOs should be able to effectively manage the link between the two of them (O'Leary, 2002).

However, without a coherent framework to manage business processes, organizations are not well prepared to avoid or solve problems related to this transition. Hence, organizations that manage their IT correctly generate returns at least 40% higher than their competitors and, for that reason, it is very important that organizations adopt an IT management framework (Ross & Weill, 2002).

IT INFRASTRUCTURE LIBRARY

In the present day, ITIL v3 consists of a set of guidelines that specify what an IT organization should do based on industry best practices. These guidelines offer advice on the definition, plan, implementation, execution, monitoring and continual improvement of the IT service management. Therefore, it is crucial not to regard ITIL as a technological project but as organizational change process (Silva & Martins, 2008).

To sum up, ITIL investment justification is a non-trivial subject and only by analyzing the investment are CIOs able to justify the value of ITIL investments. In this way, the analysis of the investment ends up being the main justification support because it produces numbers that help justifying the ITIL investment, by calculating the benefits and costs. Thus, calculating the value of the investment is part of the investment analysis, and this analysis is absolutely necessary in order to justify the investment.

Implementing ITIL

Nowadays there are multiple research case studies which support the statement that ITIL brings value (Gartner, 2006). However, CIOs are going through great difficulties so as to justify the value of ITIL implementations to their peers, as there is no pragmatic methodology in their grasp to prove the business value of ITIL implementations.

In a recent survey, 50,5% of the executives interviewed claimed that they did not approve ITIL implementations for their organizations because the business value of these implementations cannot be proven as it is depicted in figure 1.

Indeed, estimating the value of ITIL implementations is not an easy task because many variables have to be considered (Seddon, Graeser & Willcocks, 2002). Maturity level, tangible and intangible benefits and costs, organizational complexity, and cultural context are just some of the variables that can be considered. The time factor

Figure 1. Most significant barriers to ITIL adoption (Evergreen, 2006)

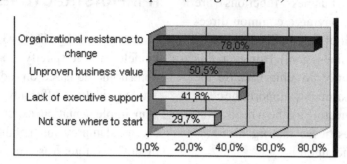

is also another important aspect to be considered in the investment evaluation process (Repenning & Sterman, 2001).

Since the value of these variables diverges greatly from organization to organization, adding up to the fact that ITIL v3 has 26 different processes, makes it is very difficult to cluster these values and, consequently, derive patterns and re-use estimations.

Thus, CIOs need a method that quantifies the intangible benefits and costs by selecting the metrics that are indispensable for computing the value of ITIL implementations. However, questions like the following one exemplify this difficulty: how measurable is customer satisfaction and increased process effectiveness? (Dos Santos, 1991; Silva & Gama, 2006). Besides, these benefits and costs take time to be realized, and if they are measured by business financial metrics, any connection with the original ITIL investment may seem tenuous, which might result in the questioning of the CIO's position as a leader. Therefore, CIOs tend to be short/mid-term thinkers as they want immediate returns, and usually do not like to take risks when it is not clear what the benefits are (Broadbent & Kitzis, 2004).

Consequently, ITIL projects that immediately fix problematic areas (e.g. incident management systems), commonly known as quick wins, are usually chosen instead of large scale ITIL implementations (University of St. Gallen, 2005). This happens because large-scale projects are more complex which originates confusion and increases

costs (Denker, 2005). Also, quick wins comprise an easier way of showing employees that ITIL works and, therefore, facilitates change that is naturally implicated in ITIL implementation projects (Silva & Martins, 2008; University of St. Gallen, 2005).

However, even if organizations observe a swift performance improvement after the quick win project is put into production, those improvements will not last forever as organizations are complex adaptive systems (Santa Fe Institute, 2005). Actually, after some time the problems that were initially solved may eventually come back and new ones might emerge, making the performance decrease yet again.

So, quick wins have early returns associated to them but, if the organization does not continue to incrementally implement the rest of the ITIL processes, then performance may become even worse than before (University of St. Gallen, 2005). On the other hand, if quick wins are completed successfully and the benefits are realized, it is much easier for the CIO to ask support for subsequent larger scale ITIL implementation projects.

Alternatively, CIOs who opt for long term ITIL implementations will experience higher returns because large scale ITIL implementations involve more abstract concepts (e.g. organization design) that systematically change the investments where the organization spends its time, which ends up making the ROI proportionally larger as it is a proactive process instead of reactive.

RELATED WORK

Currently, there is still limited academic research on appraising the value from ITIL implementations (Tiong, Cater-Steel & Tan, 2008). For this reason, ITIL estimation metrics are adapted from different investment analysis approaches which use financial metrics and other non-financial approaches, which are discussed in the following subsections.

Investment Analyses

The value of ITIL implementations can be estimated by using general investment analysis techniques because, likewise any investment, ITIL implementations still require an executive decision and financial numbers to support that decision. Thus, ITIL implementations are no different from other investments since they are treated as business decisions subject to the same investment thresholds as every business investment (Harvard Business Review, 1999).

In this manner, investment analyses provide executives with useful insights when faced with difficult investment decisions as financial metrics rank investment options against each other according to their economic value and, therefore, the decision-making process is supplied with valuable information. Another reason to calculate the value of ITIL implementations using financial metrics is due to the fact that finances and accounting practitioners still insist that every investment should be backed by verifiable metrics (Harvard Business Review, 1999).

In addition, cost benefit analyses estimate the attractiveness of an investment opportunity. However, these types of analyses have long been criticized for its inability to determine the risk and percept the value of investments of strategic nature and, therefore, are the reason for short-term decision-making focus and lack of adequate funds for large-scale IT investments. The "risk paradox" mirrors this reality: "if an organization

uses quantitative risk analysis at all, it is usually for routine operational decisions. The largest, most risky decisions get the least amount of proper risk analyses" (Hubbard, 2007).

The metrics by which IS are evaluated are divided into cost and benefit analyses and risk analyses. The metrics for cost and benefit analyses include: payback period, ROI, net present value, internal rate of return et cetera. And the risk analyses metrics include: sensitivity analysis (e.g. gross sensitivity analysis and stress testing), brainstorming, scenario planning, Monte Carlo simulation et cetera (Ballantine & Stray, 1999).

In fact, cost and benefit analyses under risk and uncertainty are the ones that embody the real value behind the estimation process since, without any quantification process concluded beforehand, some of the risk analyses can be valueless. Therefore, risk analyses are generally considered as a valuable extension of the estimation process (Stæhr, 2006).

Hence, several of the cost and benefit analysis as well as risk analysis metrics are analyzed thoroughly in the following points.

Cost and Benefit Analyses

It is important to analyze several financial metrics in terms of their main advantages and disadvantages, so as to identify which situations are more favorable to one financial metric in detriment of the others. Table 1 corresponds to the outcome of this comparison.

In summary, NPV, ROI and IRR should be used if CIOs want to understand how profitable an investment is. Likewise, EVA can also be used but only if the organization is publicly traded and the share value is an important factor for executives (as it should be). The PBP metric is good to determine how long a project will take until it compensates the initial investment.

Table 1. Comparison between financial metrics

Metrics	Advantages	Disadvantages
Net Present Value (NPV) (McCready, 2005; Harvard Business School, 2002; Gama, 2006; Dos Santos, 1991; Silvius, 2006)	- Takes under consideration the discount rate.	- Does not give any indication about the project's magnitude and risk. - Discount rate can be hard to calculate.
Return On Investment (ROI) (McCready, 2005; Harvard Business School, 2002; Silvius, 2006)	- Perfect for one-to-one project comparison. - Commonly used. - Takes under consideration the cost of capital.	- Does not give any indication about the project's magnitude. - Requires vendors to share "sensible" information. - Can only compare project with the same level of risk. - Does not recognize when the cash flows take place.
Internal Rate of Return (IRR) (McCready, 2005; Harvard Business School, 2002)	- Identifies investments with irregular profits. - Takes under consideration the discount rate.	- Not easy to compute and understand. - Does not give any indication about the project's magnitude. - Assumes that the cash inflow from an investment is reinvested at the same discount rate. - Hurdle rate varies from company to company.
PayBack Period (PBP) (McCready, 2005; Harvard Business School, 2002; Gama, 2006; Silvius, 2006)	- Expresses the time it takes for an investment to reach the 'break even' point. - Separates, in terms of risk, long-term from short-term investments.	- Does not take under consideration the discount rate. - Does not give any indication about the project's magnitude. - No information about the investment performance after the 'break even' point. - Does not identify when the cash flows take place.
Economic Value Added (EVA) (McCready, 2005; Harvard Business School, 2002; Symons, 2005)	- CIOs analyze investment with shareholder's lens. - Easy to understand. - Simple methodology. - Calculation includes cost of capital charges.	- Cannot be used by organizations that are not publicly traded. - EVA is uncertain. - Cost of capital varies from organization to organization.

Risk Analyses

In terms of sensitivity analysis, the gross sensitivity analysis reveals how sensitive the estimated ROI is to given changes in the considered variable.

In addition, stress testing consists of making an analysis of the extremes by calculating the worst/best case scenarios, and the baseline ROI is calculated by using expected values for all the variables used. Then, the ROI is recalculated by using, respectively, the smallest and the largest value for each of the variables (Stæhr, 2006; Ross, 2004).

The Monte Carlo simulation calculates the chances of success of the investment by using a normal distribution shape with a 95% confidence interval, which means that the probability that a value falls within 2σ (standard deviation) of the mean is 95%, so as to generate several scenarios through a random distribution of values, which belong to the area defined by the normal distribution curve (Hubbard, 2007; Ross, 2004).

Furthermore, several variables can be included in the Monte Carlo simulation and correlated with each others. For example, if the correlation between two variables is null then the coefficient is zero, but if there is a perfect level of correlation between two variables then the coefficient is one. If the level of correlation between two variables is high, independently of being a positive or negative r, there is more cohesion between the values assumed by the variables. On the other hand, if there is no correlation between two variables, the values are more dispersed in the Monte Carlo simulation (Rodger, Jason, 1999).

To conclude, performing risk analyses by using a Monte Carlo simulation is less limitative than using stress testing or gross sensitivity analysis, because gross sensitivity analysis only changes the values of one variable at a time and stress testing places excessive weight on very unlikely outcomes (Ross, 2004; Rodger, Jason, 1999).

IT Investment Comprehensive Approaches

Since both IS and ITIL regard organizations/systems as people, processes and technology (a slight difference comparing to the Management Information System mantra: "organization, management and technology"), an ITIL implementation can be considered an IS project. Another reason why ITIL and IS are akin is the organizational change that is associated to them, as both of them transform the organizations where they are implemented (Laudon & Laudon, 2005).

As a result, the value of ITIL implementations can be estimated by using IT investment analysis comprehensive approaches because, similarly to any IS investment, ITIL investments can be controlled and measured (Ward & Daniel, 2005).

Therefore, it is crucial to assess the real business value of ITIL implementations, which means that CIOs have to quantify the tangible benefits (e.g. sales increase, incidents reduction, production increase and workforce reduction), as well as the intangible benefits (e.g. greater insight into the relationship between users, configuration items and incidents and customer satisfaction). Even though intangible benefits are particularly difficult to quantify and measure, they definitely bring value to the organization, meaning that they must be part of the estimation process mentioned before.

For this reason, new methodologies that go beyond the traditional investment analysis, which are explained in the previous sub-section, are needed instead of focusing only on cost analysis and savings. Hence, focusing on intangible benefits as well (Violino, 1997).

However, the problem lays in the fact that CIOs must quantify these intangibles so as to give evidence that a certain investment will actually realize benefits for their organization. But, this is not an easy task, on the contrary (Violino, 1997).

Nevertheless, some authors defend that it is indeed possible to measure anything or at least to reduce the uncertainty about the value of something, by making assumptions that can help reaching an estimated value, therefore defending that the value of intangibles is not so intangible after all (Hubbard, 2007)

It is important to analyze two well-know approaches: the benefits management approach and the Val IT framework, in terms of their main advantages and disadvantages so as to identify which situations are more favorable to one approach in detriment of the other. corresponds to the outcome of this comparison.

Benefits Management

The benefits management approach is one of the available solutions for this problem, because it organizes and manages IS investments so as to actually realize the potential benefits arising from the use of IT. In fact, the benefits management approach goes beyond the aspects of IS evaluation such as financial metrics. Instead, benefits management is a comprehensive process that includes several phases. Indeed, the benefits management approach encloses the beginning and end of project management and surrounds each project (Ward & Daniel, 2005).

The advantages of the benefits management approach are (Ward & Daniel, 2005):

- CIOs and executives are able to realize

the benefits of a particular IT investment, bringing deep understanding of the business value that IT investments can provoke.

- Having the benefit of hindsight, this approach gives CIOs and executives the opportunity to make consistent and appropriate investment choices.
- If the organization embraces this methodology, the business and IT will become aligned.

And the disadvantages of the benefits management approach are (Ward & Daniel, 2005):

- It is a process and has to be used in its full extension so as to be effective.
- Requires an organization to fully adapt to the benefits management process which can cause organizational resistance, and the learning curve is also an issue.
- Many organizations have difficulties to define all the benefits.
- Requires specialists to make this approach fit with the organization.

To put it briefly, the benefits management process enables organizations to avoid benefits 'loss' and increases the number of benefits achieved by IS/IT projects. However, it is hard to change employees' attitude to embrace the benefits management "mindset".

Val IT

The purpose of the Val IT and the benefits management approaches are similar as both were designed to monitor IT investments.

The Val IT is a governance framework that consists of a set of guiding principles that provide CIOs with sufficient know-how to correctly manage IT investments, so as to generate as much value as possible from IT investments. In fact, the Val IT framework extends and complements the COBIT framework, which provides a compre-

hensive control framework for IT governance, by focusing on the investment decision and the realization of benefits parts. On the other hand, COBIT is responsible for the execution part of the IT governance framework (Symons, 2007).

The Val IT advantages are (Symons, 2007):

- Active value management.
- Initiatives evaluation is not too narrow, as Val IT business cases have to be very detailed and continually updated throughout the life cycle of an investment, so as to support the ongoing implementation and execution of a project.

And, the Val IT disadvantages are (Symons, 2007):

- Despite the availability of guidelines and case studies, few CIOs have adopted Val IT so far.
- Governance practices like reporting are very difficult to implement.
- Val IT requires a mature IT governance framework already in place.

Comparison

Both Val IT and benefits management approaches have a longer learning curve than general investment analyses. However, they have the advantage of being comprehensive processes and realizing both tangible and intangible benefits. Therefore, they can bring more long-term added value to the organization when comparing to general investment analyses, although organizational resistance can become a tough barrier to overcome.

On the other hand, considering the current financial crisis and, consequently, the IT budget cuts, it is more than ever necessary to economically justify IT investments using financial metrics.

Independent of which approach is chosen, each ITIL process has its own list of tangible and intangible benefits specified in one of the five

Figure 2. ITIL value estimation process

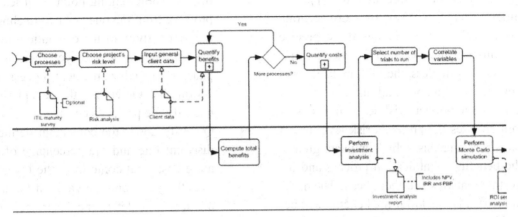

ITIL v3 books, and in order to assess the value of ITIL implementations these benefits have to be measured, but without forgetting that other variables influence the business value of the investment, for example: current maturity level of each ITIL process and dependencies between ITIL processes as well.

In conclusion, the two topics studied in this section do not constitute a satisfactory solution for the thesis' problem, because they are not prepared to make an accurate estimation of the value of ITIL implementations, as ITIL implementations involve multiple complex variables specific to ITIL which must be regarded. Nonetheless, these two approaches do provide essential insight and background for the conception of the estimation process that is described in the following section.

PROPOSED ESTIMATION PROCESS

After making a bibliographic research about general and IT-specific investment evaluation methodologies, the next logical step is to propose a solution.

In order to perform a cost benefit analysis, three actions should be included in the estimation process: determine the tangible and intangible benefits in addition to the project's costs, which embody the tangibility return of an investment,

and determine the NPV (Silvius, 2008). Subsequently, an additional sensitivity analysis should be included as the previous variables are not deterministic and, therefore, are subjected to risks and uncertainty (Stæhr, 2006).

In this research work, these steps are used with an exception. Instead of only determining the NPV, the calculation of the ROI, PBP and IRR is also included in the cost benefit analysis because they can be easily interpreted and are common financial metrics used by managers. On the other hand, the EVA is not included in the estimation process as it takes the "net operating profits after taxes" as input, which is a difficult variable to assess in the context of this research work. Also, the sensitivity analysis is performed over the ROI instead of the NPV because managers tend to value more this financial metric.

Estimation Process Description

The estimation process is represented by figure 2 and the following points explain each activity and sub-process in more detail:

- Choose the processes: the start event leads to the first activity of the process which is performed by the consultant. In this activity, the consultant determines which ITIL processes will be implemented. If a maturity survey occurs beforehand, the opportunities selection will be a lot more accurate because the consultant has more precise information about each ITIL process's maturity. Nevertheless, the ITIL maturity survey artifact is an optional input.

- Choose the project's risk level: the consultant chooses the project's risk level based on a risk analysis, which impacts greatly the benefits quantification process and investment analysis further ahead. The higher the risk is, the lower the benefits will be, and the investment is influenced as well, i.e. the higher the risk is, the higher the value of the investment will be. So, there is a downward revision of the benefits and an upward revision of the investment value, which is done on ad-hoc basis, for instance: by decreasing 10% of the benefits and increasing 10% of the value of the investment (Stæhr, 2006).

- Input general client data: the consultant inputs general client data, for example: the organization's revenue, number of employees and working hours per year.

- Quantify benefits: "prior to implementing any process improvement initiative, processes should be measured and if possible assigned a monetary value" (Tiong, Cater-Steel & Tan, 2008). Therefore, in this sub-process the benefits are quantified by analyzing the general client data gathered in the previous activity, as well as KPIs specific to each process which can be found in official literature (Brooks, 2006; Steinberg, 2006), for example: the total number of incidents, estimated average time lost in an incident per employee, etc.

- Compute total benefits: the benefits are automatically quantified by the ITIL Value Estimator through the analysis of the data that is inserted in the "quantify benefits" sub-process.

- More processes?: this gateway consists

of a decision-making point. If at least one process, from the ones that were chosen in the first activity of the estimation process, has not been processed yet, then the next phase is to analyze the next process on the waiting list. Otherwise, the next phase is to quantify the project's costs.

- Quantify costs: the consultant defines the discount rate and the percentage of operating costs that come from the investment over the years and the value of the investment, so as to determine the project's costs.

- Perform investment analysis: using the data gathered in the previous two activities, a financial analysis is made in order to assess the NPV, PBP and IRR of the investment. These values constitute the investment analysis report depicted as the output artifact of this activity.

- Select number of trials to run: in this activity the consultant selects how many scenarios will be used to perform a Monte Carlo simulation.

- Correlate variables: because some variables are correlated to others, i.e. "the state of one variable gives us the information about the likely occurrence of another" (Rodger, Jason, 1999), it is important not to ignore the correlations that exist between variables. Therefore, the consultant has to define the correlation coefficients between all the variables that enter the sensitivity analysis.

- Perform Monte Carlo simulation: to finalize the estimation process, a Monte Carlo simulation on the project's ROI is performed. However, discovering the estimated ROI by using the expected values for the project's benefits and costs is generally incorrect because of non-linearity between the variables (i.e. they are correlated). In order for the ITIL Value Estimator to be more precise and, therefore, more reliable, it is important to perform a Monte

Figure 3. Benefits quantification sub-process

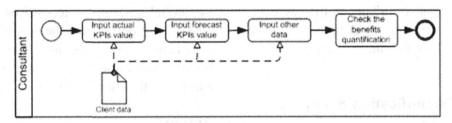

Carlo simulation since it is mathematically correct if the chosen distributions for the variables are correct. According to the "central limit theorem", since the ROI results from the sum of several variables, there are strong arguments for choosing a normal distribution. The chance that the investment will compensate is calculated by counting the number of scenarios in which the user-defined breakeven line is reached. This activity is comparable to the certainty revenue which is one of the characteristics of an investment (Silvius, 2008).

Benefits Quantification Process

This sub-process is constituted by four activities as it is illustrated in figure 3. The first activity is for the consultant to input the actual KPIs value into the ITIL Value Estimator as well as the forecast values considered to be more adequate by the consultant. Finally, other data besides the KPIs is inserted in the necessary fields and the logic behind the benefits quantification has to be checked by the consultant.

Costs Quantification Process

This sub-process, pictured in figure 4, requires the consultant to define the discount rate and the percentage of operating costs that come from the investment over the years and the value of the investment, so as to determine the project's costs.

IMPLEMENTATION

In order to realize the estimation process described in the previous section, a prototype was built with Microsoft Excel 2003 technology. Excel proved to be effective as it allows the prototype to be fully configurable, provides essential built-in functions that confer implementation flexibility as well as implementation speed, and allows powerful addIns to be incorporated into the ITIL Value Estimator.

Prototype's Development Process

The prototype's construction evolved at the same time as the development of the estimation process did, which was the result of several interactions

Figure 4. Cost quantification sub-process

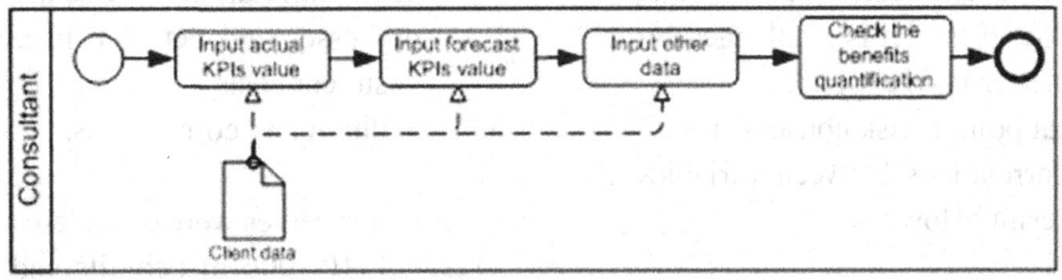

(i.e. meetings) with practitioners, insights from ITIL experts, and contributions that were introduced as a consequence of further scientific investigation. Therefore, the development process was agile.

Benefits Quantification Synopsis

The quantification of the value of each KPI is the result of human reasoning, which means that the estimation process must be prepared to accept modifications to the benefits quantification sub-process, in order to be easily adapted to the user's raison d'être.

Finally, the logic of the benefits quantification sub-process can always be challenged because it is hard to give each KPI a monetary value, despite the fact that they still can bring value to the process under analysis, as ITIL can be a business need, for instance: clients can demand suppliers to have ITIL best practices embedded into their organization, which supports the statement that an improvement in the maturity of one or more processes or the savings gained from improved KPI values, which are typically hard to quantify, bring value to the bottom-line of the organization.

Evaluation Methodology

The evaluation methodology varies according to two distinct situations: when only one process is considered for the estimation process or when multiple processes are considered.

Several questions have to be answered in order to evaluate one process:

- Which metrics are the most relevant during the benefits quantification sub-process?
- Is the logic of the KPIs challenged by the practitioner or ITIL experts?
- Until what point is risk consequential?
- Do the correlations between variables affect the result? How?

On the other hand, the evaluation methodology for several processes is focused on the consequences that derive from the dependencies that exist between processes and, consequently, the benefits adjacent to the correlation coefficients attached to these dependencies.

Action

Incident Management Process Simulation

A simulation using real KPIs' data was performed in a Portuguese state/public organization which implemented one ITIL process, the incident management process, for a period of one year.

In order to determine the real value of the incident management process it is necessary to retrieve reliable data directly from historical data and introduce it into the prototype, in order to perform the investment analysis as well as the Monte Carlo simulation. The estimated value of one or more processes is then calculated by introducing input data regarding the forecast values of the KPIs and other data, which were determined by the practitioner.

So, in this way it is possible to compare the estimator's effectiveness in a past project by comparing that project's real value and estimated value.

Simulation with Multiple Processes

A theoretical simulation with several processes was performed so as to evaluate the value of the correlations that exist between processes. The following tests were performed:

- With correlations that exist between the processes and between processes and investment costs.
- Without any correlations.

Four processes were considered and each one creates € 100.000 of benefits and the project's

Table 2. Percentages from total benefits

KPIs	Forecasted situation	Real situation
Percentage of incidents resolved without breaching one	N/A	**49,07%**
Percentage of incidents resolved within target time by priority	0,00%	N/A
Percentage of incidents re-assigned	0,13%	0,29%
Percentage of incidents incorrectly categorized	0,00%	0,00%
Percentage of calls 1st line support bypassed	3,22%	**40,22%**
Incident management process maturity	0,00%	0,01%
Number of incidents	**93,31%**	N/A
Percentage of incidents resolved by 1st line support	0,16%	1,03%
Average call time with no escalation (minutes)	0,02%	0,46%
Percentage of incidents incorrectly assigned	0,04%	0,11%
Average time for 2nd level support to respond (minutes)	1,29%	1,71%
Average time to resolve incidents (minutes)	0,27%	2,28%
Percentage of calls that are service requests	0,47%	3,42%
Percentage of incidents solved rightly the first time	0,02%	0,03%

overall investment is € 500.000, which means that the ROI mean value is -20%. The purpose of this simulation is to realize if the correlations that exist between processes pay off the superior project's investment costs or not.

Results

Incident Management Process Simulation

According to table 2, the KPI "number of incidents" has a devastating influence over the benefits quantification outcome in the simulation with estimated data with 93,31% of the monetary benefits. In contrast, the simulation with real data confirmed the existence of two high-impact KPIs, "percentage of incidents resolved without breaching one SLA" and "percentage of calls 1st line support bypassed", with 49,07% and 40,22%, respectively.

Therefore, some of the other KPIs proved to be irrelevant, but those KPIs whose percentages are linearly dependent on the "percentage of time that impacts employee productivity" could have more impact on the final result, if this percentage was set to a higher value.

So, the KPI "number of incidents" unleveraged the results of both simulations. In fact, the estimated value for this KPI is the outcome of a

Figure 5. ROI Monte Carlo simulation with (left) and without (right) correlations

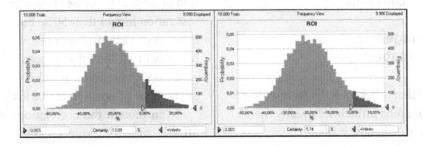

meeting with ITIL experts and the target organization's practitioner which challenged the benefits quantification. Hence, this KPI is included only in the benefits quantification of the simulation with estimated data because no real data was available at the time.

Taking a look at the risk, it influenced greatly the financial metrics included in the financial analysis. Thus, when the risk increases, the NPV and IRR decrease and the PBP increases.

Lastly, a higher level of a negative correlation between variables is associated to higher values of variance, standard deviation and skewness, which means that the Monte Carlo simulation trials tend to be more dispersed if there are negative correlations between the variables considered.

Simulation with Multiple Processes

Even though the correlations might not pay off the superior project's investment costs, there were more positive ROI scenarios in the Monte Carlo simulation with correlations than in the one without correlations, as it is illustrated in figure 5, which is caused by the fact that the standard deviation, variance and skewness are higher in the simulation with correlations than in the one without, and this causes the trials to be more dispersed in the simulation with correlations.

EVALUATION

This section is dedicated to evaluating how successful the action was so as to test out how well the proposed estimation process performed in stipulating what action to take.

Incident Management Process Simulation

The simple fact that different KPIs were utilized in the two simulations influenced greatly the effectiveness of the estimator itself.

As a consequence, different quantification logics were applied in both simulations, for instance: some KPIs are based on the employee productivity whilst others are based on the cost per incident, which is calculated by dividing the IT total costs by the total number of incidents in a period of one year. On the other hand, the employee productivity is the result of the division of the revenue by the total number of employees.

Using different forms of quantification isn't necessarily incorrect. On the contrary, it makes the estimator more correct as both forms are valid and should be taken under consideration, since the cost per incident is focused on cost reduction and the employee productivity is driven towards productivity gains.

Also, in view of the fact that the risk's influence over the investment analyses is enormous, it is important that the risk analysis is performed carefully and with the help of risk experts.

Simulation with Multiple Processes

When the correlations amongst processes are considered in order to perform a Monte Carlo simulation, there are higher chances of more positive ROI outputs being generated as a consequence.

To prove this statement, the expected loss ratio of the simulation without correlations is 7,35% higher than the one of the simulation with correlations, meaning that there are more 7,35% case scenarios with a positive ROI in the simulation that considers correlations. This result cannot be expected in situations where correlations amid processes are not considered at all.

The Monte Carlo simulation of the implementation of several processes could have an expected loss ration higher than 50%, but the fact that the benefits of each process positively influence the benefits of all the other processes decreases the expected loss ratio or, in other words, increases the number of positive scenarios.

Even though the correlations might not pay off the superior project's investment costs, it is important to consider them in the estimation process as some potential generated outputs are not neglected and, therefore, the client can be elucidated about the potential of large scale ITIL investments.

So, the benefits generated by a single process are considerably less due to the fact that the positive correlations between processes are not included in the Monte Carlo simulation.

Estimation Process Re-factorization

Taking into account the results' evaluation that is performed in the previous sub-sections, the estimation process can be re-factorized by making the following changes:

- Due to the fact that multiple interactions with the client must occur so as to improve the benefits quantification logic, this sub-process becomes cyclical.
- In case of a large scale ITIL implementation, i.e. a project with multiple processes, the dependencies between these should be checked in order to correlate the processes and this is the reason for placing a gateway after the "select the number of trials" activity. In case of being a single-process ITIL implementation, only the benefits of that process and the project's investment costs have to be correlated.

CONCLUSION

The value of ITIL is a much discussed subject these days as reducing IT costs, increasing IT performance and, at the same time, improving business performance through IT-business alignment are vital for any organization.

The related work provided enough insight to create an estimation process for assessing the value of ITIL implementations. An important acumen to be added is that ITIL investments impact dramatically the business processes' efficiency as well as the business goals' effectiveness. For this reason, the estimation process incorporates into its logic the investments' impact, plus the tangible and intangible benefits quantification as well as project's investment costs and, lastly, the risk assessment of the investment which is the ultimate outcome of the estimation process.

The estimation process was tested with data retrieved from a project that consisted of implementing the incidents management process in a state organization. The main results were that only a few KPIs have a great impact on the final benefits quantification and the project's risk has a great influence over the investment analysis and the ROI Monte Carlo simulation.

Furthermore, a theoretical exercise was performed so as to evaluate how the interconnections between processes affect the overall project's ROI. The results were revealing as the project's mean ROI can be negative but, given the fact that those processes are interconnected and interdependent, the benefits are heightened, which ends up making the investment more attractive.

FUTURE WORK

Being able to manage the IT function by using the ITIL framework cannot be done without assessing the value of ITIL implementations. Therefore, it is critical for organizations that aspire to have a state-of-the-art enterprise information systems to continue studying this chapter's theme in order to possess the necessary information when making the go/no-go decision.

Knowing that ITIL processes depend on each other, specifying the correlation coefficients between two processes is a way to include those dependencies into the estimation process, and these correlation coefficients can be derived from statistical analyses of past data or be suggested by experts. In fact, those correlations can be defined by comparing two experimental data sets, which are derived from the level of dependency that exist between processes, by using several mathematical methodologies such as the Pearson's correlation coefficient, or by associating the Pearson's correlation coefficient with the rank order coefficient (Rodger, Jason, 1999).

Another topic that needs further research is when a major operational change takes place in the IT function, for instance, when the IT department adopts a charge-back methodology for the incident management process, meaning that the IT department charges a certain amount of money per incident according to the incident's complexity and urgency. This change implies that a new KPI has to be created and quantified, but there is no way to compare the as-is with the to-be situation because the KPI is not considered in the benefits quantification before the charge-back adoption takes place. So, it is necessary to further study how these changes, whatever their range is, impact the value of ITIL implementations and, specially, what is the best way to compare the as-is with the to-be situation.

REFERENCES

Ballantine, J., & Stray, S. (1999). *Information Systems and Other Capital Investments: evaluation practices compared*. Logistics Information Management.

Broadbent, M., & Kitzis, E. (2004). *The New CIO Leader*. Cambridge, MA: Harvard Business School Press.

Brooks, P. (2006). *Metrics for IT Service Management*. San Antonio, TX: Van Haren Publishing.

Denker, A. (2005). The Challenge of Large IT Projects . In *Proceedings of World Academy of Science* (*Vol. 9*). Engineering and Technology.

Dos Santos, B. (1991). Justifying Investments in New Information Technologies. *Journal of Management Information Systems*.

Evergreen. (2006). *Developing the Business Value of ITIL*.

Gama, N. (2006). *O Business Value dos Investimentos em Sistemas de Informação*. Instituto Superior Técnico.

Gartner. (2006). The Information Technology Infrastructure Library Improves Infrastructure Investment.

Harvard Business Review. (1999). *The Business Value of IT*.

Harvard Business School. (2002). *Finance for managers*.

Hubbard, D. (2007). *How to Measure Anything: Finding the Value of Intangibles in Business*. Hoboken, NJ: John Wiley & Sons, Inc.

Laudon, K., & Laudon, J. (2005). *Management Information Systems: Managing the Digital Firm* (10th ed.). Upper Saddle River, NJ: Prentice Hall.

McCready, S. (2005). TCO, NPV, EVA, IRR, ROI, Getting the terms right. *CIOview*.

O'Leary, J. (2002). *Learn to Speak the Language of ROI*. Harvard Management Update.

Repenning, N., & Sterman, J. (2001). *Nobody ever gets credit for fixing problems that never happened: creating and sustaining process improvement*. California Management Review.

Rodger, C., Jason, P. (1999). Uncertainty & Risk Analysis. *PriceWaterHouseCoopers*.

Ross, J., & Weill, P. (2002). *Six IT Decision Your IT People Shouldn't Make*. Harvard Business Review.

Ross, S. (2004). *Introduction to Probability and Statistics for Engineers and Scientists*. Amsterdam: Elsevier Academic Press.

Seddon, P., Graeser, V., Willcocks, L. (2002). Measuring Organizational IS Effectiveness: an overview and update of senior management perspectives. *SIGMISDatabase*.

Silva, M., & Gama, N. (2006). *Activos Intangíveis dos Sistemas de Informação*. Instituto Superior Técnico.

Silva, M., & Martins, J. (2008). *IT Governance*. FCA.

Silvius, A. (2006). Does ROI Matter? Insights into the True Business Value of IT. *The Electronic Journal Information Systems Evaluation, 9*(2).

Silvius, A. (2008). The Business Value of IT: A Conceptual Model for Selecting Valuation Methods. *Communications of the IIMA, 8*(3).

Stæhr, K. (2006). *Risk and Uncertainty in Cost Benefit Analysis*. Institute for Miljøvurdering.

Steinberg, R. (2006). *Measuring ITIL*. Bloomington, IN: Trafford Publishing.

Symons, C. (2005). *Add EVA to IT Investment Analysis*. Forrester.

Symons, C. (2007). *From IT Governance to Value Delivery*. Forrester.

Tiong, C., Cater-Steel, A., & Tan, W. (2008). *Measuring Return on Investment from Implementing ITIL – A Review of the Literature*. Hershey, PA: Information Science Publishing.

University of St. Gallen. (2005). *Service-Oriented IT Management: Benefit*. Cost and Success Factors.

Violino, B. (1997). *Return on Investment*. Information Week.

Ward, J., & Daniel, E. (2005). *Benefits Management, Delivering Value from IS & IT investments*. Hoboken, NJ: Wiley Series.

Chapter 26
Information Systems Outsourcing:
Risks and Benefits for Organizations

Ana André
Technical University of Lisbon, Portugal

Fernanda Sampaio
Technical University of Lisbon, Portugal

ABSTRACT

Information Systems (IS) Outsourcing has emerged as a strategic option to be considered and has been increasingly adopted by managers. However, many contracts still fail during their initial years, meaning that Outsourcing has also been subject to strong criticism. There are advantages to Outsourcing but also significant risks associated to it, and the assessment of both is therefore of great relevance for informed decision-making. The objective of this chapter is to determine to what extent a common view about risks and benefits associated to IS Outsourcing is shared by the Portuguese market players: Service Providers, Clients and Opinion Makers. In order to accomplish this, an on-line Delphi study was conducted, combined with the Q-sort technique, which allowed to obtain the perspective of each player on the risks and benefits IS Outsourcing. Comparing these perspectives it was possible to understand that the market players don't share the same point of view.

INTRODUCTION

Driven by profit organizations are impelled to stay competitive or they risk loosing market share. Presented with an ever-changing business environment, today's organizations continuously look for more agile ways of working, capable of increasing their ability to respond to market demands. Therefore, Information Systems (IS)

Outsourcing has emerged as a strategic option to be considered and has been increasingly adopted by managers.

The Outsourcing is "considered as one of the effectiveness ways that organizations meet to balance the equation of technology evolution, costs reduction and service quality" (Maculuve & Rodrigues, 2002). Organizations are transferring a large amount of their IS functions to external providers, from logistics to human resources, so

DOI: 10.4018/978-1-61692-020-3.ch026

they can focus on their core competences (Vara-jão, 2002).

The increase in organizations' Outsourcing-related expenditure in recent years shows that Outsourcing has grown – not only in Europe but also in Portugal. IDC (2005) reveals a growth rate of 10% in Portugal, slightly lower than the 11% average in Europe. In addition it predicts a growth of 40% of Outsourcing in Portugal for the period between 2005 and 2009.

According to Gartner, quoted by Ramos (2006), 50% of Outsourcing contracts fail, being renegotiated and in 25% of the cases the contract cancellation eventually occurs. Dun & Bradstreet, also mentioned by Ramos (2006), refers that 20% to 25% of Outsourcing contracts do not succeed during their two initial years and this rate increases to 50% after five years of contract. Also, in 70% of the cases "the Service Provider did not understand adequately what was supposed to do".

There are advantages to Outsourcing but also significant risks associated to it and the assessment of both is therefore of great relevance for informed decision-making.

The objective of this chapter is to contribute to the understanding of the risks and the benefits associated to IS Outsourcing and also to determine to what extent a common view about them is shared by the Portuguese market players – Service Providers, Clients and Opinion Makers.

THEORETICAL BACKGROUND

Information Systems Outsourcing

Several authors present numerous definitions for Outsourcing, which seem to converge to the perception that is the act of contracting out services, which the organization can perform inside, to an external Service Provider by option and to focus on their core business.

Faulhaber (2005) describes Outsourcing as "the strategic use of external resources to carry out

tasks that usually are internally executed. Griffiths (1999) enhance this concept defining Outsourcing as "the strategic use of outside resources to perform activities traditionally handled by internal staff and resources". Outsourcing could engage a significant restructuring of certain activities, often including human resources transfer from a main corporation to a specialized one, usually smaller but with the necessary skills to do those activities. Outsourcing is the act of delegating or transferring some or all of the IT related decision, business processes, internal activities and services to an external provider who develop and manage those activities according to predetermined deliverables, conditions and results as established on contract (Dhar & Balakrishnan, 2006).

Outsourcing covers a wide range of options, from the strategic option of delegating total IT management to the execution of a simple function, as an answer to specific organization's needs (IDC, 2005). Rocha (2006) states that "the Outsourcing market confers different names to different kind of deals, but the boundary between them it is difficult to define". The Outsourcing degree and the way this type of arrangements are established contribute to the multiplicity of existent relationships. The IS function can be handled internally, by a subsidiary or shared with the Service Provider; or developed externally either totally or for a selection of its components. On the other hand different Provider-Client sourcing arrangements are possible from single Provider - single Client to complex relations as multiple Providers - multiple Clients (Dibbern et al., 2004).

The Historical Evolution of IS Outsourcing

The IS Outsourcing concept has been changing since its genesis. In different published papers, such as Loh & Venkatraman (1992), Lacity & Willcocks (1998), Lee et al.(2003), Dibbern et al. (2004), Sargent (2006) and Gonzalez et al.

Figure 1. Outsourcing process between the client and the service provider

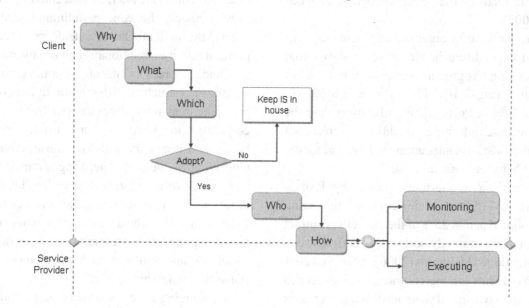

(2006b) it is possible to identify a turning point in Outsourcing contracts made till then.

During the 60's, small organizations seek hardware Outsourcing as a way to avoid costs with the acquisition of large and very expensive equipment, needed to their data processing services (Lee et al., 2003). The contract between the Blue Cross and the EDS (Electronic Data Systems), in 1963, to manage its data processing services it is considered as the genesis of IS Outsourcing (Dibbern et al., 2004) as an option for large organizations, which involved the entire data processing department and the IS people transfer to EDS (Sargent, 2006).

However it was the Kodak contract, in 1989, that marked a new generation of IS Outsourcing mega-deals (Lacity e Willcocks, 1998; Gonzalez et al., 2006b), currently known as the Kodak effect (Sargent, 2006), since it consisted on a strategic alliance with its IS partners - IBM, DEC and Businessland. This contract turned out to be of a great attention because it involved big and well-known organizations as IBM and Kodak, with an investment of 1 billion dollars deal, including assets and IS people transfer.

Nowadays, IS Outsourcing is associated to strong partnerships and alliances, where the Client and the Provider share risks and rewards (Dibbern et al., 2004).

The dissemination of successful Outsourcing contracts led to a global escalation of this practice (Varajão, 2002), as observed in other large US, Europe, Canada or Australia organizations that strategically adopted the Outsourcing (Lacity e Willcocks, 1998).

The Outsourcing Process

The Outsourcing process involves the Client and its Provider and describes the phases they go through when evaluating and implementing an Outsourcing solution. Figure 1 illustrates this process, combining suggestions from previous studies as Deloitte (2003) and Dibbern et al. (2004).

The process is divided into two major phases: the adopting Outsourcing decision and the solution implementation. During the first phase the organization weighs the advantages and disadvantages associated to Outsourcing ("why"), seeks to determine "what" to outsource and "which" is the adequate arrangement for its specific needs. Once the organization finds the answer to these questions it should undertake a careful evaluation of which way to proceed. If the decision is to go forward and adopt Outsourcing, the second phase of the process will begin, which means a provider must be selected ("who").

Both Client and Service Provider should agree on "how" to implement the chosen Outsourcing solution, negotiating a contract and implementing tools which will help them to manage the relationship. Finally as the provider delivers the service (execution), the Client should monitor the results attained for the specific outsourced function (monitoring).

During and after Outsourcing implementation organizations evaluate the results, which reflect the consequences of the Outsourcing decision, that is to say the success or failure of the arrangement and the lessons learned.

Outsourcing Risks and Benefits

Outsourcing Risks

Risk involves uncertainty hence, for the present study, the definition adopted is the probability of an event loss leading to occur.

In previous studies authors like Dhar & Balakrishnan (2006), Gewald & Hinz (2004), Bhattacharyaa et al. (2003), adopted different definitions of risk according to their line of investigation. For Dhar & Balakrishnan (2006) "risk can be interpreted as the occurrence of undesirable events". On the other hand Gewald & Hinz (2004) consider a more accurate definition of risk as a measurable probability of the negative deviation of a target value in relation to a reference value. Bhattacharyaa et al. (2003) adopt a theoretical perspective of IS Outsourcing risk, defining it as "the possibility of an unsatisfactory outcome".

Outsourcing Benefits

A benefit represents the gain attained based on an established goal. An organization adopts Outsourcing with the perspective of gaining something.

The common drivers for the organizations to outsource are to reduce and control operating costs, to improve the organization performance on its core competences, to gain access to capabilities they don't have in-house, to free internal resources for other purposes or even as a way of sharing risks with a partner company (Griffiths, 1999).

Delphi Method with Q-Sort

The Delphi method allows the analysis of qualitative data and involves a series of iterative questionnaires presented to a number of experts in a subject matter to obtain information about emerging themes and ideas, through consensus among the group of participants (Brown, 2007).

The Delphi method was devised at RAND Corporation in the 1950's (Santos & Amaral, 2004) and it was applied by the USA defence to improve the investigation based on experts forecasting (Okoli & Pawlowski, 2004).

This method was adopted in this study because the analysis of risks and benefits of Outsourcing has a strong qualitative nature and the Delphi has been the dominant approach to key IS issues research (Campos, 1998; Gottschalk et al., 2000; Gottschalk, 2001; Gonzalez et al., 2006a). Several examples may be pointed out as how the Delphi was applied to:

- investigate the drivers and inhibitors of Internet banking adoption as a channel for the delivery of financial services, by Bradley & Stewart, 2002;
- exploit the expected future role and use of four information systems and technology which gives an opportunity to improve the inter-organizational relations, by Daniel & White, 2005;

- identify success key factors for the on-line Information Services of Science and Technology Management Systems, by Santos, 2004;
- give more structure to the field of Knowledge Management and to get an outlook on developments for the next ten years, by Scholl et al., 2004;
- identify key issues of Information Systems Management in the Portuguese environment, by Campos, 1998;
- present a systemic framework of what the field of Information Systems is about, by Bacon & Fitzgerald, 2001;
- obtain Information Systems managers' view about Outsourcing in Spain, Gonzalez et al., 2006a.

It is rather usual to combine the Delphi method with sorting techniques as the Likert or the Q-sort scales.

The Likert scale is the most frequently used technique in key IS issues research, therefore became the most well-known and studied scale (Campos, 1998). In this classification, the expert judges each issue independently giving it a scale value and does not consider the issue as a part of a whole. This way, turns difficult to judge the importance of each issue relatively to the other issues, and it is common to give the extreme scale values, which contributes to obtain different issues with the same classification.

In this case the Delphi study was conducted with the Q-sort technique because it would serve the purpose of obtaining risks and benefits of Outsourcing ranked according to their importance (Okoli & Pawlowski, 2004). With this technique participants are asked to rank instead to rate and to take in consideration all issues simultaneously (Amaral et al., 2003) which prevents equal positions among listed issues.

The Delphi should be conducted through as many rounds as the necessary to achieve a reasonable level of consensus. When consensus is reached one can say the listed issues ranking is reliable (Amaral et al., 2003). The concept of a group consensus is the opinion homogeneity or consistency among the participants. In previous studies the Delphi round process has been stopped by the lack of time to proceed or the decrease of answer rates between a round to another (Santos, 2004). In this study the Kendall coefficient of agreement W was adopted as a way to evaluate the level of consensus among the experts, since it has been widely applied with the Delphi method in different knowledge areas to identify and prioritize key issues (Miguel, 2000). This Kendall's W verify the agreement among the experts, measuring the correlation of the ranked issues (Miguel, 2000). The coefficient value increase with the level of consensus, varying from 0 (without consensus) to 1 (perfect consensus) (Schmidt, 1997). This coefficient cannot be negative because when several experts are involved they can completely agree but they will not entirely disagree (Miguel, 2000).

When Kendall's coefficient is small the decision is trivial but when consensus is moderate it is difficult to come to a decision (Schmidt, 1997). Schmidt (1997) points out two criteria that can be used to stop the round process of a Delphi study:

- In case of strong consensus ($W >= 0.7$) or
- In case of absence of strong consensus among the experts, a levelling off of Kendall's W from one round to the next, which indicates a lack of progress between rounds.

Schmidt (1997) refers that for a group of more than 10 experts, even very small values of W can be significant.

EMPIRICAL STUDY METHODOLOGY

The study methodology was a qualitative survey carried out in Portugal, using the Delphi method with Q-sort, to obtain the IS market players perspective about which risks and which benefits are considered to be of most importance. Comparing these perspectives it was possible to evaluate to what extent a common view is shared by the market players.

In this research the practical application of the method followed the steps described in the next sections.

Identification of Experts

The Delphi method does not depend on a statistical and representative sample of a certain population, but on a group of qualified experts that detain a deep understanding of a specific issue (Okoli & Pawlowski, 2004). More important than the size of the experts group are their capabilities and knowledge about the issue under analysis (Saizarbitoria et al., 2006).

The participants are divided into three panels which represent the IS market players - Service Providers, Clients and Opinion Makers. The selection of the participants followed the recommendations of the Delphi method. The experts' selection for the Service Providers and Clients panels was supported by IDC Portugal (International Data Corporation), which by the nature of its activity has a collection of organizations that regularly participate on its Outsourcing studies. For the Opinion Makers panel the experts invited were authors with work published in magazines, journals, private institutions studies or conferences within this field.

The Service Providers panel was formed by 11 top managers from organizations that provide IS Outsourcing services. In general, these organizations have a business volume higher than 40 millions of Euros and more than 500 workers.

The Clients group was composed by 12 top managers from organizations that adopted IS Outsourcing. These organizations are mainly from Bank, Post and Communications, Insurance and Electricity business sectors and they have a busi-

ness volume higher than 100 millions of Euros and more than 1000 workers.

Finally, the experts who formed the Opinion Makers group were 9 elements from the academic community; from specialized press; and private institutions with published studies or conferences within this field.

Structure of Questions

The lists of risks and benefits presented to the experts were constructed based on a literature review about IS Outsourcing where risks feared by organizations and benefits they aim were identified.

The lists included a clear description of each issue to avoid misinterpretations that could bias the results and were constructed concerning with:

- Intelligibility, so they were capable of being understood;
- An unambiguous speech;
- Adequate translations, since items were a result of foreign literature review

In addition, the Transaction Costs Theory contributed to build the list of Outsourcing risks (Table 1). Trough this theory it was possible to identify risk factors associated both to the transaction (the activity outsourced) and the human behaviour of the intervenient in that transaction (Service Providers and Clients).

For the list of Outsourcing benefits (Table 2) was added information published by the Service Providers on their internet sites.

Web-Based Instrument

The Delphi study was conducted on-line, developed and turned available on the University of Minho's server (Portugal), with instructions to guide participants through the Q-sort technique.

The expert is presented to a list of issues that should be organized into three groups according

Table 1. List of outsourcing risks

Risks (and references)	Description
Existence of deficiencies on the contract. (Aubert et al., 2005; Bahli & Rivard, 2003a; Bahli & Rivard, 2003b; Dhar & Balakrishnan, 2006; Gonzalez et al., 2005a; IDC, 2005; Kakumanu & Portanova, 2006).	To draw up a contract with deficiencies may lead to amendments' costs. This deficiencies may be caused for instance by the complexity of the contract itself, by technological discontinuity, by the fast market evolution or by environmental volatility of the organization.
Unexpected costs and other hidden costs. (Aubert et al., 2005; Bahli & Rivard, 2003a; Bahli & Rivard, 2003b; Deloitte, 2005; Dhar & Balakrishnan, 2006; Kakumanu & Portanova, 2006; Varajão, 2002).	The organization inexperience about Outsourcing contracts or its weak knowledge about the activity to outsource may lead to extra costs. Frequently organizations do not define properly its IS/IT needs and may not realize the repercussions of the interdependency of the outsourced activities and the internal activities. The failure on return on investment is an example of this risk.
Organizations perform a poor cost-benefit analysis. (Gonzalez et al., 2005a; Varajão, 2002).	On an Outsourcing decision process there are some costs organizations don't consider on a cost-benefit analysis. Examples of this are costs of: suppliers selection, contract negotiation, implementation, suppliers management and, at the end of Outsourcing contracts, switching suppliers or insource.
Organization gets in the hands of the service provider organization (lock-in). (Aubert et al., 2005; Bahli & Rivard, 2003a; Bahli & Rivard, 2003b; Deloitte, 2005; Dhar & Balakrishnan, 2006; IDC, 2005; Kakumanu & Portanova, 2006; Varajão, 2002; Wright, 2004).	Some organizations face a decrease on its internal competencies, and in case of a small number of suppliers, they may not be able to switch Providers or to bring the services in-house without incurring in great expenses. Also, long term contracts, very frequent on Outsourcing deals, may became difficult for organizations to respond to market changes.
Organization has a lack of its needs fulfilled. (Aubert et al., 2005; Dhar & Balakrishnan, 2006; Gonzalez et al., 2005a; Kakumanu & Portanova, 2006; Varajão, 2002).	Although the contract fulfilment, the organization may have not specified adequately the outsourced activities or its service levels and the service could be delivered bellow expectations. Other factors may lead to this risk such as the constant changes of requirements by the organization, the lack of internal competencies to evaluate the Service Provider performance or the inexistence of mechanisms to control delivered service.
Providers don't comply with the contract. (Aubert et al., 2005; Deloitte, 2005; Dhar & Balakrishnan, 2006; Gonzalez et al., 2005a; Kakumanu & Portanova, 2006; Varajão, 2002; Wright, 2004).	The lack of compliance with the contract may occur due to: - The Provider does not know the business activity of the Client. - High rotation of human resources or skilled resources deviation to other Clients, due to an economical powerful Provider, like a monopoly position and/or with a large Clients portfolio. - As the opposite, due to an economical weak Provider, like a takeover by another company or an insolvency declaration, the organization may have to support the costs to switch Providers, since it does not have internal competencies.
Dispute and/or litigation. (Aubert et al., 2005; Bahli & Rivard, 2003b; Dhar & Balakrishnan, 2006; Varajão, 2002; Wright, 2004).	On a contractual relation the existence of a conflict is a probable event. Conflicts may have origin on defective measurement of service levels, low performance of the Provider, cultural differences or weak expertise on legal environment/aspects.
Irreversible outsourcing decision. (IDC, 2005; Gonzalez et al., 2005a; Gonzalez et al., 2006a).	An organization that adopts Outsourcing may face a too high cost to rebuilt internally the IS department in comparison with the costs of keeping the IS functions out.
IS/IT logical security failure. (Aubert et al., 2005; Dhar & Balakrishnan, 2006; Gonzalez et al., 2005a; IDC, 2004; IDC, 2005; Kakumanu & Portanova, 2006; Varajão, 2002; Wright, 2004).	On an Outsourcing contract some logical security characteristics of the IS/IT can be defined by the Provider such as rules and politics of intellectual property, privacy and confidentiality control.
Threat from opportunism by the Service Provider. (Aubert et al., 2005; Dhar & Balakrishnan, 2006; Varajão, 2002).	The Provider may take advantage of contractual gaps and charges extra fees over weak or unclear specified/unspecified services on contract.

Continued on following page

Table 1. continued

Risks (and references)	Description
Occurrence of disasters. (Aubert et al., 2005; Dhar & Balakrishnan, 2006).	The organization may incur in costs due to a loss of control over disaster recovery, loss of data or vital information, since the outsourced activities are performed outside the organization.
A lower IS/IT physical security. (Kakumanu & Portanova, 2006; Varajão, 2002; Wright, 2004).	On an Outsourcing relation the organization can assign to the Provider some IS/IT security related aspects as the control over physical access to the system, its location, the backups location and the backups system frequency.
Increasing problems on human resources management (IS staffing). (Deloitte, 2005; IDC, 2004; IDC, 2005; Varajão, 2002; Wright, 2004).	When an organization decides to outsource it may experience new human resources issues. As examples it is possible to point out the change in employee skill sets, people resistance and demotivation, potential people transfer problems or people dismissal.

to "most important", "neutral" and "less important". Within these groups the expert should choose the most and the less important issue in comparison to others until all the issues of the group are evaluated. At the end of this procedure one obtain a ranked list of issues sorted by their importance. A peculiar feature of this technique is that the certainties about the issues are at the top and at the bottom of the list since the experts have the greatest convictions about what it is "most important" and "less important" (Santos, 2004).

Number of Rounds

The common number of rounds to collect data found in previous studies is from two to four (Campos, 1998), depending on the participation rate, the time available to collect data or the structure of the Delphi study. The many the rounds the less is the participation rate (Santos & Amaral, 2004).

For the present Delphi study two rounds were conducted. For the first round the level of consensus attained for the ordered lists was low or not significant, so a second round was undertaken to attempt a consensus improvement. This second round allowed experts to review their answers and it was possible to consolidate the sorted lists from the previous round.

As shown in Table 3 there is a lack of progress from round one to round two which indicates the Delphi process can be stopped. According to Schmidt (1997) for a panel of this size even very

small values of W can be significant so the panel achieved a satisfactory consensus.

There is a levelling off of W (Table 4) between rounds which is a criteria pointed out by Schmidt (1997) to stop Delphi process. This group has low convergence for both lists.

A deeper research on previous literature has found possible causes/explanations for this result. A study carried out among the largest Spanish firms (Gonzalez et al., 2005a) shows a certain dependency between the degree of Outsourcing, the size of the organization and the risks they fear most. Gonzalez et al., 2005a found that risks are identical for different organizations independently of the activity sector they belong to. However, the significance given to risks is close related to the degree of Outsourcing and the size of the organization (measured by number of workers and business volume). These authors discovered that small organizations fear mainly the dependence on the provider while large firms show more concern about the possible opposition to Outsourcing of their IS department staff. Although the business volume of the participant organizations in the present study is the same, they have different amount of workers, which may have been an influence over the findings. Also, the degree of Outsourcing, which is another factor that contribute for this effect, is probably different among the organizations.

The findings of Gonzalez et al. (2005c) show that the size of the organization and the activity sector can influence the importance given to benefits.

Table 2. List of outsourcing benefits

Benefits (and references)	Description
Focus on core business functions. (Accenture; Capgemini; Deloitte, 2005; Gonzalez et al., 2005c; Gonzalez et al., 2006a; Griffiths,1999; HP; IBM; IDC, 2004; IDC, 2005; Kakumanu & Portanova, 2006; Novabase; Prisma; PT SI; Silva, 2002; Varajão, 2002).	Top management greater attention and dedication to the organization strategic areas by liberating the organization from time, human and financial resources consuming areas.
IS/IT service levels assurance. (Accenture; Capgemini; Deloitte, 2005; Gonzalez et al., 2005c; IDC, 2004; IDC, 2005; Silva, 2002).	The organization service levels assurance of the information and technology systems by the existence of a contract.
IS/IT risks sharing. (Deloitte, 2005; Edinfor; Griffiths, 1999; IDC, 2005; Kakumanu & Portanova, 2006; PT SI; SAP Portugal; Silva, 2002; Varajão, 2002).	Information and technology systems risks sharing or transferring to a third party by contractual guarantee.
Access to highly skilled resources. (Accenture; Deloitte, 2005; Griffiths, 1999; HP; IDC, 2004; IDC, 2005; Kakumanu & Portanova, 2006; Prisma; Silva, 2002; Varajão, 2002).	Access to highly skilled information and technology systems resources.
Costs reduction. (Accenture; Capgemini; Deloitte, 2005; Gonzalez et al., 2005c; Gonzalez et al., 2006a; Griffiths,1999; IBM; Kakumanu & Portanova, 2006; Novabase; Prisma; PT SI; Silva, 2002; Unisys; Varajão, 2002).	To acquire the same information and technology systems services with a lower cost than internally.
A higher control and accuracy over the IS/IT performance and costs. (Accenture; Griffiths, 1999; IDC, 2004; IDC, 2005; Prisma; Varajão, 2002).	A higher control and accuracy over the IS/IT performance and costs by the existence of a contract.
Improvement on Return on IS/IT Investment. (HP; SAP Portugal; NextiraOne).	Increase or early return on investment made by the organization on information and technology systems.
Higher organization productivity. (Accenture; Capgemini; SAP Portugal).	Higher organization productivity through a higher IS/IT performance.
Improvement on IS/IT management efficiency. (HP; Varajão, 2002).	An organization earns a more effective information and technology systems management.
Increase in organization flexibility. (Deloitte, 2005; Edinfor; IDC, 2005; Gonzalez et al., 2005c; Varajão, 2002).	The organization increases its ability to respond to market changes through a simplified organic structure, gain of effectiveness and a IS service level improvement.
A better adjustment of human resources needs. (Kakumanu & Portanova, 2006; Varajão, 2002).	Held up by the Provider, the organization gains a better ability to adjust its internal human resources needs and face working fluctuations.
Higher IS/IT security and reliability. (IDC, 2004; Unisys).	Higher information and technology systems security, like a better immunity against external attacks and a better access management, and higher reliability on its information and technology systems, as low failure rates or inoperability.
Simplification of the organic matrix. (Deloitte, 2005; IDC, 2004; IDC, 2005; Varajão, 2002).	The organic matrix simplification by transferring resources to the Provider.
Achievement of a standard and even organizational structure. (Accenture; Capgemini; Deloitte, 2005; IDC, 2005).	Achievement of a standard and even organizational structure by the generalized adoption of best practices and decrease of hardware and applications redundancies.
Permanent access to up to date technology. (HP; IDC, 2004; Gonzalez et al., 2005c; Gonzalez et al., 2006a; Kakumanu & Portanova, 2006; Prisma; Silva, 2002; Varajão, 2002).	Permanent access to up to date technology through the constant technological evolution performed by the supplier.
Cash flow improvement. (HP; IDC, 2004; Varajão, 2002).	Cash flow improvement of the organization due to the acquisition of information and technology systems assets by the Provider.

Table 3. Delphi rounds for service providers panel

Round	Risks	Benefits
# 1	Kendall's W = 0,44 Weak agreement among experts	Kendall's W = 0,33 Weak agreement among experts
# 2	Kendall's W = 0,39 Weak agreement among experts	Kendall's W = 0,42 Weak agreement among experts

Table 4. Delphi rounds for clients panel

Round	Risks	Benefits
# 1	Kendall's W = 0,15 Very weak agreement among experts	Kendall's W = 0,20 Very weak agreement among experts
# 2	Kendall's W = 0,23 Very weak agreement among experts	Kendall's W = 0,17 Very weak agreement among experts

Table 5. Delphi rounds for opinion makers panel

Round	Risks	Benefits
# 1	Kendall's W = 0,33 Weak agreement among experts	Kendall's W = 0,35 Weak agreement among experts
# 2	Kendall's W = 0,43 Weak agreement among experts	Kendall's W = 0,32 Weak agreement among experts

These authors say that smaller organizations often view Outsourcing as a way to facilitate access to new technologies and less as way of focusing on their core competences. In addition they found that the main reason for Service Firms to outsource is to have access to new technologies which is less important for Insurance and Financial Institutions; on the other hand Industrial Firms outsource to improve IS quality service.

For the reasons pointed out above it is possible to predict that even conducting another Delphi round it is difficult to achieve reasonable consensus among this panel, which strengths the decision of stopping the Delphi process.

The level of consensus does not change between rounds (Table 5) as it happens with the other panels so the Delphi process can be stopped. For a panel of this size even very small values of W can be significant so the panel achieved a satisfactory consensus (Schmidt, 1997).

Participation Rate and Non-Response

To invite the experts it was sent an e-mail describing the study scope and giving access to the e-Delphi, assuring to the participants confidentiality over answers and their personal and their organizational data. Santos (2004) states that to obtain a good participation rate it should be sent a personalized message to all participants with relevant information, namely the questionnaire web address and its access.

Among those who did not answered it is possible to find individuals which ignored the invitation to participate, refused to participate due to the organization policy or did not accessed the mailbox during the questionnaire period. At the end of the Delphi iterative process the participation rates attained are listed bellow:

- Service Provider panel: 55% of 20 invited experts;
- Clients group: 25% of 48 elements;
- Opinion Makers panel: 82% of 12 selected.

EMPIRICAL STUDY RESULTS AND DISCUSSION

On this section the study results, risks and benefits, are presented for each participant group: Service Providers, Clients and Opinion Makers. The comparison of their perspectives allowed to evaluate to what extent a common view is shared by the market players.

Results

Service Providers

For Service Providers group the most important risks an organization should take under consideration when adopting IS Outsourcing are: the existence of deficiencies on the contract, a poor cost-benefit analysis performed by the organization and the lack of compliance with the contract by the providers.

This panel also considers that the most important benefits to attain with IS Outsourcing are: focus on core business functions, increase in organization flexibility and access to highly skilled resources.

Clients

The Clients group consider the existence of deficiencies on the contract as the most concerning risk when it comes to outsource. This study shows that more than costs, the risk Clients fear most is the possibility of contract deficiencies. On the contrary, the IDC (2004) study among Portuguese organizations describe that 50% of participants are concerned about costs and just 40% consider the contractual issue as a barrier to outsource. Another conclusion is pointed out by the Deloitte (2005)

study that state the Service Provider performance is the greatest distress for organizations.

This panel believes that the most important benefit to achieve by Outsourcing is the organizations focus on their core business functions. This result is coincident with Gonzalez et al. (2005c) conclusions from an investigation conducted among the largest Spanish firms and it is also confirmed by 50% of the participants of an IDC (2005) study carried out among Portuguese organizations. On the contrary on a study carried out by Deloitte (2005) cost reduction is indicated by 70% of participants as the main reason to outsource; and only 35% specify focus on core business as a reason.

Opinion Makers

The Opinion Makers group think that the risks of most importance are: the existence of deficiencies on the contract, a poor cost-benefit analysis performed by organizations and the possibility of an organization getting in the hands of the service provider (lock-in).

Results demonstrate that this panel considers the greatest benefits: focus on core business functions, access to highly skilled resources and a higher control and accuracy over the IS/IT performance and costs.

Discussion

Outsourcing Risks

This study shows that the Portuguese market players share a common view about the most feared risk associated to Outsourcing (Table 6). They consider the existence of deficiencies on contract as the risk of most importance. This apprehension about contract is also shown on Gonzalez et al. (2005b) investigation where bigger organizations see a proper contract structuring as the Outsourcing relationship success key. However they don't share the same opinion about the other listed risks.

Table 6. Risks rankings for the three panel

Risks	Rank		
	Clients	Service Providers	Opinion Makers
Existence of deficiencies on the contract.	1st	1st	1st
Unexpected costs and other hidden costs.	2nd	4th	4th
Organizations perform a poor cost-benefit analysis.	3rd	2nd	2nd

Table 7. Benefits rankings for the three panel

Benefits	Rank		
	Clients	Service Providers	Opinion Makers
Focus on core business functions.	1st	1st	1st
IS/IT service levels assurance.	2nd	6th	5th
IS/IT risks sharing.	3rd	9th	12th

For the Clients group unexpected costs and other hidden costs was the second top risk compared with Service Providers and Opinion Makers where it was ranked fourth. The risk of an organization performing a poor cost-benefit analysis was the third top risk for Clients and was ranked second for Service Providers and Opinion Makers.

This classification of the second risk seems to indicate a certain consciousness of Client organizations about their "lack of experience with Outsourcing or lack of expertise with the IT operation that is intended to outsource".

On the other hand the Service Providers and Opinion Makers second risk infers they have a better perception that "on an Outsourcing decision process there are costs that organizations don't consider on the cost-benefit analysis".

Outsourcing Benefits

The Portuguese market players also share a common view about the most important benefit associated to Outsourcing (Table 7). They consider the focus on core business functions as the benefit of most importance.

On different web sites of some Service Providers as Accenture, Capgemini, IBM or Novabase

the slogan to outsource is "Outsourcing allows organizations to focus on their core competences", which in a way may have had a strong influence on the present study findings.

Besides the first top benefit the Portuguese market players don't share the same opinion about the other listed benefits.

FUTURE RESEARCH DIRECTIONS

Both the findings and some limitations of the study are referred, pointing out opportunities to future investigations. Since the existence of deficiencies on the contract is the most feared risk it would be useful to carry out case studies about IS Outsourcing contracts which failed and its lessons learned. Likewise as the organization focus on core business functions was considered to be the benefit of most importance it would be valuable to exploit ways of evaluating its accomplishment. In view of the fact that the present study involved bigger organizations it would be interesting to broaden the scope to smaller firms. In addition it is relevant to undertake a deeper analysis to understand to what extent the risks and benefits associated to

Outsourcing depend on the organizations business sector or on the Outsourcing level.

CONCLUSION

The objective of this chapter was to determine to what extent a common view about risks and benefits associated to IS Outsourcing is shared by the Portuguese market players – Service Providers, Clients and Opinion Makers. In order to accomplish this, an on-line Delphi study was conducted, combined with the Q-sort technique, which allowed to obtain each players perspective on IS Outsourcing risks and benefits.

Comparing these perspectives it was possible to understand that the market players do not share the same view. Beyond the top risk and benefit associated to Outsourcing the market players do not agree on the other listed risks and benefits ranking. They agree that the risk to fear most is the existence of deficiencies on contract and that the most important benefit is to focus on core competences.

This study also contributed to the understanding of the risks and benefits associated to IS Outsourcing and to obtain each player own perspective on IS Outsourcing risks and benefits.

REFERENCES

Accenture. (2006). Outsourcing Service. Retrieved July 2006, from http://www.accenture.com/Global/Outsourcing/default.htm

Amaral, L., Teixeira, C., & Oliveira, J. (2003). *e-Procurement: Uma reflexão sobre a situação actual em Portugal*. Caparica, Portugal: APDSI.

Aubert, B. A., Patry, M., & Rivard, S. (2005). A framework for information technology outsourcing risk management. *The Data Base for Advances in Information Systems, 36*(4), 9–28.

Bacon, C. J., & Fitzgerald, B. (2001). A systemic framework for the field of information systems. *The Data Base for Advances in Information Systems, 32*(2), 46–67.

Bahli, B., & Rivard, S. (2003a). A Validation of Measures Associated with the Risk Factors in Information Technology Outsourcing. In *Proceedings of the 36th Annual Hawaii International Conference on System Sciences* (Vol. 8, pp. 269). Washington, DC: IEEE Computer Society.

Bahli, B., & Rivard, S. (2003b). The information technology outsourcing risk: a transaction cost and agency theory-based perspective. *Journal of Information Technology, 18*(3), 211–221. doi:10.1080/0268396032000130214

Bhattacharya, S., Behara, R. S., & Gundersen, D. E. (2003). Business risk perspectives on information systems outsourcing. *International Journal of Accounting Information Systems, 4,* 75–93. doi:10.1016/S1467-0895(03)00004-6

Bradley, L., & Stewart, K. (2002). A Delphi study of the drivers and inhibitors of Internet banking. *International Journal of Bank Marketing, 20,* 250–260. doi:10.1108/02652320210446715

Brown, C. A. (2007). The Opt-in/Opt-out Feature in a Multi-Stage Delphi Method Study. *International Journal of Social Research Methodology, 10*(2), 135–144. doi:10.1080/13645570701334084

Campos, M. (1998). *Questões Chave da Gestão de Sistemas de Informação: Avaliação da Situação Nacional*. Unpublished Master dissertation, Minho University, Portugal.

Capgemini. (2006). *Outsourcing*. Retrieved July 2006, from http://www.capgemini.com/services/outsourcing/

Daniel, E. M., & White, A. (2005). The future of inter-organisational system linkages: findings of an international Delphi study. *European Journal of Information Systems, 14*(2), 188–203. doi:10.1057/palgrave.ejis.3000529

Deloitte. (2003). *Inside Outsourcing: The What, who, and how of Outsourcing IT-intensive processes*. New York: Deloitte Consulting.

Deloitte. (2005). *Calling a Change in the Outsourcing Market: The Realities for the World's Largest Organizations*. New York: Deloitte Consulting.

Dhar, S., & Balakrishnan, B. (2006). Risks, benefits, and challenges in global IT outsourcing: Perspectives and practices. *Journal of Global Information Management, 14*(3), 39–69.

Dibbern, J., Goles, T., Hirschheim, R., & Jayatilaka, B. (2004). Information systems outsourcing: a survey and analysis of the literature. *The Data Base for Advances in Information Systems, 35*(4), 6–102.

Edinfor. (2006). Retrieved July 2006, from http://www.logicacmg.com/EdinforPortuguese/350230182

Faulhaber, T. A. (2005). *Outsourcing*. Retrieved July 2006, from http://www.businessforum.com/toc.html#20

Gewald, H., & Hinz, D. (2004). A Framework for Classifying the Operational Risks of Outsourcing. In *Proceedings of the Eighth Pacific-Asia Conference on Information System*, Shanghai (pp. 986 - 999).

Gonzalez, R., Gasco, J., & Liopis, J. (2005a). Information systems outsourcing risks: a study of large firms. *Industrial Management & Data Systems, 105*(1), 45–61. doi:10.1108/02635570510575180

Gonzalez, R., Gasco, J., & Liopis, J. (2005c). Information systems outsourcing reasons in the largest Spanish firms. *International Journal of Information Management, 25*(2), 117–136. doi:10.1016/j.ijinfomgt.2004.10.002

Gonzalez, R., Gasco, J., & Llopis, J. (2005b). Information systems outsourcing success factors: a review and some results. *Information Management & Computer Security, 13*(5), 399–418. doi:10.1108/09685220510627287

Gonzalez, R., Gasco, J., & Llopis, J. (2006a). Information systems managers' view about outsourcing in Spain. *Information Management & Computer Security, 14*(4), 312–326. doi:10.1108/09685220610690790

Gonzalez, R., Gasco, J., & Llopis, J. (2006b). Information systems outsourcing: A literature analysis. *Information & Management, 43*(7), 821–834. doi:10.1016/j.im.2006.07.002

Gottschalk, P. (2001). Key issues in is management in Norway: an empirical study based on Q-methodology. *Information Resources Management Journal, 14*(2), 37–45.

Gottschalk, P., Watson, R. T., & Christensen, B. H. (2000). Global comparisons of key issues in IS management: extending key issues selection procedure and survey approach. In R. T. Watson (Ed.), *Proceedings of the 33rd Annual Hawaii International Conference on System Sciences*, Hawaii (Vol. 2).

Griffiths, D. (1999). The Theory and Practice of Outsourcing. In *48th Annual STC Conference Proceedings*. Chicago: STC.

Hewlett Packard. (2006). *Outsourcing Services*. Retrieved July 2006, from http://h20219.www2.hp.com/services/cache/9483-0-0-0-121.html

IBM. (2006). *Índice de Serviços*. Retrieved July 2006, from http://www-05.ibm.com/services/pt/portfolios/

IDC. (2004). *Caderno n° 72 - Outsourcing de Serviços de TI*. Lisboa: IDC Portugal.

IDC. (2005). *Estudo Local - Outsourcing de Serviços de TI e BPO em Portugal: Análise e Previsões 2004 - 2009*. Lisboa: IDC Portugal.

Kakumanu, P., & Portanova, A. (2006). Outsourcing: Its Benefits, Drawbacks and Other Related Issues. *Journal of American Academy of Business, 9*(2), 1–7.

Lacity, M. C., & Willcocks, L. P. (1998). An empirical investigation of information technology sourcing practices: lessons from experience. *Management Information Systems Quarterly, 22*(3), 363–408. doi:10.2307/249670

Lee, J.-N., Huynh, M. Q., Kwok, R. C.-W., & Pi, S.-M. (2003). IT outsourcing evolution: past, present, and future. *Communications of the ACM, 46*(5), 84–89. doi:10.1145/769800.769807

Loh, L., & Venkatraman, N. (1992). Diffusion of Information Technology Outsourcing: Influence Sources and the Kodak Effect. *Information Systems Research,* 334–358. doi:10.1287/isre.3.4.334

Maculuve, P., & Rodrigues, A. (2002). O Outsourcing em projectos de desenvolvimento de Sistemas de Informação: Conceitos, princípios e opinião. *Sistemas de Informação, 16,* 31–40.

Miguel, A. S. (2000). *O Risco em Projectos de Desenvolvimento de Software: Estudo Delphi em Portugal*. Paper presented at Actas da 1ª Conferência da Associação Portuguesa de Sistemas de Informação, Guimarães.

NextiraOne. (2006). *Serviços Geridos*. Retrieved July 2006, from http://www.nextiraone.pt/servicos/servicos_geridos

Novabase. (2006). *Multisourcing Services*. Retrieved July 2006, from http://www.novabase.pt/showCategory.asp?idCat=Outsourcing

Okoli, C., & Pawlowski, S. D. (2004). The Delphi method as a research tool: an example, design considerations and applications. *Information & Management, 42*(1), 15–29.

Prisma. (2006). Retrieved July 2006, from http://www.prisma.pt/1024/index.htm

PT-SI. (2006). Retrieved July 2006, from http://www.ptsi.pt/PTSI/Canais/Solucoes/Outsourcing/

Ramos, J. (2006). *Guerras no Outsourcing*. Jornal Expresso.

Rocha, V. (2006). *Valor Acrescentado dos Contratos de Outsourcing TI & BPO - O que aprendemos com os nossos Clientes*. Paper presented at Conference about Outsourcing TI & BPO, Lisboa.

Saizarbitoria, I. H., Landín, G. A., & Fa, M. C. (2006). The impact of quality management in European companies' performance: The case of the Spanish companies. *European Business Review, 18*(2), 114–131. doi:10.1108/09555340610651839

Santos, L. (2004). *Factores Determinantes do Sucesso de Adopção e Difusão de Serviços de Informação on-line em Sistemas de Gestão de Ciência e Tecnologia*. Unpublished Doctoral dissertation, Minho University, Portugal.

Santos, L. D., & Amaral, L. (2004). *Estudos Delphi com Q-Sort sobre a web: a sua utilização em sistemas de informação*. Paper presented at Actas da 5ª Conferência da Associação Portuguesa de Sistemas de Informação, Lisboa.

SAP. (2006). *Business Process Outsourcing*. Retrieved July 2006, from http://www.sap.com/services/bpo/index.epx

Sargent, A. (2006). Outsourcing relationship literature: an examination and implications for future research. In *Proceedings of the 2006 ACM SIGMIS CPR conference on computer personnel research: Forty four years of computer personnel research: achievements, challenges and the future* (pp. 280-287). Claremont, CA: ACM.

Schmidt, R. (1997). Managing Delphi surveys using nonparametric statistical techniques. *Decision Sciences, 28*(3), 763–774. doi:10.1111/j.1540-5915.1997.tb01330.x

Scholl, W., König, C., Meyer, B., & Heisig, P. (2004). The future of knowledge management: an international delphi study. *Journal of Knowledge Management, 8*(2), 19–35. doi:10.1108/13673270410529082

Silva, F. C. (2002). *O Outsourcing em Sistemas de Informação*. Paper presented at Actas da 3ª Conferência da Associação Portuguesa de Sistemas de Informação, Lisboa.

UNISYS. (2006). *End User Outsourcing and Support Services*. Retrieved July 2006, from http://www.unisys.pt/services/outsourcing/index.htm

Varajão, J. (2002). *Função de Sistemas de Informação: Contributos para a Melhoria do Sucesso da Adopção de Tecnologias de Informação e Desenvolvimento de Sistemas de Informação nas Organizações*. Unpublished Doctoral dissertation, Minho University, Portugal.

Wright, C. (2004). Top Three Potential Risks With Outsourcing Information Systems. *Information Systems Control Journal, 5*.

Chapter 27
INMATE–Innovation Management Technique:
An Innovation Management Tool with Emphasis on IT Information Technology

José Carlos Cavalcanti
Universidade Federal de Pernambuco, Brazil

ABSTRACT

The main objective of this chapter is to present an innovative tool for innovation management with emphasis to the information technology-IT management called INMATE- Innovation Management Technique. In order to arrive at this tool an analysis on the current market tools was conducted. This analysis observed that none of the existent tools gives the due importance to the role of information technology-IT for the innovation process. In this way, the chapter presents a brief discussion of two of these market tools: an international, called TEMAGUIDE, and a Brazilian, called NUGIN. Then the chapter introduces the INMATE tool with its main dimensions. Next, the chapter gives a detailed account on how the IT management is dealt inside INMATE, which is done via the concept of Enterprise Architecture, a concept from the Computing Science and Engineering. From this concept the chapter presents a methodology, in an analogy to the Structure-Conduct-Performance Paradigm (that is traditionally used on the empirical market analysis), which identifies the firm according to three linear connected approaches: its architecture, its governance, and its growth strategy.

INTRODUCTION

Nowadays is practically impossible not to deal with technology and innovation. Despite the vast amount of technology tools at our disposal, every day one sees the emergence of innovations turning obsoletes the tools we have been used to.

DOI: 10.4018/978-1-61692-020-3.ch027

In this way, the management of *innovation* ([1]) is becoming a business imperative. This condition was the main reason for the development of a research that could analyse an innovation management tool which could be simultaneously simple, fast e effective. Hence, some available tools have been assessed in order to benchmark one tool which could generate simplicity, speed and effectiveness, and more than that, it could fit to the current technology and innovation new environments, mainly to the Web 2.0 and Web 3.0 business environments.

Amongst the analysed innovation management tools one aspect called the attention: despite the current importance of the information and communications technologies, none of those tools pays the due attention to the role of these technologies to innovation. Therefore, it seemed reasonable the development of a new innovation management tool with a competitive differential in its emphasis on the information technology- IT management. In other words, a tool which paid attention to the impact of: the information content management, the information systems management, and the information and communications technology management, on the technological and organizational internal choices of the innovative firm, organization or institution.

This paper is divided into five sections. Section 2 briefly presents an international innovation management tool called TEMAGUIDE. Section 3 presents some aspects of a Brazilian innovation management tool called NUGIN. Section 4 introduces the INMATE - Innovation Management Technique, a tool conceptualized and developed by this author whose main competitive differential is its emphasis on the information technology - IT management. Section 5 presents how the information technology management is dealt inside the INMATE tool. This section is subdivided into two sub-sections: the first shows the concept of Architecture, and the second introduces the methodology of *Architecture-Governance-Enterprise Growth*, also developed by the author. Finally, section 6 presents the final conclusions.

TEMAGUIDE: AN INTERNATIONAL INNOVATION MANAGEMENT TOOL

Within the arena of the international innovation tools it is worthwhile mentioning the TEMAGUIDE tool. TEMAGUIDE, a contraction of the words Technology Management and GUIDE, is the result of a research conducted by a group of European organizations, such as Fundación COTEC (Spain), coordinator of the project, SOCINTEC, CENTRIM (from the University of Brighton, United Kingdom), IRIM (from the University of Kiel, Germany), and the Research and Development Unit of the Manchester Business School (United Kingdom). The project was financially backed by the Innovation Programme (Directorate General XIII), of the European Commission.

The basic structure of the TEMAGUIDE project contains three components: a) a description of the Technological and Innovation Management aspects from the business perspective. Its proponents look at it as being more than a description; they see it as a model that can be used either at a practical level for managing the innovation process or at an strategic level for ensuring that the Technological Management is completely integrated to business and gets the praise it deserves; b) a set of tools for assisting in specific activities of the Technological Management and the promotion of Technological Management as an important aspect of the practice of good businesses; c) a set of study cases that illustrates problems, needs and solutions from typical enterprises. These components are shown in Figure 1.

By considering that Technology Innovation is not something only related to innovating with success once or twice, but rather about frequent innovations and improvements, in other words, about enterprise *innovativeness*, TEMAGUIDE recommends a simple conceptual framework (or model) which facilitates this *innovativeness* approach. The model is based on five elements that remind the enterprise what frequently needs to be done in different points in time, and in different kinds of situations: SCAN (indicating a scan of the environment in search of signs of needs for innovation and potential opportunities), FOCUS (expressing attention and efforts in a particular strategy for business improvements and innovation, or a particular solution for a problem),

Figure 1. Components of TEMAGUIDE

Figure 2. The five elements of innovation

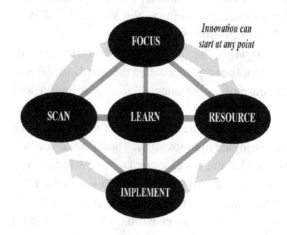

RESOURCE (showing that it must allocate resources in that strategy and prepares for what it is necessary to do to make that solution works), IMPLEMENT (pointing to the implementation of the innovation), and LEARN (indicating learning from the success experience or failure), as it is shown in Figure 2.

These five elements of the model can be supported by tools and techniques of a diversified nature, such as: a) External Information (Market Analysis, Technological Forecast, Patent Analysis, Benchmarking), b) Internal Information (Ability Auditing and Innovation, Intellectual Property Management, Environmental Assessment), c) Joint Work (Interface Management, Networks, Team Formation), d) Ideas and Problem Solution (Creativity, Value Analysis), e) Efficiency Improvements (Flexible Learning, Continuous Improvements, Change Management), e Other Techniques.

TEMAGUIDE has been publically available since 1998 e it is well recognized in the world of technological innovation management. Further details about TEMAGUIDE can be found at http://www.cotec.es. Despite being comprehensive, TEMAGUIDE does not pay the due importance to the role of information technology in its con-

ceptual design, even in the reported cases of its implementation.

NUGIN: A BRAZILIAN INNOVATION MANAGEMENT TOOL

This section briefly presents a Brazilian tool that has been recently developed called NUGIN. The word NUGIN is a contraction of *"NÚcleo de apoio ao planejamento de Gestão da Inovação em empresas de pequeno e médio porte"* (Nucleos for supporting the planning of innovation management for small and medium size enterprises), a project that had been proposed by the IEL/SC (Instituto Euvaldo Lodi/Santa Catarina), which is part of FIESC/SC System (Federação das Indústrias do Estado de Santa Catarina), in partnership with the UFSC (Universidade Federal de Santa Catarina), by means of the NEDIP (Núcleo de Desenvolvimento Integrado de Produtos), from the EMC/UFSC (Departamento de Engenharia Mecânica da UFSC), the IGTI (Núcleo de Estudos em Inovação, Gestão e Tecnologia da Informação) and the EPS/UFSC (Departamento de Engenharia de Produção e Sistemas da UFSC).

The NUGIN methodology, as described by Coral *et alli*. (2008) is based on the following assumptions:

Figure 3. Innovation management nucleos: NUGIN

a) **Innovation** must be a systematic and continuous process;
b) Adaptable to small and medium **size**s enterprise;
c) Valuation of learning;
d) Valuation of intellectual capital;
e) Systemic vision;
f) Valuation of communications and relationships;
g) **Innovation** is a fundamental element for competitiveness.

This methodology, presented in a descriptive format in Figure 3, has the objective to promote innovation within the enterprise by doing systematic identification of opportunities, ranking projects, developing technologies, products and processes, and the return of this effort to the enterprise.

Its implementation starts with the *organization* for innovation, seeking to identify the enterprise capacity for innovating in products and processes. From there, one must establish an innovation management cell (*nucleous*) within the organization. The *strategic planning* of the innovation is the result of the corporate planning of the enterprise, which analyses technology and market aspects. The *product development* process comprehends several aspects since market research until the

disposal or inactivation of the product, passing by the product and process design. The *competitive intelligence* involves all the other phases of the model, having its functions conducted in all the innovation process.

These aspects of NUGIN´s methodology, however, are also the elements that define its limitations. The methodology is not based in a proper justification for innovation; i.e., it takes for granted the need for innovation and seeks to structure the necessary knowledge for its implementation. It does not also departure from criteria that could point to the context in which the need to innovate (and where to innovate) expresses. In this way, it is difficult to perceive, *ex ante*, when the established tool ceases to contribute for the innovator´s performance. Furthermore, the methodology is essentially geared to the innovation management of goods (nothing is said for innovation issues in services products) in ongoing enterprises, and it does not provide any guidance for start ups or spin-off firms. Besides, by looking at the description on Coral *et alli* (2008), few is said in terms of intellectual property and funding concerns in dealing with innovation. Additionally, as the case of the TEMAGUIDE tool, NUGIN does not pay the due importance to the role of **information** technology in its conceptual design.

INMATE: A TOOL FOR INNOVATION MANAGEMENT WITH EMPHASIS ON INFORMATION TECHNOLOGY (IT)

This section introduces INMATE – Innovation Management Technique. This tool has its roots on the experience, for more than ten years, of teaching, research e management of science, technology and innovation of the author of this paper, as well as his perception of a worldwide scenario increasingly favorable for the support of innovation within the economic environment, but, at the same time, a lack of simple innova-

Figure 4. INMATE methodology

tion management tools and proper human capital formation for this management.

After a benchmark research on the current market tools, the INMATE methodology was conceptualized and developed in the form that is presented in Figure 4. Its main objective is to provide a tool in which enterprises, organizations and institutions could comprehend the diverse dimensions of the innovation process, and could, by themselves, take strategic decisions that best fit to their own interests. The INMATE methodology is based on the following assumptions:

a) **Innovation** is a process of perception and generation of opportunities. It is the result of a culture (entrepreneurial, organizational, or institutional) geared to the new, the disruptive, and different. It can be a systematic or a non-systematic process, depending on the context in which it reveals;

b) **Innovation** is an incentive sensitive process, mainly the economic ones. In the past it was believed that innovation could decline with competition, as long as more competition reduced monopoly rents that yielded successful innovators. Today it is perceived that the incentives of innovation depend not only to the innovation ex-post per se, but much more to the difference between post and pre-innovation rents. Hence, competition can foster innovation and growth due to the fact

that can reduce the pre-innovation rents of the firms much more than reducing its post-innovation rents. In other words, competition can enhance incremental profits of innovation, and, therefore, encourage investment geared to "*escape from competition*";

c) **Innovation** does not correlate to the **size** of the organization. It can be processed either within the large, or the medium or the small **size** enterprises, being it a start up, a spin-off, or being generated from a technology transfer;

d) **Innovation** is a multidisciplinary process that could emerge anywhere inside the organization. In order to happen it is necessary to allow the convergence of distinct knowledge, competences and cultures, and in so doing, gathering them, in a continuous and interactive way, to the innovation development process;

e) **Innovation** must align *technical rationality* (which is geared towards success) to *communicative rationality* (which is related to the understanding of the parties involved) of the same process.

The implementation of the INMATE methodology starts from what is called the *design problem*, i.e., the problem of selecting (or designing) the *innovation strategy*, followed by the definition of the *organization* that could achieve the highest performance in the context where the innovation takes place. Assuming as its starting point the perception of a business opportunity, the strategy is selected to explore such an opportunity. Hence, an *organization* should be established (and *managed*) by properly specifying the Know-What (what to do), the Know-How (how to do it), and the Know-Who (with whom to do it).

Besides the innovation strategy and the organization management, INMATE incorporates four other dimensions. Due to the information overload characteristic of the Information Era, in the current economy it is vital to any innovation process to devise a competent management of several information and communication technologies - ICT at disposal. The ICT management reflects a previous understanding, by the INMATE tool, about what an *Information Strategy* means. *Information Strategy* is understood as a composite of the *Information Content Strategy*, plus the *Information Systems Strategy*, plus the *Information and Communication Technology Strategy*. In this sense, within the INMATE methodology, the information and communication management is the information strategy management that is needed for the innovation process.

As a result of the Information Era, it is also possible to observe the emergence of different forms of relationships and relationship networks, such as personal and corporate blogs, tweets, videologs, photologs, discussion groups, widgets, amongst others. In this way, as those different forms of relationship have been enhancing labor productivity, the INMATE methodology incorporates different aspects of several relationship networks that have emerged in the last ten years. In doing so, INMATE defines its *relationship networks management* dimension which is essential to any innovation process, particularly with the recent changes in the way new knowledge is produced via *collaborative networks* for research and development.

The development of new products, processes and services comprises a vast array of aspects, starting from market research, then the phase of product (process or service) design and project, up to its obsolescence, in a dynamics movement that is known as *creative destruction*, as defined by the Austrian economist Joseph Schumpeter in the beginning of the 20th Century. This whole cycle demands a competent *product development management* in order to arrive at the established goals in the innovative strategy. This is the INMATE *product (or service) development management* dimension.

Last, but not least, there is the *marketing management* dimension. To understand the importance of this dimension to the innovation management process, and to the consequent innovative product sales, it is necessary to understand that there is a crucial difference between the current media (of the Information Era) and the media of the previous Era: it is the difference between *abundance* and *scarcity*. In the past we have had scarcity of access to information; today we see exactly the opposite, with the profusion of information, and associated means, as never seen before. This phenomenon was denominated by Prof. Barry Schwartz ([2]) as the *Paradox of Choice*, according to it the infinity of options available to humans is paralyzing and exhausting the human psyche. Therefore, in the context of information abundance it is necessary to admit the existence of an *Advertising Economics*, and fundamentally, of an emergent *Online Advertising Economics*, in which consumers are becoming increasingly more informed about the availability, variety, and quality of products and services at theirs disposal.

All these six dimensions of the INMATE methodology are covered by a conceptual apparatus of intellectual property rights which are inherent to the invention and innovation processes of products and services, particularly when technology transfer concerns are dealt with. Complementing this apparatus, the INMATE methodology defines also a parallel structure of funding models for different processes of innovation, depending on the characteristics of each innovator and the strategic trajectory established by him (or her).

THE INFORMATION TECHNOLOGY (IT) MANAGEMENT WITHIN INMATE

This section presents how the information technology- IT management works inside the INMATE. The main feature of this dimension of INMATE is provided by how the current business technological environment can be understood through the *Architecture-Governance-Enterprise Growth Analysis*, when dealing with enterprises, and

Architecture-Governance-Organizational Growth analysis, when organizations or institutions are dealt with.

In an analogy to the economic paradigm of *Structure- Conduct-Performance*, which is traditionally known in empirical market analysis, the *Architecture-Governance-Enterprise Growth analysis* was designed to describe how the enterprise, starting from its structure (or architecture), and followed by how it is governed, chooses its growth strategies. The next two sub-sections show how this analysis is viewed inside the INMATE tool.

The Enterprise Architecture Concept

As long as the enterprise (organization or institution) structures itself and grows in **size** and complexity, several factors start to inhibit its ability in solving the problem it faces. In other words, at one point in the evolution of the enterprise the factors that contributed to its structuring and business performance become numerous and complex. When one works with such complex systems, designers who face this complexity start to subdivide it into sub-systems or domains which could be less complex than the original ones.

In the case of information systems the abstraction used to deal with this complexity is named *Architecture*. An *Architecture* (in analogy to the building sector) is a project system that specifies how all the components will operate to offer the general functionality of the system. The decomposition of the enterprise into manageable parts, the definition of those parts, and the orchestration of the interaction of those parts is what is called *Enterprise Architecture*.

Professionals of information technology field, such as Iver and Gottieb (2004), focus their attention to the set of components that allows the flexible re-tooling and the creation of support environments fro different business environments. Hence, these authors developed an enterprise architecture, called *Four Domain Architecture*

(FDA), that reflects an integration of the business processes, engines, data sources (data bases and knowledge bases, for example), visualization tools, dialog managers, infrastructure, and organizational resources.

To present the FDA, the authors separate the business of creating an enterprise architecture (i.e., the processes to defining and building models of the enterprise and organizational resources requirements) from the business of doing the enterprise job (the construction and sale of goods and services) *per se*. To the former they named the *Architecture in Design (AID)*, and the latter they called *Architecture in Operation (AIO)*.

In order to offer to an enterprise a guide for decision making related to the information technology projects, the authors specified some phases. According to them there are several elements in the world of information technology that can build an enterprise architecture: networks, computers, terminals, programs, cabling, data sources, tasks, and so on. To gather these elements into domains, specific architectures of domains can be built to represent a common composite, and that could be focused in a simple and clear fashion. The authors´ four domains are: Processes Domain, Information/Knowledge Domain, Infrastructure Domain, and Organizational Domain (a detailed account of these domains can be found in Iver and Gottieb, 2004).

The *Architecture Advisory Group* (US Department of Commerce, 2004) suggests a process into seven steps to define an information technology architecture: 1. Define a Vision, Objectives and Principles (Who and what their architecture efforts will cover? What general principles the IT will guide its efforts?); 2. Characterize the state of the arts (How your office does its business, what IT is used, and how it is used?); 3. Establish a target architecture (What you wish that your IT architecture should be in the future?); 4. Determine the lags between the current and the target architecture; 5. Develop a migration plan (How would you overcome the gap between the current architecture and the target one?); 6. Implement a plan of migration and of the architecture (start to implement the plan to establish a bridge between the gaps of the IT architecture; 7. Review and update regularly (an IT architecture is a process, not a document).

The Architecture-Governance-Enterprise Growth Analysis

The IT management methodology inside the IN-MATE tool is based on three approaches: a) the *Enterprise Architecture as an Strategy* approach, which was first developed by the Massachusetts Institute of Technology (MIT) Sloan Center for Information Systems Research (US) and the IMD (Global Business School/Switzerland); the *Enterprise Governance* approach, based on the modern industrial (and services) organization theory; and, c) *Enterprise Growth* approach, based upon the economic theory of the contemporary firm. The three approaches can be briefly described as follows.

Amongst the approaches investigated by this paper in respect to enterprise architecture, one can be distinguished: that one from the MIT Sloan Center for Information Systems Research-CISR/MIT (Ross, Weil, e Robertson, 2008). After the development of a research of ten years about the IT impact on the performance of circa of 500 companies, researchers from the CISR/MIT arrived at some conclusions of enormous significance for the understanding of the role of IT on the enterprise performance.

According to the MIT's researchers the reason why some enterprises – and not others- reach a superior degree of execution and manage to explore what they do better to obtain agility and profitability, is because they have a better *execution foundation*. This *foundation for execution* consists of the IT infrastructure and of the digitalized business processes that automate central capacities

of an enterprise. The foundation for execution depends on the proper alignment between the business objectives and the IT systems using a direct logic.

First the administration defines an strategic direction; then, the IT unit, ideally in conjunction with the business administration, designs a set of solutions provided by the IT for sustaining the initiative; and, finally, the IT unit offers the applications, data and the technological infrastructure to implement the solutions. This process re-starts always when the administration defines other strategic initiative.

In reality the researchers realized that the traditional approach for IT development inside the enterprises was related to what they called the establishment of a set of *silos*, a set of applications inside the enterprise. Individually those applications worked well. Together they impeded the enterprise efforts to coordinating the processes to customers, input suppliers and workers; in other words, they did not constitute a *foundation for execution*.

To overcome this *silos* stage, and to build an efficient *foundation for execution*, Ross, Weil e Robertson (2008) proposed three key-disciplines: 1. *Operational Model*: it is the form to integrate the information assets and to establish patterns of the business process to offer goods and services to customers; 2. *Enterprise Architecture*: it is the organizational logic of the business processes and the IT infrastructure, reflecting the requirements of integration and patterns of the operational model of the enterprise; and, 3. *Model of involvement of the IT*: it is the governance mechanism systems that assures that the business projects and the IT reach their enterprise objectives either local or in general.

The *Enterprise Architecture* and the *Model of Involvement of IT* inside the enterprises are constituted in the evolution of *Maturity Stages of the Enterprise Architecture*. According to Ross, Weil e Robertson (2008) these stages are: a. Business Silos Architecture; b. Pattern Technology; c. Optimized Nucleous Architecture; and, d. Business Modularity Architecture.

The next step in the INMATE methodology is the *Enterprise Governance*, which must be understood as the enterprise (organization or institution) behavior that articulates the complex relation between the *IT Governance* and the *Corporate Governance* having in mind the business objectives. The *IT Governance* on the one hand, as understood by solution vendors and consultancy firms, is the implementation of best practices, mainly in IT services, i.e., services and support to the IT infrastructure, Data Centers operations, and so on (further details on Fernandes, Aguinaldo A. and Vladimir Ferraz de Abreu, 2008).

The *Corporate Governance*, on the other hand, is connected to the issues related to what in the Economic Science is called *asymmetric information*. As economic agents take decisions with asymmetric, imperfect and incomplete information, in their economic relations always emerge unbalances of power which could cause negative impacts in the performance of the involved parties, unless they are not properly treated.

Adriana Andrade and José Paschoal Rosseti (2007) list 10 (ten) issues associated to *Corporate Governance*: 1. size of enterprise; 2. property structure; 3. dominant sources of funding (internal or external); 4. typology of agency conflicts and harmonization of interests at play; 5. typology of legal regime of the enterprise; 6. typology of the enterprises according to group control; 7. ascendency of the enterprise after mergers and acquisitions; 8. geographical coverage of the enterprise; 9. cultural traces of the nations in which the enterprise operates; 10. legal institutions and regulatory frameworks in different parts of the world. They also present and discuss the 7 P′s of *Corporate Governance*: Property, Principles, Purpose; Power, Processes, Practices, and Permanence.

The last step in the IT management of the INMATE tool is the *Enterprise Growth*. The underline question of this step is: what determines the growth of an enterprise? This question has been addressed by several specialists for many years. In a series of newsletters published between 09/07/2007 to 13/08/2007 (see http://www.creativante.com.br), this author treated several aspects that have emerged on this subject, either from the empirical evidence side, or from the academic economics literature.

Summing up, it is possible to say that there are two types of growth models of the enterprise: a. *Stochastic Models* that point that the growth of enterprises is a pure random process (i.e., in the long-run some enterprises are lucky and tend to get a share above the average rates of growth, while other get bad luck and tend to remain at the same **size** or decline; b. *Non-Stochastic Models*. In this second kind of models there are: i. Optimization Models based in learning (passive and active); ii. Growth Models based in accumulation of human capital and those of quality ladders based on research and technology, and stochastic innovation; iii. Growth Models based in the development of the financial sector.

The approach developed inside the INMATE tool is one that filters the conditioning factors of growth (such as the macroeconomic environment) and focus on the growth strategy of the enterprise. A central concern in this approach is to model stages of growth of the enterprise. In this respect, the INMATE departures from some established models such as the *Greiner Model of Growth* (Greiner, 1972 and 1988).

Models like these from Greiner have direct correlation to the *Information Systems Maturity Models*, such as those of Nolan (1973), Gibson and Nolan (1974), which are based in the technology used and the budget of the *information systems (IS)* as indicators of maturity of the information systems management, by applying an S curve consisting of four stages: i. Initiation; ii. Contagion; iii. Control; and, iv. Maturity. Nolan´s model has been expanded in Mutsaers, Ziee and Giertz (1977). These authors described three curves in S shape as three eras of the IS management maturity: Data Processing ; Information Technology; Computer Networks.

FINAL CONCLUSIONS

As it was indicated in this paper amongst market tools for innovation management none dedicates special attention to the role of information technology – IT in its innovation processes. Such an insight catalyzed the opportunity for the development of a tool that could involve the complexity of what it is means to manage modern IT technologies in the innovation processes.

In this respect this paper showed two market innovation tools: the TEMAGUIDE and the NUGIN. Then, the INMATE- Innovation Management Technique was presented with its main assumptions and dimensions.

The central concern of this paper was to demonstrate some details (and complexity) of one dimension of INMATE: the IT management dimension. By appropriating from Computing Science and Engineering the concept of Enterprise Architecture, the paper has given special highlight to a new methodology, called *Architecture-Governance-Enterprise Growth*, which embodies an analogy to the economic paradigm of *Structure-Conduct-Performance*, which is traditionally utilized in empirical market analysis. This new methodology relies on three treatment approaches: a) the Enterprise Architecture as an Strategy approach; b) the Enterprise Governance approach; c) the Enterprise Growth approach.

Despite being presented in a brief fashion, it is hoped that this INMATE tool, with its own concepts and methodology shortly presented here, can allow a new orientation for the analysis of in-

novation processes, since these processes can not any more ignore the advances proportioned by new content, systems, and information technologies.

REFERENCES

Andrade, A., & Rosseti, J. P. (2007). *Governança Corporativa* (3rd ed.). Brasilia, Brasil: Editora Atlas.

Coral, E., Ogliari, A., & de Abreu, A. F. (2008). *Gestão Integrada da Inovação: Estratégia, Organização e Desenvolvimento de Produtos*. Brasilia, Brasil: Editora Atlas.

Fernandes, A. A., & de Abreu, V. F. (2008). *Implantando a Governança de TI: da Estratégia à Gestão dos Processos e Serviços* (2nd ed.). Brasilia, Brasil: Brasport Livros e Multimídia.

Gibson, C., & Nolan, R. (1974). Managing the Four stages of EDP Growth. *Harvard Business Review, 1*, 76–88.

Greiner, L. (1972). Evolution and revolution as organizations grow. *Harvard Business Review, 50*(4).

Greiner, L. (1998). Revolution is still inevitable. *Harvard Business Review, 3*, 62–63.

Iyer, B., & Gottieb, R. (2004). Four-Domain Architecture- FDA. *IBM Systems Journal, 43*(3).

Mutsaers, E., Zee, H., & Giertz, H. (1977). The Evolution of Information Technology. *BIK-Blad, 2*(2), 15–23.

Nolan, R. (1973). Managing the computer resource: a stage hypothesis. *Communications of the ACM, 16*(7), 399–405. doi:10.1145/362280.362284

OECD. (2005). *Oslo Manual: Guidelines for Collecting and Interpreting Innovation Data* (3rd ed.). Paris: OECD.

Ross, J. W., Weil, P., & Robertson, D. C. (2008). *Arquitetura de TI como Estratégia Empresarial*. Harvard Business Review.

U.S. Department of Commerce. (2004). *Architecture Advisory Group*. Retrieved from http://ocio.os.doc.gov/CommerceITGroups/Enterprise_Architecture_Advisory_Group/index.htm

ENDNOTES

[1]   Innovation of a *product* (good or service) or a *process* (technological, organizational, or marketing), as proposed by the OECD Oslo Manual, 2005.

[2]   See http://en.wikipedia.org/wiki/Barry_Schwartz.

Chapter 28
Analysis of IT Governance on Spanish Organizations

Alberto J. Arroyo
ALAMCIA S. L., Spain

José D. Carrillo Verdún
Universidad Politécnica de Madrid. Spain

ABSTRACT

Corporate governance is a key element today in organizations and companies. IT Governance, as a part of corporate governance, plays its role in aligning IT with the business and obtaining the maximum value, minimizing the risks. Several frameworks and guidelines have been published in order to set the basis for this discipline. The recent release of the ISO 38500 (ISO 2008) ads an effort to standardize the different elements of IT governance. Despite these efforts, none of the different frameworks or guidelines is focused on the specific characteristics of small and medium companies (SMOs), although the authors consider that their conclusions are universal. Furthermore, there is no research so far that analyzed the status of IT governance in Spanish organizations. The aim of this work is to do a research to identify the state of the art of IT governance in the Spanish small and medium organizations.

INTRODUCTION

Corporate governance is not an old issue that has already been solved. The recent credit crunch has its origins in a failure of corporate governance in the companies (Moxey 2008).Thus, corporate governance is now, more than ever, on top of the agenda of executives and governs all over the world. Just as an example, regarding the banking industry in the UK, the Chancellor of the Exche-

quer said, "it is clear that corporate governance should have been far more effective in holding bank executives to account" (Treasury 2009).

Corporate governance is based on the called "agenda issue". The agenda issue handles the different interests of shareholders and managers. While the first can focus on increasing the value of the company, the second can be more concentrated on different things, such as increasing the size of the company through mergers and acquisitions, or in an international expansion effort. This is can be

DOI: 10.4018/978-1-61692-020-3.ch028

Figure 1. Traditional model of corporate governance

Figure 2. Stakeholder model of corporate governance

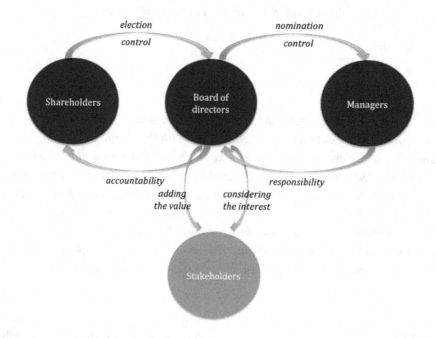

depicted on Figure 1. This is the called *traditional scheme of corporate governance* (AECA 2007).

The evolution of this agenda issue is clear, when the concern about the relationship with the stakeholders has increased on the last years, and then is not only for the board and executive management to handle the relationship with shareholders, but also with providers, clients, and even the society itself

Corporate governance (Figure 2) has gone through different stages, from defining a framework to implement specific controls (COSO 1992; COSO 2004), to the definition of code of conducts such as the Cadbury Report (Cadbury 1992) and the Turnbull Report (Turnbull 1998). Moreover, in some countries, and taking into account scandals such as Enron and Worldcom, a specific legislation has been developed to identify and establish legal responsibilities for those managers and directors who are not committing with the legal obligations (Sarbanes-Oxley 2002). But the definitively commitment with corporate governance was due to the publication of the OECD Principles of Corporate Governance in 1999, updated in 2004 (OCDE 1999; OCDE 2004).

IT governance is the discipline of corporate governance that covers information and IT assets on the organization (Weill 2003). IT governance is focusing on the way these assets are managed, organized and controlled to provide the maximum value to the organization. And this process of governing IT should be done by integrating IT into the business strategy, with an efficient management of the IT resources, and minimizing the risks; complemented by constantly monitoring the business and IT goals. Although widely accepted from the IT perspective, the concept of IT governance as a discipline of corporate governance is now accepted from on the recent codes for corporate governance (Africa 2009).

Researchers and practitioners have been working on IT governance, and different frameworks have been defined to implement and manage IT governance on companies and organizations: COBIT version 4.1 (ITGovernanceInstitute 2007), the framework defined by the CISR (Weill 2003; Ross 2006); the structures, processes and relational mechanisms (Van Grembergen 2004). And more recently the ISO 38.500 standard (ISO 2008), and other frameworks based on this standard, such as Calder-Moir (Calder 2007). One the other hand, other organizations are developing their frameworks considering this standard and other perspectives (d'Information 2005).

However, the different frameworks have been more focused on big organizations, and there is no research that deals with the specific particularities of the medium and small companies. Also, there is no research so far that covers the status of IT Governance on the Spanish organizations.

This chapter will do an approach to know the status of IT Governance in the Spanish organizations, particularly on SMOs, identify the status of IT governance mechanisms, and set the basis to define best practices for this type of organizations. This chapter describes the work done so far by the authors, which consists basically on two different research projects, which are based on questionnaires and interviews with managers of Spanish SMOs.

FROM IT GOVERNANCE TO CORPORATE GOVERNANCE

The conception of IT governance as a discipline of IT governance was done in two steps. The first consisted in separate the operation of the company to the agenda issue, and then should consider elements such as business strategy, value creation and resource utilization. This was done the first time on the report of CIMA (CIMA 2003). Corporate governance is divided in two different areas: corporate governance itself (that covers the conformance issues and the relationship between shareholders and managers) and business governance, focused on managing the business, on a strategic and tactical view.

The second step was to identify the different assets that are related to the operation of the company. This is done by Weill and Ross (Weill 2003), who identified six assets that a company should govern: human and financial resources, physical assets, intellectual property, relationships and, finally, IT and information (Figure 3).

This establishes the basis for IT governance as a discipline itself, integrated in the corporate governance. As seen in the figure, IT governance is not to be managed by the senior executive team; as a corporate discipline emanates from (and should be directed and controlled by) the board

IT GOVERNANCE

Researches and practitioners have analyzed IT governance in different ways. From a theoretical

Figure 3. Business operation as a discipline of corporate governance (adapted from CIMA)

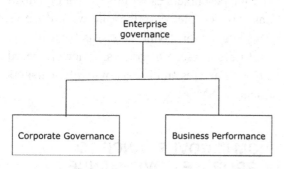

point of view, IT Governance has released COBIT version 4.1 (ITGovernanceInstitute 2007), which covers IT governance from the performance management perspective. This perspective is complemented by the Val IT framework (ITGovernanceInstitute 2006), which is more focused on the value adding of IT to the business. And also, more recently, the IT Governance Institute has released the draft for managing Risk IT framework (ITGovernanceInstitute 2009) covering the risk dimension of IT governance (Figure 4)..

The approach of the Center for Information Systems Research (Weill 2003; Ross 2006) is different, and is more in the opposite way: from the reality, from what has been done in the companies and organizations, the authors conceived a framework to implement IT Governance, taking into account the best practices that were implemented or developed in organizations with superior from IT. This framework considers three different aspects: the decision-making mechanisms and structures, the alignment processes, and communication tools and approaches. This approach has been complemented with the inclusion of the IT engagement model and the different architecture maturity stages.

Van Grembergen (Van Grembergen 2004), proposed another different framework based on three pillars: structures, processes and relational mechanisms. And other institutions such as Forrester (Symons 2005) also approached this subject by suggesting best practices to implement IT Governance. Most recently, there are two milestones to be considered. First is the publication of the ISO/IEC 38.500 (ISO 2008), covering IT Governance, and based on the Australian standard. This document is an effort to define a high level standard to implement IT Governance in the organizations, defining six principles for good corporate governance of IT, and expresses, as the standard says, desirable behaviors for the decision making process. This standard is a generic one, and there are ongoing initiatives to deeply develop the six principles through best practices.

Since the standard is generic, there is a need to define and implement this standard on the different organizations. This is when the Calder-Moir IT Governance Framework (Calder 2007) comes.

Figure 4. IT Governance as a discipline of corporate governance (adapted from CISR)

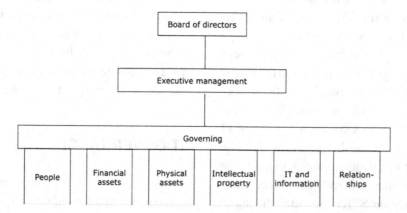

This framework is conceived to implement IT Governance from top to bottom of the organization (from the board to management), and also in the whole lifecycle, from the strategic planning to the deployment of capabilities. Clear benefits of this framework are the integration with different models, techniques and frameworks already existing (COBIT, ITIL, TOGAF, etc.). And finally, it is important to name the efforts of the Institute de la Gouvernance des Systèmes d'Information in defining its framework for IT governance (d'Information 2005), and define every one of the different techniques and tools for implementing it.

There are different definitions of IT governance. Not only this, but even it can be found, in the literature, an attempt to define this discipline considering the different frameworks and elements (Webb 2006). But, rather to define it, it is more important to understand the different elements that comprise it.

The IT Governance Institute, on its different publications (ITGovernanceInstitute 2003; ITGovernanceInstitute 2007), identified 5 key elements for IT Governance: strategic alignment, value delivery, risk management, resource management and performance management. Other institutions, such as CISR (Weill 1998; Weill 2003) consider more important aspects such as strategic alignment, organizational structures, relational mechanisms and processes. The approach of Van Grembergen (Van Grembergen 2004) is similar, basing IT governance on processes, structures and relational mechanisms. The ISO 38.500 standard considers principles such as responsibility, strategy, acquisition, performance, conformance and human behavior. And other institutions such as L'Institute de la Governance des Systêmes d'information (d'Information 2005) structure IT Governance on a different way, considering elements that have already been analyzed such as value delivery, processes, risk management and transparency and compliance, but also IT finance (budgeting and controlling), IT competencies and IT customer, more related with the operation of IT.

In the next paragraphs the different elements of IT governance are described.

Strategic Alignment

Aligning IT with the business strategy makes IT to both support the business operation and also to support the strategic of the business, in terms of business objectives.

One of the first steps to consider strategic alignment as one of the key elements was identified by Weill (Weill 1990), differentiating the value delivery of IT from the strategic and operational point of view. Nevertheless, Henderson and Venkatraman (Henderson 1999) were the first to propose a framework to align IT with the business, in which they propose the need of an IT strategy. This framework was complemented by Luftman and Brier (Luftman 1999), who identified the enablers and inhibitors of the strategic alignment of IT.

Other authors such as Weill (Weill 1998) proposed a model for the strategic alignment considering the environment, the role of IT and the strategic content, and linking it with the IT portfolio. Luftman (Luftman 2000) developed a strategic alignment maturity model, tested on 25 companies of Fortune 500, and Duffy (Duffy 2002) identified four maturity models.

Strategic alignment of IT must comprise two things in the organization. First, a clear and defined business strategy, that must have strategic lines with impact on IT. Second, an IT strategy that must consider the business strategy and its impact on IT, and also the needs, from the mid and long term point of view, of IT.

Value Delivery

From the perspective of shareholders, IT must deliver value. And this can be seen as an optimization of the investments (Weill 1998). Verifying the value delivery of IT is verifying the validity of the investments in IT, for the shareholders, the board, and the management. Weill and Broadbent (Weill 1998) established a model that allows to implement mechanisms for IT to deliver value to the business.

IT portfolio management has been seen as a key technique to align IT investments with the business strategy (Kaplan 2005; Maizlish 2005). Although this technique includes and develops elements of investment optimization, do not guarantee the real value delivery to the business. This fact is complemented with another aspect, that Weill and Broadbent called dilution of impact (Weill 1998): the value that IT investment are delivering to the business can be clearly identified on the lower level, this is at the IT infrastructure level; but this value is diluting when it comes to measure it from the business indicators perspective.

The problem is so difficult that should be treated on a framework. The IT Governance Institute has developed the Val IT framework (now on its second version (ITGovernanceInstitute 2008a), that consider not only the portfolio management but key elements as the business case.

The problem persists, and its now based in identifying best practices, not only about IT planning, IT portfolio management and IT budgeting and controlling, but also more intangible elements such as relationship management and IT communication management (d'Information 2005).

Risk Management

Corporate risk is another discipline inherent to corporate management. Initially associated to the management of financial and physical lost, it has become now, with the Enron, Worldcom and other scandals, on a discipline that has to manage risk at (and from) the board level, shareholders and executive management (CIMA 2003). The board of management should create the adequate organizational structures, as well as the appropriate risk environment, for the management of risk.

From the IT point of view, there are some frameworks and standards that cover risk regarding with aspects such as security, compliance, etc. Elieson (Elieson 2006) did a comprehensive comparison of them, and make a set of recommendations from the perspective of the IT Governance Institute and its publications.

The first attempt to define a framework for IT risk management is done by Westerman and Hunter (G. Westerman 2007), with the approach of the 4As (availability, access, accuracy, agility). Also, more recently, the release of the IT Risk Framework draft for the IT Governance Institute (Institute 2009) adds an attempt to introduce another framework for this discipline.

It is clear that the management of the risk of IT must start at the top of the organization. Risk is a matter of the whole organization, and understanding the risk appetite of the different stakeholders is the beginning, but it is also important to implement a risk based culture on the organization (G. Westerman 2007), in a way that every person must be proactive in identifying, analyzing and reporting risks.

Resource Management

Resource management is another element associated to IT governance (ITGovernanceInstitute 2007). Resources are considered applications, information, infrastructure, and people, and should be managed according with the business (and IT) strategy, in order to provide the maximum value.

The current literature points to the portfolio management (Kaplan 2005; Maizlish 2005) for the efficient management of resources in order to deliver the needed capabilities. But the management of competencies is another area in which it is necessary to insist. It is important to align human resources with the business and IT strategy; especially in the IT area this is a must.

Organizational Structures

The need to define or adequate organizational structures to implement IT governance is pointed out on Weill and Ross, when referencing decision making mechanisms. A business strategy, and an IT strategy, should have the right organizational structure to be implemented. This is also seen by Van Grembergen (Van Grembergen 2004), and other institutions (Symons 2005).

Two key concepts on IT governance should be considered when talking about organizational structures: responsibility and accountability (Weill 2003). It is important to establish accountability and responsibility in the organization for every IT initiative, not at the management level, but at the board level. Furthermore, some authors consider to define and implement the IT Governance Office (Weill 2003), that will be the delegation of the board in terms of implementing IT governance, as well as analyzing, reporting and handling IT governance issues.

IT Processes

The organizational structures need to be complemented by IT governance processes. These processes should allow to implement effective IT governance mechanisms, such as service level agreements (SLAs), but also chargeback mechanisms (Weill 2003). Van Grembergen (Van Grembergen 2004) goes beyond, identifying not only these processes, but also consider the implementation of COBIT and ITIL, as well as specific processes such as strategic decision making.

Performance Management

COBIT (ITGovernanceInstitute 2007) identifies performance management as one of the elements of IT governance, and identifies a set of processes and metrics to control it. Other authors analyzed the concept of IT balanced scorecard (Van Grembergen 2003; Van Grembergen 2008) identifying even a set of metrics and indicators for this.

THE RESEARCH

Taking this in mind, the research is divided in two phases. In the first phase, the status of IT governance is analyzed from the management point of view, trying to identify links between the state of the organization (and its structure, organization and mechanisms) and some of the elements of IT governance. The second phase was differently conceived: the aim is to identify the status of IT governance on the organizations, as well as the degree of awareness of IT governance.

The methodology used in both phases is described below:

- The definition of a questionnaire to present to managing directors/owners and IT managers (if existing) of Spanish SMOs.
- The selection and/or capturing of companies or organizations that can participate on this research.
- Questionnaire pre-test, on a small group of SMOs.
- Modification of the questionnaire, in order to incorporate the conclusions of this pre-test.
- Interviews with MDOs (managing directors/owners) of companies/organizations, in order to obtain the information of the questionnaire.
- Analysis of the information gathered.
- Identification of preliminary conclusions for IT Governance in SMOs.

The First Phase

The first phase finished last year, and did not consider the recent publications mentioned before: the standard ISO 38.500:2000 (ISO 2008) and the Calder-Moir framework (Calder 2007). The elements of IT governance were analyzed from a practical perspective. The focus was to identify best practices on organizations and the relationship with the key elements of IT governance considered:

- Strategic alignment of IT.
- Value delivery of IT.
- Organizational structures.
- Processes of IT Governance.
- Performance management.

In order to identify this, the questionnaire was focusing on obtaining information about the degree of definition and implementation of:

- The organization, in terms of departments, responsibilities, coordination mechanisms, etc.
- The business processes.
- The business strategy and reporting/monitoring mechanisms.
- The organization, processes and strategy of IT.
- The location and attributes of IT within the organization.
- IT decision making mechanisms.
- IT and the relationship with other departments/business units.

Strategy

To analyze the degree of strategic alignment on the organizations, the authors analyzed the existence of a business strategy and, eventually, an IT strategy. But this is not always present on the SMOs: instead, successful SMOs can have a clear statement of strategic goals and metrics (such as sales increase, production increase, cost cutting objectives), and a clear understanding of the implication of IT on the goals.

Processes and Organization

One of the key elements for IT governance is the existence of organizational structures that manages and drives IT, and the related processes. In

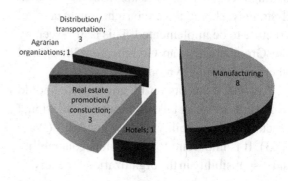

Figure 5. Industries of the organization participating on first research

the organizations, the authors searched for a well defined organizational structure, as well as a good definition and implementation of the business processes. In general, SMOs in Spain have the ISO 9.001 certification, which identifies processes and organizational structures. But this is only a threshold level of excellence; since this certification is not seen, by the managers, as a driver for a better management of the organization, and is only considered as a "must have" (needed, for example, to access to contracts with the Spanish Administration).

Balanced Scorecard

Finally, the authors looked for the existence of a balance scorecard, not only in itself, but also as an element that is timely and consistently reviewed and managed. Alternatively, the authors looked for the existence of a set of structured business objectives, monitored consistently and driving the process of decision making.

Conclusions

There were 16 organizations that participated on this phase, with different sizes and industries.

Figure 6. Size of the organizations on first research

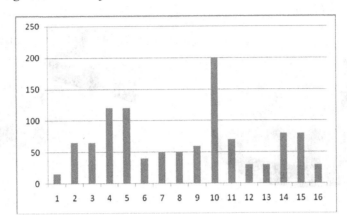

Strategic Alignment; Business and IT Goals

Only 5 of the organizations had a well-defined business strategy, with strategic lines and business goals. The figure shows the sizes of the organizations (Figures 5 and 6):

As a common element, the organizations have a very professional managing team, with a clear separation of functions. But, instead of a business strategy, the existence of a set of business objectives or goals should be considered as an alternative. Regarding this, all the companies (not the agrarian organization) had a set of business goals defined. Nevertheless, the business goals are monitored yearly, which cannot be considered as a good managing practice(Figure 7).

There was no company or organization with an IT strategy defined. But, as an alternative, the existence of IT generic goals was considered. The goals identified (on all the companies) falls under this two types:

- Implementation of information systems (ERPs as Navision or SAP) or other IT-related systems (websites).
- Systems maintenance or new functionality.

Figure 7. Organizations with a well defined business strategy

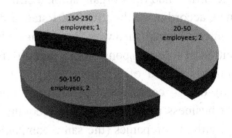

And, finally, the last aspect was the identification of IT as a key factor that drives business strategies. There were two situations identified:

- A real estate promotion company uses IT as the only channel to sell its real estate developments (by positioning its products on search engines such as Google Adwords, and a daily follow-up, optimizing the searching criteria).
- A pharmaceutical distribution company uses IT as a way to obtain key information for the strategic decision making process, on critical aspects on its value chain: stock information, and transportation routes optimization.

Figure 8. Organizations with well defined processes and organizational structure

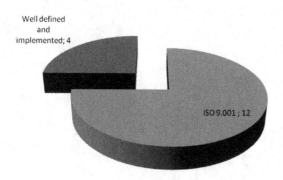

Figure 9. Responsible for the IT function

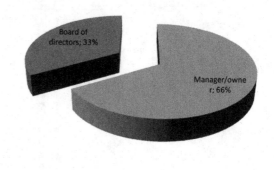

Processes and Organizations

All the SMOs had their organizational structure defined, according to the ISO 9.001 standard or in an internal established way. Regarding a clear definition of roles, responsibilities and different committees (board of directors, steering committee), only 4 companies had such definition. About business processes, the same comments apply: only 4 companies (the same companies) had the business processes clearly defined and implemented(Figure 8).

Regarding the IT function, the research tried to identify if this was performed internally or, else, was outsourced. Only 4 companies performed this function internally. Two of them were the real estate promotion and the pharmaceutical companies described above. The other two were the biggest company and a company on the interval of 51-150 employees.

The second aspect to be discovered is the person or charge responsible of IT. In general, there is not a CIO, except on three organizations. The decisions are taking (except on the agrarian organization) at the next levels:

Regarding the follow-up of IT initiatives, this is done at the same level that makes the decisions, but only on terms of budget and timing. Only in the four companies with processes and organizations well defined things such as ROI and busi-

ness indicators (contacts from the website, stocks rotation, etc.) are monitored frequently (Figure 9).

IT Governance Processes

The existence of chargeback mechanisms, and SLAs, was also analyzed. The IT function is considered as a cost center. Only on the two companies described above (real estate promotions and pharmaceutical distribution companies) the costs of IT are considered on the product pricing, and cost/benefit analysis of the IT investments are performed.

Regarding communication, there has not been identified on any of the companies communication mechanisms specifically focused on IT Governance on any company.

The Second Phase

The first phase finished last year, and did not consider the recent publications mentioned before: the standard ISO 38500 (ISO 2008) and the Calder-Moir framework (Calder 2007). The conclusion of the first phase led the author to consider a new research, a new phase, focused on identifying specific information about IT governance practices. The questionnaire was structure as follows:

Figure 10. Industry of the organizations partici-pating on the second research

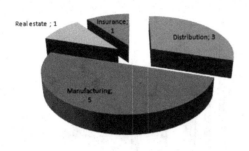

Figure 11. Size of the companies for the second research

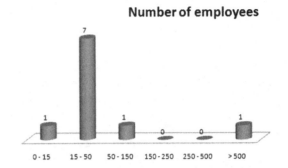

- The status and progress of IT on the companies, in terms of issues concerning IT experimented on organizations.
- Strategic alignment and value delivery.
- Best practices on IT Governance.
- Risk management.
- Decision making mechanisms.
- Knowledge of tools and frameworks of IT Governance.

The questionnaire was defined considering the first questionnaire and the different conclusions obtained on the first phase, but also questionnaires and information associated to the different Global Status Reports of IT Governance (ITGovernanceInstitute 2004; ITGovernanceInstitute 2006; ITGovernanceInstitute 2008b). This information gave the authors ideas about the structure and questions that should be included on the second questionnaire. Finally, were taken into consideration the different questionnaires included on Calder-Moir framework for both the board and the managing team.

The questionnaire has been pre-tested on 4 small and medium organizations. And the interview process is on going, and 6 new organizations have been participated so far, including a big company.

Conclusions

As said before, currently 10 organizations participated on this phase, with different sizes and industries as shown in Figures 10 and 11.

IT Status in the organizations

The first item that is discovered is regarding the status of IT in the organizations, and the problems they have. The figure shows that the main problem is focused on the relationship with suppliers and outsourcing, followed by agility problems (in developing new functionalities on the companies). Also, other problems to be considered are related to staff (insufficient or with a lack of IT skills), and IT service delivery problems. It is also important to remark the different problems existing with archiving/back-up (Figure 12).

In general, problems are remaining with the same importance that they had on the last year, and the situation has been stable.

The companies were asked to evaluate (in a scale of 1-5) the efficiency of high level actions that could help to solve these problems. The average of the efficiency is shown in the Figure 13:

The problems the companies are facing are regarding outsourcing, but there is also important

Figure 12.Problems with IT in the organizations

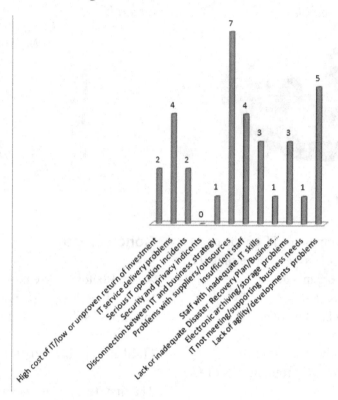

to point out the need to focus also on the management of IT resources (associated, of course, with outsourcing) but also the delivery of value of IT to the business.

Business and IT Strategy

Related with the first research, on this research the authors analyzed if the companies have a business and an IT strategy, and its relationship. This can be seen on the Figures 14 and 15:

The conclusion is clear: while organizations are concerned about managing its business with a business strategy or vision, regarding IT the situation is completely different. However, overall, the perception of the companies with regard the degree of alignment between IT and the business is good as shown in Figure 16:

Decision Making Mechanisms

The next thing was trying to identify where the IT function in the organization is, and also to understand the different decision making mechanisms that are present on the companies. In general, there is no IT department on the organization (only the big company has its own IT department), and the IT function depends of the manager. But there has been identified that the IT function depends, hierarchically, of other managing position different of the manager, in almost half of the companies. This position should be the vice-manager, or the second in charge in the company that takes care of IT (Figure 17).

Considering this information, it is clear that the sponsorships falls under the person that is in charge of the IT function: the manager/MDO, the CIO (that exists only on the big company), and the vice-manager or the second person in charge in

Figure 13.Importance of high level actions

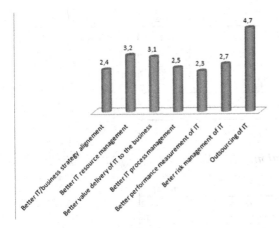

Figure 14.Business strategy status

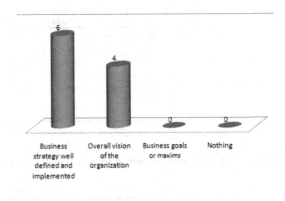

Figure 15.IT strategy status

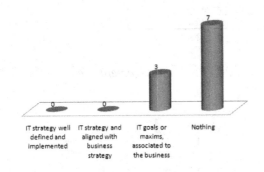

Figure 16.Degree of alignment between IT and the business

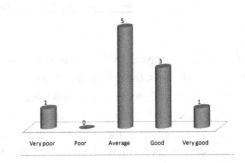

Figure 17.The dependency of the IT department

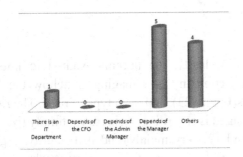

Figure 18.IT sponsorship

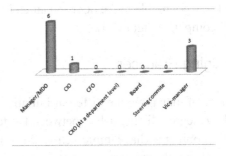

Figure 19.Who makes decision regarding IT

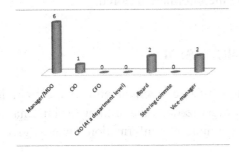

Figure 20.Accountability

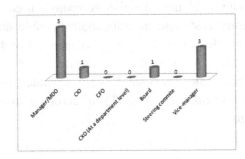

Figure 21.Project approval on IT

Tools for approving projects	TOTAL
Business case: economic and quantitative analysis	1
Business case: economic analysis	1
Business case: only costs and qualitative benefits	1
Costs, tangible and intangible benefits	7
Cost and tangible benefits	0
Cost	0
None	0

Figure 22.Other management practices on the organization

Project management practices	TOTAL
The status of any IT initiative is know in terms of schedule	8
The status of any IT initiative is know in terms of costs	10
The status of any IT initiative is know in terms of problems	10
The status of any IT initiative is know in terms of possible risks	5
There is a committee that reviews the status of any IT initiative	4
The different departments involved on IT initiatives are identified	6

the organization (Figure 18). Regarding decision making mechanisms, the results are showing that the decision is taking at the manager/MDO level, and also on the vice-manager. It is important to notice that here appears the board of directors, who makes the decision in two SMOs (Figure 19).

Interestingly, regarding accountability of the decisions, there is a slight difference and now the board is accountable of the decision taken in one small company (Figure 20).

Managing Practices

In terms of managing the different initiatives of IT, the research distinguished between the tools that the companies have implemented for project approval, and the status of some project management practices on the organizations .

Figure 21 indicates that companies used to identify costs and benefits (both tangible and intangible) when analyzing the approval of IT initiatives. And regarding management practices, the companies have knowledge of schedule, costs and problems in on-going IT projects or initiatives (Figure 22).

Figure 23.IT risk management areas

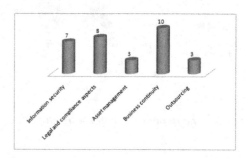

And, lastly, the authors wanted to know if the company is managing somehow the IT risks(Figure 23), and what type of risks. The risk managed is regarding business continuity (back-up and recovery, mainly) and also security. Legal and compliance aspects are important, where also important in terms of compliance with legislation about the information stored.

CONCLUSION

Although the research, in terms of incorporating more organizations and refining the information, will continue, the information gathered gives a good perception of the IT governance in SMOs in Spain. The absence of an IT strategy other than supporting the operation, and the problems with outsourcing makes indispensable to establish some type of committee to manage IT from an organization-wide perspective (somehow strategically) and to handle the different problems the companies are facing. This will allow separating, in the organizations, decision from accountability.

There is also a need to define a risk management schema that will ensure business continuity and, also, legal and compliance aspects. This is very important taking into account that, for example, while outsourcing is one of the main issues on the companies, there are few companies that are managing risk in this area.

The implementation of these practices needs to bring a win-win scenario to the companies, in which the benefits of better controlling and managing IT (and thus the business) should compensate the effort and cost to implement the structures mentioned.

REFERENCES

AECA. (2007). *Gobierno y responsabilidad social de la empresa*. Madrid: AECA.

Cadbury, A. (1992). *Report of the Committee on the Financial Aspects of Corporate Governance*. G. P. Publishing.

Calder, A. (2007). *IT Governance Pocket Guide*. Rolling Meadows, IL: IT Governance Publishing.

CIMA. (2003). *Enterprise Governance. Getting the balance right. CIMA*. IFAC.

COSO. (1992). *Internal Control - Integrated Framework*. Washington, DC: COSO.

COSO. (2004). *Enterprise Risk Management - Integrated Framework (Executive Summary)*. Washington, DC: COSO.

Duffy, J. (2002). *IT/Business alignment: Is it an option or is it mandatory? Elieson, B. D. (2006). Construction of an IT Risk Framework*. Rolling Meadows, IL: IT Governance Institute.

Henderson, J. C., & Venkatraman, N. (1999). Strategic alignment: leveraging information technology for transforming organizations. *IBM Systems Journal, 38*(2-3).

Institute de la Gouvernance des Système d'Information. (2005). *The place of IT Governance in the Enterpise Governance. Balancing Performance and Conformance*. Paris: Institute de la Gouvernance des Systèmes d'Information.

Institute of Directors of Southern Africa. (2009). *King Code Of Governance for South Africa*.

ISO. (2008). ISO / IEC 38500:2008 Corporate Governance for Information Technology.

IT Governance Institute. (2003). *Board Briefing on IT Governance* (2nd ed.). Rolling Meadows, IL: IT Governance Institute.

IT Governance Institute. (2004). *IT Governance Global Status Report*. Rolling Meadows, IL: IT Governance Institute.

IT Governance Institute. (2006). *Enterprise Value: Governance of IT Investments. The Val IT Framework*. Rolling Meadows, IL: IT Governance Institute.

IT Governance Institute. (2006). *IT Governance Global Status Report - 2006*. Rolling Meadows, IL: IT Governance Institute.

IT Governance Institute. (2007). *Control Objectives for Information and Related Technology, versión 4.1*. Rolling Meadows, IL: IT Governance Institute.

IT Governance Institute. (2008a). *Enterprise Value: Governance of IT Investments. The Val IT Framework 20*. Rolling Meadows, IL: IT Governance Institute.

ITGovernanceInstitute. (2008b). *IT Governance Global Status Report - 2008*. Rolling Meadows, IL: IT Governance Institute.

ITGovernanceInstitute. (2009). *Enterprise Risk: Identify, Govern and Manage IT Risk. The Risk IT Framework. Exposure draft*. Rolling Meadows, IL: IT Governance Institute.

Kaplan, J. (2005). *Strategic IT Portfolio Management: Governing Enterprise Transformation*. Boston: PRTM.

Luftman, J. (2000). *Assessing business-IT alignment maturity*. Communications of the Association for Information Systems.

Luftman, J., & Brier, T. (1999). *Achieving and sustaining business-IT alignment*. California Management Review.

Maizlish, B., & Handler, R. (2005). *IT Portfolio Management Step-by-step. Unlocking the Business Value of Technology*. New York: John Wiley & Sons.

Moxey, P., & Berent, A. (2008). *Corporate Governance and the Credit Crunch*. Association of Chartered Certified Accountants.

OECD. (1999). *OECD Principles of Corporate Governance*. Paris: OECD.

OECD. (2004). *OECD Principles of Corporate Governance*. Paris: OECD.

Ross, J. W., Weill, P., & Robertson, D. C. (2006). *Enterprise Architecture as Strategy. Creating a Foundation for Business Execution*. Cambridge, MA: Harvard Business School Press.

Sarbanes-Oxley Act of 2002, 49 U.S.C. §42121 (2002).

Symons, C. C. M., Oliver Young, G., & Lambert, N. (2005). *IT Governance Framework*. New York: Forrester.

Treasury, H. M. (2009). *Independent review of corporate governance of UK banking industry*.

Turnbull, N. (1998). *The Combined Code. Principes of Good Governance and Code of Best Practice*. London: The Institute of Chartered Accountants in England and Wales.

Van Grembergen, W. (2004). *Strategies for Information Technology Governance*. Hershey, PA: IGI Publishing.

Van Grembergen, W., De Haes, S., & Van Brempt, H. (2008). *Identifying and Aligning Business Goals and IT Goals*. Rolling Meadows, IL: IT Governance Institute.

Van Grembergen, W., Saull, R., & De Haes, S. (2003). *Linking the IT Balanced Scorecard to the Business Objectives at a Major Canadian Financial Group. Journal of Information Technology Cases and Applications*. JITCA.

Webb, P., Pollard, C., & Ridley, G. (2006). Attempting to define IT Governance: Wisdom or Folly? In *Proceedings of the 39th Hawaii International Conference on System Sciences*.

Weill, P. (1990). *Do computers pay-off?* ICIT Press.

Weill, P., & Broadbent, M. (1998). *Leveraging the new infrastructure*. Cambridge, MA: Harvard Business School Press.

Weill, P., & Ross, J. W. (2003). *IT Governance. How top performers manage IT decision for superior results*. Cambridge, MA: Harvard Business School Press.

Westerman, G., & Hunter, R. (2007). *IT Risk. Turning Business threats into competitive advantage*. Cambridge, MA: Harvard Business School Press.

Section 8
Collaborative, Networked and Virtual Organizations

Chapter 29
Multisite PLM Platform:
A Collaborative Design Environment

George Draghici
Politehnica University of Timisoara, Romania

Anca Draghici
Politehnica University of Timisoara, Romania

ABSTRACT

Today, product development is a result of a collaborative design process in network. Taking into consideration this fact, a National Research Network for Integrated Product and Process Engineering (INPRO) has been created. The present chapter presents the relevant items for building a PLM multisite platform for collaborative integrated product development based on the common researches developed in the INPRO project and network. The authors argue this approach by presenting the collaborative distributed design process, the product model and the PLM multisite platform for collaborative integrated product development. Based on these was built a collaborative multisite platform that join together the methodology, methods and tools for Product Lifecycle Management (PLM), Knowledge Management (KM) and Human Resources Management (HRU), examples of good practice. The core of the proposed approach is the product lifecycle model which is the base for the proposed collaborative product development methodology and the multisite PLM platform architecture. The presented research results were gained from our implication in the project "National Research Network for Integrated Product and Process Engineering – INPRO" (contract no. 243 / 08.09.2006). The model of building such collaborative design environment was inspired by the Virtual Research Laboratory for a Knowledge Community in Production (VRL-KCiP) a Network of Excellence project (contract no. FP6-507487). From 2008 the authors extended their research at the European level, in the context of a Lifelong Learning Programme, Leonardo da Vinci - Transfer of Innovation (contract nr. FR/08/LLP-LdV/TOI/117025), "Certified Integrated Design Engineer – iDesigner" in which they used the collaborative platform for the students and researchers professional qualification and certification.

DOI: 10.4018/978-1-61692-020-3.ch029

INTRODUCTION

The Specificity of Collaborative Distributed Design

The product development process has changed dramatically in the last time because of the progresses in the information and communication technology field. Nowadays, the product development is a result of a collaborative design process in network (Shpitalni, Guttman, & Bossin, 2005). Integrated product and processes development supposes to consider all the knowledge about the product lifecycle from the beginning of product design stage, by integrating the user requirements, with the quality, terms and costs constraints (Draghici, 1999), (Usher, Roy & Parsaei, 2005). Therefore, we can talk about the whole product lifecycle integration and management (Stark, 2005). The design of successful and sustainable products is increasingly linked to mastering the challenge of the complexity and multidisciplinary nature of modern products in an integrated fashion from the very earliest phases of product development.

In the same time, many product development projects require cooperation between research teams with different competence, which can be also, geographical distributed. When such a project/product team is set up, all the require knowledge must be considered to solve a certain design problem in a collaborative environment. Design engineers are increasingly confronted with the need to master several different engineering disciplines in order to get a sufficient understanding of a product or service. Competence in the major aspects of the whole product lifecycle is a key element of the skills they require to be able to conceive a product design that fulfils the requirements of all the different actors involved in the product's lifecycle as well as the constraints imposed by their individual environments. Likewise, engineering teams are getting increasingly interdisciplinary, and thus there is a strong demand

for a mutual understanding and collaboration between domain expert team members.

In the following will be explained the specificity of human resources interaction, in the new context of the collaborative distributed design process for better understand the need for building such environment. When a product is designed through the collective and joint efforts of many designers, the design process can be called as collaborative design. This work has to be done by taking into consideration the product lifecycle processes by including those dispersed functions such as design, manufacturing, assembly, test, quality and purchasing as well as those from suppliers and customers.

The main goals of such a collaborative design team might include optimizing the mechanical function of the product, minimizing the production or assembly costs, or ensuring that the product can be easily and economically serviced and maintained etc. Since a collaborative design team often works in parallels and independently using different engineering tools distributed in separate locations, even across various time zones around the world, the resulting design process may then be called distributed collaborative design.

Johansen used time-space 2D matrix to examine cooperative works (Johansen, 1998). The matrix categorizes collaboration into synchronous and asynchronous patterns, shown as Figure 1.

This space-time matrix cannot fully represent the emerging collaboration trends. For example, collaboration may happen among different geographically dispersed companies, or within the same company but between two distributed divisions. Here we extend the matrix to a three-dimensional time-location-group space, defined as O (T, L, G) to describe when, where and who are collaborating (Chen et al, 2005).

Compared to the Johansen's time-space matrix, which is a very useful and concise reference to the particular design circumstance, the proposed 3D time-location-group matrix not only looks at whether participants are in the same place, but

Figure 1. Johansen matrix (after: Johansen, 1998)

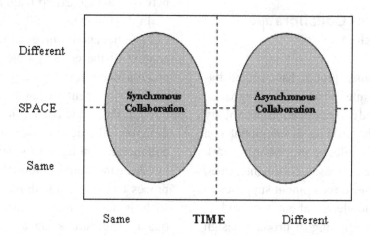

also whether they are operating (prepared, ready for the collaborative process) at the same time or not. By this 3D matrix, there can be considering whether participants are in the same company or group (Chen et al, 2005).

In the collaboration domain, enterprises are usually only concerned the security of data flow; however, the collaboration systems' architecture and their patterns should also be taken into consideration. Very often, in the domain of one enterprise, the design platforms, such as operation systems, types of network, development tools, database systems, CAD software, etc. are usually heterogeneous, whilst configurations and facilities are often different from company to company. This will result in different architectures and different system functionalities for collaborative design.

As shown in Figure 2, based on the time-coordinate, we define synchronous and asynchronous collaboration. Considering the data location, modeling kernel and functionalities of collaborative design, the tasks can be centralized or distributed. For the participants of collaborative design, it can be inter-enterprise, intra-enterprise or extra-enterprise. Due to the different patterns of collaboration models, it may result in different architectures and solutions for the realization of

distributed collaborative design frameworks and finally, environment (Chen et al, 2005).

Collaborative design issues are due to: different groups of people, often with different expertise in accord with the product life cycle phases (like design engineers, technological design engineer, manufacturing engineer, marketing experts, distribution experts, accouters or economist specialists, service and maintenance specialists, recycling specialists etc.) and that can belong to different enterprises, at different places, but having to work together in a specific product design process.

Designing complex products (such as aircrafts or automobiles) requires a tremendous collection of expertise, knowledge, technology and tools. Design resources are often distributed. Participants

Figure 2. Co-design patterns in 3-dimension

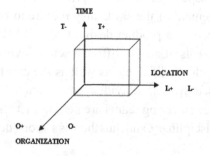

may be in different places as well. Integrated concurrent product development is realized by leveraging modern information and communication technology (ICT) to coordinate people, processes, tools and technologies. Companies (SME more often) and medium-sized suppliers are looking for an inexpensive way for geographically dispersed teams to jointly develop products together over the Internet. Traditional CAD/CAE functionalities nowadays are very often dispersed.

How can design actors manage an efficient inter-relationship (different people relationships) to attend the collaborative design process final objective?

Considering the scenario of collaborative design, a key characteristic is linked with the human relationship development in the context of their professional evolution (including their learning needs, too). For this reason there have been consider the development of the *collaborative distributed design* environment that is related to the actors-conceptor behavior (that have to be an efficient desired behavior) oriented to the design process objectives' attending (the final design solution accepted by each actor involved in the process that better satisfied customer/user).

Brief Description of the Research Organizational Context

These were strong arguments that determine the establishment of the National Research Network for Integrated Product and Process Engineering (INPRO). The idea behind such network was to overcome fragmentation by applying the network principle to research.

The INPRO network project attend strategic objectives for excellence in research, development and innovation through critical mass concentration at national level of human and materials resources of high value in the field of integrated products and process engineering in Romania and link them at the European Research Area's priorities, objectives and specific activities. The project joint 121 members (73 PhD, 37 PhD. students, 9 researchers and 2 master students) from 9 research centers, localized in different universities of Timisoara, Bucharest, Iasi, Brasov, Bacau, Suceava, Sibiu and Oradea and a national research institute. The project partners have decided to share their competencies and knowledge in the field of integrated product and process engineering. The project proposal is based on the idea of linking the Romanian scientific research to the European research using the bridge created by the participation of the Politehnica University of Timisoara, by the Integrated Engineering Research Centre, the leader of the proposed project, in the European Network of Excellence (NoE) *Virtual Research Lab for a Knowledge Community in Production* (VRL-KCiP, www.vrl-kcip.com).

The specific strategic objectives followed by the creation of the INPRO network were:

- Setting up a manufacturing knowledge base in the field of product and processes integrated engineering;
- Increasing research activities performance, stimulating excellence for facilitating the access to the EU research programs;
- Enhancing of the human resources education process by including the young PhD. students in the joint research activities and by assure the access to the disseminating activities in the INPRO network and the connection with VRL-KCiP NoE;
- Facilitating motilies inside the INPRO network (at the national level) and the VRL-KCiP NoE (at the European level);
- Better valorization of the existing material research base and research cost reduction by creating the possibility to common use of the partners' extant infrastructure;
- Managerial skills development in the scientific research field and increasing the capacity for new financial resources identification.

The operational objectives are:

- Creation, consolidation and development of the INPRO network;
- Initiation and development of jointly executed research activities;
- Spreading of excellence.

The specific strategic objectives were realized by the Joint Program of Activities. It consists of managerial aspects for organizing the INPRO network, but also the methods and tools that are used for the virtual collaborative environment development. This will support the building of a knowledge sharing culture in INPRO virtual organization.

The partners' collaboration and synergy in the national research network INPRO (Draghici & Draghici, 2007) was adapted to the actual requirements of product development. In this context, was built a collaborative multisite platform for product and its associated processes (Draghici, Savii & Draghici, 2007), (Draghici, Savii & Draghici, 2008), that join together the methodological approach, methods and tools for Product Lifecycle Management (PLM), Knowledge Management (KM) and Human Resources Management (HRU).

In this chapter are presented: the product lifecycle model which is the core of the proposed collaborative product development methodology, the human resources competencies database development, and the multisite PLM platform infrastructure.

PRODUCT LIFECYCLE MODEL

Product Model Development

Many of the world's most successful brands create breakthrough ideas that are inspired by a deep understanding of consumer's lives, their needs and constraints, and use the principles of design to innovate and build value. This is crucial

as innovation very often has to account for vast differences in cultural and socioeconomic conditions. In order to be able to do so, *design engineers* need to develop a good level of competence about the whole system they conceive, and about its environment.

For the classic "non-integrated" design methodology a lot of tools called "*Design for ...*" have been developed, which allow taking into account one specific domain (assembly, maintenance, manufacturing, etc.). Such tools are made to optimize one specific view, disregarding the fact that the global optimization of a system is in general not to be achieved by the local optimization of a series of components. Moreover, what normally has to be a constraint for the system is transformed into an objective function in these systems: Does an assembly have to be minimized, or is it sufficient to respect its operability if in another solution it can be less costly or complicated?

Integrated product design considers that the different constraints previously cited are the aim of different actors who have to control them but who "belong to the same world" (Boltanski & Thevenot, 1991). The common goal is to reduce the cost, to reduce the time to market, to take into account sustainability and to increase quality. Such actors have to work in a concurrent engineering context, having access to a common product model where they can have their own contextual views. They have to respect the just need which consists of giving a constraint on the system as soon as possible if such a constraint can be proved (Brissaud & Tichkiewitch, 2000).

Integrated product design thus does not seek to optimize one single objective, but rather aims at finding the best compromise solution under multiple, often coupled restrictions that are imposed by the actors and environments of the whole product lifecycle. They typically concern issues like manufacturability, assembly/disassembly, modularity, testability, product variant creation, environmental sustainability, product-service optimization, maintainability, cost minimization, etc. It goes without saying that Integrated Design Engineers are not supposed to master all the associated complex disciplines by themselves. They should, however, be able to understand domain experts, and be able to translate their requirements into their design tasks.

The collaborative product development model integrates knowledge from all the product lifecycle activities. For the product lifecycle representation there can be used different methods and modeling languages. Among them, there have been choose the IDEFØ (integrated Definition Method) (www. idef.com/pdf/idef0.pdf) as our preliminary research approach. This allows researchers to define the platform needs and also, its future structure.

IDEFØ is a method designed to model the decisions, actions, and activities of an organization or system. IDEFØ was derived from a well-established graphical language, the Structured Analysis and Design Technique (SADT).

The followed purpose is the deep analyze of each product lifecycle activity, under different aspects: the role of each activity, sub activities deployed, the transform parameters, the supports that allowed the development and control of an activity, the information exchange. In this context, IDEFØ method best attend the declare purpose. Each activity can be representing under a modular and graphical form, using arrows with a specific signification. One activity transforms input into output data. The activity development need assistance tools and control tools that allowed its development start or control.

For the representation of the product lifecycle model there have been used the iGrafx 2007 software (www.igrafx.com), which contained the IDEFØ module.

The superior level diagram A0 (Figure 3), has defined by the product lifecycle specific activities: needs analysis, design, manufacturing, use, disposal. There was adopted a top-bottom approach which allowed a progressive detailed from general to particular aspects for a clear and complete product lifecycle modeling. Although a product lifecycle is specific to a product, there are some basic facts, aspects, and phases that are common to almost any type of product. An Integrated Design Engineer needs this basic knowledge in order to be able to analyze and understand specific product lifecycles. The reality is however much more complex, people and departments cannot perform their tasks in isolation and one activity cannot simply finish and the next activity start. Design is an iterative process, often designs need to be modified due to manufacturing constraints or conflicting requirements.

The superior level diagram, named A0 (Figure 3), has defined by the product lifecycle specific activities:

A1 Activity: Needs analysis. The objective is to identify and formulate the needs for product development. The initiation of this activity is determinate by many factors as: a new market perception, an idea and technical and/or commercial un-satisfaction user perception. These correspond to some marketing function roles. The result of this activity is the product task book.

A2 Activity: Design. *Product design* can be defined as an entirety of activities and processes which allow us to pass from the idea of a new product (or improving an existent one) to information (drawings, programs, etc) which allow the production launching and ensure the product's use and maintenance (Perrin, 2001), (Prudhomme, 2000). Among design models the most representative is the model of Pahl and Beitz (1984), which is based on a design seen as a hierarchical, sequenced phases, the predominant logic being the convergence. At the origin of each new technical object, there is a specific problem to solve and a goal to focus on. The first phase of design consists in establishing the desired technical and economical specifications. The next phases consist of comprehending the design as a process of an increasingly defining process of adopted solution or like a bridge from a function (abstract form) to a solution (certain form). In the *conceptual design*

Figure 3. A0 Diagram: Product lifecycle activities as the base of product model

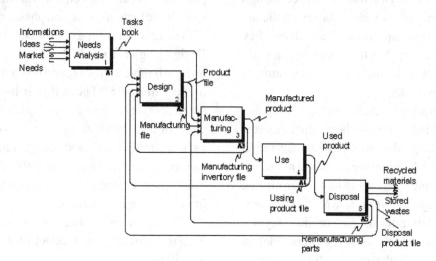

phase, after a functional analysis and a study of possible technical alternatives available for each function and sub-function a concept for the design object is usually chosen. The goal in the *embodiment design* phase is to determine the shape and the dimensions of the artifact. During the *detail design* phase are mentioned the components of the product and are formalized the papers needed for preparing the supply and manufacturing the components.

The A2 activity's inputs are the product task book and the feedback information from manufacturing, use and disposal phases. Using design methods and the study of possible alternatives there can be chosen the conceptual solution which followed the embodiment design and detailed design phases; the process planning is then, defined. Finally, is defined the product file and the manufacturing file that are needed for the following activities associated with the product manufacturing and use. Companies that design successfully have carefully crafted Product Creation Processes (PCP) that extends over all phases of product development from initial planning to customer follow-up. Their PCP is their plan for continuous improvement. The decision to develop and operate under a PCP is a corporate one. Successful operation of

a PCP requires extensive cooperation among a firm's marketing and sales, financial, design, and manufacturing organizations. In the idealized account of the PCP, everyone cooperates, desired quality is achieved, and the product succeeds in the marketplace. In practice, the process is difficult and full of conflict and risk. Converting a concept into a complex, multi-technology product involves many steps of refinement. The design process requires a great deal of analysis, investigation of basic physical processes, experimental verification, complex tradeoffs between conflicting elements, and difficult decisions. Satisfying the different and conflicting needs of function, manufacturing, use, and support requires a great deal of knowledge and skill.

A3 Activity: Manufacturing includes preparation and resources allocation for the components manufacturing deployment and for product assembly and so, it becomes ready for delivery. The information results from the manufacturing phase are included in the manufacturing management file that can be use for product design improvement.

A4 Activity: Use. The manufactured product has delivered to the user and his/her expectations have to be satisfied through the use phase. During the use phase, the product is liable to maintainable

Figure 4. Integration of PLM, ERP, SCM and CRM

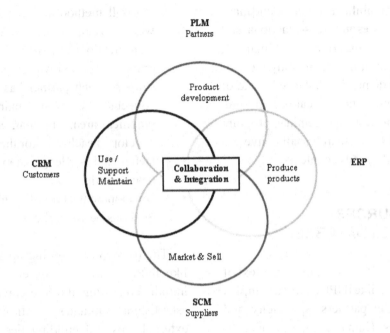

operations. In the use process all the information are record in the using product file and they had used for the product design improvement, too.

A5 Activity: Disposal. The used product is disposed, at the end of his life cycle. The first action is the disassembly and the components and materials sort in remanufacturing parts that can be inputs for other product assembly components; recycled materials that can be inputs for the supply chain; stored wastes components that have to be destroyed and storage, resulting wastes. All the output information included in the disposal product file can be use for the product re-design improvement, too. Each activity module is the object of a progressive decomposition in diagrams, which contain sub activities, till the elementary detailed level.

Collaborative Distributed Design Support and Implementation

In technical terms, collaborative product development in terms of the system- and process-oriented view elaborated in the previous chapters is based on the integration of Product Lifecycle Management (PLM), Enterprise Resource Planning (ERP), Supply Chain Management (SCM) and Customer Relationship Management (CRM) solutions (Figure 4). Integrated design engineers not only have to be able to work with these tools, but they also need to understand how they link the different teams and actors that are involved in the product lifecycle.

Although in human terms collaborative engineering is based on the support of the organization, it is very much facilitated by the awareness of each engineer about his role in the process, as well as the roles of others. Collaborative design involves product designers, manufacturing engineers, and representatives of purchasing, marketing, and field service in the early stages of design in order to reduce cycle time and improve manufacturability. This practice helps resolve what is often called the designer's dilemma, the fact that most of product cost, quality, and manufacturability are committed very early in design before more detailed information has been developed.

The key to the successful use of collaborative design concepts is the ability to organize and manage concurrent processes and cross-functional and typically distributed teams effectively. Obtaining this know-how is not a matter of studying textbooks but it rather demands a balanced blend of solid experience and of theoretical background. This is what the professional seminar program to be conceived in this research shall convey in sector- and national-specific contexts.

HUMAN RESOURCES COMPETENCIES DATABASE

The human resources data base, in the context of a virtual organization like INPRO, was a complex task considering the partners' specificity and their heterogeneous. Human resources management was linked with the organization creation, consolidation and development and, also with its sustainability.

Partners' integration and network's organization and development were activities focus on adapting the organizational activities of the network through a strategic plan, for developing and maintaining a continuous vision of industrial needs, identify the most demanding market requirements, defining the knowledge map and a competence profile regarding the current expertise of each member. In addition, there will be developed a policy to strengthen relations between the research activities. The work phases are:

- Definition of a strategic plan for the partners' integration - using the SWOT analysis method for the diagnosis of the internal and external environment regarding the INPRO network there have been elaborate the strategic priorities of the network. The procedure was applied in each year for the strategy up-date;
- Developing and maintaining a continuous living and upgraded vision on future indus-

trial needs. A marketing research by opinion poll method and a questionnaire tool were developed for the industrial needs identification regarding research, development and innovation activities and/or support. Each partner has distributed and collected the questionnaires in his geographical area. The marketing research is developed each year for the vision up-date;
- Define a knowledge map and a competence profile;
- Development of a policy to strengthen the relations between the research activities.

The roadmap for setting up such a network, like INPRO, involves the creation of a group initially consisting of 6-8 research teams or labs, establishing links and scientific cooperation with external labs and building ties with industrial partners. Obviously such a network is not primarily hierarchical in nature, and cooperation cannot be dictated from above. The topics and subjects covered and researched are extremely diverse, to some extent uncontrolled, and constantly changing. Thus we can assume that networks are adaptive and flexible but hard to manage and coordinate.

Hence, the need for ontology in networks is apparent. The ontology of the network must be much more extensive than normally required in SMEs and is more likely to capture information measured in larger companies. Furthermore, network ontology creation is not an evolutionary process. Nevertheless, networks need a clear ontology (along with a commitment to use it), first and foremost for knowledge mapping. Such a knowledge map must be created to define and classify the knowledge available in the network and to associate each knowledge topic with the labs/partners that have the appropriate expertise. Yet, the ontology must be specific to the network and limited to its scope. In this chapter, we concentrate on a specific national network, as INPRO. This network focuses on all aspects of the product life cycle, as shown schematically

Figure 5. Schematic description of the product lifecycle

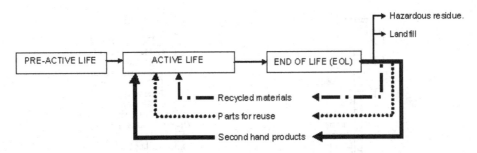

in Figure 5. Creation of this knowledge map is described here only briefly.

Product Lifecycle Ontology

Consideration of any knowledge base, knowledge-based system, or knowledge-level agent must be based upon some formal conceptualization, either implicit of explicit (Gruber & Olsen, 1994). This is true for the product lifecycle as well. That is, a body of formally represented knowledge must be based upon a conceptualization: the objects, concepts, and other entities that are assumed to exist in that area of interest and the relationships that hold among them. This type of common terminology, or ontology, is used to develop a common understanding of the information in a knowledge domain and to provide the means for automatic searching (Genesereth & Nilsson, 1987)8.

In the present research, the first step in building the product lifecycle ontology involves identifying the current competences of the members of the co-operative project, as well as industry requirements. The goal of this ontology is threefold: 1) so people can understand and describe what they do in order

for others to read about and understand it; 2) so software agents can search relevant information; and 3) so humans can examine the information as well. The ultimate goal is to achieve something that can be understood by non-experts as well by machines, so that both can codify and personalize the knowledge in the network.

Hence, a preliminary ontology for the product lifecycle was devised to determine and map the competences of the INPRO network's members. This was the second phase of the research approach for defining the input knowledge resources of the PLM multi site platform. This formal conceptualization of the product lifecycle domain was used then as the basis for applying the genetic search algorithms for selecting the required research groups. The hierarchy in the preliminary ontology was based upon discussions and interactions among experts in the field from different partners. As a result of this meeting, the following six categories were determined for the first level of the hierarchy: Design, Manufacturing, Assembly Use, Disassembly, End-of-Life (Shpitalni, Guttman, & Bossin, 2005). The initial (top level) components

Figure 6. Top level components of the product lifecycle ontology considered in the INPRO project

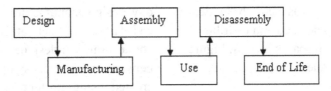

Figure 7. Sample from questionnaire used to determine group competencies

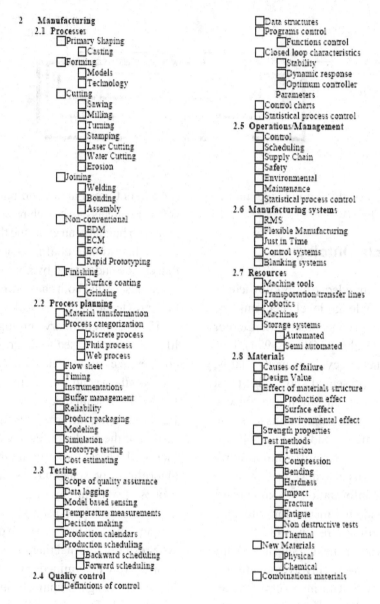

of the product lifecycle ontology are shown in Figure 6.

Based on recommendations and suggestions from colleagues and implicit knowledge of experts in the fields, each category was then sub-divided, and a questionnaire was devised and distributed among the participating research groups. Figure 7 illustrates part of the questionnaire (related to

manufacturing) circulated to determine the expertise of each group.

Six concept categories were defined, which determined the first hierarchical level in the ontology: design, manufacturing, usage/ maintenance, end of life cycle. Each category was further divided and a form was designed and distributed to the network members. A snippet from the ontology, created using Protégé (Protégé, 2007, http://

Figure 8. Snippet from the product life cycle ontology

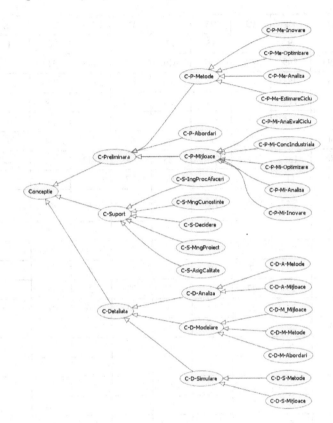

protege.stanford.edu), for the design stage, is presented in Figure 8.

Building the Knowledge/ Expertise Map

Information about the network members expertise are processed following a bottom-to-top scheme, starting from those of the persons and ending with that of the network. To be able to automate the data processing, at least partially, for each field in the form which indicates the presence of a competence, the value 1 was assigned, the rest being left with the value 0 (blank).

The first map shows the personal competencies and was created by summing the fields towards the ontology root. A synthesis of the competencies can be done by computing the percentage of the persons in the network that have competencies in each field.

Two significant values result were obtained: (1) the number of competency fields in the domain of the product life cycle for each partner (department/laboratory), and (2) the number of competency fields for each partner, grouped by products. One must note that a greater number of competencies for a person does not mean that this has a greater global level of competency than another person, with a lower number, but possibly with more impact and visibility at international level (in a narrower field). Another map shows the competencies at the network partners level (Tables 1 and 2).

The analysis of the map can yield information about the poor covered zones (empty spaces in the tables) by certain partners or at the network level, i.e. indications about the domains in which the

Table 1. Competencies at the network partners level: I Life cycle

Partner	CO	P1	P2	P3	P4	P5	P6	P7	P8	P9	INPRO
No. person	12	9	19	15	12	14	7	6	1	5	100
I. Life cycle	399	569	811	491	614	639	443	312	45	112	4435
Design	269	385	569	233	393	362	247	146	14	65	2683
>Conceptual design	96	113	141	67	134	114	101	49	5	17	837
>Detail design	143	216	353	106	221	181	77	33	9	39	1378
>Support	30	56	75	60	38	67	69	64	0	9	468
Manufacturing	86	155	189	229	185	240	182	133	30	43	1472
>Manufacturing systems	9	11	8	4	18	27	5	6	1	8	97
>Manufacturing processes	38	55	79	165	84	105	111	48	15	13	713
>Quality control	5	17	49	34	12	9	44	30	10		210
>Operation management	5	25	19	19	36	44	12	24	4	14	202
>Manufacturing support	13	32	7	5	27	28	8	12		4	136
>Management support	16	15	27	2	8	27	2	13		4	114
Utilization / Service	27	24	32	17	28	24	10	16		4	182
>Monitoring	5	3	4	4	7	2	4	2			31
>Diagnosis	3	5		1	4		2	2			17
>e-service	1		4	2	3	2					12
Maintenance	2	4		6	8	4	4	2			30
>Support	16	12	24	4	6	16		10		4	92
End of life cycle	17	5	21	12	8	13	4	17	1		98
>Disassembly		2		1	2		1	2	1		9
>Testing								1			1
>Recycling		2	3	1		1	1	1			9
>Refurbishing	1			2		1	1	1			6
>Disposal				1			1				2
>Support	16	1	18	7	6	11		12			71

network must work to gain competencies through the training procedures of human resources.

Creating the Database with the Network's Human Resources Competencies

The data from the forms were extracted in a neutral format (CSV), and then used to create a usual database (by importing data from CSV text files). For the Microsoft Access application, splitting the data into three tables was necessary, because of the great number of fields (255+255+253). The three tables were linked by relations using key fields. In order to find the person with certain competencies, a usual Access query is launched (Figure 9) or using SQL.

An Internet based interrogation is in train to be finished, using MySQL. This creates the possibility to query the (sole) competencies database by each partner, from his office or from anywhere an Internet link exists.

Table 2. Competencies at the network partners level: II Products

Partner	CO	P1	P2	P3	P4	P5	P6	P7	P8	P9	INPRO
Person	12	9	19	15	12	14	7	6	1	5	100
II. Products	**17**	**18**	**17**	**23**	**26**	**40**	**24**	**17**		**3**	**185**
Manufacturing systems	9	13	12	6	18	15	12	10		1	96
Sheet metal proc.	1			1		2	2	3			9
Home appliances				5		7	4				16
Medical equipment	1					1					2
Automobiles	1	1		3	3	5	1				14
Tools and dies	4	3	2	5	5	3	3	3		2	30
Industrial		1	3	1		2	1	1			9
Micro-electro-mechanical equipment				2		1					3
Optoelectronic equip.	1					1					2
Furniture						1	1				2
Cloths						2					2

Figure 9. An Access query about competencies

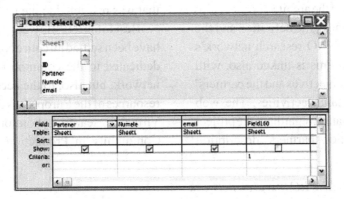

THE ARCHITECTURE OF THE MULTISITE PLM PLATFORM

Based on the preliminary researches concerning the product lifecycle representation and the human resources competencies capitalization and explore, there have been developed the collaborative multisite PLM platform. The main objective and motivation of this approach was to build a collaborative environment for the product design process. The PLM multisite architecture for the collaborative product development is based on the integration of the Product Lifecycle Management (PLM), Enterprise Resource Planning (ERP), Supply Chain Management (SCM) and Customer Relationship Management (CRM) solutions (CIMdata, 2002).

The INPRO universities partners' PLM platform and the potential industrial partners have been connected through Internet/Intranet and they built the multisite PLM platform of the collaborative product development in network. A client-server architecture has been used inside the network (Figure 10). It consists of a four servers cluster,

Figure 10. The collaborative product development network infrastructure – IT architecture

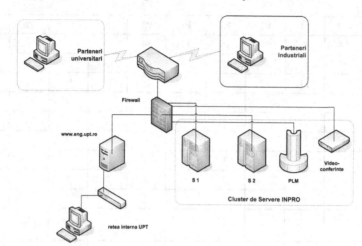

for: Internet/Intranet (S1), databases (S2), PLM and videoconference system. This is the core of the information technology (IT) architecture definition and design.

A preliminary stage of the architecture development process includes also, the definition and the configuration of the INPRO research network's web page (Figure 11). This is linked also, with the project operational objectives and the partners' integration in the research activities. The web page consists of information regarding: the project objectives and activities, partners' description (link to their own web pages), conferences (scientific events), workshops and meetings that are organized by the partners, research results (with public interest) and the link to the Intranet section that was restricted to the network members only.

Beside the INPRO web page development there have been settled an entire communication system dedicated to the common research work in the network, but also, to the access at some research resources of the European Network of Excellence, Virtual Research Laboratory for a Knowledge Community in Production (www.vrl-kcip.org),

Figure 11. Detail of the INPRO research network web page

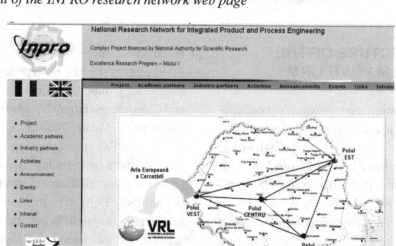

Table 3. CAD/CAM and PDM systems of each partner involved in the multisite PLM platform

Partners Systems	CO	P1	P2	P3	P4	P5	P6	P7	P8	P9	INPRO
CAD/CAM	8	7	5	8	6	6	6	5	2	6	59
CATIA	1	1	1	1	1	1	1	1		1	9
ProEngineer		1					1			1	3
SolidWorks	1	1		1	1					1	5
Inventor				1		1	1		1		4
AutoCAD	1	1		1		1	1	1	1	1	8
SolidEdge	1		1	1		1	1	1			6
NX			1	1			1	1			4
Tecnomatix	1				1	1					3
DELMIA		1			1					1	3
Other	3	2	2	2	2	1		1		1	14
PDM	1		1	1	1	1	1			1	7
Teamcenter	1		1	1	1	1	1			1	7

in the European Research Area (see Figure 11). Also, with the support of the videoconference system the collaboration was possible.

The INPRO partners' PLM platforms architecture design has included a large diversity of software. To illustrate the large variety of information technology applications used in such context, the list of CAD/CAM and PDM systems of each partner involved in the PLM multisite platform is shown in Table 3.

The most important problem that has to be solved between partners was the compatibility of the design format/representation because of the existing of the different design software. Finally, the Teamcenter Community software solution was the option for harmonizing the design parts delivered by the partners and that have conduct to a final product.

In collaborative product development, partners have to exchange their product data with other partners in order to update their digital mock-up (DMU). It represents an effective problem for data exchange because each partner has to translate other partner's data to the format of his own CAD and PDM systems. A solution for this problem

has been presented in (Guyot et al, 2007). This solution has been adapted for the PLM multisite platform architecture design.

To translate the meta-data into common format and send those to partners there have been built an exchange architecture integrated to the new PDM. The solution is to use a PDM interface that extracts all the DMU's data in a storage files with an internal format. This interface is the same for all projects. After extraction, storage files are filtering and translating into project's common format.

The use of a generic PDM interface limits the application customizations for each project: instead of extracting data with the translator of each project, there has been build one interface for all projects. Furthermore, data extraction in internal format allows the project coordinator to run other internal processing on DMU's. On the other hand, the translation depends on common format so that it cannot be the same development for all projects. Now, the aim is to reduce developments between the different translation processes.

Figure 12 has shown the mechanism of data exchange between partners in a collaborative project. The aim of the new system is to use the

Figure 12. The data exchange mechanism

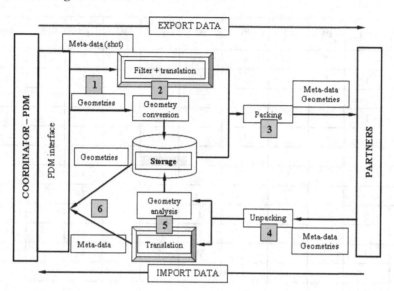

same steps for each project and to reuse mechanisms between projects. So, in the Figure 6, these different steps have depicted. During an export phase, PDM interface extracts geometric data and the whole product's meta-data (phase 1). Two different translators (phase 2) translate geometric data and meta-data to the common format. When all data are translated, they are packed and sent to partners (phase 3). During an import phase, partner's data are unpacked (phase 4) and meta-data are translated (phase 5). PDM interface imports translated meta-data and partners' geometric data (phase 6).

CONCLUSIONS AND FUTURE WORK

In the framework of the National Research Network for Integrated Product and Process Engineering (INPRO) it was built a collaborative multisite PLM platform for the product development and its associated processes. The proposed product collaborative development model integrates knowledge from the entire product lifecycle. There have been discussed the product conceptual design phase and there have been presented.

In the paper has presented the main aspects that reflect the achieved stage of the project of building the collaborative product development network: the product life cycle model, the network members' expertise, and the PLM multisite platform infrastructure. The product life cycle model is the base of the collaborative design methodology that has adopted for the PLM multisite platform. The model of collaborative product development integrated the whole lifecycle. For identifying the persons with the required competencies for a specific project, an Access or an Internet usually query has launched, using MySQL. The universities partners' PLM platforms and the potential industrial partners have connected through Internet/Intranet, constituting the PLM multisite platform of the collaborative product development network.

The future research work is related to the INPRO networks resources valorization in the context of the Certified Integrated Design Engineer - iDesigner project (FR/08/LLP-LdV/TOI/117025) which deals with the creation of a professional modular qualification program with certification for the new job role of an integrated design engineer. This transfer of innovation (ToI) project integrates and transfers the results of other

Table 4. The skills set definition of integrated design engineers in the iDesigner project (together with partners' involvement in their development)

Skill units	Skill elements	Partner's responsibility
Process competence	• Product lifecycle process, value chain	GNP
	• Design Process Innovation	PUT
	• Change Management Process	ISCN
Systems engineering	• Understanding and Design of Complex Product	GNP
	• Requirement Engineering	ISCN
	• Validation and Improvement of Design Models	PUT
	• Capitalization on Design Knowledge over different products and domains	GNP
Knowledge management and sharing	• Formalization of design knowledge	GNP
	• Sharing of design knowledge	GNP
Collaborative distributed design	• Working in distributed engineering teams	UPT
	• Communication with experts from different fields	UPT
	• Design process moderation	UPT
Responsible (aware) design (case studies)	• Sustainable design	GNP
	• Safety conscious design	ISCN
	• Security conscious design	ISCN
	• Health conscious design	All partners
	• Testability conscious design	All partners
	• Maintainability conscious design	PUT
	• Product/service co-design	GNP

former EU projects and the only Network of Excellence in Manufacturing and Innovation (VRL-KCiP that have been transform in the EMIRAcle association) but also, some past national projects developed by the partners.

The new results will be transferred to the market in form of job role based training and certificates. The iDesigner project's partners are: Institute Polytechnique de Grenoble (coordinator) – France (GNP), Poznan University of Technology – Poland (PUT), Politehnica University of Timisoara – Romania (UPT), International Software Consulting Network (ISCN) – Austria and the European Manufacturing and Innovation Research Association a cluster leading excellence (EMIRAcle) – Belgium that is responsible with the dissemination activities and results.

The qualification and certification of integrated design engineers addresses itself at experienced design engineers (as the INPRO network's members can be considered together with master programs or PhD. students that belong to the partners universities) who want to complement and/or certify their advanced design skills. The students typically aim at a senior or principal engineer position in their design teams, but also, for managing positions. The certificate, however, is not supposed to certify the student's capabilities as a design team manager. One of the biggest challenges is to conceive a training program that covers the complete skills set in a maximum of three weeks.

Table 4 shows a skill set which provides the basis of our future research and development activities. It is the result of an initial consolidation of our experiences in research, education, as well as in collaboration with industry. Although we consider this skill set already stable, it is supposed to evolve in the course of the project as we involve experts from different industrial sectors, and get the feedback from partners in industry and academia and from students of initial training seminars.

We consider the skill units process competence, systems engineering, knowledge management and sharing, and collaborative distributed design, largely independent of specific industrial sectors, whereas under responsible (aware) design we subsume more specialized skills, which are supposed to be trained using case-studies mainly. As will be developed in the future (2010-2011), the training and certification concept is modular, so that students (target groups) will be able to choose those specialized skills that are relevant to their professions. Most of the competences that are indicated in Table 4 are closely linked to lifecycle engineering knowledge and skills.

AKNOWLEDGMENT

We would like to thanks to our research partners that give us constant support and encourage us to develop the PLM multisite platform as a national collaborative design environment. The presented researches have been developed under the financial support of the CEEX program in Romania during the project: "National Research Network for Integrated Product and Process Engineering – INPRO" (contract no. 243 / 2006) and the Virtual Research Laboratory for a Knowledge Community in Production (VRL-KCiP) a Network of Excellence project (contract no. FP6-507487). From 2008 we extend our researches at the European level, in the context of a Lifelong Learning Programme, Leonardo da Vinci - Transfer of Innovation (contract nr. FR/08/LLP-LdV/TOI/117025), "Certified Integrated Design Engineer – iDesigner" in which we use the collaborative platform for the students and researchers professional qualification and certification.

REFERENCES

Boltanski, L., & Thevenot, L. (1991). *De la justification, les économies de grandeur*. Paris: Gallimard.

Brissaud, D., & Tichkiewitch, S. (2000). Innovation and manufacturability analysis in an integrated design context. *Computers in Industry, 43*, 111–121. doi:10.1016/S0166-3615(00)00061-0

Chen, X., Fuh, J., Wong, Y., Lu, Y., Li, W., & Qiu, Z. (2005). An Adaptable Model for Distributed Collaborative Design. *Computer-Aided Design & Applications, 2*(1-4), 47–55.

CIMdata. (2002). *Product Lifecycle Management. Empowering the Future of Business*. CIMdata report. Retrieved September 23, 2009, from http://www.cimdata.com/PLM/plm.htm

Draghici, A., & Draghici, G. (2007). Romanian Research Network for Integrated Product and Process Engineering. In F.-L. Krause (Ed.), *The Future of Product Development, Proceedings of the 17th CIRP Design Conference* (pp. 341-350). Berlin: Springer.

Draghici, G. (1999). *Ingineria integrata a produselor*. Timisoara, Romania: Eurobit Publisher.

Draghici, G., Savii, G., & Draghici, A. (2007). Platform for Collaborative Product and Processes Development. In B. Katalinic (Ed.), *Annals of DAAAM for 2007 & Proceedings of the 18th International DAAAM Symposium* (pp. 253-254). Vienna, Austria: DAAAM International.

Draghici, G., Savii, G., & Draghici, A. (2008). Building a Collaborative Product Development Network. In *Design Synthesis, Conference abstracts of the 18th CIRP Design Conference*, Enschede, The Netherlands (pp. 24).

Genesereth, R., & Nilsson, N. J. (1987). *Logical Foundations of Artificial Intelligence*. San Mateo, CA: Morgan Kaufmann Publishers.

Gruber, T. R., & Olsen, G. R. (1994). An Ontology for Engineering Mathematics. In J. Doyle, P. Torasso, & E. Sandewall (Eds.), *Fourth International Conference on Principles of Knowledge Representation and Reasoning*. Bonn, Germany: Morgan Kaufmann.

Guyot, E., Ducellier, G., Eynard, B., Girard, Ph., & Gallet, T. (2007). Product data and digital mock-up exchange based on PLM, *Product Lifecycle Management, Assessing the industrial relevance* [Genève, Switzerland: Interscience Enterprises Ltd.]. *PLM-S, P3*, 243–252.

iGrafx, Enabling Process Excellence, Retrieved June 20, 2008, from www.igrafx.com

Integration Definition for Function Modeling (IDEF0). (1993). *Category of Standard: Software Standard, Modelling Techniques*. Retrieved May 13, 2009, from http://www.idef.com/pdf/idef0.pdf

Johansen, R. (1998). *Groupware: Computer Support for Business Teams*. New York: The Free Press.

Pahl, G., & Beitz, W. (1984). *Engineering Design*. London: Design Council.

Perrin, J. (2001). *Concevoir l'innovation industrielle. Méthodologie de conception de l'innovation*. Paris: CNRS Editions.

Protégé. (2007). *The Protégé Ontology Editor for Knowledge Acquisition System*. Retrieved from http://protege.stanford.edu

Prudhomme, G. (2000). Analyse Fonctionnelle et démarche de conception . In Drăghici, G., & Brissaud, D. (Eds.), *Modélisation de la connaissance pour la conception et la fabrication intégrées* (pp. 7–30). Timisoara, Romania: Editura Mirton.

Shpitalni, M., Guttman, G., & Bossin, D. (2005). Forming Task-Oriented Groups in Networks based on Knowledge Mapping. In *Proceedings of the 15th International CIRP Design Seminar*, Shanghai, China, May 22-26.

Stark, J. (2005). *Product Lifecycle Management: Paradigm for 21st Century Product Realization*. London: Springer-Verlag.

Usher, J. M., Roy, U., & Parsaei, H. (2005). *Integrated Product and Process Development: Methods, Tools, and Technologies*. New York: John Wiley & Sons, Inc.

Chapter 30
Virtual Center for Entrepreneurship Development

Anca Draghici
"Politehnica" University of Timisoara, Romania

Monica Izvercianu
"Politehnica" University of Timisoara, Romania

George Draghici
"Politehnica" University of Timisoara, Romania

ABSTRACT

This chapter shows a preliminary approach for building a virtual center for entrepreneurship development that will be implemented in a university research network in Romania. The authors argue the most relevant aspects that conduct us to an organizational information system design, implementation and management with double role: education/training (entrepreneurial skills development for students) and research (about the entrepreneurship phenomena at regional and national level but in relation of the global economy). The following items are presented: (1) the training needs for business creation - based on a preliminary market research developed with subjects with technical and economical background and that allow the identification of the entrepreneurial knowledge; (2) the university entrepreneurial education as a process of knowledge transfer; (3) preliminary design and architecture of the virtual center for entrepreneurship. Finally, some relevant conclusions and the future researches directions are presented.

INTRODUCTION

Europe needs to foster the entrepreneurial drive more effectively, even in this crisis period. It needs more new and thriving firms willing to embark on creative or innovative ventures. Encouraging the enterprise spirit is a key to achieving these objectives. Education can contribute to encouraging entrepreneurship, by fostering the right mindset, by raising awareness of career opportunities as an entrepreneur or a self-employed person, and by providing the relevant business skills (European Commission reports, 2008).

The conclusion of the European Commission report in 2008, regarding entrepreneurship teaching was that it is not yet sufficiently integrated in higher education institutions' curricula. Available data show that the majority of entrepreneurship

DOI: 10.4018/978-1-61690-020-3.ch030

courses are offered in business and economic studies. The diffusion of entrepreneurship is particularly weak in some of the Member States that joined the European Union (EU) in and after 2004.

However, it is questionable whether business schools are the most appropriate place to teach entrepreneurship: innovative and viable business ideas are more likely to arise from technical, scientific and creative studies. In this context, the challenge is to build inter-disciplinary approaches, making entrepreneurship education accessible to all students specialization curricula, creating teams for the development and exploitation of business ideas, mixing students from economic and business studies with students from other faculties and with different backgrounds (by interdisciplinary training modules or courses).

Entrepreneurial skills and attitudes provide benefits to society, even beyond their application to business activity. In fact, personal qualities that are relevant to entrepreneurship, such as creativity and a spirit of initiative, can be useful to everyone, in their working activity and in their daily life. "The European Commission found that there is today in most European Union Member States — although in varying degrees — a policy commitment at governmental/ministerial level to promote the teaching of entrepreneurship in the education system" (European Commission reports, 2008).

In the context of this paper, human resources training regarding their entrepreneurship competencies development have to be amplifying in the high education period and it has to continue with training during all professional life (as vocational training) with the support of the dedicated lifelong learning programs.

Encouraging the entrepreneurial spirit and behavior are key elements to create jobs and improving competitiveness and economic growth (Draghici & Draghici, 2006), (European Commission reports, 2008). If it is to make a success of the Lisbon strategy for growth and employment,

universities needs to stimulate the entrepreneurial mindsets of young people, encourage innovative business start-ups, and foster a culture or an environment that is friendlier to entrepreneurship and to the growth of small and medium-sized enterprises (SMEs). However, the benefits of entrepreneurship education are not limited to start-ups, innovative ventures and new jobs. The Bologna process can have a positive effect on the way entrepreneurial knowledge are spread. So, in the knowledge based society universities have to play an enhanced role in innovation as entrepreneurs. This paper presents some important aspects of knowledge transfer processes developed by universities to become entrepreneurial and to increase their implication and contributions to human resources development at the local/regional economic level. These mechanisms are expected to contribute to economic development through universities roles: education, research and knowledge transfer to society (Izvercianu & Draghici, 2008).

Entrepreneurship refers to an individual's ability to turn ideas into action and is therefore a key competence for all, helping young people to be more creative and self-confident in whatever they undertake (Tornatzky et al., 2002). At higher education level, the primary purpose of entrepreneurship education should be to develop entrepreneurial capacities and mindsets. In this context, entrepreneurship education programs can have different objectives, such as: developing entrepreneurial drive among students (raising awareness and motivation); training students in the skills they need to set-up a business and manage its growth; developing the entrepreneurial ability to identify and exploit opportunities (Draghici & Draghici, 2006), (Tornatzky et al., 2002).

The paper will debate the following items: (1) the university entrepreneurial education as a process of knowledge transfer based on the knowledge map competencies for the engineer graduate student profile (engineering and management specialization); (2) the training needs for business creation - based on a preliminary market research developed with subjects with technical and economical background and that allow the identification of the entrepreneurial knowledge; (3) preliminary design and architecture of the virtual center for competencies/expertise evaluation CE@ANPART (based on a web platform concept) that will highlight the role of the information technology in the proposed activities and the propose specific steps and arrangements for the entrepreneurship education innovation. Finally, some relevant conclusions will be presented.

The presented research results were gained from our implication in two national projects: *"Partnership for Excellence Research in Developing Entrepreneurial Skills and a Competitive Human Capital in the Innovation and Knowledge-Based Economy and Society – CE@ANPART"* (contract no. 91069/2007) and *"Comparative Researches Concerning Knowledge Management in Romanian Engineering Education - UNIKM"* (contract no. 92074/2008).

Since 2009 we extend our researches at the European level, in the context of a Lifelong Learning Programme, Leonardo da Vinci (503021-LLP-1-2009-1-BE-LEONARDO-LMP): *"Certified EU Researcher – Entrepreneur - ResEUr"*. Taking into consideration this European project, we shall present some perspective of our research, too.

ENTREPRENEURSHIP COMPETENCIES NEED AND DEVELOPMENT – A MARKETING SURVEY

Market Survey for the Training Needs Identification

In the following are presented the most relevant research results started since 2007 because our involvement in the FORCREST project (Izver-

cianu, 2007), in the framework of Leonardo da Vinci Program where 9 European countries were partners in this collaboration: Spain, Germany, France, Ireland, United Kingdom, Italy, Czech Republic, Hungary and Romania. The research motivation and objectives were to detect the knowledge gaps of the undergraduate students from technical and economics universities, in the area of business creation, during their involvement in the high education programs. The research methodologies were: phenomenological group analysis and investigation based on questionnaires (using the non-directly centered group interview method). The questionnaire structure consist the following items (the subjects were faced with real or imaginary situation of being entrepreneur and were encouraged to give their comments – answers on those particular items): drawing-up a business plan, technical study, financial-economic study, innovation management, project management, environment impact study, managerial skills and communication skills.

The research scenario that was design and test in the context of the Leonardo da Vinci project was re-apply with new subjects to identify the dynamics of the entrepreneurial behavior and the students' interests in different skills education. The survey results allow us to outline the subjects' behavior/profile in business creation and development processes. The comparative results for target groups as well as their different needs are briefly presented in the following. Final analysis and conclusions affects the curricula improvement mainly in the MBA program at the "Politehnica" University of Timisoara in Romania.

The identification of the training needs for the human resources involved in the industrial environment (which was the case of the sample subjects), has the following objectives (research objectives): (1) identification of the vocational training requirements of the persons that work in industrial enterprises; (2) searching for the vocational training requirements of the managers

Table 1. Entrepreneurial competencies that have to be developed, for the technical group (with engineering background, results from the open questions' answers)

Research or questionnaire items that were analyze:	Entrepreneurial competencies required to be developed (training lines that were identify):
Drawing-up a business plan	Business idea; Human capital; Market and competition; Marketing / Distribution; Opportunities and risks; Business management; Economic and financial viability; Legal frame of the company
Technical study	Production system; Production strategies; Distribution plant; Production and know-how; Operations plan: logistics, quality; Prototyping; Outsourcing
Financial-economic study	Indicators of business viability; Project scheduling; Economic quantification; Cash flows; Aids/Subventions and support instruments
Companies creation simulation	Case studies (companies creation)
Innovation management	Knowledge management; Basic concepts of innovation; Business strategy and technology strategy; Data mining; Technology forecast; Technology alertness; Research and development, research classes, Research and development steps; Tools for the innovation management
Project management	Planning tools and projects management; Teams organisation; Project culture; Short-term planning; Objectives management; Cost engineering; Financial management; Human resources and PM; Security management and health at work; Contracting system; Communication management; Control; Total quality of the project; Simulator of projects management
Environment impact study	Basic concepts about sustainability; Models of sustainable growth; Business ethics; Planning of environmental management; Environmental impact; Competition and sustainable development; Profit and sustainable development; Control of the environmental management; Environmental policy of the EU; Economic setting and business repercussions on the environment; Strategic approach of the sustainable development; Case studies
Managerial skills	Leadership; Team management and motivation; Team working; Negotiations and conflict resolution; Change management; Time management; Motivation techniques; Communication in the company; Emotional intelligence; Strategic and operation planning
Communication skills	Communication skills; Networking; Business negotiation; Business ethics

that request and finance the training programs. These objectives have risen from a vast analysis developed upon 28 enterprises from the West part of Romania, regarding the vocational training of their human resources, in the context of our country's integration in the European Union.

The market survey has referred to the training needs of human resources with technical and economical background, in order to acquire the knowledge regarding the process of business opportunities creation and development and also, to train them for the trials they will confront with for business creation, to aware them on sustainable development implications, and to offer them the necessary competencies. 155 subjects were involved in the survey and they belong to two target groups: 80 subjects were graduates, under-

graduates or undertaking master of science courses with technical background – this was the technical group; 75 subjects were graduates, undergraduates, undertaking master of science courses or from SMEs with economical background – this was the economic group (Izvercianu, 2007), (Izvercianu & Draghici, 2007).

Some relevant conclusions were elaborated regarding the entrepreneurial training development need (). For our present and future research, the conclusions regarding the technical group (with engineering background) are briefly presented in Table 1. The research has underlined the lack of minimal entrepreneurial skills in the structure of university curricula and the need for specific tools development for the entrepreneurship competencies/expertise development and/or evaluation.

Entrepreneurship Education as Knowledge Transfer Process in University

Knowledge management is vital for a university to be able to develop its own knowledge, to come up with new knowledge and to react to the work environment in a way that should both meet the organization scopes and to adapt to all perturbations occurring in that work environment. Consequently, knowledge management is becoming a strategic process that enables universities to keep up with all changes in the knowledge society, to improve their competitiveness and evolve to excellence. Within this framework has been developed the UNIKM project (UNIKM, 2009) and its research activities. The general objectives of the project are the sustain of research and development activities, carried out in collaboration by the consortium members (universities of Oradea, Cluj-Napoca, Timisoara and Bucharest together with a research institute for economic and social researches in Romania), for the development of a knowledge management based environment in engineering education institutions, for new approach and innovation generation in teaching and research activities, as well as the effectiveness and efficiency improvement of their services. Some research results gained in this project will be presented in the following.

In the knowledge based society universities play an enhanced role in innovation as entrepreneur. They retains the traditional academic roles of social reproduction and extension of certified knowledge, but placed them in a broader context as part of its new role in promoting innovation. Based on the tri-lateral networks and hybrid organizations model there have been developed a framework to analyze how universities developed their implication and contribution to local (regional) economic development (Etzkowitz and Leydesdorff, 2000), (Tornatzky, et. al., 2002), (Draghici, et. al., 2009) (Figure 1).

The Innovation U framework encompasses the boundary-spanning structures that reflect the universities relations with industry, local state and government through: programs development activities of state and local economic development organizations, industrial advisory boards and councils with business community. These mechanisms are expected to contribute to economic development by producing *locally captured (technological) outcomes*. These outcomes can be structured in three university roles: education (smart people), research (new knowledge) and the knowledge transfer to society (entrepreneurship, knowledge, technology, know-how).

The entrepreneurial outcome can be considered as a result of the enterprising university-industry-government relationship. According to Ropke (1998) the university itself, as an organization, can become entrepreneurial, the university members can become entrepreneurs and the university interaction with the region can follow entrepreneurial patterns.

In accord with the above considerations, the first research aim was to overview the activities type that are carried out by university in the field of knowledge transfer and that can be considered for entrepreneurship education as knowledge capitalization processes. In accord with the references (Ropke, 1998), (Tornatzky et al., 2002), the ten most mentioned activities are shown in Table 2. These knowledge transfer activities were analyzed in the case of the "Politehnica" University of Timisoara, Romania (Draghici, et. al., 2009).

The identification of the knowledge transfer activities allowed their characterization by translating into a scale of increasing mutual obligations or increasing cooperation and integration of the "actors" on the market (Figure 2). The mechanisms of knowledge transfer evolve linked with the stages of cooperation from the traditional knowledge transfer organization (the first stage) and the virtual knowledge transfer organization (the last stage). This virtual knowledge transfer

Figure 1. Innovation U: Conceptual Framework

Industry			
Industrial enables Mission, vision and goals; Faculty culture and rewards	→	**Partnering mechanism and facilitators** Industry research partnership; Industry education and training; Industry extension and technical assistance; Entrepreneurship development; Technology transfer; Career services and placement.	
University system			
Partnerships with economic development organizations			

Locally captured technological outcomes
New knowledge
Smart people
State of the art knowledge
Technology
Entrepreneurial

→ **Economic development**

organization can cover the exploitation of a collective intellectual property portfolio or joint projects for specific research areas.

Each activity presented in table 1 can be relevant for the entrepreneurial education process in universities but these activities have to be correlated with knowledge transfer intimate process that is developed through the learning process (Figure 3). Entrepreneurship education seeks to provide students with the knowledge, skills and motivation to encourage entrepreneurial success in a variety of settings (Draghici, et. al., 2009).

The researches regarding the knowledge transfer mechanism, together with the state-of-art study of the specific methods and tools (developed under the UNIKM project) have been the premise of the CE@ANPART virtual center for entrepreneurship development.

Entrepreneurial Competencies Training: The Case Study of "Politehnica" University of Timisoara, Romania

The preliminary research studies have identified a strong need for more entrepreneurship education but it is not possible to meet this demand fully with the current staff involved in entrepreneurship studies or business studies, in general. The use of action-oriented teaching methods is crucial for developing entrepreneurial competencies, but this is labor intensive and costly, and requires specific training. Funding can be obtained by applications in national research projects because entrepreneurship is a national priority, too.

Professors have to be trained for entrepreneurship (inside/outside the university). Professors should have a better understanding of entrepreneurship education, and of the range of aims, methods and contents. There is also, a need to graduate enough PhD. students in entrepreneurship, to build-up new and modern teaching resources.

After the market research, a few seminars were organized in the university with training and consulting experts and also, with some successful entrepreneurs from the West part of Romania. The aim of these meetings was to reform the license studies and curricula in the university (in particular at the Faculty of Management in Production and Transportation), in accord with the market trends and needs. Experts were, asked to identify factors of success for integrating entrepreneurship into higher education, for spreading it across the curriculum of different fields of study (Izvercianu & Draghici, 2008).

While public policies and the overall outside environment can play an important role in ensuring that the entrepreneurship teaching can be spread

Table 2. List of the 10 most mentioned knowledge transfer activities in universities

No.	Knowledge transfer activities	Description
1	Patents and licensing	Concerns the exploitation of intellectual property. Through patents an institute for higher education can protect its intellectual property and if a patent is guaranteed it can be commercialized through sales of the patent or a license.
2	Spin-off and enterprise creation	A spin-off company is a new company whose formation was dependent on the use of intellectual property that was created and/or developed at a Public Research Organization; spin-off is the entrepreneurial route to commercializing knowledge of public research, both intellectual property and non-intellectual property based.
3	University-industry networks	Describes the dynamic two-way interaction between university and industry in collaborative networks.
4	International cooperation	University cooperation with public and private organizations beyond national borders.
5	European affairs	Management, acquisition and monitoring of European projects and European funding.
6	Continuous professional development	Comprises the post-initial education programs aiming at improving the capability and realizing the full potential of professionals at work.
7	Alumni affairs	Management of alumni contacts.
8	National subsidies	National government programs and policies intended to encourage certain types of research programs and other specified university activities.
9	Regional subsidies	Regional government programs and policies intended to encourage certain types of research programs and other specified university activities.
10	Grants	Are provided by the government or other non-profit organizations to encourage (individual) development or growth in a particular area.

Figure 2. Integration and cooperation activitities extention of knowledge transfer activities

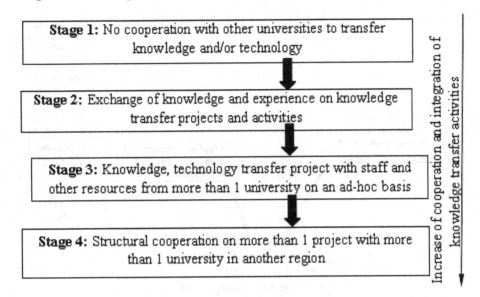

Figure 3. The mechanism of knowledge transfer through education/learning

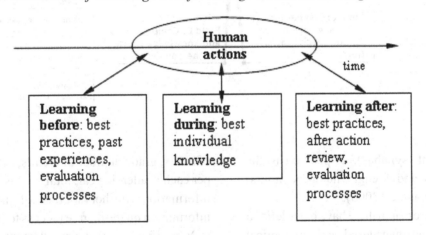

effectively, at the higher education institutions level, a success factor is the extent through which traditional lecturing are with substantial element of active self-learning. The ultimate success factor is transformation into an "entrepreneurial university", characterized by a diffused entrepreneurial culture. Many universities are clearly moving in that direction, but are still far from this end goal.

As a research result a knowledge map has been built that define the graduate student expertise profile at "Politehnica" University of Timisoara, Romania (http://www.upt.ro) by considering the existing situation of the Faculty of Management in Production and Transportation (Figure 4) that train specialists with technical (engineering) and managerial (economical) background. It is obviously the tendency of entrepreneurial education as an objective in the learning process. For each sub-competencies there have been attached the corresponding teaching subjects that have been

Figure 4. The competencies knowledge map for the graduate student profile

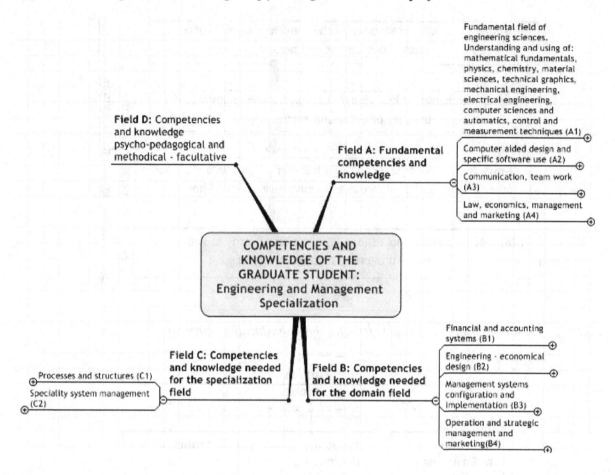

define as content (syllabus), as position in the education process and as length (number of hours) (Izvercianu & Draghici, 2008).

Based on this research there have been defined the content of the managerial and economical subjects' syllabus to develop the entrepreneurial education as a process of knowledge transfer.

The most relevant result of this study was the diploma supplement form (in Romanian and English languages) that is attached to each student diploma. The chapters of this form are: information identifying the holder; information on the study program; information on the level of the study program; information on the contents and gained results (program detail results as: number

of hours, grade number of credits; average grade per each academic year, total credits); additional information (further sources of information); information on the degree (access to further studies); certification of the supplement (authorized signatures and stamps); information on the national education system.

One more idea arises from the experts and professors debates: the need of lifelong learning programs in the field of entrepreneurial competencies development and update. This market need has been analyze and conduct us to develop a project for building a virtual center for entrepreneurship as it will be described in the following.

PRELIMINARY ARCHITECTURE OF THE CE@ANPART VIRTUAL CENTER FOR ENTREPRENEURSHIP DEVELOPMENT

CE@ANPART Project Description – the Context of the Virtual Center Development

The CE@ANPART project (CE@ANPART, 2009) proposes to have a competitiveness accession by developing a partnership for excellence research in the field of entrepreneurial abilities and competitive human capital on knowledge and innovation-based economy and society. The results of this project is materialized into innovative services for the educational and economical environment, as well as through assessment and development services for the entrepreneurial abilities and for the competences of entrepreneurial management on the basis of the tools developed inside this project. Another materialization of this project is the establishment of research results implementation mechanisms which must ensure sustainability through the CE@ANPART portal.

The results of the project will contribute to the improving of competitiveness and to the promotion of the entrepreneurial behavior, to the development of organizational culture based on innovation and entrepreneurial spirit within the systems of economy, education and research. All this are addressed to the beneficiaries target groups (students and master students) as well as to young highly qualified researchers (PhD students, young researchers from inside and outside university).

At the same time, the project ranges with the latest researches and concerns at the European level, taking into account that one of the suggestions of the *"Oslo Agenda for Entrepreneurship Education"* claims that "it should develop a common framework of the desirable results of entrepreneurial education – the development of capabilities, abilities, individual mentalities and it should encourage the use of these capabili-

ties, contributing this way to the development of both economy and society ". The project aims at promoting the reinforcement of education in the development of one Lisbon agreement Key Competences: KC7 Entrepreneurship at a national level and especially among young people.

The project's results contribute to the increase of competitiveness and promotion of entrepreneurial behavior, the organizational culture development based on innovation and entrepreneurial spirit in the economy's systems, of education and research.

The Approach Motivation of the Information System Development

Beside the aspect of "capacity building" effects of the network, the question of sustainability has to be considered to reach a long term partnership among all participants involved in the CE@ANPART project. To do so the broad expertise, the technical infrastructure and the distributed locations of the partners can be used to reach a high number of "clients" - students all over the country. The research network (developed under the CE@ANPART project and linked with the UNIKM network's project) develops training modules on different levels of education and offer its services to interested target groups (Adelsberger et al., 2002).

The demand for entrepreneurial education is permanently rising and not limited to a certain age, degree or job position. Even among retired people there is a demand for continuous education to extend their personal knowledge and skills in the field of new practices of their own business administration (intrapreneurial skills development are also consider to be developed). The detected target groups for educational services are shown in Figure 5. In general, one can identify four major groups for scientific education (Niemann et al. 2004), (Niemann et al. 2003).

The "qualifying education" is meant as an education for students who are enrolled in the

Figure 5. Potential target groups for the CE@ANPART virtual center

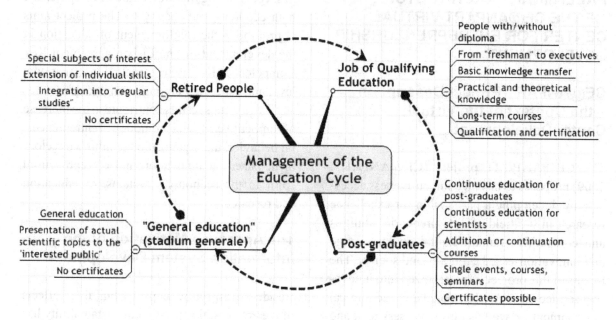

university or any other educational institution to get a scientific degree. This also includes people who already have a degree and study on to reach a higher or an additional degree. The group of "Post graduates and Scientist" requires activities to reach a higher level of personal knowledge and skills in specific and selected fields. This additional knowledge are necessary to master daily job requirements. The education is offered on a continuous or continual basis. The third group includes students of any age and any social level. These courses are open to everybody. Such courses offer a platform to learn and discuss about the latest research results and allow people to join lectures which are not related to their core subjects. The objective of such courses is to extend one's individual general knowledge base and create expert forums. The fourth group consists mainly of retired persons who are still interested in learning and extending their personal knowledge and skills. The main objective of this group is not to hunt for certificates, but to keep contact with current questions and results of research. These

types of students are, frequently integrated into the schedule of undergraduate courses.

As can be seen in Figure 4, the different target groups for scientific education call for a holistic approach to master the entire range of students. On the other hand the management of education cycles requires individual programs to meet the various demands of all groups. Delivering adequate education modules to such different target groups calls for adequate organizational structures and resources of the educational institution.

The key conditions for a network with virtual structures are courses which are offered in modules. A modular structure provides flexibility and faster reaction to turbulent market conditions. The modules can be delivered "on demand", in different languages and from the partner of the network that is most competent.

The network activities are managed by a *broker* who keeps contact with network partners and configures the course portfolio (Figure 6). She/He determines the form of education course and the necessary support activities (materials, communication channels, etc.) delivered and

Figure 6. The concept of the virtual center for entrepreneurship competencies assessment and development

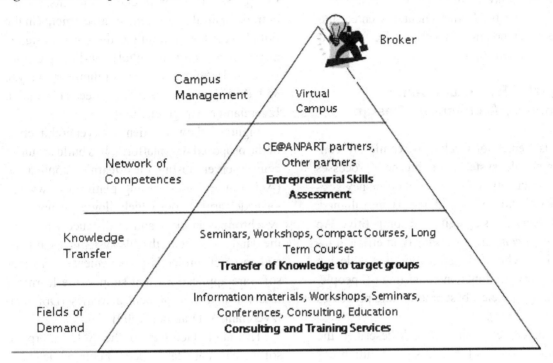

provided on the web platform (Niemann et al. 2003), (Niegemann et al. 2004).

The construction of such a web-based model ensures the system's flexibility, because new courses can be established "on demand" and – if necessary - at short notice. The broker establishes – based on the specific field of demand – a course offer to meet this demand. She/He chooses the adequate form of teaching (seminar, workshop...) and decides about the channel of knowledge transfer (internet, face-to-face...). In a third and fourth step, the location and the course tutors are established. The course tutors determine the contents of the courses and are responsible for the delivery of adequate materials. So, the approach to generate a course is a mixture of a bottom-up and a top-down strategy.

This open broker organization supports the demand for fast reaction to market requirements and allows integrating many partners and experts (Figure 6). Especially for international research co-operations or education networks the systems

offers a high degree of flexibility (Westkämper, 2006). In this modular organization each partner teaches courses in their specific fields of core competence. The system provides a high level of independence concerning location and content of courses. The synchronizations of different courses and co-ordination are subject to the broker.

The existing technical infrastructure also, enables the CE@ANPART partners in the network to offer tele-based courses via videoconference, so that the courses can be offered at many physical locations at the same time ("any time-any place potential"). It is also an option charge a fee from participants for some selected courses or trainings that will help to make the system independent from public funding.

The CE@ANPART virtual center will therefore ensure the permanent spreading of current research results and will open a gate to offer further educational or training services to different target groups. The efforts will also foster the deep integration of the network into the society and to open further links between researchers if we consider the Entrepreneurial Centers that will be developed in the location of each partner involved in the project.

CE@ANPART Virtual Center Preliminary Architecture Design

There is tremendous value in seamlessly connecting people, systems, and business processes across organization. Operational efficiency goes up, operational costs go down. Better aligned, the company can stay agile and competitive. An *integration competence center* is an efficient information technology application that is design to share services function consisting of: people, technology, policies, best practice and processes (Lenzerini, 2002).

In this context, our approach described the preliminary study of the existing solutions of integration competencies centers, their structure and users facilities analysis with the aim of building the CE@ANPART virtual center. This define a unique products/services offer on the market through information and communication technologies and will support, encourage, qualify and certified the entrepreneurial competencies (Draghici, Izvercianu & Draghici, 2009).

The preliminary researches showed that there is still an acute need for training and consulting services in this field. The virtual center development process started from two ideas: (1) the design of a special section dedicated to entrepreneurial training (e-learning system for competencies development and evaluation, WWW based courses support system) and consulting (portal of entrepreneurship resources, business services, library) on the existing web page of the CE@ANPART project, and (2) the development of the virtual conference system that will be a powerful tool for the collaborative learning and research between the partners involved in the project (the universities of Iasi – the coordinator, Cluj-Napoca, Timisoara and Sibiu, but also, some local indus-

trial partners) and for the clients/students. For the entrepreneurial competencies assessment (in the initial stage before training) there was designed a special section that includes on-line questionnaires and other facilities that preliminary analyze and identify the clients training needs (Draghici, Izvercianu & Draghici, 2009).

Figures 7 show the client – server architecture of the proposed web platform. It is build around a central server, hosting the e-learning application (AeL Enterprise e-learning platform (www.advancedelearning.com, which allow asynchronous, synchronous in class and at distance learning), the database system, the file system (documents and research project's management) and other software applications that support the learning, research and management activities (Draghici, Izvercianu & Draghici, 2009).

The main facilities of the AeL Enterprise software that are developed for entrepreneurship training and evaluation are: asynchronous study, virtual class and library, training record (including the evaluation tests of gain competencies), reports (regarding the training process evolution), administration, and discussion forum. The business consulting session is a client-server oriented architecture approach that integrates three entities: the services need – client (user friendly interface), the information technology system (server) and the services data base (integration at the service level with the flexible and quick response to add/change actions).

Figure 8 describes the connections, via Internet, of the video-conferences systems that are located to each university partner. The video-conference system allow: collaborative project sections, collaborative learning sections, virtual conferences etc.

The first facilities that have been created on the CE@ANPART virtual campus are related to the self assessment of the future clients/students. A capability adviser has been build for this. It consists of two main entities: (1) assess your skills and (2) view the learning steps and sign in

Figure 7. The CE@ANPART virtual center preliminary architecture

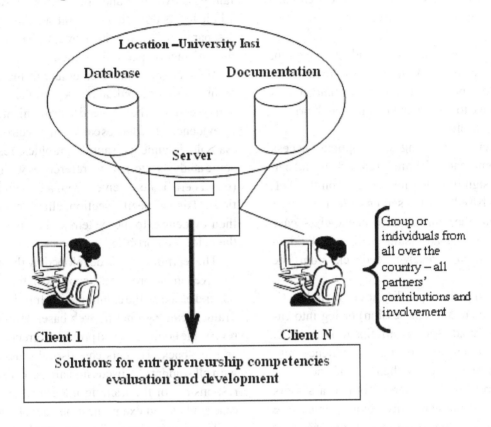

Figure 8. The CE@ANPART virtual center – representation of the network IT tool

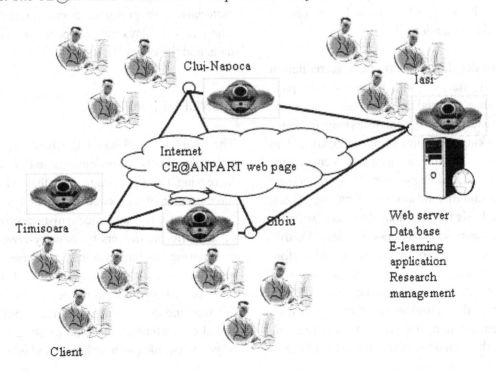

for the courses. This part of the virtual campus allows the client to:

- Log in the capability adviser section, browse the skills tree, assess their skills against performance criteria, upload evidences to prove their skills, and print a skills profile;
- Select the learning steps options, access recommended learning references, and can call sign in to log into courses on the AeL web based training server system;
- Attend the courses, perform exercises, case studies, upload results of their individual works, and receive feedback from the trainers;
- Switch to the capability adviser window (if they complete one session) or log into capability adviser as participant and upload their homework results as evidence into the system to prove their competence;
- Inform the assessors. Formal assessors log into the capability adviser, assess the evidence, the performance criteria, and produce a formal skills profile of the client. The results of the formal assessors are display separately.

Course developers (as trainers, accreditation institutions, etc.) log into an e-working space where course material development work can be shared in a team. The system offers team management, working scenarios, version control, and an interface to export the training and reference materials in the AeL training system. Also, trainers can enter and administrate a skill card on-line, which forms the basis for the client skills assessment.

The self assessment process includes a skill tree with skills units, learning elements, and performance criteria. After the client select the option of self test against certain performance criteria he/she will be invited to complete a multiple choice test. The system automatically checks the answers and scores with a standard evaluation scale of poor/ fair/good/excellent and not applicable. After the whole test is done, client could see the results in a separate window with percent chart showing the satisfaction per skill element.

If the client wants to enter any formal assessment or formal accreditation (beyond the scope of a self assessment) he/she need to prove his/her skills by evidences. Evidences can be any electronic files (sample documents, sample graphics, results of some analysis, etc.) or any references with details (e.g. a certificate received from a certain institution). Using a specific section, clients can upload their evidences to the system and build this way the evidence portfolio.

The learning pool is developed by the trainers involved in the project in accord with their expertise and based on the client specific training needs. Trainers can log into the web based training and review the homework and provide correction notes and feedback. Trainers can also, discuss results with all students in discussion areas. Trainers are responsible of the training materials, exercises, case studies and exam questions development.

The examination facilities (multiple choice test questionnaires) are defined based on the learning materials and the performance criteria established. The exam displays general personal and exam data, and the client ID.

CONCLUSION

The chapter has debated the new role of the university in the knowledge based society for increasing the knowledge transfer process for the entrepreneurship education. The knowledge transfer activities and mechanism are the core of an efficient university-industry-government relationship for entrepreneurial outcomes increasing. Based on a marketing research, there have been described the training needs for business creation and development and for complete the actual competencies (base on existing abilities) of young people (with technical and economical background) to become successful entrepreneurs. Also, there have been presented the preliminary architecture of the virtual center for entrepreneurship development. The research results and consequences were focused on: (a) Adjustments of the university curricula; (b) Identification and description of those activities that can be carried out by universities in the field of knowledge transfer and that can be considered for entrepreneurship education, too (especially for the technical education); (c) The CE@ANPART virtual center design as an answer to the market demand and with the support of an university partnership for research (Draghici, Izvercianu & Draghici, 2009). Future researches will be developed for building the virtual center for competencies/expertise evaluation CE@ANPART and test all the functionalities with real clients – entrepreneurs (the information system development and test). Some comparative researches will identify the correlations and differences of knowledge management in engineering education institutions in Romania (under the UNIKM project).

FUTURE RESEARCHES

Also, future researches will be developed at the European level, in the context of a Lifelong Learning Programme, Leonardo da Vinci (503021-LLP-1-2009-1-BE-LEONARDO-LMP): "*Certified EU Researcher – Entrepreneur*", also call by acronym ResEUr. The motivation for this project proposal lies in the lack of a European-wide valid set of training modules and certification of entrepreneurial skills of young academic people. Europe is far from exploiting its potential of successful entrepreneurship in higher education, because it often fails to mobilize the right innovative resources and young brains. The proposed project aims at delivering to innovative researchers the qualification to determine if their work and/or their ideas have a market potential, as well as to

be able to create a commercial interest for what they are doing (ResEUr, 2009).

This new project results envisaged are a skill set which clearly describes the skills/competencies required for a researcher to turn his ideas into marketable products, and thus to be able to create a sustainable enterprise. For all the skill elements training material will be provided in several languages and in an e-learning environment. A pool of test questions will be defined, which provides the basis for the certification of students. All these elements will be verified with a number of students in the context of initial trainings and certifications. The partners involved in this project are: EMIRAcle, European Manufacturing and Innovation Research Association a cluster leading excellence – association established after the Belgian law in 2008 (www.emiracle.eu, the promoter and coordinator of the project); Politehnica University of Timisoara, Romania; Institute Polytechnique de Grenoble, France; International Software Consulting Network Ltd. (ISCN) Wicklow, Ireland; proHUMAN Cooperation and Business Management Ltd. Maribor, Slovenia and Skills International GmbH Grossklein, Austria;

By its very composition, the proposed consortium will be able to have a significant impact on a European level. To give examples, the applicant organization EMIRAcle unites a large pool of leading universities, who are all very active in leading-edge research as well as in organizing influential and recognized international conferences. Members are able to pre-select researchers based on a long-term observation of their works. ISCN as coordinator of the EuroSPI initiative runs a PhD selection program, where a number of international PhD students are assessed based on the innovation potential of their contributions to the topic of software and innovation process improvement. Grenoble INP has established a "*House of Entrepreneurship*", which is dedicated to mobilize researchers to turn their research results into successful innovations on the market. UPT has gained a lot of experience in the entrepreneurship filed because of the CE@ANPART project and thei have developed the Entrepreneurship Center.

The main objectives and priorities of the common future research are:

- Increasing Europe's entrepreneurial and innovation power via a modern training and certification program in the lifelong learning programs area;
- To implement European-wide validity of both qualification and certification. The system established over years by the European Certification and Qualification Association provides an ideal platform to achieve this goal (ECQA, 2009);
- Entrepreneurship is much more attractive than its image in many EU Member States. ResEUr shall provide an attractive and high-quality access to it particularly for researchers;
- ResEUr focuses on key qualifications for researchers to become successful entrepreneurs. It positions itself complementary to the generic trainings and support programs for new entrepreneurs;
- A clearly described curriculum and one European certification standard for all levels of education, will promote quality assurance in all sectors of education;
- ResEUr qualification will be based on the use of "Best Practices" and "Lessons Learned" to a large extent by using practical examples and real life cases.

The future researches expected impact are mainly manifested in the following key aspects (in the context of the ResEUr project):

- Establishment of a complete and consistent self-assessment, training and certification platform for entrepreneurial competences of researchers on the European level. This will have a positive impact on the knowledge interoperability in the European economy of SMEs, especially for the development of new business and radical innovation;
- Development of a European competence network of experts for entrepreneurial skills and of certified entrepreneurs, which will feed back experiences and best practices into the qualification and certification program;
- Increasing the success rate of young entrepreneurs on the European level by targeted systematic development and certification of their competences in terms of understanding and mastering the keys to judge if ideas and/or research results are innovative;
- Support and encouragement of entrepreneurial culture and spirit of young, highly educated and gifted with huge potential, students (graduates, masters, PhD students and young researchers) by giving them the opportunity to have an EU-wide recognized qualification and certificate in this field in addition to their specific university diploma. The demand for these researches is especially strong in the information technology area, where often hi-tech business ideas get obsolete or common practice very quickly.;

A specific impact group refers to the young researchers in the manufacturing area who are confronted with the particular challenge of massive outsourcing of production (and increasingly also development) to low-wage countries notably in Asia. Without a qualification, the new project researches wants to establish, Europe risks to lose their potential to create the innovations that are the key to bringing manufacturing competences and capacities back to Europe. These predominant two target groups can be optimally impacted by the proposed consortium.

ACKNOWLEDGMENT

The presented research results were gained from our implication in two national projects: "Partnership for excellence in research for the entrepreneurial skills and competitive human capital development in the knowledge and innovation base society - CE@ANPART" (contract no. 91069/2007 with National Center for Programmes Management - CNMP) and "Comparative researches concerning knowledge management in Romanian engineering education - UNIKM" (contract no. 92074/2008 with National Center for Programmes Management - CNMP). From 2009 we extend our researches at the European level, in the context of a Lifelong Learning Programme, Leonardo da Vinci (503021-LLP-1-2009-1-BE-LEONARDO-LMP): "Certified EU Researcher – Entrepreneur", project financed by the European Commision. This will allowed the European qualification and certification of the research-entrepreneur competencies using the link to a training and examination web platform. The present chapter is also, connected with the dEUcert project (Dissemination of European Certification Schema ECQA, 505101-LLP-1-2009-1-AT-KA4-KA4MP), that has been funded with support from the European Commission, also. This chapter and communication reflects the views only of the authors, and the Commission cannot be held responsible for any use which may be made of the information contained therein.

REFERENCES

Adelsberger, H., Collis, B., & Pawlowski, J. M. (2002). *Handbook on Information Technologies for Education and Training*. Berlin: Springer.

AeL Enterprise. (2007). *SIVECO Romania*. Retrieved April 12, 2007, from http://www.advancedelearning.com

CE@ANPART. (2009). *Partnership for Excellence Research in Developing Entrepreneurial Skills and a Competitive Human Capital in the Innovation and Knowledge-Based Economy and Society*. Retrieved December 12, 2009, from http://www.ceanpart.lx.ro/index.htm

Draghici, A., & Draghici, G. (2006). New business requirements in the knowledge-based society . In Cunha, M. M., Cortes, B. C., & Putnik, G. D. (Eds.), *Adaptive Technologies and Business Integration: Social, Managerial and Organizational Dimensions* (pp. 2111–2243). Hershey, PA: Idea Group Publishing.

Draghici, A., Foldvary-Schramko, K., Vartolomei, M., & Suciu, S. (2009). Exploring Trans-University Knowledge Transfer - A New Approach for Knowledge Management in Engineering Education. In C. Rusu (Ed.), *Management of Technological Changes: Proceedings of the 6th International Conference on Management of Technological Changes* (Vol. 2, pp. 461-464). Alexandroupolis, Greece: Democritus University of Thrace.

Draghici, A., & Izvercianu, M. (2009). The University Entrepreneurship Education. *Review of Management and Economic Engineering*, *8*(1), 27–35.

Draghici, A., Izvercianu, M., & Draghici, G. (2009). Virtual Center for Entrepreneurial Competencies Assessment and Development – Preliminary Architecture Design. In M. M. Cruz-Cunha, J. E. Quintela Varajão, L. A. Martins do Amaral (Eds.), *Proceedings of the CENTERIS 2009 - Conference on ENTERprise Information Systems – aligning technology, organization and people* (pp. 153-164). Barcelos, Portugal: Instituto Politecnico do Cavado e do Ave.

Draghici, A., Vartolomei, M., Foldvary-Schramko, K., & Suciu, S. (2009). Entrepreneurial University Development through the Knowledge Sharing Culture Development. In C. Rusu (Ed.), *Management of Technological Changes: Proceedings of the 6th International Conference on Management of Technological Changes* (Vol. 2, pp. 465-468). Alexandroupolis, Greece: Democritus University of Thrace.

ECQA. (2009). *European Certification & Qualification Association*. Retrieved December 20, 2009, from http://www.ecqa.org/index.php?id=7

EMIRAcle. (2008). *European Manufacturing and Innovation Research Association a cluster leading excellence*. Retrieved November 12, 2009, from http://www.emiracle.eu

Etzkowitz, L., & Leydesdorff, M. (2000). The Dynamics of Innovation: from National Systems and Model 2 to a Triple Helix of University-Industry-Government Relation. *Research Policy*, *29*(2), 109. doi:10.1016/S0048-7333(99)00055-4

European Commission. (2008). *Helping to Create an Entrepreneurial Culture – A Guide on Good Practice in Promoting Entrepreneurial Attitudes and Skills through Education*. Retrieved June 22, 2008, from http://europa.eu.int/comm/enterprise/entrepreneurship/support_measures/training_education/index.htm

European Commission. (2008). *Directorate-General for Enterprise and Industry: Entrepreneurship in Higher Education, Especially Within Non-Business Studies – Final Report of the Expert Group*. Retrieved June 22, 2008, from http://europa.eu.int/comm/enterprise/entrepreneurship/support_measures/index.htm

Izvercianu, M. (2007). *Research Regarding the Training Needs Identification for Business Creation*. Report in the Leonardo da Vinci program Sustainable enterprises development – FOR-CREST. ES/03/B/F/PP-149101.

Izvercianu, M., & Draghici, A. (2007). Vocational Training Requirements' Analysis for Industrial Romanian Enterprises . In Karwowski, W., & Trzcielinski, S. (Eds.), *Value Stream Activities Management* (pp. 567–574). Pznan, Poland: International Ergonomics Association.

Izvercianu, M., & Draghici, A. (2008). The University Entrepreneurship Education. The Case of Politehnica University of Timisoara. In M. G. Simion & I. Talpasanu (Eds.), *Proceeding of the 3rd Annual Congress of the American Romanian Academy of Arts and Sciences (ARA)* (pp. 238-241). Boston: Wentworth Institute of Technology.

Izvercianu, M., & Draghici, A. (2008). The Entrepreneurship Education as Part of Human Resources Development. In J. Han & P. Holejsovska (Eds.), *Proceedings of the 10th International Conference on the Modern Information Technology in the Innovation Processes of the Industrial Enterprises* (*MITIP 2008*) (pp. 200-206). Pilsen, Czech Republic: University of West Bohemia.

Lenzerini, M. (2002). A Theoretical Perspective . In *PODS 2002* (pp. 243–246). Data Integration.

Niegemann, H., Hessel, S., & Hochscheid-Mauel, D. (2004). *Kompendium E-Learning*. Berlin: Springer.

Niemann, J., Galis, M., Ciupan, C., & Westkämper, E. (2003). The e-Virtual Professor - an International Network of Universities for Computer Assisted Learning Education in Mechanical Engineering . *Marine Engineering*, *3*(1-2), 200–206.

Niemann, J., Galis, M., Stolz, M., Legg, L., & Westkämper, E. (2004). E-Teach Me: An e-Learning Platform for Higher Education in Manufacturing Engineering. *Academic Journal of Manufacturing Engineering*, *2*(1), 1–9.

ResEUr. (2009). *Certified EU Researcher – Entrepreneru*. Retrieved December 20, 2009, from http://www.vrl-kcip.org/spip.php?article591

Ropke, F. (1998). *The Entrepreneurial University: Innovation, Academic Knowledge Creation and Regional Development in a Globalize Economy.* Working paper of the Department of Economics, Philips University Marburg, Germany.

Tornatzky, G. (2002). *Innovation U: New University Roles in a Knowledge Economy.* Research Triangle Park, NC: Southern Growth Policy Board.

UNIKM. (2009). *Comparative Researches Concerning Knowledge Management in Romanian Engineering Education.* Retrieved December 20, 2009, from http://imtuoradea.ro/unikm/index_en.htm

Westkämper, E. (2006). Manufuture - Key Technology for Manufacturing Innovation and Environmental Sustainability, Discussion Paper - Academic Perspective. In B.-W. Choi (Ed.), *IMS International: Proceedings of the IMS Vision Forum 2006* (pp. 90-97). Seoul, Korea: Korea Cheong-Moon-Gak Publishers.

Chapter 31
Collaborative Demand and Supply Planning Networks

Hans-Henrik Hvolby
Aalborg University, Denmark

Kenn Steger-Jensen
Aalborg University, Denmark

Erlend Alfnes
Norwegian University of Science and Technology, Norway

Heidi C. Dreyer
Norwegian University of Science and Technology, Norway

ABSTRACT

The focus of manufacturing planning and control has gradually expanded from (in-house) production activities towards all manufacturing and logistic activities in the supply chain. Planning of in-house operations is still very important, but the trends towards increased use of outsourcing and mass customisation require that customers and suppliers are able to exchange information frequently to cut down costs and lead time while quickly adapting their manufacturing and logistics operations to market/customer requirements. Many vendors offer systems to plan and control in-house operations, whereas only a few large vendors (such as Oracle, SAP and I2) offer supply chain planning systems. This limits the ability for SMEs to exploit the supply chain planning options. This chapter discuss current supply chain planning solutions and presents a more simple and adaptive concept to be used in both SMEs and larger enterprises. The research presented in this chapter is funded by the EU Union via the EmpoSME, ValuePole projects, and by the Research Council of Norway via the SFI Norman project.

INTRODUCTION

Most manufacturing companies face strong competition and continuowus changes in market and customer requirements. Planning are frequently affected by the actions of suppliers and customers in their supply networks such as changes to orders that are already in production or re-planning caused by lack of materials or resources. Often, decisions have to be made without having a complete, real time overview of possible options and associated

DOI: 10.4018/978-1-61692-020-3.ch031

consequences. The result is typically excess inventories, too long lead times, too low customer satisfaction and poor resource utilisation.

Supply networks are dynamic and hard to define, and a single company is often part of several different supply networks simultaneously. An increasing level of customisation combined with demands for high quality, low costs, short and precise delivery times, and high flexibility represents a significant challenge to managing operations in networks.

Although these challenges will apply to companies of all sizes, they are particularly true for SMEs due to the following characteristics:

- The network are typically non-hierarchical
- They have limited staff available for specialist roles in planning and decision making
- They have limited resources available to invest in Advanced Planning Systems
- They require flexible tools which let them exploit the advantage of typically being flexible and easier to manage than larger enterprises

Observation shows that information exchange is often limited to order placements without any kind of information visibility or other communication between network partners. Thus network effects of individual decisions are often not possible to neither intercept nor predict. This implies that planning and control at any network partner is currently executed with incomplete information about status among the other network partners and without the possibility to see the full consequences of decisions being made. Additionally, the planning and control task will vary with regards to scope and complexity challenging the traditional planning and control approaches, and existing methodologies, tools and knowledge.

The paper briefly discusses three major areas for manufacturing in non-hierarchical networks. After this a more simple and adaptive alternative approach to existing APS solutions is presented, and finally the approach is positioned in a broader perspective titled "Work Bench Concept" to be used in both SMEs and larger enterprises.

COLLABORATION IN NON-HIERARCHICAL NETWORKS

Typical for SMEs is that they operate in non-hierarchical networks, characterised by power being distributed among members, and the absence of one or several dominant actors that dictate plans or impose a centralised planning perspective (Harland et al., 2001). In such networks each member participates in multiple supply chains and all members are more or less equal in status and therefore no member has the power to dictate the others (Jagdev and Thoben, 2001). The core part of each network might form what could be titled as a Virtual Enterprise to share skills or core competencies and resources in order to better respond to business opportunities.

Coordination and collaboration between the companies is vital in such networks. Collaboration refers to the activities and environment related to the "joint planning and execution of supply chain activities" (Ayers, 2006), and is therefore an essential element in planning activities in a network perspective. Collaboration is using cooperative efforts in order to meet mutual goals, exchanging information, developing improvement in partnership (Ayers, 2006). A manufacturing network is fully coordinated when all decisions are aligned to accomplish global system objectives (Sahin and Robinson 2002); of course when this occurs decisions have already crossed the company's boundaries, meeting articulated and complex contexts (Danese et al., 2004). Several collaborative models for coordination networks activities have been developed. The aim of models such as collaborative planning, forecasting and replenishment (CPFR), vendor managed inventory (VMI) and automated replenishment programs (ARP) is

Table 1. Examples of E-Business impacts on supply chain integration and business processes (Lee & Whang, 2001)

Dimensions of SC Integration	Business Processes			
	Procurement	Order Fulfilment	Product Design	Post-Sales Support
Information Integration	Supplier information sharing	Information sharing across the supply chain	Design data sharing, product change plan sharing	Customer usage data linkages
Planning Synchro-nisation	Co-ordinated replenishment	Collaborative planning and co-ordination, demand and supply management	Synchronised new product introduction and rollover plans	Service supply chain planning co-ordination
Workflow Co-ordination	Paperless procurement, auctions, auto replenishment, auto payment	Workflow automation with contract manu-facturers or logistics providers, replenishment services.	Product change management automation, collaborative design	Auto replenishment of consumables
New Business Models	Market exchanges, auctions, secondary markets	Click-and-mortar models, supply chain restructuring, market intelligence & demand management	Mass customisation, new service offerings	Remote sensing & diagnosis, auto-test, downloadable upgrades
Monitoring and Measurement	Contract agreement compliance monitoring	Logistics tracking, order monitoring	Project monitoring	Performance measurement and tracking

to achieve seamless inter-organisational interfaces by specifying control principles and operations models for the flow of materials and information (Holweg et al., 2005).

Collaboration in the network is decentralised and each actor performs individual planning, with the aim of optimising operations in a local perspective. Companies in non-hierarchical networks face challenges that make collaboration difficult. Firstly, the networks themselves are dynamic and hard to define, and a single company is often part of several different manufacturing networks simultaneously. The focal company and other network members frequently face situations with conflicting interest and trade-off situations. A typical scenario is when orders from different networks compete for scarce resources and deadlines and delivery times are short. Frequently, these requirements cannot be fulfilled because there is a lack of information about the current state of the production and network processes. In addition, customers might request changes to orders that are already in production, making it difficult to make quick decisions based on a complete, real time overview

of possible options and associated consequences. Secondly, products are becoming more and more sophisticated and intelligent, with service and value added elements embedded in the products themselves. Further, with an increasing level of customisation, and demands for high quality, low costs, short and precise delivery times, and high flexibility, the management of the operations in the networks represents a significant challenge.

Other examples of E-Business Impacts on Supply Chain Integration and Business Processes are seen in Table 1.

One would imagine that the main improvements from implementing information exchange solutions would be a reduction of resources to enter/update information in the ERP-system, but experiences from Electrolux in Australia shows that even more time is released from (not) answering all kind of order related questions on the phone, not only in the administration but also in the production.

MANUFACTURING PLANNING AND CONTROL

The essential task of *manufacturing planning and control* is to efficiently manage the flow of materials, the utilisation of people and equipment and to respond to customer requirements by utilising the capacity of suppliers and internal resources to meet customer demand (Vollmann et al., 2005). *Planning* across non-hierarchical networks is a complicated and complex task due to conflicting objectives and continuously changing demand. In such a case, the planning and scheduling issues will have to face the challenge of coordinating systems that do not fully share all relevant information between companies (Alvarez, 2007).

Distributed planning in non-hierarchical networks has to be performed in a setting where relevant information from several IT systems are integrated and up to date, and can be accessed in real time from anywhere in the network. This information visibility depends on the exchange of critical data required for the efficient management and control of the flow of products, services and related information between members in the network (Handsfield and Nichols, 2002). Each node should ideally be able to see the real time situation in the network, downstream as well as upstream, from boardroom to shop floor, enabled by *automatic data acquisition*. Although *information visibility* and *system integration* are regarded as keys for enabling collaboration, very few networks have successfully achieved this (Quinn, 2003).

The dominating techniques and systems for planning and control (e.g. Enterprise Resource Planning - ERP, Manufacturing Execution Systems - MES) do not support the need for a network perspective. They have a single-company focus and mainly support centralized production and planning and control (Alvarez, 2007). This makes network planning difficult and inefficient. This amplifies the need for supply chains to rely on flexible, adaptable and responsive planning and

decision support tools across the entire network (Özbayrak, 2006).

ADVANCED PLANNING AND SCHEDULING

Advanced Planning and Scheduling (APS) systems introduced the benefits of constraint-based planning and optimization to the business world and enabled companies to optimize plans according to financial and other strategic objectives. APS seeks to find feasible, near optimal plans unlike traditional Enterprise Resource Planning (ERP) systems (Stadtler & Kilger, 2005). APS takes into account constraints at enterprise level as well as at plant level. Materials and capacity issues are considered simultaneously, and manufacturing, distribution, and transportation issues are integrated. Many ERP and APS systems make it possible to include suppliers and customers in the planning procedure and thereby optimize a whole supply chain on a real-time basis (Wortmann, 1998; Vollmann et al., 2004; Kennerly & Neely, 2001).

Therefore, APS does not substitute but supplement existing ERP systems. The ERP system handles the basic activities and transactions such as customer orders and accounting whereas the APS system focus on the operational activities related to decision-making, planning, scheduling and control of a supply chain and related management activities, which are not explicitly well covered in ERP systems. APS has the capability to simulate different scenarios for decision support, to plan and to schedule on-line as well as off-line. Planning and scheduling is by nature a proactive process, which can initiate an event in another area of the business or at partners based on the workflow control.

APS is the most comprehensive system for supply chain planning and control today. Although APS aims at automating and computerizing the planning processes by use of simulation and optimization, the decision-making is still made by planners with insight in the particular supply chain and know how on the system constraints but likewise important: a feeling for feasibility of created plans. Thus, APS aim to bridge the gap between the supply chain complexity and the day-to-day operative decisions. This requires, however, that planners are able to model and setup decision rules for the planning and optimization.

According to Petroni (2002) there are several problems involved in using planning software such as high complexity, lack of training and knowledge among managers and personnel, low-data accuracy, and lack of support from the software vendor. Early adopters of APS report significant reductions in cycle time, resource and inventory load (OM Control, 2001; Schell, 2002; Hess, 2002). A study by Funk (2001) however, showed that only 20% of the APS installations investigated were successful (based on a threshold of achieving 70% of projected gain to become a success).

In spite of the supply chain functionality, most APS implementations are limited to a single organization or a single manufacturing site. A few cases can be found in literature on successful supply chain implementations. Gupta et al. (2002), for example, describe a decision support system which helps Pfizer to plan their distribution network. Another study from the Vita Group show an increase in delivery accuracy from 79 up to 99% while reducing lead time from 5-7 days to zero and reducing the planning resources by 30% (Works Management, 2008).

THE WORK BENCH CONCEPT

As pointed out by the US National Institute of Standards and Technology, the 20th century, competitive advantage was defined by the production and labour capabilities of individual original equipment manufacturers (OEMs). In the mid 90s, OEMs sought to reduce those costs by distributing those capabilities across a global supply chain. Competitive advantage is now seen as the combined capabilities of the suppliers that make up the OEMs' supply chain. Therefore, the only way to improve competitive advantage is to improve those combined capabilities through better integration – that is information exchange across the supply chain. The challenge is to develop and demonstrate an open, standards-based, testing and integration infrastructure that enables the automated exchange of information across the supply chain. This infrastructure will provide the foundation for new types of collaboration and management and it will help propel both OEMs and SMEs to a better competitive position in the global marketplace.

The Work Bench Concept is an alternative approach to enable such an infrastructure supporting supply chain planning where decentralised planning decisions are made with regards to individual company operations – but with a network perspective. The main functionality is to operate and manage existing SMEs manufacturing networks. The work bench comprises components for integration of information systems, visualisation of the planning and production situation, communication to enable cooperative decision making under uncertainty, optimisation of plans and simulation of the decisions, network diagnostics and performance monitoring among others. This involves a number of challenges such as providing members access to network-wide real time information (Wang and Wei, 2007), enable visualisation of the available information (Boyson et al., 2003), secure the interaction between advanced ICT based decision support tools and human decision making (Barthélemy et al., 2002), and creating a coordinated and collaborative environment (Deek et al., 2003) for planning and decision making. The state of the art, major challenges and identified requirements are listed in Table 2.

In the following section a supply chain planning approach to solve requirement 2 (Techniques for solving distributed and dynamic planning) is presented.

Table 2. State of the art, challenges and requirements for future supply chain planning solutions

State of the art	• Collaborative practices and methodologies have been developed for coordination between long term supply chain partners. Examples include Vendor Managed Inventory and Collaborative Planning, Forecasting and Replenishment (Holweg et al., 2005). • Predominant manufacturing planning and control techniques are based on centralized production control, with infinite capacity, constant lead time and fixed routings in the single company (Alvarez, 2007). • Decision support tools for network planning and execution are based on optimisation and simulation such as Advanced Planning and Scheduling, Strategic Network Planning etc. (Turban, 2007)
Challenges and conflicts	Existing collaborative practices and methodologies: • Are not supported by low cost ICT-systems • Have a single-company perspective, fail to provide collaborative planning for the network and fail to include the non-hierarchical perspective • Are restricted to centralized planning and control, and lack flexibility and real-time information. • Are out of reach for most SMEs due to the centralized control, high complexity and high cost • Assume centralized control in hierarchical networks and consensus between stakeholders Furthermore, the tools does not: • Address uncertainty and risk adequately • Support a more diversified classification of tasks to enable improved planning results based on a more holistic view. • Enable effective human interaction in decision making • Include presentation and real time information from network • Support an "individual" real-time plan generation

Requirements	1. Planning and control techniques and principles with the capability to handle conflicting objectives, dynamic networks and distributed decision making
	 2. Techniques for solving distributed and dynamic planning.
	 3. Full integration with dashboard solutions, allowing real-time decision support with advanced what-if capabilities and graphical, interactive planning boards
	 4. Simple ICT-supported collaborative methodologies for non-hierarchical network collaboration which:
	    • Consider new manufacturing planning and control techniques for non-hierarchical networks
	    • Explicitly address operational (and selected tactical and strategic issues) as well as operational uncertainties and risk, and cope with the dynamicity and complexity of manufacturing systems
	    • Automate routine tasks, leaving human schedulers to concentrate on exceptions handling

A NEW SUPPLY CHAIN PLANNING APPROACH

Whilst the planning and optimisation procedure used in Advanced Planning and Scheduling systems is the current state-of-the-art for a single company or a hierarchical supply chain/network, planning among individual companies belonging to several non-hierarchical networks require other solutions. The reason for this is quite simple: an APS system need to have a joint goal and clear constrains for the planning engine to work, and this is not obtainable when dealing with several non-hierarchical networks. Furthermore, the hierarchical demand planning approach is based on the premise of aggregation and disaggregation which is reflected in the master demand schedule as well as the structures for capacity and material,

the bill-of-resources and bill-of-materials structure. Today's APS systems planning and control capability depends on the ability to aggregate and disaggregate plans and the data they are based on. This makes the structure of the planning foundation critical, unfortunately a simple linear disaggregation of information is not always possible due to the nature of the planning foundation and the multiple usage purposes of the information contained herein.

We therefore present a relative simple solution based on individual ERP or APS plans in the respective companies followed by improvements in between partners. It is assumed that requests from customers (customer orders) have been accepted as far as possible by the ERP/APS system, possibly based on customer priorities (se below) in case of resource or materials shortage.

However, such a plan is normally based on standard customer lead-times to allow the individual ERP-plans to create realistic plans at the first attempt. The option of optimising the joint plan is therefore primarily based on the difference in between standard customer lead-time and actual lead-times in the company.

Solving the challenges related to collaboration in Non-hierarchical network is not new. A concept of Extended Value Chain Management (EVCM) is introduced by Görlitz (2002) as an add-on to the existing ERP-system. The idea is that the EVCM acts as a broker in between a customer and suitable suppliers in the market place. For the broker to identify one or more suppliers each SMEs needs to register on the market place. This solution, however, does not support the option of adjusting plans in between a customer and a supplier to enable a mutual (optimal) solution.

The outmost simple solution is therefore to allow partners to (manually) view the (production) plan and based on this utilise/request the available "free space". A more far-reaching solution would be to allow customers to also move low priority jobs in order to create extra "free space" and thereby make way for more orders. This solution requires that jobs and customers are segmented and assigned a given priority such as illustrated in Table 3.

Assigning customer priority is a manual task. Job priorities need to be assigned automatically to allow the system to work without consuming extra resources. High priority jobs are typically related to bottleneck resources or customer orders with little or no slack. Low priority jobs could either be related to customer orders with slack or it could be stock orders. Cancellation or reduction of stock orders (jobs) might lead to higher costs depending on the details (in case of high setup costs the ERP-system might generate a stock order in connection with a customer order to reduce the total costs).

The planning approach could work in a more or less manual version where the customer-initiated changes are updated manually, but a more integrated approach would be more beneficial for all parties but also more costly. In both cases the production plan needs to be generated individually for each partner, allowing him to only view details of own orders/jobs whereas other orders/jobs only appear as a coloured (red/yellow/green) anonymous job. Further, no matter how information is changed in the system, the partners in the network likely request to keep track of the changes made. VMI vendors have already invented solutions for this and could be used as an initial source for ideas.

A strong combination of EVCM and the concept described above might lead to a more automated Collaborative Demand and Supply Planning (CDSP) model. This requires that standard interfaces are developed in between the ERP-systems and the CDSP, at least in selected areas such as items and order specifications. The process of exchanging data involves three steps:

Table 3. Job and customer priority rules

Jobs: Customers:	High priority (red)	Medium priority (yellow)	Low priority (green)
High priority	Orders are unlikely to be moved (customer requests change)	Orders might be moved (customer requests change)	Orders can be moved (customer initiate change)
Medium priority	Orders can't be moved	Orders are unlikely to be moved (customer requests change)	Orders might be moved (customer requests change)
Low priority	No access to view plans		

- electronic data interchange through a message broker
- matching relations (e.g. dealing with different item id's, date-formats, units, time-zones etc)
- process integration (in case of systems integration)

One might ask why any company should allow customers to make changes to current production plans and the answer is quite simple: to be attractive and flexible and thereby increase their competitiveness for high- and medium-priority customers. A simple comparison with our own diary would immediately create an understanding of the potential of segmenting and colouring our appointments - avoiding that we are left out of important meetings/activities because of minor/moveable arrangements.

CONCLUSION

In the highly competitive market that most companies find themselves in it is vital to organise the manufacturing and supply chain operations in the best possible way. The first step in this development process is to organise the internal operations in an appropriate and fruitful way, but for most companies there are similar improvements to be made by involving supply chain partners in the planning process. Information access and visibility, new planning and control principles, collaborative mechanisms and new information tools have to be developed in order to meet the particular challenges of SMEs in non-hierarchical networks. The paper discusses the current state of the art applications and outlines a new approach titled "Work Bench" to further improve the planning with special focus on non-hierarchical networks. Especially a simple approach to align production plans is presented.

ACKNOWLEDGMENT

We would like to acknowledge the other partners (SINTEF, Frauenhofer, IMI, ISOIN and UNIBG) of the PLANET FP7 proposal for valuable contribution.

REFERENCES

Alvarez, E. (2007). Multi-plant production scheduling in SMEs. *Robotics and Computer-integrated Manufacturing*, *23*, 608–613. doi:10.1016/j.rcim.2007.02.006

Ayers, J. B. (2006). *Handbook of supply chain management* (2nd ed.). New York: Auerbach Publications.

Brown, G., Keegan, J., Vigus, B., & Wood, K. (2001). The Kellogg company optimizes production, inventory and distribution. *Interfaces*, *31*(6), 1–15.

IOM Control. (2001). ERP survey. *Institute Operation Management*, *27*(8).

Danese, P., Romano, P., & Vinelli, A. (2004). Managing business processes across supply networks: the role of coordination mechanisms. *Journal of Purchasing and Supply Management*, *10*, 165–177. doi:10.1016/j.pursup.2004.11.002

Funk, G. (2001). Enterprise integration: join the successful 20%. *Hydrocarbon Processing, 80*(4).

Görlitz, O., Neubert, R., Teich, T., & Benn, W. (2002). Extended Value Chain Management on Electronic Marketplaces. *International Journal of e-Business Strategy Management, 3*(3).

Gupta, V., Peter, E., Miller, T., & Blyden, K. (2002). Implementing a distribution-network decision-support system at Pfizer/Warner-Lambert. *Interfaces, 32*(4), 28–45. doi:10.1287/inte.32.4.28.54

Handsfield, R. B., & Nichols, E. L. (2002). *Supply Chain Redesign: Transforming Supply Chains into Integrated Value Systems*. Upper Saddle River, NJ: Prentice Hall.

Harland, C. M., Lamming, R. C., & Zheng, J. J. (2001). A taxonomy of supply networks. *Journal of Supply Chain Management*, 37.

Hess, E. (2002 May). Make advanced planning & scheduling work for your company. *APS*.

Holweg, M., Disney, S., Holmström, J., & Småros, J. (2005). Supply Chain Collaboration: Making Sense of the Strategy Continuum. *European Management Journal*, 23, 170–181. doi:10.1016/j.emj.2005.02.008

Jagdev, H. S., & Thoben, K. D. (2001). Anatomy of enterprise collaborations. *Production Planning and Control*, 12, 437–451. doi:10.1080/09537280110042675

Kennerly, M., & Neely, A (2001 February). Enterprise resource planning: analysing the impact. *Integrated Manufacturing System*, 103-113.

Lee, H. L., & Whang, S. (2001). E-Business and Supply Chain Integration. *Stanford Global Supply Chain Management Forum*. Retrieved from http://www.stanford.edu/group/scforum/Welcome/EB_SCI.pdf

Özbayrak, M., Papadopouloub, T., & Samarasb, E. (2006). A flexible and adaptable planning and control system for an MTO supply chain system. *Robotics and Computer-integrated Manufacturing*, ▪▪▪, 22.

Petroni, A. (2002). Critical factors of MRP implementation in small and medium-sized firms. *International Journal of Operations & Production Management*, 22(3), 329–348. doi:10.1108/01443570210417623

Quinn, F. (2003). The Elusive Goal of Integration. *Supply Chain Management Review*, 7.

Sahin, F., & Robinson, E. P. (2002). Flow coordination and information sharing in supply chains: review, implications and directions for future research. *Decision Sciences*, 33(4), 1–32. doi:10.1111/j.1540-5915.2002.tb01654.x

Schell, D. (2002). Overcoming intricacies of ERP system implementation. *Integrated Solutions*, 2.

Stadtler, H., & Kilger, C. (2005). *Supply Chain Management and Advanced Planning – Concepts, Models, Software and Case Studies* (3rd ed.). Berlin: Springer.

Vollmann, T. E., Berry, W. L., Whybark, D. C., & Jacobs, R. F. (2005). *Manufacturing Planning and Control for Supply Chain Management*. Boston: McGraw-Hill.

Works Management. (2008). *IT in practice Planning & scheduling, Growing in stature*. Retrieved April 2009, from http://www.worksmanagement.co.uk/articles/12830/Growing-in-stature.pdf

Wortmann, J. C. (1998). Evolution of ERP systems. In Bititci, U. S., & Carrie, A. S. (Eds.), *Strategic Management of the manufacturing value chain* (pp. 11–23). Boston, MA: Kluwer Academic.

Compilation of References

Abu-Shanab, E., & Al-Tarawneh, H. (2009). Production Information Systems Usability . In Martins do Amaral, A. (Ed.), *M. Cruz-Cunha, E. Qintela Varajão* (pp. 43–53). Ofir, Portugal: CENTERIS.

Accenture. (2006). Outsourcing Service. Retrieved July 2006, from http://www.accenture.com/Global/Outsourcing/default.htm

Adamson, C., & Venerable, M. (1998). *Data Warehouse Design Solutions*. Danvers, MA: John Wiley & Sons.

Adelsberger, H., Collis, B., & Pawlowski, J. M. (2002). *Handbook on Information Technologies for Education and Training*. Berlin: Springer.

Adelson, E. H. (2000). *Lightness perceptions and lightness illusions. The new cognitive sciences* (Gazzaniga, M., Ed.). 2nd ed.). Cambridge, MA: MIT Press.

AECA. (2007). *Gobierno y responsabilidad social de la empresa*. Madrid: AECA.

AeL Enterprise. (2007). *SIVECO Romania*. Retrieved April 12, 2007, from http://www.advancedelearning.com

Afuah, A. (1998). *Innovation Management*. Oxford, UK: Oxford University Press.

Agarwal, R. (2000). Individual acceptance of information technologies . In Zmud, R. (Ed.), *Framing the domains of IT management* (pp. 85–104). Cincinnati, OH: Pinnaflex Education Resources, Inc.

Agarwal, R., & Prasad, J. (1998). A conceptual and operational definition of personal innovativeness in the domain of information technology. *Information Systems Research, 9*(2), 204–215. doi:10.1287/isre.9.2.204

Agarwal, R., & Prasad, J. (1999). Are Individual Differences Germane to the Acceptance of New Information Technologies? *Decision Sciences, 30*(2), 361–391. doi:10.1111/j.1540-5915.1999.tb01614.x

Agarwal, R., Raha, A. R., & Ghosh, B. (2000). Our experience and learning in ERP implementation. *ACM SIGSOFT Software Engineering Notes, 25*(2).

Agarwal, S., & Studer, R. (2006). Automatic Matchmaking of Web Services. In *International Conference on Web Services (ICWS'06)*.

Agrawal, S., Dashora, Y., Tiwari, M. K., & Son, Y. J. (2008). Interactive Particle Swarm: A Pareto-Adaptive Metaheuristic to Multiobjective Optimization. *IEEE Transactions on Systems, Man and Cybernetics – Part A, 38*(2), 258-277.

Aguinis, H. (2004). *Regression Analysis for Categorical Moderators*. New York: The Guilford Press.

Aickelin, U. (1999). *Genetic Algorithms for Multiple-Choice Problems*. Unpublished doctoral dissertation, University of Wales, Swansea.

Ajzen, I. (1991). The theory of planned behavior. *Organizational Behavior and Human Decision Processes, 50*, 179–211. doi:10.1016/0749-5978(91)90020-T

Ajzen, I. (2002). Perceived behavioral control, self-efficacy, locus of control and the theory of planned behavior. *Journal of Applied Social Psychology, 32*, 1–20. doi:10.1111/j.1559-1816.2002.tb00236.x

Ajzen, I., & Madden, T. J. (1986). Prediction of good-directed behavior: attitudes, intentions and perceived behavioral control. *Journal of Experimental Social Psychology, 22*, 453–474. doi:10.1016/0022-1031(86)90045-4

Akers, S. B. (1956). A graphical approach to production scheduling problems. *Operations Research, 4*, 244–245. doi:10.1287/opre.4.2.244

Akkermans, H., & Van Helden, K. (2002). Vicious and virtuous cycles in ERP implementation: a case study of interrelations between critical success factors. *European Journal of Information Systems, 11*(1), 35–46. doi:10.1057/palgrave/ejis/3000418

Aksin, O. Z., & Harker, P. T. (2003). Capacity sizing in the presence of a common shared resource: Dimensioning an inbound call center. *European Journal of Operational Research, 147*(3), 464–483. doi:10.1016/S0377-2217(02)00274-6

Aksin, O. Z., Véricourt, F., & Karaesmen, F. (2008). Call center outsourcing contract design and choice. *Management Science, 54*(2), 354–368. doi:10.1287/mnsc.1070.0823

Aktunc, O., Dronavallli, S., & Tanik, M. (2008). Rapid prototyping of digital enterprises using content management systems. In *IEEE 2008 Southeastcon* (pp. 231–235).

Alavi, M., & Leidner, D. E. (2001). Review: Knowledge management and knowledge management systems: Conceptual foundations and research issues. *Management Information Systems Quarterly, 25*(1), 107–136. doi:10.2307/3250961

Alberts, L. K. (1993). *YMIR: An Ontology for Engineering Design*. PhD thesis, University of Twente.

Al-Kahtani, M. A., & Sandhu, R. (2002). A model for attribute-based user-role assignment. In *Computer Security Applications Conference 2002* (pp. 353–362).

Allport, F. H. (1962). A structuronomic conception of behavior: Individual and collective. *Journal of Abnormal and Social Psychology, 64*, 3–30. doi:10.1037/h0043563

Al-Mashari, M., Al-Mudimigh, A., & Zairi, M. (2003). Enterprise Resource Planning: a taxonomy of critical factors. *European Journal of Operational Research, 146*, 352–364. doi:10.1016/S0377-2217(02)00554-4

Alshare, K., Grandon, E., & Miller, D. (2004). Antecedents of computer technology usage: considerations of the technology acceptance model in the academic environment. *Journal of Circuits. Systems and Computers, 19*(4), 164–180.

Alter, S. (1999). The effects of State Street on electronic commerce and the Internet: The year in review. *Wilmer Hale*. Retrieved July 25, 2009, from http://www.wilmerhale.com/publications/whPubsDetail.aspx?publication=618

Alvarez, E. (2007). Multi-plant production scheduling in SMEs. *Robotics and Computer-integrated Manufacturing, 23*, 608–613. doi:10.1016/j.rcim.2007.02.006

Alves-Mazzotti, A. J., & Gewandsznajder, F. (1999). *O método nas ciências naturais e sociais: pesquisa quantitativa e qualitativa*. São Paulo, Brasil: Thomson.

Amaral, L., Teixeira, C., & Oliveira, J. (2003). e-Procurement: *Uma reflexão sobre a situação actual em Portugal*. Caparica, Portugal: APDSI.

Ambrose, S. H. (2001). Paleolithic technology and human evolution. *Science, 291*, 1748–1753. doi:10.1126/science.1059487

American National Standards Institute (ANSI). (2007). [Industrial automation systems - Concepts and rules for enterprise models.]. *ISO, 14258*, 1998.

American Psychological Association. (2001). *Publication Manual of the American Psychological Association* (5th ed.). Washington, DC: Author.

Amor, D. (2001). *The E-Business (R)evolution: Living and Working in an Interconnected World* (2nd ed.). Englewood Cliffs, NJ: Prentice Hall.

Anderson, D. (2000). *Managing Information Systems*. New York: Prentice Hall.

Anderson, E. W., & Sullivan, M. W. (1993). The antecedents and consequences of customer satisfaction for firms. *Marketing Science*, *12*, 125–143. doi:10.1287/mksc.12.2.125

Andrade, A., & Rosseti, J. P. (2007). *Governança Corporativa* (3rd ed.). Brasilia, Brasil: Editora Atlas.

Andrés, C. (2001) *Programación de la Producción en Talleres de Flujo Híbridos con Tiempos de Cambio de Partida Dependientes de la Secuencia: Modelos, Métodos y Algoritmos de Resolución: Aplicación a Empresas del Sector Cerámico*. Unpublished doctoral dissertation, Universidad Politécnica de Valencia, Valencia.

Ang, J. S. K., Sum, C. C., & Yeo, L. N. (2002). A multiple-case design methodology for studying MRP success and CSFs. *Information & Management*, *39*(4), 271–281. doi:10.1016/S0378-7206(01)00096-9

Angerman, W. S. (2004). *Coming Full Circle with Boyd's OODA Loop Ideas: An Analysis of Innovation Diffusion and Evolution*. Washington, DC: Storming Media.

Antao, R., et al. (2005). *Quantifying the Value, Effectiveness, Efficiency, and Security of IT Controls*. IT Process Institute. Retrieved from http://www.itpi.org/docs/ITPI_Controls_Bench-marking_Survey_Initial_Findings_v0817.pdf

Arakji, R. Y., & Lang, K.-R. (2007). Digital consumer networks and producer-consumer collaboration: innovation and product development in the digital entertainment industry. In *Proceedings of the 40th Annual Hawaii International Conference on System Sciences (HICSS'07)* (pp. 211c-211c). doi: 10.1109/HICSS.2007.173

Argyris, C. (1977 September). Double Loops Learning in Organizations. *Harvard Business Review*.

Arroyo, J., & Armentano, V. (2005). Genetic local search for multi-objective flowshop scheduling problems. *European Journal of Operational Research*, *167*, 717–738. doi:10.1016/j.ejor.2004.07.017

Artz, K. W. (1999). Buyer-Supplier Performance: The Role of Asset Specificity, Reciprocal Investments and Relational Exchange. *British Journal of Management*, *10*, 113–126. doi:10.1111/1467-8551.00114

Asch, S. E. (1956). Studies of Independence and Submission to Group Pressure. A Minority of One Against a Unanimous Majority. *Psychological Monographs*, 70.

Ashby, W. R. (1956). *An Introduction to Cybernetics*. London: Chapman & Hall.

Aubert, B. A., Patry, M., & Rivard, S. (2005). A framework for information technology outsourcing risk management. *The Data Base for Advances in Information Systems*, *36*(4), 9–28.

Auramaki, E., Lehtinen, E., & Lyytinen, K. (1988, April). A speech-act-based office modeling approach. *ACM Transactions on Office Information Systems*, *6*(2), 126–152. doi:10.1145/45941.214328

Auster, E., & Choo, W. (1994). How Senior Managers Acquire and Use Information in Environmental Scanning. *Information Processing & Management*, *30*(5), 607–618. doi:10.1016/0306-4573(94)90073-6

Avramidis, A. N., & L'Ecuyer, P. (2005). *Modeling and simulation of call centers*. Paper presented at the Proceedings of the 2005 Winter Simulation Conference.

Awalt, D., & McUmber, R. (2004). *Secrets of Great Architects*. Retrieved November 15, 2009, from http://msdn.microsoft.com/en-us/library/aa480041(lightweight).aspx

Ayers, J. B. (2006). *Handbook of supply chain management* (2nd ed.). New York: Auerbach Publications.

Azvine, B., Cui, Z., & Nauck, D. D. (2005). Towards real-time business intelligence. *BT Technology Journal*, *23*(3), 214–225. doi:10.1007/s10550-005-0043-0

Azvine, B., Cui, Z., Nauck, D. D., & Majeed, B. (2006). *Real Time Business Intelligence for the Adaptive Enterprise*.

Bacon, C. J., & Fitzgerald, B. (2001). A systemic framework for the field of information systems. *The Data Base for Advances in Information Systems*, *32*(2), 46–67.

Bagchi, T. P. (1999). *Multiobjective Scheduling by Genetic Algorithms*. Dordrecht, The Netherlands: Kluwer Academic Publishers.

Bahli, B., & Rivard, S. (2003a). A Validation of Measures Associated with the Risk Factors in Information Technology Outsourcing. In *Proceedings of the 36th Annual Hawaii International Conference on System Sciences* (Vol. 8, pp. 269). Washington, DC: IEEE Computer Society.

Bahli, B., & Rivard, S. (2003b). The information technology outsourcing risk: a transaction cost and agency theory-based perspective. *Journal of Information Technology*, *18*(3), 211–221. doi:10.1080/0268396032000130214

Baker, K. R. (1975). A comparative study of flow shop algorithms. *Operations Research*, *23*, 62–73. doi:10.1287/opre.23.1.62

Bakos, J. Y., & Brynjolfsson, E. (1993). Information technology, incentives, and the optimal number of suppliers. *Journal of Management Information Systems*, *10*(2), 37–53.

Balakrishnan, V., & Das, A. (2009). Analysis of critical problems in ERP implementation to enhance SOA for energy and utilities - a case study. In *SEFBIS Professional Journal of the Scientific and Educational Forum on Business Information Systems* (pp. 18-29).

Ballantine, J., & Stray, S. (1999). *Information Systems and Other Capital Investments: evaluation practices compared*. Logistics Information Management.

Baltzan, P., & Phillips, A. (2008). *Business Driven Information Systems*. New York: McGraw-Hill/Irwin.

Barabba, V. (2004). *Surviving Transformation: Lessons from GM's Surprising Turnaround*. Oxford, UK: Oxford University Press.

Barbara, Wixom, & Watson. (2001). An Empirical Investigation of the Factors Affecting Data Warehousing Success. *Management Information Systems Quarterly*, *25*(1), 17–41. doi:10.2307/3250957

Barbosa, R. (2002). Inteligência Empresarial: uma avaliação de fontes de informação sobre o ambiente organizacional externo. *DataGramaZero, Revista de Ciência da Informação, 3*(6). Retrieved October 2007, from http://www.dgz.org.br/dez02/F_I_art.htm

Barlow, H. A., & Burke, M. E. (1999). The organization as an information system: Signposts for new investigations. *East European Quarterly, 4*, 549–556.

Barn, B. S., & Oussena, S. (2009). BPMN, Toolsets, and Methodology: A Case Study of Business Process Management in Higher Education. In G. A. Papadopoulos et al. (Eds.), *Information System development* (pp. 685-693). Berlin: Springer Science + Business Media. doi. 10.1007/b137171_71

Barothy, T., Peterhans, M., & Bauknecht, K. (1995). Business Process Reengineering: emergence of a new research field. *ACM SIGOIS Bulletin, 16*, 3–10. doi:10.1145/209891.209892

Baroudi, J. J., Olson, M. H., & Ives, B. (1986). An empirical study of the impact of user involvement on system usage and information satisfaction. *Communications of the ACM, 29*, 232–238. doi:10.1145/5666.5669

Baumeister, R. F., Campbell, J. D., Krueger, J. I., & Vohs, K. D. (2005 January). Exploding the self-esteem myth. *Scientific American.*

Ben Cheikh, A., Saidi, R., Front, A., & Rieu, D. (2009). Variability integration in multi-view business process design. In *Proceedings of the 13th IBIMA conference on Knowledge management and Innovation in Advancing Economics*, Marrakesh, Morocco.

Benjamins, R., & Gomez Perez, A. (1999). Overview of Knowledge, Sharing and Reuse Components: Ontologies and Problem-Solving Methods. In *Proceedings of the IJCAI-99 workshop on Ontologies and Problem-Solving Methods (KRR5)*, Stockholm, Sweden (pp. 1-15).

Benzecri, J. P. (1979). Sur le calcul des taux d'inertie dans l'analyse d'un questionnaire. *Les Cahiers de l'Analyse des Donnees, 3*, 377–384.

Berners-Lee, T. (2005). *Uniform Resource Identifier (URI), Generic Syntax*. Retrieved from http://labs.apache.org/webarch/uri/rfc/rfc3986.html/

Berners-Lee, T., Hendler, J., & Lassila, O. (2001, May 17). The Semantic Web. *Scientific American Magazine*.

Bernroider, E. (2008). IT governance for enterprise resource planning supported by the DeLone-McLean model of information system success. *Information & Management, 45*(5), 257–269. doi:10.1016/j.im.2007.11.004

Bernroider, E. W. N., & Leseure, M. J. (2005). *Enterprise resource planning (ERP) diffusion and characteristics according to the system's lifecycle: A comparative view of small-to-medium sized and large enterprises*. Working papers on information processing and Information Management. Institute of information processing and information management. Vienna University of Economics and Business Administration.

Bernroider, E., & Koch, S. (2001). ERP selection process in midsize and large organizations. *Business Process Management Journal, 7*(3), 251–257. doi:10.1108/14637150110392746

Bernson, S., & Standing, C. (2008). *Information Systems: A Business Approach*. New York: John Wiley and Sons.

Betz, C. T. (2007). *Architecture and Patterns for IT Service Management, Resource Planning, and Governance: making shoes for the Cobbler's children*. San Francisco, CA: Morgan Kaufman Publishers.

Beyerlein, M., Freedmau, S., McGee, C., & Moran, L. (2003). *Beyond Teams Building: The Collaborative Organization*. San Francisco: Jossey-bass/Pfeiffer.

Bhattacharya, S., Behara, R. S., & Gundersen, D. E. (2003). Business risk perspectives on information systems outsourcing. *International Journal of Accounting Information Systems, 4*, 75–93. doi:10.1016/S1467-0895(03)00004-6

Bhattacherjee, A. (2001). Understanding information systems continuance: an expectation–confirmation model. *Management Information Systems Quarterly, 25*, 351–370. doi:10.2307/3250921

Bhattacherjee, A., & Premkumar, G. (2004). Understanding changes in belief and attitude toward information technology usage: A theoretical model and longitudinal test. *Management Information Systems Quarterly, 28*(2), 229–254.

Bhattacherjee, A., & Sanford, C. (2006). Influence process for information acceptance: An elaboration likelihood model. *Management Information Systems Quarterly, 28*(4), 805–825.

Biere, M. (2003). *Business Intelligence for the Enterprise*. New York: IBM Press.

Bingi, P., Sharma, M. K., & Godla, J. K. (1999). Critical issues affecting an ERP implementation. *Information Systems Management, 16*(3), 7. doi: 1907155

Bio, S. R. (1996). *Sistemas de Informação: um enfoque gerencial*. São Paulo, Brasil: Atlas.

Blazewicz, J., Ecker, K., Pesch, E., Schmidt, G., & Weglarz, J. (2007). *Handbook on Scheduling*. Berlin: Springer.

Bloom, N., Dorgan, S., Dowdy, J., & Van Reenen, J. (2007). Management practice and productivity. *The Quarterly Journal of Economics, 122*(4), 1351–1408. doi:10.1162/qjec.2007.122.4.1351

Bohr, N. (1955). Science and the unity of knowledge . In Leary, L. (Ed.), *The unity of knowledge* (pp. 44–62). New York: Doubleday.

Bolloju, N., Khalifa, M., & Turban, E. (2002). Integrating knowledge management into enterprise environments for the next generation decision support. *Decision Support Systems, 33*, 163–176. doi:10.1016/S0167-9236(01)00142-7

Boltanski, L., & Thevenot, L. (1991). *De la justification, les économies de grandeur*. Paris: Gallimard.

Booth, D., Champion, I. M., Ferris, C., Haas, H., McCabe, F., Newcomer, E., & Orchard, D. (2004). *Web Services Architecture*. Retrieved from http://www.w3.org/TR/ws-arch/

Borgman, C. L. (1989). All users of information retrieval systems are not created equal: an exploration into individual differences. *Information Processing and Management: an International Journal*, 25(3), 237–251. doi:10.1016/0306-4573(89)90042-3

Borst, W. N. (1997). *Construction of Engineering Ontologies*. Enshede, The Netherlands: Centre for Telematica and Information Technology, University of Twente.

Botta-Genoulaz, V., & Millet, P. A. (2005). A Classification for Better Use of ERP Systems. *Computers in Industry*, 56(6), 537–587.

Botta-Genoulaz, V., Millet, P.-A., & Grabot, B. (2005). A survey on the recent reserach literature on ERP systems. *Computers in Industry*, 56(6), 510–522. doi:10.1016/j.compind.2005.02.004

Bradbury, J. A., Branch, K. M., & Malone, E. L. (2003). *An evaluation of DOE-EM Public Participation Programs (PNNL-14200)*. Richland, WA: Pacific Northwest National Laboratory.

Bradley, L., & Stewart, K. (2002). A Delphi study of the drivers and inhibitors of Internet banking. *International Journal of Bank Marketing*, 20, 250–260. doi:10.1108/02652320210446715

Brancheau, J. C., & Wetherbe, J. C. (1990). The adoption of spreadsheet software: testing innovation diffusion theory in the context of end-user computing. *Information Systems Research*, 1(2), 115–143. doi:10.1287/isre.1.2.115

Brehm, N., & Marx Gómez, J. (2005). Standardization approach for Federated ERP systems based on Web Services. In *1st International Workshop on Engineering Service Compositions*, Amsterdam.

Brehm, N., & Marx Gómez, J. (2007). The Web Service-based combination of data and logic integration in Federated ERP systems. In *Proceedings of 18th IRMA International Conference - Managing Worldwide Operations and Communications with Information Technology (IRMA'2007)*, Vancouver, Canada (pp. 1559-1564).

Brehm, N., Lübke, D., & Marx Gómez, J. (2007). Federated Enterprise Resource Planning (FERP) System . In *Handbook of Enterprise Systems Architecture in Practice* (pp. 294–297). Hershey, PA: IGI Global.

Brehm, N., Mahmoud, T., Marx-Gomez, J., & Memari, A. (2008). Towards Intelligent Discovery of Enterprise Architecture Services (IDEAS). *Journal of Enterprise Architecture*, 4(3), 26–37.

Brehm, N., Marx Gómez, J., & Strack, H. (2007). Request-Response-Evaluation Infrastructure for trusted Web Service-based ERP Systems . In Rautenstrauch, C. (Ed.), *Die Zukunft der Anwendungssoftware – die Anwendungssoftware der Zukunft* (pp. 83–93). Aachen, Germany: Shaker.

Breitner, C. A. (1997). *Data Warehousing and OLAP: Delivering Just-In-Time Information for Decision Support*.

Brissaud, D., & Tichkiewitch, S. (2000). Innovation and manufacturability analysis in an integrated design context. *Computers in Industry*, 43, 111–121. doi:10.1016/S0166-3615(00)00061-0

Broadbent, M., & Kitzis, E. (2004). *The New CIO Leader*. Cambridge, MA: Harvard Business School Press.

Bromiley, P., & Cummings, L. L. (1991). *Transaction Costs in Organizations with Trust*. Working Paper, Department of Strategic Management and Organization, Carlson School of Management, University of Minnesota.

Brooks, P. (2006). *Metrics for IT Service Management*. San Antonio, TX: Van Haren Publishing.

Brown, C. A. (2007). The Opt-in/Opt-out Feature in a Multi-Stage Delphi Method Study. *International Journal of Social Research Methodology*, 10(2), 135–144. doi:10.1080/13645570701334084

Brown, G., Keegan, J., Vigus, B., & Wood, K. (2001). The Kellogg company optimizes production, inventory and distribution. *Interfaces*, 31(6), 1–15.

Brown, J., & Duguid, P. (2000). *The Social Life of Information*. Boston: Harvard Business Press.

Brown, R. (2008). *Plan B 3.0, Mobilizing to Save Civilization*. New York: Earth Policy Institute.

Brucker, P. (1988). An efficient algorithm for the job-shop problem with two jobs. *Computing, 40*, 353–359. doi:10.1007/BF02276919

Brucker, P. (2004). *Scheduling Algorithms*. Berlin: Springer.

Bruijn, J. D., Domingue, G., Fensel, D., Lausen, H., Polleres, A., Roman, D., & Stollberg, M. (2007). *Enabling Semantic Web Services, the Web Service Modeling Ontology*. Berlin: Springer.

Brusoni, S., & Tronchetti-Provera, S. (2005). The limits to specialization: Problem solving and coordination in 'Modular Networks.' [Retrieved from ABI database.]. *Organization Studies, 26*(12), 1885–1907. doi:10.1177/0170840605059161

Brynjolfsson, E., & Hitt, L. M. (1997). Information technology and internal firm organization: an exploratory analysis. [Retrieved from ABI database.]. *Journal of Management Information Systems, 14*(2), 81–101.

Brynjolfsson, E., Malone, T. W., Gurbaxani, V., & Kambil, A. (1994). Does information technology lead to smaller firms? [Retrieved from JSTOR database.]. *Management Science, 40*(12), 1628–1650. doi:10.1287/mnsc.40.12.1628

Bülbül, K., Kaminsky, P., & Yano, C. (2004). Flow shop scheduling with earliness, tardiness, and intermediate inventory holding costs. *Naval Research Logistics, 51*, 407–445. doi:10.1002/nav.20000

Burke, E. K., Landa-Silva, J. D., & Soubeiga, E. (2003). Hyperheuristic Approaches for Multiobjective Optimization. In *The Fifth Metaheuristics International Conference* (pp. 052.1-052.6). Kyoto: The University of Tokyo.

Burstein, F., & Holsapple, C. (Eds.). (2008). *Handbook on Decision Support Systems*. Berlin: Springer-Verlag.

Burstein, M., Martin, D., McDermott, D., McGuinness, D., McIlraith, S., Paolucci, M., et al. (2004). Bringing Semantics to Web Services: The OWL-S Approach. In *Proceedings of the First International Workshop on Semantic Web Services and Web Process Composition (SWSWPC 2004)*, July 6-9, San Diego, California, USA. Retrieved from http://www.daml.org/services/owl-s

Burton-Jones, A., & Gallivan, M. J. (2004). *Towards a deeper understanding of system usage in organizations: a multilevel perspective*. Working paper, Computer Information Systems Department J. Mack Robinson College of Business Georgia State University.

Burton-Jones, A., & Gallivan, M. J. (2007). Toward a deeper understanding of system usage in organizations: A multilevel perspective. *Management Information Systems Quarterly, 31*(4), 657–679.

Busemeyer, J., & Trueblood, J. (2009). Comparison of quantum and Bayesian inference models. In P. Bruza, D. A. Sofge, W. F. Lawless, K. Van Rijsbergen & M. Klusch (Eds.), *Quantum Interaction. Third International Symposium, QI-2009*. Berlin: Springer-Verlag.

Bussler, C., & Fensel, D. (2002). The Web Service Modeling Framework WSMF. *Electronic Commerce Research and Applications, 1*(2).

Bussler, C., Fensel, D., Keller, U., Kifer, M., Lausen, H., Oren, E., & Roman, D. (2004). *Web Service Modeling Ontology (WSMO)*. Retrieved from http://www.wsmo.org/2004/d2/v1.0/

Cabral, L., Domingue, J., Hakimpour, F., Motta, E., & Sell, D. (2004). A platform and infrastructure for creating WSMO based Semantic Web Services . In *WSMO Implementation Workshop*. Frankfurt, Germany: IRS III.

Cabral, L., Domingue, J., Hakimpour, F., Motta, E., & Sell, D. (2005). Semantic Web Service Composition in IRS III: The Structured Approach. In *International IEEE Conference on E-Commerce Technology*, Universität Münchin, Germany.

Cadbury, A. (1992). *Report of the Committee on the Financial Aspects of Corporate Governance*. G. P. Publishing.

Calder, A. (2007). *IT Governance Pocket Guide*. Rolling Meadows, IL: IT Governance Publishing.

Campbell, H. G., Dudek, R. A., & Smith, M. L. (1970). A Heuristic Algorithm for the n Job, m Machine Sequencing Problem. *Management Science, 16*(10), 630–637. doi:10.1287/mnsc.16.10.B630

Campos, M. (1998). *Questões Chave da Gestão de Sistemas de Informação: Avaliação da Situação Nacional*. Unpublished Master dissertation, Minho University, Portugal.

Campos, V. (1992). *TQC: Controle da qualidade total (no estilo Japonês)*. Rio de Janeiro, Brasil: Block.

Campos, V. (2002). *Gerenciamento pelas Diretrizes (Hoshin Kanri)*. Belo Horizonte, Brasil: Editora de Desenvolvimento Gerencial.

Capgemini. (2006). *Outsourcing*. Retrieved July 2006, from http://www.capgemini.com/services/outsourcing/

Cardoso, J. (2000). *Unified Customer Interaction™: Gestão do Relacionamento num Ambiente Misto de Interacção Self e Assistida*. Lisboa: Centro Atlântico.

Cardoso, J., Hepp, M., & Lytras, M. (2007). *The Semantic Web: Real-World Applications from Industry*. Berlin: Springer.

Carley, K. M. (2002). Simulating society: The tension between transparency and veridicality. In *Social Agents: ecology, exchange, and evolution*. Chicago: University of Chicago, Argonne National Laboratory.

Carlier, J., & Rebaï, I. (1996). Two branch and bound algorithms for the permutation flow shop problem. *European Journal of Operational Research, 90*, 238–251. doi:10.1016/0377-2217(95)00352-5

Carter, S. (2007). *The New Language of Business. SOA & WEB 2.0*. New York: IBM Press.

Carton, F., & Adam, F. (2008). ERP and Functional Fit: How Integrated Systems Fail to Provide Improved Control. *The Electronic Journal Information Systems Evaluation, 11*(2), 51 – 60. Retrieved from http://www.ejise.com

Casati, F., & Shan, M.-C. (2001 May). Models and Languages for Describing and Discovering E-Services (Tutorial). In *Proceedings of the International ACM SIGMOD Conference on Management of Data*, Santa Barbara, CA.

CE@ANPART. (2009). *Partnership for Excellence Research in Developing Entrepreneurial Skills and a Competitive Human Capital in the Innovation and Knowledge-Based Economy and Society*. Retrieved December 12, 2009, from http://www.ceanpart.lx.ro/index.htm

Cebeci, U. (2009). Fuzzy AHP-based Decision Support System for Selecting ERP Systems in Textile Industry by Using Balanced Scorecard. *Expert Systems with Applications, 36*(5), 8900–8909. doi:10.1016/j.eswa.2008.11.046

Chan, J. O. (2005). Toward a unified view of customer relationship management. *The Journal of American Academy of Business, 6*(1), 32–38.

Chandramouli, R. (2001). A framework for multiple authorization types in a healthcare application system. In *17th Annual Computer Security Applications Conference (ACSAC)* (pp. 137-148).

Chang, P. C., Chen, S. H., & Liu, C. H. (2007). Sub-population genetic algorithm with mining gene structures for multiobjective flowshop scheduling problems. *Expert Systems with Applications, 33*, 762–777. doi:10.1016/j.eswa.2006.06.019

Chang, P. C., Hsieh, J.-C., & Lin, S. G. (2002). The development of gradual priority weighting approach for the multi-objective flowshop scheduling problem. *International Journal of Production Economics, 79*, 171–183. doi:10.1016/S0925-5273(02)00141-X

Chang, S. (2004). ERP life cycle implementation, management and support: implications for practice and research. In *Proceedings of the 37th Annual Hawaii International Conference on System Sciences (HICCS 04)*, Big Island, Hawaii (pp. 80227-80237).

Chankong, V., & Haimes, Y. Y. (1983). *Multiobjective Decision Making Theory and Methodology*. New York: Elsevier Science.

Charnes, A., & Cooper, W. (1961). *Management Models and Industrial Applications of Linear Programming.* New York: John Wiley and Sons.

Chatterjee, D., Grewal, R., & Sambamurthy, V. (2002). Shaping up for ecommerce: Institutional enablers of the organizational assimilation of Web Technologies. *Management Information Systems Quarterly, 26*(2), 65–89. doi:10.2307/4132321

Chaudhuri, S., & Dayal, U. (1997). An overview of data warehousing and OLAP technology. *SIGMOD Record, 26*(1), 65–74. doi:10.1145/248603.248616

Checkland, P. (2000). Soft systems methodology: a thirty year retrospective. *Systems Research, 17*(S1), S11–S58. doi:10.1002/1099-1743(200011)17:1+<::AID-SRES374>3.0.CO;2-O

Chen, X., Fuh, J., Wong, Y., Lu, Y., Li, W., & Qiu, Z. (2005). An Adaptable Model for Distributed Collaborative Design. *Computer-Aided Design & Applications, 2*(1-4), 47–55.

Chen, Y., & Chien, S. (2009). Investigating factors influencing the use of E-Government service. In *Proceedings of the Americas Conference on Information Systems* (pp. 695).

Cheung, C., & Limayem, M. (2005). Understanding continuance of advanced internet-based learning technologies: the role of satisfaction, prior behavior, and habit. In *Proceeding of Pacific Asia Conference on Information Systems* (pp. 1323-1332).

Chi, L., Hartono, E., Holsapple, C., & Li, X. (2008). Organizational decision support systems: Parameters and benefits . In Burstein, F., & Holsapple, C. (Eds.), *Handbook on Decision Support Systems 1: Basic Themes* (pp. 433–468). Berlin: Springer-Verlag. doi:10.1007/978-3-540-48713-5_22

Chikofsky, E., & Cross, J. I. (1990). Reverse-engineering and design recovery: a taxonomy. *IEEE Software, 7*, 13–17. doi:10.1109/52.43044

Chitura, T., Mupemhi, S., Dube, T., & Bolongkikit, J. (2008). Barriers to Electronic Commerce Adoption in Small and Medium Enterprises: A Critical Literature Review. *Journal of Internet Banking and Commerce, 13*(2), 1–13.

Choo, W. (2002). *Information management for the intelligent organization: the art of scanning the environment.* Medford, NJ: Information Today, Inc.

Choo, W. (2006). *A Organização do conhecimento: como as organizações usam a informação para criar significado, construir conhecimento e tomar decisões.* São Paulo, Brasil: Editora Senac São Paulo.

Chou, S. W., & Chen, Pi-Yu, (2009). The influence of individual difference on continuance intentions of enterprise resource planning (ERP). *Int. J. Human-Computer Studies,* 1-31.

Christensen, E., Curbera, F., Meredith, G., & Weerawarana, S. (2001). *Web services description language (WSDL) 1.1.* Retrieved from http://www.w3.org/TR/2001/NOTE-wsdl-20010315

CIMA. (2003). *Enterprise Governance. Getting the balance right. CIMA.* IFAC.

CIMdata. (2002). *Product Lifecycle Management. Empowering the Future of Business.* CIMdata report. Retrieved September 23, 2009, from http://www.cimdata.com/PLM/plm.htm

Cimpian, E., Moran, M., Oren, E., Vitvar, T., & Zaremba, M. (2005). *Overview and Scope of WSMX.* Technical report. Retrieved from http://www.wsmo.org/TR/d13/d13.0/v0.2/

Ciurana, J., Garcia-Romeu, M., Ferrer, I., & Casadesus, M. (2008). A Model for Integrating Process Planning and Production Planning and Control in Machining Processes. *Robotics and Computer-integrated Manufacturing, 24*, 532–544. doi:10.1016/j.rcim.2007.07.013

Clement, L., Hately, A., von Riegen, C., & Rogers, T. (2004). *UDDI version 3.0.2.* UDDI Spec Technical Committee Draft. Retrieved from http://uddi.org/pubs/uddi_v3.htm

Coase, R. H. (1937). The Nature of the Firm. [Retrieved from ABI database.]. *Economica*, *4*, 386–405. doi:10.1111/j.1468-0335.1937.tb00002.x

Cockburn, A. (1998). Basic use case template. *Humans and technology.* Retrieved from http://members.aol.com/acockburn/papers/uctempla.htm

Coello, C., & Mariano, C. (2002). Algorithms and Multiple Objective . In Ehrgott, M., & Gandibleux, X. (Eds.), *Multiple Criteria Optimization. State of the Art Annotated Bibliographic Surveys* (pp. 277–331). Boston: Kluwer Academic Publishers.

Cohen, E. (Ed.). (2002). *Challenges of Information Technology Education in the 21st Century.* Hershey, PA: Idea Group Publishing.

Cohen, H. S. (1980). *Measuring and modeling user satisfaction with telephone switching and transmission performance.* Paper presented at the 9th International Symposium on Human Factors in Telecommunications, Red Bank, New Jersey.

Cohen, L. (1995). *Time-frequency analysis: theory and applications.* Upper Saddle River, NJ: Prentice Hall Signal Processing Series.

Cohen, W., & Levinthal, D. (1990). Absorptive Capacity: A new perspective on learning and innovation. *Administrative Science Quarterly*, *35*(1), 128–152. doi:10.2307/2393553

Collins, J. (2001). *Why some companies make the leap... and others don't.* Sydney, Australia: Random House.

Cooper, R. B., & Zmud, R. W. (1990). Information Technology Implementation Research: A Technological Diffusion Approach. *Management Science*, *36*(2), 123–139. doi:10.1287/mnsc.36.2.123

Coral, E., Ogliari, A., & de Abreu, A. F. (2008). *Gestão Integrada da Inovação: Estratégia, Organização e Desenvolvimento de Produtos.* Brasilia, Brasil: Editora Atlas.

COSO. (1992). *Internal Control - Integrated Framework.* Washington, DC: COSO.

COSO. (2004). *Enterprise Risk Management - Integrated Framework (Executive Summary).* Washington, DC: COSO.

Courtois, A., Pillet, M., & Martin-Bonnefous, C. (2006). *Gestão da Produção* (5th ed.). Lisboa, Portugal: Lidel.

Crounse, B. (2004). Collaborative Health-Better information better care-A special presentation for Microsoft Partners.

Cruz, C., Rodrigues, E., & Nagano, M. (2007) Análise do relacionamento da gestão do conhecimento e as práticas para melhoria da qualidade: Estudo de caso em uma empresa de alta tecnologia. *Revista Gestão Industrial*, *3*(2), 45-56. Retrieved Febraury 2008, from http://www.pg.cefetpr.br/ppgep/revista/revista2007/vol2/artigo/V3N2B4.pdf

Curtis, B., Kellner, M., & Over, J. (1992). Process Modeling. *Communications of the ACM*, *35*, 75–90. doi:10.1145/130994.130998

Curtis, G., & Cobham, D. (2008). *Business Information Systems: Analysis, Design, and Practice.* New York: Financial Times Management.

Czyzak, P., & Jaszkiewicz, A. (1998). Pareto Simulated Annealing–A metaheuristic technique for multiple objective combinatorial optimization. *Journal on Multi-Criteria Decision Analysis*, *7*, 34–47. doi:10.1002/(SICI)1099-1360(199801)7:1<34::AID-MCDA161>3.0.CO;2-6

Dabholkar, P. A., Shepard, C. D., & Thorpe, D. I. (2000). A comprehensive framework for service quality: An investigation of critical conceptual and measurement issues through a longitudinal study. *Journal of Retailing*, *76*, 139–173. doi:10.1016/S0022-4359(00)00029-4

Daft, R. (2003). *Management.* New York: Dryden Press.

Daft, R. L., & Lengel, R. H. (1986). Organizational information requirements, media richness and structural design. *Management Science*, *32*(5), 554–571. doi:10.1287/mnsc.32.5.554

Damij, N., Damij, T., Grad, J., & Jelenc, F. (2008). A methodology for business process improvement and information system development. In *Information and Software Technology*. Amsterdam: Elsevier. doi:10.1016/jinfsof.2007.11.004

Danaher, P. J., & Rust, R. T. (1996). Indirect financial benefits from service quality. *Quality Management Journal*, 3(2), 63–75.

Danese, P., Romano, P., & Vinelli, A. (2004). Managing business processes across supply networks: the role of coordination mechanisms. *Journal of Purchasing and Supply Management*, 10, 165–177. doi:10.1016/j.pursup.2004.11.002

Daniel, E. M., & White, A. (2005). The future of inter-organisational system linkages: findings of an international Delphi study. *European Journal of Information Systems*, 14(2), 188–203. doi:10.1057/palgrave.ejis.3000529

Daniels, R. L., & Chambers, R. J. (1990). Multiobjective flow-shop scheduling. *Naval Research Logistics*, 37, 981–995. doi:10.1002/1520-6750(199012)37:6<981::AID-NAV3220370617>3.0.CO;2-H

Davenport, T. (1996). *Holistic management of mega-package change: The case of SAP*. Boston: Center of Business Innovation, Ernest & Young LLP.

Davenport, T. (1998). *Ecologia da Informação: por que só a tecnologia não basta para o sucesso na era da informação*. São Paulo, Brasil: Futura.

Davenport, T. (1998). Putting the Enterprise into the Enterprise System. *Harvard Business Review*, 76(4), 121–131.

Davenport, T. (2000). *Mission Critical*. Boston: Harvard Business School Press.

Davenport, T. (2000). *Mission Critical: Realizing the Promise of Enterprise Systems*. Boston: Harvard Business School Press.

Davenport, T. H., & Prusak, L. (2000). *Working Knowledge*. Boston, MA: Harvard Business School Press.

Davenport, T., & Prusak, L. (1998). *Conhecimento Empresarial: como as organizações gerenciam o seu capital intelectual*. Rio de Janeiro, Brasil: Campus.

Davis, F. D. (1989). Perceived usefulness perceived ease of use, and user acceptance of information technology. *Management Information Systems Quarterly*, 13(3), 319–340. doi:10.2307/249008

Davis, F. D., Bagozzi, R. P., & Warshaw, P. R. (1989). User acceptance of computer technology: a comparison of two theoretical models. *Management Science*, 35, 982–1003. doi:10.1287/mnsc.35.8.982

Davis. (1993). User acceptance of information technology: system characteristics, user perceptions and behavioral impacts. *International Journal of Man - Machine Studies, 38*, 475-487.

Dawes, R. M., Faust, D., & Meehl, P. E. (1989). Clinical versus actuarial judgment. *Science, 243*(4899), 1668–1674. doi:10.1126/science.2648573

De Boer, F. S., Bonsangue, M. M., Groenewegen, L. P. J., Stam, A. W., Stevens, S., & Van Der Torre, L. (2005). Change impact analysis of enterprise architectures. In *Proceedings of the 2005 IEEE International Conference on Information Reuse and Integration (IRI-2005)* (pp. 15-17).

de Oliveira, A. (2004). *Análise do investimento em sistemas e tecnologias da informação e comunicação*. Lisboa, Portugal: Sílabo.

De Pablos Heredero, C., & De Pablos Heredero, M. (2008). Elements that can explain the degree of success of ERP systems implementation. In Cruz-Cunha, M. M. (Ed.), *Social, Managerial and Organizational Dimensions of Enterprise Information Systems*. Hershey, PA: IGI Publishing.

Dekkers, J., Versendaal, J., & Batenburg, R. (2007). *Organizing for Business intelligence: A Framework for aligning the use and development of information*. Paper presented at the Merging and Emerging Technologies, Processes and Institutions.

Deloitte Consulting. (1999). *ERPs Second Wave* [Report]. Deloitte Consulting. Retrieved from http://www.deloitte.com

Deloitte. (2003). *Inside Outsourcing: The What, who, and how of Outsourcing IT-intensive processes*. New York: Deloitte Consulting.

Deloitte. (2005). *Calling a Change in the Outsourcing Market: The Realities for the World's Largest Organizations*. New York: Deloitte Consulting.

DeLone, W. H., & McLean, E. R. (1992). Information Systems Success: The Quest for the Dependent Variable. *Information Systems Research, 3*(1), 60–95. doi:10.1287/isre.3.1.60

DeLone, W. H., & McLean, E. R. (2003). The DeLone and McLean model of information systems success: A ten-year update. *Journal of Management Information Systems, 19*(4), 9–30.

DeLone, W., & McLean, E. (1992). Information Systems Success: The Quest for the Dependent Variable. *Information Systems Research, 3*(1), 60–95. doi:10.1287/isre.3.1.60

Demarco, T. (1997). *The Deadline*. New York: Dorset House Publishing.

den Hamer, P. (2005). *De organisatie van Business Intelligence*. Den Haag, Nederland: SDU Publishers.

Denker, A. (2005). The Challenge of Large IT Projects . In *Proceedings of World Academy of Science* (Vol. 9). Engineering and Technology.

Department of Statistics. Jordan. (2008). *Statistics related to the Jordanian Industrial Sector*. Retrieved from http://www.dos.gov.jo/dos_home_a/gpd.htm

Deslauriers, J. P. (1991). *Recherce qualitative: Guide Pratique*. New York: McGraw-Hill.

Devaraj, S., & Kohli, R. (2003). Performance Impacts of Information Technology: Is Actual Usage the Missing Link? *Management Science, 49*, 273–289. doi:10.1287/mnsc.49.3.273.12736

Dhar, S., & Balakrishnan, B. (2006). Risks, benefits, and challenges in global IT outsourcing: Perspectives and practices. *Journal of Global Information Management, 14*(3), 39–69.

Dibbern, J., Goles, T., Hirschheim, R., & Jayatilaka, B. (2004). Information systems outsourcing: a survey and analysis of the literature. *The Data Base for Advances in Information Systems, 35*(4), 6–102.

Dietz, J. L. (2006). *Enterprise Ontology: Theory and Methodology* (1st ed.). Berlin: Springer. doi:10.1007/3-540-33149-2

Dietz, J. L. G. (2006). *Enterprise Ontology: Theory and Methodology*. Delft, The Netherlands: Springer. doi:10.1007/3-540-33149-2

DiMaggio, P. J., & Powell, W. W. (1983). The Iron Cage Revisited: Institutional Isomorphism and Collective Rationality in Organizational Fields. *American Sociological Review, 48*(2), 147–160. doi:10.2307/2095101

Dishaw, M. T., & Strong, D. M. (1999). Extending the technology acceptance model with task–technology fit constructs. *Information & Management, 36*(1), 9–21. doi:10.1016/S0378-7206(98)00101-3

Dixon, D. R. (1999). The behavioral side of information technology. *International Journal of Medical Informatics, 56*(1-3), 117–123. doi:10.1016/S1386-5056(99)00037-4

Dorn, J., Girsch, M., Skele, G., & Slany, W. (1996). Comparison of iterative improvement techniques for schedule optimization. *European Journal of Operational Research, 94*, 349–361. doi:10.1016/0377-2217(95)00162-X

Dos Santos, B. (1991). Justifying Investments in New Information Technologies. *Journal of Management Information Systems*.

Draghici, A., & Draghici, G. (2006). New business requirements in the knowledge-based society . In Cunha, M. M., Cortes, B. C., & Putnik, G. D. (Eds.), *Adaptive Technologies and Business Integration: Social, Managerial and Organizational Dimensions* (pp. 2111–2243). Hershey, PA: Idea Group Publishing.

Draghici, A., & Draghici, G. (2007). Romanian Research Network for Integrated Product and Process Engineering. In F.-L. Krause (Ed.), *The Future of Product Development, Proceedings of the 17ᵗʰ CIRP Design Conference* (pp. 341-350). Berlin: Springer.

Draghici, A., & Izvercianu, M. (2009). The University Entrepreneurship Education. *Review of Management and Economic Engineering, 8*(1), 27–35.

Draghici, A., Foldvary-Schramko, K., Vartolomei, M., & Suciu, S. (2009). Exploring Trans-University Knowledge Transfer - A New Approach for Knowledge Management in Engineering Education. In C. Rusu (Ed.), *Management of Technological Changes: Proceedings of the 6th International Conference on Management of Technological Changes* (Vol. 2, pp. 461-464). Alexandroupolis, Greece: Democritus University of Thrace.

Draghici, A., Izvercianu, M., & Draghici, G. (2009). Virtual Center for Entrepreneurial Competencies Assessment and Development – Preliminary Architecture Design. In M. M. Cruz-Cunha, J. E. Quintela Varajão, L. A. Martins do Amaral (Eds.), *Proceedings of the CENTERIS 2009 - Conference on ENTERprise Information Systems – aligning technology, organization and people* (pp. 153-164). Barcelos, Portugal: Instituto Politecnico do Cavado e do Ave.

Draghici, A., Vartolomei, M., Foldvary-Schramko, K., & Suciu, S. (2009). Entrepreneurial University Development through the Knowledge Sharing Culture Development. In C. Rusu (Ed.), *Management of Technological Changes: Proceedings of the 6th International Conference on Management of Technological Changes* (Vol. 2, pp. 465-468). Alexandroupolis, Greece: Democritus University of Thrace.

Draghici, G. (1999). *Ingineria integrata a produselor*. Timisoara, Romania: Eurobit Publisher.

Draghici, G., Savii, G., & Draghici, A. (2007). Platform for Collaborative Product and Processes Development. In B. Katalinic (Ed.), *Annals of DAAAM for 2007 & Proceedings of the 18th International DAAAM Symposium* (pp. 253-254). Vienna, Austria: DAAAM International.

Draghici, G., Savii, G., & Draghici, A. (2008). Building a Collaborative Product Development Network. In *Design Synthesis, Conference abstracts of the 18ᵗʰ CIRP Design Conference,* Enschede, The Netherlands (pp. 24).

Dragstra, P. (2005). *Enterprise Architecture: The select process of an Enterprise Architecture Toolset to support understanding and the governing Enterprise*. Unpublished master dissertation, Department of Mathematics and Computing Science.

Drucker, P. (2000). O advento da Nova Organização . In *Gestão do Conhecimento. Harvard Business Review. (A. C. da Cunha Serra, Trad.)*. Rio de Janeiro, Brasil: Campus.

Druker, P. (1993). *Post-Capitalism Society*. Oxford, UK: Butherworth-Heinemann.

Dudek, R. A., Panwalkar, S. S., & Smith, M. L. (1992). The lessons of flowshop scheduling research. *Operations Research, 40*, 7–13. doi:10.1287/opre.40.1.7

Duffy, J. (2002). *IT/Business alignment: Is it an option or is it mandatory? Elieson, B. D. (2006). Construction of an IT Risk Framework*. Rolling Meadows, IL: IT Governance Institute.

Eck, B. T., & Pinedo, M. (1993). On the minimization of the makespan subject to flowtime optimality. *Operations Research, 41*, 797–801. doi:10.1287/opre.41.4.797

ECQA. (2009). *European Certification & Qualification Association*. Retrieved December 20, 2009, from http://www.ecqa.org/index.php?id=7

Edinfor. (2006). Retrieved July 2006, from http://www.logicacmg.com/EdinforPortuguese/350230182

Edmondson, A. (2008, July). The competitive Imperative of Learning. *Harvard Business Review, 86*(7/8).

Ehrgott, M. (2000). Approximation algorithms for combinatorial multicriteria optimization problems. *International Transactions in Operational Research, 7*, 5–31. doi:10.1111/j.1475-3995.2000.tb00182.x

Ehrgott, M., & Gandibleux, X. (2001). Bounds and bound sets for biobjective Combinatorial Optimization problems . In Köksalan, M., & Zionts, S. (Eds.), *Multiple Criteria Decision Making in the New Millennium (5th ICMCDM), LNEMS 507* (pp. 241–253). Berlin: Springer.

Ehrgott, M., & Gandibleux, X. (2002). Multiobjective Combinatorial Optimization: Theory, Methodology, and Applications . In Ehrgott, M., & Gandibleux, X. (Eds.), *Multiple Criteria Optimization: State of the Art Annotated Bibliographic Surveys* (pp. 369–444). Boston: Kluwer Academic Publishers.

Ehrgott, M., & Wiecek, M. (2005). Multiobjective Programming . In Figueira, J., Greco, S., & Ehrgott, M. (Eds.), *Multiple Criteria Decision Analysis* (pp. 667–722). New York: Springer.

Eleftheriadou, D. (2008). Small - and Medium-Sized Enterprises Hold the Key to European Competitiveness: How to Help Them Innovate through ICT and E-business. *The Global Information Technology Report 2007-2008.* World Economic Forum European Commission. (2003). *SME Definition: Recommendation 2003/361/EC Regarding the SME Definition.*

Elsawah, S., Abdelfattah, A., & Rasmy, M. H. (2008). A quantitative model to predict the Egyptian ERP Implementation Success Index. *Business Process Management, 14*(3), 288–306. doi:10.1108/14637150810876643

Emelichev, V. A., & Perepelista, V. A. (1992). On cardinality of the set of alternatives in discrete many-criterion problems. *Discrete Mathematics and Applications, 2*(5), 461–471. doi:10.1515/dma.1992.2.5.461

EMIRAcle. (2008). *European Manufacturing and Innovation Research Association a cluster leading excellence*. Retrieved November 12, 2009, from http://www.emiracle.eu

Ende, J., Jaspers, F., & Gerwin, D. (2008). *Involvement of system firms in development of complementary products: The influence of novelty.* Technovation.

Engels, G., Forster, A., Heckel, R., & Thone, S. (2005). Process Modeling in UML . In Dumas, M., Van der Aalst, S. M. P., & ter Hofstede, M. (Eds.), *Process aware information systems* (pp. 85–117). Hoboken, NJ: John Wiley and Sons. doi:10.1002/0471741442.ch5

Eriksson, L. T., & Hultman, J. (2005). One digital leap or a step-by-step approach? - An empirical study of e-commerce development among Swedish SMEs. *International Journal of Electronic Business, 3*(5), 447–460. doi:10.1504/IJEB.2005.008519

Esteves, J., & Pastor, J. (2001). Analysis of critical success factors relevance along SAP implementation phases. In *Proceedings of the Seventh Americas Conference on Information Systems* (pp. 1019-1025).

Etzkowitz, L., & Leydesdorff, M. (2000). The Dynamics of Innovation: from National Systems and Model 2 to a Triple Helix of University-Industry-Government Relation. *Research Policy, 29*(2), 109. doi:10.1016/S0048-7333(99)00055-4

European Commission. (2008). *Directorate-General for Enterprise and Industry: Entrepreneurship in Higher Education, Especially Within Non-Business Studies – Final Report of the Expert Group.* Retrieved June 22, 2008, from http://europa.eu.int/comm/enterprise/entrepreneurship/ support_measures/index.htm

European Commission. (2008). *Helping to Create an Entrepreneurial Culture – A Guide on Good Practice in Promoting Entrepreneurial Attitudes and Skills through Education.* Retrieved June 22, 2008, from http://europa.eu.int/comm/enterprise/entrepreneurship/support_measures/training_education/index.htm

Evans, M. G. (1985). A Monte Carlo study of the effects of correlated method variance in moderated multiple regression analysis. *Organizational Behavior and Human Decision Processes, 36,* 302–323. doi:10.1016/0749-5978(85)90002-0

Evergreen. (2006). *Developing the Business Value of ITIL.*

Ewusi-Mensah, K. (2003). *Software Development Failures.* Cambridge, MA: MIT Press.

Falkowski, G., Pedigo, P., Smith, B., & Swamson, D. (1998). A recipe for ERP success. Beyond Computing. *International Journal of Human-Computer Interaction, 16*(1), 5–22.

Fan, J., & Fang, K. (2006). ERP Implementation and Information Systems Success: A Test of DeLone and McLean's Model. In *PICMET2006 Conference proceedings,* July 2006,Turkey (pp. 9-13).

Faulhaber, T. A. (2005). *Outsourcing.* Retrieved July 2006, from http://www.businessforum.com/toc.html#20

Fayyad, U., & Uthurusamy, R. (1996). Data mining and knowledge discovery in databases. *Communications of the ACM, 39*(11), 24–26. doi:10.1145/240455.240463

Ferguson, M. (1996). Tools and Techniques for Analyzing and Mining Warehouse Data. *InfoDB, 9*(3), 13–18.

Fern, E. F. (1982). Why do focus groups work: a review and integration of small group process theories . In Mitchell, A. (Ed.), *Advances in Consumer Research* (*Vol. 9,* pp. 444–451). St. Louis, MO: Association for Consumer Research.

Fernandes, A. A., & Abreu, V. F. (2008). *Implantando a Governança de TI: da estratégia à gestão dos processos e serviços.* São Paulo, Brasil: Brasport.

Fernandes, A. A., & de Abreu, V. F. (2008). *Implantando a Governança de TI: da Estratégia à Gestão dos Processos e Serviços* (2nd ed.). Brasilia, Brasil: Brasport Livros e Multimídia.

Fernandez, M., Gomez-Perez, A., & Juristo, N. (1997 March). Methontology: from Ontological Art towards Ontological Engineering. In *Proceedings of the AAAI97 Spring Symposium Series on Ontological Engineering,* Stanford, USA (pp. 33–40).

Fichman, R. G., & Kemerer, C. F. (1999). The illusory diffusion of innovation: an examination of the assimilation gaps. *Information Systems Research, 10*(3), 255–275. doi:10.1287/isre.10.3.255

Finney, S., & Corbett, M. (2007). ERP implementation: a compilation and analysis of critical success factors. *Business Process Management Journal, 13*(3), 329–347. doi:10.1108/14637150710752272

FIPA-Tunisia (The Foreign Investment Promotion Agency). (2007). Key figures: Economic Data: GNP/GDP. Retrieved October, 16, 2008, from http://www.investintunisia.tn/site/en/article.php?id_article=846

Fishbein, M., & Ajzen, I. (1975). *Belief, attitude, intention and behavior: An introduction to theory and research.* Reading, MA: Addison-Wesley Publishing Company.

Fisher, D. M., Fisher, S. A., & Kiang, M. Y. (2004). Evaluating mid-level ERP software. *Journal of Computer Information Systems, 45*(1), 38–46.

Fitzgerald, L., & Kiel, G. (2001). *Applying a consumer acceptance of technology model to examine adoption of online purchasing.* Retrieved February 2004, from http://130.195.95.71:8081/WWW/ANZMAC2001/anzmac/AUTHORS/pdfs/Fitzgerald1

Florida, R. (2002). *The Rise of the Creative Class.* New York: Basic Books.

Fortin, M.-F. (1999). *O Processo de Investigação: Da concepção à realização.* Porto, Portugal: Lusociência - Edições Técnicas e Científicas, Lda.

Fox, M. S., Barbuceanu, M., Gruninger, M., & Lin, J. (1997). *An Organization Ontology for Enterprise Modeling.* Enterprise Integration Laboratory - Department of Mechanical and Industrial Engineering, University of Toronto.

Framinan, J. M., Leisten, R., & Ruiz-Usano, R. (2002). Efficient heuristics for flowshop sequencing with the objectives of makespan and flowtime minimisation. *European Journal of Operational Research, 141,* 559–569. doi:10.1016/S0377-2217(01)00278-8

França, J., & Vasconcellos, A. (2007). *Manual para Normalização de Publicações técnico-científicas.* Belo Horizonte, Brasil: UFMG.

French, S. (1982). *Sequencing and Scheduling: An Introduction to the Mathematics of the Job Shop.* Chichester, UK: Ellis Horwood.

Frey, B. S. (1993). Shirking or work morale? The impact of regulating. *European Economic Review, 37*(8), 1523–1532. doi:10.1016/0014-2921(93)90120-Y

Frielink, A. B. (1961). *Auditing automatic data processing.* Amsterdam: Elsevier.

Fui-Hoon, F., Zuckweiler, K. M., & Lee-Shang, J. (2003). ERP implementation: Chief Information Officers' Perceptions on Critical Success Factors. *International Journal of Human-Computer Interaction, 16*(1), 5–22. doi:10.1207/S15327590IJHC1601_2

Funk, G. (2001). Enterprise integration: join the successful 20%. *Hydrocarbon Processing, 80*(4).

Gaballa, A., & Pearce, W. (1979). Telephone sales manpower planning at Qantas. *Interfaces, 9*(3), 1–9. doi:10.1287/inte.9.3.1

Gable, G., & Stewart, G. (1999). SAP R/3 implementation issues for small to medium enterprises. In *Americas Conference on Information Systems*, Milwaukee, WI (pp. 779-781).

Galbraith, J. R. (1974). Organization design: An information processing view. *Interfaces,*28–36. doi:10.1287/inte.4.3.28

Gama, N. (2006). *O Business Value dos Investimentos em Sistemas de Informação.* Instituto Superior Técnico.

Gamma, E., Helm, R., Vlissides, J., & Johnson, R. E. (1993). Design Patterns: Abstraction and Reuse of Object-Oriented Design. In *Proceedings of the 7th European Conference on Object-Oriented Programming* (LNCS 707, 406-431).

Gandibleux, X., Mezdaoui, N., & Fréville, A. (1997). A tabu search procedure to solve multiobjective combinatorial optimization problems. *Lecture Notes in Economics and Mathematical Systems, 455,* 291–300.

Gans, N., & Zhou, Y.-P. (2003). A call-routing problem with service-level constraints. *Operations Research, 51*(2), 255–271. doi:10.1287/opre.51.2.255.12787

Gans, N., & Zhou, Y.-P. (2007). Call-Routing Schemes for Call-Center Outsourcing. *Manufacturing & Service Operations Management, 9*(1), 33–50. doi:10.1287/msom.1060.0119

Gans, N., Koole, G., & Mandelbaum, A. (2003). Telephone call centers: tutorial, review and research prospects. *Manufacturing & Service Operations Management, 5*(2), 79–141. doi:10.1287/msom.5.2.79.16071

García Bravo, D. (2000). *Sistemas de información en la empresa. Conceptos y aplicaciones.* Madrid: Pirámide.

Garey, M. R., & Johnson, D. S. (1979). *Computers and Intractability: A Guide to the Theory of NP-Completeness.* San Francisco: Freeman.

Garrido, P. (2008). Collective intelligence . In Putnik, G., & Cunha, M. (Eds.), *Encyclopedia of Networked and Virtual Organizations* (pp. 280–287). Hershey, PA: Information Science Reference.

Garrido, P., & Faria, N. (2008). Design of a social decision support system for organizations. In J. Boaventura (Ed.), *Proceedings of Controlo 2008 – Eight Portuguese Conference on Automatic Control* (pp. 802-807). Vila Real, Portugal: UTAD. Retrieved November 26, 2009, from http://hdl.handle.net/1822/9788

Gartner. (2006). The Information Technology Infrastructure Library Improves Infrastructure Investment.

Garvin, D. (2000). Construindo a Organização que Aprende . In *Gestão do Conhecimento. Harvard Business Review. (A. C. da Cunha Serra, Trad.).* Rio de Janeiro, Brasil: Campus.

Garvin, D., Edmondson, A., & Gino, F. (2008 March). Is Yours a Learning Organization? *Harvard Business Review.*

Geiger, M. (2007). On operators and search space topology in multi-objective flow shop scheduling. *European Journal of Operational Research, 181,* 195–206. doi:10.1016/j.ejor.2006.06.010

Genesereth, R., & Nilsson, N. J. (1987). *Logical Foundations of Artificial Intelligence*. San Mateo, CA: Morgan Kaufmann Publishers.

George, J. F. (2008). The nature of organizational decision support systems . In Burstein, F., & Holsapple, C. (Eds.), *Handbook on Decision Support Systems 1: Basic Themes* (pp. 415–432). Berlin: Springer-Verlag. doi:10.1007/978-3-540-48713-5_21

Gershenfeld, N. (2000). *The physics of information technology*. Cambridge, UK: Cambridge University Press.

Gewald, H., & Hinz, D. (2004). A Framework for Classifying the Operational Risks of Outsourcing. In *Proceedings of the Eighth Pacific-Asia Conference on Information System,* Shanghai (pp. 986 - 999).

Gibert, J. (2003a). The IT Management Status Quo and the 5 Year Challenge. IT Physician Heal Thyself. *bITa-Center.* Retrieved June 20, 2007 from http://archive.bita-center.com/bitalib/bita/jg_art1.pdf

Gibert, J. (2003b). Concepts of a Unified Framework and Mapping Existing IT Frameworks.[s. l.]: IT Physician Heal Thyself. *bITa-Center.* Retrieved June 20, 2007 from http://archive.bita-center.com/bitalib/bita/jg_art2.pdf

Gibert, J. (2003c). Mapping IT Governance and the IT Value Chain onto a Unified Framework. [s. l.]: IT Physician Heal Thyself. *bITa-Center.* Retrieved June 20, 2007 from http://archive.bita-center.com/bitalib/bita/jg_art3.pdf

Gibert, J. (2003d). End to End Service Management: a case study. [s. l.]: IT Physician Heal Thyself. *bITa-Center.* Retrieved June 20, 2007 from http://archive.bita-center.com/bitalib/bita/jg_art4.pdf

Gibert, J. (2003e). The UPF Support Dimension. [s. l.]: IT Physician Heal Thyself. *bITa-Center.* Retrieved June 20, 2007 from http://archive.bita-center.com/bitalib/bita/jg_art5.pdf

Gibert, J. (2003f). The UPF Enabling Dimension. [s. l.]: IT Physician Heal Thyself. *bITa-Center.* Retrieved June 20, 2007 from http://archive.bita-center.com/bitalib/bita/jg_art6.pdf

Gibert, J. (2003g). UPF The Way Forward. [s. l.]: IT Physician Heal Thyself. *bITa-Center.* Retrieved June 20, 2007 from http://archive.bita-center.com/bitalib/bita/jg_art7.pdf

Gibson, C. F., & Nolan, R. L. (1974). Managing the four stages of EDP growth. *Harvard Business Review, 52*(1), 76–88.

Gibson, C., & Nolan, R. (1974). Managing the Four stages of EDP Growth. *Harvard Business Review, 1*, 76–88.

Gile, K. (2003). *Business intelligence and redefining the analytic end user.* Forrester Research.

Gilsing, V., Beerkens, B., & Vanharverbeke, W. (in press). Exploration and exploitation in technology-based alliance networks . In Therin, F. (Ed.), *Handbook of Research on Techno-entrepreneurship.* Northampton, MA: Edward Elgar Publishing.

Giorgini, P., Rizzi, S., & Garzetti, M. (2005). Goal-oriented requirement analysis for data warehouse design. In *Proc. DOLAP* (pp. 47-56).

Gnaim, K. (2005). Innovation is one of Quality aspects. *Quality in Higher Education, 1*(2).

Gomez, M. (2009). Corporate Environmental Management Information Systems - The next Generation . In *Abu-Shanab, unpublished introductory talk with powerpoint transparencies.* Ofir, Portugal: CENTERIS.

Gonzalez, R., Gasco, J., & Liopis, J. (2005a). Information systems outsourcing risks: a study of large firms. *Industrial Management & Data Systems, 105*(1), 45–61. doi:10.1108/02635570510575180

Gonzalez, R., Gasco, J., & Liopis, J. (2005c). Information systems outsourcing reasons in the largest Spanish firms. *International Journal of Information Management, 25*(2), 117–136. doi:10.1016/j.ijinfomgt.2004.10.002

Gonzalez, R., Gasco, J., & Llopis, J. (2005b). Information systems outsourcing success factors: a review and some results. *Information Management & Computer Security, 13*(5), 399–418. doi:10.1108/09685220510627287

Gonzalez, R., Gasco, J., & Llopis, J. (2006a). Information systems managers' view about outsourcing in Spain. *Information Management & Computer Security, 14*(4), 312–326. doi:10.1108/09685220610690790

Gonzalez, R., Gasco, J., & Llopis, J. (2006b). Information systems outsourcing: A literature analysis. *Information & Management, 43*(7), 821–834. doi:10.1016/j.im.2006.07.002

González, T., & Johnson, D. B. (1980). A new algorithm for preemptive scheduling of trees. *Journal of the Association for Computing Machinery, 27*, 287–312.

Goodhue, D. L., & Thompson, R. L. (1995). Task-technology fit and individual performance. *Management Information Systems Quarterly, 19*(2), 213–236. doi:10.2307/249689

Gopi, M., & Ramayah, T. (2007). Applicability of theory of planned behavior in predicting intention to trade online some evidence from developing country. *International Journal of Emerging Markets, 2*(4), 348–360. doi:10.1108/17468800710824509

Gordon, V., Proth, J. M., & Chu, C. (2002). A survey of the state of the art of common due date assignment and scheduling research. *European Journal of Operational Research, 139*, 1–25. doi:10.1016/S0377-2217(01)00181-3

Görlitz, O., Neubert, R., Teich, T., & Benn, W. (2002). Extended Value Chain Management on Electronic Marketplaces. *International Journal of e-Business Strategy Management, 3*(3).

Gottschalk, P. (2001). Key issues in is management in Norway: an empirical study based on Q-methodology. *Information Resources Management Journal, 14*(2), 37–45.

Gottschalk, P. (2007). *Business Dynamics in Information Technology.* Hershey, PA: Idea Group.

Gottschalk, P., Watson, R. T., & Christensen, B. H. (2000). Global comparisons of key issues in IS management: extending key issues selection procedure and survey approach. In R. T. Watson (Ed.), *Proceedings of the 33rd Annual Hawaii International Conference on System Sciences,* Hawaii (Vol. 2).

Goulart, I. (2002). Estudos exploratórios em psicologia organizacional e do trabalho . In Goulart, I. (Ed.), *Psicologia organizacional e do trabalho, teoria, pesquisa e temas correlatos.* São Paulo, Brasil: Casa do Psicólogo.

Grabowski, J., & Wodecki, M. (2004). Some local search algorithms for no-wait flow-shop problem with makespan criterion. *Computers & Operations Research, 32*, 2197–2212. doi:10.1016/j.cor.2004.02.009

Graham, R. L., Lawler, E. L., Lenstra, J. K., & Rinnooy Kan, A. H. G. (1979). Optimization and approximation in deterministic sequencing and scheduling: A survey. *Annals of Discrete Mathematics, 5*, 287–326. doi:10.1016/S0167-5060(08)70356-X

Grant, R. M. (1994). Toward a knowledge-based theory of the firm. *Strategic Management Journal, 17*(Special Issue: Knowledge and the Firm), 109–122. Retrieved December 3, 2009, from http://www.jstor.org/stable/2486994

Gray, P. (2008). The nature of group decision support systems . In Burstein, F., & Holsapple, C. (Eds.), *Handbook on Decision Support Systems 1: Basic Themes* (pp. 415–432). Berlin: Springer-Verlag. doi:10.1007/978-3-540-48713-5_19

Greenacre, M. (1984). *Theory and applications of correspondence analysis.* London: Academic Press.

Greenfield, A., Patel, J., & Fenner, J. (2001, November). Online Invoicing for Business-to-Business Users. *Information Week, 863*, 80–82.

Greiner, L. (1972). Evolution and revolution as **organiza**tions grow. *Harvard Business Review, 50*(4).

Greiner, L. (1998). Revolution is still inevitable. *Harvard Business Review, 3*, 62–63.

Grembergen, W. V. (2004). *Strategies for Information Technology Governance.* Hershey, PA: Idea Group Publishing.

Griffith, T. L., Zummato, R. F., & Ayman, L. (1999). Why new technologies fail? *Industrial Management (Des Plaines), 41*(3), 29–34.

Griffiths, D. (1999). The Theory and Practice of Outsourcing. In *48th Annual STC Conference Proceedings*. Chicago: STC.

Grover, G., Teng, J., Segars, A. H., & Fiedler, K. (1998). The influence of information technology diffusion and business process change on perceived productivity: The IS executive's Perspective. *Information & Management*, *34*, 14–159. doi:10.1016/S0378-7206(98)00054-8

Gruber, T. R. (1993). A Translation Approach to Portable Ontology Specifications. *Knowledge Acquisition*, *5*(2), 199–220. doi:10.1006/knac.1993.1008

Gruber, T. R. (1993). *Welcome to the SRKB working group*. Retrieved January 15, 2008 from http://www-ksl.stanford.edu/email-archives/srkb.messages/0.html

Gruber, T. R. (1995). Toward principles for the design of ontologies used for knowledge sharing. *International Journal of Human-Computer Studies*, *43*(5-6), 907–928. doi:10.1006/ijhc.1995.1081

Gruber, T. R., & Olsen, G. R. (1994). An Ontology for Engineering Mathematics. In J. Doyle, P. Torasso, & E. Sandewall (Eds.), *Fourth International Conference on Principles of Knowledge Representation and Reasoning*. Bonn, Germany: Morgan Kaufmann.

Guarino, N. (1996). Understanding, Building, and Using Ontologies. In *Proceedings of the 10th Knowledge Acquisition for Knowledge-Based Systems Workshop*, Alberta, Canada.

Guarino, N., & Giaretta, P. (1995). Ontologies and Knowledge Bases: Towards a Terminological Clarification . In Mars, N. (Ed.), *Towards Very Large Knowledge Bases: Knowledge Building and Knowledge Sharing* (pp. 25–32). Amsterdam: IOS Press.

Gunton, T. (1998). *Infrastructure: Building a Framework for Corporate Information Handling*. New York: Prentice Hall.

Guo, Y., Tang, S., Tong, Y., & Yang, D. (2006). Triple-Driven Data Modeling Methodology in Data Warehousing: A Case Study. In *Proc. of ACM 9th International Workshop on Data Warehousing and OLAP (DOLAP)*, Arlington,Virginia, USA (pp. 59-66).

Gupta, J. N. D. (1972). Heuristic Algorithms for Multistage Flowshop Scheduling Problem. *AIIE Transactions*, *4*(1), 11–18.

Gupta, J. N. D., Neppalli, V. R., & Werner, F. (2001). Minimizing total flow time in a two-machine flowshop problem with minimum makespan. *International Journal of Production Economics*, *69*(3), 323–338. doi:10.1016/S0925-5273(00)00039-6

Gupta, S., & Keswani, B. (2008). *Exploring the Factors That Influence User Resistance to the Implementation of ERP*. Hyderabad, India: The ICFAI University Press.

Gupta, V., Peter, E., Miller, T., & Blyden, K. (2002). Implementing a distribution-network decision-support system at Pfizer/Warner-Lambert. *Interfaces*, *32*(4), 28–45. doi:10.1287/inte.32.4.28.54

Guyot, E., Ducellier, G., Eynard, B., Girard, Ph., & Gallet, T. (2007). Product data and digital mock-up exchange based on PLM, *Product Lifecycle Management, Assessing the industrial relevance* [Genève, Switzerland: Interscience Enterprises Ltd.]. *PLM-S*, *P3*, 243–252.

Gyampah, A. K. (2007). Perceived usefulness, user involvement and behavioral intention: An empirical study of ERP implementation. *Computers in Human Behavior*, *23*, 1232–1248. doi:10.1016/j.chb.2004.12.002

Gyampah, A. K., & Salam, A. M. (2004). An extension of the technology acceptance model in an erp implementation Environment. *Information & Management*, *41*, 731–745. doi:10.1016/j.im.2003.08.010

Haller, M., Jenichl, G., & Küng, J. (1998). *Data Mining, Multidimensional Databases and the Web for a Better Interpretation of Data*. Paper presented at the 5th International Conference IDG'98

Hammer, M. (1990). Reengineering work: don't automate. *Harvard Business Review*, *68*, 104–112.

Han, J., & Kamber, M. (2006). *Data Mining: Concepts and Techniques*. Morgan Kaufmann.

Han, S. W. (2004). ERP - Enterprise resource planning: A cost-based business case and implementation assessment. *Human Factors and Ergonomics in Manufacturing, 14*(3), 239–256. doi:10.1002/hfm.10066

Handschuh, S., & Staab, S. (2003). *Annotation for the Semantic Web*.

Handsfield, R. B., & Nichols, E. L. (2002). *Supply Chain Redesign: Transforming Supply Chains into Integrated Value Systems*. Upper Saddle River, NJ: Prentice Hall.

Hapke, M., Jaszkiewicz, A., & Slowinski, R. (1998). Interactive Analysis of multiple-criteria project scheduling problems. *European Journal of Operational Research, 107*(2), 315–324. doi:10.1016/S0377-2217(97)00336-6

Hardgrave, B. C., Davis, F. D., & Riemenschneider, C. K. (2003). Investigating determinants of software developers to follow methodologies. *Journal of Management Information Systems, 20*(1), 123–151.

Harland, C. M., Lamming, R. C., & Zheng, J. J. (2001). A taxonomy of supply networks. *Journal of Supply Chain Management, 37*.

Harmon, P. (2003). *Business Process Change*. San Francisco: Morgan Kaufmann.

Harmon, P. (2007). *Business Process Change: a guide for business managers and BPM and six sigma professionals*. Burlington, MA: Morgan Kaufman Publishers.

Harrington, J. (1991). *Business process improvement: the breakthrough strategy for total quality, Productivity and Competitiveness*. New York: McGraw Hill.

Harvard Business Review. (1999). *The Business Value of IT*.

Harvard Business School. (2002). *Finance for managers*.

Hasson, U., Nir, Y., Levy, I., Fuhrmann, G., & Malach, R. (2004). Intersubject Synchronization of Cortical Activity During Natural Vision. *Science, 303*, 1634–1640. doi:10.1126/science.1089506

Haupt, R. (1989). A survey of priority rule-based scheduling. *Operational Research Spektrum, 11*, 3–16. doi:10.1007/BF01721162

Hawkins, L., Meier, T., Nainis, W. S., & James, H. M. (2001). *The evolution of the call center to customer contact center: ITSC - Information Technology Support Center*.

He, Z. L., Wong, P. K., & Kam, P. K. (2004). Exploration vs. Exploitation: An Empirical Test of the Ambidexterity Hypothesis. *Organization Science, 15*(4), 481–494. doi:10.1287/orsc.1040.0078

Hedman, J. (2003). *On Enterprise Systems Artifacts: Changes in Information Systems Development and Evaluation. Lund Studies in Informatics, No. 2*. Lund, Sweden: Department of Informatics.

Hedman, J., & Borell, A. (2003). ERP systems impact on organizations. In Grant, G. (Ed.), *ERP & Data Warehousing in organizations: issues and challenges* (pp. 1–21). Hershey, PA: Idea Group Publishing.

Hedman, J., & Borell, A. (2004). Narratives in ERP systems evaluation. *Journal of Enterprise Information Management, 17*(4), 283–290. doi:10.1108/17410390410548698

Heisenberg, W. (1999). Language and reality in modern physics. In *Physics and philosophy. The revolution in modern science* (pp. 167-186). New York: Prometheus Books. (Original manuscript published in 1958).

Henderson, J. C., & Venkatraman, N. (1993). Strategic alignment: Leveraging information technology for transforming organizations. *IBM Systems Journal, 32*(1), 4–16. doi:10.1147/sj.382.0472

Henderson, J. C., & Venkatraman, N. (1999). Strategic alignment: leveraging information technology for transforming organizations. *IBM Systems Journal, 38*(2-3).

Hess, E. (2002 May). Make advanced planning & scheduling work for your company. *APS*.

Hevner, A. R., March, S. T., Park, J., & Ram, S. (2004). Design science in information systems research. *Management Information Systems Quarterly, 28*(1), 75–106.

Hewlett Packard. (2006). *Outsourcing Services*. Retrieved July 2006, from http://h20219.www2.hp.com/services/cache/9483-0-0-0-121.html

Hitt, L. M., Wu, D. J., & Xiaoge, Z. (2002). Investment in Enterprise Resource Planning: Business Impact and Productivity Measures. *Journal of Management Information Systems, 19*(1), 71–98.

Ho, C.-Y., Lin, Y.-M., & City, J.-L. (2002). The Relationship between ERP Pre-implementation Decision and Implementation Risks on ERP Projects. In *Proceedings of the First Workshop on Knowledge Economy and Electronic Commerce*.

Ho, J. C., & Chang, Y.-L. (1991). A new heuristic for the n-job, m-machine flowshop problem. *European Journal of Operational Research, 52*, 194–202. doi:10.1016/0377-2217(91)90080-F.

Holland, C. P., & Light, B. (1999, May). A critical success factors model for ERP implementation. *IEEE Software*, 30–36. doi:10.1109/52.765784

Holloway, S. (2006). *Potential of RFID in the Supply Chain*. Chicago, IL: Solidsoft Ltd.

Holman, D., Batt, R., & Holtgrewe, U. (2007). *The Global Contact Center Report: International Perspectives on Management and Employment*.

Holmqvist, M. (2004). Experiential Learning Processes of Exploitation and Exploration Within And Between Organizations: An Empirical Study of Product Development. *Organization Science, 15*(1), 70–81. doi:10.1287/orsc.1030.0056

Holsapple, C. W., & Joshi, K. D. (2001). Organizational knowledge resources. *Decision Support Systems, 31*, 39–54. doi:10.1016/S0167-9236(00)00118-4

Holsapple, C. W., & Joshi, K. D. (2003). A Knowledge Management Ontology. In Holsapple, C. W. (Ed.), *Handbook on Knowledge Management* (Vol. 1, pp. 89–124). Lexington, KY: Springer.

Holsapple, C. W., & Singh, M. (2003). The Knowledge Chain Model: Activities for Competitiveness . In Holsapple, C. W. (Ed.), *Handbook on Knowledge Management* (Vol. 2, pp. 215–251). Lexington, KY: Springer.

Holten, R. (2003). Specification of management views in information warehouse projects. *Information Systems, 12*, 709–751. doi:10.1016/S0306-4379(02)00080-7

Holweg, M., Disney, S., Holmström, J., & Småros, J. (2005). Supply Chain Collaboration: Making Sense of the Strategy Continuum. *European Management Journal, 23*, 170–181. doi:10.1016/j.emj.2005.02.008

Hoogervorst, J. (2004). Enterprise architecture: Enabling integration, agility and change. *International Journal of Cooperative Information Systems, 13*(3), 213–233. doi:10.1142/S021884300400095X

Hoogeveen, H. (2005). Multicriteria Scheduling. *European Journal of Operational Research, 167*, 592–623. doi:10.1016/j.ejor.2004.07.011

Hoogeveen, J. A. (1992). *Single-Machine Bicriteria Scheduling*. Unpublished doctoral dissertation, CWI, The Netherlands Technology, Amsterdam.

Hopkins, J. (2008). *Eating the IT Elephant: Moving from Greenfield Development to Brownfield*. New York: IBM Press.

Hori, M. (2001). The Development of IT and a New Work Format for Women in Japan . In *Proceedings of t-world 2001, The 8th*. International Assembly on Telework.

Hori, M. (2003). *Society of Telework and Working women*. Tokyo: Chuo University.

Hori, M., & Ohashi, M. (2001). Information Technology and The Possibility of Women's Work: A New Work Format for Women in Japan. In *The 6th International ITF Workshop and Business Conference Working in the New Economy*, Amsterdam.

Hori, M., & Ohashi, M. (2004a). Implementing Adaptive Collaborative Telework in Public Administration . In Cunningham, P., & Cunningham, M. (Eds.), *eAdoption and the Knowledge Economy:Issues, Applications, & Case Studies* (pp. 708–714). Amsterdam: IOS Press.

Hori, M., & Ohashi, M. (2004b). Telework Changes Working Style for Japanese Women. In *Proceedings of AWEEB, International Workshop on Advanced Web Engineering for E-Business*, Frankfurt, Germany.

Hori, M., & Ohashi, M. (2004c). Telework and Mental Health-Collaborative Work to Maintain and Manage Mental Health. In *Proceedings of the the 37ᵗʰ Annual Hawaii International Conference on System Sciences*, Hawaii.

Hori, M., & Ohashi, M. (2005a). Applying XML Web Services into health care management. In *Proceedings of the 38ᵗʰ Annual Hawaii Conference on System Science*, Hawaii.

Hori, M., & Ohashi, M. (2005b). Adaptive Collaboration: The Road Map to Leading Telework to a More Advanced and Professional Working Format. *The Journal of the IPSI BgD Transaction on Advanced Research Issues in Computer and Engineering*, 6-42.

Hori, M., & Ohashi, M. (2006a). The Municipality's Role for Building of the Regional Health & Medical Welfare Information Services System. *Jounal of Policy & Culture, 13*.

Hori, M., & Ohashi, M. (2006b). On the Study of Collaborative Telework in the Infosocionomics Society. *Jounal of Policy & Culture, 13*.

Hori, M., & Ohashi, M. (2006c). Citizen-Centric s-Healthcare Management Based on the XML Web Services . In Cunningham, P., & Cunningham, M. (Eds.), *Exploiting the Knowledge Economy: Issues, Applications, & Case Studies* (pp. 957–964). Amsterdam: IOS press.

Hori, M., Ohashi, M., & Ssuzuki, S. (2005). Citizen-Centric Approach and healthcare Management Based on XML Web Services. In *Proceedings of the 12ᵗʰ European Conference on Information Technology Evaluation* (pp. 241).

Horrocks, I. (2008). Ontologies and the semantic web. *Communications of the ACM, 51*(12), 58–67. doi:10.1145/1409360.1409377

Horsky, D., & Rao, M. R. (1984). Estimation of attribute weights from preference comparison. *Management Science, 30*(7), 801–822. doi:10.1287/mnsc.30.7.801

Hsieh, J. J. P., & Wang, W. (2007). Explaining Employees' Extended Use of Complex Information Systems. *European Journal of Information Systems, 16*(3), 216–227. doi:10.1057/palgrave.ejis.3000663

Hssain, A., Djeraba, C., & Descotes-Genon, B. (1993). Production Information Systems Design. In *Proceedings of Int Conference on Industrial Engineering and Production Management (IEPM-33)*, Mons, Belgium, June 1993.

Hsu, C., & Rattner, L. (1990). Information Modeling for Computerized Manufacturing. *IEEE Transactions on Systems, 20*(4).

Hu, Y., Sun, X., Wei, P., & Yang, Q. (2008 September). Applying Semantic Web Services to Enterprise Web. In *The 6th International Conference on Manufacturing Research (ICMR08)*, Brunel University, UK.

Huang, G., & Lim, A. (2003). Fragmental Optimization on the 2-Machine Bicriteria Flowshop Scheduling Problem. In B. Werner (Ed.), *Proceedings: 15th IEEE International Conference on Tools with Artificial Intelligence* (pp. 194-198). Sacramento: IEEE Computer Society.

Huang, Z., & Palvia, P. (2001). ERP implementation issues in advanced and developing countries. *Business Process Management, 7*(3), 276–284. doi:10.1108/14637150110392773

Hubbard, D. (2007). *How to Measure Anything: Finding the Value of Intangibles in Business*. Hoboken, NJ: John Wiley & Sons, Inc.

Huber, G. P. (2003). *The necessary nature of future firms: Attributes of Survivors in a changing World*. San Francisco: Sage.

Huber, G. P. (2003). *The necessary nature of future firms: Attributes of survivors in a changing world*. Thousand Oaks, CA: Sage.

Hughes, J., & Lang, K.-R. (2006). Transmutability: Digital decontextualization, manipulation, and recontextualization as a new source of value in the production and consumption of culture products. In *Proceedings of the 39th Annual Hawaii International Conference on System Sciences (HICSS'06)* (pp. 165a-165a). doi: 10.1109/HICSS.2006.511

Hung, S. Y. (2003). Expert versus novice use of the executive support systems: an empirical study. *Information & Management, 40*(3), 177–189. doi:10.1016/S0378-7206(02)00003-4

Hunton, J., Lippincott, B., & Reck, J. (2003). Enterprise Resource Planning Systems: Comparing Firm Performance of Adopters and Nonadopters. *Accounting Information Systems, 4*, 165–184. doi:10.1016/S1467-0895(03)00008-3

Iandoli, L., Klein, M., & Zollo, G. (2008). *Can We Exploit Collective Intelligence for Collaborative Deliberation? The case of the Climate Change Collaboratorium.* CCI Working Paper 2008-002. Cambridge, MA: Center for Collective Intelligence, MIT Sloan School of Management. Retrieved from http://papers.ssrn.com/sol3/papers.cfm?abstract_id=1084069

IBM. (2005). Component Business Models: Making Specialization Real. *IBM Institute for Business Value.* Retrieved April 10, 2009, from http://www-935.ibm.com/services/us/index.wss/ibvstudy/imc/a1017908?cntxt=a1003208

IDC. (2004). *Caderno nº 72 - Outsourcing de Serviços de TI.* Lisboa: IDC Portugal.

IDC. (2005). *Estudo Local - Outsourcing de Serviços de TI e BPO em Portugal: Análise e Previsões 2004 - 2009.* Lisboa: IDC Portugal.

Ifinedo, P. (2007). An empirical study of ERP success evaluations by business and IT mangers. *Information Management & Computer Security, 15*(4), 270–282. doi:10.1108/09685220710817798

Ifinedo, P. (2007). Interactions between organizational size, culture, and structure and some IT factors in the context of ERP success assessment: an exploration investigation. *Journal of Computer Information Systems, 27*(4), 28–44.

Ifinedo, P., & Nahar, N. (2007). ERP systems success: an empirical analysis of how two organizational stakeholder groups prioritize and evaluate relevant measures. *Enterprise Information Systems, 1*(1), 25–48. doi:10.1080/17517570601088539

Ignall, E., & Schrage, L. E. (1965). Application of the branch-and-bound technique to some flow-shop scheduling problems. *Operations Research, 13*, 400–412. doi:10.1287/opre.13.3.400

iGrafx, Enabling Process Excellence, Retrieved June 20, 2008, from www.igrafx.com

Indulska, M., Recker, J., Rosemann, M., & Green, P. (2009). Business process modeling: current issues and future challenges. In P. van Eck et al (Eds.), *Advanced Information System Engineering* (LNCS 5565, pp. 501-514). Berlin: Springer Verlag.

Institute de la Gouvernance des Système d'Information. (2005). *The place of IT Governance in the Enterpise Governance. Balancing Performance and Conformance.* Paris: Institute de la Gouvernance des Systèmes d'Information.

Institute of Directors of Southern Africa. (2009). *King Code Of Governance for South Africa.*

Integration Definition for Function Modeling (IDEF0). (1993). *Category of Standard: Software Standard, Modelling Techniques.* Retrieved May 13, 2009, from http://www.idef.com/pdf/idef0.pdf

IOM Control. (2001). ERP survey. *Institute Operation Management, 27*(8).

Irani, Z., Hlupic, V., & Giaglis, G. (2000). Business Process reengineering: a design perspective. *International Journal of Flexible Manufacturing Systems, 12*, 247–252. doi:10.1023/A:1008103931482

Isermann, H. (1977). The enumeration of the set of all efficient solutions for a linear multiple objective program. *Operational Research Quarterly, 28*(3), 711–725.

Ishibuchi, H., & Murata, T. (1998). A multi-objective genetic local search algorithm and its application to flowshop scheduling. *IEEE Transactions on Systems, Man and Cybernetics – Part C, 28*(3), 392-403.

Ishibuchi, H., Misaki, S., & Tanaka, H. (1995). Modified simulated annealing algorithms for the flow shop sequencing problem. *European Journal of Operational Research, 81*, 388–398. doi:10.1016/0377-2217(93)E0235-P

ISO. (2008). ISO/IEC 38500:2008 Corporate Governance for Information Technology.

ITGovernanceInstitute. (2008b). *IT Governance Global Status Report - 2008*. Rolling Meadows, IL: IT Governance Institute.

ITGovernanceInstitute. (2009). *Enterprise Risk: Identify, Govern and Manage IT Risk. The Risk IT Framework. Exposure draft*. Rolling Meadows, IL: IT Governance Institute.

Iyer, B., & Gottieb, R. (2004). Four-Domain Architecture- FDA. *IBM Systems Journal, 43*(3).

Izvercianu, M. (2007). *Research Regarding the Training Needs Identification for Business Creation*. Report in the Leonardo da Vinci program Sustainable enterprises development – FORCREST. ES/03/B/F/PP-149101.

Izvercianu, M., & Draghici, A. (2007). Vocational Training Requirements' Analysis for Industrial Romanian Enterprises. In Karwowski, W., & Trzcielinski, S. (Eds.), *Value Stream Activities Management* (pp. 567–574). Pznan, Poland: International Ergonomics Association.

Izvercianu, M., & Draghici, A. (2008). The Entrepreneurship Education as Part of Human Resources Development. In J. Han & P. Holejsovska (Eds.), *Proceedings of the 10th International Conference on the Modern Information Technology in the Innovation Processes of the Industrial Enterprises (MITIP 2008)* (pp. 200-206). Pilsen, Czech Republic: University of West Bohemia.

Izvercianu, M., & Draghici, A. (2008). The University Entrepreneurship Education. The Case of Politehnica University of Timisoara. In M. G. Simion & I. Talpasanu (Eds.), *Proceeding of the 3rd Annual Congress of the American Romanian Academy of Arts and Sciences (ARA)* (pp. 238-241). Boston: Wentworth Institute of Technology.

Jackson, T. L. (2006). *Hoshin Kanri for the Lean Enterprise: Developing Competitive Capabilities and Managing Profit*. Florence, KY: Productivity Press.

Jafari, S. M., Osman, M. R., Yusuff, R. M., & Tang, S. H. (2006). ERP Systems Implementation In Malaysia: The Importance Of Critical Success Factors. *International Journal of Engineering and Technology, 3*(1), 125–131.

Jagdev, H. S., & Thoben, K. D. (2001). Anatomy of enterprise collaborations. *Production Planning and Control, 12*, 437–451. doi:10.1080/09537280110042675

Jasperson, J. S., Carter, P. E., & Zmud, R. W. (2005). A Comprehensive Conceptualization of Post-Adoptive Behaviors Associated with Information Technology Enabled Work Systems. *Management Information Systems Quarterly, 2*(3), 525–557.

Jasperson, J., Carter, P. E., & Zumd, R. W. (2005). A comprehensive conceptualization of post-adoptive behaviors associated with information technology enabled work systems. *Management Information Systems Quarterly, 29*(3), 525–557.

Jaszkiewicz, A. (2004). A Comparative Study of Multiple-Objective Metaheuristics on the Bi-Objective Set Covering Problem and the Pareto Memetic Algorithm. *Annals of Operations Research, 13*, 135–158. doi:10.1023/B:ANOR.0000039516.50069.5b

Jaszkiewicz, A., & Ferhat, A. B. (1999). Solving multiple criteria choice problems by interactive trichotomy segmentation. *European Journal of Operational Research, 113*(2), 271–280. doi:10.1016/S0377-2217(98)00216-1

Jean, G. (2000). *L'urbanisation du Business des Systèmes d'Information*. Paris: Hermes Science Publications.

Jennex, M. E., & Olfman, L. (2003). Organizational Memory . In Holsapple, C. W. (Ed.), *Handbook on Knowledge Management* (*Vol. 1*, pp. 207–234). Lexington, KY: Springer.

Jennings, M. (2005). *Business: Its Legal, Ethical and Global Environment.* Brentford: South-Western.

Jerez-Gómez, P., Céspedes-Lorente, J., & Valle-Cabrera, R. (2005). Organizational Learning and Compensation Strategies: Evidence from the Spanish Chemical Industry. *Human Resource Management, 44*(3), 279–299. doi:10.1002/hrm.20071

Johansson, B., & Newman, M. (2009). Competitive Advantage and Enterprise Resource Planning (ERP) Systems: Some Conflicts in the Value-Chain. In *Americas Conference on Information Systems (AMCIS) 2009*, San Francisco.

Johnson, S. M. (1954). Optimal two- and three-stage production schedules with setup times included. *Naval Research Logistics, 1*, 61–68. doi:10.1002/nav.3800010110

Jones, D. F., Mirrazavi, S. K., & Tamiz, M. (2002). Multi-objective meta-heuristics: An overview of the current state of the art. *European Journal of Operational Research, 137*, 1–9. doi:10.1016/S0377-2217(01)00123-0

Jongho, K., Woojong, S., & Heeseok, L. (2003). Hypermedia modeling for linking knowledge to data warehousing system. *Expert Systems with Applications, 24*, 103–114. doi:10.1016/S0957-4174(02)00088-X

Joslin, E. O. (1968). *Computer selection.* London: Addison-Wesley.

Kakumanu, P., & Portanova, A. (2006). Outsourcing: Its Benefits, Drawbacks and Other Related Issues. *Journal of American Academy of Business, 9*(2), 1–7.

Kalling, T. (1999). *Gaining competitive advantage through information technology: a resource-based approach to the creation and employment of strategic IT resources.* Lund, Germany: Lund Business Press.

Kaplan, J. (2005). *Strategic IT Portfolio Management: Governing Enterprise Transformation.* Boston: PRTM.

Karaarslan, N., & Gundogar, E. (2009). An Application for Modular Capability-based ERP Software Selection Using AHP Method. *International Journal of Advanced Manufacturing Technology, 42*(9-10), 1025–1033. doi:10.1007/s00170-008-1522-5

Karahanna, E., Straub, D. W., & Chervany, N. I. (1999). Information Technology Adoption Across Time: Across-Sectional Comparison Of Pre-Adoption and Post-Adoption Beliefs. *Management Information Systems Quarterly, 23*, 183–213. doi:10.2307/249751

Karimi, J., Somers, T. M., & Bhattacherjee, A. (2007). The Impact of ERP Implementation on Business Process Outcomes: A Factor-Based Study. *Journal of Management Information Systems, 24*(1), 101–134. doi:10.2753/MIS0742-1222240103

Karsak, E. E., & Ozogul, C. O. (2009). An Integrated Decision Making Approach for ERP System Selection. *Expert Systems with Applications, 36*(1), 660–667. doi:10.1016/j.eswa.2007.09.016

Kartiwi, M., & MacGregor, R. C. (2007). Electronic Commerce Adoption Barriers in Small to Medium-Sized Enterprises (SMEs) in Developed and Developing Countries: A Cross-Country Comparison. *Journal of Electronic Commerce in Organizations, 5*(3), 35–51.

Kasper, H. (2000). *O Processo de Pensamento Sistêmico: um estudo das principais abordagens a partir de um quadro de referencia proposto.* Unpublished master dissertation, Universidade Federal do Rio Grande do Sul.

Ke, W., & Wei, K. K. (2006). Organizational Learning Process: Its Antecedents and Consequences in Enterprise System Implementation. *Journal of Global Information Management, 14*(1), 1–22.

Keil, M., & Tiwana, A. (2006). Relative importance of evaluation criteria for enterprise systems: a conjoint study. *Information Systems Journal, 16*(3), 237–262. doi:10.1111/j.1365-2575.2006.00218.x

Kelley, G. (Ed.). (2009). *Selected Readings on Information Technology Management.* Hershey, PA: IGI Global.

Kelley, H. H. (1992). Lewin, situations, and interdependence. *The Journal of Social Issues, 47*, 211–233. doi:10.1111/j.1540-4560.1991.tb00297.x

Kennerly, M., & Neely, A (2001 February). Enterprise resource planning: analysing the impact. *Integrated Manufacturing System*, 103-113.

Kenny, D. A., Kashy, D. A., & Bolger, N. (1998). Data analysis in social psychology . In Gilbert, D. T., Fiske, S. T., & Lindzey, G. (Eds.), *The handbook of Social Psychology* (Vol. 1, pp. 233–268). Boston: McGraw-Hill.

Kerschberg, L. (2001). Knowledge Management in Heterogeneous Data Warehouse Environments. In *3rd International Conference on Data Warehousing and Knowledge Discovery (DaWaK 01)*, Munich, Germany (LNCS 2114, pp. 1–10). Berlin: Springer.

Kimball, R. (2008). *The Data Warehouse Lifecycle Toolkit* (2nd ed.). New York: John Wiley & Sons.

Kirschner, P., Shum, S., & Carr, C. (Eds.). (2003). *Visualizing Argumentation: Software tools for collaborative and educational sense-making.* London: Springer-Verlag.

Klein, H., & Myers, M. (1999). A set of principles for conducting and evaluating interpretive field studies in information systems. *Management Information Systems Quarterly, 23*(1), 67–93. doi:10.2307/249410

Klein, M. (2007). *Achieving Collective Intelligence via Large-Scale On-Line Argumentation.* CCI Working Paper No. 2007-001. Cambridge, MA: Center for Collective Intelligence, MIT Sloan School of Management. Retrieved December 14, 2009, from http://papers.ssrn.com/sol3/papers.cfm?abstract_id=1040881

Knowles, J., & Corne, D. (2002). On Metrics Comparing Nondominated Sets. In IEEE (Ed.), *Proceedings of the 2002 Congress on Evolutionary Computation* (pp. 711-716). New York: IEEE.

Koch, C. (2001). *ERP-systemer: erfaringer, ressourcer, forandringer.* København, Danmark: Ingeniøren-bøger.

Koole, G., & Mandelbaum, A. (2002). Queuing models of call centers: an introduction. *Annals of Operations Research, 113*, 41–59. doi:10.1023/A:1020949626017

Korten, S. (2009). *Agenda for a New Economy.* San Francisco: Berrett-Koehler.

Koubarakis, M., & Plexousakis, D. (2000). A Formal Model for Business Process Modeling and Design. In *Advanced Information System Engineering* (LNCS 1789, pp. 142-156). Berlin: Springer.

Koulamas, C. (1998). A new constructive heuristic for the flowshop scheduling problem. *European Journal of Operational Research, 105*, 66–71. doi:10.1016/S0377-2217(97)00027-1

Kumar, K., & Van Hillegersberg, J. (2000). ERP experiences and evolution. *Communications of the ACM, 43*(4), 22–26. doi:10.1145/332051.332063

Kumar, V., Maheshwari, B., & Kumar, U. (2002). Enterprise resource planning systems adoption process: a survey of Canadian organizations. *International Journal of Production Research, 40*(3), 509–523. doi:10.1080/00207540110092414

Kumar, V., Maheshwari, B., & Kumar, U. (2003). An investigation of critical management issues in ERP implementation: empirical evidence from Canadian organizations. *Technovation, 23*(10), 793–807. doi:10.1016/S0166-4972(02)00015-9

Kyriakopoulos, K., & Moorman, C. (2004, September). Tradeoffs in marketing exploitation and exploration strategies: The overlooked role of market orientation. *International Journal of Research in Marketing, 21*(3), 219–240. doi:10.1016/j.ijresmar.2004.01.001

Lacity, M. C., & Willcocks, L. P. (1998). An empirical investigation of information technology sourcing practices: lessons from experience. *Management Information Systems Quarterly, 22*(3), 363–408. doi:10.2307/249670

Lageweg, B. J., Ixnstra, J. K., & Rinnooy Kan, A. H. G. (1978). A general bounding to minimize makespan/total flowtime of jobs. *European Journal of Operational Research, 155*, 426–438.

Laha, D., & Chakraborty, U. K. (2007). An efficient stochastic hybrid heuristic for flowshop scheduling. *Engineering Applications of Artificial Intelligence, 20,* 851–856. doi:10.1016/j.engappai.2006.10.003

Laha, D., & Chakraborty, U. K. (2008). An efficient heuristic approach to flowtime minimization in permutation flowshop scheduling. *International Journal of Advanced Manufacturing Technology, 38,* 1018–1025. doi:10.1007/s00170-007-1156-z

Laha, D., & Chakraborty, U. K. (2009). A constructive heuristic for minimizing makespan in no-wait flowshop scheduling. *International Journal of Advanced Manufacturing Technology, 41,* 97–109. doi:10.1007/s00170-008-1454-0

Lai, J., Ong, Ch., Yang, Ch., & Tang, W. (2005). Factors influencing employees' usage behavior of KMS in e-business. In *Proceedings of the Pacific Asia Conference on Information Systems* (pp. 126-137).

Lall, V., & Teyarachakul, S. (2006). Enterprise Resource Planning (ERP) System selection: A Data Envelopment Anaysis (DEA) approach. *Journal of Computer Information Systems, 47*(1), 123–127.

Landa-Silva, J. D., Burke, E. K., & Petrovic, S. (2004). An Introduction to Multiobjective Metaheuristics for Scheduling and Timetabling. *Lecture Notes in Economics and Mathematical Systems, 535,* 91–129.

Langefors, B. (1977). Information System Theory. *Information Systems, 2,* 207–219. doi:10.1016/0306-4379(77)90009-6

Langer, A. M. (2007). Business Process Reengineering . In *Analysis and design of Information Systems* (pp. 268–280). London: Springer.

Lankhorst, M. (2005). *Enterprise Architecture at Work.* New York: Springer.

Lankhorst, M. (2009). *Enterprise architecture at work: Modelling, communication and analysis.* Berlin: Springer-Verlag GmbH.doi:10.1007/978-3-642-01310-2

Larsen, M., & Myers, M. D. (1998). When Success Turns into Failure: A Package-Driven Business Process Re-engineering project in the Financial Services Industry. *The Journal of Strategic Information Systems, 8,* 395–417. doi:10.1016/S0963-8687(00)00025-1

Laudon, K., & Laudon, J. (2005). *Management Information Systems: Managing the Digital Firm* (10th ed.). Upper Saddle River, NJ: Prentice Hall.

Laudon, K., & Laudon, J. (2009). *Management Information Systems* (11th ed.). Englewood Cliffs, NJ: Prentice Hall.

Laudon, K., Laudon, J., & Laudon, K. (2005). *Management Information Systems.* New York: Prentice Hall.

Laudon, K., Laudon, J., & Laudon, K. (2007). *Essentials of Management Information Systems.* New York: Prentice Hall.

Law, C. C. H., & Ngai, E. W. T. (2007). ERP system adoption: An exploratory study of the organizational factors and impacts of ERP success. *Information & Management, 444*(4), 418–432. doi:10.1016/j.im.2007.03.004

Law, C. C. H., & Ngai, E. W. T. (2007). ERP systems adoption: An exploratory study of the organizational factors and impacts of ERP success. *Information & Management, 44,* 418–432. doi:10.1016/j.im.2007.03.004

Lawler, E. L., Lenstra, J. K., & Rinnooy Kan, A. H. G. (1993). Sequencing and scheduling: Algorithms and complexity . In Graves, S. C., Rinnooy Kan, A. H. G., & Zipkin, P. H. (Eds.), *Handbooks in Operations Research and Management Science, 4, Logistics of Production and Inventory* (pp. 445–524). Amsterdam: Elsevier. doi:10.1016/S0927-0507(05)80189-6

Lawless, W. F., Bergman, M., & Feltovich, N. (2005). Consensus-seeking versus truth-seeking. *Practice Periodical of Hazardous, Toxic, and Radioactive Waste Management, 9*(1), 59–70. doi:10.1061/(ASCE)1090-025X(2005)9:1(59)

Lawless, W. F., Bergman, M., Louçã, J., Kriegel, N. N., & Feltovich, N. (2007). A quantum metric of organizational performance: Terrorism and counterterrorism. *Computational & Mathematical Organization Theory, 13*, 241–281. doi:10.1007/s10588-006-9005-4

Lawless, W. F., Castelao, T., & Ballas, J. A. (2000). Virtual knowledge: Bistable reality and the solution of ill-defined problems. *IEEE Systems Man, and Cybernetics, 30*(1), 119–126. doi:10.1109/5326.827482

Lawless, W. F., Howard, C. R., & Kriegel, N. N. (2008b). A quantum real-time metric for NVO's . In Putnik, G. D., & Cuhna, M. M. (Eds.), *Encyclopedia of Networked and Virtual Organizations*. Hershey, PA: Information Science Reference. doi:10.4018/978-1-59904-885-7.ch083

Lawless, W. F., Sofge, D. A., & Goranson, H. T. (2009). Conservation of Information: A New Approach to Organizing Human-Machine-Robotic Agents Under Uncertainty. In P. Bruza, D. A. Sofge, W. F. Lawless, K. Van Rijsbergen & M. Klusch (Eds.), *Quantum Interaction. Third International Symposium, QI-2009*. Berlin: Springer-Verlag.

Lawless, W. F., Whitton, J., & Poppeliers, C. (2008a). Case studies from the UK and US of stakeholder decision-making on radioactive waste management. *Practice Periodical of Hazardous, Toxic, and Radioactive Waste Management, 12*(2), 70–78. doi:10.1061/(ASCE)1090-025X(2008)12:2(70)

Lebart, L., Morineau, A., & Warwick, K. M. (1984). *Multivariate Descriptive Statistical Analysis: Correspondence Analysis and Related Techniques for Large Matrices*. New York: J. Wiley & Sons.

Lee, H. L., & Whang, S. (2001). E-Business and Supply Chain Integration. *Stanford Global Supply Chain Management Forum*. Retrieved from http://www.stanford.edu/group/scforum/Welcome/EB_SCI.pdf

Lee, H. L., Padmanabhan, V., & Whang, S. (1997). Information Distortion in Supply Chain: The Bullwhip Effect. *Management Science, 43*(4), 546–558. doi:10.1287/mnsc.43.4.546

Lee, J.-N., Huynh, M. Q., Kwok, R. C.-W., & Pi, S.-M. (2003). IT outsourcing evolution: past, present, and future. *Communications of the ACM, 46*(5), 84–89. doi:10.1145/769800.769807

Lee, R. M. (1988, April). Bureaucracies as deontic systems. *ACM Transactions on Office Information Systems, 6*(2), 87–108. doi:10.1145/45941.45944

Lee, Y. W., & Strong, D. M. (2004). Knowing-why about data processing and data quality. *Journal of Management Information Systems, 20*(3), 13–39.

Lee, Y., Kozar, K. A., & Larsen, K. R. T. (2003). The technology acceptance model: past, present, and future. *Communications of the AIS, 12*(50), 752–280.

Lengnick-Hall, C. A., Lengnick-Hall, M. L., & Abdinnour-Helm, S. (2004). The role of social and intellectual capital in achieving competitive advantage through enterprise resource planning (ERP) systems. *Journal of Engineering and Technology Management, 21*(4), 307–330. doi:10.1016/j.jengtecman.2004.09.005

Lenzerini, M. (2002). A Theoretical Perspective . In *PODS 2002* (pp. 243–246). Data Integration.

Leonard-Barton, D. (1998). *Nascentes do Saber*. Rio de Janeiro, Brasil: Fundação Getúlio Vargas.

Lessig, L. (1999). *Code and other laws of cyberspace*. New York: Basic Books.

Lessig, L. (2001). *The future of ideas, The fate of the commons in a connected world*. New York: Random House.

Leung, J. Y.-T., & Young, G. H. (1989). Minimizing schedule length subject to minimum flow time. *SIAM Journal on Computing, 18*, 314–326. doi:10.1137/0218022

Levenburg, N. M., Schwarz, T. V., & Motwani, J. (2005). Understanding adoption of internet technologies among SMEs. *Journal of Small Business Strategy, 16*(1), 51–69.

Levine, J. M., & Moreland, R. L. (1998). Small groups . In Gilbert, D. T., Fiske, S. T., & Lindzey, G. (Eds.), *Handbook of Social Psychology* (*Vol. 2*, pp. 415–469). Boston, MA: McGraw-Hill.

Levy, M., Powell, P., & Worrall, L. (2005). Strategic Intent and E-Business in SMEs: Enablers and Inhibitors. *Information Resources Management Journal*, *18*(4), 1–20.

Liang, H., Saraf, N., Hu, Q., & Xu, W. (2007). Assimilation of Enterprise Systems: The Effect of Institutional Pressures and the Mediating Role of Top Management. *Management Information Systems Quarterly*, *31*(1), 59–87.

Liao, C. J., Yu, W. C., & Joe, C. B. (1997). Bicriterion scheduling in the two-machine flowshop. *The Journal of the Operational Research Society*, *48*, 929–935.

Liao, X. W., Li, Y., & Lu, B. (2007). A model for selecting an ERP system based on linguistic information processing . *Information Systems*, *32*(7), 1005–1017. doi:10.1016/j.is.2006.10.005

Liles, D. H., & Presley, A. R. (1996). Enterprise modeling within an enterprise engineering framework. In *Proceedings of the 28th conference on Winter simulation* (pp. 993-999). Coronado, CA: IEEE Computer Society. doi: 10.1145/256562.256882

List, B., & Korherr, B. (2006). An evaluation of conceptual business Process Modeling Languages. In *Proceedings of the 2006 ACM Symposium on Applied Computing* (pp. 1532 - 1539).

Liu, J., & Reeves, C. R. (2001). Constructive and composite heuristic solutions to the $P//\Sigma C_i$ scheduling problem. *European Journal of Operational Research*, *132*, 439–452. doi:10.1016/S0377-2217(00)00137-5

Lo, C., Tsai, C., & Li, R. (2005, January). A Case Study of ERP Implementation for Opto-Electronics Industry. *International Journal of The Computer . The Internet and Management*, *13*(1), 13–30.

Loh, L., & Venkatraman, N. (1992). Diffusion of Information Technology Outsourcing: Influence Sources and the Kodak Effect. *Information Systems Research*, 334–358. doi:10.1287/isre.3.4.334

Lomnicki, A. (1965). Branch-and-bound algorithm for the exact solution of the three-machine scheduling problem. *Operational Research Quarterly*, *16*, 89–100. doi:10.1057/jors.1965.7

Lopes, M. (2007). *Panorama do Desenvolvimento da Siderurgia Brasileira*. Instituto Brasileiro de Siderurgia. Retrieved November 2007, from http://www.abmbrasil.com.br

Loukil, T., Teghem, J., & Tuyttens, D. (2005). Solving multi-objective production scheduling problems using metaheuristics. *European Journal of Operational Research*, *161*, 42–61. doi:10.1016/j.ejor.2003.08.029

Lu, K., & Sy, C. (2008). *A real-time decision-making of maintenance using fuzzy agent*. Expert Systems with Applications.

Ludke, M., & Andre, M. (1986). *Pesquisa em educação: abordagens qualitativas*. São Paulo, Brasil: EPU.

Luftman, J. (2000). *Assessing business-IT alignment maturity*. Communications of the Association for Information Systems.

Luftman, J., & Brier, T. (1999). *Achieving and sustaining business-IT alignment*. California Management Review.

Mabert, V. A., & Venkatraman, M. A. (1998). Special Research Focus on Supply Chain Linkages: Challenges for Design and Management in the 21st Century. *Decision Sciences*, *29*(3), 537–550. doi:10.1111/j.1540-5915.1998.tb01353.x

Mabert, V., Soni, A., & Venkatamara, M. (2003). Enterprise Resource Planning: managing implementation process. *European Journal of Operational Research*, *146*(2), 302–314. doi:10.1016/S0377-2217(02)00551-9

Macdonald-Ross, M. (1977). How Numbers Are Shown: A Review of Research on the Presentation of Quantitative Data in Texts. *Audio-Visual Communication Review*, *25*, 359–409.

Maculuve, P., & Rodrigues, A. (2002). O Outsourcing em projectos de desenvolvimento de Sistemas de Informação: Conceitos, princípios e opinião. *Sistemas de Informação*, *16*, 31–40.

Maddalena, A. (2004). Pattern Based Management: Data Models and Architectural Aspects. In W. Lindner et al. (Eds.), *EDBT 2004 Workshops* (LNCS 3268, pp. 54–65).

Maes, R., Rijsenbrij, D., Truijens, O., & Goedvolk, H. (2000). *Redefining business–IT alignment through a unified framework*. White paper.

Mahmood, M. A., Burn, J. M., Gemoets, L. A., & Jacquez, C. (2000). Variables affecting information technology end-user satisfaction: a meta-analysis of the empirical literature. *International Journal of Human-Computer Studies, 52*, 751–771. doi:10.1006/ijhc.1999.0353

Mahmoud, T., & Marx Gómez, J. (2008a). Semantic Web Services Process Mediation Using WSMX Concepts. In *Proceedings 20th International Conference on Systems Research, Informatics and Cybernetics (InterSymp-2008)*, Baden-Baden, Germany.

Mahmoud, T., & Marx Gómez, J. (2008b). *Integration of Semantic Web Services Principles in SOA to Solve EAI and ERP Scenarios*.

Mahmoud, T., & Marx Gómez, J. (2009). Towards Process Mediation in Semantic Service Oriented Architecture. In *Handbook of Research on Social Dimensions of Semantic Technologies and Web Services*. Hershey, PA: IGI Global.

Maizlish, B., & Handler, R. (2005). *IT Portfolio Management Step-by-step. Unlocking the Business Value of Technology*. New York: John Wiley & Sons.

Malhotra, A., Gosain, S., & El Sawy, O. A. (2005, March). Absorptive Capacity Configurations in Supply Chains: Gearing for Partner-Enabled Market Knowledge Creation. *Management Information Systems Quarterly, 29*(1), 145–187.

Malhotra, A., Peterson, D., & Gao, S. Sperberg-McQueen. C. M. & Thompson, H. (2009). *W3C XML Schema Definition Language (XSD) 1.1 Part 2: Datatypes*. Retrieved from http://www.w3.org/TR/xmlschema11-2/

Malie, M., Duffy, N., & van Rensburg, A. C. J. (2008). Enterprise resource planning solution selection criteria in medium-sized South African companies. *South African Journal of Industrial Engineering, 19*(1), 17–41.

Malinowski, E., & Zimányi, E. (2006). Hierarchies in a multidimensional model: From conceptual modeling to logical representation. *Data & Knowledge Engineering, 59*, 348–377. doi:10.1016/j.datak.2005.08.003

Mandal, P., & Gunasekaran, A. (2002). Issues in implementing ERP: A case study. *European Journal of Operational Research*, 274–283.

Mandelbaum, A., & Zeltyn, S. (2007). *Service Engineering of Call Centers: Research, Teaching, Practice*. Haifa, Israel: Faculty of Industrial Engineering and Management, Technion.

Mangan, J., Lalwani, C., & Butcher, T. (2008). *Global Logistics and Supply Chain Management*. Hoboken, NJ: John Wiley & Sons, Inc.

March, J. G. (1991, February). Exploration and Exploitation in Organizational Learning. *Organization Science, 2*(1), 71–87. doi:10.1287/orsc.2.1.71

Marconi. M & Lakatos, E. (1988). *Técnicas de Pesquisa*. São Paulo, Brasil: Editora Atlas.

Markus, M. L., & Keil, M. (1994). If we build it, they will come: designing information systems that people want to use. *Sloan Management Review, 35*(4), 11–25.

Markus, M. L., & Tanis, C. (2000). The Enterprise System Experience: From Adoption to Success . In Zmud, R. W. (Ed.), *Framing the Domains of IT Management: Projecting the Future through the Past* (pp. 173–207). Cincinnati: Pinnaflex, Educational Resources Inc.

Markus, M. L., Tanis, C., & Fenema, P. C. V. (2000). Multisite ERP implementations. *Communications of the ACM, 43*(4), 42–46. doi:10.1145/332051.332068

Massetti, B., & Zmud, R. W. (1996). Measuring the extent of EDI usage in complex organizations: Strategies and illustrative examples. *Management Information Systems Quarterly, 20*(3), 331. doi:10.2307/249659

Mathieson, K. (1991). Predicting user intentions: comparing the technology acceptance model with the theory of planned behavior. *Information Systems Research, 2*, 173–191. doi:10.1287/isre.2.3.173

Maximilien, E., & Munindar, P. (2004). *Towards Autonomic Web Services Trust and Selection.* New York: ACM.

McCormack, K. P., & Johnson, W. C. (2003). *Supply Chain Networks and Business Process Orientation.* Boca Raton, FL: St. Lucie Press.

McCrea, B. (2008). ERP: Gaining Momentum. *Logistic Management,* November 2008, pp. 44-46.

McCready, S. (2005). TCO, NPV, EVA, IRR, ROI, Getting the terms right. *CIOview.*

McDonald, W. J. (1992). The influence of moderator philosophy on the content of focus group sessions: a multivariate analysis of group session content . In Kumar, V. (Ed.), *Enhancing Knowledge Development in Marketing* (Vol. 3, pp. 540–545). Chicago, IL: American Marketing Association.

McDonald, W. J. (1994). Provider perceptions of focus group research use: a multicountry perspective. *Journal of the Academy of Marketing Science, 22*(3), 265–273. doi:10.1177/0092070394223007

McGee, J., & Prusak, L. (1994). *Gerenciamento estratégico da informação.* Rio de Janeiro, Brasil: Campus.

McGuinness, D. L. (1998). Ontologies Come of Age . In Fensel, D., Hendler, J., Lieberman, H., & Wahlster, W. (Eds.), *Spinning the Semantic Web: Bringing the World Wide Web to Its Full Potential.* Cambridge, MA: MIT Press.

McLeod, R. (2000). *Management information systems.* Mexico City: Prentice Hall.

McLeod, R., & Schell, G. (2003). *Management Information Systems.* New York: Prentice Hall.

Meihoefer, H. J. (1969). The Utility of the Circle as an Effective Cartographic Symbol. *Canadian Cartographer, 6,* 105–117.

Meihoefer, H. J. (1973). *The Visual Perception of the Circle in Thematic Maps: Experimental Results.*

Merchants. (2007). *Global Contact Centre Benchmarking Report.* New York: Dimension Data Group.

Merriam-Webster. (2008). *Ontology word In Merriam-Webster Dictionary online.* Retrieved February 1, 2009, from http://www.m-w.com/dictionary/ontology

Michalewicz, Z., Schmidt, M., Michalewicz, M., & Chiriac, C. (2007). *Adaptive Business Intelligence.* Berlin: Springer.

Microsoft Corporation. (2003). Clinical Systems Integration Reference Implementation for Microsoft [*Guide.*]. *The Office,* 2003.

Microsoft Corporation. (2004). *BizTalk Acceleration for HL7.*

Microsoft Corporation. (2004). *Path to Profitability reduces Costs and Increase revenues with InfoPath.*

Microsoft Corporation. (2009a). *Home: Microsoft's Health Solutions.* Retrieved from http://www.microsoft.com/japan/smallbiz/healthcare/default.mspx

Microsoft Corporation. (2009b). *Cast studies: Medical support and welfare cases.* Retrieved from http://www.microsoft.com/japan/showcase/industry/medical.aspx

Microsoft Corporation. (2009c). *Case Studies: Nihoe Prefectural Hospital.* Retrieved from http://www.microsoft.com/japan/showcase/ninohe_hospital.mspx

Microsoft. (2003). *Microsoft Business Solutions.* Retrieved from http://www.microsoft.com/business solutions

Miguel, A. S. (2000). *O Risco em Projectos de Desenvolvimento de Software: Estudo Delphi em Portugal.* Paper presented at Actas da 1ª Conferência da Associação Portuguesa de Sistemas de Informação, Guimarães.

Miles, M. B., & Huberman, A. M. (1994). *Qualitative Data Analysis* (2nd ed.). Thousand Oaks, CA: Sage Publications.

Minella, G., Ruiz, R., & Ciavotta, M. (2007). A review and evaluation of multi-objective algorithms for the flowshop scheduling problem. *INFORMS Journal on Computing, 20,* 451–471. doi:10.1287/ijoc.1070.0258

Ministry of Health, Labour and Welfare. (2000-2001). *Annual Report on Health, Labour and Welfare*. Tokyo, Japan.

Mintzberg, H. (1983). *Structure in Fives-Designing Effective Organizations*. Upper Saddle River, NJ: Prentice Hall Inc.

Mirchandani, D. A., & Motwani, J. (2001). Understanding small business electronic commerce adoption: an empirical analysis. *Journal of Computer Information Systems*, *41*(3), 70–73.

MIT–CCI. (2006). *Home page – MIT Center for Collective Intelligence*. Retrieved December 15, 2009, from http://cci.mit.edu/index.html

Mitra, N. (2003). *SOAP version 1.2 part 0: Primer*. W3C Recommendation. Retrieved from http://www.w3.org/TR/soap12-part0/

Mokotoff, E. (2009). Minimizing the Makespan and Total Flow Time on the Permutation Flow Shop Scheduling Problem. In J. Blazewicz, M. Drozdowski, G. Kendall & B. McCollum (Eds.), *Proceedings of the 4th Multidisciplinary International Conference on Scheduling: Theory and Applications* (pp. 479-506). Dublin: The University of Nottingham.

Møller, C. (2005). ERP II: a conceptual framework for next-generation enterprise systems? *Journal of Enterprise Information Management*, *18*(4), 483–497. doi:10.1108/17410390510609626

Monforte Moreno, M. (1995). *Sistemas de información para la dirección*. Madrid: Pirámide.

Monma, C. L., & Rinnooy Kan, A. H. G. (1983). A concise survey of efficiently solvable special cases of the permutation flow-shop problem. *RAIRO Recherche Opérationelle*, *17*, 105–119.

Moor, J. H. (1985). What is computer ethics? *Metaphilosophy*, *16*(4), 266–275. doi:10.1111/j.1467-9973.1985.tb00173.x

Moore, G., & Benbasat, I. (1991). Development of an instrument to measure the perceptions of adopting an information technology innovation. *Information Systems Research*, *2*(3), 192–222. doi:10.1287/isre.2.3.192

Morabito, V., Pace, S., & Previtali, P. (2005). ERP Marketing and Italian SMEs. *European Management Journal*, *23*(5), 590–598. doi:10.1016/j.emj.2005.09.014

Morley, C., Hugues, J., Lebland, B., & Hugues, O. (2005). *Processus métier et Systèmes d'Information*. Paris: Dunod.

Morrison, E., & Milliken, F. (2000). Organizational silence: a barrier to change and development in a pluralistic world. *Academy of Management Review*, *25*(4), 706–725. doi:10.2307/259200

Moss, T. (2004). *Reliability Data Handbook*. New York: ASME.

Motwani, J., Mirchandani, M., & Gunasekaran, A. (2002). Successful implementation of ERP Projects: evidence from two case studies. *International Journal of Production Economics*, *75*, 83–96. doi:10.1016/S0925-5273(01)00183-9

Mourtzis, D., Papakostas, N., Makris, S., Xanthakis, V., & Chryssolouris. (2008). Supply chain modeling and control for producing highly customized products. *Manufacturing Technology Journal*.

Moxey, P., & Berent, A. (2008). *Corporate Governance and the Credit Crunch*. Association of Chartered Certified Accountants.

Moyaux, T., & Chaib-draa, B. (2007, May). Information sharing as a coordination mechanism for reducing the bullwhip effect in supply chain. *IEEE Transactions on Systems, Man, and Cybernetics*, *37*(3), 396–409. doi:10.1109/TSMCC.2006.887014

Muehlen, M. Z., & Ho, D. T.-Y. (2006). Risk management in the BPM lifecycle. In *Proceedings of The workshop Business Process Design: Past Present and Future* (LNCS 3812, pp. 454-466). Berlin: Springer.

Mulej, M. (1974). The Dialectical Theory . In *Slovene*. Ljubljana, Slovenia: University of Ljubljana.

Mulej, M. (2007). Systems theory: A worldview and/ or a methodology aimed at requisite holism/realism of humans' thinking, decisions and action. *SRBS*, *24*(3), 347–357.

Mulej, M. (at al.). (2003). Informal systems thinking or systems theory. *Cybernetics and Systems*, *34*(2), 71–92. doi:10.1080/01969720302868

Mulej, M. (et al.) (2000). *Basic of Systems Theory*. Maribor, Slovenia: FEB.

Mulej, M., & Kajzer, S. (1998). Ethics of Interdependence and the Law of Requisite Holism . In Rebernik, M., & Mulej, M. (Eds.), *STIQE '98* (pp. 56–67). Maribor, Slovenia: ISR.

Mulej, M., Likar, B., & Potocan, V. (2005). Increasing the capacity of companies to absorb inventions from research organizations and encouraging people to innovate. *Cybernetics and Systems*, *36*(5), 491–512. doi:10.1080/01969720590944276

Murata, T., Ishibuchi, H., & Tanaka, H. (1996). Multi-Objective Genetic Algorithm and its Applications to Flowshop Scheduling. *Computers & Industrial Engineering*, *30*(4), 957–968. doi:10.1016/0360-8352(96)00045-9

Musaji, Y. (2005). ERP Post-implementation Problems. *Information Systems Control Journal*, *4*. Retrieved September 21, 2008 from http://www.isaca.org/Template. cfm?Section=Home&Template=/ContentManagement/ ContentDisplay.cfm&ContentID=26149

Muscatello, J., & Parente, D. (2006). Enterprise Resource Planning (ERP), A Post--Implementation Cross-Case Analysis. *Information Resources Management Journal*, *19*(3), 61–80.

Mutsaers, E., Zee, H., & Giertz, H. (1977). The Evolution of **Information** Technology. *BIK-Blad*, *2*(2), 15–23.

Myers, M. D. (1997). Qualitative Research in Information Systems. *Management Information Systems Quarterly*, *21*(2), 241–242. doi:10.2307/249422

Nagar, A., Heragu, S. S., & Haddock, J. (1995b). A Branch and Bound approach for a two machine flowshop scheduling problem. *The Journal of the Operational Research Society*, *46*, 721–734.

Nagar, J., Haddock, J., & Heragu, S. S. (1995a). Multiple and bicriteria scheduling: A literature survey. *European Journal of Operational Research*, *81*, 88–104. doi:10.1016/0377-2217(93)E0140-S

Nah, F. F. H., & Delgado, S. (2006). Critical success factors for enterprise resource planning implementation and upgrade. *Journal of Computer Information Systems*, *46*(SI), 99-113.

Nah, F. F., Tan, X., & The, S. H. (2004). An empirical investigation on end-users' acceptance of enterprise systems. *Information Resources Management Journal*, *17*(3), 32–53.

Nah, F., & Delgado, S. (2006). Critical Success Factors for ERP Implementation and Upgrade. *Journal of Computer Information Systems*, *46*(5), 99–113.

Nah, F., Lau, J., & Kuang, J. (2001). Critical factors for successful implementation of enterprise systems. *Business Process Management*, *7*(3), 285–296. doi:10.1108/14637150110392782

Nauck, D., Spott, M., & Azvine, B. (2003). SPIDA—A Novel Data Analysis Tool. *BT Technology Journal*, *21*(4), 104–112. doi:10.1023/A:1027339722343

Nawaz, M., Enscore, E. E. Jr, & Ham, I. (1983). A heuristic algorithm for the m machine, n job flowshop sequencing problem. *OMEGA . The International Journal of Management Science*, *11*, 91–95.

Neches, R., Fikes, R., Finin, T., Gruber, T., Patil, R., Senator, T., & Swartout, W. R. (1991). Enabling Technology for Knowledge Sharing. *AI Magazine*, *12*(3), 36–56.

Negash, S., & Gray, P. (2003). *Business Intelligence*. Paper presented at the Ninth Americas Conference on Information Systems.

Nemati, H. R., Steiger, D. M., Iyer, L. S., & Herschel, R. T. (2002). Knowledge Warehouse: An Architectural Integration of Knowledge Management, Decision Support, Artificial Intelligence and Data Warehousing. *Decision Support Systems, 33*(2), 143–161. doi:10.1016/S0167-9236(01)00141-5

Nemati, H. R., Steiger, D. M., Iyer, L. S., & Herschel, R. T. (2002). Knowledge warehouse: an architectural integration of knowledge management, decision support, artificial intelligence and data warehousing. *Decision Support Systems, 33*(2), 143–161. doi:10.1016/S0167-9236(01)00141-5

Neppalli, V. R., Chen, C. L., & Gupta, J. N. D. (1996). Genetic algorithms for the two-stage bicriteria flowshop problem. *European Journal of Operational Research, 95,* 356–373. doi:10.1016/0377-2217(95)00275-8

Nevo, D., & Wand, Y. (2005). Organizational memory information systems: a transactive memory approach. *Decision Support Systems, 39,* 549–562. doi:10.1016/j.dss.2004.03.002

Nevu, D., & Wade, M. R. (2007). How to avoid Disappointment by Design. *Communications of the ACM, 50*(4).

Newell, A. (1981). *The Knowledge Level.* AI Magazine.

Newell, A., & Simon, H. A. (1972). *Human Problem Solving.* Englewood Cliffs, NJ: Prentice-Hall.

NextiraOne. (2006). *Serviços Geridos.* Retrieved July 2006, from http://www.nextiraone.pt/servicos/servicos_geridos

Ngai, E. W. T., Law, C. C. H., & Wat, F. K. T. (2008). Examining the critical success factors in the adoption of enterprise resource planning. *Computers in Industry, 59*(6), 548–564. doi:10.1016/j.compind.2007.12.001

Nicolas, R. (2004). Knowledge management impacts on decision making process. *Journal of Knowledge Management, 8*(1), 20–31. doi:10.1108/13673270410523880

Niegemann, H., Hessel, S., & Hochscheid-Mauel, D. (2004). *Kompendium E-Learning.* Berlin: Springer.

Niemann, J., Galis, M., Ciupan, C., & Westkämper, E. (2003). The e-Virtual Professor - an International Network of Universities for Computer Assisted Learning Education in Mechanical Engineering . *Marine Engineering, 3*(1-2), 200–206.

Niemann, J., Galis, M., Stolz, M., Legg, L., & Westkämper, E. (2004). E-Teach Me: An e-Learning Platform for Higher Education in Manufacturing Engineering. *Academic Journal of Manufacturing Engineering, 2*(1), 1–9.

Nolan, R. (1973). Managing the **computer** resource: a stage hypothesis. *Communications of the ACM, 16*(7), 399–405. doi:10.1145/362280.362284

Nonaka, I. (1986). A Dynamic Theory of Organizational Knowledge Creation. *Organization Science, 5*(1), 14–37. doi:10.1287/orsc.5.1.14

Nonaka, I. (2000). A empresa criadora de conhecimento . In *Gestão do Conhecimento. Harvard Business Review. (A. C. da Cunha Serra, Trad.).* Rio de Janeiro, Brasil: Campus.

Nonaka, I., & Takeuchi, H. (1997). *Criação de Conhecimento na Empresa: como as empresas japonesas geram a dinâmica da inovação.* Rio de Janeiro, Brasil: Campus.

Novabase. (2006). *Multisourcing Services.* Retrieved July 2006, from http://www.novabase.pt/showCategory.asp?idCat=Outsourcing

Nowicki, E., & Zdrzałka, S. (1990). A survey of results for sequencing problems with controllable processing times. *Discrete Applied Mathematics, 26,* 271–287. doi:10.1016/0166-218X(90)90105-L

Nunamaker, J. F. Jr, & Deokar, A. V. (2008). GDSS parameters and benefits . In Burstein, C., & Holsapple, C. (Eds.), *Handbook on Decision Support Systems 1: Basic Themes* (pp. 392–415). Berlin: Springer-Verlag. doi:10.1007/978-3-540-48713-5_20

Nunnally, J. C. (1967). *Psychometric Theory.* New York: McGraw-Hill.

Nunnally, J. C. (1978). *Psychometric Theory* (2nd ed.). New York: McGraw-Hill.

Nunnally, J. C. (1978). *Psychometric Theory*. New York: McGraw-Hill.

O'Dell, C., & Grayson, J. C. (2003). Identifying and Transferring Internal Best Practices . In Holsapple, C. W. (Ed.), *Handbook on Knowledge Management* (pp. 601–622). Lexington, KY: Springer.

O'Leary, J. (2002). *Learn to Speak the Language of ROI*. Harvard Management Update.

OECD. (1999). *OECD Principles of Corporate Governance*. Paris: OECD.

OECD. (2001). *Health at Glance*.

OECD. (2002). *OECD employment outlook*.

OECD. (2004). *OECD Principles of Corporate Governance*. Paris: OECD.

OECD. (2005). *Oslo Manual: Guidelines for Collecting and Interpreting Innovation Data* (3rd ed.). Paris: OECD.

Oh, W., & Pinsonneault, A. (2007). On the Assessment of the Strategic Value of Information Technologies: Conceptual and Analytical Approaches. *Management Information Systems Quarterly*, *31*(2), 239–265.

Ohashi, M. (2003). *Knowledge-Based Collaborative Work*. The Report of Supplementary Budget Project of the Ministry of Post and Telecommunications.

Ohashi, M. (2003). *Public iDC and c-Society*. Tokyo: Kogaku Tosho.

Ohashi, M. (2003). *The Report of Society for the Advance Study on e-Society*. The Society of the Basis for e-Community.

Ohashi, M. (2003). *Time Business*. Tokyo: NTT Publication.

Ohashi, M. (2004).The Report of the Advanced Studies for the Social Capital of e-Society. *The Society of the Basis for the e-Community*.

Ohashi, M. (2005). *XML Web Services for Next Generation & A view of Citizen Centric*. Tokyo: Kinokuniya Co. Ltd.

Ohashi, M., & Hori, M. (2005). *The Theory of Economics for Network Societ*. Tokyo: Kinokuniya Co.

Ohashi, M., & Nagai, M. (2001). *Internet Data Center Revolution*. Tokyo: Impress.

Ohashi, M., Sasaki, K., & Hori, M. (2004). On the Study of Knowledge Structualization and Adaptive process Based on Project Based Learning. *Journal of Policy Studies*, *11*, 55–78.

Okhuysen, G. A., & Eisenhardt, K. M. (2002). Integrating knowledge in groups: How formal interventions enable flexibility. *Organization Science*, *13*(4), 370–386. doi:10.1287/orsc.13.4.370.2947

Okoli, C., & Pawlowski, S. D. (2004). The Delphi method as a research tool: an example, design considerations and applications. *Information & Management*, *42*(1), 15–29.

Oliver, R. L. (1980). A cognitive model for the antecedents and consequences of satisfaction. *JMR, Journal of Marketing Research*, *17*, 460–430. doi:10.2307/3150499

Onwubolu, G., & Davendra, D. (2006). Scheduling flow shops using differential evolution algorithm. *European Journal of Operational Research*, *171*, 674–692. doi:10.1016/j.ejor.2004.08.043

Orlikowski, W. J. (1992). The duality of technology: rethinking the concept of technology in organization. *Organization Science*, *3*(3), 398–427. doi:10.1287/orsc.3.3.398

Orlikowski, W. J., & Baroudi, J. J. (1991). Studying information technology in organizations: research approaches and assumptions. *Information Systems Research*, *2*, 1–28. doi:10.1287/isre.2.1.1

Osman, I. H., & Potts, C. N. (1989). Simulated Annealing for Permutation Flowshop Scheduling. *OMEGA . The International Journal of Management Science*, *17*(6), 551–557.

Ouellet, M.-C., & Morin, C. M. (2004). Cognitive behavioral therapy for insomnia associated with traumatic brain injury: a single-case study. *Archives of Physical Medicine and Rehabilitation*, *85*, 1298–1302. doi:10.1016/j.apmr.2003.11.036

OWL-S. (2004). Semantic Markup for Web Services. W3C Member Submission, November 2004. Retrieved from http://www.w3.org/Submission/2004/SUBM-OWL-S-20041122/

Özbayrak, M., Papadopouloub, T., & Samarasb, E. (2006). A flexible and adaptable planning and control system for an MTO supply chain system. *Robotics and Computer-integrated Manufacturing*, •••, 22.

Ozsomer, A., & Gencturk, E. (2003). A Resource-Based Model of Market Learning in the Subsidiary: The Capabilities of Exploration and Exploitation. *Journal of International Marketing*, *11*(3), 1–29. doi:10.1509/jimk.11.3.1.20157

Pagarkar, M., Natesan, M., & Prakash, B. (2005). *RFID in Integrated Order Management Systems*. Chennai, India: Tata Consultancy Services.

Pahl, G., & Beitz, W. (1984). *Engineering Design*. London: Design Council.

Panwalkar, S. S., & Iskander, W. (1977). A survey of scheduling rules. *Operations Research*, *25*, 45–61. doi:10.1287/opre.25.1.45

Papazoglou, M., & Van Den Heuvel, W. (2007). Business process development life cycle methodology. *Communications of the ACM*, *50*, 79–85. doi:10.1145/1290958.1290966

Parasuraman, A., & Zinkhan, G. M. (2002). Marketing to and serving customers through the internet: an overview and research agenda. *Journal of the Academy of Marketing Science*, *30*(4), 286–295. doi:10.1177/009207002236906

Parker, B. (1998). Evolução e Revolução: Da Internacionalização à globalização . In Caldas, M., Fachin, R., & Fischer, T. (Eds.), *Handbook de Estudos Organizacionais. Modelos de Análise e Novas Questões em Estudos Organizacionais* (*Vol. 1*). São Paulo, Brasil: Atlas.

Parker, D. (1988). Ethics for Information Systems Personnel. *Journal of Information Systems Management*, *5*, 44–48. doi:10.1080/07399018808962925

Parker, R. G. (1995). *Deterministic Scheduling Theory*. New York: Chapman & Hall.

Parthasarathy, S., & Rajendran, C. (1997). An experimental evaluation of heuristics for scheduling in a real-life flowshop with sequence-dependent setup times of jobs. *International Journal of Production Economics*, *49*, 255–263. doi:10.1016/S0925-5273(97)00017-0

Pastore, S. (2006). Web Content Management Systems: using Plone open source software to build a website for research institute needs. In *Digital Telecommunications, ICDT '06. International Conference* (pp. 24-29).

Pasupathy, T., Rajendran, C., & Suresh, R. K. (2006). A multi-objective genetic algorithm for scheduling in flow shops to minimize the makespan and total flow time of jobs. *International Journal of Advanced Manufacturing Technology*, *27*, 804–815. doi:10.1007/s00170-004-2249-6

Patnayakuni, R., Rai, A., & Seth, N. (2006). Relational Antecedents of Information Flow Integration for Supply Chain Coordination. *Journal of Management Information Systems*, *23*(1), 13–49. doi:10.2753/MIS0742-1222230101

Patni Americas, Inc. (2008). *Thought Paper: Global Data Synchronization: A Foundation Block for Realizing RFID Potential*. Cincinnati, OH: Patni Americas, Inc. Retrieved July 24, 2008, from http://www.patni.com/resource-center/collateral/RFID/tp_RFID_Global-Data-Synchronization.html

Patton, M. Q. (2002). *Qualitative Research and Evaluation Methods*. Thousand Oaks, CA: Sage Publications.

Pedersen, M. K., & Larsen, M. H. (2001). Distributed knowledge management based on product state models - the case of decision support in health care administration. *Decision Support Systems*, *31*(1), 139–158. doi:10.1016/S0167-9236(00)00124-X

Pelanda, M. L. (2006). *Modelos de Governança de Tecnologia da Informação adotados no Brasil: um estudo de casos múltiplos*. Unpublished master dissertation, Universidade Metodista de São Paulo, São Bernárdo do Campo.

Perrin, J. (2001). *Concevoir l'innovation industrielle. Méthodologie de conception de l'innovation*. Paris: CNRS Editions.

Petroni, A. (2002). Critical factors of MRP implementation in small and medium-sized firms. *International Journal of Operations & Production Management, 22*(3), 329–348. doi:10.1108/01443570210417623

Pfeffer, J., & Fong, C. T. (2005). Building Organization Theory from First Principles: The Self-Enhancement Motive and Understanding Power and Influence. *Organization Science, 16*(4), 372–388. doi:10.1287/orsc.1050.0132

Philips, E., & Vriens, D. (1999). *Business Intelligence, Marketing Wijzer.* Amsterdam: Kluwer Bedrijfsinformatie B.V.

Pijpers, G., Bemelmans, T., Heemstra, F., & Montfort, K. v. (2001). Senior executives' use of information technology. *Journal of Information and Software Technology, 43*, 959–971. doi:10.1016/S0950-5849(01)00197-5

Pinedo, M. L. (2002). *Scheduling: Theory, Algorithms, and Systems.* New Jersey: Prentice Hall.

Pirttimäki, V., & Hannula, M. (2003). Process models of business intelligence. *Frontiers of e-business research,* 250-259.

Pirttimäki, V., Lönnqvist, A., & Karjaluoto, A. (2006). Measurement of Business Intelligence in a Finnish Telecommunications Company. *Electronic Journal of Knowledge Management, 4*(1), 83–90.

Pitoura, E., & Bhargava, B. (1999). Data Consistency in Intermittently Distributed Systems. *IEEE Transactions on Knowledge and Data Engineering, 11*(6), 896–915. doi:10.1109/69.824602

Plaza, M., & Rohlf, K. (2008). Learning and Performance in ERP Implementation Projects: A Learning-curve Model for Analyzing and Managing Consulting Costs. *International Journal of Production Economics, 115*(1), 72–85. doi:10.1016/j.ijpe.2008.05.005

Plazaola, L., et al. (2006). A Metamodel for Strategic Business and IT. Alignment Assessment. In *Proceedings of the 41st Annual Hawaii International Conference on System Sciences (HICSS 2008)*, Hawaii.

Plouffe, C., Hulland, J., & Vandenbosch, M. (2001). Research report: richness versus parsimony in modeling technology adoption decisions-understanding merchant adoption of a smart card-based payment system. *Information Systems Research, 12*(2), 208–222. doi:10.1287/isre.12.2.208.9697

Plut, D. (2009). *Planet in Slovenija pred izzivi globalizacije in sonaravnega razvoja.* Ljubljana, Slovenia: University of Ljubljana.

Potocan, V. (1997). A New Perspectives on Business Decision Making. *Management, 2*(1), 13–24.

Potocan, V. (2003). *Business Organization.* Maribor, Slovenia: DOBA.

Potocan, V. (2005). Holistic information support for virtual business organization. *Journal of business and economics research, 3*(11), 25-36.

Potocan, V. (2008). Reliability of information . In Engemann, K., & Lasker, G. (Eds.), *Advances in decision technology and intelligent information systems* (*Vol. 9*, pp. 21–25). Windsor, Ontario: IIAS.

Potocan, V., & Kuralt, B. (2007). Synergy in business: Some new suggestions. *The Journal of American Academy of Business, 12*(11), 199–204.

Potts, C. N. (1980). An adaptive branching rule for the permutation flow-shop problem. *European Journal of Operational Research, 5*, 19–25. doi:10.1016/0377-2217(80)90069-7

Potts, C. N., Shmoys, D. B., & Williamson, D. P. (1991). Permutation vs. non-permutation flow shop schedules. *Operations Research Letters, 10*, 281–284. doi:10.1016/0167-6377(91)90014-G

Power, D. J. (1995–2009). Decision Support Systems Resources. *DSSResources.COM.* Retrieved December 10, 2009, from http://dssresources.com/

Power, D. J. (2002). *Decision Support Systems: Concepts and resources for managers.* Westport, CO: Quorum Books.

Prahalad, C. (1997). A Organização Reestruturável . In *A Organização do Futuro: como preparar as empresas de amanhã*. São Paulo, Brasil: Futura.

Prahalad, C. K. (2008). *The new age of innovation: Driving Co-Created Value Through Global Network*. New York: McGraw Hill.

Prahalad, C., & Hamel, G. (1998). A Competência Essencial da Corporação . In Montgomery, C. A., & Porter, M. E. (Eds.), *Estratégia A Busca da Vantagem Competitiva*. Rio de Janeiro, Brasil: Elsevier Editora.

Premkumar, G., Ramamurthy, K., & Liu, H. (2008). Internet messaging: An examination of the impact of attitudinal, normative, and control belief systems. *Information & Management*, 45, 451–457. doi:10.1016/j.im.2008.06.008

Prisma. (2006). Retrieved July 2006, from http://www.prisma.pt/1024/index.htm

Protégé. (2007). *The Protégé Ontology Editor for Knowledge Acquisition System*. Retrieved from http://protege.stanford.edu

Prudhomme, G. (2000). Analyse Fonctionnelle et démarche de conception . In Drăghici, G., & Brissaud, D. (Eds.), *Modélisation de la connaissance pour la conception et la fabrication intégrées* (pp. 7–30). Timisoara, Romania: Editura Mirton.

Prusak, L. (2001). Where did knowledge management come from? *IBM Systems Journal*, 40(4), 1002–1007. doi:10.1147/sj.404.01002

PT-SI. (2006). Retrieved July 2006, from http://www.ptsi.pt/PTSI/Canais/Solucoes/Outsourcing/

Quinn, F. (2003). The Elusive Goal of Integration. *Supply Chain Management Review*, 7.

Raden, N. (2004). Dashboarding ourselves. *Intelligent Enterprise*, 7(8).

Raghu, T. S., & Vinze, A. (2007). A business process context for Knowledge Management. *Decision Support Systems*, 43, 1062–1079. doi:10.1016/j.dss.2005.05.031

Rai, A., Patnayakuni, R., & Seth, N. (2006, June). Firm Performance Impacts of Digitally Enabled Supply Chain Integration Capabilities. *Management Information Systems Quarterly*, 30(2), 225–246.

Rainville-Pitt, S., & D'Amour, J. (2007). Using a CMS to create fully accessible websites. In *Proceedings of the 2007 international Cross-Disciplinary Conference on Web Accessibility (W4a)* (Vol. 225).

Rajendran, C. (1992). Two-stage flowshop scheduling problem with bicriteria. *The Journal of the Operational Research Society*, 43(9), 879–884.

Rajendran, C. (1993). Heuristic algorithm for scheduling in a flowshop to minimize total flowtime. *International Journal of Production Economics*, 29, 65–73. doi:10.1016/0925-5273(93)90024-F

Rajendran, C. (1995). Heuristics for scheduling in flowshop with multiple objectives. *European Journal of Operational Research*, 82, 540–555. doi:10.1016/0377-2217(93)E0212-G

Rajendran, C., & Ziegler, H. (1997). An efficient heuristic for scheduling in a flowshop to minimize total weighted flowtime of jobs. *European Journal of Operational Research*, 103, 129–138. doi:10.1016/S0377-2217(96)00273-1

Rajendran, C., & Ziegler, H. (2004). Ant-colony algorithms for permutation: flowshop scheduling. *European Journal of Operational Research*, 155, 426–438. doi:10.1016/S0377-2217(02)00908-6

Rajendran, C., & Ziegler, H. (2005). Two ant-colony algorithms for minimizing total flowtime in permutation flowshops. *Computers & Industrial Engineering*, 48, 789–797. doi:10.1016/j.cie.2004.12.009

Rajendran, C., & Ziegler, H. (2009). A Multi-Objective Ant-Colony Algorithm for Permutation Flowshop Scheduling to Minimize the Makespan and Total Flowtime of Jobs . In Chakraborty, U. K. (Ed.), *Computational Intelligence in Flow Shop and Job Shop Scheduling* (pp. 53–99). Berlin: Springer-Verlag. doi:10.1007/978-3-642-02836-6_3

Ralaivao, J., & Darmont, J. (2007). Knowledge and Metadata Integration for Warehousing Complex Data. In *6th International Conference on Information Systems Technology and its Applications (ISTA 07)*, Kharkiv, Ukraine.

Ramos, J. (2006). *Guerras no Outsourcing*. Jornal Expresso.

Rao, S. S. (2000). Enterprise resource planning: business needs and technologies. *Industrial Management & Data Systems, 100*(1-2), 81–88. doi:10.1108/02635570010286078

Rasmy, M. H., Tharwat, A., & Ashraf, S. (2005). Enterprise resource planning (ERP) implementation in the Egyptian organizational. *BNET Business Network*, 1-13.

Rathman, R. G., Johnsen, J., & Wen, H. J. (2005). Alignment of business Strategy and IT Strategy: A Case Study of A Fortune 50 Financial Services Company. *Journal of Computer Information Systems, 45*(2), 1–8.

Razmi, J., Sangari, M. S., & Ghodsi, R. (2009). Developing a Practical Framework for ERP Readiness Assessment Using Fuzzy Analytic Network Process. *Advances in Engineering Software, 40*(11), 1168–1178. doi:10.1016/j.advengsoft.2009.05.002

Recker, J., & Rosemann, M. (2007). Integration of models for understandinding continuance of process modeling techniques. In . *Proceedings of the Americas Conference on Information Systems, 14*, 1–11.

Reeves, C. R. (1993). Improving the Efficiency of Tabu Search for Machine Scheduling Problems. *The Journal of the Operational Research Society, 44*(4), 375–382.

Reeves, C. R. (1995). A Genetic Algorithm for Flowshop Sequencing. *Computers & Operations Research, 22*, 5–13. doi:10.1016/0305-0548(93)E0014-K

Repenning, N., & Sterman, J. (2001). *Nobody ever gets credit for fixing problems that never happened: creating and sustaining process improvement*. California Management Review.

Report, S. S. A. (2006). *SSA ERP on SOA Platform*. SSA Global and IBM. Retrieved from http://www.ssaglobal.com

ResEUr. (2009). *Certified EU Researcher – Entrepreneru*. Retrieved December 20, 2009, from http://www.vrl-kcip.org/spip.php?article591

Rezende, D. A., & Abreu, A. F. (2002). *Modelo de Alinhamento Estratégico da Tecnologia da Informação ao Negócio Empresarial*. Paper presented at the meeting of the XXII Encontro Nacional de Engenharia de Produção, Curitiba.

Ribeiro, R., Batista, F., Paulo, J., Mamede, N., & Pinto, H. S. (2006). Cooking an Ontology. In *Proceedings of the 12th International Conference on Artificial Intelligence: Methodology, Systems, Applications*.

Rieffel, E. G. (2007). Certainty and uncertainty in quantum information processing. In *Quantum Interaction: AAAI Spring Symposium*, Stanford University, AAAI Press.

Rinnooy Kan, A. H. G. (1976). *Machine Scheduling problems: Classification, Complexity and Computations*. The Hague: Martinus Nijhoff.

Riquelme, H. (2002). Commercial Internet Adoption in China: Comparing the experiences of small, medium and large businesses. *Internet Research: Electronic Networking Applications and Policy, 12*(3), 276–286. doi:10.1108/10662240210430946

Rizzi, S. (2003). Open problems in data warehousing: 8 years later. In *Proc. DMDW*.

Rizzi, S. (2007). Conceptual Modeling Solutions for the Data Warehouse. In Wrembel, R., & Koncilia, C. (Eds.), *Data Warehouses and OLAP: Concepts, Architectures and Solutions*. Hershey, PA: IRM Press.

Robey, D., Ross, J. W., & Boudreau, M.-C. (2002). Learning to Implement Enterprise Systems: An Exploratory Study of the Dialectics of Change. *Journal of Management Information Systems, 19*(1), 17–46.

Rocha, V. (2006). *Valor Acrescentado dos Contratos de Outsourcing TI & BPO - O que aprendemos com os nossos Clientes*. Paper presented at Conference about Outsourcing TI & BPO, Lisboa.

Rodger, C., Jason, P. (1999). Uncertainty & Risk Analysis. *PriceWaterHouseCoopers.*

Rodriguez, M. (2004). Advances towards a general-purpose societal-scale human-collective problem-solving engine. In *Proceedings of the International Conference on Systems, Man and Cybernetics* (Vol. 1, pp. 206-211). The Hague, Netherlands: IEEE SMC. Retrieved December 12, 2009, from http://arxiv.org/abs/cs/0501004

Rodriguez, M. A., Steinbock, D. J., Watkins, J. H., Gershenson, C., Bollen, J., Grey, V., & deGraf, B. (2007). Smartocracy: social networks for collective decision making. In *Proceedings of HICSS '07 – The 40th Annual Hawaii International Conference on System Sciences.* Washington, DC: IEEE Computer Society.

Rodriguez, M., & Steinbock, D. (2004). A social network for societal-scale decision-making systems. In *North American Association for Computational Social and Organizational Science Conference Proceedings 2004.* Retrieved November 26, 2009, from http://arxiv.org/abs/cs.CY/0412047

Rodriguez, M., & Steinbock, D. (2006). *The Anatomy of a Large Scale Collective Decision Making System.* Technical Report LA-UR-06-2139. Los Alamos National Laboratory. Retrieved from http://markorodriguez.com/Articles_files/ci-anatomy.pdf

Rodriguez, M., & Watkins, J. (2009). Revisiting the age of enlightenment from a collective decision making systems perspective. *First Monday, 8*(4). Retrieved December 12, 2009, from http://www.uic.edu/htbin/cgiwrap/bin/ojs/index.php/fm/article/view/2584/2250

Rogers, E. M. (1983). *Diffusion of Innovation* (3rd ed.). New York: Free Press.

Rogers, E. M. (1995). *The Diffusion of Innovation* (4th ed.). New York: Free Press.

Rolland, C. (2007). Capturing System Intentionality with Maps . In *Conceptual Modeling in Information System Engineering* (pp. 141–158). Berlin: Springer. doi:10.1007/978-3-540-72677-7_9

Rolland, C., & Prakash, N. (2000). Bridging the Gap Between Organisational Needs and ERP Functionality. *Requirements Engineering, 5*(3), 180–193. doi:10.1007/PL00010350

Ropke, F. (1998). *The Entrepreneurial University: Innovation, Academic Knowledge Creation and Regional Development in a Globalize Economy.* Working paper of the Department of Economics, Philips University Marburg, Germany.

Rosario, J. G. (2000 May). On the leading edge: critical success factors in ERP implementation projects. *Business World*, 21-27.

Ross, J. W., Weil, P., & Robertson, D. C. (2008). *Arquitetura de TI como Estratégia Empresarial.* Harvard Business Review.

Ross, J. W., Weill, P., & Robertson, D. C. (2006). *Enterprise Architecture as Strategy. Creating a Foundation for Business Execution.* Cambridge, MA: Harvard Business School Press.

Ross, J., & Weill, P. (2002). *Six IT Decision Your IT People Shouldn't Make.* Harvard Business Review.

Ross, S. (2004). *Introduction to Probability and Statistics for Engineers and Scientists.* Amsterdam: Elsevier Academic Press.

Rothaermel, F. T., & Deeds, D. L. (2004, March). Exploration and Exploitation Alliances in Biotechnology: A System of New Product Development. *Strategic Management Journal, 25*(3), 201–221. doi:10.1002/smj.376

Ruiz, R. (2003). *Técnicas Metaheurísticas para la Programación Flexible de la Producción.* Unpublished doctoral dissertation, Universidad Politécnica de Valencia, Valencia.

Ruiz, R., & Maroto, C. (2005). A comprehensive review and evaluation of permutation flowshop heuristics. *European Journal of Operational Research, 165*, 479–494. doi:10.1016/j.ejor.2004.04.017

Ruiz-Díaz, F., & French, S. (1983). A survey of multi-objective combinatorial scheduling. In French, S., Hartley, R., Thomas, L. C., & White, D. J. (Eds.), *Multi-Objective Decision Making* (pp. 59–77). New York: Academic Press.

Rummler, G., & Brache, A. P. (1994). *Melhores Desempenhos das Empresas*. São Paulo, Brasil: Makron Books.

Saaty, T. L. (1980). *The Analytic Hierarchy Process.* New York: McGrawHill.

Sahin, F., & Robinson, E. P. (2002). Flow coordination and information sharing in supply chains: review, implications and directions for future research. *Decision Sciences, 33*(4), 1–32. doi:10.1111/j.1540-5915.2002.tb01654.x

Saizarbitoria, I. H., Landín, G. A., & Fa, M. C. (2006). The impact of quality management in European companies' performance: The case of the Spanish companies. *European Business Review, 18*(2), 114–131. doi:10.1108/09555340610651839

Salazar, E. (2006). Content Management for the Virtual Library. *Information Technology and Libraries, 25*(3), 170–175.

Samavi, R., Yu, E., & Topaloglu, T. (2008). Strategic reasoning about business models: a conceptual modeling approach. *Information Systems and E-Business management, 7, 171-198.*

Samuelson, D. A. (1999). Predictive dialing for outbound telephone call centers. *Interfaces, 29*(5), 66–94. doi:10.1287/inte.29.5.66

Sanchez, R. (1995). Strategic Flexibility in Product Competition. *Strategic Management Journal, 16*, 135–159. doi:10.1002/smj.4250160921

Sanders, N. R. (2008). Pattern of information technology use: The impact of buyer-supplier coordination and performance. *Journal of Operations Management, 26*, 349–367. doi:10.1016/j.jom.2007.07.003

Santhanam, R., Sasidharan, S., Meharia, P., Brass, D., & Sambamurthy, V. (2009). Improving the success of enterprise information system implementation - current findings and future research. In *SEFBIS Professional Journal of the Scientific and Educational Forum on Business Information Systems* (pp. 29-42).

Santos, L. (2004). *Factores Determinantes do Sucesso de Adopção e Difusão de Serviços de Informação on-line em Sistemas de Gestão de Ciência e Tecnologia.* Unpublished Doctoral dissertation, Minho University, Portugal.

Santos, L. D., & Amaral, L. (2004). *Estudos Delphi com Q-Sort sobre a web: a sua utilização em sistemas de informação.* Paper presented at Actas da 5ª Conferência da Associação Portuguesa de Sistemas de Informação, Lisboa.

SAP. (2006). *Business Process Outsourcing.* Retrieved July 2006, from http://www.sap.com/services/bpo/index.epx

SAP. (2006). *SAP Customer Success Story.* Retrieved from http://www.sap.com

Sarbanes-Oxley Act of 2002, 49 U.S.C. §42121 (2002).

Sargent, A. (2006). Outsourcing relationship literature: an examination and implications for future research. In *Proceedings of the 2006 ACM SIGMIS CPR conference on computer personnel research: Forty four years of computer personnel research: achievements, challenges and the future* (pp. 280-287). Claremont, CA: ACM.

Sayin, S., & Karabati, S. (1999). A bicriteria approach to the two-machine flow shop scheduling problem. *European Journal of Operational Research, 113*, 435–449. doi:10.1016/S0377-2217(98)00009-5

Schell, D. (2002). Overcoming intricacies of ERP system implementation. *Integrated Solutions, 2.*

Schmidt, R. (1997). Managing Delphi surveys using nonparametric statistical techniques. *Decision Sciences, 28*(3), 763–774. doi:10.1111/j.1540-5915.1997.tb01330.x

Scholl, W., König, C., Meyer, B., & Heisig, P. (2004). The future of knowledge management: an international delphi study. *Journal of Knowledge Management, 8*(2), 19–35. doi:10.1108/13673270410529082

Schreiber, G., Akkermans, H., Anjewierden, A., de Hoog, R., Shadbolt, N., van de Velde, W., & Wielinga, B. (2000). *Knowledge Engineering and Management - the CommonKADS Methodology.* Cambridge, MA: MIT Press.

Schultheis, R., & Sumner, M. (1998). *Management Information System.* Boston: McGraw Hill.

Schulz, A. (1996). *Scheduling and Polytopes.* Unpublished doctoral dissertation, Technical University of Berlin, Berlin.

Scott, J. E., & Vessey, I. (2000). Implementing Enterprise Resource Planning Systems: The Role of Learning from Failure. *Information Systems Frontiers, 2*(2), 213. doi:10.1023/A:1026504325010

Seddon, P., Graeser, V., Willcocks, L. (2002). Measuring Organizational IS Effectiveness: an overview and update of senior management perspectives. *SIGMISDatabase.*

Sedera, D., & Tan, T. C. F. (2007). Reconceptualizing Usage for Contemporary Information Systems Success. In *European Conference of Information Systems (ECIS).*

Seeley, M., & Targett, D. (1999). Patterns of senior executives' personal use of computers. *Information & Management, 35*(6), 315–330. doi:10.1016/S0378-7206(99)00002-6

Selen, W. J., & Hott, D. D. (1986). A mixed-integer goal-programming formulation of the standard flow-shop scheduling problem. *The Journal of the Operational Research Society, 12*(37), 1121–1128.

Serafini, P. (1992). Simulated annealing for multiple objective optimization problems. In *Proceedings of the Tenth International Conference on Multiple Criteria Decision Making, vol. 1* (pp. 87-96). Taipei.

Shang, S., & Seddon, P. B. (2002). Assessing and managing the benefits of enterprise systems: the business manager's perspective. *Information Systems Journal, 12*(4), 271–299. doi:10.1046/j.1365-2575.2002.00132.x

Shaw, W. (2007). *Business Ethics.* New York: Wadsworth Publishing.

Shmoys, D. B., & Tardos, É. (1993). An approximation algorithm for the generalized assignment problem. *Mathematical Programming, 62,* 461–474. doi:10.1007/BF01585178

Shpitalni, M., Guttman, G., & Bossin, D. (2005). Forming Task-Oriented Groups in Networks based on Knowledge Mapping. In *Proceedings of the 15th International CIRP Design Seminar,* Shanghai, China, May 22-26.

Shutzberg, L. (2004). *Radio Frequency Identification (RFID) In The Consumer Goods Supply Chain: Mandated Compliance or Remarkable Innovation?* Norcross, GA: Rock-Tenn Company.

Siemieniuch, C. E., Waddell, F. N., & Sinclair, M. A. (1999). The role of partnership in supply Chain management for fast-moving consumer goods: A case study. *International Journal of Logistics, 2*(1), 87–101. doi:10.1080/13675569908901574

Silva, F. C. (2002). *O Outsourcing em Sistemas de Informação.* Paper presented at Actas da 3ª Conferência da Associação Portuguesa de Sistemas de Informação, Lisboa.

Silva, M. (2005). *Microsoft Project 2003.* FCA.

Silva, M., & Gama, N. (2006). *Activos Intangíveis dos Sistemas de Informação.* Instituto Superior Técnico.

Silva, M., & Martins, J. (2008). *IT Governance.* FCA.

Silvius, A. (2006). Does ROI Matter? Insights into the True Business Value of IT. *The Electronic Journal Information Systems Evaluation, 9*(2).

Silvius, A. (2008). The Business Value of IT: A Conceptual Model for Selecting Valuation Methods. *Communications of the IIMA, 8*(3).

Simchi-Levi, D., Kaminsky, P., & Simchi-Levi, E. (2004). *Managing the Supply Chain: The Definitive Guide for the Business Professional.* New York: McGraw-Hill.

Simon, H. A. (1976). *Administrative Behavior.* New York: The Free Press.

Sin, C. C. S. (1989). *Some topics of parallel-machine scheduling theory.* Unpublished doctoral dissertation, University of Manitoba, Winnipeg.

Singla, A. (2005). Impact of ERP Systems on Small and Mid Sized Public Sector Enterprises. *Journal of Theoretical and Applied Information Technology,* 119-131.

Sivrikaya-Serifoglu, F. S., & Ulusoy, G. (1998). A bicriteria two machine permutation flowshop problem. *European Journal of Operational Research, 107,* 414–430. doi:10.1016/S0377-2217(97)00338-X

Slovic, P., Flynn, J. H., & Layman, M. (1991). Perceived risk, trust, and the politics of nuclear waste. *Science, 254,* 1603–1607. doi:10.1126/science.254.5038.1603

Slovic, P., Layman, M., Kraus, N., & Flynn, J. Chalmers, J., & Gesell, G. (2001). Perceived risk, stigma, and potential economic impacts of a high-level nuclear waste repository in Nevada. In J. Flynn, P. Slovic, & H. Kunreuther (Eds.), *Risk, Media and Stigma* (pp. 87-106). London: Earthscan.

Smadi, S. (2001). Employees' Attitudes Towards the Implementation of the Japanese Model Kaisen for Performance Improvement and Meeting Competitive Challenges in The Third Millennium: The Jordanian Private Industrial Sector. *Abhath Al-Yarmouk,* 313-335.

Smith, A. (2009). New framework for enterprise information systems. *International Journal of CENTERIS, 1*(1), 30–36.

Smith, A. (2009). New framework for enterprise information systems. *International Journal of CENTERIS, 1*(1), 30–36.

Smith, F. O. (2008 May). Oracle Says It Will Leapfrog Competitors in Manufacturing Intelligence. *Manufacturing Business Technology,* 26-29.

Smith, W. K., & Tushman, M. L. (2005). Managing strategic contradictions: A top management model for managing innovation streams. *Organization Science, 16*(5), 522–536. doi:10.1287/orsc.1050.0134

Soja, P. (2006). Success Factors in ERP Systems Implementations: Lessons From Practice. *Journal of Enterprise Information Management, 19*(6), 646–661. doi:10.1108/17410390610708517

Somers, T. M., & Nelson, K. G. (2004). A Taxonomy of Players and Activities across the ERP Project Life Cycle. *Information & Management, 41*(3), 257–278. doi:10.1016/S0378-7206(03)00023-5

Somers, T. M., & Nelson, K. G. (2004). A taxonomy of players and activities across the ERP project life cycle. *Information & Management, 41*(3), 257–278. doi:10.1016/S0378-7206(03)00023-5

Sommers, G., & Nelson, C. (2003). A taxonomy of players and activities across the ERP project life cycle. *Information & Management, 41*(3), 257–278. doi:10.1016/S0378-7206(03)00023-5

Son, J. Y., Narasimhan, S., & Riggins, F. J. (2005). Effects of Relational Factors and Channel Climate on EDI Usage in the Customer-Supplier Relationship. *Journal of Management Information Systems, 22*(1), 321–353.

Song, I.-Y., Rowen, W., Medsker, C., & Ewen, E. (2001). An analysis of many-to-many relationships between fact and dimension tables in dimensional modeling. In *Proceedings of the Third International Workshop on Design and Management of Data Warehouses (DMDW'2001),* Interlaken, Switzerland.

Souer, J., Honders, P., Versendaal, J., & Brinkkemper, S. (2007). Defining operations and maintenance in web engineering: a framework for cms-based web applications. In *Digital Information Management, 2007. ICDIM '07. 2nd International Conference* (Vol. 1, pp. 430-435).

Souer, J., Luinenburg, L., Versendaal, J., van de Weerd, I., & Brinkkemper, S. (2008). Engineering a design method for web content management implementations. In *Proceedings of the 10th international Conference on information integration and Web-Based Applications & Services (iiWAS '08)* (pp. 351-358).

Speier, C., & Venkatesh, V. (2002). The hidden minefields in the adoption of sales force automation technologies. *Journal of Marketing, 65*, 98–111. doi:10.1509/jmkg.66.3.98.18510

Srinivas, N., & Deb, K. (1995). Multiobjective function optimization using nondominated sorting genetic algorithms. *Evolutionary Computation, 2*(3), 221–248. doi:10.1162/evco.1994.2.3.221

Srinivasan, R., Lilien, G. L., & Rangaswamy, A. (2002). Technological opportunism and radical technology adoption: An application to e-business. [Retrieved from ABI database.]. *Journal of Marketing, 66*(3), 47–60. doi:10.1509/jmkg.66.3.47.18508

Srivardhanaa, T., & Pawlowski, S. D. (2007). ERP systems as an enabler of sustained business process innovation: A knowledge-based view. *The Journal of Strategic Information Systems, 16*(1), 51–69. doi:10.1016/j.jsis.2007.01.003

Stacey, R. (2000). *Strategic Management & Organisational Dynamics – The challenge of complexity* (3rd ed.). Harlow, UK: Pearson Education.

Stachura, M. E., Astapova, E. V., Tung, H. L., Sofge, D. A., Grayson, J., Bergman, M., et al. (2009). Conservation of information (COI), Geospatial and operational developments in e-Health and Telemedicine for virtual and rural communities. In M. Manuela Cunha, Antonio Tavares & Ricardo Simoes (Eds.), *Handbook of Research on Developments in e-Health and Telemedicine*. Hershey, PA: IGI.

Stadtler, H., & Kilger, C. (2005). *Supply Chain Management and Advanced Planning – Concepts, Models, Software and Case Studies* (3rd ed.). Berlin: Springer.

Stæhr, K. (2006). *Risk and Uncertainty in Cost Benefit Analysis*. Institute for Miljøvurdering.

Standish Group. (1996). *Unfinished Voyages*. Retrieved July 20, 2008, from http://www.standishgroup.com/sample_research/unfinished_voyages_1.php

Standish Group. (1998). *Chaos: A recipe for success*. Retrieved July 20, 2008, from http://www.standishgroup.com/sample_research/PDFpages/chaos1998.pdf

Standish Group. (2006). *Projects success rate*. Retrieved December 20, 2008, from http://www.standishgroup.com/quarterly_reports/pdf_copy/q1_2007_sample.pdf

Stark, J. (2005). *Product Lifecycle Management: Paradigm for 21st Century Product Realization*. London: Springer-Verlag.

Steinberg, R. (2006). *Measuring ITIL*. Bloomington, IN: Trafford Publishing.

Stenmark, D. (2002). Information vs. Knowledge: The Role of intranets in Knowledge Management. In *Proceedings of the 35th Hawaii International Conference on System Sciences*.

Stevens, G. C. (1990). Successful Supply Chain Management. *Management Decision, 28*(8), 25–30. doi:10.1108/00251749010140790

Stewart, D. W., & Shamdasani, P. N. (1990). *Focus Group: Theory and Pratice*. Newbury Park, CA: Sage Publications.

Stigler, G. (1971). The theory of economic regulation. [Retrieved from ABI database.]. *The Bell Journal of Economics and Management Science, 2*, 3–21. doi:10.2307/3003160

Stratman, J. K., & Roth, A. V. (2002). Enterprise resource planning (ERP) competence constructs: two-stage multi-item scale development and validation. *Decision Sciences, 33*(4), 601–628. doi:10.1111/j.1540-5915.2002.tb01658.x

Straub, D., Limayem, M., & Karahanna-Evaristo, E. (1995). measuring systems usage: Implications for IS theory testing. *Management Science, 41*(8), 1328–1342. doi:10.1287/mnsc.41.8.1328

Strauss, A., & Corbin, J. (1990). *Basics of Qualitative Research: Grounded Theory Procedures and Techniques*. Newbury Park, CA: Sage Publications.

Studer, R., Benjamins, V. R., & Fensel, D. (1998). Knowledge engineering: principles and methods. *IEEE Transactions on Data and Knowledge Engineering, 25*(1-2), 161–197. doi:10.1016/S0169-023X(97)00056-6

Studer, R., Grimm, S., & Abecker, A. (2007). *Semantic Web Services: Concept, Technologies and Applications.* Heidelberg, Germany: Springer.

Subramani, M. (2004, March). How Do Suppliers Benefit From Information Technology Use in Supply Chain Relationships? *Management Information Systems Quarterly, 28*(1), 45–73.

Sudzina, F. (2007). Importance of EPR selection criteria in Slovak companies. *Manažment v teórii a praxi, 3*(4), 4-20.

Sukaviriya, N., Sinha, V., Ramachandra, T., Mani, S., & Stolze, M. (2007). User-Centered Design and Business Process Modeling: Cross Road in Rapid Prototyping Tools. In C. Baranauskas et al. (Eds.), *Human-Computer Interaction – INTERACT 2007* (LNCS 4662, pp. 165-178). Berlin: Springer.

Summer, M. (1999). Critical success factors in enterprise wide information management systems projects. In *Proceedings of 5th Americas Conference on Information Systems* (pp. 232-234).

Sunstein, C. (2006). *Infotopia: How many minds produce knowledge?* New York: Oxford University Press.

Swartout, W. R., Neches, R., & Patil, R. (1994). Knowledge sharing: Prospects and challenges . In Fuchi, K., & Yokoi, T. (Eds.), *Knowledge Building and Knowledge Sharing* (pp. 102–109). Amsterdam: IOS Press.

Symons, C. (2005). *Add EVA to IT Investment Analysis.* Forrester.

Symons, C. (2007). *From IT Governance to Value Delivery.* Forrester.

Symons, C. C. M., Oliver Young, G., & Lambert, N. (2005). *IT Governance Framework.* New York: Forrester.

Szajna, B. (1996). Empirical evaluation of the revised technology acceptance model. *Management Science, 42*(1), 85–92. doi:10.1287/mnsc.42.1.85

T'kindt, V., & Billaut, J.-C. (2001). Multicriteria scheduling problems: a survey. RAIRO- . *Operations Research, 35*, 143–163. doi:10.1051/ro:2001109

T'kindt, V., & Billaut, J.-C. (2006). *Multicriteria scheduling: Theory, Models and Algorithms* (2nd ed.). Berlin: Springer.

T'kindt, V., Gupta, J. N. D., & Billaut, J.-C. (2003). Two machine flowshop scheduling problem with a secondary criterion. *Computers & Operations Research, 30*(4), 505–526. doi:10.1016/S0305-0548(02)00021-7

T'kindt, V., Monmarche, N., Tercinet, F., & Laugt, D. (2002). An ant colony optimization algorithm to solve a 2-machine bicriteria flowshop scheduling problem. *European Journal of Operational Research, 142*(2), 250–257. doi:10.1016/S0377-2217(02)00265-5

Taillard, E. (1990). Some efficient heuristic methods for the flor shop sequencing problem. *European Journal of Operational Research, 47*, 67–74. doi:10.1016/0377-2217(90)90090-X

Taillard, E. (1993). Benchmark for basic scheduling problems. *European Journal of Operational Research, 64*, 278–285. doi:10.1016/0377-2217(93)90182-M

Takahashi, M., Herman, G., Ito, A., Nemoto, K., & Yates, J. (2009). *The Role of Online Community in Relation to Other Communication Channels in a Business Development Case.* CCI Working Paper 2009-002. Cambridge, MA: Center for Collective Intelligence, MIT Sloan School of Management. Retrieved December 14, 2009, from http://cci.mit.edu/publications/CCIwp2009-02.pdf

Takeda, Y., et al. (2006). Avoidance of Performance Bottlenecks Caused By HTTP Redirect in Identity Management Protocols. In *Proceedings of the 2006 ACM Workshop on Digital Identity Management*, Alexandria, Virginia, USA (pp. 5-32).

Talbi, E.-G., Rahoual, M., Mabed, M. H., & Dhaenens, C. (2001). A Hybrid Evolutionary Approach for Multicriteria Optimization Problme: Application to the Flow Shop . In Zitzler, E., Deb, K., Thiele, L., Coello, C. A. C., & Corne, D. (Eds.), *Evolutionary Multi-Criterion Optimization (EMO 2001), LNCS 1993* (pp. 416–428). Berlin: Springer. doi:10.1007/3-540-44719-9_29

Tallon, P. (2008). A process-oriented perspective on the alignment of information technology and business strategy. *Journal of Management Information Systems, 24*(3), 227–268. doi:10.2753/MIS0742-1222240308

Tan, X., & Siau, K. (2006). Understanding modeling method by IS developers: a theoretical model and an empirical test. In *Twenty-Seventh International Conference on Information Systems* (pp. 937-947).

Targowsky, A. (2009). *How to Transform the Information Infrastructure of Enterprises into Sustainable, Global-oriented and to Monitor and Predict the Sustainability of Civilization. Unpublished introductory talk with power-point transparencies, CENTERIS 2009*. Portugal: Ofir.

Taylor, G. (2008). *Evolution's Edge: The Coming Collapse and Transformation of our World*. Gabriola Island: New Society Publishers.

Taylor, S., & Todd, P. (1995). Assessing IT Usage: The Role of Prior Experience. *Management Information Systems Quarterly, 19*(1), 25.

Taylor, S., & Todd, P. A. (1995). Understanding information technology usage: a test of competing models. *Information Systems Research, 6*, 144–179. doi:10.1287/isre.6.2.144

Tchokogué, A., Bareil, C., & Duguay, C. R. (n.d.). Key lessons from the implementation of an ERP at Pratt & Whitney Canada. *Int. J. Production Economics*. doi: 10.1016

Teng, J. T. C., Grover, V., & Guttler, W. (2002). Information technology innovations: General diffusion patterns and its relationships to innovation characteristics. *IEEE Transactions on Engineering Management, 49*(1), 13–27. doi:10.1109/17.985744

Theodorou, P., & Giannoula, F. (2008). Manufacturing strategies and financial performance- The effect of advanced information technology: CAD/CAM systems. *The International Journal of Management Science, 36*, 107–121.

Tichy, N., & Cohen, E. (2002). *Leadership Engine*. New York: Harper.

Tiong, C., Cater-Steel, A., & Tan, W. (2008). *Measuring Return on Investment from Implementing ITIL – A Review of the Literature*. Hershey, PA: Information Science Publishing.

Tornatzky, G. (2002). *Innovation U: New University Roles in a Knowledge Economy*. Research Triangle Park, NC: Southern Growth Policy Board.

Tornatzky, L. G., & Fleischer, M. (1990). *The processes of technological innovation*. Lexington, MA: Lexington Books.

Toth, G. (2008). *Resnično odgovorno podjetje (in Slovene)*. Ljubljana: GV.

Tracy, M., & Wiersema, F. (1993). Customer intimacy and other value principles. *Harvard Business Review, 71*(1), 84–93.

Trari, A. (2008). مكتبة جامعة اليرموك. Retrieved from http://library.yu.edu.jo/

Treasury, H. M. (2009). *Independent review of corporate governance of UK banking industry*.

Tremblay, M. C., Fuller, R., Berndt, D., & Studnicki, J. (2007). Doing more with more information: Changing healthcare planning with OLAP tools. *Decision Support Systems, 43*(4), 1305–1320. doi:10.1016/j.dss.2006.02.008

Trivinos, A. (1987). *Introdução à pesquisa em ciências sociais: a pesquisa qualitativa em educação*. São Paulo, Brasil: Atlas.

Trkman, P. (2009). The critical success factors of business process management. *International Journal of Information Management*. doi:.doi:10.1016/j.ijinfomgt.2009.07.003

Tsai, W., & Hung, S. (2008). E-Commerce Implementation: An Empirical Study of the Performance of Enterprise Resource Planning Systems Using the Organizational Learning Model. *International Journal Of Management, 25*(2).

Tsalgatidou, A., & Junginger, S. (1995). Modeling in the reengineering process. *ACM SIGOIS Bulletin, 16*, 17–24. doi:10.1145/209891.209896

Tsoukas, H., & Vladimirou, E. (2001). What is organizational knowledge? *Journal of Management Studies, 38*(7), 972–993. doi:10.1111/1467-6486.00268

Tufte, E. R. (2001). *The Visual Display of Quantitative Information*. Cheshire, CT: Graphics Press.

Tung, H. L., Marshall-Bradley, T., Wood, J., Sofge, D. A., Grayson, J., Bergman, M., & Lawless, W. F. (2009). Enterprise Information Systems: Two Case Studies. In M. Manuela Cunha, Eva F. Oliveira, Antonio J. Tavares, & Luis G. Ferreira (Eds.), *Handbook of Research on Social Dimensions of Semantic Technologies and Web Services*. Hershey, PA: IGI.

Turban, E., Aronson, J. E., Liang, T. P., & Sharda, R. (2007). *Decision Support and Business Intelligence Systems*. Englewood Cliffs, NJ: Pearson Education International.

Turban, E., Leidner, D., McLean, E., & Wetherbe, J. (2008). *Information Technology for Management* (6th ed.). Hoboken, NJ: John Wiley.

Turnbull, N. (1998). *The Combined Code. Principes of Good Governance and Code of Best Practice*. London: The Institute of Chartered Accountants in England and Wales.

Turoff, M., & Hiltz, S. (1982). Computer support for group versus individual decisions. *IEEE Transactions on Communications, 30*(1), 82–91. doi:10.1109/TCOM.1982.1095370

Turoff, M., Hiltz, S. R., Cho, H.-K., Li, Z., & Wang, Y. (2002). Social decision support systems (SDSS). In *Proceedings of the 35th Hawaii International Conference on System Sciences*. Retrieved November 26, 2009, from http://www.hicss.hawaii.edu/HICSS_35/HICSSpapers/PDFdocuments/CLCSC03.pdf

Turoff, M., Hiltz, S., Baghat, A., & Rana, A. (1993). Distributed group support systems. *Management Information Systems Quarterly, 17*(4), 399–417. doi:10.2307/249585

U.S. Department of Commerce. (2004). *Architecture Advisory Group*. Retrieved from http://ocio.os.doc.gov/CommerceITGroups/Enterprise_Architecture_Advisory_Group/index.htm

Ulrich, P. (1997). *Integrative Wirtschaftsethik*. Berlin: Paul Haupt.

Ulungu, E. L. (1993). *Optimisation Combinatoire MultiCritère: Détermination de l'ensemble des solutions efficaces et méthodes interactives*. Unpublished doctoral dissertation, Université de Mons-Hainaut, Mons.

Ulungu, E. L., & Teghem, J. (1994). Multiobjective Combinatorial Optimization problems: A survey. *Journal of Multi-Criteria Decision Analysis, 3*, 83–104. doi:10.1002/mcda.4020030204

Umble, E. J., Haft, R. R., & Umble, M. M. (2003). Enterprise Resource Planning: implementation procedures and critical success factors. *European Journal of Operational Research, 146*, 241–257. doi:10.1016/S0377-2217(02)00547-7

Umble, E. J., Haft, R. R., & Umble, M. M. (2003). Enterprise resource planning: implementation procedures and critical success factors. *European Journal of Operational Research, 146*(2), 241–257. doi:10.1016/S0377-2217(02)00547-7

Umble, E. J., Haft, R. R., & Umble, M. M. (n.d.). Enterprise resource planning: Implementation procedures and critical success factors (pp.). *European Journal of Operational Research, 146*, 241–257.

UNIKM. (2009). *Comparative Researches Concerning Knowledge Management in Romanian Engineering Education*. Retrieved December 20, 2009, from http://imtuoradea.ro/unikm/index_en.htm

UNISYS. (2006). *End User Outsourcing and Support Services*. Retrieved July 2006, from http://www.unisys.pt/services/outsourcing/index.htm

University of St. Gallen. (2005). *Service-Oriented IT Management: Benefit*. Cost and Success Factors.

Upton, D. M., & McAfee, M. M. (2000). A path-based approach to information technology in manufacturing. *International Journal of Technology Management, 20*(3/4), 354–372. doi:10.1504/IJTM.2000.002876

Uschold, M., & Gruninger, M. (1996). Ontologies: principles, methods and applications. *Journal of Knowledge Engineering Review, 11*(2), 93–155. doi:10.1017/S0269888900007797

Uschold, M., & King, M. (1995). Towards a Methodology for Building Ontologies. In *Proc. of IJCAI95's Workshop on Basic Ontological Issues in Knowledge Sharing.*

Uschold, M., King, M., Moralee, S., & Zorgios, Y. (1996). *The Enterprise Ontology.* Retrieved June 14, 2007, from http://www.aiai.ed.ac.uk/~oplan/documents/1996/96-enterprise-ontology.pdf van Heijst, G., Schreiber, A. T., & Wielinga, B. J. (1996). Using Explicit Ontologies in KBS Development. *International Journal of Human and Computer Studies, 46*(2/3),183-292.

Usher, J. M., Roy, U., & Parsaei, H. (2005). *Integrated Product and Process Development: Methods, Tools, and Technologies.* New York: John Wiley & Sons, Inc.

Vaishnavi, V. K., & Kuechler, W. (2007). *Design Science Research Methods and Patterns: Improving and Innovating Information & Communication Technology.* Retrieved from http://home.aisnet.org/displaycommon.cfm?an=1&subarticlenbr=279

van Beek, D. (2006). *De Intelligente Organisatie, prestatieverbetering en organisatieontwikkeling met Business Intelligence.* Amsterdam: Tuteint Nolthenius.

Van Den Hoven, J. (2004). Data architecture standards for the effective enterprise. *Information Systems Management, 21*(3), 61–64. doi:10.1201/1078/44432.21.3.20040601/82478.9

van der Aalst, W. M. P., & ter Hofstede, A. H. M. (2005). YAWL: Yet Another Workflow Language. *Information Systems, 30*(4), 245–275. doi:10.1016/j.is.2004.02.002

Van der Aalst, W. M. P., van Dongen, B. F., Herbst, J., Maruster, J., Schimm, G., & Weijters, A. J. M. M. (2002). Workflow Mining: A Survey of Issues and Approaches. *Journal of Data and knowledge engineering, 47,* 237-267. doi:10.1016/S0169-023X(03)00066-1

Van Grembergen, W. (2004). *Strategies for Information Technology Governance.* Hershey, PA: IGI Publishing.

Van Grembergen, W., De Haes, S., & Van Brempt, H. (2008). *Identifying and Aligning Business Goals and IT Goals.* Rolling Meadows, IL: IT Governance Institute.

Van Grembergen, W., Saull, R., & De Haes, S. (2003). *Linking the IT Balanced Scorecard to the Business Objectives at a Major Canadian Financial Group. Journal of Information Technology Cases and Applications.* JITCA.

Van Waarden, F. (2001). Institutions and innovation: The legal environment of innovating firms. [Retrieved from ABI database.]. *Organization Studies, 22*(5), 765–795. doi:10.1177/0170840601225002

Varadharajan, T. K., & Rajendran, C. (2005). A multi-objective simulated-annealing algorithm for scheduling in flowshops to minimize the makespan and total flowtime of jobs. *European Journal of Operational Research, 167,* 772–795. doi:10.1016/j.ejor.2004.07.020

Varajão, J. (2002). *Função de Sistemas de Informação: Contributos para a Melhoria do Sucesso da Adopção de Tecnologias de Informação e Desenvolvimento de Sistemas de Informação nas Organizações.* Unpublished Doctoral dissertation, Minho University, Portugal.

Varian, H. R. (2001). High-technology industries and market structure. In *Proceedings of Federal Reserve Bank of Kansas City* (pp. 65-101). Retrieved from ABI database.

Varian, H. R., Farrell, J. V., & Shapiro, C. (2004). *The economics of information technology: An introduction.* Boston: Cambridge University Press.

Vassiliadis, P., Bouzeghoub, M., & Quix, C. (2000). Towards quality-oriented data warehouse usage and evolution. *Information Systems, 25*(2), 89–115. doi:10.1016/S0306-4379(00)00011-9

Venkatesh, V., & Davis, F. D. (2000). A theoretical extension of the technology acceptance model: four longitudinal field studies. *Management Science, 45*(2), 188–204.

Venkatesh, V., & Morris, M. G. (2000). Why don't men stop to ask for directions? Gender, social influence, and their role in technology acceptance and usage behavior. *Management Information Systems Quarterly, 24*, 115–137. doi:10.2307/3250981

Vergara, S. (2007). *Projetos e relatórios de pesquisa em administração* (8ª ed.). São Paulo, Brasil: Atlas Editora.

Verma, A., & Kapur, P. (Eds.). (2006). *Quality, Reliability and Information Technology*. Oxford, UK: Alpha Science.

Verville, J., & Halingten, A. (2003). A six-stage model of the buying process for ERP software. *Industrial Marketing Management, 32*(7), 585–594. doi:10.1016/S0019-8501(03)00007-5

Vieira, M. (2004). Por uma boa pesquisa (qualitativa) em administração . In Vieira, M., & Zouain, M. (Eds.), *Pesquisa qualitativa em administração*. Rio de Janeiro, Brasil: Editora FGV.

Violino, B. (1997). *Return on Investment*. Information Week.

Vitt, E., Luckevich, M., & Misner, S. (2002). *Making Better Business Intelligence Decisions Faster*. Redmond, WA: Microsoft Press.

Vollmann, T. E., Berry, W. L., Whybark, D. C., & Jacobs, R. F. (2005). *Manufacturing Planning and Control for Supply Chain Management*. Boston: McGraw-Hill.

Wagner, E., & Newell, S. (2007). Exploring the Importance of Participation in the Post-Implementation Period of an ES Project: A Neglected Area. *Journal of the Association for Information Systems, 8*(10), 508–524.

Walsham, G. (1995). The Emergence of Interpretivism in IS Research. *Information Systems Research, 6*(4), 376–394. doi:10.1287/isre.6.4.376

Wang, E., Shih, S. P., Jiang, J. J., & Klein, G. (2008). The consistency among facilitating factors and ERP implementation success: A holistic view of fit. *Journal of Systems and Software, 81*(9), 1609–1621. doi:10.1016/j.jss.2007.11.722

Wang, M., Chan, C., Chang, S., & Yang, Y. (2007). Effects of online shopping attitudes, subjective norms and control beliefs on online shopping intentions: a test of the theory of planned behavior. *International Journal of Management, 24*(2), 296–302.

Wang, T., & Hu, J. (2008). An Inventory control systems for product with optional components under service level and budget constraints. *European Journal of Operational Research, 189*, 41–58. doi:10.1016/j.ejor.2007.05.025

Wang, W. (2005). Factors influencing employees' deep usage of information systems. In *Proceedings of the Pacific Asia Conference on Information Systems* (pp. 30-43).

Wang, W., & Hsieh, P.-A. (2006). Beyond routine: Symbolic adoption, extended use, and emergent use of complex information systems in the mandatory organizational context. In *Proceedings of the Twenty- Seventh Conference on Information Systems*, Milwaukee, 2006 (pp. 732-750).

Wang, W., Hsieh, J., Butler, J., & Hsu, S. (2008). Innovative Complex Information Technologies: A Theoretical Model And Empirical Examination. *Journal of Computer Information Systems*, (Fall): 27–36.

Ward, J., & Daniel, E. (2005). *Benefits Management, Delivering Value from IS & IT investments*. Hoboken, NJ: Wiley Series.

Watkins, J., & Rodriguez, M. (2008). A survey of web-based collective decision making systems . In Nayak, R., Ichalkaranje, N., & Jain, L. (Eds.), *Evolution of the Web in Artificial Intelligence Environments* (pp. 245–279). Berlin: Springer-Verlag. doi:10.1007/978-3-540-79140-9_11

Webb, P., Pollard, C., & Ridley, G. (2006). Attempting to define IT Governance: Wisdom or Folly? In *Proceedings of the 39th Hawaii International Conference on System Sciences*.

Wei, C. C., Chien, C. F., & Wang, M. J. J. (2005). An AHP-based approach to ERP system selection. *International Journal of Production Economics, 96*(1), 47–62. doi:10.1016/j.ijpe.2004.03.004

Weill, P. (1990). *Do computers pay-off?* ICIT Press.

Weill, P., & Broadbent, M. (1998). *Leveraging the new infrastructure*. Cambridge, MA: Harvard Business School Press.

Weill, P., & Ross, J. W. (2003). *IT Governance. How top performers manage IT decision for superior results*. Cambridge, MA: Harvard Business School Press.

Welling, L., & Thompson, L. (2005). *PHP and MySQL Web development* (3rd ed.). Indianapolis, IN: Sams Publishing.

Westerman, G., & Hunter, R. (2007). *IT Risk. Turning Business threats into competitive advantage*. Cambridge, MA: Harvard Business School Press.

Westkämper, E. (2006). Manufuture - Key Technology for Manufacturing Innovation and Environmental Sustainability, Discussion Paper - Academic Perspective. In B.-W. Choi (Ed.), *IMS International: Proceedings of the IMS Vision Forum 2006* (pp. 90-97). Seoul, Korea: Korea Cheong-Moon-Gak Publishers.

WFMC (The Workflow Management Coalition). (1999). *Terminology and Glossary*. Technical report.

White, S. A. (2004). Process modeling notations and Workflow Patterns . In Fisher, L. (Ed.), *Workflow Handbook* (pp. 265–294). Lighthouse Point, FL: Future Strategies.

Wickens, C. D. (1992). *Engineering psychology and human performance* (2nd ed.). Columbus, OH: Merrill Publishing.

Wielinga, B. J., & Schreiber, A. T. (1993). Reusable and sharable knowledge bases: A European perspective. In *Proceedings International Conference on Building and Sharing of Very Large-Scaled Knowledge Bases* (pp. 103–115). Tokyo, Japan: Japan Information Processing Development Center.

Wielinga, B., Schreiber, A. T., & Jansweijer, W. F. (1995). The KACTUS View on the 'O' Word. In *IJCAI Workshop on Basic Ontological Issues in Knowledge Sharing* (pp. 159-168).

Wier, B., Hunton, J., & Hassab Elnaby, H. R. (2007). Enterprise resource planning systems and non-financial performance incentives: The joint impact on corporate performance. *International Journal of Accounting Information Systems, 8*(3), 165–190. doi:10.1016/j.accinf.2007.05.001

Wier, B., Hunton, J., & Hassab Elnaby, H. R. (2007). Enterprise resource planning systems and non-financial performance incentives: The joint impact on corporate performance. *International Journal of Accounting Information Systems, 8*(3), 165–190. doi:10.1016/j.accinf.2007.05.001

Wierzbicki, A. P. (1980). A methodological guide to the multiobjective optimization. In K. Iracki, K. Malanowski, & S. Walukiewicz (Eds.), *Optimization Techniques (9th IFIP COT 1979)* (LNCS 22, pp. 99-123). Berlin: Springer.

Wikipedia. (2009). *Groupthink*. Retrieved November 26, 2009, from http://en.wikipedia.org/wiki/Groupthink

Willcocks, L. P., & Sykes, R. (2000). Enterprise resource planning: the role of the CIO and it function in ERP. *Communications of the ACM, 43*(4), 32–38. doi:10.1145/332051.332065

Williamson, O. E. (1981). The economics of organization: The transaction cost approach. [Retrieved from ABI database.]. *American Journal of Sociology, 87*(3), 548–577. doi:10.1086/227496

Williamson, O. E. (1985). *The Economic Institutions of Capitalism*. New York: The Free Press.

Williamson, O. E. (1996). *The Mechanisms of Governance*. New York: Oxford University Press.

Williamson, O., & Winter, S. (Eds.). (1991). *The nature of the firm: origins, evolution and development*. New York: Oxford University Press.

Wilson, J. M. (1989). Alternative formulation of a flow shop scheduling problem. *The Journal of the Operational Research Society, 40*(4), 395–399.

Winograd, T. (1987). A language/action perspective on the design of cooperative work. *Human-Computer Interaction, 3*(1), 3–30. doi:10.1207/s15327051hci0301_2

Wodecki, M., & Bozejko, W. (2002). Solving the Flow Shop Problem by Parallel Simulated Annealing. In Goos, G., Hartmanis, J., & van Leeuwen, J. (Eds.), *Parallel Processing and Applied mathematics (PPAM 2001), LNCS 2328* (pp. 236–244). Berlin: Springer.

Wohed, P., Van der Aalst, W. M. P., Dumas, M., ter Hofstede, A. H. M., & Russell, N. (2006). On the suitability of BPMN for business process modeling. In S. Dustdar, J. L. Fiadeiro, & A. Sheth (Eds.), *Business Process Management* (LNCS 4102, pp. 161-176). Berlin: Springer Verlag.

Wong, S. T. C., Hoo, K. S., Knowlton, R. C., Laxer, K. D., Cao, X., & Hawkins, R. A. (2002). Design and Applications of a Multimodality Image Data Warehouse Framework. *Journal of the American Medical Informatics Association, 9*, 239–254. doi:10.1197/jamia.M0988

Wood, J., Tung, H. L., Marshall-Bradley, T., Sofge, D. A., Grayson, J., & Lawless, W. F. (2009). Applying an Organizational Uncertainty Principle: Semantic Web-Based Metrics. In M. M. Cunha, Eva Oliveira, Antonio Tavares & Luis Ferreira (Eds.), *Handbook of Research on Social Dimensions of Semantic Technologies and Web Services*. Hershey, PA: IGI.

Works Management. (2008). *IT in practice Planning & scheduling, Growing in stature*. Retrieved April 2009, from http://www.worksmanagement.co.uk/articles/12830/Growing-in-stature.pdf

Wortmann, J. C. (1998). Evolution of ERP systems . In Bititci, U. S., & Carrie, A. S. (Eds.), *Strategic Management of the manufacturing value chain* (pp. 11–23). Boston, MA: Kluwer Academic.

Wright, C. (2004). Top Three Potential Risks With Outsourcing Information Systems. *Information Systems Control Journal, 5*.

Wu, J., & Wang, Y. (2006). Measuring ERP Success: The Ultimate Users' View. *International Journal of Operations & Production Management, 26*(8), 882–903. doi:10.1108/01443570610678657

Wu, J., & Wang, Y. (2006). Measuring ERP Success: The Ultimate Users' View. *International Journal of Operations & Production Management, 26*(8), 882–903. doi:10.1108/01443570610678657

IBM. (2006). *Índice de Serviços*. Retrieved July 2006, from http://www-05.ibm.com/services/pt/portfolios/

IT Governance Institute. (2003). *Board Briefing on IT Governance* (2nd ed.). Rolling Meadows, IL: IT Governance Institute.

IT Governance Institute. (2004). *IT Governance Global Status Report*. Rolling Meadows, IL: IT Governance Institute.

IT Governance Institute. (2006). *Enterprise Value: Governance of IT Investments. The Val IT Framework*. Rolling Meadows, IL: IT Governance Institute.

IT Governance Institute. (2006). *IT Governance Global Status Report - 2006*. Rolling Meadows, IL: IT Governance Institute.

IT Governance Institute. (2007). *Control Objectives for Information and Related Technology, versión 4.1.* Rolling Meadows, IL: IT Governance Institute.

IT Governance Institute. (2008a). *Enterprise Value: Governance of IT Investments. The Val IT Framework 20*. Rolling Meadows, IL: IT Governance Institute.

ITPI. (2005). *IT Controls Benchmarking Survey: quantifying the value, effectiveness, efficiency and security of IT controls*. Retrieved February 11, 2008, from http://www.itpi.org/docs/ITPI_Controls_Benchmarking_Survey_Initial_Findings_v0817.pdf

Johansen, R. (1998). *Groupware: Computer Support for Business Teams*. New York: The Free Press.

Jordan Industrial Cities. (2008). *Statistics from the website of the JIC*. Retrieved from http://www.jci.org.jo

OMG (Object Management Group). (2006). *Business Process Modeling Notation Specification.* Retrieved from http://www.omg.org

OMG (Object Management Group). (2007). *Business Process Definition Metamodel Specification.* Retrieved from http://www.omg.org

Web Services Initiative. (2005). *Web Services Application Guideline.*

Web Services Initiative. (2007). *The Report of Web2.0 and Citizen Centric Technology.*

Xu, L., & Brinkkemper, S. (2007). Concepts of product software. *European Journal of Information Systems, 16*(5), 531–541. doi:10.1057/palgrave.ejis.3000703

Yagmahan, B., & Yenisey, M. M. (2008). Ant colony optimization for multi-objective flow shop scheduling problem. *Computers & Industrial Engineering, 54,* 411–420. doi:10.1016/j.cie.2007.08.003

Yagoubi, M. (2004). HRM in Tunisia . In Kamoche, K., Debrah, Y., Horwitz, F., & Muuka, G. N. (Eds.), *Managing Human Resources in Africa.* London: Routledge.

Yang, M., Chang, W., Yarnk, K., Cheng, T., Luo, W., Hsu, S., & Yang, P. (2008). *Proceedings of the 2008 3rd international Conference on innovative Computing information and Control.*

Yeh, J. (2007). How the organizations change in ERP implementation. In *Proceedings of the Americas conference.*

Yen, Ch., Yen, Ch., & Hsu, J. (2008). An implementation of Web Based PDM with Open Source CMS. In *Virtual Environments, Human-Computer Interfaces and Measurement Systems, VECIMS 2008. IEEE Conference* (pp. 162-165).

Yetton, P., Martin, A., Sharma, R., & Johnston, K. (2000). A model of information systems development project performance. *Information Systems Journal, 10*(4), 263–289. doi:10.1046/j.1365-2575.2000.00088.x

Yi, M. Y., & Davis, F. D. (2001). Improving computer training effectiveness for decision technologies behavior modeling and retention enhancement. *Decision Sciences, 32*(3), 521–544. doi:10.1111/j.1540-5915.2001.tb00970.x

Yin, R. (2001). *Estudo de caso: planejamento e métodos.* Porto Alegre, Brasil: Bookman.

Yin, R. (2008). *Case study research: Design and methods.* San Francisco: Sage Pub.

Yin, R. K. (2003). *Case study Research: Design and Methods.* London: Sage Publications.

Yoon, C. Y. (2008). *A structural model of end-user computing competency and user performance.* Knowledge-Based Systems.

Yu, C. S. (2005). Causes influencing the effectiveness of the post-implementation ERP system. *Industrial Management & Data Systems, 105*(1), 115–132. doi:10.1108/02635570510575225

Yu, E. S. K., & Mylopoulos, J. (1994). From E-R to "A-R" - Modelling strategic actor relationships for business process reengineering. In *13-th Int. Conf. on the Entity-relationship Approach*, December 13-16, 1994, Manchester, UK.

Yu, H. (2005). *Content and Workflow Management for Library Web Sites: Case Studies.* Hershey, PA: Information Science Publishing.

Yusuf, Y., Gunasekaran, A., & Abthorpe, M. S. (2004). Enterprise information systems project implementation: A case study of ERP in Rolls-Royce. *International Journal of Production Economics, 87,* 251–266. doi:10.1016/j.ijpe.2003.10.004

Zaheer, A., & Venkatraman, N. (1995). Relational governance as an interorganizational Strategy: An empirical test of the role of trust in economic change. *Strategic Management Journal, 16*(5), 373–392. doi:10.1002/smj.4250160504

Zeng, L., Xu, L., Shi, Z., Wang, M., & Wu, W. (2006a). *Techniques, Process, and Enterprise Solutions of Business Intelligence.* Paper presented at the Conference on Systems, Man, and Cybernetics Taipei, Taiwan.

Zhang, L., & Matthew, K. O. Lee, Zhang, Z., & Banerjee, P. (2003). Critical success factors of enterprise resource planning systems implementation success in china. In *Proceedings of the 36th Hawaii International Conference on System Sciences*.

Zhu, K., & Kraemer, K. L. (2005). Post-Adoption Variations in Usage and Value of E-Business by Organizations: Cross-Country Evidence from the Retail Industry. *Information Systems Research, 16*(1), 61–84. doi:10.1287/isre.1050.0045

Zitzler, E. (1999). *Evolutionary Algorithms for Multiobjective Optimization: Methods and Applications*. Unpublished doctoral dissertation, Swiss Federal Institute of Technology, Zurich.

Zitzler, E., & Thiele, L. (1999). Multiobjective evolutionary algorithms: A comparative case study and the strength pareto approach. *IEEE Transactions on Evolutionary Computation, 3*, 257–271. doi:10.1109/4235.797969

Zviran, M., Pliskin, N., & Levin, R. (2005). Measuring user satisfaction and perceived usefulness in the ERP context. *Journal of Computer Information Systems*, 43–52.

About the Contributors

Cruz-Cunha, Maria Manuela is currently an Associate Professor in the School of Technology at the Polytechnic Institute of Cavado and Ave, Portugal. She holds a Dipl. Eng. in the field of Systems and Informatics Engineering, an M.Sci. in the field of Information Society and a Dr.Sci in the field of Virtual Enterprises, all from the University of Minho (Portugal). She teaches subjects related with Information Systems, Information Technologies and Organizational Models to undergraduated and post-graduated studies. She supervises several PhD projects in the domain of Virtual Enterprises and Information Systems and Technologies. She regularly publishes in international peer-reviewed journals and participates on international scientific conferences. She serves as a member of Editorial Board and Associate Editor for several International Journals and for several Scientific Committees of International Conferences. She has authored and edited several books and her work appears in more than 70 papers published in journals, book chapters and conference proceedings. She is the co-founder and co-chair of CENTERIS – Conference on ENTERprise Information Systems.

Varajão, João Eduardo is professor of information systems management and software engineering at the University of Trás-os-Montes e Alto Douro and visiting professor at EGP – University of Porto Business School. He graduated in 1995, received his master degree in Computer Science in 1997 and, in 2003, received his PhD in Technologies and Information Systems, from University of Minho (Portugal). He supervises several Msc and PhD thesis in the information systems field. His current research includes information systems management and enterprise information systems. He has over 100 publications, including books, book chapters, refereed publications, and communications at international conferences. He serves as associate editor and member of editorial board for international journals and has served in several committees of international conferences. He is the co-founder and co-chair of CENTERIS – Conference on ENTERprise Information Systems. He is also a member of AIS, IEICE and APSI.

* * *

Alfnes, Erlend is associate professor at the Department of Production and Quality Engineering at the Norwegian University of Science and Technology, and a senior researcher at SINTEF Technology Management. Alfnes has 10 years experience from national and international research projects, and is currently the leader of two national research projects. His research interests are within production planning and control, supply chain management, and enterprise reengineering. He is lecturing master courses in Enterprise Resource Planning Systems, Manufacturing strategy, and Systems engineering.

Almeida, Ricardo João Costa born in 1974 and graduated in 1997 on Management Software Engineering at Universidade Portucalense Infante D. Henrique, has an MsC at Universidade de Aveirto in the area of order decision making considering production capacity. Currently he is a PhD student from MIT Portugal EDAM Program and Researcher at Inesc Porto (one of the main research and technology transfer institutes in Portugal). He also is an assistant professor at Universidade Lusófona do Porto. Before heading for the PhD study, he had 2 major professional experiences on Portuguese software market, acting as a software developer (Microsoft technologies) and project manager. One of his major challenges was as a software development director for almost 9 years, applying their software to almost 130 industrial companies.

Alves, Gabriela is a widely-experienced professional. Since 1999 she has been working for Arcelor-Mittal - the largest steel company in the world - supporting projects in areas such as human resources, quality, safety and procurement. Currently she is Continuous Improvement manager in North America responsible for special projects focusing on cost reduction, incentive plans implementation and information management. Before that she was general manager at Brazilian Human Resource Association. In 2006 she finished a post-graduation in Business Management at Fundação Dom Cabral (FDC) and in 2008 she obtained her Master of Administration at FEAD Centro de Gestão Empreendedora in Minas Gerais, Brazil.

André, Ana has a degree in Industrial Production Engineering from Faculty of Sciences and Technology, New University of Lisbon, Portugal, since 1996. She holds a post graduation in Systems and Information Technology for Organizations from ISEG - School of Economics and Management, Technical University of Lisbon, Portugal, since 2004 and received her Master Degree in Science on Management Information Systems also from ISEG, in 2008. Her research area for dissertation was Information Systems Outsourcing and its risks and benefits and her interests also includes business process management and process modelling. She worked for 3 years defining functional requirements of business information systems and works for 4 years in business process consultancy at the postal company CTT - Correios de Portugal, S.A. She presented her research at the CENTERIS2009 (Conference on Enterprise Information Systems), organised by Polytechnic Institute of Cávado and Ave and University of Trás-os-Montes and Alto Douro, in Portugal.

Angeles, Rebecca is Full Professor, Management Information Systems Area, Faculty of Business Administration, University of New Brunswick Fredericton, Canada. Her research publications have appeared in such publications as Information & Management, Decision Support Systems, Supply Chain Management: An International Journal, Industrial Management & Data Systems, International Journal of Integrated Supply Management, International Journal of Management and Enterprise Development, International Journal of Value Chain Management, International Journal of Physical Distribution & Logistics Management, Logistics Information Management, Journal of Business Logistics, among others. Her research interests are in the areas of radio frequency identification, supply chain management issues, outsourcing and its consequences on supply chains, electronic trading partnership management issues, electronic business, business-to-business exchanges, electronic trading partnerships, electronic data interchange (EDI), Internet-EDI, and interorganizational systems, and innovative education approaches in Management Information Systems.

Astapova, Elena V. is associate director for research and technology at the Medical College of Georgia (MCG) Center for Telehealth. Dr. Astapova came to MCG in 2004 from Siberian Medical University School of Public Health and Healthcare where she was an assistant professor where she developed a course in medical informatics and telemedicine. She is a 1994 graduate of Russia*s Siberian Medical University Department of Bio-Medical Cybernetic. She completed her Ph.D. in general oncology and medical informatics in 1998 at Tomsk Scientific Center of Russian Academy of Medical Sciences, Cancer Research Institute. In 2002, she was a Carnegie Research Fellow at MCG*s Center for Telehealth. Her professional interests include using telecommunications for information collection and management as well as for health care delivery.

Azevedo, Américo Lopes de born in 1965 and graduated in 1988 from Faculty of Engineering of University of Porto (FEUP), has a PhD in the area of collaborative planning systems in the context of networking enterprises. Currently he is an Associate Professor at FEUP and Research Unit Manager at Inesc Porto (one of the main research and technology transfer institutes in Portugal). He assumed several R&D project contract responsibilities with European Union and Portuguese public institutions and enterprises and also, he has been reviewer and evaluator of several international R&D Industrial projects and member of several scientific programmes committees. He is author of many articles in international journals and technical publications and he has been active in preparing and participating in R&D projects involving industrial companies as well as has been supervising several PhD and M.Sc research thesis. His main R&D interests are in the domain of Enterprise Cooperation Networks (Interoperability, Business Networking, and Alignment and Business Process Management), Supply Chain Management and Operations Management.

Birry, Dalia is a teaching assistant at the Business Administration department, Faculty of Commerce, Alexandria University.

Cavalcanti, José Carlos is a Civil Engineer- Universidade Federal de Pernambuco- UFPE- 1981. MSc in Urban and Regional Planning - Universidade Federal do Rio de Janeiro- UFRJ- 1986. PhD in Economics- University of Manchester-England-1991. Lecturer of Economics of the Universidade Federal de Pernambuco. Author of many articles related to Information and Communication Technologies-ICTs. Ex-President of the Pernambuco Science and Technology Agency- FACEPE (1999-2002). Founder Member of the Board of the Porto Digital, Information Techology Park of Pernambuco (2000-2006). Ex-Secretary for Technology, Innovation and Higher Education- Pernambuco State Government (2003-2006). Consultant in the field of Information and Communication Technologies. Creator of the blog for Information and Communication Technology Economics: http://jccavalcanti.wordpress.com. Founder of the innovation and technology economics start-up firm: http://www.creativante.com.br

Cheikh, Ansem Ben is Ph.D. Student in Information Systems at the Laboratory of Informatics of Grenoble (LIG) and Pierre Mendès France University (Grenoble, France). She took her master's research degree in 2008 at the Joseph Fourier University. She took in 2005 an engineering degree from the Tunisia Polytechnic School on computer and telecom sciences. Her research areas include information systems engineering, business process management and event driven business processes. She works during her thesis under the project DéSIT of the Region Rhône Alpes (France) on developing a pervasive information system based on business processes and applied for intelligent transportation systems.

Dajci, Fjorentina Angjellari earned her MA and PhD in Economics from Kansas State University in 2005. She has over five years of teaching experience at the university level, teaching a variety of courses in economics, statistics, econometrics, finance, accounting, and business management for the University of Phoenix, Rollins College, Indiana University, Globe Institute of Technology in New York City, Kansas State University and University of Tirana. Her research focuses on the interrelations between economic growth, institutions, social capital, civil society and social networks, both at national and regional levels. She has published a book chapter and has several undergoing research projects. Dr. Angjellari-Dajci has found conjectures between her research interests, teaching, and community service in teaching multidisciplinary courses, where students were engaged in community and research based service learning projects on the regional economic impact of social capital networks on the quality of life in Central Florida.

Deus, Flávio Elias Gomes de received his BS in Electrical Engineering from Federal University of Goiás, in 1998, MS in Electrical Engineering from University of Brasília, in 2001, and Ph.D. in Electrical Engineering from the University of Brasília, in 2006. He was also Visiting Scholar in Information Science and Telecommunications at University of Pittsburgh, USA, from 2004 to 2005. He was Coordinator of the Network and Support Services unit from the University of Brasilia's Data Processing Center, in 2007. He worked in software development projects primarily on the following themes: electronic document management system, use case description and Web services development, in 2008. He is currently Associate Professor in the Department of Electrical Engineering, University of Brasilia, Brazil. His research interests include information technologies, wireless and sensors networks, fault tolerant systems, software development process, among other related topics.

Draghici, Anca is professor at Politehnica University of Timisoara (UPT) - Romania, Management Faculty, Department of Economical and Social-Humanities Sciences. Her teaching subjects are Ergonomics, Human Resources Management and Knowledge Management. Her research field of interest is linked with the impact of the knowledge based society upon the social / human dynamics / evolution and the organizational behavior. She regularly publishes and participates on international scientific conferences. She is director of several national and international research projects that were developed in partnership. She is member of the UPT team in the European Manufacturing and Innovation Research Association a cluster leading excellence – association established after the Belgian law, in 2008 (www.emiracle.eu).

Draghici, George is Professor at Politehnica University of Timisoara (UPT) - Romania, the Mechanical Engineering Faculty. He is the Director of the Integrated Engineering Research Centre and PhD. advisor in the field of Industrial Engineering. His teaching subjects are Manufacturing Engineering and Integrated Engineering. His research field is Integrated Product and Processes Engineering. He has published more than 150 articles in scientific journals and proceedings of international conferences organized in Romania, Hungary, Poland, France, UK and Canada. He is member of the UPT team in the European Manufacturing and Innovation Research Association a cluster leading excellence – association established after the Belgian law, in 2008 (www.emiracle.eu).

Dreyer, Heidi C. gained a Ph.D. degree in logistics from the Norwegian University of Science and Technology, NTNU in 1997. She works as a Professor at NTNU at the department of Production and Quality Engineering. Additionally she holds a position as senior research scientist at SINTEF Technology and Science. Her research interest relates to logistics in the supply chain and network context specifically related to design, planning and control and collaboration issues. How to utilize ICT and information sharing is a central subject in her research activities. Establishment, development and success factors of third party logistics alliances was the topic in her doctoral dissertation. She lectures across different master programs and levels mostly in the area of Supply Chain Management and Production Logistics. She has been a guest lecturer at several universities teaching in the fields of logistics and has supervised students in the field of supply chain management. Through her research activities she has gained broad experience as research and project leader. Her research is presented in journal articles and through conference papers with referee.

Elragal, Ahmed is an Associate Professor of Information Systems at the German University in Cairo (GUC). Dr. Elragal has got his PhD in Decision Support Systems from the University of Plymouth in the UK, 2001. He has more than 20 conference papers and journal articles published in enterprise systems and business intelligence. Also, he has been doing IS consulting in various sectors including retail, food manufacturing, and printing. He is a member of ACM and AIS.

Enriquez, Leticia Borrajo is a Computer Researcher in the Technological Research Institute of the Systems Laboratory, of the Department of Electronics and Computer Science, University of Santiago de Compostela. Received his Bachelor Degree of Computer Science from the University of Vigo in 2003. She is currently writing her final project to receive the 5th year engineering degree (Master of Computer Science). From July 2006 to September 2007 she was working at CERN in the Information Technology Department and the Engineering Department. Leticia Borrajo is a member of the Systems Laboratory, a research unit integrated in the Technological Research Institute of the University of Santiago de Compostela since 2007. Her research activities are focused on: Internet applications and Web Information Systems.

Front, Agnès is Assistant Professor in Grenoble University (France) since 1998 and member of LIG (Laboratory of Informatics of Grenoble) in SIGMA team. She obtained a PhD in Computer Science from Joseph Fourier University. Her main research interests concern reused-based information system engineering: pattern based approaches, component based development methods, business process modeling and management, MDE approaches for transformation and coherence between models, etc. She is co-responsible of a working group of the GDR I3 and member of the executive comity of INFORSID association. Since 2008, she is member of the computer science department of CNU (French National University Committee).

Garrido, Paulo was born in 1955, at Porto, Portugal. He graduated in electrical engineering at University of Porto, in 1979. He received his PhD in informatics from University of Minho (UM), in 1994. He is presently a tenured Associate Professor at UM School of Engineering. He has been working at UM since 1982, first on automatic control and intelligent systems, researching on the integration of logic programming and neural networks (PhD thesis). His research then turned to human learning. Concurrently, he has collaborated with Paulo Salgado in fuzzy logic research. Since 2006, he focused his research on collective intelligence and its application to organizations. This research, in collaboration with Nelson Faria, led to the conversational approach to organizational decision support systems, presented in this book. Currently, he is pursuing other lines of development for collective intelligence as open design, modelling markets as collective intelligence devices, and advanced organizational production modes with Goran Putnik.

Gómez, Jorge Marx studied computer engineering and industrial engineering at the University Of Applied Science Of Berlin (Germany). He was a lecturer and researcher at the Otto-von-Guericke-University Magdeburg where he also obtained PhD degree in business information systems with the work "Computer-Based Approaches to Forecast Returns of Scrapped Products to Recycling". In 2004, he received his habilitation for the work "Automated Environmental Reporting through Material Flow Networks" at the Otto-von-Guericke-University Magdeburg. From 2002-2003, he was a visiting professor for business informatics at the Technical University of Clausthal (Germany). In October 2005, he became a full professor of business information systems at the Oldenburg University (Germany). Professor Marx Gómez's research interests include business information systems, business intelligence, e-commerce, Web intelligence, material flow management systems, life cycle assessment, eco-balancing, environmental reporting, recycling program planning, disassembly planning and control, simulation, and neuro-fuzzy-systems.

Gonçalves, António Leonardo (MSc) is an Associate Professor at the Systems and Informatics Department of Polytechnic Institute of Setúbal responsible for the courses in Computing over the Internet. He is a PhD student at Technical University of Lisbon on subject of Enterprise Architectures and Theory of Organized Activity. He was involved in several research programmes of the European Community, such as SPECS (Specification and Programming Environment for Communication Software) project is a completed part of the RACE (Research and Development in Advanced Communications in Europe) and project CTS3/FDT regarding conformance testing services for LOTOS and SDL tools.

Gonçalves, Ramiro is an Associate Professor of Computer Science at the Trás-os-Montes University, Vila Real, Portugal. He received his PhD in Computer Science from Trás-os-Montes University, Portugal. He has fifteen years of experience as information systems' technology consultant. His current research focuses on electronic commerce and management information systems.

Grayson, James M., Ph.D., is a tenured Associate Professor of Management Science and Operations at the Hull College of Business Administration at Augusta State University. He received a Bachelor of Science degree from the United States Military Academy at West Point, an MBA with a Marketing emphasis from the University of North Texas, and then a Ph.D. in Management Science with an Information Systems minor also from the University of North Texas. Jim brings to his research considerable industry experience including about twelve years at Texas Instruments contributing in quality engineering, quality and reliability assurance management, supplier management, subcontractor management, software quality engineering management, statistical consulting, total quality management and a joint venture management (Ti - Martin Marietta). Jim also worked as a Project Manager for an engineering consulting firm and as a Signal Corps officer in the U.S. Army in the United States and Europe. His research interests are diverse and range from unique approaches to organizational structure to applying management science methods to financial planning to operations management.

Hedman, Jonas is Associate Professor at Copenhagen Business School, Denmark. Currently he works at Center for Applied ICT where he had a Post Doc position, within the DREAMS project. Prior coming to Denmark he held a position as Senior Lecture at University College of Borås, Sweden. He holds a Ph.D. in information systems from Informatics, School of Economics and Management, Lund University, Sweden where he also earned his Master and Bachelor degrees. His research interest are in the areas of Enterprise Systems, business models, information system usage, information systems integration and disintegration in the context of mergers and acquisitions, wireless technologies, and cashless society.

Heredero, Carmen de Pablos is a Professor in the Business Administration Area at the Rey Juan Carlos University in Madrid, Spain from 1994. She is responsible for the PhD in Business Administration. She is specialised in the impact of information technologies over organisational systems where she develops main research. She has chaired Doctoral Dissertations and Projects on the impact of information and communication technologies in organisational performance. She has presented communications in different international venues and has published in specialised journals. She has also worked as a consultant in the area of IS management at Primma Consulting.

Heredero, Mónica de Pablos is an Associate Professor in the Business Administration Area at the Rey Juan Carlos University in Madrid, Spain from 2001. She is teaching and doing research in the impact of new technologies in Organizations, especially in the area of ERPs and CRMs. She is also the CIO for the InSitu Group in Spain. She has been project leader in the SAP ERP implementations in different industries in the international context. She has published on the impact of ERP over organisational final performance.

Hori, Mayumi is a professor at Graduate School and Faculty of Business Management, Hakuoh University, Japan. She receives BE. and ME degree in economics form Rikkyo University, Japan and Dr. Policy Studies degree from Chuo University, Japan. Her research activity covers telework(e-work). She is a director of The Infosocionomics Society in Japan. She published many books and presents a lots of papers at the international conferences regarding e-health and a flexible working by telework.

Hvolby, Hans Henrik is professor at the Centre for Logistics, Aalborg University in Denmark and visiting professor at University of South Australia. He holds a Ph.D. in Manufacturing Information Systems and has published more than 100 peer-reviewed papers and serves as associate editor and European of two international journals and editorial board member of 5 international journals. He is originator or partner in 13 research projects raising national research funding to a value of 14,7 million DKK (2 million €) and European research funding to a value of 14 million DKK (1,9 million €). He has organised more than 30 seminars and workshops, amongst others the SMESME International Conference in 2001. Accepted to organise the MITIP International Conference in 2010. Published 97 peer-reviewed publications since 1993. His research areas include manufacturing information systems (MRP, ERP, APS, VMI), Logistics, Supply Chain Planning, Supply Chain Integration, Value Chain Management and Order Management (BPR).

Izvercianu, Monica is professor at Politehnica University of Timisoara – Romania and Dean of the Management Faculty. Her teaching subjects are related to Marketing sciences. Her research fields of interest are: entrepreneurship development and organization competitiveness. She regularly publishes and participates on international scientific conferences and manages several national and international research projects. Since 1996 she is the president of the Romanian Consortium of Engineering - Economics that join together the universities responsible staff of the engineering and management specialization.

Jávega, Alberto J. Arroyo, Managind director and owner of ALAMCIA. Degree on Computer Science by the Universidad Politécnica de Madrid. Executive MBA. Former manager in Accenture. Huge professional experience on defining and establishing management models both in big and small companies. On the last years is focusing his research on the mechanisms of implementing and managing IT Governance on companies and organizations, specifically on SMEs. Member of ISACA.

Jelen, Jonatan is a former executive manager with companies in Paris and New York, is currently a business owner and avid entrepreneur. He is also Assistant Professor of Business at Parsons The New School for Design. He regularly teaches at USST in Shanghai, China, and to the Faculty of Economics of the University of Zagreb, Croatia. Jon's research interests are in Social Entrepreneurship, Leadership, Chinese Business Education, and the Nature of the Firm. Dr. Jelen earned a JD in Germany, MBAs from Ecole Supérieure de Commerce de Paris, Heriot-Watt University, Scotland, and Baruch College; LLMs from University of Pau, France, University of Paris II, Panthéon-Assas, and Fordham University School of Law, and and MPhil in Business from the City University of New York Graduate School and University Center. His first PhD is from University of Pau, France and he is s PhD candidate in Business/Computer Information Systems at Baruch College.

Jensen, Kenn Steger gained a Ph.D. in Enterprise Resource Planning (ERP) and Advanced Planning and Scheduling (APS) Information Systems at Aalborg University in 2004 and a M.Sc. degree in Industrial Management from Aalborg University in 2000. He has been Associate Professor of Supply Chain Integration at Aalborg University since 2004. His research interests are within supply chain planning and manufacturing planning and control theory in general. Working areas are within modeling and solving inter-organizational decision and KPI, planning, scheduling and optimization problems; Information systems as APS, ERP, SFC, MES and integration. Lecturing across different master programmers in areas as, manufacturing planning and control theory, scheduling theory, shop floor control theory and systems, ERP-systems, APS-systems, IT-systems development, Design of IT-systems, Management Sciences and Operational Research.

Johansson, Björn is Associate Senior Lecturer at the Department of Informatics at School of Economics and Management, Lund University. Before that he had a Post Doc position for three years at Center for Applied ICT at Copenhagen Business School, within the 3gERP project (http://www.3gERP.org). He holds a PhD and a Licentiate degree in Information Systems Development from the Department of Management & Engineering at Linköping University and a Bachelor degree in Business Informatics from Jönköping International Business School. He defended his doctoral thesis "Deciding on Sourcing Option for Hosting of Software Applications in Organisations" in 2007. He is a member of the IFIP Working Group on Diffusion, Adoption and Implementation of Information and Communication Technologies (IFIP TC8 WG8.6), the IFIP Working Group on Enterprise Information Systems (IFIP TC8 WG8.9) and the research networks: VITS Work practice development, IT usage, Coordination and Cooperation and KiO Knowledge in Organizations.

Junior, Humberto Abdalla received his BS in Electrical Engineering from Federal University of Pernambuco, in 1972, MS in Electrical Engineering from the Catholic University of Rio de Janeiro, in 1976, PhD in Telecommunications from Universuté of Limoges, in1982, post-doctoral fellowship by the Center National D Etudes des Telecommunications, in1989 and post-doctoral fellowship by the Center National D Etudes des Telecommunications, in 1993. He is currently Full Professor in the Department of Electrical Engineering, University of Brasilia, Brazil. Has experience in Electrical Engineering with emphasis on Telecommunications. His research interests include Phase Linear, non-minimum phase, Bessel polynomial, telecommunication systems, information technology, change management.

Kolakovic, Marko, after an early consulting and corporate management career in Croatia's reforming economy in the 90s, Marko Kolakovic advanced to an academic career, first at the Faculty of Law, and is now Associate Professor of Business and Economics at the University of Zagreb, Faculty of Economics, Graduate School of Economics and Business. He directs the Program in Entrepreneurship at the School, consults for various ministries of the Croatian government, and leads various projects and grants in the field of Entrerpreneurship research and practice in Croatia and neighboring Central European countries. He has published extensively in European and international journals on the topics of his expertise in entrepreneurship, and the role of networked organizations, virtualized firms, and intellectual capital in the new economy. Dr. Kolakovic obtained his BA, MSc, and PhD in Economics at the Graduate School of Economics and Business of the Faculty of Economics at the University of Zagreb.

Kouki, Rafa is a member of the Interuniversity Research Centre on Enterprise Networks, Logistics and Transportation (CIRRELT). She holds a PhD in Administration Sciences From Université Laval, Canada, an MBA and a B.Com. in management information systems and operations management from the University of Ottawa, Canada. Her current research interests include enterprise resource planning (ERP) systems assimilation and success assessment, global IT management and strategies for integration and coordination of business processes.

Larsson, Christian, Industrial Engineer from the University of Lulea, Sweden. Consultant Partner of INOVA, a consultancy specialized in R+D and innovation management, with a renowned track record in the years 2005-2009. More than 15 years of experience in different industrial sectors, holding posts such as Head of Knowledge Management and Project Chief at Dalphi-Metal Spain, SA., Project engineer at Televés and Production engineer at Triab Engineering, Sweden. Specialized in new product development, R&D and innovation management. Focus on achieving results from the R&D activities in companies and on successful inter-firm Technology Transfer and from Universities and Centres of Technology. Key Fields of Expertise: Creativity and idea generation, Innovation Management Techniques, Innovation Process, Open Innovation, Product development, Technology Transfer, setting up and managing complex international R&D projects, R&D funding.

Lawless, William F. is a Professor of Mathematics and Psychology. He has a PhD in Social Psychology that was granted in 1992 from Virginia Tech, and a Masters Degree in Mechanical Engineering (LSU, 1977). He is a Professional Engineer with a rating in Nuclear Waste Management and he is a Senior member of IEEE. His research interests are in organizational theory, organizational performance and metrics, and in mathematical models of organizations. He has published over 36 articles and book chapters, over 110 peer-reviewed proceedings and abstracts, and he has received about $1.4 million in research grants. He was a founding member of Department of Energy's Savannah River Site Citizens Advisory Board (1994-2000; 2003-2007) where he authored or coauthored over 100 sets of recommendations. He is also a past member of the European Trustnet hazardous decisions group.

Lenart, Gregor is a teaching assistant and senior researcher at the Faculty of Organizational Science, University of Maribor. He received his PhD in the MIS field from Faculty of Organizational Sciences at University of Maribor, Slovenia in 2003. He is a member of eCenter and head of the eCollaboration Laboratory. His current research includes computer supported collaborative work, group support systems and knowledge management. He is also actively involved in several EU research projects focusing on mobile commerce and e-business. He has published over 50 papers in journals and conference proceedings.

Levy, Meira is a post-doctoral fellow at the Ben-Gurion Univerity of the Negev and an adjunct lecturer and researcher at the University of Haifa. She holds a Ph.D. from the Department of Education in Technology and Science of the Technion – Israel Institute of Technology. She holds a Master degree from the Faculty of Industrial Engineering and Management and her Bachelor degree is from the Faculty of Computer-Science, both of the Technion. Meira has over 20 years of experience in the high-tech industry in development and management positions. Her research interests combine her professional background with her research in the cognitive science discipline: knowledge engineering and management, both from human and technological perspectives, including: KM audit and requirements analysis methodologies; modeling and design of knowledge systems; embedding KM frameworks within business processes (e.g. decision making); identifying KM culture barriers; and distance learning in general, and in computer science in particular.

Lopez, Pedro Jose Saco is a Professor of the Department of Electronics and Computer Science, University of Santiago de Compostela. Received his PhD Degree in Physics from the University of Santiago de Compostela in 1996 and became a Professor in 2000. Prof. Saco is a member of the Systems Laboratory, a research unit integrated in the Technological Research Institute of the University of Santiago de Compostela. His research activities are focused on: Multimedia, Internet applications and Web Information Systems. As a brief summary of his academic and research activities, he has participated in about 20 national and international research projects. He has led about 21 R&D activities supported by private organizations, enterprises and government. He has published more than 10 papers in several research fields. Besides, he actively collaborated in the organization of several National and International Congress in different fields such as Remote Sensing or Biomedical Engineering.

Mahmoud, Tariq studied Information Engineering at Al-Baath University (Syria) and is currently a research assistant at the working group of business information systems at the Carl von Ossietzky University of Oldenburg (Germany). He is working on his PhD thesis at the Department of Computer Science in Oldenburg. His research work focuses on applying semantics on SOA-enabled ERP solutions, information security, and Semantic Web.

Mokotoff, Ethel is PhD and Professor of Economics (Mathematics for Economists) at the University of Alcalá, in Spain. Her research interests are: Combinatorial Optimization: Scheduling Theory, Multicriteria Decision and Preference Aggregation Methods. She has been working in several research projects concerning Scheduling Theory and Multicriteria Decision Making, and now she is the main researcher of the project untitled Modelling and Optimization Techniques for a Sustainable Development: Multicriteria Decision Making and Group Decision Techniques (2008-2011), supported by the Science and Innovation Council of Spain. She is the author of a book, chapters in other books, and many articles published at international journals, like European Journal of Operational Research, Annals of Operations Research, TOP, Asia-Pacific Journal of Operations Research, etc. She acts as reviewer for Computers and Operations Research, European Journal of Operational Research, Computational Optimization and Applications, Asia Pacific Journal of Operational Research, International Journal of Systems Science, SIAM Journal on Discrete Mathematics, Computers and Mathematics with Applications, Robotics and Computer Integrated Manufacturing, Omega, etc.

Molinaro, Luis Fernando Ramos received his BS in Electrical Engineering from the University of Brasilia, in 1979, MS in Electrical Engineering from State University of Campinas, in 1981 and Ph.D. in Electrical Engineering from the University of São Paulo, in 1991. He is currently Associate Professor II at the University of Brasilia, acting on the following areas: telecommunications, video conferencing, education, communication networks, process management and management of IT organizations. He worked in consulting and training for Compaq, HP, Solectron, IBM, Brasil Telecom. His research interests include information technologies, information systems, software engineering, enterprise architecture design, modeling and integration, collaboration and networked and virtual organizations.

Mulej, Matjaz was born on Jan., 20, 1941, in Maribor, Slovenia; living in Maribor, Slovenia. Retired from University of Maribor, Faculty of Economics & Business, Maribor, as Professor Emeritus of Systems and Innovation Theory. +1.500 publications in +40 countries (see: IZUM – Cobiss, 08082). Visiting professor abroad for15 semesters. Author of the Dialectical Systems Theory (see: François, 2004, International Encyclopedia ..) and Innovative Business Paradigm for catching-up countries. Member of New York Academy of Sciences (1996), European Academy of Sciences and Arts, Salzburg (2004), European Academy of sciences and Humanities, Paris (2004), president of IFSR (International Federation for Systems Research with 37 member associations). Many Who is Who entries. M.A. in Development Economics, Doctorates in Systems Theory and in Management.

Neto, Annibal Affonso received his BS in Electrical Engineering from Federal University of Santa Catarina, in 1987, specialization in Information Science from the University of Brasília, in 1995, specialization in Marketing from California State University, in1996, an MS from the University of Brasilia, in1993 and Ph.D. in Business Administration from Federal University of Minas Gerais, in 2003. He worked at the Banco do Brasil, serving as advisor to the presidency. He is currently professor in the Department of Production Engineering, University of Brasilia. He has experience in Management and Consulting, with emphasis on strategy and marketing. His research interests include strategic planning, structure modeling, quality management, process management, organizational diagnosis and strategic planning.

Neves, Jorge Tadeu de Ramos is Economist and Metallurgical Engineer; Professional experience in Brazil at EXXON and CASTROL; Diplôme d'Etudes Approfondies (DEA) and Doctorate degree in Industrial Engineering and Technological Innovation Management in France; Sabbatical year (2001) at Université de Montréal in Canada; Associate Professor at Universidade Federal de Minas Gerais (UFMG) and Fundação Pedro Leopoldo; Invited Professor at Fundação Dom Cabral (FDC); Executive Editor of two important academic journals in Information Studies and Management.

Ohashi, Masakazu is a professor at Graduate School and Faculty of Policy Studies, Chuo University, Japan. He received BE, BS, ME, and Dr.Eng. degree from Chuo University, Japan. His research activity covers the system for the next generation networking social systems and Social Design. He is a vice-president of The Infosocionomics Society in Japan. He is a member of UN/CEFACT TBG6. He is the top executive of Time Business Form and was chair of Web Services Initiative in Japan. He published many books and presents a lots of papers at the international conferences regarding of the next generation social systems and Social Design.

Oliveira, Pedro graduated in 2007 and received a master degree in 2009, both in Computer Science and Engineering, from the Technical University of Lisbon. During this period, Pedro attended the Management of Technology course, for one semester, at the Delft University of Technology. Pedro's master thesis subject was focused on assessing the value of ITIL and was written in close cooperation with Accenture. Since 2009 Pedro has been working in an energy utilities company – EDP (Energias de Portugal) and has been involved in: smart grid systems implementation, work force management and IS architecture planning.

Páscoa, Carlos Jorge Ramos is a PhD Student supervised by Dr. José Tribolet at IST/UTL - Instituto Superior Técnico, Technical University of Lisbon, in the area of Information Systems and Organizational and Design Engineering. He works for the Portuguese Air Force and teaches Organizational and Design Engineering at the Air Force Academy.

Pellerin, Robert is associate professor in the Department of Mathematics and Industrial Engineering at École Polytechnique de Montreal. He holds degrees in engineering management (B.Eng.) and industrial engineering (Ph.D.). He has practiced for more than 12 years in reengineering projects and ERP systems implementation including 10 years as a project manager He is also a certified professional in Operations Management (CPIM). His current research interests include enterprise system adoption, implementation, and integration. He is a member of the CIRRELT research group.

Potocan, Vojko born 1962, is an Associate Professor of organization and management on the Faculty of Economics and Business (FEB), Department of Organization and Informatics, University of Maribor, Slovenia. He teaches (on the graduate level, on the undergraduate level, and in doctoral program) in three universities in Slovenia and in three universities abroad (Germany, Croatia and Czech Republic). He takes part in different foreign scientific conferences and realized a number of study visits on abroad (University of Gent, Belgium; University of Greenwich, London, UK; University of Economics, Vienna, Austria). He was 3 times a visiting professor abroad and gave about eight further seminars at foreign universities. He has published +450 texts (+350 in foreign languages in 32 countries), including 8 books, and edited proceedings and textbooks. His research interests include Organization and Management.

Poulin, Diane is full professor of management at Université Laval, Canada and is presently a visiting professor at the École Polytechnique Fédérale de Lausanne, Switzerland. She co-authored several articles and books in the field of strategic management and network enterprises. She intervenes also as a consultant for several public and private organisations. Her current research interests include strategic management, network enterprise, strategic alliances, organisational design and technological innovation. She is a member of the CIRRELT research group.

Pucihar, Andreja is an Assistant Professor in e-business and management of information systems (MIS) at the Faculty of Organizational Sciences, University of Maribor. She received her PhD in the MIS field from Faculty of Organizational Sciences at University of Maribor, Slovenia in 2002. Since 1995, she has been involved in eCenter and its several research and e-commerce activities. She is a head of eMarkets Laboratory and contact person for Living laboratory for research fields of eMarkets, eSMEs and eGovernment. She is involved into several EU projects focusing on e-business and e-government and intensively cooperates with industry. Her current research includes: e-marketplaces, e-business, supply chain management, e-government and new e-business models. She has published over 100 papers in journals and conference proceedings. She is a conference chair of annual international conference "Bled eConference" (http://BledConference.org).

Raaij, Bas van MSc. is Senior Consultant at Capgemini. As a business analyst and project leader he focuses on Business Information Management (BIM): how to use information to monitor organizational performance and how to make sure the strategic goals remain feasible? Bas writes articles on this topic and supervises students during their graduation process. Bas also plays a significant role in the development of the Capgemini Intelligent Enterprise research.

Ramos, Karoll Haussler Carneiro received his BS in Business Administration from University of Brasilia, in 2006, and habilitation in Business and Public Administration from University of Brasilia, in 2009, MS in Electrical Engineering from the University of Brasilia, in 2009. She is currently a researcher at the Nucleo de Multimidia e Internet in the Department of Electrical Engineering, University of Brasilia, Brazil. Consultant in the development of Enterprise Architecture and Business Process Management. She is currently researcher in the Department of Electrical Engineering, University of Brasilia, Brazil. Her research interests include strategic planning, information technologies, enterprise architecture design, component business model, IT human resource, management of change.

Ridder, Martijn van de MSc. is Senior Consultant at Capgemini in the field of Business Information Management. At several clients in multiple industries he helps organizations to maximize the added value of information. His experience varies from Business Intelligence (BI) tool implementations to setting up BI governance models and facilitating organizational performance improvement initiatives. Martijn likes to link these experiences to science through research and publications. Currently he is one of the main drivers of Sustainability Reporting and the Intelligent Enterprise research at Capgemini.

Rieu, Dominique is full professor at Pierre Mendès France University (UPMF) in Grenoble (France). She is vice-president in charge of Information System at UPMF and joint director of Laboratory of Informatics of Grenoble (LIG). Her main research interests concern information systems engineering (reuse, traceability and variability), development methods (process modeling, process reuse and component based development methods) and business process management. She is responsible of the theme «engineering for and by models in information systems» of GDR I3 (Information, Interaction, Intelligence) and president of INFORSID, the French association of researchers and industrials in Information System.

Rijo, Rui is an Associate Professor of Computer Science at the Polytechnic Institute of Leiria. He has more than ten years of experience as contact centers' technology consultant in Tokyo (Japan), Macau (China), Hong-Kong (China), São Paulo (Brazil), Kuala Lumpur (Malaysia), Madrid (Spain), Amsterdam

(Holland) and Lisbon (Portugal). His current research interests include project management, software engineer, and voice over IP communications.

Sampaio, Fernanda is an assistant professor of the Department of Management at the ISEG - School of Economics and Management, Technical University of Lisbon, Portugal. She currently teaches lectures of Graduation and Master Degrees namely Information Systems, Information Technologies, Information Systems Research Methods, and Organizational Changes and Information Systems Integration. She holds a PhD from Technical University of Lisbon. She is member of a research centre Advance. Her current research interests are in information systems development, business process management, organizational change, information systems integration and outsourcing process. Her publications have appeared in some conferences related to Information Systems.

Serra, José Manuel Correia (MSc) is a CEO of OLISIPO (www.olisipo.pt), a Portuguese information technology services company, and a CEO of SQS Portugal (www.sqs.pt), a subsidiary of SQS Group, that is the largest independent provider of software testing and quality management services. He is involved in several research programs in the business environment and in the enterprise strategies and architectures. He is interested in issues concerning competency management and the innovation environments. He was a publisher of several magazines about technology, innovation and management in companies and government organizations, financial, health, utilities and telecommunication industries.

Serra, Natalia Baikova Correia (MSc) is an Associate Professor at the Systems and Informatics Department of Polytechnic Institute of Setúbal responsible for the courses in Advanced Programming. She is an PhD student at Technical University of Lisbon on subject of Enterprise Architectures and Competency Modelling and Management. She was involved in several research programs of the European Communitie, such as SPECS (Specification and Programming Environment for Communication Software) and SCORE (Service Creation in an Object-Oriented Reuse Environment) projects as a completed part of the RACE (Research and Development in Advanced Communications in Europe).

Shanab, Emad Ahmed Abu earned his PhD degree in business administration, majoring in MIS area in 2005 from Southern Illinois University – Carbondale, USA. He is an instructor at the MIS department in Yarmouk University, where he teaches courses like operations research, e-commerce, e-government, introductory courses in MIS, Production information systems and legal issues of computing (for both bachelor and master degrees). His research interests are in the area of technology acceptance, E-government, enterprise systems applications, E-learning, GDSS, and strategic issues of information systems. His bachelor degree is in civil engineering from Yarmouk University in Jordan (1984), and an MBA from Wilfrid Laurier University in Canada (1995). He is now the Head of the Quality Assurance office in Oman College of Management & Technology in Oman.

Silva, João Mello da received his BS in Mechanical Engineering by the University of Sao Paulo, in 1969, MS in Systems Analysis and Applications by the National Space Research Institute ,in 1971, MS in Operations Research by the Case Western Reserve University, in 1973 and PhD in Operations Research by the Case Western Reserve University degree, in 1975. Has experience in the area of Production Engineering and Information and Communications Services, with emphasis in ICT Services Planning and Business involving ICT Services Providers. His areas of interest include business engineering, project management, risk management and engineering education. At the moment he is an Associate Professor at the Faculty of Technology of the University of Brasilia, where he currently holds the position of Coordinator of the Production Engineering area at the University of Brasilia.

Silva, Miguel Mira da graduated in 1989 and received a master degree in 1993, both in Computer Systems, from the Technical University of Lisbon. In 1997 Miguel received a PhD in Computing Science from the University of Glasgow in Scotland and in 2005 a prestigious master in management "Sloan Fellowship" from the London Business School. Since 1998 Miguel has been Professor of Information Systems in the Technical University of Lisbon, senior researcher at the INESC research institute and an IT management consultant. In 2007 Miguel started a research group at INOV to focus on IT Governance and in 2008 he started another group to implement information systems. Miguel has supervised dozens of master students and one PhD student that graduated in 2008. Miguel has written four thesis, four books and more than 50 research papers, most published in international journals and conferences.

Silva, Nuno Furtado da graduated in Computation (1992) and received a master degree in Computer Science (1996), respectively from Portucalense (Porto) and Minho (Braga) Universities. Nuno received the Eng. António de Almeida Foundation award for academic achievement upon graduation. He was Assistant Lecturer in Portucalense University (1992/93), Portucalense Technical Institute (1993/94), and Minho University (1994/95). Nuno joined CPC-IS (Porto) in 1996 as Information Systems Analyst. Later in 1996, he joined Accenture Consultancy. Since 1996, Nuno participated in more than 30 projects (mostly for Financial Services, but also for Oil, Energy, and Industrial sectors). He managed more than 16 projects, covering several aspects of IT& IS, among other: Systems Integration, Custom Development for Core Systems and Transactional Sites, Implementation Strategy, Assessments, Strategic Planning, Organization, Workforce, Unit Setup, Service Management, and Governance. Since September 2009, Nuno is an independent Management and Technology Consultant.

Sofge, Donald A. is Computer Scientist within the Natural Computation Group at the Naval Research Laboratory, Don Sofge applies nature-inspired computing paradigms to challenging problems in sensing, artificial intelligence, and control. He is an internationally recognized expert in computational intelligence and non-traditional forms of computation including quantum computing, neural networks, and evolutionary computation, and he has authored or co-authored approximately 50 peer-reviewed publications including journal articles, book chapters, conference proceedings, an edited textbook, and several dozen conference papers. His research is currently focused on applying various nature-inspired computing paradigms to teams of agents, studying the means and limitations of collective intelligence in teams and other groups, and exploring emergent behaviors for swarm-based control of distributed autonomous robotic systems.

Sousa, Pedro Manuel Moreira Vaz Antunes de (PhD) is an Associate Professor at IST/UTL - Instituto Superior Técnico, responsible for the courses in Information and Enterprise Architecture. He is also a researcher at Center for Organizational Design and Engineering (CODE) of INOV - INESC INOVAÇÃO, where he has more than 70 articles and presentations on subject of Enterprise Architectures and IT Alignment. He also works as senior consultant of link consulting (www.link.pt), an Aitec company. During the past seven years he has been involved in more than 20 professional projects on Enterprise Architectures both in public and private sector, mostly in finance and telecommunication industries in Portugal, Luxemburg and Brazil.

Spruit, Marco is an Assistant Professor in the Organisation & Information research group at the Institute of Information and Computing Sciences of Utrecht University. His information systems research revolves around Knowledge Discovery processes to help achieve organisational goals through Data Mining techniques, Business intelligence methods, Linguistic Engineering techniques and Web 2.0 technologies. Additionally, he investigates Information Security models and Cloud Computing frameworks as infrastructural safeguards and enablers for Knowledge Discovery processes. Marco initiated his Knowledge Discovery research agenda while performing his PhD in Quantitative Linguistics at the University of Amsterdam. In 2005 he was awarded an ALLC Bursary Award for this work.

Stachura, Max E. Director Center for Telehealth, Tenured Professor: Medical College of Georgia Departments of Medicine and Physiology, School of Medicine; Department of Physiological and Technological Nursing, School of Nursing; and School of Graduate Studies. Graduated Hamilton College and Harvard Medical School. Previous faculty service: State University of New York (Buffalo) and University of Chicago. NIH Career Development Award (1976-81). Chief, Section of Metabolic and Endocrine Disease at MCG and Augusta VA Medical Center (1981-95). School of Medicine Outstanding Faculty Member (1987). Director, Center for Telehealth since 1995. Georgia Research Alliance Eminent Scholar in Telemedicine since 1998. Principal Investigator on NIH, VA, US Departments of Energy and Defense, and Foundation grants. Published more than 240 journal articles, book chapters, and abstracts. Associate Editor for three professional journals. Visiting Professor at several US universities and internationally. Advisory Board: iCons in Medicine and several companies. Immediate past-president: Alliance for Public Technology.

Sudzina, Frantisek is an assistant professor in information systems at Copenhagen Business School, Denmark. He received his master degree in economics and business management and PhD in sectoral and intersectoral economies from the University of Economics Bratislava, Slovakia in 2000 and 2003, respectively. He received his bachelor and master degrees in mathematics from Safarik University Kosice, Slovakia in 2002 and 2004 respectively. He received his bachelor and master degrees in computer science from Safarik University Kosice, Slovakia in 2005 and 2006 respectively. Currently, he pursues his master degree in bioinformatics at Copenhagen University, Denmark. His research interests include information systems (enterprise systems, business intelligence, Web 2.0 applications, information strategy, open source software, data mining), and quantitative methods (econometrics, operations research, statistics). He has published over 100 papers in journals and conference proceedings.

Tarawneh, Heyam Abdel Razzaq Al earned her bachelor degree in psychology from Jordan University (1987), and a high diploma in special needs education from the same university. She is pursuing her master degree in education psychology at Yarmouk University, Irbid Jordan. Since 1987, she has been working in the Ministry of Education as a counselor in more than one school, currently at Safieh Ben Abdel-Muttaleb School in Irbid, Jordan. Mrs. Al-Tarawneh has participated in many counseling workshops and conducted many lectures in schools and arranged many activities. She is interested in behavioral aspects of technology, the role of women in leadership positions, and emotional intelligence issues.

Tijsen, Rick MSc is a recently graduated master student from Utrecht University. During his master studies on Business Informatics, he gained broad knowledge on the business side of IT. Among others his MSc thesis research on Business Intelligence end-user adoption has provided him with a profound knowledge and insights on the organizational side of Business Intelligence. In his daily profession as a Business Intelligence consultant, Rick aspires to put this knowledge to practice, while operating on the edge between IT and business. His research interests are focused on gaining a deeper understanding of the role of technology in business.

Tribolet, José Manuel (PhD, M.I.T.) is Full Professor of Information Systems at IST/UTL - Instituto Superior Técnico, Technical University of Lisbon, responsible for the courses in Enterprise Information Systems and Organizational Engineering, and President of INESC, the largest Portuguese private research institute. He is senior researcher at the Center for Organizational Design and Engineering (CODE) of INOV - INESC INOVAÇÃO, where he has, since 2000, more than 100 publications on Enterprise Architecture, Enterprise Engineering and Governance. Under his supervision, 4 Ph.D. theses have been successfully defended in 2007 and 2008, with 4 more coming up for defense in the next 3 years. He also works as private executive counselor for top executives in business and public administration. Among is present commitments is counseling the Attorney General on the architecture and deployment of the next generation information systems of the Portuguese Justice System.

Tung, Hui Lien is an Assistant Professor of Mathematics and Computer Science at Paine College. She has a Masters Degree in Information Science (State University of New York-Albany, 2000) and a Masters Degree in Education (National-Louis University, IL, 1990). Her research interests are in MIS, metrics of organizational information systems and performance, e-Government, IT in eHealth, Systems Analysis and Design and database. She has published several Journal articles, book chapters, peer-reviewed proceedings and conference papers.

Verdún, José D. Carrillo. Ph. D. in Computer Science, and Ingeniero de Montes by the Universidad Politécnica de Madrid. MBA (CEPADE, e IESE). Professor Principal on the Facultad de Informática, Universidad Politécnica de Madrid, and responsible of Doctoral Thesis. Academic director of the Masters in Audit and Security organized by the Universidad Politécnica de Madrid, and the ALI from 2.001. ISACA Academic Advocate. Honorary Teacher of the Sociedad de Estudios Internacionales from 1.998. President of the Software Metrics Association (AEMES) from 1.997. Board member of ISBSG (Information Systems Benchmarking Software Group). Expert in Technological Innovation on the Fundación COTEC. Member of AESPLAN (Spanish Association of Planning) and AECA (Spanish Association of Accounting and Business Administration).

Vila, Alberto Casal da, Industrial engineer from the Universidad Politécnica de Madrid and graduate in innovation by IMD-MIT. Chairman of BlueMobility Systems, company specialized in electric vehicles recharging infrastructures. Founder and Managing Partner of INOVA, a consultancy specialized in R+D and innovation management, with a renowned track record in the years 2005-2009, in different industrial sectors. More than 30 years of experience in automotive. COO and responsible for international development of the Dalphimetal-TRW Group Spain, and Managing Director of DYTECH-ENSA. In both companies carrying out significant expansion plans based on internationalization of operations and technological development of new products, in the areas of passive safety and emissions control. Began his career in PSA Citroen-Vigo, where he was latterly responsible of the industrial planning of new vehicles. Key Fields of Expertise: Technology and Innovation Management, Innovation Process techniques, Open Innovation, Product development, Technology Transfer, and Entrepreneurship.

Wood, Joseph C. is the chief of a research department at an Army Medical Center. He is a physician and is board certified in Internal Medicine, Endocrine, Diabetes and Metabolism. He has a PhD in Endocrinology that was granted in 1991 from the Medical College of Georgia, and a Doctor of Medicine from the George Washington University School of Medicine in 1995. He is an academic clinician and is on the teaching staff at his institution. His research interests are experimental therapeutics in bone and soft tissue wound healing, thyroid cancer and in organizational theory, organizational performance and metrics. He has published over 8 articles and book chapters, over 38 peer-reviewed proceedings and abstracts, and he has received about $750,000 in research grants. He is a fellow in the American College of Physicians and a Fellow in the American Association of Clinical Endocrinologists.

Yañez, Jose Manuel Cotos is a Professor of the Department of Electronics and Computer Science, University of Santiago de Compostela. PhD in Physics from the University of Santiago de Compostela from November 1993, develops his research in Computer Science. His research interests are Geographic Information Systems, and its extension to GRID computing environments focusing on the development of architectures and tools for the development of GRID computing environments for research projects in satellite image processing. Within its research activity has led 3 doctoral theses related to the integration of monitoring and control using geographic information systems and various artificial intelligence tools, plus 3 degree dissertations. He has published over 10 articles with impact and participated in 30 conferences. He is currently the principal investigator of USC's participation in 3 research national projects and 2 autonomous ones. He has also participated in more than 30 research contracts with companies and institutions.

Index